# MAPPING JUDAH'S FATE IN EZEKIEL'S ORACLES AGAINST THE NATIONS

# ANCIENT NEAR EASTERN MONOGRAPHS

*General Editors*
Alan Lenzi
Juan Manuel Tebes

*Editorial Board:*
Reinhard Achenbach
Roxana Flammini
Esther J. Hamori
Steven W. Holloway
René Krüger
Steven L. McKenzie
Martti Nissinen
Graciela Gestoso Singer

Number 15

# MAPPING JUDAH'S FATE IN EZEKIEL'S ORACLES AGAINST THE NATIONS

Lydia Lee

Atlanta

Copyright © 2016 by Lydia Lee

All rights reserved. No part of this work may be reproduced or transmitted in any form or by any means, electronic or mechanical, including photocopying and recording, or by means of any information storage or retrieval system, except as may be expressly permitted by the 1976 Copyright Act or in writing from the publisher. Requests for permission should be addressed in writing to the Rights and Permissions Office, SBL Press, 825 Houston Mill Road, Atlanta, GA 30329 USA.

Library of Congress Cataloging-in-Publication Data

Names: Lee, Lydia, author.
Title: Mapping Judah's fate in Ezekiel's oracles against the nations / by Lydia Lee.
Description: Atlanta : SBL Press, [2016] | Series: Ancient Near East monographs ; number 15 | Includes bibliographical references and index.
Identifiers: LCCN 2016040614 (print) | LCCN 2016040853 (ebook) | ISBN 9781628371512 (pbk. : alk. paper) | ISBN 9780884141839 (hardcover : alk. paper) | ISBN 9780884141808 (ebook)
Subjects: LCSH: Bible. Ezekiel, XXV-XXXII--Criticism, interpretation, etc.
Classification: LCC BS1545.52 .L44 2016 (print) | LCC BS1545.52 (ebook) | DDC 224/.406--dc23
LC record available at https://lccn.loc.gov/2016040614

Printed on acid-free paper.

Dedicated to my foes, friends, and family,
all of whom have led me on a journey of self-discovery

# TABLE OF CONTENTS

**Acknowledgements**..................................................................................xi

**Abbreviations**.......................................................................................xiii

**Prologue: A Journey of Self-Discovery**..............................................1

**Chapter One: Setting the Course**........................................................7
1. Navigating the Landscape.....................................................................8
　1.1. The "Implicit Hope" Focus................................................................8
　1.2. The "Hubris" Focus.........................................................................14
　1.3. The "Oblique Judgment" Focus......................................................17
2. Identifying the Obstacles....................................................................23
　2.1. Ideological Overgeneralization......................................................23
　2.2. Contextual Isolation.......................................................................33
3. Marking the New Path........................................................................35
　3.1. Semantic Links, Textual Allusions, and Rhetorical Impacts............40
　3.2. Wider Influences beyond Ezek 25–32............................................44

**Chapter Two: The Dispossession of the Promised Land in Ezek 25**....51
1. The Ominous Beginning.....................................................................53
　1.1. The First Proof-Saying...................................................................54
　1.2. The Second Proof-Saying..............................................................56
　1.3. The Third Proof-Saying..................................................................57
　1.4. The Fourth Proof-Saying................................................................58
　1.5. The Fifth Proof-Saying...................................................................61
2. The Allusions to the Promised Land and Divine Retribution.............63
　2.1. The "Possession"............................................................................64
　2.2. The "Glory of the Land".................................................................68
　2.3. The "Vengeance"............................................................................71

2.4. The "Stretching-Hand" and "Cutting-Off"..................................73
3. The Rhetorical Impact..................................................................76
   3.1. The Territorial Resemblances between the Nations and Judah..........77
   3.2. The Shared Judgment between the Nations and Judah....................77

**Chapter Three: The Destruction of the Jerusalem Temple and Priesthood in Ezek 26–28............................................................................79**
1. The Allocation of the Perfect Beauty..............................................83
   1.1. The Proof-Sayings..................................................................84
   1.2. The Dirges............................................................................86
2. The Allusions to the Israelite Sanctuary and Priesthood........................89
   2.1. The Conflation of the Tabernacle and First Temple Images............89
   2.2. The Enumeration of the Jewels on the High Priestly Pectoral..........95
3. The Rhetorical Impact.................................................................102
   3.1. The Foreboding Beauty..........................................................102
   3.2. The Exalted Glory.................................................................105
      3.2.1. The All-Encompassing Trade List......................................105
      3.2.2. The Divine Cherub..........................................................107
   3.3 The Destruction *in toto*........................................................118
      3.3.1. The Final Blow by the East Wind......................................118
      3.3.2. The Profanation of the Tyrian King...................................120

**Chapter Four: The Death of Judah in Ezek 29–32..........................123**
1. The Shaping of Egypt as YHWH's Enemy......................................127
   1.1. The Crocodile/Dragon Monster................................................127
   1.2. The Broken Arm...................................................................135
   1.3. The Chthonic Cedar..............................................................139
2. The Allusions to Judah as Egypt's Ally..........................................144
   2.1. The Crushed Reed to the House of Israel..................................145
   2.2. The People of the Covenant Land............................................147
   2.3. The Multitude......................................................................154
   2.4. The Cedar and the Vine.........................................................158
3. The Rhetorical Impact.................................................................165
   3.1. Destruction.........................................................................167
   3.2. Exile..................................................................................170
   3.3. Death.................................................................................171
   3.4. Restoration.........................................................................175

**Chapter Five: Exploring the Afterlives........................................183**
1. Summary................................................................................184
2. Affirming the Oblique Judgment..................................................186
   2.1. The Beginning of the Fateful Siege..........................................188

2.2. The Arrival of the Terrifying News..........................................193
3. Transforming the Oblique Judgment...............................................197
   3.1. In Opposition to the Mountains of Israel...................................198
      3.1.1. The Magnified Hostility..................................................200
      3.1.2. The Magnified Desolation................................................204
   3.2 Not an Ally, but an Enemy....................................................207
      3.2.1. The Previous Ally........................................................209
      3.2.2. The Present Enemy.......................................................217

**Epilogue: Implications of the Study**..................................................223

**Bibliography**..................................................................................231

**Indexes**.........................................................................................257

# ACKNOWLEDGEMENTS

This monograph is a revised version of my doctoral thesis submitted to Georg-August-Universität Göttingen in April 2014. The completion of the thesis is impossible without the assistance of my *Doktorvater*, Dr. Nathan MacDonald, my *Doktormutter*, Prof. Annette Zgoll, and the third committee member, Prof. Hermann Spieckermann. Special thanks are due to Dr. Nathan MacDonald. Working as one of the doctoral research assistants in his Sofja-Kovalevskaja Research Team in Göttingen, "Unity and Diversity in Early Jewish Monotheisms" allowed me to test and exchange ideas at various local and international conferences. Summaries of my research were presented at the doctoral colloquiums in Göttingen (June 2012, May 2013), at the Society of Biblical Literature meetings held in Amsterdam and Chicago (July 2012, November 2012), and at the graduate meetings in Lausanne (June 2012, June 2014). The intellectually challenging research job introduced me to other ingenious colleagues in Göttingen, including Dr. Sonja Ammann, Dr. Rob Barrett, Dr. Ken Brown, Dr. Mette Bundvad, Reed Carlson, Dr. Izaak de Hulster, Dr. (des.) Paul Michael Kurtz, Dr. Matt Lynch, Roberto Piani, and Dr. Harald Samuel. All of them have offered me different kinds of incentives to complete the doctoral thesis as well as possible.

My heartfelt gratitude goes to another group of people, whose precious encouragements, critical insights, and technical support have helped the book see the light of day. Prof. Ian Young, my Honors supervisor at the University of Sydney, who has always believed in me and shown me the way, kindly proofread an earlier version of Prologue and Chapter One. Prof. Shani Tzoref, who had introduced me to the fascinating world of the Second Temple Literature during my undergraduate studies, helpfully commented on a previous version of Chapter Five and Epilogue. Prof. Mark Leuchter's passion for the prophetic literature is so contagious that I have been infected by it ever since I undertook an undergraduate course taught by him. Dr. Carla Sulzbach, Dr. Rachelle Gilmour, Dr. Nickolas Roubekas, and Dr. Safwak Marzouk selflessly shared their insights and tirelessly proofread my work, either in part or in whole. Dr. Selim Adalı deserves credit and thanks for showing interests in my chapter on Gog and for pointing me to many valuable references. The feedback of the editors and reviewers of my articles at *Zeitschrift für die alttestamentliche Wissenschaft* (on Ezek 25) and *Journal for the Study of the Old Testament* (on Ezek 28) has helped sharpen my argument in various sections of the book. Parts of those articles are reused in chapters two and three with the permission of the editors. I am indebted to Prof. Herrie van Rooy and Prof. Hans van Deventer for accepting me as a postdoctoral research fellow at the North-West University in South Africa, where I completed the final editing before publication. I cannot express enough thanks to Prof. Alan Lenzi, the General Editor of the SBL Ancient Near Eastern Monograph Series, who graciously accepted the manuscript, went through it with efficiency and erudition, and drew my attention to various relevant ancient Near Eastern materials. The anonymous reviewers of my manuscript provided highly useful comments for the improvement of my arguments. Nicole Tilford, the Production Manager of the SBL Press, went to great lengths in supervising my preparation of the printer-ready manuscript. Participating in this innovative online open-access endeavour has brought me much satisfaction and joy.

Devoting countless days and nights to the study of ancient texts can be tedious without the loving support of a family. Throughout my doctoral studies, my parents, Kau and Mu Tan Lee, kept me in their prayers. My brother, Paul Lee, and my sister, Esther Lee, constantly cheered me up with words of encouragements. My brothers and sisters in Christ from the Göttingen Chinese Christian Congregation and the Potchefstroom International Church (RC Potch Bult) have melted my heart with their warmth and made me feel at home in the foreign countries. The gratitude list would be incomplete without mentioning the sacrificial love of my husband, Zhiyang Liu, who patiently and joyfully looked after my practical needs over a long period of time, so as to free me up for academic research.

Reflecting on the writing and production of this book has made me realized the importance of all of the aforementioned people in shaping and enriching my life. They all have led me on a journey of self-discovery, teaching me to revisit the past and to embrace not only the good but also the bad experiences in life. I thus dedicate this study to all of them.

Οἴδαμεν δὲ ὅτι τοῖς ἀγαπῶσιν τὸν θεὸν πάντα συνεργεῖ εἰς ἀγαθόν, τοῖς κατὰ πρόθεσιν κλητοῖς οὖσιν.

Lydia Lee
Potchefstroom
Heritage Day 2016

# ABBREVIATIONS

| | |
|---|---|
| AASF | Annales Academiae scientiarum fennicae |
| ÄAT | Ägypten und Altes Testament |
| AB | Anchor Bible |
| *ABR* | *Australian Biblical Review* |
| ABS | Archaeology and Biblical Studies |
| *Ag. Ap.* | *Against Apion* |
| *AHw* | *Akkadisches Handwörterbuch.* W. von Soden. 3 vols. Wiesbaden, 1965–1981 |
| ANEM | Ancient Near East Monographs/Monografías sobre el Antiguo Cercano Oriente |
| *ANEP* | *The Ancient Near East in Pictures Relating to the Old Testament.* Edited by James B. Pritchard. Princeton: Princeton University Press, 1954 |
| *ANET* | *Ancient Near Eastern Texts Relating to the Old Testament.* Edited by J. B. Pritchard. 3rd ed. Princeton: Princeton University Press, 1969 |
| *ANF* | *Ante-Nicene Fathers.* Edited by A. Roberts and J. Donaldson. 1885–1887. 10 vols. Repr., Peabody: Hendrickson, 1994. |
| *Ant.* | *Jewish Antiquities* |
| AOAT | Alter Orient und Altes Testament |
| AoF | Altorientalische Forschungen |
| *ASTI* | *Annual of the Swedish Theological Institute* |
| ATD | Das Alte Testament Deutsch |
| *AUSS* | *Andrews University Seminary Studies* |
| BA | *Biblical Archaeologist* |
| BBB | Bonner biblische Beiträge |
| *BBR* | *Bulletin for Biblical Research* |
| BEATAJ | Beiträge zur Erforschung des Alten Testaments und des antiken Judentum |
| BETL | Bibliotheca ephemeridum theologicarum lovaniensium |

| | |
|---|---|
| BEvT | Beiträge zur evangelischen Theologie |
| BHS | *Biblia Hebraica Stuttgartensia*. Edited by K. Elliger and W. Rudolph. Stuttgart: Deutsche Bibelgesellschaft, 1983 |
| Bib | *Biblica* |
| BibInt | *Biblical Interpretation* |
| BibInt | Biblical Interpretation Series |
| BibOr | Biblica et orientalia |
| BIES | *Bulletin of the Israel Exploration Society (=Yediot)* |
| Bijdr | *Bijdragen: Tijdschrift voor filosofie en theologie* |
| BN | *Biblische Notizen* |
| b. Sanh. | Babylonian Talmud Sanhedrin |
| BZAW | Beihefte zur Zeitschrift für die alttestamentliche Wissenschaft |
| CAD | *The Assyrian Dictionary of the Oriental Institute of the University of Chicago*. Chicago: The Oriental Institute of the University of Chicago, 1956–2006 |
| CBC | Cambridge Bible Commentary |
| CBET | Contributions to Biblical Exegesis and Theology |
| CBQ | *Catholic Biblical Quarterly* |
| CBQMS | Catholic Biblical Quarterly Monograph Series |
| CC | Continental Commentaries |
| CEV | Contemporary English Version |
| ConBOT | Coniectanea biblica: Old Testament Series |
| COS | *The Context of Scripture*. Edited by William W. Hallo. 3 vols. Leiden: Brill, 1997–2002 |
| CTJ | *Calvin Theological Journal* |
| DDD | *Dictionary of Deities and Demons in the Bible*. Edited by Karel van der Toorn, Bob Becking, and Pieter W. van der Horst. Leiden: Brill, 1995. 2nd rev. ed. Grand Rapids: Eerdmans, 1999 |
| DSSSE | *Dead Sea Scrolls: Study Edition*. Edited by F. G. Martínez and E. J. C. Tigchelaar. Leiden: Brill, 1997–1998 |
| EA | El-Amarna tablets. According to the edition of Jørgen A. Knudtzon. *Die el-Amarna-Tafeln*. Leipzig: Hinrichs, 1908–1915. Repr., Aalen: Zeller, 1964. Continued in Anson F. Rainey, *El-Amarna Tablets, 359–379*. 2nd rev. ed. Kevelaer: Butzon & Bercker, 1978 |
| EdF | Erträge der Forschung |
| EncJud | *Encyclopaedia Judaica*. Edited by Fred Skolnik and Michael Berenbaum. 2nd ed. 22 vols. Detroit: Macmillan Reference USA, 2007 |
| ESV | English Standard Version |
| ETL | *Ephemerides theologicae lovanienses* |
| FAT | Forschungen zum Alten Testament |

| | |
|---|---|
| FB | Forschung zur Bibel |
| FRLANT | Forschungen zur Religion und Literatur des Alten und Neuen Testaments |
| GNB | Good News Bible |
| *HALOT* | *The Hebrew and Aramaic Lexicon of the Old Testament*. Ludwig Koehler, Walter Baumgartner, and Johann J. Stamm. Translated and edited under the supervision of Mervyn E. J. Richardson. 4 vols. Leiden: Brill, 1994–1999 |
| HAT | Handbuch zum Alten Testament |
| HDR | Harvard Dissertations in Religion |
| HKAT | Handkommentar zum Alten Testament |
| HSM | Harvard Semitic Monographs |
| HSS | Harvard Semitic Studies |
| *HTR* | *Harvard Theological Review* |
| HTS | Harvard Theological Studies |
| *HUCA* | *Hebrew union College Annual* |
| ICC | International Critical Commentary |
| *IEJ* | *Israel Exploration Journal* |
| *JBL* | *Journal of Biblical Literature* |
| *JNES* | *Journal of Near Eastern Studies* |
| *JNSL* | *Journal of Northwest Semitic Languages* |
| JPS | Tanakh: The Holy Scriptures: The JPS Translation according to the Traditional Hebrew Text |
| JSJSup | Supplements to the Journal for the Study of Judaism |
| *JSOT* | *Journal for the Study of the Old Testament* |
| JSOTSup | Journal for the Study of the Old Testament: Supplement Series |
| *JSS* | *Journal of Semitic Studies* |
| *JSSEA* | *Journal of the Society for the Study of Egyptian Antiquities* |
| Jub. | Jubilees |
| J.W. | Jewish War |
| KAT | Kommentar zum Alten Testament |
| *KTU* | *Die keilalphabetischen Texte aus Ugarit*. Edited by Manfried Dietrich, Oswald Loretz, and Joaquín Sanmartín. Münster: Ugarit-Verlag, 2013. 3rd enl. ed. of *KTU: The Cuneiform Alphabetic Texts from Ugarit, Ras Ibn Hani, and Other Places.* Edited by Manfried Dietrich, Oswald Loretz, and Joaquín Sanmartín. Münster: Ugarit-Verlag, 1995 (= CTU) |
| *LÄ* | *Lexikon der Ägyptologie*. Edited by Wolfgang Helck, Eberhard Otto, and Wolfhart Westen dorf. Wiesbaden: Harrassowitz, 1972 |
| LAE | Life of Adam and Eve |
| LHBOTS | The Library of Hebrew Bible/Old Testament Studies |
| LXX | Septuagint |

| | |
|---|---|
| Midr. Ps | Midrash Psalms |
| *MIO* | *Mitteilungen des Instituts für Orientforschung* |
| MT | Masoretic Text |
| NASB | New American Standard Bible |
| NEchtB | Neue Echter Bibel |
| NET | New English Translation |
| NIBCOT | New International Biblical Commentary on the Old Testament |
| NICOT | New International Commentary on the Old Testament |
| NKJV | New King James Version |
| *NTT* | *Norsk Teologisk Tidsskrift* |
| OAN | Oracles against the Nations |
| OBO | Orbis biblicus et orientalis |
| ÖBS | Österreichische biblische Studien |
| OTG | Old Testament Guides |
| OTL | Old Testament Library |
| *OtSt* | *Oudtestamentische Studiën* |
| PEQ | Palestine Exploration Quarterly |
| Pesiq. Rab. | Pesiqta Rabbati |
| Pirqe R. El. | Pirqe Rabbi Eliezer |
| *PRSt* | *Perspectives in Religious Studies* |
| PTMS | Pittsburgh Theological Monograph Series |
| *RB* | *Revue biblique* |
| *RevQ* | *Revue de Qumran* |
| RIA | *Reallexikon der Assyriologie*. Edited by Erich Ebeling et al. Berlin: de Gruyter, 1928– |
| RINAP | The Royal Inscriptions of the Neo-Assyrian Period |
| SBLDS | Society of Biblical Literature Dissertation Series |
| SBLRBS | Society of Biblical Literature Resources for Biblical Study |
| SBLSP | Society of Biblical Literature Seminar Papers |
| SBS | Stuttgarter Bibelstudien |
| SCS | Septuagint and Cognate Studies Series |
| SHBC | Smyth & Helwys Bible Commentary |
| *SJOT* | *Scandinavian Journal of the Old Testament* |
| STDJ | Studies on the Texts of the Desert of Judah |
| SVTP | Studia in Veteris Testamenti pseudepigraphica |
| *TDOT* | *Theological Dictionary of the Old Testament*. Edited by G. Johannes Botterweck and Helmer Ringgren. Translated by John T. Willis et al. 8 vols. Grand Rapids: Eerdmans, 1974–2006 |
| *Them* | *Themelios* |
| TSAJ | Texte und Studien zum antiken Judentum |
| *TynBul* | *Tyndale Bulletin* |
| UBL | Ugaritisch-biblische Literatur |
| *UF* | *Ugarit-Forschungen* |

| | |
|---|---|
| VAB | Vorderasiatische Bibliothek |
| *VT* | *Vetus Testamentum* |
| VTSup | Supplements to Vetus Testamentum |
| Vulg. | Vulgate |
| WAW | Writings from the Ancient World |
| WBC | Word Biblical Commentary |
| WMANT | Wissenschaftliche Monographien zum Alten und Neuen Testament |
| WUNT | Wissenschaftliche Untersuchungen zum Neuen Testament |
| *WW* | *Word and World* |
| YOSR | Yale Oriental Series, Researches |
| *ZA* | *Zeitschrift für Assyriologie* |
| *ZAW* | *Zeitschrift für die alttestamentliche Wissenschaft* |
| *ZDMG* | *Zeitschrift der deutschen morgenländischen Gesellschaft* |

# PROLOGUE

# A JOURNEY OF SELF-DISCOVERY

> No man is an Iland, intire of itselfe; every man is a peece of the Continent, a part of the mained; if a Clod bee washed away by the Sea, Europe is the lesse, as well as if a Promontorie were, as well as if a Manor of thy friends or of thine owne were; any mans death diminishes me, because I am involved in Mankinde; And therefore never send to know for whom the bell tolls; It tolls for thee.
> John Donne

Ezekiel 25–32 possesses a rich tapestry of imagery of foreign nations. These eight chapters of prophecies paint a lush landscape, in which all sorts of ancient nations come to life. Here, Ammon and Moab scorn and taunt; Edom and Philistia execute vengeance; the beautiful Tyre, decorated with merchandise from many countries, proudly possesses all her splendor and glory, but is ultimately destroyed by the east wind and overthrown into oblivion; and the monstrous Egypt, comparable to a tall cosmic tree or a ferocious lion, finally enters a shameful fate in the netherworld with the uncircumcised and the pierced.

This collection of prophecies within the book of Ezekiel belongs to the literary terrain of the so-called Oracles against the Nations (OAN). Concerned with the mystical past, disputed present, and oft-disastrous future of the specifically named nations other than Israel and Judah, the OAN sprawl over the Latter Prophets. These texts, as in Isa 13–23, Jer 46–51, Ezek 25–32, Amos 1–2, Zeph 2–3, and Zech 9, appear as a collection within the prophetic books. Sometimes, they occupy the entire prophetic book, as is the case with Nahum and Obadiah, which indict Nineveh and Edom respectively. The OAN in no way represent a specific *Gattung* or genre, and the content often plays a far more important role than the form in defining the OAN.¹ This is because the OAN display diverse structures and forms, be it a proof-saying,² an invitation to flight or flee,³ a dirge (קינה),⁴ or an utterance (משא).⁵ They comprise a significant percentage of word count, covering 13.6 percent of the corpus of the Latter Prophets.⁶ If one would include all doom passages against the nations, including Isa 34, Ezek 35, 38–39, and Joel 4, the percentage would probably increase to 15–20 percent.⁷ That is to say, nearly a fifth of the Latter Prophets would consist of the OAN.

Despite its statistical prominence in the Hebrew Bible, Fechter rightly acknowledges that the OAN in general remain an alien or unfamiliar acre in

---

¹ For this consensus, see B. Huwyler, *Jeremia und die Völker: Untersuchungen zu den Völkersprüchen in Jeremia 46–49*, FAT 20 (Tübingen: Mohr Siebeck, 1997), 2; R. Albertz, *Die Exilszeit: 6. Jahrhundert v. Chr.*, Biblische Enzyklopädie 7 (Stuttgart: Kohlhammer, 2001), 145–46; D. L. Christensen, *The Transformations of the War Oracle in Old Testament Prophecy: Studies in the Oracles against the Nations*, HDR 3 (Missoula: Scholars Press, 1975), 1; A. Hagedorn, *Die Anderen im Spiegel: Israels Auseinandersetzung mit den Völkern in den Büchern Nahum, Zefanja, Obadja und Joel*, BZAW 414 (Berlin: de Gruyter, 2011), 11; B. C. Jones, *Howling over Moab: Irony and Rhetoric in Isaiah 15–16*, SBLDS 157 (Atlanta: Scholars Press, 1996), 56–57.

² E.g., Amos 1–2; Ezek 25; 26:1–6, which usually include a reason for judgment and a statement of judgment. Cf. J. B. Geyer, "Mythology and Culture in the Oracles against the Nations," *VT* 36 (1986): 129–45, here 130–32.

³ This form is typical of the Jeremianic oracles. The invitations to flee include Jer 48:6–8, 28; 49:8, 30; 50:8–10; 51:6, 45. The invitations to fight include Jer 46:3–6, 9–10; 49:14–15, 28–29, 31–33; 50:14–15, 16, 21–23, 26–27, 29–30; 51:3–4, 11–12, 27–29. See also Isa 13:2; 21:2b, 5b; Jer 5:10; 6:4–6; Hos 5:8; Joel 4:9–12, 13; Mic 4:13; Obad 1. For more details, see R. Bach, *Die Aufforderungen zur Flucht und zum Kampf im alttestamentlichen Prophetenspruch*, WMANT 9 (Neukirchen: Neukirchener Verlag, 1962), 15–22, 51–69.

⁴ E.g., Ezek 27; 28; 32. Cf. the משל in Isa 14.

⁵ E.g., Nah 1:1; Hab 1:1; Zech 9:1, but especially in Isa 13–23 (e.g., 13:1; 14:28; 15:1; 17:1; 19:1; 21:1, 11, 13; 22:1; 23:1). The texts to which משא is attached display a diversity of styles and structures. For more explications, see B. B. Margulis, "Studies in the Oracles against the Nations" (PhD diss., Brandeis University, 1966), 200–222; G. H. Jones, "An Examination of Some Leading Motifs in the Prophetic Oracles against Foreign Nations" (PhD diss., University of Wales, 1970), 50–55; Jones, *Howling*, 62–76.

⁶ P. R. Raabe, "Why Prophetic Oracles against the Nations?" in *Fortunate the Eyes That See: Essays in Honor of David Noel Freedman in Celebration of His Seventieth Birthday*, ed. A. B. Beck et al. (Grand Rapids: Eerdmans, 1995), 236.

⁷ Ibid., 236–37.

the wider landscape of biblical scholarship.⁸ On one level, none of these texts appears as part of a liturgical reading or sermon in churches. On another level, they rarely feature in a biblical course taught at a tertiary institution. Fechter thus questions if the exclusion of this large part of the biblical traditions is executed with justice. Independent of Fechter's study, Boadt comes to a similar conclusion: "Rarely does the commentator integrate the oracles against the nations into a summary of the prophet's theology."⁹ Their observations are indeed justified when Westermann's classic study entitled *Grundformen prophetischer Rede* dedicates only one out of 149 pages to the biblical OAN, so that the reader gets the impression that the corpus is not part of the original prophetic judgment or that it is an insignificant part of the prophetic books in general.¹⁰ A later period has witnessed the writing of one English dissertation on Ezek 25–32 completed by Strong (1993) and the publication of a German monograph on Ezekiel's OAN composed by Premstaller (2005).¹¹ Still, their studies do not alleviate the general indifference shown toward this corpus within the book of Ezekiel. This neglect is amply demonstrated when Schmid's introduction to the book of Ezekiel in the recently published *T&T Clark Handbook of the Old Testament* (2006, Eng. 2012) barely mentions the collection of the OAN.¹²

Even if references are made to the OAN, commentators generally assume the corpus' vitriolic tone and nationalistic spirit. Having compared the OAN

---

⁸ F. Fechter, *Bewältigung der Katastrophe: Untersuchungen zu ausgewählten Fremdvölkersprüchen im Ezechielbuch*, BZAW 208 (Berlin: de Gruyter, 1992), 1, n. 2.

⁹ L. Boadt, "Rhetorical Strategies in Ezekiel's Oracles of Judgment," in *Ezekiel and His Book: Textual and Literary Criticism and Their Interrelation*, ed. J. Lust; BETL 74 (Leuven: Leuven University Press, 1986), 196. This isolated status of the OAN is also observed by P. C. Beentjes, "Oracles against the Nations, a Central Issue in the 'Later Prophets,'" *Bijdr* 50 (1989): 204–5.

¹⁰ He characterizes the OAN in the Hebrew Bible simply as the judgment proclamation to Israel's enemy. C. Westermann, *Grundformen Prophetischer Rede*, 5th ed., BEvT 31 (München: Kaiser, 1978), 147–48.

¹¹ J. T. Strong, "Ezekiel's Oracles against the Nations within the Context of His Message" (PhD diss., Union Theological Seminary of Virginia, 1993); V. Premstaller, *Fremdvölkersprüche des Ezechielbuches*, FB 104 (Würzburg: Echter, 2005).

¹² This neglect of the OAN is despite the fact that the author of the introduction acknowledges that "the book of Ezekiel is widely and correctly considered the most tightly structured prophetic book of the Old Testament" (452). For the introduction, see K. Schmid, "The Book of Ezekiel," in *T&T Clark Handbook of the Old Testament*, ed. J. C. Gertz et al., trans. J. Adams-Maßmann (New York: T&T Clark International, 2012), 451–65. This textbook first appeared in 2006 in German as *Grundinformation Altes Testament: Eine Einführung in Literatur, Religion und Geschichte des Alten Testaments*, ed. J. C. Gertz et al. (Göttingen: Vandenhoeck & Ruprecht, 2006).

in Jer 46–51 with the rest of the prophetic book, Schwally claims that YHWH in the OAN section appears thoroughly as the "Rachegott," which is an image incompatible with the compassionate and merciful God portrayed elsewhere in the book.[13] Pfeiffer famously condemns all OAN in the Hebrew Bible as "ardently nationalistic and fanatically intolerant."[14] Even in an attempt to redeem the moral reading of Nahum, Nysse still issues a pessimistic assessment: "The oracles against the nations are not safe to read, and no amount of explanation can make them so."[15] In short, these oracles in the Hebrew Bible are either blatantly ignored or deeply feared.

Looking beyond this sense of alienation and estrangement, this study explores one important dimension of Ezek 25–32, which has not yet received sustained attention: *Ezekiel 25–32 highlights the commonality between Judah and the nations, by deploying the doom oracles of the nations as the implicit pronouncements concerning the dispossession of the Judean land, the destruction of the Jerusalem temple and priesthood, and the demise of Judah.*

To justify this argument, I will examine the concrete lexical features of Ezek 25–32, taking into consideration both the diachronic (temporal) and synchronic (spatial) aspects of the features. That is to say, this study will pay attention to the synchronic space occupied by the literary features used to construct the imagery of Ammon, Moab, Edom, Philistia, Tyre, and Egypt in Ezek 25–32. At the same time, the study will explore the possible textual allusions to Judah or the pre-exilic house of Israel embedded in the lexemes used in Ezek 25–32. A more detailed explication of how the synchronic and diachronic aspects of the texts aid in a deeper appreciation of the rhetorical impacts created by the texts will be found in Chapter One.

The subsequent chapters deal with the focal texts for examination, including the oracles against Transjordan and Philistia in Ezek 25, the dirges against Tyre in chapter 26–28, and the prophecies against Egypt in chapters 29–32. The goal is not to deal with every facet of all these oracles, but to pay attention to the major literary allusions embedded in Ezekiel's OAN that have received less sustained attention, to highlight the unstable boundary between Judah and

---

[13] F. Schwally, "Die Reden des Buches Jeremia gegen die Heiden XXV, XLVI–LI," *ZAW* 8 (1888): 177–217, esp. 204: "In 46 bis 49 dagegen tritt Jahve durchgehends als Rachegott auf, welcher die Heiden unabänderlichem Untergang geweiht hat." In comparison with the other materials concerning foreign nations such as Isa 15, 16, 24, Obadiah, and Ezek 25–32, 38–39, Schwally claims that Jeremiah's OAN share characteristics with the OAN found in other prophetic books (207–13). Subsequently, Schwally passes the judgment that Jeremiah's OAN, like the other OAN in the Hebrew Bible, are more likely to be late, postexilic, and spurious.

[14] R. H. Pfeiffer, *Introduction to the Old Testament* (New York: Harper, 1941), 443.

[15] R. W. Nysse, "Keeping Company with Nahum: Reading the Oracles against the Nations as Scripture," *WW* 15 (1995): 412–19, here 412.

the nations in these passages, and to emphasize their common characteristics and shared judgment.

Chapter Two examines Ezek 25, which inaugurates a series of prophecies against the nations in the middle of the prophetic book. I will argue that this chapter with prophecies against Transjordan and Philistia contains an oblique judgment against the land of Judah. The lexical features of the oracles in Ezek 25, such as "possession" (מורשה) and "the glory of the land" (צבי ארץ) are linked to the traditions related to the Promised Land. The language of judgment applied to the nations reflects knowledge of the divine punishments applied to Jerusalem in Ezek 14 and 24. Taken as a whole, the dispossession of the neighboring countries in chapter 25 implicitly affirms the dispossession of the territory of the kingdom of Judah.

Chapter Three centers on the two dirges lifted up over Tyre in Ezek 27 and 28. It will be argued that these dirges reveal extensive connections to the traditions related to the Israelite sanctuary and priesthood pictured in Exod 28, 39, numerous passages of 1 Kings and 2 Chronicles, as well as Ezek 16. With the sudden downfall of Tyre and its ruler in the two dirges, the common lexemes are contextualized in a way that brings suspense, anxiety, and apprehension toward the fate of Jerusalem's cultic sphere.

From Chapter Four comes an analysis of the portrayals of Egypt and Pharaoh in Ezek 29–32. It will be argued that the lexical features of the oracles against Egypt allude to various historical alliances between Egypt and Judah. The lexemes are contextualized in the Egypt oracles in an indirect manner, not only to announce the shared exile, destruction, and demise of Egypt and Judah, but also to anticipate the future restoration of Israel as a nation with Egypt being kept at bay.

The dispossession of the land of Judah, the destruction of the First Temple, and the demise of the kingdom of Judah, weaved intricately into Ezek 25, 26–28, and 29–32 respectively, elicit response and counter-response in later layers of the book of Ezekiel. Chapter Five thus moves beyond Ezek 25–32 and places the attention on the surrounding literary contexts of Ezek 25–32, which include the chronological markers in 24:1 and 33:21, as well as the Seir and the Gog oracles in chapters 35 and 38–39. Representing later editorial activities within the book of Ezekiel, they interpret chapters 25–32 in two directions. One chooses to reinforce the oblique judgment focus by framing Ezek 25–32 with the chronological formulas that accentuate the siege and fall of Jerusalem. Another selects, adapts, and reconfigures the lexical features found in Ezek 25–32, in order to polarize the fate of the nations with that of the restored house of Israel. The aim of this polarization is to herald hope and salvation for the house of Israel.

The Epilogue will return to examine the accusations, which have been mentioned in the Prologue, and which judge all the OAN as vitriolic, xenophobic, intolerant, particularistic, unsafe to read, and thus best to be ignored.

How should we respond to such challenges in reading the biblical texts? Do Ezekiel's OAN really lend themselves to such criticisms? Let us then begin the quest for answers in the subsequent chapters.

# CHAPTER ONE

# SETTING THE COURSE

> The oracles against the nations are not safe to read, and no amount of explanation can make them so.
> Richard W. Nysse

> In der gegenwärtigen kirchlichen Praxis der öffentlichen Verkündigung (z.B. in Predigt und Unterricht) spielen diese Texte überhaupt keine Rolle; nicht einer von ihnen ist als (Teil einer) Perikope einer gottesdienstlichen Lesung oder Predigt vorgesehen. Auch im Rahmen der Lehrpläne begegnen nur ganz selten einmal Hinweise darauf. M.W. ist kein einziger dieser Texte als Lerninhalt vorgesehen. Es sei dahingestellt, ob dieses Ausklammern großer Teile der biblischen Überlieferung mit Recht vollzogen wird.
> Friedrich Fechter

This chapter will situate the present study within a broader scholarly treatment of materials relevant to Ezek 25–32. It will be shown that a vast majority of scholars has presupposed either a contrasting or a parallel status between the nations and YHWH's people. These assumptions too often overgeneralize or constrain the rhetorical roles of Ezek 25–32, without explaining the corpus' relation with the surrounding judgment oracles against Judah in chapters 24 and 33 or clarifying the separation of this corpus from the Mount Seir oracles in chapter 35 and the Gog oracles in chapters 38–39. My approach to these difficulties will be paying attention to the collection's synchronic connections with the surrounding literary contexts and its diachronic links to past traditions and sources. This will justify the main argument fleshed out in this study: The OAN in Ezek 25–32 predominantly, but not exclusively, conveys a message of judgment that highlights the commonality between Judah and the nations, so that the doom of the nations also hints at the dispossession of the Promised Land, the destruction of the Jerusalem temple and priesthood, and the demise of Judah. This message of oblique judgment for the house of Judah generates a lens to view Ezek 25–32 more integrally with the surrounding passages concerning the fall of Judah (chapters 24, 33), and also accounts for the dramatic transformations of the nations into the enemy *par excellence* of the restored house of Israel (chapters 35, 38–39).

## 1. NAVIGATING THE LANDSCAPE

For over half a century, several biblical exegetes, despite the general neglect of or controversy surrounding the OAN in the field of biblical studies, have indeed delved into the analysis of Ezekiel's OAN from a variety of angles, and they have come to different conclusions about the rhetorical meanings and purposes of this corpus. Despite their differences in detail, their conclusions can roughly be categorized into three foci: The "implicit hope," the "hubris" and the "oblique judgment" foci.

Being the foci, they do not exclude each other necessarily. That means, a scholar who focuses on the "implicit hope" rhetoric can still embrace elements of "oblique judgment" in the oracles, albeit to a lesser degree.[1] Moreover, the categorizations of these foci in this section are based on the different rhetorical functions purported for Ezekiel's OAN. In other words, within each of the following rhetorical foci, varied textual approaches possibly exist side by side. It should also be noted that the following survey does not aim to be exhaustive but rather illuminative for the major trend in each focus.[2] More detailed discussions of the scholarly works related to each of the chapters of Ezekiel's OAN will appear in due course in the main body of the study.

### 1.1. THE "IMPLICIT HOPE" FOCUS

According to the advocates of the "implicit hope" focus, the message of the OAN in chapters 25–32 stands in stark contrast with the message of judgment addressed to Judah in the rest of Ezekiel. With the destruction of the foreign nations, the OAN function rhetorically to provide indirect hope for the house

---

[1] For example, J. Strong's dissertation posits that Ezek 29–32 is an indirect judgment against Judah, while Ezek 25 contains a message of indirect salvation for Judah. Thus, his evaluation of Ezekiel's OAN embraces both the first and the third foci ("Ezekiel's Oracles," esp. 6).

[2] Another extensive monograph on Ezekiel's OAN is Fechter, *Bewältigung*. For the moment, this survey of scholarship will not deal with Fechter's monograph directly, since his approach that separates the "original" oracles from the later expansions seems to be too atomistic to provide any emphasis on a particular focus and is thus difficult to be placed in any of the above foci.

of Israel in Ezekiel. Underlying this focus are thus the assumed antagonistic and opposing roles between Israel and the nations. This assumption is perhaps influenced by different theories that have emerged after World War II to account for the origins of the OAN in the Hebrew Bible.[3] The origins of the OAN, according to these theories, can be traced back to various historical contexts that seek the destruction of Israel's political enemies.

In 1950, Bentzen posited a cultic origin for the OAN in Amos 1:2–2:16.[4] For him, Amos's OAN is analogous to the ritual of the second millennium Egyptian execration texts that pronounce doom over and against foreign rulers and other political enemies. Bentzen observes that "the oracles [Amos 1–2] are arranged in an order resembling that of the Egyptian execration texts, following the corners of the world."[5] Also, he notes that the enumerations of the nations in both sets of texts "take special care of their own country, denouncing single traitors and other criminals and so purging the country of all sorts of iniquity."[6] On the basis of these similarities, he postulates that Amos 1–2 has a similar cultic background to that of the Egyptian execration texts. Further influenced by Mowinckel's New Year festival theory,[7] Bentzen locates this cultic background of Amos 1–2 in an enthronement ritual in Israel, in which the celebrated victory of YHWH over "Chaos" or the "foes of God" symbolizes "a festival against the political enemies among Israel's neighbours."[8] In short, the foreign nations, in Bentzen's view, stand diametrically opposite to God's chosen people. His cultic theory is subsequently followed

---

[3] For a survey of these various propositions, see D. L. Petersen, "The Oracles against the Nations: A Form-Critical Analysis," SBLSP (1975): 39–61; D. R. Ulrich, "Proleptic Intrusions of the Final Judgment in Ezekiel's Oracles against the Nations" (PhD Dissertation, Westminster Theological Seminary, 1996), 5–37; S. M. Paul, *Amos: A Commentary on the Book of Amos*, Hermeneia (Minneapolis: Fortress Press, 1991), 7–11; Jones, "Examination," 1–28.

[4] A. Bentzen, "The Ritual Background of Amos 1:2–2:16," *OtSt* 8 (1950): 85–99.

[5] Ibid., 90.

[6] Ibid., 91.

[7] S. Mowinckel treats the foreign nations as the historicized equivalents of the "primeval ocean" and the "power of chaos." He justifies this treatment by citing Ps 46:2–4, 7–8 [Eng. 46:1–3, 6–7], where the uproar of the "nations" (גוים) and the staggering of the "kingdoms" (ממלכות) correspond to the uproar of the "waters" (מים) and the trembling of the "mountains" (הרים). See S. Mowinckel, *The Psalms in Israel's Worship*, trans. D. R. Ap-Thomas, 2 vols. (Oxford: Blackwell, 1962), 1:136–39, 151–54.

[8] Bentzen, "Ritual Background," 93.

and expanded by a few scholars on the one hand,[9] and criticized by several on the other.[10]

In 1966 Margulis, following a group of Israeli scholars (Haran, Seeligmann, and Kaufmann), adopted an alternative theory of the origins of the OAN—the war oracle hypothesis.[11] While Bentzen's cultic theory is based primarily on analogous extrabiblical materials, Margulis derives the origin of the OAN from other biblical texts and reads the OAN as part of the literary heritage of pre-classical prophecy. In fact, Margulis follows Haran, who, in a comparative literary analysis of Isa 15–16 and Jer 48, argues that both compositions are elaborations of the so-called "Song of Mošlim," a war oracle

---

[9] Bentzen's position is followed by G. Fohrer, though Fohrer calls for the dissociation of the form from its original setting in the established institution ("Prophetie und Magie," *ZAW* 78 [1966]: 25–47, esp. 40–44). Bentzen's study also generates an interest in the relationship of treaty curses and the OAN, as demonstrated in H. G. Reventlow, *Das Amt des Propheten bei Amos*, FRLANT 80 (Göttingen: Vandenhoeck & Ruprecht, 1962), 111; F. C. Fensham, "Common Trends in Curses of the Near Eastern Treaties and Kudurru-Inscriptions Compared with Maledictions of Amos and Isaiah," *ZAW* 75 (1963): 155–75; D. R. Hillers, *Treaty-Curses and the Old Testament Prophets*, Sacra scriptura antiquitatibus orientalibus illustrate 16 (Roma: Pontifical Biblical Institute, 1964).

[10] See M. Weiss, "The Pattern of the "Execration Texts" in the Prophetic Literature," *IEJ* 19 (1969): 150–57; S. M. Paul, "Amos 1:3–2:3: A Concatenous Literary Pattern," *JBL* 90 (1971): 398; Albertz, *Exilszeit*, 146–47. They raise three main criticisms against Bentzen's analogy of the biblical OAN with the Egyptian execration texts. First, the OAN considered by Bentzen are restricted to one collection in Amos only and cannot be generalized easily to the rest of the biblical OAN. Second, the fixed geographical structure—south (Nubians), north (Asiatics), west (Libyans), and lastly Egypt—is not unique to the Egyptian execration texts but can also be found in other Egyptian documents, magical or otherwise. Third, the directional order of the nations in Amos appears to be a result of a progressive redactional activity and is entirely different from that in the Egyptian execration texts: northeast (Aram), southwest (Philistia), northwest (Tyre), southeast (Edom, Ammon, Moab), and finally Judah and Israel.

[11] The works of these Israeli scholars are summarized and elucidated in Margulis, "Studies," 15–19. Other proponents of the war oracle hypothesis include Christensen, *Transformations*; Albertz, *Exilszeit*, 147–48; Y. Hoffman, "From Oracle to Prophecy: The Growth, Crystallization and Disintegration of a Biblical Gattung," *JNSL* 10 (1982): 75–81; A. C. Hagedorn, "Looking at Foreigners in Biblical and Greek Prophecy," *VT* 57 (2007): 432–48; N. K. Gottwald, *All the Kingdoms of the Earth: Israelite Prophecy and International Relations* (Minneapolis: Fortress Press, 2007), 49. Meanwhile, J. H. Hayes favours a diversity of forms, original intentions and possible *Sitze im Leben* of the OAN ("The Oracles against the Nations in the Old Testament: Their Usage and Theological Importance" [PhD diss., Princeton Theological Seminary, 1964], 39–81; "The Usage of Oracles against Foreign Nations in Ancient Israel," *JBL* 87 [1968]: 81–92).

reflected in Num 21:27–30.[12] While the origin of Num 21:27–30 is a matter of debate,[13] what Margulis seeks to prove is that this war oracle exerts "the most significant single literary influence" on the OAN tradition.[14] Central to Margulis' more expansive endeavour is the exploration of the war-related motifs such as fire, captivity, exile, dispossession, destruction, and lamentation that link Num 21 to other OAN in the Hebrew Bible.[15] On the basis of these parallels, Margulis concludes that "the literary prototype of, and the source of direct influence, upon the O.A.N. tradition, is the ancient Israelite war-taunt literature or Mošlim tradition, principally, and fragmentarily, represented by the Song of the Mošlim in Numbers 21."[16] The numerous war-related motifs in the received form of the OAN leads to his conclusion that "the constant and abiding concern of the O.A.N. tradition is with Israel's historical, political and military foes."[17]

Christensen's *The Transformations of the War Oracle in Old Testament Prophecy: Studies in the Oracles against the Nations* (1975) presents a more sophisticated view of the war oracle hypothesis. In his extensive doctoral thesis, Christensen draws attention to the antagonism between the Israelites and Syrians in 1 Kgs 20:28. Observing several formal similarities, Christensen suggests that the OAN in Amos 1–2 and Jer 46–51 are oracles derived from

---

[12] The term Mošlim is derived from the Hebrew participle (המשלים) in Num 21:27. It is generally agreed that they are the reciters of proverbs, parables, and riddles found, for instance, in 1 Sam 24:14; 1 Kgs 20:11; Num 23–24; Ezek 17:2–12. Margulis applies the expression "Song of Mošlim" specifically to Num 21:27–30. See also M. Haran, "An Archaic Remnant in Prophetic Literature," *BIES* 13 (1946/47): 7–15, cited in Christensen, *Transformations*, 5; Paul, *Amos*, 7. For more detailed explications of this term, see J. Milgrom, *Numbers: The Traditional Hebrew Text with the New JPS Translation*, JPS Torah Commentary (Philadelphia: Jewish Publication Society of America, 1990), 181; B. A. Levine, *Numbers: A New Translation with Introduction and Commentary*, 2 vols., AB 4, 4A (New York: Doubleday, 1993, 2000), 2:102–3.

[13] Some consider the song to be of Amorite origin, while others argue it to be of Israelite origin. For more discussions and bibliography about this debate, see Margulis, "Studies," 115, n. 2; P. J. Budd, *Numbers*, WBC (Waco: Word, 1984), 245.

[14] Margulis, "Studies," 22. Interestingly, some German scholars are more reticent about the dependence of other OAN on Num 21:27–30. For instance, U. Fistill notes the similarities and disjunctions between Num 21:28–29 and Jer 48:45–46, but then he is of the opinion that Jer 48:45–46 fits the context of chapter 48 better, while Num 21:27–30 seems like a later insertion into its present context in chapter 21. He thus tentatively raises the possibility that Jer 48:45–46 might be a better witness to an earlier tradition than Num 21:27–30 (*Israel und das Ostjordanland: Untersuchungen zur Komposition von Num 21,21–36,13 im Hinblick auf die Entstehung des Buches Numeri*, ÖBS 30 [Frankfurt am Main: Lang, 2007], 72).

[15] Margulis, "Studies," 80–199.

[16] Ibid., 368.

[17] Ibid., 367.

an earlier speech form of the war oracle in passages such as 1 Kgs 20:28.[18] He is prudent enough to stress that the rhetoric of the OAN can be different from the original war oracle. In fact, he envisions two major stages of transformations of the war oracle:

> In Amos 1–2 the earlier war oracle has been transformed into a judgment speech against the nations of the idealized Davidic Empire, with particular focus on Israel. In the hands of Jeremiah, following the defeat of Judah and the exile of King Jehoiachin in 597, the war oracle experienced another transformation as the focus of attention shifted from judgment on the national foes of Yahweh, the suzerain of the nations, to the preservation of the Divine Warrior's people in exile and their ultimate restoration to Zion.[19]

In his words, the war oracle, in the tenth–eighth centuries BCE, was first turned into "the literary mode of a prophetic judgment speech against both military foes and the nation of Israel, together with her political allies" as attested in Amos 1–2.[20] At the beginning of the sixth century BCE, it moved further into "the trans-historical realms of early apocalyptic" as attested in Jeremiah's OAN.[21] As such, Christensen's work displays a flexibility that allows the roles of the foreign nations to take on different significances at various stages of historical development of the OAN.

Probably under the influence of various hypotheses about the origins of the OAN that often maintain the antagonistic roles of the foreign nations in relation to YHWH's people, several exegetes of Ezekiel affirm that Israel's ultimate deliverance is embedded within the judgment upon the nations. Block's two-volume commentary on the book of Ezekiel (1997, 1998) forcefully puts forward such an "implicit hope" message. According to Block, the whole of Ezek 25–32 represents "the judgment of the enemies of God's people,"[22] and "the nations addressed by Ezekiel all represented the enemies of Israel."[23] He further observes that "the words of hope inserted in Ezekiel 28:24–26 function as a fulcrum, dividing Ezekiel's oracles against foreign nations into two sensitively balanced halves, virtually identical in length" (ninety-seven verses in each half).[24] This symmetrical structure enclosing the

---

[18] Christensen, *Transformations*, 31–32, 71.
[19] Ibid., 15.
[20] Ibid., 283.
[21] Ibid.
[22] D. I. Block, *The Book of Ezekiel*, 2 vols., NICOT (Grand Rapids: Eerdmans, 1997–1998), 1:3.
[23] Ibid., 1:4.
[24] Ibid.

salvific fulcrum leads to his assertion that the whole composition of Ezekiel's OAN functions as a "backhanded message of hope" for the house of Israel.[25]

Eichrodt (1970), Fuhs (1986, 1988), and Albertz (2003) emphasize another literary trait within Ezekiel's OAN. They accept as axiomatic the claim that Ezekiel shares with Isa 1–39 and the LXX of Jeremiah a tripartite eschatological structure.[26] As such, Ezekiel comprises three major units, which delineate an evolution toward the salvation of God's people: After the judgment oracles against Israel and Jerusalem in Ezek 1–24, chapter 25 starts with a series of judgments against foreign nations, which glides into a message of hope and restoration found in chapters 33–48. This structure, as Eichrodt puts it, represents "the prophet's mighty forward march from judgment to salvation" and reflects "the history of salvation" in the current shape of the prophetic book.[27] This tripartite eschatological schema, in the words of Fuhs, "geht zurück auf ein zweigliedriges Schema »Unheil - Heil« in zeitlicher Abfolge..., indem nach Gerichtsworten über Israel solche über die Völker eingefügt wurden, die man als Vorbereitung für das Heil Israels verstand."[28] Likewise, Albertz claims that this tripartite arrangement shares a similar literary function with Ezek 38–39, Joel 4, and Zech 14, all of which announce "die eschatologische Konzeption der nachexilischen Zeit," "daß Israels endgültige Rettung erst aufgrund eines großen Völkergerichts stattfinden könne."[29] In a nutshell, those who assert a tripartite eschatological structure for the book of Ezekiel assume that Israel's salvation in chapters 33–48 comes at the expense of the divine retribution executed on the foreign nations in chapters 25–32.

Taken as a whole, this group of scholars, despite their differences in detail, presupposes that the message of judgment of the nations in the OAN heralds

---

[25] Ibid.

[26] On the pervasive scholarly consensus about this tripartite eschatological structure in the prophetic books, see T. D. Mayfield, *Literary Structure and Setting in Ezekiel*, FAT 2/43 (Tübingen: Mohr Siebeck, 2010), 25.

[27] W. Eichrodt, *Ezekiel: A Commentary*, trans. C. Quin, OTL (Philadelphia: The Westminster Press, 1970), 21–22.

[28] H. F. Fuhs, *Ezechiel 1–24*, NEchtB 7 (Würzburg: Echter-Verlag, 1984), 7. Eventually Fuhs in the second volume of his commentary on Ezekiel seems to soften his position and considers only Ezek 25 as conveying the indirect message of hope for the house of Israel, as he states: "Gericht über die Feinde bedeutet Heil für Israel, so in Jes und Jer. In Ez trifft das nur für die Worte gegen die unmittelbaren Nachbarn Israels zu ($25^{1-17}$)" (*Ezechiel 25–48*, NEchtB 22 [Würzbrug: Echter-Verlag, 1988], 135). He considers the status of Tyre and Egypt as different from that of the nations in Ezek 25. Since Tyre and Egypt are represented more as the enemy of Babylon and less as the enemy of Israel in the book of Ezekiel, he thus concludes: "Mit ihrem Widerstand gegen Babel halten Tyrus und Ägypten Jahwes Gericht an Israel auf. Deshalb muß er gebrochen werden" (135).

[29] Albertz, *Exilszeit*, 149.

glimpses of light, hope, and salvation for the house of Israel. These scholars assume that the nations and God's chosen people are diametrically opposed to one another.

1.2. THE "HUBRIS" FOCUS

Unlike those who adhere to the "implicit hope" focus, commentators who posit the "hubris" focus do not emphasize nor conceive the relation between Judah and the foreign nations in opposing terms. Instead, those who concentrate on the self-exaltations of the nations in Ezekiel's OAN highlight more of the guilt and judgment of the nations, independent of those committed by Judah, and they view the nations as standing side by side with Judah under the universal judgment of YHWH.

Zimmerli's monumental commentaries on Ezekiel (1969, Eng. 1979, 1983) are considered to be his *magnum opus*.[30] In this two-volume set, Zimmerli is of the opinion that the OAN in chapters 25–32 had broken up the original connection between 24:25–27 and 33:12–13 and were inserted into their current position in the book.[31] Employing a form-critical approach, he divides these eight chapters of oracles into three main groups: Chapter 25, chapters 26–28, and chapters 29–32.[32] He dates the collection of the oracles against Egypt and Pharaoh in chapters 29–32 and the oracles against Tyre in 26:1–28:19 earlier than the oracles against Judah's neighbouring nations in chapter 25.[33] With regard to the predominant message in Ezekiel's OAN, Zimmerli bases his view on the first two groups of oracles, which can be dated earlier.[34] Even though he allows an "implicit hope" rhetoric to come into play specifically in the prophecies against the Transjordanian nations and Philistia in

---

[30] Besides his commentaries, most of his essays on Ezekiel are collected in *Gottes Offenbarung: Gesammelte Aufsätze zum Alten Testament*, 2nd ed. (München: Chr. Kaiser Verlag, 1963). The translated collection in English is entitled *I AM Yahweh* (Atlanta: John Knox, 1982). In these essays, Zimmerli never specifically elaborated upon the OAN as he did with other topics within the prophetic book.

[31] W. Zimmerli, *A Commentary on the Book of the Prophet Ezekiel*, 2 vols., Hermeneia (Philadelphia: Fortress Press, 1979, 1983), 1:72.

[32] Zimmerli posits a "school of the prophet" who took part in the ongoing process of "updating tradition" to preserve the prophecies of Ezekiel (ibid., 1:68–74; idem, "Das Phänomen der 'Fortschreibung' im Buche Ezechiel," in *Prophecy: Essays Presented to Georg Fohrer on His Sixty-Fifth Birthday 6 September 1980*, ed. J. A. Emerton [Berlin: de Gruyter, 1980], 174–91).

[33] Zimmerli, *Ezekiel*, 1:72–73.

[34] Ibid., 1:60–61, 72–73.

chapter 25,[35] he still concludes sweepingly that the charge of hubris is "a stereotypical feature of the prophetic oracles against foreign nations."[36] He further justifies this focus on hubris by stressing the size of the second and third group of oracles, in which Ezekiel attacks Egypt and Tyre primarily because of their excessive pride. Egypt is accused of its overweening arrogance (e.g., 29:19; 30:4, 10, 15; 31:2, 18; 32:12, 16) and the Tyrian ruler of his "pretension of behaving like God" (28:1–10).[37] With this emphasis on the arrogance of the nations, Zimmerli, however, seems to be puzzled by the link between the OAN and the prophet's own message about the house of Israel. He questions Ezekiel's concern for the hubris of the foreign nations, when "nothing is said of the prophet's task to be a prophet to the nations" (cf. 3:6).[38]

Greenberg (1983, 1997), another towering figure in the scholarship on Ezekiel, is famous for his stress on a synchronic perspective on Ezekiel. Different from the form-critical approach displayed by Zimmerli, Greenberg emphasizes reading the book of Ezekiel as a unified whole written by "an individual authorial mind and hand."[39] Despite that, like Zimmerli, Greenberg

---

[35] His view on Ezekiel 25 is rather ambiguous. On the one hand, Zimmerli suggests that chapter 25 heralds "a new act of mercy by Yahweh towards his people and his mocked and despised land (36:13)" (ibid., 1:61). On the other hand, he stresses not YHWH's mercy to his people, but the "self-righteousness" of the Transjordanian states as the motivation of divine judgment (ibid., 2:19–20).

[36] Ibid., 1:60.

[37] Ibid., 1:61.

[38] *Contra* Jeremiah's commission as a prophet to the nations (Jer 1:2–10). See ibid., 1:60.

[39] M. Greenberg, *Ezekiel 1–20: A New Translation with Introduction and Commentary*, AB 22 (Garden City: Doubleday, 1983), 396; idem, "What Are Valid Criteria for Determining Inauthentic Matter in Ezekiel?" in *Ezekiel and His Book: Textual and Literary Criticism and Their Interrelation*, ed. J. Lust, BETL 74 (Leuven: Leuven University Press, 1986), 123–35. Greenberg is not the first to postulate the single authorship of Ezekiel, which has been in view since the nineteenth century. E.g., S. R. Driver claims: "No critical question arises in connexion with the authorship of the book, the whole from the beginning to end bearing unmistakably the stamp of a single mind" (*An Introduction to the Literature of the Old Testament* [New York: Charles Scribner's Sons, 1891; repr., Gloucester: Peter Smith, 1972], 279). Cf. R. Smend, *Der Prophet Ezechiel*, Kurzgefasstes exegetisches Handbuch zum Alten Testament 8 (Leipzig: S. Hirzel Verlag, 1880), XVI, XXI. A minority view assumes a single authorship but claims the book is Pseudepigraphy produced by a later writer from the Persian or Hellenistic periods. E.g., L. Zunz, "Bibelkritisches," *ZDMG* 27 (1875): 676–88; J. Becker, "Erwägungen zur Ezechielischen Frage," in *Künder des Wortes: Beiträge zur Theologie der Propheten*, ed. L. Ruppert et al. (Würzbrug: Echter, 1982), 137–49; C. C. Torrey, *Pseudo-Ezekiel and the Original Prophecy*, YOSR 18 (New Haven: Yale University Press, 1930), 108–12. On the influence of Greenberg's holistic

also highlights the central theme of hubris in Ezek 26–32. In Greenberg's opinion, chapters 26–28 display the insolence of Tyre through Tyre's pompous wealth and through the Tyrian ruler's striving to become an equal of YHWH.[40] As he sums up, "from the beginning the prophet associated Tyre's gloating over Jerusalem's ruin with her boundless self-exaltation."[41] By positing the concept of hubris, he aims to distance the punishments inflicted on Tyre from what he terms as "an outburst of patriotic petulance on Ezekiel's part."[42] Commenting on the slaying of the Nile monster in Ezek 29:1–16, Greenberg claims: "The main issue of the oracle is Egypt's pride as epitomized in the boastful self-sufficiency of Pharaoh."[43] Also, the fall of the cosmic tree in another Egypt oracle in Ezek 31, according to him, conveys first and foremost a message concerning "the downfall of the proud" to assert YHWH's sovereignty over the nations.[44] Even more severe than Zimmerli, Greenberg stresses that no material hope is offered in Ezek 25. In spite of the nations' gloating and vengeance upon Jerusalem in Ezek 25, "no material advantage to Israel results from it [the act of judgment on the nations]."[45] Ezekiel's characteristic concern remains not the material interest of Israel, but "the injured majesty of God."[46] The transgressions committed by all the nations, in Greenberg's opinion, belong to the violations of "a universal principle" or "a universal morality."[47] These violations have everything to do with God's sovereignty, but signify "no particular favor toward the victimized Judahites."[48]

Following Greenberg's "holistic interpretation," Premstaller's monograph on Ezekiel's OAN (2005) focuses on the received shape of the MT Ezek 25–32 and the other smaller collections in 21:33–37; 35; 38–39.[49] He perceives the hubris of the foreign nations as the most direct challenge to YHWH's universal sovereignty and supremacy. For instance, in his analysis of Ezek 28:1–

---

model, see also K.-F. Pohlmann, *Ezechiel: Der Stand der theologischen Diskussion* (Darmstadt: Wissenschaftliche Buchgesellschaft, 2008), 33–48.

[40] M. Greenberg, *Ezekiel 21–37: A New Translation with Introduction and Commentary*, AB 22A (Garden City: Doubleday, 1997), 540–41, 577–78.

[41] Ibid., 541.

[42] Ibid., 540.

[43] Ibid., 610.

[44] Ibid., 645.

[45] Ibid., 526.

[46] Ibid., 527.

[47] Ibid., 577, 593, 611.

[48] Ibid., 611.

[49] Premstaller states his methodology clearly: "Wie die Mongraphien von H.D. Van Dijk, L. Boadt und M.A. Corral sowie auf den Spuren der „holistic interpretation" von M. Greenberg und D.I. Block beschränkt sich die Textanalyse dabei auf den vorliegenden Endtext ..." (*Fremdvölkersprüche*, 8).

10, he claims: "Jeder vergleichbaren Selbstverherrlichung und Arroganz wird JHWH damit ein Ende bereiten."[50] Subsequently, in an overview of the reasons for judgment against Tyre, Premstaller stresses that Tyre's hubris constitutes one of the main reasons for the impending divine judgment: "Die Gründe, weshalb Tyrus das göttliche Gericht auf sich lädt, sind somit zugleich wirtschaftspolitischer Natur als auch darin zu finden, dass Tyrus als Symbol menschlicher Hybris galt."[51] Thereafter, throughout his monograph, Premstaller highlights the universal sovereignty of YHWH in light of the arrogant provocations of the nations. In regard to the oracle against Sidon in Ezek 28, Premstaller concludes: "Als der Herr der Geschichte wie aller Nationen macht JHWH hier keinen Unterschied."[52] In the summary to the punishment on Egypt in Ezek 31, he similarly states: "Grundbotschaft von c.31 ist es ja auch, dass JHWH nicht nur als Gott Israels für sein Volk sowie für die mit ihm in Verbindung stehenden Nachbarstaaten zuständig ist, sondern in gleicher Weise weltweit für alle Reiche und deren Herrscher."[53] He does not seem to draw a distinction between the concerns of Ezek 25–32 and those found within the smaller collections in 21:33–37; 35; 38–39. In the conclusion of his monograph, Premstaller unequivocally stresses the universal sovereignty of YHWH as the main message throughout the whole courpus of the OAN, which serves to justify the divine judgment on both YHWH's people and the nations: "Den Völkersprüchen des Ezechielbuches liegt die Überzeugung zu Grunde, dass JHWH nicht nur über sein eigenes Volk herrscht, sondern in seiner Allmacht auch die anderen Völker kontrolliert."[54] In short, according to Premstaller, the concept of hubris offers the most important reason for judgment that allows YHWH to extend his judgment beyond Judah and to other nations.

To sum up, the advocates of the "hubris" focus concentrate less on the interactions or conflicts between the nations and the kingdom of Judah. The hubris of the nations has little to do with their offenses against Judah, but poses the most direct challenge toward YHWH's universal sovereignty. These scholars perceive the nations and Judah as standing side by side under YHWH's all-encompassing judgment.

1.3. THE "OBLIQUE JUDGMENT" FOCUS

If the "hubris" focus fully recognizes the nations and Judah as *separate*, standing *independently of each other* under the universal judgment of YHWH, the focus on the "oblique judgment" rhetoric presents the relation of the nations

---

[50] Ibid., 103.
[51] Ibid., 121.
[52] Ibid., 133.
[53] Ibid., 184–85.
[54] Ibid., 261.

and Judah in a much more complex, intricate, disturbing, and unsettling light. Exegetes have begun to highlight bits and pieces of information, which demonstrate the shared characteristics between the foreign nations and Judah, and thus Ezekiel's OAN can also contain indictments directed obliquely at the people in Jerusalem, the capital city of the kingdom of Judah.

With regard to Ezek 25, Schwagmeier (2004) briefly comments that the judgment upon the Transjordanian nations and Philistia is linked linguistically to the punishment upon Judah in chapters 1–24. Schwagmeier's main interest lies in the textual differences between the Masoretic and Greek traditions. As such, his monograph pays more attention to the materials related to Ezek 36–39, where the differences between the MT and P967 are the greatest.[55] Despite that, his study still provides stimulating insights into the lexemes and hermeneutics of other chapters in the book of Ezekiel. In particular, he cites the lexical correspondences between 24:21 and 25:3, where the noun מקדש "sanctuary" is paired with the root חלל "to profane."[56] Furthermore, he notices the lack of date formula at the beginning of chapter 25. On this basis, he asserts the connections between Ezek 25 and the rest of the Judah and Ammon oracles found in previous chapters of Ezekiel: "Ez 25 gibt sich der Leserschaft somit durch die Ammonitertextbrücke (25,1ff/21,23ff) und die erwähnten Leitwortberührungen als mit dem vorderen Teil des Buches verbunden zu erkennen."[57] Having stressed this fluid boundary between the judgment oracles in chapter 25 and the preceding prophecies in the same prophetic book, he further sums up: "In diesem Zusammenhang gelesen, wird dem Leser deutlich, daß es Israel wie den Völkern ergeht (vgl. 25,8) und den Völkern wie Israel, was auch die Dreiheit der Adressaten in 25,3 und die Dreiheit in 21, 2.7 nahelegt."[58] In short, the fate of Judah, in his opinion, is akin to the fates of the other nations.[59] Schwagmeier's perspective, nevertheless, is an anomaly among a vast majority of scholars who insist on an "implicit hope" message in Ezek 25.[60]

---

[55] P. Schwagmeier, "Untersuchungen zu Textgeschichte und Entstehung des Ezechielbuches in masoretischer und griechischer Überlieferung" (PhD diss., Universität Zürich, 2004), 42–43. He is of the opinion that P967 attests to an older form of the book of Ezekiel than the MT (313–17).

[56] Ibid., 261.

[57] Ibid.

[58] Ibid.

[59] Even though H. G. Reventlow observes several lexical and formal connections between Ezek 25 and the rest of the prophetic book, he spares little space to discuss the meaning of these connections in the received context, and briefly draws the conclusion that the foreign nations incur YHWH's wrath due to their acts of undermining the divine election of Israel (*Wächter über Israel: Ezechiel und seine Tradition*, BZAW 82 [Berlin: Töpelmann, 1962], 139–43).

[60] E.g., L. C. Allen, *Ezekiel 20–48*, WBC 29 (Waco: Word Books, 1990), 69; J. A. Bewer, *The Book of Ezekiel in the Authorized Version with Introductions and Critical*

As for Ezekiel's Tyre oracles, the portrayal of the Tyrian king especially in 28:11–19 attracts much scholarly attention. In 1964, Yaron observed the link of the Tyrian figure to the Israelite priesthood. The list of precious stones worn by the Tyrian king in the MT of Ezek 28:13, as he notes, reflects "an astonishing similarity" with the concentrated accumulation of the precious stones inlaid upon the high priest's pectoral in Exod 28:17–20; 39:10–13, albeit with minuses and in a different order.[61] According to Yaron, the similarities between Ezek 28 and the two excerpts in Exodus can be easily accounted for, since "in the Ancient Near East the king fulfilled many cultic functions."[62] He further concludes that "it is quite conceivable that the Palestinian princelets before the Israelite conquest of Canaan were equipped with such a pectoral, taken over by the Davidic ruler of Jerusalem."[63] In short, he thinks that Ezek 28 represents a Canaanite story that has been adopted by the Israelites. Such a mythological interpretation of Ezek 28 in relation to the Canaanite traditions makes Yaron stand in the same line with the Ugaritic scholar Marvin Pope, who famously suggests that the (reconstructed) Ugaritic myth concerning the deposed El and his subsequent exile into the underworld forms the background of the downfall of the Tyrian king in Ezek 27.[64] This has become a standard view in scholarship.[65]

---

*Notes*, 2 vols., Harpers Annotated Bible 9 (New York: Harper, 1954), 5; B. Gosse, "Le Recueil d'Oracles contre les Nations d'Ezéchiel XXV-XXXII dans la Rédaction du Livre d'Ezéchiel," *RB* 93 (1986): 535–62, esp. 546; Block, *Ezekiel*, 2:3–4; Fuhs, *Ezechiel 25–48*, 135; Strong, "Ezekiel's Oracles," 170.

[61] Both of the Exodus passages list out twelve precious stones: Ruby, topaz, emerald, turquoise, sapphire, diamond, jacinth, agate, amethyst, beryl, onyx, and jasper. The MT of Ezek 28:13 does not contain jacinth, agate, and amethyst, and arranges the rest of the nine stones in a different order. See K. Yaron, "The Dirge over the King of Tyre," *ASTI* 3 (1964): 28–57, esp. 35.

[62] Yaron justifies his position by citing biblical examples such as Gen 14:18–20; Ps 110:4; Judg 8:24–28; 1 Sam 14:24, 34, 35; 2 Sam 6; Amos 7:13 ("Dirge," 39–40). However, he does not include any ancient Near Eastern sources outside the Hebrew Bible to support his statement.

[63] Ibid., 40.

[64] M. H. Pope, *El in the Ugaritic Texts*, VTSup 2 (Leiden: Brill, 1955), 97–102. See the objection to Pope's thesis in O. Loretz, "Der Wohnort Els nach ugaritischen Texten und Ez 28,1–2.6–10," *UF* 21 (1989): 259–67.

[65] For further examples of interpreting Ezek 28 as derived from either the Mesopotamia or the Canaanite-Phoenician traditions, see G. Widengren, *Sakrales Königtum im Alten Testament und im Judentum*, Franz-Delitzsch Vorlesungen 1952 (Stuttgart: Kohlhammer, 1955), 26–33; idem, "Early Hebrew Myths and Their Interpretation," in *Myth, Ritual, and Kingship*, ed. S. H. Hooke (Oxford: Clarendon Press, 1958), 165–76; H. Gunkel, *Schöpfung und Chaos in Urzeit und Endzeit* (Göttingen: Vandenhoeck und Ruprecht, 1921), 148–49; J. Herrmann, *Ezechiel*, KAT 11 (Leipzig: Deichert,

In 1987, Wilson wrote an article, in which he tentatively accepted this extrabiblical origin of Ezek 28. He affirms that: "On somewhat firmer ground is the argument advanced by Marvin Pope, who interprets Ezekiel 28 against the background of the El myths embedded in the Ugaritic texts."[66] Wilson, however, is careful to state that such a background does not explain the rhetorical functions of the MT in an Israelite context. Instead of focusing on the ancient Near East materials, he makes use of LXX Ezek 28:13, which lists all of the precious jewels mentioned in Exod 28:17–20; 39:10–13, in order to support and illumine the reading in the corresponding passage in the MT. Upon comparison of the two versions, he rather hastily jumps to the conclusion that the explicit reference to the priestly breastplate in MT Ezek 28:13 means "to *identify* the figure in the garden as the Israelite high priest."[67] He claims further that the dirge in chapter 28 must be read as an oblique oracle addressed to the "upper-class bureaucrats and priests taken into captivity during the first deportation."[68] Wilson then concludes briefly that the text was later reinterpreted upon its later attachment to a genuine anti-Tyrian oracle in vv. 1–10, so that "the original point of the unit became less clear."[69] A similar conclusion was independently reached by Bogaert earlier in 1983.[70] Recent commentators, however, are more preoccupied with the presentations of the Tyrian king as either an angelic being or a primal man than with the link of the Tyrian king to the Israelite priesthood.[71]

---

1924), 182–84; J. Morgenstern, "The Mythological Background of Psalm 82," *HUCA* 14 (1939): 111–14.

[66] R. R. Wilson, "The Death of the King of Tyre: The Editorial History of Ezekiel 28," in *Love and Death in the Ancient Near East: Essay in Honor of Marvin H. Pope*, ed. J. H. Marks and R. M. Good (Guilford: Four Quarters, 1987), 213.

[67] Ibid., 214. Emphasis mine.

[68] Ibid.

[69] Ibid.

[70] P.-M. Bogaert, "Montagne Sainte, Jardin d'Éden et Sanctuaire (Hiérosolymitain) dans un Oracle d'Ézéchiel contre le Prince de Tyr (Éz 28,11–19)," *Homo Religiosus* 9 (1983): 146: "Il me paraît donc permis de proposer, à côté d'autres explications de la complainte contre le roi de Tyr, celle selon laquelle il s'agirait à l'origine d'un oracle contre Jerusalem, ultérieurement retrouné contre Tyr." Bogaert suggests that behind the oracle witnessed by the LXX is an earlier version which has been directed initially against the high priest of Jerusalem, and which transforms later into a dirge over the ruler of Tyre after Israel has found itself in exile.

[71] E.g., G. A. Anderson, "Ezekiel 28, the Fall of Satan, and the Adam Books," in *Literature on Adam and Eve: Collected Essays*, ed. G. A. Anderson et al., SVTP 15 (Leiden: Brill, 2000), 133–47; J. Barr, "'Thou Art the Cherub:' Ezekiel 28:14 and the Post-Ezekiel Understanding of Genesis 2–3," in *Priests, Prophets and Scribes: Essays on the Formation and Heritage of Second Temple Judaism in Honour of Joseph Blenkinsopp*, ed. E. Ulrich et al., JSOTSup 149 (Sheffield: JSOT Press, 1992), 213–23; D. E. Callender Jr., "The Primal Man in Ezekiel and the Image of God," SBLSP (1998):

Strikingly unique and distinctive vocabulary shared between Ezekiel's Egypt and Judah oracles occupy scholarly discussions of Ezek 29–32. In an article entitled "The Rhetorical Strategies in Ezekiel's Oracles of Judgment" written in 1986, Boadt judges these vocabulary correspondences as "hardly an accidental coincidence since almost all of these are unique to Ezekiel in the Bible."[72] In particular, "the assemblage of terminology in this passage [Ezek 17]," in his opinion, "brings to mind rather the description of the great cedar tree in Ezekiel 31."[73] Both oracles employ specialized words such as "treetop" (צמרת), "planting place" (מטע) and "boughs" (דליות), which are rarely found elsewhere in the Hebrew Bible.[74] On this basis, Boadt suggests that the linguistic connections illustrate "the comparison between Zedekiah and the Egyptian pharaoh, that both are guilty of the same charge, a divine hubris."[75] Boadt's articulation of this point of view, however, remains limited in scope, being confined to only six out of the nineteen pages of the article.

The fullest and most recent exposition of the dialogue between the Judah and Egypt oracles in Ezekiel is Marzouk's monograph. According to Marzouk's central thesis, the monstrification of Egypt in Ezek 29–32 can be explained by the idolatrous and adulterous intimacy between Egypt and Israel in chapters 20 and 23.[76] For Marzouk, Egypt poses a danger concerning the assimilation of Israel's religious identity. He further justifies this thesis by pointing to the "similar terminology" and "shared language" used to describe both Egypt and Israel.[77] Daringly, Marzouk asserts:

> The shared language as a literary device amplifies the similarities between Israel and Egypt in terms of their moral chaos and in terms of the judgment that falls upon them. The shared language portrays Egypt as Israel's double and thus it underlines the common elements of the shared identity between Egypt and Israel.[78]

---

606–25; C. A. Newsom, "A Maker of Metaphors: Ezekiel's Oracles against Tyre," in *"The Place is Too Small for Us:" The Israelite Prophets in Recent Scholarship*, ed. R. P. Gordon, Sources for Biblical and Theological Study 5 (Winona Lake: Eisenbrauns, 1995), 191–204.

[72] Boadt, "Rhetorical Strategies," 182–200, esp. 198.

[73] Ibid., 193.

[74] Ibid., 193–94.

[75] Ibid., 194. Unlike the scholars in the category of the "hubris" focus, Boadt views hubris as not only a characteristic of the nations, but also that of the kingdom of Judah.

[76] S. A. Marzouk, *Egypt as a Monster in the Book of Ezekiel*, FAT 2/76 (Tübingen: Mohr Siebeck, 2015), 115–53.

[77] Ibid., 118.

[78] Ibid. Marzouk also states: "Shared language brings to the fore some shared elements of identity between Egypt and Israel" (124).

Since Egypt in Ezekiel is portrayed more as a political and religious ally of Judah than as an oppressor,[79] the judgment upon Egypt in chapters 29–32 is intricately linked to the punishments upon Judah. Despite the fact that Marzouk does not discuss his analyses of the Egypt oracles in relation to the Tyre, Transjordan, and Philistia oracles in Ezekiel, Marzouk's work still offers the best recent attempt in articulating the breaking down of the boundary of identity between Egypt and Judah in Ezekiel. In the end, Egypt becomes the *alter ego* of Judah.[80]

Up to this point, our survey of the scholarship, categorized into three foci, opens up a wide array of possibilities for the interpretation of Ezek 25–32. The stress on the "implicit hope" rhetoric, though generalizing the opposition between foreign nations and Judah in Ezekiel's OAN too much, has the potential to clarify a few late additions within Ezek 25–32 that anticipate the identity reformulation and reconstruction central in later chapters of the same prophetic book. The emphasis on the "hubris" of the nations, while too often reading the OAN in isolation from the larger context of the book, draws out the challenge of the nations to YHWH's sovereignty in several passages and highlights a central concern for the universal recognition of YHWH by all nations. Meanwhile, the "oblique judgment" model reminds us to take into account other oracles that display semantic links to the OAN, pointing out the instability of identity boundary and the intricate dependence of "us" on the "others." Yet, the discovery remains limited in scope, one group of studies seldom engages or interacts with another, and it remains to be seen if this "oblique judgment" focus can be justified as the predominant message across Ezek 25–32. It is precisely at this point that we need to provide a fuller account of the positives and negatives related to each focus.

---

[79] "The prophet's discourse on the exodus event neither recalls an oppression and liberation nor does it speak of the parting of the sea as Second Isaiah does (Isa 51:8–10). The prophet, rather, remembers Israel's time in Egypt in terms of idolatry (Ezekiel 20:5–9) and 'adultery' (23:1–4)..." (ibid., 29).

[80] For other examples of the "Israelitization" of the foreigners or the "Otherization" of the Israelites in the Hebrew Bible, see E. Ben Zvi, "Othering, Selfing, 'Boundarying' and 'Cross-Boundarying' as Interwoven with Socially Shared Memories: Some Observations," in *Imagining the Other and Constructing Israelite Identity in the Early Second Temple Period*, ed. E. Ben Zvi and D. V. Edelman, LHBOTS 456 (London: Bloomsbury, 2014), 20–40. As Ben Zvi wisely observes, "these sites and narratives shaped a discursively significant series of 'in-between' realms that communicated and socialized the community in terms of ternary systems rather than simple, clear-cut Us vs. Them systems of categorization" (21).

## 2. Identifying the Obstacles

As noted, several commentators in the "implicit hope" focus work from a putative war or cultic origin of Ezekiel's OAN. The important insight of these hypotheses about the origins of the OAN, in my view, lies in their emphasis on the wider connections between these oracles and the ancient cultures from which they are derived. The OAN, according to these hypotheses, are to be understood in terms of either cultic practices or war settings in ancient Israel. By detecting shared formal features among texts, the hypotheses provide lenses to view the OAN as a result of continuous literary creativity, whether more broadly in ancient Near Eastern cultural milieus, or more narrowly within the biblical texts themselves.

In the survey of the "hubris" focus, we have observed that the scholars there tend to place the OAN independent of the Judah oracles, and they thus understand YHWH's acts of judgment to be applied in a parallel or non-intersecting line to both the nations and Judah. The transgressions committed by the nations belong to the violations of a universal standard of morality, while the kingdom of Judah is mainly judged because of their violations of the particular covenant with YHWH. This position has the advantage of providing a reason that justifies YHWH's extension of his sovereignty not only over Judah, but also over all other nations.

In what follows, however, I will note that the "implicit hope" focus and the "hubris" focus cannot adequately explain the rhetorical functions of Ezek 25–32. At one end of the spectrum, I will argue, the "implicit hope" focus falls prey to a danger of over-generalizing the contrast between the nations and Judah that is either absent or not evident in many parts of the oracles. At the other end of the spectrum, the "hubris" focus unwarrantedly isolates and confines Ezekiel's OAN to only one literary factor (hubris), without considering other motifs that link to the surrounding passages of the same prophetic book. The critique of both approaches will then prepare us for a fuller exposition of the potential of the "oblique judgment" focus that offers a more integral reading of Ezek 25–32 within the literary context of the same book.

### 2.1. Ideological Overgeneralization

The discussions concerning the impact of the hypothesized origins upon the OAN too often display a generalizing tendency, and thus exaggerate the animus between the nations and God's people. More perceptively, proponents of the war oracle theory including Christensen and Hoffman stress the power of transformations, such that the content of the OAN, as in Amos 1–2, could become an epitome of Israel's fate.[81] For them, the canonical prophets were

---

[81] Christensen, *Transformations*, 283; Hoffman, "Oracle," 81.

capable of employing and manipulating the traditional genres innovatively to convey a message of oblique judgment to the house of Israel. The present collections of the OAN thus represent a stage of development distant from their hypothesized origins; whatever generic constraints and typical settings that might have belonged to the oracles at some early stages can be loosened and transformed in various ways.[82] Nonetheless, the importance of this transformed rhetoric has not been sufficiently stressed. Thus, having compared the OAN in the Hebrew Bible innovatively with the Greek prophecies against foreigners, Hagedorn, an advocate of the war oracle theory, concludes sweepingly that "the context of war seems to be an important point of reference" in both compositions, and subsequently "the announcement of doom for the other [foreign nations] serves as an implicit announcement of salvation for the group that hears the oracles."[83] Underlying this "implicit message of salvation" is his general conviction that "the nations represent Israel's enemy" in all biblical OAN.[84]

Similarly, Block's view to judge the whole OAN to be about the implicit hope for Israel falls prey to overgeneralization. It is true that Ezek 28:24–26 draws a contrast between the destruction of all those who have scorned Israel (v. 24) and the restoration of the house of Israel (v. 25).[85] The pericope's presupposition of the exile before the ingathering of the house of Israel points to the fact that this promise of restoration might be a secondary element, and thus might indicate a later attempt in casting the destructions of the nations as a proclamation of an implicit hope for Israel.[86] This attempt, however, does not automatically reduce the whole composition of Ezekiel's OAN to be about the implicit hope for the house of Israel. We need to avoid generalizing the message found in a single textual unit to the whole OAN in the prophetic book. In fact, Block's conclusion highlights the deeply entrenched ideological presupposition that all foreign nations are enemies of God's people.

---

[82] Petersen cautions: "To identify the original function of a genre or tradition is not to explain the use to which the genre or tradition is put by a later writer" ("Oracles," 55).

[83] Hagedorn, "Foreigners," 448. Even though he does indicate that Judah was envisioned as the foreign enemy in certain texts (439), he does not elaborate on this, nor takes this into account in his conclusion.

[84] Ibid., 438.

[85] Another messenger formula in v. 25 breaks the oracle directed mainly against Sidon in vv. 20–24 from the unit concentrating on the regathering of the house of Israel (vv. 25–26).

[86] N. Mendecki dates vv. 25–26 as post-deuteronomistic (ca. 300 B.C.E.), as in Ezek 34:25–30 and 39:23–29 ("Postdeuteronomistische Redaktion von Ez 28, 25–26?" *BN* 73 [1994]: 66–73). On the secondary nature of this more upbeat textual unit (Ezek 28:20–24, 25–26), see Zimmerli, *Ezekiel*, 2:100–101; Eichrodt, *Ezekiel*, 387–98; Fechter, *Bewältigung*, 260–81.

Such a presupposition also underlines the view that Ezekiel, like First Isaiah and LXX Jeremiah, follows the tripartite eschatological structure, which in turn implies that Israel's salvation comes at the expense of the divine acts of judgment on the foreign nations.[87] Nevertheless, the points of demarcation within the tripartite structure are far from clear-cut. Rightly, Sweeney questions such a rigid theological understanding of the structure across the Major Prophets.[88] Even though a tripartite eschatological structure is applicable to First Isaiah, Sweeney points out that the present form of Isa 1–39 does not constitute a full prophetic book.[89] Also, the MT of Jeremiah displays a very different arrangement from the eschatological structure in the LXX, with the OAN coming after chapter 45, instead of after 25:13 as in the LXX.[90] The beginning of the third major section within the book of Ezekiel is similarly problematic. In fact, when viewed as a whole, instead of being followed immediately by promises of restoration, Ezek 25–32 is sandwiched between chapters 24 and 33, which accentuate the siege and fall of Jersualem respectively. After the destruction of the foreign nations, the restoration of Israel is

---

[87] We have surveyed the positions of Eichrodt, Fuhs, and Albertz in the foregoing section about the "implicit hope" focus.

[88] M. A. Sweeney, "The Assertion of Divine Power in Ezekiel 33:21–39:29," in idem, *Form and Intertexuality in Prophetic and Apocalyptic Literature*, FAT 45 (Tübingen: Mohr Siebeck, 2005), 156–72, here 156–57.

[89] The complex textual development of the book of Isaiah can be glimpsed from U. F. Berges, *The Book of Isaiah: Its Composition and Final Form*, trans. M. C. Lind (Sheffield: Sheffield Phoenix Press, 2012), 509–11. He suggests that chapters 1–32* and 40–52* in Isaiah were initially two independent core texts that were later joined by chapter 33 in the middle of the fifth century in Jerusalem. The subsequent additions in the order of chapters 34–35; 60–62; 36–39; 24–27 came later to shape the present book of Isaiah.

[90] Also, the MT places the vision of the cup of wrath (25:15–38) before the oracles against Egypt, Philistia, Moab, Ammon, Edom, Damascus, Kedar, Hazor, Elam, and Babel. The LXX places the vision of the cup of wrath (32) at the end of the oracles against Elam, Egypt, Babylon, Philistia, Edom, Ammon, Kedar, Hazor, Damascus, and Moab. Cf. E. Tov, "The Literary History of the Book of Jeremiah in the Light of Its Textual History," in *Empirical Models for Biblical Criticism*, ed. J. H. Tigay (Philadelphia: University of Pennsylvania Press, 1985), 211–37; K. Schmid, "The Book of Jeremiah," in *T&T Clark Handbook of the Old Testament*, ed. J. C. Gertz et al., trans. J. Adams-Maßmann (New York: T&T Clark International, 2012), 431–33; W. McKane, *A Critical and Exegetical Commentary on Jeremiah*, 2 vols., ICC (Edinburgh: T&T Clark, 1986), 1:xv–xxxi; 2:clxiv; G. Fischer, "Jer 25 und die Fremdvölkersprüche: Unterschiede zwischen hebräischem und griechischem Text," *Bib* 72 (1991): 474–99; C. J. Sharp, " 'Take another Scroll and Write:' A Study of the LXX and the MT of Jeremiah's Oracles against Egypt and Babylon," *VT* 47 (1997): 487–516.

not as immediately effective as often considered. This calls into question assertions that the destruction of the foreign nations stands in a causal relation to the restoration of Israel.

In fact, if we peruse ancient historiography related to the sixth century BCE, a period that is contemporaneous to the literary setting of the book of Ezekiel, the relations between Judah and some nations are cast in a rather ambiguous light and do not necessarily exude animosity. In the sixth year of Nebuchadrezzar's reign (599–598 BCE), the Ammonites indeed served with the Chaldeans in suppressing Jehoiakim's rebellion (2 Kgs 24:2), and perhaps in return for this service the Ammonites were given a free hand in Gilead (Jer 49:2).[91] Despite that, a few years later, in 593 BCE, Ammon was listed in a group of foreign nations who sent their representatives to Jerusalem during the reign of Zedekiah the son of Josiah (Jer 27:3).[92] The foreign envoys probably arrived there to hatch a plan with the king of Judah to rebel against Babylon. This prompted Jeremiah the prophet to point out the futility of rebelling against the dominion of Babylon, since YHWH had given all the nations to Nebuchadnezzar the king of Babylon (Jer 27:4–8).[93] Ammon probably remained in this anti-Babylonian pact, since Ezek 21:23–28 (Eng. 21:18–23) shows how difficult it was for the king of Babylon to decide whether to attack Jerusalem or "Rabbah of the Ammonites."[94] In addition, 2 Kgs 25:4–5 narrates Zedekiah's evident attempt to flee to Transjordan.[95] Jer 40:11–12 records refugees from Judah who found asylum in Ammon. Taken altogether, Ammon was likely an important ally of Judah in its attempt to break away from Babylon.

Moab's relation with Judah was also not always fueled with enmity during the sixth century BCE. It is true that the Moabites, like the Ammonites, were

---

[91] O. Lipschits, *The Fall and Rise of Jerusalem: Judah under Babylonian Rule* (Winona Lake: Eisenbrauns, 2005), 52–53; B. Oded and L. I. Rabinowitz, "Ammon, Ammonites," *EncJud* 2:86; J. M. Miller and J. H. Hayes, *A History of Ancient Israel and Judah*, 2nd ed. (London: SCM Press, 2006), 467.

[92] For the dating of the meeting to the first year of the reign of King Zedekiah (597 BCE), see Miller and Hayes, *History*, 469–70. For the dating of the meeting to 593 BCE on the basis of the title of Jer 28, which refers instead to the fourth year of the reign of King Zedekiah, see Lipschits, *Fall*, 64, n. 98; Oded and Rabinowitz, "Ammon," 86.

[93] Miller and Hayes, *History*, 470; Lipschits, *Fall*, 71.

[94] Miller and Hayes, *History*, 475; Lipschits, *Fall*, 72; Oded and Rabinowitz, "Ammon," 86.

[95] For the suggestion that Zedekiah was fleeing specifically to Ammon, see Miller and Hayes, *History*, 476; Lipschits, *Fall*, 78, n. 155. This is justified in light of the fact that Ba'alis, king of Ammon later supported Ishmael, the son of Nethaniah, and allowed the latter to take refuge in Ammon after the murder of Gedaliah son of Ahikam, the Babylonian deputy in Judah (Jer 41:15).

included in the auxiliary forces of the Chaldeans in suppressing Jehoiakim's rebellion (2 Kgs 24:2).[96] Other poetical texts, the specific historical settings of which are often unclear, generally treat Moab as an enemy of God's people.[97] Still, like Ammon, Moab later took part in the conspiracy against Babylon in 593 BCE (Jer 27:3).[98] The relationship between Moab and Judah was so close that Moab became one of the lands to which the Judahites had fled after the second capture of Jerusalem by the Babylonians and when the government was in the hands of Gedaliah (Jer 40:11–12).[99] We do not know the ultimate fate of Moab for sure, but Jer 48:7 mentions that Chemosh, the national god of Moab, went into exile.[100] Furthermore, if we can believe the account of Josephus, the Moabites, along with the Ammonites, were attacked by Nebuchadnezzar in the twenty-third year of his reign, "on the fifth year after the destruction of Jerusalem" (582 BCE), probably due to their rebellions against Babylon.[101] In light of this, Moab, in the first half of the sixth century BCE, likely formed a united front with Judah against Babylon's hegemony.

Edom's relation with Judah was perhaps more antagonistic than that of Ammon or Moab in the early sixth century BCE, but then the intensity of the animosity of Edom against Judah during this period remains controversial. Outside the Hebrew Bible, Arad Ostraca 24 and 40 seem to reflect the Judahites' worries about Edomite activity in the region.[102] These two ostraca, addressed to a certain Malchiah, record the military movement in Ramat-

---

[96] M. Avi-Yonah and B. Oded, "Moab," in *EncJud* 2:403; J. M. Miller, "Moab and the Moabites," in *Studies in the Mesha Inscription and Moab*, ed. J. A. Dearman, ABS 2 (Atlanta: Scholars Press, 1989), 20–21; Miller and Hayes, *History*, 467.

[97] E.g., Exod 15:14–15; Ps 83:1–8; Amos 2:1–3; Isa 15–16; Jer 48:1–47.

[98] Avi-Yonah and Oded, "Moab," 403; Miller, "Moab," 21.

[99] Miller, "Moab," 21.

[100] Bartlett, J. R., "The Moabites and Edomites," in *Peoples of Old Testament Times*, ed. D. J. Wiseman (Oxford: Clarendon Press, 1973), 243.

[101] "For on the fifth year after the destruction of Jerusalem, which was the twenty-third of his reign, Nebuchadnezzar made an expedition against Coelesyria; and when he had possessed himself of it, he made war against the Ammonites and Moabites" (Josephus, *Ant.* 10.180–85). Cf. Oded and Rabinowitz, "Ammon," 86; Avi-Yonah and Oded, "Moab," 403.

[102] For translations, commentary, and bibliography of the two ostraca, see *COS* 3.43K–L:84–85; Y. Aharoni, *Arad Inscriptions: Judean Desert Studies* (Jerusalem: Israel Exploration Society, 1981), 46–49, 69–74; F. W. Dobbs-Allsopp et al., *Hebrew Inscriptions: Texts from the Biblical Period of the Monarchy with Concordance* (New Haven: Yale University Press, 2005), 47–53, 69–75; S. Aḥituv, *Echoes from the Past: Hebrew and Cognate Inscriptions from the Biblical Period*, trans. A. F. Rainey, Carta Handbook (Jerusalem: Carta, 2008), 126–33, 142–45.

negeb to meet the threat from Edom.[103] Yet, the dating of the ostraca is subject to scholarly debate. Some suggest a dating in a later period under the reign of Zedekiah.[104] However, this dating is less likely, given that Jer 27:1 and 28:1 mention an anti-Babylonian coalition among Edom, Judah, and a number of other states exactly during the reign of Zedekiah. The ostraca, according to Dobbs-Allsopp and Lemaire, should rather be dated during the reign of Jehoiakim, around 599/598 BCE,[105] when YHWH launched raiding parties against Jehoiakim in Jerusalem (cf. 2 Kgs 24:2).[106] Within the Hebrew Bible, Ps 137:3, Lam 4:21–22, and Obad 11:13–14 refer to the Edomites' participation in the fall of Jerusalem. A later text, 1 Esd 4:42–46, explicitly condemns the Edomites for burning the Jerusalem temple during the invasion of Babylon. Most scholars consider these descriptions of Edom's crimes against Judah in the sixth century BCE as historical facts.[107] Yet, Edom peculiarly emerges in Jer 40:11 as one of the nations that provided refuge for some Judahites following the Babylonian onslaught. Without denying the fact that the negative portrayals might have been prompted by some historical actions of Edom, several commentators such as Dicou and Assis highlight that these polemics against Edom could have been greatly exaggerated, given that Edom functioned increasingly in several late biblical and Second Temple literature as a metaphor to represent all the non-Israelite nations in order to affirm Israel's election.[108]

---

[103] The reference to Edom in Arad ostracon 24 is confirmed by the last line in the reverse side, which displays: "lest Edom should go there" (פן תבא אדם שמה). The third feminine verb assures that אדם refers to a nation and not a common noun "man, person."

[104] See Y. Aharoni, "The Negeb of Judah," *IEJ* 8 (1958): 26–38, who dates the ostraca a few years later under Zedekiah.

[105] Dobbs-Allsopp et al., *Hebrew Inscriptions*, 53; A. Lemaire, "Edom and the Edomites," in *The Books of Kings: Sources, Composition, Historiography and Reception*, ed. André Lemaire and Baruch Halpern, VTSup 129 (Leiden: Brill, 2010), 238.

[106] Following the Syriac version, we read "Edom" instead of "Aram" in 2 Kgs 24:1–2. See Lemaire, "Edom," 237, who notes that there was no longer any Aramaen kingdom at this time.

[107] B. C. Cresson, "The Condemnation of Edom in Postexilic Judaism," in *The Use of the Old Testament in the New and Other Essays: Studies in Honor of William Franklin Stinespring*, ed. J. M. Efird (Durham: Duke University Press, 1972), 125–48; B. Glazier-McDonald, "Edom in the Prophetical Corpus," in *You Shall Not Abhor an Edomite for He Is Your Brother: Edom and Seir in History and Tradition*, ed. D. V. Edelman, ABS 3 (Atlanta: Scholars Press, 1994), 23–32; M. Haller, "Edom im Urteil der Propheten," in *Vom Alten Testament: Karl Marti zum 70. Geburtstage Gewidmet*, ed. K. Budde, BZAW 41 (Gießen: Töpelmann, 1925), 109–17; M. A. Corral, *Ezekiel's Oracles against Tyre: Historical Reality and Motivations,* BibOr 46 (Roma: Pontifical Biblical Institute, 2002), 55; Lemaire, "Edom," 237–40.

[108] B. Dicou, *Edom, Israel's Brother and Antagonist: The Role of Edom in Biblical Prophecy and Story*, JSOTSup 169 (Sheffield: JSOT Press, 1994), 204; E. Assis, "Why Edom? On the Hostility towards Jacob's Brother in Prophetic Sources," *VT* 56 (2006):

Little is known of the historical roles of Philistia during the fall of Jerusalem. The Philistine cities Ashdod, Ekron, and Gaza likely benefited from the defeat of Judah by Sennacherib in 701 BCE, by gaining several Judahite cities in the Shephelah.[109] During the seventh century BCE, under Assyrian rule, the Philistine cities enjoyed great prosperity.[110] Thereafter, Ashdod and Gaza were destroyed by the Egyptians,[111] and Ashkelon and Ekron by the Babylonians.[112] Apparently, some Philistine cities continued to exist under Babylonian rule, but their political roles were so weak that, not surprisingly, representatives from Philistia were absent at the Jerusalem meeting in 593 BCE.[113] A later text, Neh 4:1 [Eng. 4:7], lists the Ashdodites, along with the Ammonites and the Arabs, as present in Jerusalem to impede the repairs of Jerusalem's walls after the return from Babylon. 1 Maccabees knows of a temple of Dagon in Ashdod (10:83–84; 11:4). In light of these later texts, Machinist is of the opinion that "the Philistines are not simply memories from older tradition, but still existent, in some historical form, through the postexilic period

---

1–20. To an extreme, J. R. Bartlett, "Edom and the Fall of Jerusalem, 587 B.C.," *PEQ* 114 (1982): 13–24; J. M. O'Brien, "Edom as (Selfish) Brother," in *Challenging Prophetic Metaphor: Theology and Ideolgy in the Prophets* (Louisville: Westminster John Knox, 2008), 153–73, deny Edom as being responsible for the destruction of Judah and Jerusalem in 587 BCE.

[109] *ANET*, 288a, records the words of Sennacherib after his siege of Jerusalem: "His [Zedekiah's] towns which I had plundered, I took away from his country and gave them (over) to Mitinti, king of Ashdod, Padi, king of Ekron, and Sillibel, king of Gaza." Cf. Ezek 16:27; Greenberg, *Ezekiel 1–20*, 282; Zimmerli, *Ezekiel*, 2:18; Corral, *Ezekiel's Oracles*, 56, 91.

[110] For an overview of the reconstructed history of Philistia under the Assyrian rule, see Lipschits, *Fall*, 8–9.

[111] According to Herodotus, *History*, 2.157, the Egyptians besieged Ashdod for 29 years until they captured the city. See also Herodotus, *History*, 2:159: "[Necho] with his land army met and defeated the Syrians at Magdolus, taking the great Syrian city of Cadytis." The Syrians are identified as the Babylonians, while Cadytis is identified as Gaza. Lipschits finds further support of the Egyptian attack on Gaza during this period in Jer 47:1. Cf. Lipschits, *Fall*, 28, 50, n. 46.

[112] The conquest of Ashkelon by Nebuchadnezzar in 604–603 BCE is cited in Miller and Hayes, *History*, 443–44: "In the first year [604/603 B.C.E.] of Nebuchadnezzar in the month of Sivan he mustered his army and went to the Hatti-territory.... He marched to the city of Askelon and captured it in the month of Kislev. He captured its king and plundered it and carried off [spoil from it ...] He turned the city into a mound and heaps of ruins and then in the month of Sebat he marched back to Babylon." See also Lipschits, *Fall*, 40–41. Around the same time, Adon the Philistine king of Ekron wrote to Pharaoh requesting aid to resist the impending Babylonian forces. See *COS* 3.54:132–34; B. Porten, "The Identity of King Adon," *BA* 44 (1981): 36–52.

[113] Miller and Hayes, *History*, 469–70.

of Achaemenid Persian domination."[114] The territorial dispute in the Shephelah region during the seventh century BCE must have been retained in the Judahite mind during or after the fall of Jerusalem, but the political status of the Philistine cities very likely went into decline after the Assyrian rule.

As for Tyre's role during the fall of Jerusalem, the present circumstances do not allow an exact evaluation, but Tyre likely functioned as a dominant power against the rising hegemony of Babylon during the sixth century BCE.[115] The representative from this Phoenician city-state also came to Jerusalem in 593 BCE (Jer 27:3). It is likely that Tyre maintained its animus toward Babylon, since Ezek 29:17–20 notes that Nebuchadnezzar immediately besieged Tyre after he had invaded Jerusalem, but was ultimately unsuccessful in his attempt to conquer Tyre.[116] "He and his army had no wages from Tyre for the labor that he had performed against it" (29:18). There is only one external document outside the Hebrew Bible, which explicitly mentions the siege laid on Tyre by Nebuchadnezzar. Citing Menander Ephesus, the Roman Jewish historian Josephus states: "Nabuchodonor besieged Tyre for thirteen years in the days of Ithobal, their king; after him reigned Baal, ten years."[117] Since the reigning period of Ithobal remains uncertain, there are thus different attempts to synchronize Menander's statement with specific events.[118] Josephus himself dates the onset of the siege to the seventh year of Nebuchadnezzar, the same year that Nebuchadnezzar first laid siege on Jerusalem (598/597 BCE).[119] On the other hand, Wiseman surmises that the beginning of a siege would have been at the outset of Nebuchadnezzar's incursions against Egypt, as early as 603/602 BCE, when a strategic goal would have been to neutralize the fleets of Tyre and Sidon supporting Egypt.[120] There is still another possibility raised by Odell for the siege to have begun in 585 BCE, since several Neo-Babylonian texts suggest that Tyre was under the control of Babylon by 570 BCE.[121] In any event, these varied dates proposed for the siege laid on Tyre leave the exact causes and impacts of that siege for further debates and discussions. If Tyre did indeed resist the rising hegemony of Babylon, then

---

[114] P. Machinist, "Biblical Traditions: The Philistines and Israelite History," in *The Sea Peoples and Their World: A Reassessment*, ed. E. D. Oren, University Museum Monograph 108 (Philadelphia: University of Pennsylvania Museum, 2000), 57.

[115] Fuhs, *Ezechiel 25–48*, 140–41; Zimmerli, *Ezekiel*, 2:24; Odell, *Ezekiel*, SHBC16 (Macon: Smyth & Helwys, 2005), 334.

[116] Lipschits, *Fall*, 66, n. 108; 72.

[117] Josephus, *Ag. Ap.*, 1.21. Noted by Odell, *Ezekiel*, 333.

[118] Odell, *Ezekiel*, 333.

[119] Josephus, *Ag. Ap.*, 1.21.

[120] D. J. Wiseman, *Nebuchadrezzar and Babylon: Schweich Lectures in Biblical Archaeology* (Oxford: Oxford University Press, 1983), 26–28, cited in Corral, *Ezekiel's Oracles*, 60; Odell, *Ezekiel*, 333.

[121] Odell, *Ezekiel*, 333, shares the same view with Lipschits, *Fall*, 66–67.

Judah would have viewed Tyre rather favorably in order to secure its own national survival from the Babylonian depredations.

Egypt's relations with Judah during the sixth century BCE come across as cordial in several sources.[122] Papyrus Rylands IX, 14:16–19 provides a glimpse of the political climate shortly after Egypt's successful campaign against Nubia in 593 BCE that reflects the Egyptian interest in the Levant.[123] It describes an expedition of Psammetichus II (594–589 BCE) in the following manner:

> In the fourth regnal year of Pharaoh Psamtek Neferibre they sent to the great temples of Upper and Lower Egypt, saying, "Pharaoh (Life, Prosperity, Health) is going to the Land of Palestine. Let the priests come with the bouquets of the gods of Egypt to take them to the Land of Palestine."[124]

Clearly, this campaign was of a religious nature, and it was apparently not a military campaign. As Lipschits states, "it might nevertheless have had propaganda value ..., and it is reasonable to assume that hope of liberation from Babylonain subjugation was awakened throughout the region."[125] Further biblical and extrabiblical accounts support the assumption that Egypt played a significant role in Judah's campaign against Babylon in the final years of Zedekiah's reign. In Ezek 17:15, there is an appeal for military strength to be sent from Egypt to help Zedekiah in the revolt against Babylon.[126] Jer 37:5–11 records the arrival of Egypt's troops sent by the new Pharaoh, Apries (Hophra, 589–570 BCE), that caused the temporary withdrawal of Babylon's army at the height of the Babylonian siege against Jerusalem.[127] Nevertheless, Jere-

---

[122] On the historical background of the Judeo-Egyptian alliance, see B. U. Schipper, *Israel und Ägypten in der Königszeit: Die kulturellen Kontakte von Salomo bis zum Fall Jerusalems*, OBO 170 (Freiburg: Universitätsverlag, 1999), 242–46; A. Malamat, "The Kingdom of Judah between Egypt and Babylon: A Small State within a Great Power Confrontation," *ST* 44 (1990): 65–77; Miller and Hayes, *History*, 446–48, 468–77; Marzouk, *Egypt*, 30–33; Corral, *Ezekiel's Oracles*, 46–49; Strong, "Ezekiel's Oracles," 55–58.

[123] Miller and Hayes, *History*, 473; Lipschits, *Fall*, 63–64.

[124] F. L. Griffith, *Catalogue of the Demotic Papyri in the John Tylands Library*, 3 vols. (Manchester: Manchester University Press, 1909), 2:64–65. For the original transcription and a German translation, see G. Vittmann, *Der demotische Papyrus Rylands 9*, ÄAT 38 (Wiesbaden: Harrassowitz, 1998, 164–65).

[125] Lipschits, *Fall*, 63, n. 97. Cf. Schipper, *Israel*, 242–44; Corral, *Ezekiel's Oracles*, 46–47; Marzouk, *Egypt*, 32; Miller and Hayes, *History*, 474.

[126] Zimmerli, *Ezekiel* 1:365; Eichrodt, *Ezekiel*, 227; J. Blenkinsopp, *Ezekiel*, IBC (Louisville: John Knox Press, 1990), 80–81.

[127] Lipschits, *Fall*, 75. Cf. Schipper, *Israel*, 245; Miller and Hayes, *History*, 475; Corral, *Ezekiel's Oracles*, 48–49.

miah responded negatively to this Egyptian assistance by warning that: "Pharaoh's army, which set out to help you, is going to return to its own land, to Egypt. And the Chaldeans shall return and fight against this city; they shall take it and burn it with fire" (37:7–8). Lachish ostracon 3 seems to supplement and confirm the intervention of an Egyptian army in Judah.[128] The ostracon is dated immediately before the beginning of the Babylonian siege of Lachish, perhaps in the autumn of 589 (or 588) BCE.[129] It reports that a certain Coniah, son of Elnathan, commander of the army, traveled to Egypt, presumably to make a request for military assistance: "The commander of the army, Coniah the son of Elnathan, has gone down to go into Egypt."[130] In short, according to the above ancient historiography, Egypt was a major political and military ally of Judah to resist the domination of Babylon in the Levant.

As seen, the ancient historiography outside Ezekiel presents the nations having various kinds of relations with Judah during the sixth century BCE. Most of these nations, including Ammon, Moab, Tyre, and Egypt, engaged in different forms of alliances with Judah against the rising hegemony of Babylon. Edom's aggressions against Judah seem to be plausible given the more prevalent evidence recorded in the ostraca and several biblical texts, but the aggressions as recorded in some later Jewish sources might be slightly exaggerated. Philistia, despite previous territorial disputes, appeared to play no active role in the fall of Jerusalem. In this light, it is highly problematic to adopt a reductionism that generalizes all these nations mentioned in Ezek 25–32 as the historical enemies of the kingdom of Judah during the early sixth century BCE. If the nations mentioned in Ezek 25–32 are not all enemies of Judah, it is then even less plausible to judge the destruction of the nations in Ezek 25–32 as serving only an implicit herald of the upcoming hope and restoration for the house of Israel. To complicate the matter even further, the historical relationship between Judah and the nations also fluctuated from time to time. Ezekiel's OAN are an editorial product, which, having undergone a long process of compilation, can reflect changing attitudes from different historical standpoints. Even then, we cannot exclude the possibility that the changing historical roles of the nations do not necessarily dictate the literary functions of Ezekiel's OAN. The portrayals of the foreign nations expressed by the collection of the OAN within the book of Ezekiel can contain ideological concerns different from those reconstructed from other historiography. As such, we need to examine the rhetoric of Ezek 25–32 on a case-by-case basis, rather than putting forward a blanket judgment that demands the

---

[128] Corral, *Ezekiel's Oracles*, 49; Dobbs-Allsopp et al., *Hebrew Inscriptions*, 308.

[129] *COS* 3:78; Schipper, *Israel*, 245; Miller and Hayes, *History*, 442; Lipschits, *Fall*, 64.

[130] *COS* 3:79; *ANET*, 322. Cf. Dobbs-Allsopp et al., *Hebrew Inscriptions*, 308–14; Aḥituv, *Echoes*, 62–69.

destruction of all these foreign nations to stand in a causal relationship with the upcoming hope and restoration for the house of Israel.

## 2.2. CONTEXTUAL ISOLATION

If the scholars who advocate the "implicit hope" reading of Ezekiel's OAN expose their false assumption that all the nations are necessarily enemies of Judah, the commentators who promote the "hubris" focus of Ezekiel's OAN face the challenge of unwarrantedly isolating the depictions of the fates of the nations from the surrounding literary contexts that pronounce judgment to Judah. With his focus on the self-exaltation of the nations in Ezekiel's OAN, Zimmerli reflects his puzzlement: Why should Ezekiel be bothered about the vanity of the other nations, when "nothing is said of the prophet's task to be a prophet to the nations"?[131] We can pose a similar question to Greenberg: Why does a prophet, whose mission is to warn of the covenant sins of Judah, switch, all of a sudden, to judge the foreign nations according to a "universal principle" against arrogance, with "no particular favor toward the victimized Judah"?[132] Both Zimmerli and Greenberg consider hubris as an offense that cannot be correlated with the trangressions or the fate of Judah.[133]

Their focus on the "hubris" of the nations unnecessarily constrains the rich characterizations of the nations within Ezekiel's OAN. Hubris, as Zimmerli also admits, is not the sole reason for judgment in Ezek 25.[134] The nations in the chapter are judged for laughing at the "house of Judah when they went into exile" (v. 3), for mocking "the house of Judah as all the nations" (v. 8), for "taking vengeance" (v. 12), and for "destroying with everlasting/ancient enmity" (v. 15). Their *Schadenfreude* as depicted in chapter 25 reflects less of their own self-exaltations and more of the sufferings of Judah. Even though Greenberg correctly notes that the actions of the nations invoke the "injured majesty of Yahweh,"[135] and even if "no material advantage to Israel,"[136] as Greenberg suggests, is to be found in Ezek 25, it is farfetched to judge the whole of Ezek 25 as totally devoid of any particular concerns for the house of Judah. Thus, within the OAN of Ezekiel, various references to the house of

---

[131] Zimmerli, *Ezekiel*, 1:60.

[132] Greenberg, *Ezekiel 21–37*, 611.

[133] So also D. E. Gowan, *When Man Becomes God: Humanism and "Hybris" in the Old Testament*, PTMS 6 (Eugene: Pickwick Publications, 1975), 42, who claims: "Ancient Israel understood pride to be a universal characteristic of man without any special relationship to the peculiar demands of Yahweh upon his covenant people."

[134] Zimmerli states that "the oracles against the immediate neighbors of the house of Israel: Ammon (cf. 21:33), Moab, Edom, the Philistines in ch. 25 (and 35) are fully related to the prophet's own message about the house of Israel" (*Ezekiel*, 1:61).

[135] Greenberg, *Ezekiel 21–37*, 527.

[136] Ibid., 526.

Judah are found. Tyre's comment "concerning Jerusalem" (על ירושלים) constitutes one of the reasons for divine judgment against the Phoenician city-state (26:2).[137] "Judah and the land of Israel" are listed in the extensive trade network of Tyre (27:17).[138] Egypt is directly accused of having been only "a staff of reed to the house of Israel" (29:6).[139] All these statements provide further indications that the fates of the nations are not judged according to a universal principle against hubris that is without any particular concern for the house of Judah.

The surrounding literary contexts outside of Ezek 25–32 likewise affirm the varied intricate interactions between Judah and the foreign nations. In the horrifying account of Ezek 16, Jerusalem is condemned for commiting harlotry with "the Egyptians" (v. 26), "the Assyrians" (v. 28), and "the land of merchants—Chaldea" (v. 29).[140] YHWH further punishes the adulterous city of Jerusalem by delivering it to "the daughters of the Philistines, who are ashamed of your lewd conduct" (v. 27). Egypt, in particular, continues to play a major role in the political aberration of the house of Judah, leading the latter to rebel against the Babylonian domination (17:15). Their alliance can be traced to the time of Israel's exodus from Egypt, when Israel defiles itself with "the idols of Egypt" (20:7). Even in the exile, the people of YHWH try to emulate the nations "by worshipping wood and stone" (20:32).[141] These repeated failures of YHWH's people finally prompt him to send out his tool of judgment—"the sword of the king of Babylon," which will not only destroy the city of Jerusalem, but will also annihilate the neighbouring "Rabbah of the sons of Ammon" (21:23–28; Eng. 21:18–23).[142] The mockery of the nations,

---

[137] The preposition על can be translated either in a neutral sense—"with regard to, concerning," or in a hostile sense—"against." Cf. *HALOT* 1:826. For the latter translation, see Block, *Ezekiel*, 2:34. For the former translation, see Zimmerli, *Ezekiel*, 2:26; Eichrodt, *Ezekiel*, 365; J. W. Wevers, *Ezekiel*, The Century Bible (London: Nelson, 1969), 201.

[138] The juxtaposition with "Judah" indicates that "the land of Israel" here refers to the northern kingdom that was destroyed by the Assyrians. Elsewhere in 40:2; 47:18, the latter refers to the entire region west of Jordan. See Zimmerli, *Ezekiel*, 2:66; Block, *Ezekiel*, 2:75.

[139] The reed imagery here is likely to be derived from Isa 36:6 (=2 Kgs 18:21). For more details, see Chapter Four.

[140] The image of the adulterous Jerusalem is developed more fully in Ezek 23.

[141] For the dependence of Ezek 20:32 on Deut 4:27–28; 28:36, 64, see J. Gile, "Deuteronomy and Ezekiel's Theology of Exile," in *For Our Good Always: Studies on the Message and Influence of Deuteronomy in Honor of Daniel I. Block*, ed. J. S. DeRouchie et al. (Winona Lake: Eisenbrauns, 2013), 293–95.

[142] For the suggestion that Ezek 21:33–35a [Eng. 28–30a] is a direct address to the Ammonites, see Odell, *Ezekiel*, 271–74. The pronouncements against Ammon are fleshed out more fully in 25:1–7.

and especially that of Edom and Mount Seir, against YHWH's people is echoed abundantly in the later chapters in Ezek 35:15; 36:5 (cf. 25:12–14). The references to the nations are not restricted only to Ezekiel's OAN, but sprinkled in various layers of the texts of Ezekiel. In light of all this, it seems that the foreign nations play an active role in the rise and fall of Judah, and thus it is possible to read Ezekiel's prophecies concerning both groups in light of each other. The hubris of the nations, interpreted as a challenge to the sovereignty of YHWH, can be understood only when the fate of YHWH's people is also taken into account.

I therefore express my reservation when Zimmerli comments: "Die Fremdvölkerworte von Ez 25–32…zeigen im Einzelnen wenig Berührung mit der spezifischen Botschaft an Israel. … Im Ganzen aber behält die Völkerverkündigung Ezechiels etwas Schematisches und läßt sich nicht mit den persönlichen Umgang Jahwes mit seinem eigenen Volk vergleichen."[143] As seen at the beginning of this chapter, his comment is only the tip of the iceberg of the general scholarly inability to integrate the OAN in Ezekiel with the rest of the book. By viewing hubris as a separate reason for judgment that is applicable to the foreign nations only, the prophecies against the foreign nations are singled out from the rest of the book of Ezekiel. It is not that the scholars who embrace the "hubris" focus are wrong. In fact, they rightly highlight several pericopes in the OAN where the self-exaltation of the nations is clearly the central issue. The problem is that they often do not go far enough to view the chatisements of the nations as relevant also to the fate of Judah. If we read Ezekiel's OAN through the lens of "hubris" only, the chastisements carried out against the foreign nations remain contextually independent of, and lacking much interaction with, the rise and fall of Jerusalem in the surrounding passages. We need other literary links and contexts to shed light on, to elucidate, and to enrich the present context of the OAN. This is precisely the point where the "oblique judgment" focus can be of use, and help illumine a new path in understanding Ezekiel's OAN.

3. MARKING THE NEW PATH

Contrary to the "hubris" focus, the "oblique judgment" focus seems to be able to overcome the contextual isolation and promise a closer and more integral reading of Ezekiel's OAN. The "oblique judgment" reading of Ezekiel's OAN

---

[143] W. Zimmerli, *Grundriß der alttestamentlichen Theologie*, Theologische Wissenschaft 3 (Stuttgart: Kohlhammer, 1972), 187.

draws our attention more closely to the judgment of Judah. Upon closer reading, except for the date in 29:17,[144] all the chronological markers that congregate within Ezekiel's OAN mark the days around the fall of Jerusalem.[145] The chronological formulas in Ezek 29:1; 31:1 can be dated to the year 588 BCE;[146] the date formula in 26:1, due to the missing month, points to either 587 or 586 BCE;[147] and the date formulas in 32:1, 17 belong to the year 586 BCE. In addition, chapters 25–32 are enclosed by two chapters accentuating the day when "the king of Babylon has laid siege to Jerusalem" (24:2) and the day when "the refugees came to me, saying, 'the city has been taken'" (33:21). In other words, paying attention to the "oblique judgment" rhetoric has the potential to account for the concentrated references to the calamity that befell Jerusalem and the peculiarities where the restoration of Israel is not immediately in view.

Contrary to the ideological overgeneralization prevalent in the arguments for the "implicit hope" focus, the most attractive promise held out by the "oblique judgment" of the text is that many of its advocates such as Boadt and Marzouk have grounded their arguments on the concrete linguistic connections within and beyond the book of Ezekiel.[148] The judgment language found

---

[144] The chronological formula in 29:17 is dated to 572 BCE and is far removed from the fall of Jerusalem. The following oracle attached to this formula is an update of Ezekiel's oracle concerning Tyre in Ezek 26:7–14 (Zimmerli, *Ezekiel*, 2:102).

[145] For a detailed examination of these chronological markers in Ezekiel, see Chapter Five.

[146] This date in 29:1 has been related to the occasion when Pharaoh Hophra (588–570 BCE) made his army march to relieve Jerusalem and thus prompted Nebuchadnezzar to lift the siege of Jerusalem temporarily (cf. Jer 37:3–10). See W. R. Albright, "The Seal of Eliakim and the Latest Preexilic History of Judah, with Some Observations on Ezekiel," *JBL* 51 (1932): 77–106, esp. 94; Blenkinsopp, *Ezekiel*, 127–28; G. A. Cooke, *Ezekiel: A Critical and Exegetical Commentary on the Book of Ezekiel*, ICC (Edinburgh: T&T Clark, 1951), 325. Against the above position, Zimmerli argues that "in the immediately following oracle in vv 3–6 there is not the slightest indication of this" (*Ezekiel*, 2:110).

[147] The year number in MT Ezek 26:1 causes problems for many commentators, since the "eleventh year" seems to precede the fall of Jerusalem, while the narrative starting from v. 2 presupposes the fall of Jerusalem (cf. Wevers, *Ezekiel*, 147; Allen, *Ezekiel 20–48*, 73–75; Gosse, "Recueil," 554–57). Unlike the MT, Codex Alexandrinus reads the year number as the "twelfth year."

[148] These verbal parallels are particularly prevalent within the prophetic books. For instance, T. E. Fretheim observes that various special linguistic features in Jeremiah's OAN also appear in the oracles concerning Judah (*Jeremiah*, SHBC 15 [Macon: Smyth & Helwys, 2002], 555–649, esp. 583, 605, 609). Such a literary phenomenon within the prophetic books has been observed as early as the beginnings of biblical interpretation. On the semantic parallels of Obad 3 and Jer 49:16, Rabbi Isaac in the Talmud

in Ezekiel's OAN often echo those found in the prophecies against Judah in the rest of the book. Schwagmeier's meticulous study confirms the important role of the terminological connections in MT Ezekiel, more so than that in the LXX.[149] For instance, while the term ארז "cedar" in the MT links both chapters 17 and 31 together, the LXX renders the term differently in both chapters, as κέδρος (17:3, 22, 23) and κυπάρισσος (31:3, 8; cf. 27:24) respectively.[150] In another example, the reference to the פליט is an important element that connects chapter 33 to the previous chapters in MT Ezek 1–24 (e.g., 14:22; 24:26–27; 33:21–22). Meanwhile, the LXX again provides different translations for this term, as ἀνασωθείς in 33:21 and as ἀνασῳζόμενος in 24:26–27.[151] Taking these and other examples together, Schwagmeier concludes that the LXX "funktioniert anders. Stichtwortberührungen und Leitwörte etwa spielen ganz offenkundig nicht die große Rolle, die sie im hebräischen Text spielen."[152] It is widely recognized that the MT of Ezekiel displays numerous points of linguistic contact with the book of Jeremiah, Deuteronomy, the priestly writings, and the Holiness Code.[153] For instance, Jeremiah and Ezekiel both share the same interest in the motif of an enemy from the north (צפון).[154] They both share the polemic against false prophets and the rejection of intermediary figures to avert the disaster that is predicted for Jerusalem.[155] In addition, Ezekiel's expression of exile (הפיץ בגוים וזרה בארצות) "to scatter among the nations and to

---

explained: "The same communication is revealed to many prophets, yet no two prophets prophesy in the identical phraseology" (b. Sanh. 89a). Early church fathers attributed the semantic parallels among the prophets to the fact that they all had been "given utterance through one and the same spirit" (*Theophilus to Antolycus* 2.35; cf. 2.9 [*ANF* 2:94–121, esp. 97, 108], noted by R. L. Schultz, *The Search for Quotation: Verbal Parallels in the Prophets*, JSOTSup 180 [Sheffield: Sheffield Academic Press, 1999], 20).

[149] Schwagmeier, "Untersuchungen," 119–24.
[150] Ibid., 121.
[151] Ibid.
[152] Ibid., 124.
[153] For an overview of the scholarship on these connections, see Zimmerli, *Ezekiel*, 1:41–52; A. Klein, *Schriftauslegung im Ezechielbuch: Redaktionsgeschichtliche Untersuchungen zu Ez 34–39*, BZAW 391 (Berlin: de Gruyter, 2008), 17–23.
[154] E.g., Jer 1:13–15; 4:6; 6:1, 22; 10:22; 13:20; 15:12; 46:6, 10, 20, 24; 47:2; 50:3, 9, 41; 51:48; Ezek 26:7; 38:6, 15; 39:2. On the discussion of this motif in Jeremiah and Ezekiel, see ibid., 132–39.
[155] There are other parallels in Jeremiah and Ezekiel. For the portrayals of Jerusalem as the unfaithful female figure, see Jer 2–3; Ezek 16, 23. For the polemic against the false prophets, see Jer 2:8, 26, 30b; 4:9; 5:12–14, 30–31; 6:13–15; 8:11; 14:13–17; 23:9–32, 33–40; 37:19. For further expositions, see D. Vieweger, *Die literarischen Beziehungen zwischen den Büchern Jeremia und Ezechiel*, BEATAJ 26 (Frankfurt am Main: Peter Lang, 1993), 19–36. For a critique of Vieweger's methodology, see Klein, *Schriftauslegung*, 19–20.

disperse among the countries") seems to be a fusion of the deuteronomic and Holiness Code locutions.[156] In this light, the verbal connections between Ezekiel and other biblical texts in the MT of Ezekiel abound, and they are potential evidence for us to take the other biblical passages more concretely into account, when we explore the rhetorical functions of Ezek 25–32. On the one hand, this focus on language is restrictive enough to prioritize the biblical texts under examination, and thus minimizes using other generalizing concepts or hypotheses to predetermine the meaning of the present texts. On the other hand, this focus on language is also expansive enough, as common vocabulary and phraseology provide powerful, solid, and verifiable evidence to bring in other texts for comparison and contrast.[157] Therefore, I have more sympathy with the method used and the outcome derived by the scholars in the "oblique judgment" focus.

All these discoveries in the scholarship on Ezekiel are highly suggestive, but remain limited in scope. None of the full-length monographs on Ezekiel's OAN engages fully with the aforementioned studies, nor does any of them deal adequately with the lexical connections embedded in the corpus. Premstaller's monograph places most of the semantic links between Ezekiel's OAN and the rest of the Hebrew Bible in the footnotes, and it lacks discussion of the rhetorical impact of these significant links in the received literary context of Ezekiel.[158] Fechter's investigation omits Ezek 30–32 completely, and his diachronic approach to the texts remains limited to the inner development of chapters 25–29, without probing the larger role of chapters 25–32 within the prophetic book.[159] Even though Strong's dissertation does emphasize the implicit indictment of the house of Judah in the Egypt oracles, his discussions of

---

[156] Cf. הפיץ בעמים in Deut 4:27; 28:64 and זרה בגוים in Lev 26:33. See Gile, "Deuteronomy," 287–306, who builds on the insight of M. A. Lyons, *From Law to Prophecy: Ezekiel's Use of the Holiness Code*, LHBOTS 507 (London: Bloomsbury, 2009); R. L. Kohn, *A New Heart and a New Soul: Ezekiel, the Exile and the Torah* JSOTSup 358 (London: Sheffield Academic Press, 2002).

[157] Cf. R. Nurmela, "The Growth of the Book of Isaiah Illustrated by Allusions in Zechariah," in *Bringing Out the Treasure: Inner Biblical Allusion in Zechariah 9–14*, ed. M. J. Boda and M. Floyd, LHBOTS 370 (London: Bloomsbury, 2003), 245–59, here 247.

[158] Pohlmann criticizes Premstaller's monograph as being too paraphrastic of the biblical texts: "Darauf folgen unter „Inhalt" umfangreichere Darlegungen, die allerdings häufig kaum mehr als Textparaphrasierungen darstellen" (*Ezechiel*, 106).

[159] According to Fechter's reconstruction, several texts (25:1–5; 26:1b–5a; 27*; 28:11–19* and 29:1–5*) came into being around 587 BCE and are thus considered to be the oldest layers (287). They were later expanded in multi-staged redaction with different purposes in mind. For instance, the oracle against Moab in 25:8–11 is an expansion of the original oracle in 25:1–5 in order to be a more recent "Beitrag zur Frage nach dem Erwählungsgedanken" (290). The Tyre oracle in 26:7–14, which

the shared vocabulary and phraseology between the Egypt and Judah oracles remain rather sporadic.[160]

None of the studies that observe lexical allusions within Ezekiel's OAN synthesizes the results as a coherent whole. Schwagmeier's observations of the lexical connections and the absent element of hope for Israel in chapter 25 are tremendously insightful and leave room for further exploration.[161] Yet, his monograph contains only a perfunctory survey of MT Ezek 25–32,[162] while dedicating more attention to Ezek 36–39, where the differences between the MT and P967 remain the greatest.[163] Likewise, Yaron, Wilson, and Bogaert deal only with a particular Tyre oracle,[164] while the research from Boadt and Marzouk scrutinize the semantic allusions within the Egypt oracles more specficially.[165] Studies on one chapter of the OAN seldom interact with studies on another, and little space is devoted to explore the significance of the vocabulary correspondences for the hermeneutics of the texts in question.

Few have fully discussed the rhetorical impacts generated by the lexical allusions in Ezek 25–32, let alone conceptualized the precise types of divine judgment directed obliquely at the house of Judah in these texts. Having noted the overwhelming lexical connections between Ezek 27 and the biblical texts describing the Israelite tabernacle or Solomon's temple, Geyer barely discusses the rhetorical functions of these connections and merely suggests that the shared terminology arises due to the similar architectural structures for the

---

names Nebuchadnezzar as the destroyer of Tyre, is a more concrete update of the former judgment oracle in 26:1b–5a (290). The text shows that Nebuchadnezzar is the divine tool of judgment. Fechter further identifies the restoration oracles in Ezek 28:25–26 and 29:13–16a as belonging to the younger redactional layer. Similar restoration visions also appear in some of the latest texts of the prophetic book, including Ezek 34:25–30; 36; 37:25–28; 39:25–29 as well as some other passages in chapters 40–48 (304). For Fechter, the younger redactional layer reflects an apocalyptic *Tendenz* (103).

[160] See Strong, "Ezekiel's Oracles," 54–133.

[161] See nn. 56–58; Schwagmeier, *Untersuchungen*, 261.

[162] A brief overview of chapters 25–32 is subsumed with chapters 1–24 under the section entitled "Relieflesung von Ez 1–32" in ibid., 241–72.

[163] Ibid., esp. 272–317. In fact, his whole monograph focuses more on the other manuscript traditions of Ezekiel than the MT.

[164] For the focus on Ezek 28:11–19, see Yaron, "Dirge," 28–57; Wilson, "Death," 211–18; P.-M. Bogaert, "Le Chérub de Tyr (Ez 28, 14.16) et l'Hippocampe de ses Monnaies," in *Prophetie und geschichtliche Wirklichkeit im alten Israel* (Stuttgart: Kohlhammer, 1991), 29–38; idem, "Montagne," 131–53.

[165] E.g., the discussion of the Egypt oracles in Boadt, "Rhetorical Strategies," 182–200, is only a part of his wider analysis of Ezekiel's oracles of judgment (including chapters 4–7; 15–19). Marzouk's extensive dissertation on Egypt's oracles does not include the Tyre, Transjordan, and Philistia oracles in Ezekiel.

temples in Tyre and Jerusaelm.¹⁶⁶ Having listed only two short pages of lexical connections between the oracles against the nations and those against Judah, Boadt quickly jumps to the conclusion: "Just as both foreign kings will be destroyed for these divine pretensions, so Israel must expect destruction for its own hubris when it breaks the covenant it has made with Babylon at Yahweh's will."¹⁶⁷ While Boadt's conclusion might be right in the end, the way he derives the conclusion seems to be hasty, since semantic parallels do not necessarily serve to highlight similarities, they can also act to underline a contrast. Marzouk deserves credit for explaining the verbatim correspondences more thoroughly in light of Ezekiel's perceptions of not only the political alliance, but also the idolatrous bonding between Egypt and Judah.¹⁶⁸ Still, his discussion is limited to the Egypt oracles, without extending to other oracles against the nations. All in all, simply putting a blanket judgment that the nations and the house of Judah share the same fate of divine judgment is not enough. We also need to explore the surrounding literary context in order to uncover the more specific ideology that motivates this perception of shared judgment within Ezek 25–32, and to view this ideology more comprehensively in light of the later reception of Ezek 25–32 within the book.

Questions that await more exploration include: (1) Can we find more of those lexical parallels in other parts of the OAN and the rest of the book? What are the literary criteria that can be used to detect significant morphological resemblances useful to our study of Ezek 25–32? (2) How do we explain the strikingly similar language, form, and content? What kinds of literary dependence or historical tradition do these literary parallels reveal? (3) How can these traditions as illustrated by the connections help shed light on the rhetorical functions of Ezekiel's OAN in its present shape within the MT book? (4) How can the later reception of Ezek 25–32 found in the rest of the book illuminate the readings we have derived from Ezek 25–32?

3.1. SEMANTIC LINKS, TEXTUAL ALLUSIONS, AND RHETORICAL IMPACTS

The studies by Tooman, Lyons, Sommer, Gile, Seiler, and Schultz are especially enlightening and useful to answer the first two sets of questions, which are concerned with the criteria of finding lexical parallels among texts and of

---

¹⁶⁶ J. B. Geyer, "Ezekiel 27 and the Cosmic Ship," in *Among the Prophets: Language, Image and Structure in the Prophetic Writings*, ed. P. R. Davies and D. J. A. Clines, JSOTSup 144 (Sheffield: JSOT Press, 1993), 105–26, here 124. Cf. Odell, *Ezekiel*, 346–47, who claims that the vocabulary in Ezek 27 should be seen as referring to common trade goods in the ancient world, and that "not too much should be made of the sacral connections."

¹⁶⁷ Boadt, "Rhetorical Strategies," 197–98.

¹⁶⁸ Marzouk, *Egypt*, esp. 119–25.

determining the direction of dependence among them.[169] Synthesizing and building on their insights, three main criteria are available to determine the semantic links that are not "simply due to chance," but likely the result of "purposeful borrowing."[170] The first is the *rarity and distinctiveness* of a literary element, common among a few texts.[171] For example, the phrase "perfect beauty" (כְּלִילַת יֹפִי) is a rare expression within the Hebrew Bible. The related forms surface only in the descriptions of Jerusalem (Ps 50:2; Lam 2:15; Ezek 16:14) and Ezekiel's prophecies against Tyre (Ezek 26–28).[172] Such rare occurrences invite comparison between the beauty of Tyre and that of Jerusalem. The second indication of significant semantic links is the *accumulation of several shared elements* among the texts.[173] One special kind of accumulation is called the "inversion" or "Seidel's Law," which inverts "the order of elements in the borrowed locution."[174] Ezekiel 8:2 and 1:27–28 illustrate this principle of "inversion." Both visions, as pointed out by Tooman, contain the same four

---

[169] W. A. Tooman, *Gog of Magog*, FAT 2.52 (Tübingen: Mohr Siebeck, 2011), 27–35; M. A. Lyons, "Marking Innerbiblical Allusion in the Book of Ezekiel," *Bib* 88 (2007): 245–50; B. D. Sommer, *A Prophet Reads Scripture: Allusion in Isaiah 40–66*, Contraversions: Jews and Other Differences (Stanford: Stanford University Press, 1998), 6–31; idem, "Exegesis, Allusion and Intertextuality in the Hebrew Bible: A Response to Lyle Eslinger," *VT* 46 (1996): 479–89; J. Gile, "Ezekiel 16 and the Song of Moses: A Prophetic Transformation?" *JBL* 130 (2011): 87–108, esp. 95–99; S. Seiler, "Intertextualität," in *Lesarten der Bibel: Untersuchungen zu einer Theorie der Exegese des Alten Testaments*, ed. H. Utzschneider and E. Blum (Stuttgart: Kohlhammer, 2006), 275–293; Schultz, *Search*, 222–39.

[170] Gile, "Ezekiel 16," 95, makes this distinction. So also G. D. Miller, "Intertextuality in Old Testament Research," *Currents in Biblical Research* 9 (2011), 283–309, here 284; B. M. Levinson, *Legal Revision and Religious Renewal in Ancient Israel* (Cambridge: Cambridge University Press, 2008), 102–3.

[171] Cf. Tooman, *Gog*, 27–28; Gile, "Ezekiel 16," 97; Miller, "Intertextuality," 295; Sommer, "Exegesis," 484–85.

[172] See Ezek 27:3–4, 11; 28:12. For more details, see Chapter Three.

[173] Tooman names this principle "Multiplicity" (*Gog*, 28–29). Meanwhile, Seiler calls this principle "Addition" ("Intertextualität," 282; cf. J. Helbig, *Intertextualität und Markierung: Untersuchungen zur Systematik und Funktion der Signalisierung von Intertextualität*, Beiträge zur neueren Literaturgeschichte 3.141 [Heidelberg: Winter, 1996], 98, 101–2). Listed by Seiler, other examples that illustrate the principle of accumulation are the creation statements in Psalms, which display manifold connections to Gen 1–2. E.g., Ps 136:5 // Gen 1:7–8; Ps 136:6 // Gen 1:9–10; Ps 136:7–9 // Gen 1:14–18; Ps 104:2 // Gen 1:6–8; Ps 104:8 // Gen 1:9; Ps 104:14 // Gen 1:11–12, 29–30; Ps 104:25 // Gen 1:20; Ps 104:29 // Gen 2:7; Ps 104:30 // Gen 2:7.

[174] W. A. Tooman, "Ezekiel's Radical Challenge to Inviolability," *ZAW* 121 (2009): 501; idem, *Gog*, 31; Lyons, "Allusion," 245–46. For the bibliography on "Seidel's Law," see also B. M. Levinson, *Deuteronomy and the Hermeneutics of Legal Innovation* (New York: Oxford University Press, 1997), 18–19.

locutions: "like the appearance of amber" (כעין חשמל), "from the appearance of his loins and upward' (ממתניו ולמעלה), "from the appearance of his loins and downward" (ממראה מתניו ולמטה), and "like the appearance of fire" (כמראה אש). However, Ezek 8:2 displays the four locutions found in 1:27 in an inverted order. As Tooman puts it, this "dense constellation of identical locutions" identifies the "mysterious being [in 8:2] with the divine Presence (כבוד יהוה; 1,28)."[175] The third helpful hint of lexical links is the conflation of *multiple elements from different texts* in one single text under examination.[176] In such a case, the direction of dependence can often be ascertained rather quickly, since the text where the conflation takes place is usually the later text. Ezekiel 27, taken as an example, reflects language that is used elsewhere in relation to the Jerusalem temple in Ezek 16.[177] The same chapter 27 of Ezekiel also employs language that is applied especially to the construction of the tabernacle in the wilderness in the priestly literature of the Pentateuch.[178] Moreover, the Tyrian merchant ship in the lament of Ezek 27 resembles the imagery of the First Temple in the book of Kings and Chronicles.[179] Taken as a whole, the Tyrian ship in Ezek 27 thus embodies various elements that belong to the Israelite tabernacle or temple in other biblical passages. Based on the pattern of this conflation, it is likely that Ezek 27 adopts elements of the Israelite sanctuary depicted elsewhere in the Hebrew Bible and reconfigures them to build its own imagery of the Tyrian ship.

When ascertaining the direction of inner biblical allusions, we have to be aware of two kinds of scenarios. On the one hand, it is possible for the semantic links to indicate a direct dependence of one text on a prescursor text. The portrayal of Pharaoh in Ezek 29:6b–7 as "a staff of reed to the house of Israel" that breaks and tears all men who lean on it possesses dense lexical and imagery correspondences to the portrayal of Pharaoh in Isa 36:6 (= 2 Kgs 18:21). In this case, the pre-exilic literary setting of Isa 36 does not preclude a pre-exilic date of composition, and so Ezek 29, which reflects an exilic literary setting, is likely to be directly dependent on Isa 36.[180] On the other hand, it is also possible that the correspondences do not justify the knowledge by one

---

[175] Tooman, "Radical Challenge," 501; idem, *Gog*, 31.

[176] Cf. Seiler, "Intertextualität," 282, who cites Helbig, *Intertextualität*, 98–100.

[177] E.g., Ezek 27:3 and 16:14 share the combination of יפה and כלל; Ezek 27:7, 16, 24 share the references to רקמה and שש; both Ezek 27:17 and 16:13, 19 refer to דבש ושמן. For more details, see Chapter Three.

[178] E.g., קרש in Ezek 27:6 also appears in Exod 26; 36; 39:33; 40:18; Num 3:36; 4:31. For more details, see Chapter Three.

[179] E.g., The combination of ברושים and ארז appears consistently in the building of the First Temple in 1 Kgs 5:13, 22, 24; 6:15, 18, 20, 34; 9:11 [Heb.]; 2 Chr 2:7. Other occurrences of the combination are found in Is 14:8; Ezek 31:8. For more details, see Chapter Three.

[180] For a more detailed discussion, see Chapter Four.

text of other specific texts under comparison, but simply point to a larger common cultural milieu.[181] The expression of Tyre as the "perfect beauty" in Ezek 27:3–4, 11 is widely thought to be related to Jerusalem's beauty in Ezek 16:14. Since this phrase is applied more frequently to Jerusalem in the Hebrew Bible, appearing also in Ps 50:2 and Lam 2:15, it is more likely that the phrase is a stereotypical reference to Jerusalem rather than to Tyre. It is thus likely that Ezek 27 is alluding not to one specific instance in Ezek 16:14, but to this whole cultural tradition about Jerusalem.[182] All in all, it has to be noted in advance that the weighing of of the verbatim correspondences and litearay dependence between texts is "an art, not a science."[183] When more of the aforementioned three criteria are met by two or more well-defined passages, the case for literary dependence becomes more likely to be *bona fide*. The first three chapters of my study will deal with the salient cases where the semantic links between Ezek 25–32 can be established, and where it can be proven that Ezek 25–32 is alluding to earlier traditions or precursor texts.

Recognizing vocabulary correspondences and literary dependence among texts is only the first step in the exercise of intertextual reading.[184] More important to the present study is to answer the third question, which is concerned with the rhetorical impacts the textual allusions generate in one or more of the related texts.[185] I will assume that the precursor texts or common traditions

---

[181] Sommer, *Prophet*, 32. Cf. Seiler, "Intertextualität," 280, who highlights: "Denn daneben besteht noch die Möglichkeit, dass bestimmte Formulierungen oder Themen bereits so sehr zum allgemeinen Traditionsgut geworden sind, dass von einem bewussten Bezug auf einen Prätext nicht mehr gesprochen werden kann. Außerdem können Beziehungen von den RezipientInnen selbst hergestellt werden, die von den AutorInnen nicht beabsichtigt waren."

[182] For a more detailed discussion, see Chapter Three. A similar argument for the literary, but not lexical, connection between John 1:14 and Exod 34:6 is put forward in K. Brown, "Temple Christology in the Gospel of John: Replacement Theology and Jesus as the Self-Revelation of God" (Master diss., Trinity Western University, 2010), 26–27. Likewise, F. E. König treats a repeated phrase such as כשד משדי יבוא "it will come like destruction from the Almighty" in Isa 13:6 and Joel 1:15 as an idiomatic expression which has its origin in the "unconscious creative soul of the language [*Sprachseele*]" ("Gibt es ‚Zitate' im Alten Testament?" *NKZ* 28 [1908]: 734–46, here 739). In the nineteenth century, C. P. Caspari has already listed seven different ways to account for verbal parallels in different passages, without reducing all the verbal parallels to solely reflections of borrowed and borrowing texts ("Jesajanische Studien. I. Jeremia ein Zeuge für die Aechtheit von Jes. c. 34," *Zeitschrift für die gesammte lutherische Theologie und Kirche* 4 (1843): 1–73, esp. 4–8; summarized in Schultz, *Search*, 23).

[183] Sommer, *Prophet*, 35. Gile suggests that the proof for a literary dependence involves "a cumulative argument" ("Ezekiel 16," 89).

[184] Miller, "Intertextuality," 299.

[185] Ibid.

hovering behind Ezek 25–32 can be integrated purposefully within the received contexts and thus illumine the present rhetorical functions of Ezek 25–32. A diachronic awareness of the sources and traditions behind the received texts can help draw out rhetorical distinctiveness inherent within the present OAN of the book of Ezekiel. At the same time, we need to be familiar with the synchronic forms and structures that contextualize and give new meanings to the precursor texts and common traditions. That is to say, the same locutions used in another set of sources or traditions can serve to convey different nuances and meanings in the received context of Ezek 25–32. Following Assmann's categorizations, Seiler suggests that intertextual connections within the Hebrew Bible can perform the functions to comment, to imitate, or to criticize.[186] While a literary comment understands the precursor text as "canonical," which can only be cited without further interpretations or criticisms,[187] a literary imitation often leads to further exegesis. For instance, Qoh 5:3–4 belongs to this second category in that it imitates the statement concerning vows to God in Deut 23:22–24.[188] The parallels between the two passages indicate an exegetical advancement, such that the requirement to make a vow to God in Deuteronomy is now being generalized to be the universally wise and reasonably moral action in Qoheleth. On the other hand, Jer 4:23–28 belongs to the third category. The passage shares intertextual links with Gen 1 but stands in an antithetical light to the situation described in Genesis. Jeremiah records the havoc wreaked in the land of Judah as the chaotic תהו ובהו, a reversal of the creation narrative.[189] In short, different textual allusions, placed in their respective literary contexts, can bear a wide array of rhetorical impacts, resulting in either a comparison or a contrast. The synchronic arrangement of a received text provides anchorage for the diachronic traditions alluded to by the text, while the diachronic traditions alluded to add a deeper layer of meaning that is below the surface of the synchronic text and thus help establish the dominant rhetorical functions of Ezek 25–32.

3.2. WIDER INFLUENCES BEYOND EZEK 25–32

If Ezek 25–32 can draw on key words and phrases from earlier traditions, reconfigure them in the received context, and thus accommodate them to its own innovations, it is also possible for Ezek 25–32 to become "the content of

---

[186] Seiler, "Intertextualität," 286. For the basic functions of intertextuality in the Hebrew Bible, see also the detailed discussion in Sommer, *Prophet*, 23–31. Sommer's position is summarized in Miller, "Intertextuality," 301–3.

[187] Seiler, "Intertextualität," 286. This understanding is similar to Sommer's idea of "echoes," which "do not suggest any altered understanding of the passage in which they appear" (*Prophet*, 31).

[188] Seiler, "Intertextualität," 286.

[189] Ibid., 287.

the tradition" (the putative *traditum*), which provides stock phrases for the later reinterpretations in the "long and varied process of transmission" (the putative *traditio*).[190] This leads us to question four, which inquires after the reception of Ezek 25–32 within the same prophetic book.

The works from scholars such as Fishbane (1985) and Levinson (1997, 2008) have highlighted the "midrashic dimension" of the biblical corpus.[191] That is to say, the Hebrew Bible, on its own terms, is not a fixed and static entity, but, like the midrash, displays the literary phenomenon of rewriting. Earlier traditions within the biblical book can be reused and reinterpreted by later authors in a wide array of ways to give the traditions new contexts and meanings. This idea has influenced Klein (2008, 2010) and Spieckermann (2012). They argue at length that the phenomenon of reception does not begin outside of the Hebrew Bible, but has already begun during the very composition of the Masoretic texts.[192] Working on the salvation oracles in Ezek 34–37, Klein rejects viewing the corpus as a static collection of prophetic words, but insists that the collection "geht ... auf eine anfängliche literarische Komposition zurück, an die sich midraschartige Fortschreibungen angelegt haben. Diese Nachinterpretationen bedienen sich vorliegender Texte, die aufgenommen, weitergeführt, umgearbeitet und neu interpretiert werden."[193] She further concludes: "Insofern ist die Schriftauslegung im Ezechielbuch alttestamentlicher Vorläufer der Auslegungsliteratur in Qumran und der jüdische Bibelexegese im Midrasch."[194] Similarly, Spieckermann emphasizes the fluid boundary between the synthesis and supplementation taking place both within and outside the biblical texts, and suggests that the reception history continues the

---

[190] M. Fishbane, *Biblical Interpretation in Ancient Israel* (Oxford: Clarendon Press, 1985), 6, see also 10–13, 408–9.

[191] Fishbane, *Biblical Interpretation*; Levinson, *Deuteronomy*. See also the extensive bibliography on "inner-biblical exegesis" amassed in Levinson, *Legal Revision*, 95–181.

[192] Both utilize this approach to bridge the gap between the search for origins of the biblical texts, which characterizes much of nineteenth century biblical scholarship, and the study of reception history, which focuses on the influences the texts generate. See Klein, *Schriftauslegung*, 3, and H. Spieckermann, "From Biblical Exegesis to Reception History," *Hebrew Bible and Ancient Israel* 3 (2012): 327–50.

[193] Klein, *Schriftauslegung*, 407. She is using Ezek 34–37 as an example to illustrate the dynamic composition of the whole book of Ezekiel.

[194] Ibid., 408. In this manner, she affirms the insight of the seminal article written in I. L. Seeligmann, "Voraussetzungen der Midraschexegese," in *Congress Volume: Congress of the International Organization for the Study of the Old Testament, Copenhagen 1953*, VTSup 1 (Leiden: Brill, 1953), 150–81. In this latter article, Seeligmann finds analogy between the production of the biblical texts and the midrashic exegesis.

task of biblical exegesis.[195] As he states: "Interpretation of biblical texts does not begin only at the point of canonization. Rather, interpretation is already the *raison d'être* of the genesis of biblical texts."[196] There is no doubt that the present corpus of Ezekiel evinces multiple stages of redactional activities.[197] Some later prophecies of Ezekiel receive from earlier prophecies of Ezekiel, in order to produce new contexts for understanding.

Following this trend in biblical scholarship, the end of my study will discuss how Ezek 25–32 was received in later layers of the same prophetic book. This search for influences beyond Ezek 25–32 can in turn shed light on the previous literary analyses of Ezek 25–32, and thus reinforce or challenge the latent meanings embedded in Ezek 25–32. To illustrate this point, we can cite some extrabiblical examples of the reception of Ezekiel, which illumine the rhetorical meanings of several sections within the Masoretic book of Ezekiel in two main ways.

On the one hand, the reception materials and the precursor texts can display points of continuity. For instance, it has been widely recognized that several Dead Sea Scrolls, such as the *Description of the New Jerusalem* and the *Songs of the Sabbath Sacrifice*, which outline a huge temple or city in the eschatological era, where angelic beings perform their prayer service, do not name the temple or city described as Jerusalem. What can be deduced is that the historical Jerusalem plays no role in these texts. Historically speaking, the sectarian strifes during the Second Temple Period might have prompted the Qumranic aversion to the historical Jerusalem, where other sectarian groups

---

[195] Spieckermann, "Biblical Exegesis," 327.

[196] Ibid., 349.

[197] That the biblical texts have undergone stages of development is made highly plausible by the "variant literary editions," which display additions, omissions, or other structural differences. Such variations, for instance, exist among the books of Esther, Exodus, Judges, and Psalms. For more discussions of the fluid and pluriform state of the biblical text in the BCE period, see also I. Young, "The Dead Sea Scrolls and the Bible: The View from Qumran Samuel," *ABR* 62 (2014): 14–30; E. Ulrich, "Multiple Literary Editions: Reflections toward a Theory of the History of the Biblical Text," in *Dead Sea Scrolls and the Origins of the Hebrew Bible* (Grand Rapids: Eerdmans, 1999), 99–120; E. Tov, *Textual Criticism of the Hebrew Bible* (Minneapolis: Fortress Press, 1992), 320–349; idem, *The Greek and Hebrew Bible: Collected Essays on the Septuagint*, VTSup 72 (Leiden: Brill, 1999), 151–160; idem, "The Lucianic Text of the Canonical and Apocryphal Sections of Esther: A Rewritten Biblical Book," *Textus* 10 (1982): 1–25; K. De Troyer, *The End of the Alpha Text of Esther: Translation and Narrative Technique in MT 8:1–17, LXX 8:1–17, and at 7:14–41*, SCS 48 (Atlanta: Society of Biblical Literature, 2000), 346; K. Brown, *The Vision in Job 4 and Its Role in the Book*, FAT 2/75 (Tübingen: Mohr Siebeck, 2015), 221, n. 265.

thrived and prevailed.[198] Despite their differences in detail, scholars such as Newsom, Mizrahi, and Odell point to the structural and terminological influences of Ezek 40–48 on the *Songs of the Sabbath Sacrifice*.[199] Meanwhile, Fujita and García Martínez highlight the formal and lexical affinities between Ezek 40–48 and the *Description of the New Jerusalem*.[200] With these textual affinities and allusions in mind, further points of continuity between the two groups of texts are revealed. Remarkably, Ezek 40–48, like the aforementioned Dead Sea Scrolls, does not identify the restored city as "Jerusalem" or "Zion" at all.[201] The descriptions of the ideal temple in these chapters of Ezekiel appear to deliberately avoid mentioning any use of the building materials

---

[198] For the sectarian negative attitude toward the historical Jerusalem, see F. García Martínez, "New Jerusalem at Qumran and in the New Testament," in *The Land of Israel in Bible, History and Theology: Studies in Honour of E. Noort*, ed. J. van Ruiten and J. C. de Vos, VTSup 124 (Leiden: Brill, 2009), 285–86.

[199] For the influences of Ezek 40–48 on the *Songs of the Sabbath Sacrifice*, see C. A. Newsom, *Songs of the Sabbath Sacrifice: A Critical Edition*, HSS 27 (Atlanta: Scholars Press, 1985), 53. In addition to the influence of Ezekiel, arguments are also made for the influences of the temple descriptions of Kings and Chronicles on the *Songs of the Sabbath Sacrifice*. See N. Mizrahi, "The Songs of the Sabbath Sacrifice and Biblical Priestly Literature: A Linguistic Reconsideration," *HTR* 104 (2011): 33–58; M. S. Odell, "Creeping Things and Singing Stones: The Iconography of Ezekiel 8:7–13 in Light of Syro-Palestinian Seals and the Songs of the Sabbath Sacrifice," in *Images and Prophecy in the Ancient Eastern Mediterranean*, ed. M. Nissinen and C. E. Carter, FRLANT 233 (Göttingen: Vandenhoeck & Ruprecht, 2009), 200–201.

[200] For a detailed discussion of the shared vocabulary between Ezek 40–48 and the *New Jerusalem*, see S. Fujita, *The Temple Theology of the Qumran Sect and the Book of Ezekiel: Their Relationship to Jewish Literature of the Last Two Centuries B.C.* (Ann Arbor: Univ. Microfilms, 1983), 306–15. For the studies on the *New Jerusalem* text, see F. García Martínez, "The 'New Jerusalem' and the Future Temple of the Manuscripts from Qumran," in *Qumran and Apocalyptic: Studies on the Aramaic Texts from Qumran*, STDJ 9 (Leiden: Brill, 1992), 180–213; idem, "New Jerusalem," in *Encyclopedia of the Dead Sea Scrolls* 2:606–610; L. DiTommaso, *The Dead Sea: New Jerusalem Text: Contents and Contexts*, TSAJ 110 (Tübingen: Mohr Siebeck, 2005).

[201] In contrast to Isaiah that has 49 occurrences of "Zion" and Jeremiah that mentions "Zion" 19 times, Ezekiel makes no reference to "Zion" at all. The absence of "Jerusalem" is also striking, given its repeated appearance in chapters 1–39, and given that T. A. Rudnig has helpfully detected other terminological, stylistic and thematic connections between Ezek 40–48 and 1–39 (*Heilig und Profan: Redaktionskritische Studien zu Ez 40–48*, BZAW 287 [Berlin: de Gruyter, 2000], 52–64, esp. 63). Cf. J. Galambush, *Jerusalem in the Book of Ezekiel*, SBLDS 130 (Atlanta: Scholars Press, 1992), 145; M. Konkel, *Architektonik des Heiligen: Studien zur zweiten Templevision Ezechiels (Ez 40–48)*, BBB 129 (Berlin: Philo, 2001), 223.

or coverings such as שׁשׁ and רקמה, which have previously appeared in the description of the Jerusalem sanctuary in chapter 16.[202] Instead, Ezek 40–48 simply describes the ideal temple as built from "wood" (עץ). In this way, the vision in Ezekiel creates a distance between the restored temple and the past Jerusalem temple. Reading the vision of Ezekiel in light of the *Description of the New Jerusalem* and the *Songs of the Sabbath Sacrifice* makes us aware of how the "eschatologization" of the temple is also present within the very traditions of the MT. Recognizing the allusions reused in the later texts can thus go a long way to explaining heretofore unnoticed interpretations of the older texts.

On the other hand, the reception materials and the percursor texts can also display points of divergence. That is to say, when dealing with the reception of Ezekiel's OAN, we must not assume an unbroken linear progression of a metanarrative. Instead, the fluid textual traditions can engage in a meaningful "discourse of differences." To illustrate this possibility of a meaningful divergence, we can turn to a significant Greek witness to Ezekiel—P967. This Greek papyrus attests to a different chapter order than in the MT, having 36:1–23; 38–39; 37; 40–48. This means, the Gog oracles (chapters 38–39) in P967 are placed before the vision concerning the resurrection of the dry bones in chapter 37. Also, the papyrus presents a version that is shorter than the MT at various places. Several significant passages of the MT such as 12:26–28, 32:24–26, and 36:23bβ–38 are missing in P967.[203] The different chapter orders in the MT and P967 reflect different kinds of eschatological outlook in two major aspects. First, the MT places the restoration of Israel in Ezek 37 straight after YHWH's call for the nations' recognition in 36:23a. By contrast,

---

[202] The terms such as "embroidery" (רקמה), "fine linen" (שׁשׁ), and "fine leather" (תחשׁ) in Ezek 16:10 can also be found in the construction of the tabernacle in passages such as Exod 25:5; 26:14, 36; 27:16; 28:39; 35:7, 23, 35; 36:37; 38:18; 39:29; Num 4:6, 8, 10. The similarities between the clothing of Lady Jerusalem and the building materials of the Israelite sanctuary are also noted in Zimmerli, *Ezekiel*, 1:340–41; Block, *Ezekiel*, 1:485; Galambush, *Jerusalem*, 95.

[203] On the differences and minuses in P967, see J. Lust, "Major Divergences between LXX and MT in Ezekiel," in *The Earliest Text of the Hebrew Bible: The Relationship between the Masoretic Text and the Hebrew Base the Septuagint Reconsidered*, ed. A. Schenker, SCS 52 (Atlanta: Society of Biblical Literature, 2003), 83–92; A. S. Crane, *Israel's Restoration: A Textual-Comparative Exploration of Ezekiel 36–39*, VTSup 122 (Leiden: Brill, 2008), 207–64; S. S. Scatolini, "Ezek 36, 37, 38 and 39 in Papyrus 967 as Pre-Text for Re-Reading Ezekiel," in *Interpreting Translation*, BETL 192 (Leuven: Leuven University Press, 2005), 331–57, esp. 338–40; Schwagmeier, "Untersuchungen," 239-316; Klein, *Schriftauslegung*, 59–77; Tooman, *Gog*, 77–83. For a survey of the critical scholarship on P967, see I. A. Lilly, *Two Books of Ezekiel: Papyrus 967 and the Masoretic Text as Variant Literary Editions*, VTSup 150 (Leiden: Brill, 2012), 28–62.

P967 places the battle with Gog (Ezek 38–39) straight after the declaration of YHWH to demonstrate his holy name among the nations (Ezek 36:23a). That is to say, whereas P967 presents YHWH's vindication of his holiness through the defeat of Gog and Gog's allies, the MT seeks the knowledge of divine holiness via Israel's restoration.[204] Second, the vision of the dry bones in the MT expects a historical restoration of the nation, whereas P967 places the resurrection of the dry bones in Ezek 37 after the cosmic battle with Gog in Ezek 38–39. From the different arrangement, Crane surmises that the dry bones in P967 Ezek 37:1–14 includes Israel's slain following the battle with Gog.[205] The vision of the dry bones in P967 seemingly indicates both a physical/individual and a national/moral resurrection. The direction of influences between the MT and P967 remains a highly contentious issue. On the one hand, scholars such as Lust, Crane, Scatolini, and Schwagmeier suggest that P967 represents an older *Vorlage* than that of the MT.[206] On the other hand, the discovery of the Masada Ezekiel manuscript, which dates earlier than P967 but bears close resemblances with the MT,[207] prompts Patmore to take a more critical stance on the chronological priority of the *Vorlage* of P967.[208] Lilly

---

[204] Cf. Schwagmeier, "Untersuchungen," 292: "In p967 gewinnen die Völker diese Erkenntnis nun aber nicht an Jhwhs Handeln an Israel, sondern am Eingreifen Gottes gegen sie selbst."

[205] Crane, *Restoration*, 251.

[206] J. Lust, "Ezekiel 36–40 in the Oldest Greek Manuscript," *CBQ* 43 (1981): 517–33, esp. 521–25; idem, "Divergences," 83–92; idem, "The Use of Textual Witnesses for the Establishment of the Text: The Shorter and Longer Texts of Ezekiel: An Example: Ez 7," in *Ezekiel and His Book: Textual and Literary Criticism and Their Interrelation*, ed. J. Lust, BETL 74 (Leuven: Leuven University Press, 1986), 7–20; idem, "Messianism in LXX-Ezekiel: Towards a Synthesis," in *The Septuagint and Messianism*, ed. M. A. Knibb (Leuven: Peeters, 2006), 417–30; Crane, *Restoration*, 236-50, 257–63; Scatolini, "Papyrus 967," 331–57; Schwagmeier, "Untersuchungen," 313–17, 368. In a later article, Lust changes his view and comments that both P967 and the proto-MT Masada fragments were circulating at the same time ("Ezekiel's Utopian Expectations," in *Flores Florentino: Dead Sea Scrolls and Other Early Jewish Studies in Honour of Florentino García Martínez*, ed. A. Hilhorst et al. [Leiden: Brill, 2007], 404).

[207] The Masada Ezekiel manuscript contains 35:11–38:14 and is dated earlier than 70 CE. For further information, see S. Talmon, "1043–2220 (MasEzek) Ezekiel 35:11–38:14," in *Masada VI: The Yigael Yadin Excavations 1963–1965: Hebrew Fragments from Masada* (Jerusalem: Israel Exploration Society and the Hebrew University of Jerusalem, 1999), 59–75; E. Tigchelaar, "Notes on the Ezekiel Scroll from Masada (MasEzek)," *RevQ* 22/86 (2005): 269–75; Schwagmeier, *Untersuchungen*, 101–3, 354.

[208] H. M. Patmore contends that P967 and the proto-MT manuscript from Masada demonstrate that "the 'longer' (i.e., Masoretic) and 'shorter' (i.e., Greek) texts were in circulation *concurrently and in Hebrew* for at least 200 years" ("The Shorter and

attempts to mediate between the two positions. She criticises Lust for overstating his case "by implying that the status of textual priority extends to all of p967's textual features."[209] On the other hand, Lilly is cautious of Patmore's over-reliance on fragmented Hebrew manuscripts to determine the textual tradition for the MT.[210] Instead of envisioning the *Vorlagen* of P967 and MT floating at the same time independently of each other, Lilly posits their mutual influences.[211] In any case, the above examples taken from Ezek 36–39 helpfully illustrate that the divergences among textual traditions need not be explained as merely accidental or due to *parablepsis*. Rather, the differences can be viewed as imbued with ideological meanings and as a result of divergent actions and reactions among a host of textual traditions.

The reception materials of Ezekiel's OAN are not restricted to extrabiblical sources, but can also be found within the Hebrew Bible. What the above examples accomplish is to illustrate how various interpretations of the biblical texts have come alive by allowing the texts to converse with their reception. With appropriately clarified purpose for comparison, examining the intersection of redaction and reception can point to tensions and harmony, reveal aspects of the subjects that may not be obvious when looked at in isolation, and cement the results derived from within a selected group of biblical texts.[212] Investigating the reception materials that are found beyond Ezek 25–32 ultimately brings us back to and sheds light on the focal texts, sharpening our perspectives on the rhetorical functions of Ezek 25–32 within the book.

Having set the course with a scholarly review and a discussion of the methodology to be used, we can now embark on a journey to the textual world of Ezek 25–32.

---

Longer Texts of Ezekiel: The Implications of the Manuscript Finds from Masada and Qumran," *JSOT* 32 [2007]: 231–42, here 241).

[209] Lilly, *Two Books*, 21. On the same page, she also thinks that it is problematic for Crane to conflate P967 and Old Greek. In the conclusion, she criticises both Lust and Crane for having "swung the pendulum too far in the other direction, declaring p967's text to be earlier than the MT" (302).

[210] Ibid., 24. However, Lilly courteously agrees with Patmore, when she states that "it is still too early to establish textual priority between P967 and MT's texts" (25).

[211] Ibid., 302–3. Her position is not dissimilar from the view presented in M. Popović, "Prophet, Book and Texts: Ezekiel, Pseudo-Ezekiel and the Authoritativeness of Ezekiel Traditions in Early Judaism," in *Authoritative Scriptures in Ancient Judaism*, ed. Idem, JSJSup 141 (Leiden: Brill, 2010), 227–51, esp. 244, 247.

[212] Cf. B. A. Strawn, "Comparative Approaches: History, Theory, and the Image," in *Method Matters: Essays on the Interpretation of the Hebrew Bible in Honor of David L. Petersen*, ed. J. M. LeMon and K. H. Richards, SBLRBS 56 (Atlanta: Society of Biblical Literature, 2009), 117.

# CHAPTER TWO

# THE DISPOSSESSION OF THE PROMISED LAND IN EZEK 25

בן אדם ארץ כי תחטא לי למעל מעל ונטיתי ידי עליה ושברתי לה מטה לחם והשלחתי בה רעב והכרתי ממנה אדם ובהמה

"Son of man, if a country sins against me by committing unfaithfulness, then I will stretch out my hand against it, and I will break its staff of bread, and I will send famine upon it, and I will cut off man and beast from it."

Ezek 14:13

לכן כה אמר אדני יהוה ונטתי ידי על אדום והכרתי ממנה אדם ובהמה ונתתיה חרבה מתימן ודדנה בחרב יפלו

Therefore, thus has the Lord YHWH declared, "And I will stretch out my hand against Edom, and I will cut off man and beast from it, and I will lay it waste. From Teman even to Dedan they will fall by the sword."

Ezek 25:13

Ezekiel 25, the first of the series of Ezekiel's OAN, is marked by severe invectives against the neighboring nations of Judah—Ammon, Moab, Edom, and Philistia. Ammon is inveighed due to its mockery of YHWH's profaned sanctuary, the land of Israel, and the house of Judah (vv. 3, 6); Moab is judged because it mocks the house of Judah that it is like all the other nations (v. 8); Edom is accused of taking vengeance against the house of Judah (v. 12); the Philistines are impugned for taking vengeance with a spiteful heart due to their ancient hatred (v. 15). The malicious *Schadenfreude* and the acts of vengeance executed against Judah form the reasons for divine judgment of these foreign nations.

In light of this, most exegetes suggest that chapter 25 leaves behind the message of retribution for Judah in Ezek 1–24, heralding instead an implicit hope and salvation for Israel.¹ Accordingly, Allen boldly claims that the role of Ezek 25 is "to bring reassurance to the Judeans, in a round-about way."² Gosse argues that the mockery of the Transjordanian states marks a shift of Ezekiel's prophetic mission toward a declaration of salvation for Israel, where God begins to defend Israel against the foreign enemies.³ Strong stresses that the actions of the nations in chapter 25 motivate YHWH to clear out the enemies, to defend his people and to "affirm Yahweh's promise of the land to Israel."⁴

These scholars pay too much attention to the victimized postion of the Judahite land in the reasons for judgment. As such, they do not account for why the subsequent announcements of judgment against the Transjordanian nations and Philistia do not concretely envisage the promise to restore the land of Israel. YHWH vows to ride roughshod over the Ammonite and Moabite cities and lands by handing them over not to the house of Judah, but to the unidentified "sons of the east" (vv. 4, 10). Moreover, YHWH will execute his vengeance, laying waste the lands, cities, and seacoasts, cutting off men and animals from the Edomite and Philistine territories (vv. 7, 13–14, 16–17). Still, the house of Judah is in no way promised that it will regain its territorial sovereignty or be compensated fully from all the catastrophes that befell the nations. It is no wonder that Greenberg remarks briefly but perceptively that

---

¹ E.g., Blenkinsopp, *Ezekiel*, 108–9; Eichrodt, *Ezekiel*, 362; Block, *Ezekiel*, 1:3–4; Bewer, *Ezekiel*, 5; Albertz, *Exilszeit*, 150; Fuhs, *Ezechiel 25–48*, 135.

² Allen, *Ezekiel 20–48*, 69.

³ Gosse states: "La jubilation, le dédain et le mépris des nations qui se sont manifestés à la suite de la chute de Jérusalem provoquent, en faveur d'Israël, le retournement de Dieu contre les nations" ("Recueil," 535–62, esp. 546). According to Gosse, Ezek 25 historically displays a different function from that of the Tyre and Egypt oracles in chapters 26–32. The Tyre and Egypt oracles align with Ezekiel's prophetic mission before the fall of Jerusalem. These oracles function mainly to deter Judean resistance against the Babylonian dominion, and thereby announce the certainty of judgment against Judah. On the other hand, the oracles in Ezek 25, in Gosse's opinion, reflect Ezekiel's prophetic mission after the fall of Jerusalem. Here, the judgment upon Judah is completed, and therefore YHWH can start defending Israel against the mockery of the foreign nations.

⁴ Strong, "Ezekiel's Oracles," 170. Viewing Ezek 25–32 as a whole, he claims that the OAN bolster the promise of the land and Zion's doctrine of YHWH's kingship (25). He further asserts that, "Ezekiel 25 consists of a collection of three oracles that were delivered later than the collection of oracles against Egypt and served as indirect salvation oracles for the house of Israel" (132). Having analyzed the reasons for judgment in Ezek 25, he concludes that "Ezekiel ultimately chose the nations in order to formulate in the terms of the conquest tradition a series of foreign nations oracles that proclaim Israel's restoration to the land" (143).

what is at stake in Ezek 25 is not Israel's interest, but YHWH's "injured majesty."[5] Odell helpfully highlights that the house of Judah "in no way benefits from Yahweh's assault on the nations."[6] They advocate a more pessimistic but sober reading that views the message of Ezek 25 as less about hope for Israel.[7] What goes unnoticed for both Greenberg and Odell is that many lexical features that describe the characteristics and judgment of the nations in Ezek 25 find parallels elsewhere in the book of Ezekiel and the rest of the Hebrew Bible.

In this chapter, we will first familiarize ourselves with the form and content of the present oracles, noting in particular the absence of the hopeful promise of a restoration of God's people in the statements of the judgment against the neighboring nations. Having done so, I will argue that many lexical features found in Ezek 25 draw inspiration from the traditions related to the Promised Land and the divine judgment executed against Jerusalem. These parallels provide clues to the possible sources of inspiration behind Ezek 25, which in turn affect our understanding of the passage's current rhetoric. In their current literary context in Ezek 25, the parallels create a rhetorical impact so radical that the house of Judah, though victimized, does not receive territorial compensation. This chapter will conclude that Ezek 25 forms an oblique rhetoric, affirming not only the dispossession of the belligerent nations, but also that of Judah.

## 1. THE OMINOUS BEGINNING

Contrary to the argument by many commentators for implicit hope in Ezek 25, the material compensations for the house of Judah hardly play a role in the proof-sayings against the Transjordanian nations and Philistia. At the very beginning, Ezek 25 already evinces a premonition of imminent doom. The chapter begins with the prophetic word formula, "And the word of YHWH came to me saying" (ויהי דבר יהוה אלי לאמר, v. 1).[8] YHWH then commands the prophet to set his face against the Ammonites (vv. 2–3a) in order to pronounce

---

[5] Greenberg, *Ezekiel 21–37*, 527. He states: "Instead the nations' mocking and victimizing Israel is presented as in some way an injury to God" (525).

[6] Odell, *Ezekiel*, 324.

[7] For a similar view of Ezek 25, see Schwagmeier, "Untersuchungen," 261. He comments briefly that the lack of a date formula at the beginning of Ezek 25 indicates that the judgment upon the neighboring nations should be linked to that of Judah depicted in chapter 24.

[8] For F.-L. Hossfeld, the prophetic word formula in Ezekiel is "das wichtigste Anfangssyntagma," signaling the beginning of a macrotext unit (*Untersuchungen zu Komposition und Theologie des Ezechielbuches*, FB 20 [Würzburg: Echter, 1977], 10).

judgment over them. The expression "set your face against" (שִׂים פָּנֶיךָ [עַל]אֶל) is rare but characteristic of Ezekiel.[9] It appears in the context when YHWH issues his statement of judgment not only to other foreign nations, but also to Judah.[10] This thus brings an ominous tone to the proof-sayings that unfold subsequently. Although the reasons for judgment of Ammon, Moab, Edom, and Philistia, signaled by the conjunction "because" (יַעַן),[11] presuppose the misery of the house of Judah, the subsequent announcements of judgment, signaled by the conjunction "therefore" (לָכֵן),[12] focuses on the centrality of YHWH's judgment, and not Judah's territorial interests. Throughout the proof-sayings, little promise of restoration is offered to the victimized house of Judah.

## 1.1. THE FIRST PROOF-SAYING

In the first proof-saying (25:3b–5), the silence about the future fate of Judah is intriguing, when בְּנֵי עַמּוֹן—treated as both the population of a nation "the Ammonites" and the name of the country "Ammon"[13]—are directly accused of victimizing the house of Judah. In v. 3b, the country is condemned for its mockery of YHWH's sanctuary (מִקְדָּשִׁי), the land of Israel (אַדְמַת יִשְׂרָאֵל), and the house of Judah (בֵּית יְהוּדָה).[14] The paralinguistic exclamation "aha" clearly

---

[9] Ezek 6:2; 13:17; 21:2, 7; 25:2; 28:21; 29:2; 35:2; 38:2. Outside of Ezekiel, a similar expression appears less frequently in Lev 20:5; Jer 21:10; 44:11, where YHWH becomes the grammatical subject and the object is connected with the preposition בְּ instead of אֶל or עַל.

[10] For the hostility signified by this expression, see K. Schöpflin, *Theologie als Biographie im Ezechielbuch: Ein Beitrag zur Konzeption alttestamentlicher Prophetie*, FAT 36 [Tübingen: Mohr Siebeck, 2002], 74–78; Block, *Ezekiel*, 1:34; Strong, "Ezekiel's Oracles," 152; Fechter, *Bewältigung*, 71–73.

[11] Ezek 25:3, 6, 8, 12, 15.

[12] Ezek 25:4–5, 7, 9–11, 13–14, 16–17.

[13] In the Hebrew Bible, בְּנֵי עַמּוֹן occurs more than 104 times, and can be used in a context that is in association with either the country names or the inhabitants of the surrounding nations. Therefore, based on the surrounding context, the Hebrew term can be translated as either "Ammon" or "Ammonites." E.g., Judg 10:6, 11; 1 Sam 14:47; 2 Sam 8:11b–12 (=1 Chr 18:11); 1 Kgs 11:33; 2 Kgs 23:13; 24:2; Jer 9:25 (Eng. 9:26); 25:19–23; 40:11; Amos 1–2. For further explications, see D. I. Block, "Bny 'Mwn: The Sons of Ammon," *AUSS* 22 (1984): 197–212.

[14] Zimmerli suggests that the triad of the sanctuary, the house of Judah, and the land of Israel forms a concentric circle (*Ezekiel*, 2:563–565). Judah is not set in contrast to the old northern kingdom, but is rather subsumed and included within Israel. H. G. M. Williamson also follows this inclusive understanding of Israel in Ezekiel ("The Concept of Israel in Transition," in *The World of Ancient Israel*, ed. R. E. Clements [Cambridge: Cambridge University Press, 1989], 141–61, esp. 144). As such, in this chapter, we will refer to God's people most of the time as "the house of Judah,"

marks Ammon's intention of derision, which adds to the villainous nature of Ammon.[15] With its distinctive lexical connections to 24:21, where the profaned sanctuary is also in view, Ammon's taunt clearly presupposes the misery of Judah.[16]

Yet, the subsequent announcement of judgment in 25:4–5 does not envision any benefit gained by Jerusalem.[17] Instead, YHWH will deliver Ammon as a "possession" (מורשה) into the hand of "the sons of the east" (בני קדם).[18] Scholars tend to focus on the *identity* of these "sons of the east," seeking to specify their geographical location on the map. On the one hand, a majority of scholars identify these "sons of the east" with the tribe of Arab and Aramaean stock who roamed the desert east of Ammon.[19] On the other hand, Schwagmeier notes the prominent role of the king of Babylon as the conqueror in the book of Ezekiel, and posits the view that the "sons of the east" should be identified with Babylon.[20] However, it is more helpful to focus on the *rhetorical function* of these sons of the east. The possessors from the *east* signify a rhetorical contrast with Judah in the *west* of Ammon. Not the latter but the former will enjoy the agricultural products of the land.[21] Rabah will turn into "a pasture for camels," and Ammon will be "a resting-place for flocks."[22] The

---

but we will also bear in mind that Ezekiel mostly perceives Judah as an integral part of the larger "house of Israel."

[15] The term "aha" (האח) appears in the context of mockery and derision in Ezek 26:2; 36:2; Ps 35:21, 25; 40:16. Isa 44:16 uses the term to designate the self-satisfaction of an idolater, whereas Job 39:25 relates this term to the sound of a horse in battle. Cf. Gosse, "Recueil," 544.

[16] Both 24:21 and 25:3b attest to the pairing of "sanctuary" (מקדש) and the verbal root "to profane" (חלל). In 24:21, YHWH is the grammatical subject of the act of desecration. On the other hand, in 25:3b, an impersonal *niphal* is used for the verb חלל. In the latter passage, this might indicate a *passivum divinum*, noted by Premstaller, *Fremdvölkersprüche*, 37. The pairing of מקדש and חלל also appears in Ezek 7:24; 23:39, but the grammatical subject of the act of profanation is the people of Judah.

[17] By contrast, Isa 11:14, Jer 49:2, and Zeph 2:8–9 all announce that the Ammonites will be subjugated under Israel.

[18] Other biblical references to the בני קדם include Gen 29:1; Judg 6:3, 33; 7:12; 8:10; 1 Kgs 5:10 [Eng. 4:30]; Isa 11:14; Jer 49:28; Job 1:3.

[19] Cooke, *Ezekiel*, 282; Fuhs, *Ezechiel 25–48*, 137; Fechter, *Bewältigung*, 78; Premstaller, *Fremdvölkersprüche*, 37; Zimmerli, *Ezekiel*, 2:13; Eichrodt, *Ezekiel*, 357; Block, *Ezekiel*, 2:17; Gottwald, *Kingdoms*, 323.

[20] Schwagmeier, "Untersuchungen," 262, n. 949. See the appearances of Babylon in Ezek 12:13; 17:12 (2x), 16, 20; 19:9; 21:19, 21; 24:2; 26:7; 29:18, 19; 30:10, 24, 25 (2x); 32:11.

[21] For a similar view, see Odell, *Ezekiel*, 327.

[22] רבה and בני עמון are usually juxtaposed together to form a construct phrase. E.g., Ezek 21:25 [Eng. 21:20]; 2 Sam 12:26, 27; 17:27; Deut 3:11; Jer 49:2. So Block, *Ezekiel*, 2:14, n. 27; Greenberg, *Ezekiel 21–37*, 519; Premstaller, *Fremdvölkersprüche*, 38.

ultimate aim of the punishments executed upon Ammon is marked not by any benefit for the house of Judah, but by the recognition formula at the end of v. 5, which states: "And you will know that I am YHWH."[23]

## 1.2. The Second Proof-Saying

Even in the second proof-saying (25:6–7), where the mockery expressed by Ammon toward the land of God's people is further elaborated, future compensations for the house of Judah are not mentioned. Signified by the prophetic word formula (כי כה אמר אדני יהוה), Ammon is indicted for having clapped its hands and stamped its feet over the devastated land of Israel (v. 6).[24] Elsewhere in Ezek 6:11 and 21:19, 22 [Eng. 21:14, 17], clapping hands and stamping feet are associated with YHWH's commissioning of the prophet to vent his wrath against his people.[25] In contrast to the fury, gloom and severity pervading these previous contexts, the same gestures of Ammon in 25:6 are accompanied by light-hearted and frivolous verb and noun—"to rejoice" (שמח) and "contempt" (שאט).[26]

Despite this humiliation, the subsequent announcement of judgment (v. 7) does not mention the way the land of Israel licks its wounds, but focuses only on YHWH's dealings with the Ammonites. Here, a series of first person verbs characterizes YHWH's assertions against Ammon: "I have stretched out my hand against you," "and I will deliver you as a booty to the nations,"[27] "and I will cut you off from the peoples," "and I will destroy you from the countries,"

---

[23] This formula employs the second masculine plural form, addressing בני עמון as the population of a nation.

[24] Unlike the previous pericope, which utilizes either a masculine plural or a feminine singular form, the present pericope uses the second masculine singular suffix to address Ammon. While Zimmerli thinks this shift to the 2ms pronominal suffix has no apparent reason (*Ezekiel*, 2:13), Block attributes this change to the shift in focus from the land of Ammon to the human population as a collective (*Ezekiel*, 2:18).

[25] The gestures opening the paragraph (6:11) are immediately followed by YHWH's venting his wrath against the people in the next verse (וכליתי חמתי בם, v. 12). Similarly, YHWH's clapping of hands in 21:22 [Eng. 21:17] associates him with the appeasement of his wrath (והנחתי חמתי).

[26] Within different contexts in the Hebrew Bible, clapping, as expressed through verbs such as נכה, ספק, תקא, and מחא, can designate various moods, such as joy and celebration (e.g., Ps 47:2 [Eng. 47:1]; 98:8; Isa 55:2; 2 Kgs 11:12), gloating (e.g., Ezek 25:6; Nah 3:19), derision (e.g., Job 27:23; Lam 2:15) or anger (Num 24:10). See also K. G. Friebel, *Jeremiah's and Ezekiel's Sign-Acts*, JSOTSup 283 (Sheffield: Sheffield Academic Press, 1999), 255–56, 301–3; Schöpflin, *Theologie*, 40–41.

[27] The *Kethib* reads לבג, which is meaningless, and we should follow the *Qere* to read לבז "as a booty."

and ultimately "I will eliminate you."[28] As indicated by the recognition formula ("Thus you will know that I am YHWH") appearing at the end of the proof-saying, all these severe acts of judgment intend to lead Ammon to acknowledge YHWH. In all this, the territorial interests or compensations for the house of Israel are not in view.

1.3. THE THIRD PROOF-SAYING

The absence of any hopeful elements for the house of Judah persists even in the third proof-saying (25:8–11), where YHWH turns his judgment toward Moab.[29] Moab is accused of deflating the house of Judah,[30] likening it to the other nations (ככל הגוים). Fechter remarks that "In diesem Satz drückt sich eine Infragestellung des Erwählungsgedankens aus."[31] Similarly, Eichrodt claims that Moab's statement is "a clear refutation of that nation's claim to a special position as the bearer of a message from God."[32] If we look more closely, the statement is more than an attack on the elect status of the house of Judah; it is a direct assault of YHWH's dignity and his sovereignty over his people. Outside Ezekiel, the phrase ככל הגוים appears once in Deuteronomy and twice in 1 Samuel.[33] There, the Israelites are "like all the nations" for wanting a king for themselves. At the foundation of these passages, YHWH's supremacy is challenged by the demand of Israel. Unlike the aforementioned passages, Ezek 25 is certainly not concerned with the issue that the exiles want a king for themselves. Yet, the supremacy of YHWH over Israel is similarly challenged when Moab has mocked the exiles. A more immediate comparison with the statement made by Moab concerning the house of Judah appears in Ezek 20:32,

---

[28] This phrase "I will eliminate you" (אשמידך) comes without a *waw* conjunction and is thus an asyndetic construction. Also, given that נטיתי את ידי עליך is parallel to אשמידך, the phrase והאבדתיך מן הארצות is parallel to והכרתיך מן העמים, and ונתתיך לבג לגוים disrupts the parallelism in the verse. Therefore, it was often treated as a gloss. E.g., Zimmerli, *Ezekiel*, 2:8, and Eichrodt, *Ezekiel*, 356. See also the explanation in Block, *Ezekiel*, 2:14, n. 36.
[29] The MT's inclusion of Seir alongside Moab is not attested in the LXX. The content in vv. 8–11 also does not touch on Seir. More likely, the inclusion of Seir is a later gloss, anticipating the oracle against Edom in 25:12–14 and 35 (cf. v. 15). On the suggestion that the insertion of the gloss might indicate an increasing hatred towards Edom, see Zimmerli, *Ezekiel*, 2:8. On the other hand, Allen, *Ezekiel 20–48*, 65; Block, *Ezekiel*, 2:19, suggest that the gloss is to draw attention to parallels with the Edom and the Seir oracles (25:12–14; 35:2–9).
[30] The LXX has "the house of Israel and Judah" (οἶκος Ισραηλ καὶ Ιουδα).
[31] Fechter, *Bewältigung*, 86.
[32] Eichrodt, *Ezekiel*, 360.
[33] Deut 17:14; 1 Sam 8:5, 20. Cf. Zimmerli, *Ezekiel*, 2:14; Block, *Ezekiel*, 2:20; Premstaller, *Fremdvölkersprüche*, 41.

where the exiles claim that "to be like the nations" means not only the loss of territorial identity by living abroad, but also the loss of Judah's religious identity by worshipping "wood and stone" (עץ ואבן).³⁴ Moab, in Ezek 25:8, reflects the inner thinking of the exiles (20:32) almost verbatim.³⁵ If this loss of religious identity is what is in the meaning of the words of Moab, YHWH's retaliation can then be interpreted as an attempt to claim responsibility, to defend, and to assert his sovereignty over the fate of his people.

Perplexingly, the following declaration of judgment does not give any hint that YHWH will assert his authority by regathering the exiles back to the land (25:9–11). Instead, YHWH presupposes the status of the cities of Moab as the "glory of the land" (צבי ארץ). Specific cities at the "flank of Moab," including Beth-jeshimoth, Baal-meon, and Kirjathaim, further qualify and clarify the phrase צבי ארץ (v. 9).³⁶ Instead of handing the lands over to the house of Judah, the cities are declared as a possession to the "sons of the east" just like the land of Ammon, which will no longer be remembered among the nations (v. 10).³⁷ The ultimate aim in delivering the divine judgment is to draw attention to YHWH's majesty—to make the nations know that "I am YHWH" (v. 11b).

## 1.4. THE FOURTH PROOF-SAYING

As in the previous proof-sayings, the material compensations for the house of Judah play little role in the fourth and fifth proof-sayings (25:12–14, 15–17).

---

³⁴ Deut 4:27–28; 28:36, 64 also utilize this distinctive Hebrew apposition. Deut 4:28 juxtaposes the "wood and stone" with "gods, the work of the hands of man" (אלהים מעשה ידי אדם); whereas 28:36, 64 parallel "wood and stone" with "other gods" (אלהים אחרים). Thus, according to these deuteronomic passages, worshipping wood and stone amounts to worshipping other gods.

³⁵ Within the book of Ezekiel, these are the only two places (20:32 and 25:8), where Judah is made directly comparable with other nations (גוים). The cases in 20:32 and 25:8, where the exile of the Judahites is at issue, represent the *effect* of YHWH's judgment. Cf. Ezek 11:12, where Judah abandons YHWH's statutes and ordinances and acts according to the ordinances of the nations (כמשפטי הגוים), which becomes the *cause* of YHWH's judgment.

³⁶ "The flank of Moab" (כתף מואב) literally means "the shoulder of Moab." The word can be used figuratively as a designation of territory. So Josh 15:8, 10–11; 18:12–13, 16, 18–19; Isa 11:14. See Zimmerli, *Ezekiel*, 2:8.

³⁷ The third feminine singular verb תזכר clearly indicates an understanding of בני עמון as a geographical designation—"Ammon/the land of Ammon". The phrase על בני עמון and the subsequent reference to בני עמון in v. 10 are considered as secondary elements, which reflect a conscious attempt to link the oracle of Moab to the preceding proof-sayings about Ammon (vv. 1–5). See Eichrodt, *Ezekiel*, 356.

These oracles targeting Edom and Philsitia stand out from the rest of the oracles in chapter 25, by being characterized with the *Leitwort*—נקם.[38] Edom is accused of acting with bitter vengeance (בנקם נקם) against the house of Judah, the intensity of which is further reinforced by another *figura etymologica*— "and they have incurred grievous guilt" (ויאשמו אשום, v. 12).[39] Despite the culpability of Edom, the exact nature of Edom's crime is not spelled out.[40] Elsewhere in Ezekiel, the crime of Edom is always specified. What is at issue in Ezek 16:57 is the *Schadenfreude* of Edom. A later tradition in Ezek 35 elaborately paints Mount Seir as the aggressor of the Israelite land, specifying Seir's enduring hostility (v. 5), bloodshed (v. 6), drive to expand (v. 10), anger, envy, hatred (v. 11), and arrogant speech (v. 13).[41] By contrast, Ezek 25 does not indict Edom in terms of either its mockery or the land issue, but only uses the generic language of "vengeance" (נקם) and "guilt" (אשם) to convey an antagonistic attitude toward Edom. Without specifying Edom's actions, the accusations of Edom in Ezek 25 remain impersonal and abstract.

In light of the rather bland reasons for judgment, the focus of attention is drawn to YHWH's acts of punishment (25:13–14). In response to Edom's act of vengeance, YHWH decides to retaliate by stretching out his hand against (על+יד+נטה) Edom and to cut off (man and beast) from the land (*hiphil* of the verb כרת+מן+[אדם+בהמה]). He will execute his vengeance (נקמתי) through the

---

[38] For the terminological and structural parallels between both the Edom and the Philistia oracles, see W. T. Koopmans, "Poetic Reciprocation: The Oracles against Edom and Philistia in Ezek. 25:12–17," in *Verse in Ancient Near Eastern Prose*, ed. J. C. de Moor et al., AOAT 42 (Krevelaer: Butzon & Bercker, 1993), 113–22. Similarly, Fuhs remarks that "Die Worte gegen Edom ¹²⁻¹⁴ und Philistäa ¹⁵⁻¹⁷ gehören formal und inhaltlich zusammen. Sie stehen unter dem Leitwort Rache, das sowohl die Begründung wie die Ankündigung des Gerichts beherrscht" (*Ezechiel 25–48*, 139).

[39] Related forms of the verbal root אשם "to incur guilt" occurs several other times in Ezekiel to denote the concept of sins in Judah or in the restored Israel. E.g., Ezek 22:4; 40:39; 42:13; 44:29; 46:20. Outside of Ezekiel, the noun also describes human guilt, acting in a similar way to the verb חטא "to sin." E.g., Gen 26:10; Jer 51:5 and Ps 68:22 [Eng. 69:21]. See D. Kellermann, "אשם," *TDOT* 1:429–437; *HALOT*, 1:95–96.

[40] Similarly, Isa 34:5–8 and 63:1–4 announce YHWH's vengeance against Edom without specifying its crime against Jerusalem. See Assis, "Edom," 3; O'Brien, "Edom," 158–59.

[41] Such details of Edom's actions against Israel in Ezek 35 are perhaps due to the literary function of chapters 35–36. J. Lust explains that the function of chapters 35–36 is different from that of 25:12–14 ("Edom–Adam in Ezekiel, in the MT and LXX," in *Studies in the Hebrew Bible, Qumran, and the Septuagint Presented to Eugene Ulrich*, ed. P. W. Flint et al., VTSup 101 [Leiden: Brill, 2006], 396). He cites Allen, who sees the oracle against Edom as serving "as a dark backcloth to enhance the revelation of Israel's glorious salvation" (*Ezekiel 20–48*, 171).

hand of Israel, in order to fulfil his anger and wrath (v. 14). Too often, commentators seize upon the reference to "my people Israel" (עמי ישראל) in v. 14, stating that YHWH's retribution against Edom means a promise of restoration for Israel. Peels, for instance, quickly concludes "that the Israel nearly eliminated in 586 will one day have a *national* existence again."[42] Eichrodt claims that this verse is inserted later on the basis that it reflects a "relapse into nationalist vindictiveness," which is incompatible with Ezekiel's attitude toward divine justice as expressed elsewhere in the prophetic book.[43] With the same reason, Fuhs describes the oracle against Edom in Ezek 25:12–14 as "[e]in Machwerk, aus dem nicht prophetisches Geistwort, sondern nationalistischer Ungeist spricht."[44] All these interpretations seem to assume that a restoration in the form of a sovereign nation with a people's own territory comes directly at the expense of the destructions of the foreign nations.

This relationship between YHWH and Israel in v. 14, in my opinion, is not expressed in terms of territorial compensation at all. In v. 14a, the reference to Israel only suggests a means to achieve YHWH's vengeance, as Peels also admits.[45] The verbal phrase ונתתי את נקמתי should be connected with באדום,[46] whereas the expression ביד is not to be rendered literally as "in the hand of" in the sense of exercising complete control over the enactment of vengeance, but rather metaphorically as a preposition "through" in the sense of acting as an instrument. This expression is to highlight the instrumental role of Israel in carrying out YHWH's vengeance. The instrumental role of Israel is further justified by the next part of the same verse (v. 14b). In generic language, the clause remarks that "they (Israel) will act in Edom according to my anger and according to my wrath" (ועשו באדום כאפי וכחמתי). Like "the sons of the east" who are the agent of divine punishment to receive Ammon and Moab as a "possession" (מורשה, vv. 4, 10), whatever Israel does serves only to fulfil YHWH's anger and wrath against Edom. The third part of the same verse (v.

---

[42] Italics mine. See H. G. L. Peels, *The Vengeance of God: The Meaning of the Root NQM and the Function of the NQM-Texts in the Context of Divine Revelation in the Old Testament*, OtSt 31 (Leiden: Brill, 1995), 190.

[43] Eichrodt, *Ezekiel*, 362.

[44] Fuhs, *Ezechiel 25–48*, 139. Similarly, A. Bertholet states: "Hier spricht recht deutlich der Israelit, dem der Hass gegen das Brudervolk im Blute steckt" (*Hesekiel*, HAT 1.13 [Tübingen: Mohr Siebeck, 1936], 134). So also Wevers, *Ezekiel*, 198; Cooke, *Ezekiel*, 285. Cf. the more reserved position in Zimmerli, *Ezekiel*, 2:18, who states that: "At any rate, this statement can be connected only with difficulty with the rest of Ezekiel's preaching."

[45] Peels, *Vengeance*, 190.

[46] The construction ב+נקמה+נתן (+ object of vengeance) is also used in immediate proximity. Thus 25:17b reads: "And they will know that I am YHWH when I inflict my vengeance upon them" (ותדעו כי אני יהוה בתתי את נקמתי בם). Cf. Num 31:3; Judg 15:7; 1 Sam 18:25; Ps 149:7; Jer 5:9, 29; 9:9 [Eng. 9:8]; 50:15.

14c) further confirms the centrality of YHWH's vengeance, and not Israel's territorial interests. Different from most of the other recognition formulas in Ezek 25, the recognition formula in v. 14c merges YHWH himself and YHWH's vengeance, reading, "they will know my vengeance."[47] Hence, Edom's knowledge of YHWH is attained exclusively through YHWH's vengeance. In this specific case, the ultimate aim of YHWH's retribution is not to restore the land of Judah, but to bring the nations to recognize YHWH's power.[48]

1.5. THE FIFTH PROOF-SAYING

The fifth proof-saying issued against the Philistines (25:15–17), like the preceding proof-saying about Edom, does not play up the tensions and conflicts with Judah. In v. 15, the Philistines are accused of taking bitter vengeance (וינקמו נקם), acting out of "contempt in soul" (שאט בנפש) and "everlasting/ancient enmity" (איבת עולם).[49] In particular, the phrase "with contempt in soul" (בשאט בנפש) is lexically linked to 25:6, where Ammon derides the devastation with all its contempt in soul (בכל שאטך בנפש).[50] There, the target of Ammon's mockery is explicitly the land of Israel. It is thus possible that the victim of Philistia's vengeance is the land of Israel. Despite this, the object of the Philistines' vengeance remains peculiarly absent.[51] The prophetic books, as noted by Gordon, commonly express territory as the heart of the struggle between Israel and Philistia.[52] Isaiah 9:12 pictures the Syrians from the east and the

---

[47] Normally, the recognition formulas in Ezekiel, as in 25:5, 8, 11, attest the form of "and you will know that I am YHWH" (וידעתם כי אני יהוה) or "and they will know that I am YHWH" (וידעו כי אני יהוה). Variant forms in connection to YHWH's נקם appear in 25:14 and 25:17.

[48] Cf. J. T. Strong, "Ezekiel's Use of the Recognition Formula in His Oracles against the Nations," *PRSt* 22 (1995): 115–34, who suggests that the appearances of the recognition formulas within the OAN do not indicate a sense of "internationalism" or "universalism" where YHWH aims to establish a covenantal relationship with the indicted foreign nations. Rather, what is being urged to be recognized by the nations is YHWH's reputation before these nations as a powerful god.

[49] In Ezek 35:5, Mount Seir is also accused of acting against the sons of Israel with איבת עולם.

[50] Within the Hebrew Bible, the verbal root שאט "to despise, to show contempt" appears only in Ezek 16:57; 25:6, 15; 28:24, 26; 36:5. For its meaning, see D. Bodi, *The Book of Ezekiel and the Poem of Erra*, OBO 104 (Freiburg: Universitätsverlag, 1991), 69–71.

[51] The English translation in NIV and the German translation in *Gute Nachricht Bibel* less accurately makes Judah the object of vengeance and destruction.

[52] R. P. Gordon, "The Ideological Foe: The Philistines in the Old Testament," in *Biblical and Near Eastern Essays*, ed. C. McCarthy, JSOTSup 375 (London: T&T

Philistines from the west as having devoured Israel. Similarly, Ezek 16:57 observes how YHWH ravaged the land of Judah while the Philistines witnessed this event favourably.[53] This highlight of the territorial struggle between Philistia and Israel/Judah, as exemplified by other biblical texts, could have been emulated by the short oracle against the Philistines in Ezek 25. Still, 25:15 does not polemicize the differences or the tensions between the Philstines and the Judahites. The reason for judgment in this verse appears to be more abstract and impersonal by the repetitious usage of נקם.[54] What can be ascertained is only the negative evaluation of such vengeance, evident through the use of the abstract words such as "despite in soul" (שאט בנפש) and "everlasting/ancient enmity" (איבת עולם).

The subsequent announcement of judgment of Philistia (vv. 16–17), as in the oracle about Edom, focuses on the centrality of YHWH's vengeance, and not Israel's territorial interests. YHWH vows to stretch out his hand against the Philistines, to cut off the Cherethites and to destroy the remnant of the seacoast (v. 16, cf. vv. 7, 13). Against Philistia, YHWH will execute "great vengeance" (נקמות גדלות) with wrathful rebukes (v. 17a).[55] As in the Edom oracle, the stress on YHWH's vengeance in the oracle against Philistia goes hand in hand with the use of the recognition formula. In v. 17b, the recognition formula (וידעו כי אני יהוה), as observed by Zimmerli, is further expanded by a statement summarizing the preceding description concerning the divine vengeance (בתתי את נקמתי בם).[56] This supplementary clause, consisting of a suffixed infinitive joined by ב, shows that YHWH's action on the Philistines does not serve the restoration of the land of Israel, but forms the foundation for the targeted recognition.

In light of this preliminary survey, I cannot concur with scholars who advocate Ezek 25 as a chapter heralding the restoration hope for Israel. Following the above synchronic exploration, there is a discrepancy between the reasons for judgment and the announcements of judgment in Ezek 25. While the reasons for judgment of the foreign nations generally affirm the sufferings and

---

Clark International, 2004), 22–36, here 24–25. So also P. Machinist, "Biblical Traditions," 67–69.

[53] Cf. Isa 11:14; Obad 19; Zeph 2:6–7; Zech 9:7, which envision Israel's victory over Philistia.

[54] For instances, 1 Sam 24:13b; Ps 79:10; Isa 35:3–4 also render נקם abstractly. So W. Dietrich, "Rache: Erwägungen zu einem alttestamentlichen Thema," *EvT* 36 (1976): 450–72, here 463–64. Cf. the comment on Ezek 25 made by Greenberg, *Ezekiel 21-37*, 523: "Specificity and color diminish as the oracle unfolds."

[55] בתוכחות חמה "with wrathful rebukes" is missing in the LXX. Wevers, *Ezekiel*, 199, suggests that it is a late gloss.

[56] W. Zimmerli, "Knowledge of God according to the Book of Ezekiel," in *I Am Yahweh*, ed. W. Brueggemann, trans. D. W. Stott (Atlanta: John Knox, 1982), 29–98, esp. 38.

the victimized position of the house of Judah, the announcements of judgment neglect to mention the name of Judah. The latter do not present any land restoration or material benefits for the house of Judah that would come with the destruction of the neighboring nations. Instead, the punishments of the nations repeatedly draw attention to the nations' recognition of YHWH.

Now, the question arises as to why the announcements of judgment of these neighboring nations stay consistently mute about any material compensation for the house of Israel. In order to answer this, we must delve deeper into the possible background sources that influence and shape the ideology of Ezek 25.

## 2. THE ALLUSIONS TO THE PROMISED LAND AND DIVINE RETRIBUTION

Undeniably, the whole of Ezek 25 attests to a complex compositional history, hinted at by the frequent shift of personal addresses and literary style. The opening statement in vv. 1–3a initiated by the divine word formula ("And the word of YHWH came to me saying") is directed only at the Ammonites and not at other neighboring nations of Judah.[57] As such, according to Zimmerli, the subsequent judgment oracles against Ammon (vv. 3b–5, 6–7), clothed in the second person form, are likely to be the original complex within chapter 25.[58] Afterwards, starting from v. 8, there is a shift to the third person address in the oracle about Moab. Zimmerli persuasively deduces that such a shift makes the Moab oracle a secondary expansion of the preceding oracle against Ammon.[59] Meanwhile, a starkly impersonal tone and the *Leitwort* נקם characterizing the Edom-Philistia oracles (vv. 12–17) make the oracles stand out from the rest of the proof-sayings in chapter 25. Still, the two oracles about Edom and Philistia contain several lexical connections to the previous oracles about Ammon, including the phrase שאט נפש (v. 15, cf. v. 6) as well as the stretching-hand and cutting-off motifs (vv. 13, 16, cf. v. 7). As such, Zimmerli concludes that the pair of the Edom-Philistia oracles must have been added at a later stage, perhaps at the same time with the second oracle against Ammon (vv. 6–7) or the Moab oracle (vv. 8–11).[60] Despite their differences in detail, most commentators follow Zimmerli in understanding chapter 25 as having

---

[57] Zimmerli, *Ezekiel*, 2:11.

[58] Even within the Ammon oracles, there are constant shifts of the gender of the pronominal suffixes, from the third masculine plural suffix (עליהם) in v. 2b and the masculine plural imperative (שמעו) in v. 3, to the second feminine suffix in vv. 3b–4, and lastly to the second masculine singular suffix used in vv. 6–7.

[59] Zimmerli, *Ezekiel*, 2:11.

[60] Ibid.

undergone a continuous process of *Fortschreibung*.⁶¹ It is thus highly possible that the lexical features in chapter 25 can point to a range of background sources that were gathered and reused to convey a meaningful idea in the received form of the chapter.

In this section, I will move beyond the inner development of Ezek 25, trying to find a wider range of background sources that inspired or motivated the current rhetoric of chapter 25. This search for background sources will be guided mainly by the concrete lexical connections that the oracles build with these other biblical passages. Certainly not all morphologically identical or similar linguistic elements are significant in the analysis of the rhetorical functions of chapter 25. As discussed in Chapter One, I will focus on elements that are rare, or distinctive, or that accumulate or conflate in a certain pattern. We will discover that these literary elements in chapter 25 bear resemblances to the traditions related to the Promised Land and the divine judgment against Jerusalem.

## 2.1. THE "POSSESSION"

In Ezek 25, the fact that Ammon and Moab are given to the sons of the east as a "possession" (מורשה) is striking (vv. 4, 10).⁶² This *hiphil* participle of ירש is found rarely in the Hebrew Bible. Besides the seven occurences in Ezekiel, מורשה appears once in Exodus, and once in Deuteronomy.⁶³ All occurrences of this noun, except Ezek 25:4, 10 and Deut 33:4, explicitly refer to the Promised Land.⁶⁴ Hence, Exod 6:8 links the noun to the land promise in the Abraham tradition (cf. Gen 15:3, 4, 7, 8).⁶⁵ Similarly, in Ezek 11:5; 33:24, the inhabitants of Jerusalem, who remain in the land after the devastation wrought

---

⁶¹ So also Eichrodt, *Ezekiel*, 361–64; Fuhs, *Ezechiel 25–48*, 140; Allen, *Ezekiel 20–48*, 66–67; Gottwald, *Kingdoms*, 324; Strong, "Ezekiel's Oracles," 144–149; Fechter, *Bewältigung*, 52–54.

⁶² On the significance of the word מורשה in the Hebrew Bible, see Premstaller, *Fremdvölkersprüche*, 37, n. 70; Lust, "Edom-Adam," 390; Kohn, *New Heart*, 38; C. A. Strine, *Sworn Enemies: The Divine Oath, the Book of Ezekiel, and the Polemics of Exile*, BZAW 436 (Berlin: de Gruyter, 2013), 186–90, D. Frankel, *The Land of Canaan and the Destiny of Israel*, Siphrut 4 (Winona Lake: Eisenbrauns, 2011), 40.

⁶³ Ezek 11:15; 25:4, 10; 33:24; 36:2, 3, 5; Exod 6:8; Deut 33:4.

⁶⁴ Note the *hiphil* of the verb ירש appears in the context of conquest, possession, and return to the Promised Land (Num 14:24; 33:53; Josh 8:7; 17:12; Judg 1:19, 27; Obad 17; Ezra 9:12). Only in three poetic contexts (Exod 15:9; Job 13:26, 1 Sam 2:7), the *hiphil* of ירש conveys a more metaphorical meaning. In short, the term generally refers to or presupposes the concept of land/territory of Israel.

⁶⁵ In Gen 15, the related verbal form of ירש appears in the context, where the land is promised to Abraham. Cf. R. Rendtorff, "Genesis 15 im Rahmen der theologischen Bearbeitung der Vätergeschichten," in *Werden und Wirken des Alten Testaments:*

by the Babylonians, seek to claim the land as their "possession" (מורשה) by referring to the Abrahamic covenant. Yet, Ezekiel immediately refutes the claim as a false sense of security, which will not stop the sword and the beasts brought by YHWH (33:24).[66] The true claim of possession, according to 11:17, lies with the regathered exiles.[67] In 36:2–5, מורשה is again used for the land of Israel. This time the right to possess the land is claimed by the external enemies—the Edomites.[68] Again, the Edomites are denied the right of possession, which ultimately lies with the house of Israel (36:12). Overall, in these passages of Ezekiel, the land of Israel as a מורשה is deemed to be so unique, such that both the inhabitants of Jerusalem and the Edomites vie to gain it, but are ultimately denied the right to possess it.

Different from the aforementioned passages, Deut 33:4 does not employ this noun as a designation of the land of Israel, but as a reference to the Mosaic Torah. This verse in Deuteronomy is part of the so-called "Blessing of Moses," the composition of which is rather complex.[69] Lohfink, who rejects this interpretation of מורשה, insists that the concrete land possession is intended in Deut

---

*Festschrift für Clas Westermann*, ed. R. Albertz et al. (Göttingen: Vandenhoeck & Ruprecht, 1980), 74–81, cited in Strine, *Enemies*, 186. On the literary connections between Exod 6:2–8 and Ezekiel (esp. chapter 20), see Lust, "Edom-Adam," 390; idem., "Exodus 6,2–8 and Ezekiel," in *Studies in the Book of Exodus: Redaction-Reception-Interpretation*, ed. M. Vervenne, BETL 126 (Leuven: Leuven University Press, 1996), 209–24.

[66] Strine states: "Whereas Gen 15 uses ירש in an overwhelmingly positive sense, all seven instances of מורשה in Ezekiel are negative" (*Enemies*, 186).

[67] On the polemic against the Abraham tradition and its claims to possess the land in Ezek 11:15 and 33:24, see Strine, *Enemies*, 181–90, esp. 188; S. Japhet, *From the Rivers of Babylon to the Highlands of Judah: Collected Studies on the Restoration Period* (Winona Lake: Eisenbrauns, 2006), 101–3; D. Rom-Shiloni, "Ezekiel as the Voice of te Exiles," *HUCA* 76 (2005): 1–45.

[68] On the basis of the common uses of the term מורשה and its related forms in Ezek 11:15; 33:24; 35:10; 36:2, Lust, "Edom-Adam," 389, sees an assimilation of the Edomites (35:10; 36:2) with the inhabitants of Jerusalem (11:15; 36:2–3). Lust concludes that Edom in Ezek 35 is "a nickname for the inhabitants of Jerusalem, as opposed to 'real Israel' in exile or in the diaspora" (400). His position is subsequently followed by Strine, *Enemies*, 193–99.

[69] M. E. Biddle suggests at least three significant stages of composition: (1) The blessings in vv. 6–25 seem to be pre-Deuteronomic, perhaps in the early monarchic period. (2) The psalms in vv. 2–5, 26–29, which bear no clear marks of Deuteronomic influence, are added at a second phase to frame the blessings (e.g., this is the only occasion of Deuteronomy's use of the word Sinai rather than Horeb). (3) As indicated by the references to Moses in the third person (e.g., 33:1), a post-Deuteronomic editor incorporates the psalm/blessing composition to the core of Deuteronomy (*Deuteronomy*, SHBC 4 [Macon: Smyth & Helwys, 2003], 491–92).

33:4.[70] Yet, given the focus on the Sinai theophany (v. 2), the references to "fiery law" (אשדת, v. 2),[71] "words" (מדברת, v. 3), and the parallelism with "law" (תורה, v. 4) in the surrounding context, it is more likely that the מורשה here refers to the Mosaic Torah. Nevertheless, this understanding of מורשה should not be separated completely from the concept of the covenantal land. This verse may be a later addition to Deuteronomy,[72] in order to qualify and downplay "the indispensable character of life on the the land."[73] Hence, the מורשה in Deut 33:4 likely presupposes the concept of the Promised Land.

All this makes the designation of the lands of Ammon and Moab as a מורשה in Ezek 25:4, 10 even more starkly out of place. In fact, it is my conjecture that the ideology reflected by the מורשה in 25:4 is akin to the Israelite conquest tradition in Deut 2–3.[74] In these two chapters of Deuteronomy, the nominal form מורשה does not appear, but the verbal root ירש figures prominently.[75] In Deut 3:20, Israel is promised a territorial possession (ירושה).[76] Still, their possession is not the only allotment under God's contract. In Deut 2:5, 9, 19, Edom, Moab, and Ammon each occupy a possession (ירושה).[77] Explicitly,

---

[70] N. Lohfink, "ירש," *TDOT* 6:376.

[71] Rabbinic reading splits the word into two—אש דת, having the phrase "fiery law." The LXX has it as ἄγγελοι μετ' αὐτοῦ, probably derived from אשרו אלים "with him messengers/angels" (noted by Biddle, *Deuteronomy*, 495).

[72] G. Braulik claims: "Der Hinweis auf die Tora des Mose dürfte erst in einer späteren Fassung eingefügt worden sein" (*Deuteronomium: 2.16, 18–34,12*, NEchtB 28 [Würzburg: Echter-Verlag, 1992], 238).

[73] Frankel, *Land*, 40.

[74] On Deut 2–3, see D. A. Glatt-Gilad, "The Re-Interpretation of the Edomite-Israelite Encounter in Deuteronomy II," *VT* 47 (1997): 441–55; P. D. Miller, "The Wilderness Journey in Deuteronomy: Style, Structure, and Theology in Deuteronomy 1–3," in *Israelite Religion and Biblical Theology: Collected Essays*, JSOTSup 267 (Sheffield: Sheffield Academic Press, 2000), 572–92; B. A. Anderson, *Brotherhood and Inheritance: A Canonical Reading of the Esau and Edom Traditions*, LHBOTS 556 (New York: T&T Clark, 2011), 157–68. N. Lohfink, "Darstellungkunst und Theologie in Dtn 1,6–3,29," *Bib* 41 (1940): 105–34, esp. 127–31; D. Preuss, *Deuteronomium*, EdF 164 (Darmstadt: Wissenschaftliche Buchgesellschaft, 1982), 75–80; J. C. Gertz, "Kompositorische Funktion und literarhistorischer Ort von Deuteronomium 1–3," in *Deuteronomistischen Geschichtswerke*, ed. M. Witte, BZAW 365 (Berlin: de Gruyter, 2006), 103–23. See also the detailed bibliography in E. Otto, *Deuteronomium 1–11* (Freiburg im Breisgau: Herder, 2012), 408–11.

[75] Deut 2:5, 9, 12, 19, 21, 22, 24, 31; 3:12, 18, 20. Cf. 1:8, 21, 39.

[76] Lohfink considers this noun synonymous with נחלה (*TDOT* 6:376).

[77] A similar concept of the divine giving of lands to the nations is found in Deut 32:8.

YHWH is made responsible for the giving (נתן) of these territories to the foreign nations.[78] Consequently, Israel is instructed to avoid any armed conflicts with Edom, Moab, and Ammon.[79] The divine endowment of the land to the foreign nations is made comparable to Israel's possession of the land (Deut 2:12). In this way, the Promised Land is juxtaposed, and stands on par, with the allotments of the foreign nations. Unlike the aforementioned passages from Genesis, Exodus, and Ezekiel, the Abraham covenant is not cited in this Deuteronomic text in order to stress the uniqueness of the Israelite territory.[80] In Deuteronomy, the land of Israel is juxtaposed with the territories of Ammon, Moab, and Edom as equally under the divine contract. Likewise, Ezek 25 envisions the lands of the Ammonites and Moabites to be no different from the covenantal land, such that each of these foreign lands can be called a מורשה. In this manner, Ezek 25 is different from the rest of the מורשה passages in the Hebrew Bible, which directly or indirectly apply the term to the Promised Land only. Instead, Ezek 25 aligns more with the ideology reflected in Deut 2–3, which applies a related form of ירש to compare the Promised Land with the foreign territories.

This rhetorical comparison is further intensified by the *parallelismus membrorum* formed by "fruit" (פרי) and "milk" (חלב) in Ezek 25:4b. The pair of words characterizes the wealth in the land of the Ammonites, which will subsequently be devoured by the sons of the east.[81] Elsewhere within the Hebrew Bible, the same pair of words appears only in Num 13:27 when the spies came back to report on the Promised Land: "We went in to the land where you sent us; and it certainly does flow with milk (חלב) and honey, and this is its fruit (פריה)."[82] The comparison is not exact, but the rarity of this pair in the Hebrew

---

[78] On the theological significance of נתן in Deuteronomy, see Lohfink, "Dtn 12,1 und Gen 15,18: Das dem Samen Abrahams geschenkte Land als der Geltungsbereich der deuteronomischen Gesetze," in *Die Väter Israels*, ed. M. Görg (Stuttgart: Katholisches Bibelwerk, 1989), 183–210.

[79] On the divergent portrayals of Edom in Num 20:14–21 and Deut 2:2–8, see N. MacDonald, "Edom and Seir in the Narratives and Itineraries of Numbers 20-21 and Deuteronomy 1–3," in *Deuteronomium—Tora für eine neue Generation*, ed. G. Fischer et al. (Wiesbaden: Harrasowitz, 2011), 83–104. While Num 20 has Esau refusing Israel passage and forcing them to go around their country, Deut 2 presents a friendlier picture that allows Israel passing through Edom with payment.

[80] Miller, "Wilderness," 582, thinks this is to break "the potential hubris and misunderstanding of God's gift of the land to Israel." A similar view can be found in Glatt-Gilad, "Re-interpretation," 442.

[81] On the association of milk with wealth, see also Isa 60:16, which refers to the riches of the world. More often it is used to describe the wealth in the Promised Land. So. Cf. A. Caquot, "חלב," *TDOT* 4:389.

[82] Cf. the fruit gathered by the spies in Deut 1:25. The LXX translates Ezek 25:4 with an unusual clause: πίονται τὴν πιότητά σου "They will drink your fatness." J. W.

Bible reinforces the connections between the two passages. Individual appearances of חלב and פרי in the Hebrew Bible also point to this connection with the land of Israel. While the noun חלב appears quite often in the biblical descriptions of the Promised Land,[83] the noun פרי appears in passages in the book of Ezekiel that are related to either the land of Judah or the restored land of Israel.[84] In other words, a land flowing with milk and fruit characterizes the Promised Land more often than a foreign territory. Following this observation, the representation of the Ammonite and Moabite territories abounding in "milk" and "fruit" in the passages that presuppose the destruction of Jerusalem likely allude to the imagery of the pre-exilic Promised Land.

To summarize, the characterizations of a land as a "possession" (מורשה) flowing with "milk" and "fruit" find echoes in the biblical traditions about the Promised Land (e.g., Deut 2–3; Exod 6; Num 13). These descriptions of the Promised Land are then applied to characterize the foreign lands of Ammon and Moab in the proof-sayings of Ezek 25.

2.2. THE "GLORY OF THE LAND"

Like the oracle against Ammon, the oracle against Moab reflects language closely related to the Promised Land. As noted, the Moabite territory is also called a "possession" (מורשה), ready to be given to the sons of the east (25:10, cf. v. 4). What has not yet been discussed is that YHWH presupposes the status of the cities of Moab as the "glory of the land" (צבי ארץ, v. 9).

A similar phrase, which combines צבי with a territorial noun, appears in Ezek 20:6, 15 and describes the Promised Land during the Israelite march to the Canaanite region. Ezekiel 20:6, 15 pictures the land of Israel to be the glory of all lands, flowing with milk and honey.[85] It is a land that is spied out specifically by YHWH for his people, after he has brought them out from

---

Olley, *Ezekiel: A Commentary Based on Iezekiēl in Codex Vaticanus*, Septuagint Commentary Series 7 (Leiden: Brill, 2009), 411, states that the related form πιότης is "often being used generally of rich provision in the land or temple [Gen 27:28, 39; Ps 35:9 (36:8); 64:12 (65:10)]." A clear connection to the chosen land is thus evident through the selection of the word.

[83] Cf. Exod 3:8, 17; 13:5; 33:4; Lev 20:24; Num 13:27; 14:8; 16:13–14; Deut 6:3; 11:9; 26:9, 15; 27:3; 31:20; Josh 5:6; Jer 11:5; 32:22; Ezek 20:6, 15 (noted by Fechter, *Bewältigung*, 74, 79; Caquot, *TDOT* 4:389; Strong, "Ezekiel's Oracles," 159).

[84] Ezek 17:8–9, 23; 19:12, 14; 34:27; 36:30; 47:12 (noted by Fechter, *Bewältigung*, 74, 79). Cf. Deut 7:13, which describes the bearing of the fruit as a sign of divine blessing on the Promised Land. On the theological meaning of פרי in relation to the land, see B. Kedar-Kopfstein, "פרה," *TDOT* 12:90.

[85] In v. 6 and v. 15, the LXX has "it is a honeycomb" (κηρίον ἐστὶν), instead of "the glory of all the lands."

Egypt.⁸⁶ This affirmation of the land's special status dramatizes the subsequent exile among the nations (20:23), showing how in a reverse fashion the city of Jerusalem will become a disgrace before the nations and a mockery to all the countries (22:4).⁸⁷ In a similar vein, Jeremiah assigns צבי to the house of Israel, recounting its past glory, calling the land of Israel "the most beautiful of the nations" (3:19). This elect status of the territory is to contrast with Israel's subsequent treacherous departure from YHWH (3:20). Isaiah employs a similar phrase to denote the proud kingdoms, such as Babylon (13:19), Tyre (23:9), and Israel (28:1, 4), but they will all come under God's judgment. For Isaiah, the expression ultimately is applicable only for the elect remnant who will receive the true glory (Isa 4:2; 28:5). One way or another, the term צבי in the aforementioned examples is linked to the glorious status of a chosen territory, kingdom, or people.⁸⁸ Calling the Moabite cities as the "glory of the land" thus indicates a special effort that is made in Ezek 25 to connect the land of Moab with the Promised Land.

This effort is further confirmed by the names of three specific towns in the oracle—Beth-jeshimoth (בית הישימת),⁸⁹ Baal-meon (בעל מעון),⁹⁰ and Kirjathaim (קריתים)⁹¹—which qualify and clarify the phrase צבי ארץ (25:9). The locations of these three Moabite towns are not in the heartland of Moab. Instead, they are the border towns in the northern region of Moab, which was more open to the outside world and was much better known to the biblical

---

⁸⁶ With YHWH as the grammatical subject, "to spy out" (תור) also appears in Deut 1:33. There YHWH seeks out a camping place for his people in the wilderness. This verbal root appears frequently in the spy narrative in Num 13:2, 16–17, 21, 25, 32; 14:6–7, 34, 36 and 38.

⁸⁷ On the consensus that צבי היא לכל הארצות in Ezek 20:6, 15 is a special expression in reference to the Promised Land, see Zimmerli, *Ezekiel*, 2:16; Reventlow, *Wächter*, 141; Eichrodt, *Ezekiel*, 361; Block, *Ezekiel*, 2:21; H. Madl, "צבי," *TDOT* 12:237. This understanding makes the application of the expression צבי ארץ upon foreign nations in Ezek 25 more provocative.

⁸⁸ In a later tradition, in Dan 8:9; 11:16, 41, 45, צבי becomes a code name for the Promised Land. The term צבי also has a secondary meaning as "gazelle" in Deut 12:15, 22; 14:4; 15:22; 2 Sam 2:18; 1 Kgs 5:3; Isa 13:14; Prov 6:5; Song 2:9, 17; 8:14; Ezra 2:57; Neh 7:59. Cf. *HALOT* 2:998; Madl, *TDOT* 12:236-38.

⁸⁹ Cf. Num 33:49; Josh 12:3; 13:20. Beth-jeshimoth is situated in the south of the Plains of Moab, to the north-east of the Dead Sea.

⁹⁰ Baal-meon is more fully named Beth-baal-meon in Josh 13:17 and appears also in Num 32:38; Jer 48:23. It is located by the Dead Sea a few miles inland.

⁹¹ Here, the *Kethib* has it as קריתמה, while the *Qere* reads קריתימה. Kiriathaim occurs in Gen 14:5 and appears as a Reubenite territory in Num 32:37; Josh 13:19 and occurs later in the oracle against Moab in Jer 48:1, 23. It is to the south of Baal-meon.

writers.⁹² It belongs to a region that is hotly disputed between the Israelites and the Moabites. Both the biblical materials and the Mesha inscription record the ancient Israelite elements in this disputed region. According to the biblical materials, the Moabites were expelled from the region north of the river Arnon by the Amorite king Sihon, who ruled in Heshbon.⁹³ Moses then conquered all of this region from the Amorites,⁹⁴ and assigned the conquered tableland to the tribes of Gad and Reuben.⁹⁵ Dated to the ninth century BCE, lines 10-11 of the Mesha inscription read: "And the men of Gad lived in the land of Ataroth from ancient times, and the king of Israel built Ataroth for himself."⁹⁶ Subsequently, as indicated by the Mesha inscription, Mesha king of Moab strove to reclaim the region that included the two cities—Baal-meon and Kirjathaim, then under the possession of the Omride dynasty in Israel (lines 9–10, 30).⁹⁷ Consequently, Zimmerli clarifies that these regions in Ezek 25 belong to that territory "which in the course of history was disputed between Israel and Moab and which obviously lay in particular fashion within a Judean's field of vision."⁹⁸

Indeed, it is peculiar that the Moabite territory is called the "glory of the land," which is an expression more commonly reserved for the chosen land of Israel (cf. Jer 3:29; Ezek 20:23). The boundary between the Moabite territory

---

⁹² The inaccessible waters of the *Mūjib* (biblical Arnon River) and the *Ḥesā* (biblical Zered River) form natural barriers to divide Moab into the northern area (the region north of Arnon) and the southern Moabite plateau. The southern plateau is isolated by the geographical barriers mentioned above. For more details of the geographical description of this land, see Miller, "Moab," 2, 299 (map). On the more specific locations of the Moabite towns, see also J. A. Dearman, "Historical Reconstruction and the Mesha Inscription," in *Studies in the Mesha Inscription and Moab*, ed. J. A. Dearman, ABS 2 (Atlanta: Scholars Press, 1989), 175–77; Block, *Ezekiel*, 2:21; S. Fisch, *Ezekiel: Hebrew Text and English Translation with an Introduction and Commentary* (London: Soncino Press, 1964), 170; Miller, "Moab," 27–28.

⁹³ Num 21:27–35; cf. Isa 15–16; Jer 48. Noted by Avi-Yonah and Oded, "Moab," 401.

⁹⁴ Cf. Num 21:13, 15, 24; 22:36; 33:44; Deut 2:26–37; Judg 11:12–28.

⁹⁵ Cf. Num 32:37–38; Josh 12:3; 13:17, 19–20. Noted by Miller, "Moab," 3, 16–19; Avi-Yonah and Oded, "Moab," 401.

⁹⁶ Translations of the Mesha Inscription can be found in *ANET*, 320–21; *COS* 2.23:137–38; K. P. Jackson, "The Language of the Meshaᶜ Inscription," in *Studies in the Mesha Inscription and Moab*, ed. J. A. Dearman, ABS 2 (Atlanta.: Scholars Press, 1989), 97–98. Among the numerous obscure notations in the genealogies of 1 Chr 1–8, there is also mention of a Moabite ruler of the Judahite descent (1 Chr 4.22). Cf. Miller, "Moab," 3, 18.

⁹⁷ King Mesha is also mentioned in 2 Kgs 3:4. The king of Moab is said to rebel again the king of Israel after the death of Ahab (2 Kgs 1:1; 3:5).

⁹⁸ Zimmerli, *Ezekiel*, 2:15–16. Cf. Greenberg, *Ezekiel 21–37*, 251; Eichrodt, *Ezekiel*, 361; Odell, *Ezekiel*, 328; Block, *Ezekiel*, 2:21.

and the Promised Land become even more blurry, when the cities of Moab, which are to be dispossessed, do not lie in the heartland of Moab, but are the frontier cities, of which the Israelites once claimed possession (cf. Num 21:21–31; 32:37–38; Deut 2:26–37; Josh 12:3; 13:17, 19–20).[99]

## 2.3. THE "VENGEANCE"

As noted, the proof-sayings against Edom and Philistia are different from the rest of chapter 25 in terms of their stress on YHWH's vengeance, which is highlighted by the repeated usage of the lexeme נקם.[100] Related forms of the verbal root נקם already occur four times in just two verses of the announcements of the divine judgment (vv. 14, 17). Related forms of the root נקם occur twelve times in the whole book of Ezekiel, but are concentrated only in chapters 24 and 25.[101] As such, the role of the lexeme in the oracles against Edom and Philistia deserves further exploration.[102]

Based on the distinctive distribution of the term within the book of Ezekiel, the inhabitants of Jerusalem, alongside Edom and Philistia, are the only other group of people who suffer YHWH's vengeance. Willfully, the inhabitants of Jerusalem have exposed their blood guilt on a smooth bare rock, with no dust to cover it (24:7).[103] In response, at the beginning of the siege placed on Jerusalem, YHWH announces his vengeance (נקם) against the Jerusalemites by

---

[99] Ezekiel seems to reject all Israelite claims to the Transjordan. Even in the later vision of an ideal land of Israel in 47:13–48:29, there is no reference to the Transjordan (noted also by Block, *Ezekiel*, 2:21). In this manner, Ezekiel is closer to other biblical texts, which assume that Moab extended as far north as Heshbon and Elealeh (see Num 21:20, for example, and the oracles concerning Moab in Isa 15–16 and Jer 48). Cf. Miller, "Moab," 3; Block, *Ezekiel*, 2:69; Zimmerli, *Ezekiel*, 2:16.

[100] On נקם in the Hebrew Bible, see Dietrich, "Rache," 450–72; G. E. Mendenhall, "The 'Vengeance' of Yahweh," in *The Tenth Generation: The Origins of the Biblical Tradition* (Baltimore: Johns Hopkins University Press, 1976), 69–104; W. T. Pitard, "Amarna *ekēmu* and Hebrew 'Naqam,' " *Maarav* 3 (1982): 5–25; E. Lipinski, "נקם," *TDOT* 10:1–9.

[101] Ezek 24:8; 25:12, 14, 15, 17. This is the second highest distribution of the term in the Hebrew Bible, coming after Jeremiah (18x). Cf. Jer 5:9, 29; 9:8; 11:20; 15:15; 20:10, 12; 46:10; 50:15 (2x), 28 (2x); 51:6, 11 (2x), 36 (2x). For a list of statistical and grammatical analysis of נקם in the Hebrew Bible, see Peels, *Vengeance*, 24.

[102] *Contra* Fechter, *Bewältigung*, 37, who finds no links between Ezek 24 and 25: "Von einem Bezug" [zu Ez 24] "ist in Ez 25 nichts zu merken."

[103] Contrary to the prescription in Lev 17:13, which states that whenever an animal or a bird is hunted and eaten, its blood must be covered with earth, lest it induce the wrath of God, the guarantor of life. Cf. D. I. Block, "Ezekiel's Boiling Cauldron: A Form-Critical Solution to Ezekiel XXIV 1–14," *VT* 41 (1991): 30; Lyons, *Law*, 73–74, 115–16.

raising up wrath (חמה, 24:8).¹⁰⁴ He will expose and advertise Jerusalem's sins by placing the blood the city has shed on a bare rock (24:8). The blood on the exposed rock becomes the perpetual witness and evidence to the crime committed,¹⁰⁵ and the divine vengeance signifies YHWH's legal right to exact retribution on his people.¹⁰⁶ In short, the concentrated distribution of נקם in Ezek 24 and 25 binds the judgment on Edom and Philistia closer to that on Jerusalem.

With regard to the direction of dependence, 25:12–17 and 24:3–14 are likely to have influenced each other. The Edom and Philistia oracles, due to their constant references to vengeance (נקם), stand apart from the rest of the oracles in Ezek 25 and were probably added at a later date than the oracles against Ammon and Moab. Given that the literary setting of the oracles in Ezek 25 generally presupposes the fall of Jerusalem, it is thus likely that the Edom and Philistia oracles came into existence after the fall of Jerusalem. On the other hand, YHWH's vengeance (נקם) on Jerusalem (24:6–8) appears in the context when the fall of Jerusalem has not yet been viewed as coming into fruition.¹⁰⁷ Yet, in comparison to the rest of chapter 24, the pericope in vv. 6–8 is the only textual unit that refers to the Hebrew noun נקם and thus likely indicates a later attempt to link the divine vengeance on Jerusalem to that on Edom and Philistia. On this basis, both 24:6–8 and 25:12–17 probably attest to a case of mutual influence. The loaded term נקם in both pericopes draws shocking attention to the wound inflicted mercilessly on not only the Jerusalemites, but also the Edomites and the Philistines.

---

¹⁰⁴ The parallelism of נקם/חמה also appears in 25:14, 17 to denote divine judgment agaisnt Edom and Philistines. Cf. Peels, *Vengeance*, 130, who cites H. F. Fuhs, "Ez 24: Überlegungen zu Tradition und Redaktion des Ezechielbuches," in *Ezekiel and His Book*, ed. J. Lust, BETL 74 (Leuven: Leuven University Press, 1986), 266.

¹⁰⁵ On the blood from the ground becoming a witness to the crime committed, and a reminder of the injustice unavenged, see Gen 4:10; Job 16:18. Cf. J. Byron, "Abel's Blood and the Ongoing Cry for Vengeance," *CBQ* 73 (2011): 743–56; Block, "Cauldron," 31.

¹⁰⁶ Cf. Lev 26:25; Isa 1:21–26; Jer 51:34–47. On the legal connotation of God's נקם, see Pitard, "Amarna *ekēmu*," 17–19. In the Hebrew Bible, God is usually the explicit or implicit subject of vengeance. E.g., Deut 32:43; 1 Sam 24:13 [Eng. 24:12]; 2 Kgs 9:7; Isa 1:24; Jer 15:15; 46:10; 51:36; Ps 149:7. For further examples and explications, see Lipinski, "נקם," 9; Peels, *Vengeance*, 274–76.

¹⁰⁷ The pot and flesh imagery in 24:6–8 finds its parallel in 11:5–12, which is another prediction of divine retribution on the inhabitants in Jerusalem.

## 2.4. THE "STRETCHING-HAND" AND "CUTTING-OFF"

Another literary feature confirming the link to the judgment of Jerusalem is one pattern of retribution in 25:13, 16 (cf. 25:7).[108] Repeatedly, YHWH stretches out his hand against (על+יד+נטה) the Ammonites, the Edomites, and the Philistines, in order to cut off (man and beast) (*hiphil* of the verb כרת+מן+[אדם+בהמה]) from the lands. This pattern of combination consists of both the "stretching-hand" and "cutting-off" elements. Each of the elements in the combination appears independently of each other in other passages within the Hebrew Bible, while the combined elements can only be found in the judgment announced to the exiles and Jerusalem in Ezek 14:1–11, 12–23 and in the retribution applied on the foreign nations in chapter 25.[109]

To the extent of my research, none of the scholars of Ezekiel has noticed this specific conflation of the "stretching-hand" and "cutting-off" motifs in chapters 14 and 25.[110] Within the book of Ezekiel, 21:8–9 (Eng. 21:3–4), 29:8 and 35:7 attest to the cutting-off motif, while the stretching of YHWH's hand is also found in 6:14 (against the house of Israel) and 35:3 (against Mount Seir). However, none of these five passages, unlike chapters 14 and 25, juxtaposes the cutting-off and stretching-hand motifs. Outside of Ezekiel, the stretching-hand motif surfaces independently of the cutting-off motif in both pentateuchal and prophetic materials.[111] In the plague stories of Exodus, YHWH's outstretched hand is paralleled by his salvific act of bringing his people out of Egypt (Exod 7:5),[112] while the prophetic traditions utilize the

---

[108] With this pattern of retribution, the second speech against Ammon (25:6–7) stands closer to the Edom and the Philistia oracles (25:12–17). Cf. Premstaller, *Fremdvölkersprüche*, 33; Zimmerli, *Ezekiel*, 2:11.

[109] K.-F. Pohlmann also notices the common motif of the "cutting off (men and animals)" in Ezek 14:12–20; 25:13 and 29:8, but he does not notice the motif used in the book of Ezekiel is distinctively juxtaposed with the "stretching-hand" motif (*Das Buch des Propheten Hesekiel (Ezechiel): Kapitel 20–48*, ATD 22.2 [Göttingen: Vandenhoeck & Ruprecht, 2001], 368).

[110] Some scholars observe other examples of Ezekiel's conflation techniques. E.g., Ezek 25:7 combines the clause "It will cut off your livestock" (Lev 26:22) with the clause "You will perish among the nations" (Lev 26:38), so that it reads: "I will cut you off from the peoples, and make you perish among the lands." Cf. Gile, "Deuteronomy," 292. For other examples of Ezekiel's conflation, see Lyons, *Law*, 95–97.

[111] On the stretching-hand motif in the Hebrew Bible in general, see, for instance, K. Martens, "'With a Strong Hand and an Outstretched Arm:' The Meaning of the Expression byd ḥzqh wbzrw' nṭwyh," *SJOT* 15 (2001): 123–41; H. Simian, *Die theologische Nachgeschichte der Prophetie Ezechiels*, FB 14 (Würzburg: Echter Verlag, 1974), 180–82; Kohn, *New Heart*, 33.

[112] וידעו מצרים כי אני יהוה בנטתי את ידי על מצרים והוצאתי את בני ישראל מתוכם. Cf. Exod 7:19; 8:1, 2, 13 [Eng. 8:5, 6, 17]; 9:22; 10:12, 21, 22; 14:16, 26, 27. Note the passages in the plague narratives where the stretching-hand motif appears are mostly attributed

synonymous motif not in a context that promises salvation for the elect, but in a context that highlights the totalizing aspect of divine judgment, which is applied even to God's own people.[113] The cutting-off motif, or the so-called הכרית formula, independent of the stretching-hand motif, features prominently in the Holiness Code (H, i.e., Lev 17–26) and in several prophetic materials outside of Ezekiel to associate the divine judgment with the act of "cutting off" (*hiphil* of the verb כרת).[114] While the הכרית formula in H is directed against the Israelites themselves,[115] the prophetic materials employ the formula indiscriminately to speak of the divine judgment upon both foreigners and God's people.[116] None of these aforementioned passages juxtaposes the "cutting-off" motif with the "stretching-hand" motif.

This makes the juxtaposition of the two motifs in Ezek 14 and 25 even more significant. Having threatened to cut off the idolater from the congregation, YHWH announces the stretching out of his hand against any prophet who speaks falsely in his name (14:8–9). In response to the unfaithfulness of Jerusalem,[117] YHWH vows to stretch out his hand against it, in order to bring a famine, a sword, and a plague, and to "cut off from it both man and beast" (14:13, 17, 19; cf. 14:21).[118] A similar juxtaposition is evident in Ezek 25. In chapter 25 YHWH also stretches out his hand in order to execute judgment, and to "cut off human and beast" from the relevant territory (26:7, 13, 16).[119] However, Ezek 25 differs from chapter 14 in that the targets of judgment are

---

to the P-source. Cf. the table in B. S. Childs, *Exodus*, OTL (Philadelphia: The Westminster Press, 1974), 131.

[113] E.g., Jer 6:12; 15:6; 21:5; 51:25 (cf. Ezek 6:14; 14:9).

[114] For further explanation of the cutting-off motif in the Hebrew Bible, see W. Zimmerli, "Die Eigenart der prophetischen Rede des Ezechiel," *ZAW* 66 (1954): 13–19; Reventlow, *Wächter*, 141; D. J. Wold, "Kareth Penalty in P: Rationale and Cases," SBLSP 1 (1979): 1–25; J. Joosten, *People and Land in the Holiness Code: An Exegetical Study of the Ideational framework of the Law in Leviticus 17–26*, VTSup 67 (Leiden: Brill, 1996), 79–82.

[115] See Lev 17:10; 20:3, 5, 6.

[116] The prophetic materials utilize the formula more loosely. E.g., Isa 9:13; 10:7; 14:22; Jer 9:21; 36:29; 44:7; Nah 1:14; 2:13; Zeph 1:3; 3:6; Amos 1:5, 8; 2:3; Mic 5:9–14 [Eng. 5:10–15].

[117] In Ezek 14:13 lies the reason for divine judgment on the Jerusalemites. The country has committed unfaithfulness (למעל מעל). This *figura etymologica* appears again in 15:8 (מעלו מעל) as the reason for judgment of Judah. On other lexical ties between 14:12–23 and 15:1–8, see Block, *Ezekiel 1–24*, 438.

[118] The triad of famine, sword, and plague can also be found in Ezek 5:12; 6:11–12; 7:15; 12:16; 33:27, all of which are oracles against Jerusalem/Mountains of Israel.

[119] In 25:7, the object of YHWH's cutting-off is simply the Ammonite territory, whereas a play on words והכרתי את כרתים is evident in 25:16. Only 26:13 mentions the object of judgment as "human and beast." Cf. Eichrodt, *Ezekiel*, 356.

not the exiles or inhabitants of Jerusalem, but rather the Ammonites, Edomites, and Philistines.

In addition to the aforementioned juxtaposition, portions of the same two chapters in Ezekiel contain a more expanded form of the הכרית formula than that found in H.[120] Ezek 14:13, 17, 19, 21 and 25:13, unlike H, apply the הכרית formula not only to human beings but also to animals. Instead of mentioning just the "man" (איש) or "person, breath" (נפש) being cut off,[121] or just the "beast" (בהמה) being destroyed,[122] the הכרית formula in Ezek 14 and 25 encompasses both "human and beast" (אדם ובהמה).[123] Through this wider scope of the application of the הכרית formula in Ezek 14 and 25, YHWH's anger against Jerusalem is expressed and felt more intensely.

Given the distinctive juxtaposition and expansion of the "stretching-hand" and "cutting-off" motifs in Ezek 14 and 25, the two chapters are unmistakably linked. Chapter 25 was probably aware of, if not contemporaneous with, chapter 14. Even though both the "stretching-hand" and "cutting-off" motifs appear in Ezek 14, the two motifs are juxtaposed closely only in v. 13. By contrast, the two motifs are juxtaposed closely whenever they appear in Ezek 25. In this light, the literary style in the oracles against Edom and Philistia appears more formulaic and developed than that in the prophecy against Jerusalem. It can be ascertained that the Edom and the Philistia oracles represent later insertions into Ezek 25, and their literary setting presents the fall of Jerusalem as *fait accompli*. On the other hand, the literary setting of Ezek 14 appears more ambiguous.[124] The first part of the oracle (14:1–11) focuses on the abominations committed possibly by the first wave of exiles who has arrived in Babylon in 597 BCE. There is no mention of the impending fall of Jerusalem. The second half of the oracle warns of the upcoming destruction of a rebellious land (14:12–20). It is not until 14:21 that Jerusalem is identified specifically as the land suffering the destruction. The textual unit in 14:12–20, in

---

[120] Another example of Ezekiel's expansion can be seen in its use of the scattering motif. Lev 26:33 reads "And you I will scatter among the nations." On the other hand, Ezekiel attests to a more elaborate form: "I will disperse you among the nations and scatter you among the lands" (12:15; 20:33; 22:15; 29:12; 30:23, 26; 36:19). Cf. Lyons, *Law*, 92. For the possible deuteronomistic influence on this expression, see Gile, "Deuteronomy," 290.

[121] E.g., Lev 17:4, 9, 10.

[122] E.g., Lev 26:22.

[123] The juxtaposition of "human" (אדם) and "beast" (בהמה) is also characteristic of Jeremiah in a context that describes the empty land of Judah devastated by the Chaldeans (e.g., Jer 32:43; 36:29). Cf. Zeph 1:3; Zech 2:8 [Eng. 2:4]. Elsewhere the pair occurs in Lev 27:28; Ps 36:7, albeit in the non-judgment contexts.

[124] Due to the ambiguous literary setting, Ezek 14:1–11 is considered to have emerged either before or after the fall of Jerusalem. Cf. Eichrodt, *Ezekiel*, 179; Zimmerli, *Ezekiel*, 1:306.

which the "stretching-hand" and "cutting-off" motifs concentrate, thus likely emerged even before the fall of Jerusalem, while 14:21–23 respresents the expansion that took place after the fall of Jerusalem.[125] Taking all the aforementioned into consideration, the "cutting-off" and the "stretching-hand" motifs in Ezek 25 were probably composed later and were dependent on the looser formulas in chapter 14. The reuse of these motifs in the announcements of judgment against Edom and Philistia (and perhaps Ammon) in Ezek 25 invite comparisons with the judgment upon God's chosen city and people.

### 3. The Rhetorical Impact

With the above survey in mind, I now draw attention to the rhetorical impact generated by the textual allusions in Ezek 25 to the traditions concerning the Promised Land and the divine judgment of Jerusalem. A comparison with the post-modern rendition of Ezek 25:17 in the American film "Pulp Fiction" directed by Quentin Tarantino in 1994 sharpens the main message of our foregoing analysis of Ezek 25.[126] In the film, the gangster protagonist Jules recites his own version of Ezek 25:17, with fury and self-righteousness, before he executes someone:

> The path of the righteous man is beset on all sides by the inequities of the selfish and the tyranny of evil men. Blessed is he who, in the name of charity and good will, shepherds the weak through the valley of the darkness. For he is truly his brother's keeper and the finder of lost children. And I will strike down upon thee with great vengeance and furious anger those who attempt to poison and destroy my brothers. And you will know I am the Lord when I lay my vengeance upon you.

In the citation, the good and evil people belong to clearly demarcated categories. "The righteous man" is set in contrast with "the evil men," and Jules considers himself to be the former, looking after "the weak through the valley of the darkness," and being endowed with the right to act "with great vengeance and furious anger" on any man he deems wicked. In fact, the last line of the citation reflects the size of his ego as he claims to embody the justice of

---

[125] On the view that 14:21–23 represent a later addition, see Wevers, *Ezekiel*, 114; Pohlmann, *Ezechielstudien: Zur Redaktionsgeschichte des Buches und zur Frage nach den ältesten Texten*, BZAW 202 (Berlin: de Gruyter, 1992), 6–11. On the lexical ties between vv. 12–20 and vv. 21–23, see Block, *Ezekiel*, 1:441.

[126] For a useful summary of the relationship between the film and Ezek 25:17, see A. Reinhartz, *Scripture on the Silver Screen* (Louisville: Westminster John Knox, 2003), 97–113.

God himself. Contrary to Jules's rendition, we find a different picture of good and evil in the MT of Ezek 25. Despite the victimized position of Judah, Ezek 25 blurs both the physical and ideological boundaries between Judah and the menacing nations, by highlighting their territorial resemblances, and by stressing their shared judgment.

3.1. THE TERRITORIAL RESEMBLANCES BETWEEN THE NATIONS AND JUDAH

The reasons for judgment of Ammon and Moab present the two nations' merciless mockery of the sanctuary of Jerusalem, the land of Israel, and the house of Judah (25:3, 6, 8). Yet, when the tension is built, YHWH does not retaliate in a way that brings material compensations for the house of Judah. Instead, he hands the Ammonite land and the Moabite cities to the "sons of the east," and thus denies Judah in the west as the beneficiary of the deprivation of the Transjordanian states (vv. 4, 10).

Moreover, YHWH renders the neighboring territories comparable to the Promised Land. Hence, the Ammonite territory is labelled as the "possession" abounding in "milk" and fruit" (Ezek 25:4). All of these expressions and characterizations, as noted, are applied elsewhere primarily to the land of Israel (cf. Exod 6:8; Num 13:27; Ezek 11:15; 33:24; 36:2–3, 5). Meanwhile, the Moabite towns—"the glory of the land"—do not lie in the heartland of Moab, but in the frontier region that was hotly disputed between Israel and Moab (Ezek 25:9). In this manner, the prophecies issued against Ammon and Moab surprisingly relativize the Judahite land's former glory and bring it to the same level as the territories of other neighboring nations.

3.2. THE SHARED JUDGMENT BETWEEN THE NATIONS AND JUDAH

The two proof-sayings in Ezek 25:12–17, as observed, do not emphasize the conflicts between Judah and the Edom/Philistia. The reasons for judgment on the latter are captured by a more impersonal and abstract concept of "vengeance" (vv. 12, 15), and the object of Philistia's act of vengeance remains vague and elusive (v. 15). In the announcements of divine judgment, the house of Israel is only an instrument to punish Edom (v. 14), and the recognition formulas repetitively affirm that only YHWH has the right to vengeance (vv. 14, 17).

In addition, the foregoing survey reveals that the expressions related to YHWH's vengeance, "stretching-hand," and "cutting-off" in Ezek 25:12–17 bear disturbing resemblances to the divine punitive actions against God's people in Ezek 14 and 24. Given the direction of dependence, and viewed in its current literary arrangement, the acts of divine judgment in chapter 25 have an escalating and an equalizing effect. The expressions concerning YHWH's "stretching-hand" and "cutting-off" recall the doom predicted for Jerusalem in chapter 14, while YHWH's vow to execute his vengeance on Edom and Philistia distinctively evokes the divine vengeance upon Jerusalem in 24:8. Coming straight after these grim predictions for the fate of Jerusalem, the divine acts of punishment in 25:12–17 bring the chosen city down to an equal level with the other foreign lands. All nations now stand on an equal footing with Jerusalem under the divine judgment.

The end of "Pulp Fiction" brings Jules to think in a way closer to our interpretation of Ezek 25. Pointing his gun at the robber, Ringo, Jules ponders over the meaning of his rendition of Ezek 25:17 and provides different ways of understanding it in his current situation. He finally decides: "The truth is you're the weak. And I'm the tyranny of evil men. But I'm tryin', Ringo. I'm tryin' real hard to be the shepherd." Instead of killing Ringo, Jules concludes that he is not innocent enough to execute justice, and so he lets Ringo escape. This last scene strangely echoes the message of judgment embedded in Ezek 25. Undeniably, YHWH's offensives against the Transjordanian lands and Philistia reflect a special link between the fate of Judah and the honour of YHWH. Unconventionally, the solution to this crisis is not to redeem Jerusalem. Comparing the territories and punishments of the foreign nations with those of God's people, Ezek 25 implicitly affirms that Jerusalem has become a contaminated city like the other foreign nations.

# Chapter Three

# The Destruction of the Jerusalem Temple and Priesthood in Ezek 26–28

ויצא לך שם בגוים ביפיך כי כליל הוא בהדרי אשר שמתי עליך נאמ אדני יהוה
And your renown went forth among the nations because of your beauty, for it was perfect through the splendor that I had bestowed on you, the declaration of the Lord YHWH.

Ezek 16:14

צור את אמרת אני כלילת יפי בלב ימים גבליך בניך כללו יפיך
O Tyre, you said, "I am perfect in beauty." Your borders were in the heart of the seas; your builders perfected your beauty.

Ezek 27:3b–4

After the judgment pronounced against the Transjordanian nations and Philistia in Ezek 25, the destruction of the beauty of Tyre dominates chapters 26–28. Out of all nations described in Ezekiel's OAN, Tyre is uniquely and consistently characterized as a perfect beauty that brings admiration. The exclamation of Tyre—"I am perfect in beauty" (אני כלילת יפי, 27:3b)—finds its confirmation when the builders have all contributed precious materials from various far-flung countries to decorate and furnish Tyre, which is now metaphorized as a merchant ship (27:4–25a). Identified as a cherub that is "perfect in beauty" (כליל יפי) and "full of wisdom" (מלא חכמה, 28:12), the Tyrian royal is lavished with precious stones (28:13). Yet, the perfect beauty of both the Tyrian ship and king does not protect them from meeting their tragic ends. The former is ultimately wrecked by the east wind (27:26), while the latter corrupts his wisdom, is cast down from the mountain of *Elohim*, and is consumed by fire (28:16–18).

Commentators have come up with various reasons for the destruction of Tyre's perfect beauty. One group of scholars links the tragic fate of Tyre's perfect beauty to its hubris. Tyre not only haughtily claims to possess the perfect beauty (27:3), its ruler even boldly asserts his own divinity, sitting in the seat of *Elohim*, in the heart of the seas (28:2). According to these commentators, the self-acclamations made by Tyre and its ruler are thus concrete evidence of hubris and arrogance, which alone lead to the outpouring of the divine castigation upon Tyre.[1] Hence, regarding the fate of Tyre in Ezekiel, Fohrer concludes:

> Seine eigene Überheblichkeit wird es in den Abgrund führen—ein Beispiel dafür, daß solche stolze Anmaßung und solch falsches Vertrauen eine verderbenbringende Gefahr bilden und daß entgegen dieser Gottwidrigkeit Jahwe sich als Herr aller Völker und Menschen erweisen wird.[2]

In a similar vein, Greenberg thinks that the sustained theme in the prophecies against Tyre is its hubris, a universal immorality, without any particular concern for Israel.[3] Certainly, arrogance is a common and stereotypical accusation of the foreign nations in the Hebrew Bible.[4] Nonetheless, to focus only on the hubris of Tyre seems to cast Tyre's perfect beauty too quickly in a negative light. Too often, commentators overlook the elaborate details that have gone into the oracles that acknowledge and affirm the beauty of Tyre, exemplified, for instance, by the extensive trade network of Tyre detailed in 27:12–25a. Also, the wide-ranging lament and wailing upon the loss of Tyre's beauty seems to be melancholic and sincere enough (26:15–18; 27:28–36). Therefore, one wonders if there is something more substantial at stake than an overgeneralized accusation of hubris in Ezekiel's Tyre oracles.

A growing number of commentators now see the tragic end of Tyre's beauty as more seriously related to its oppression of Jerusalem. That is to say, these exegetes do not stress Tyre's *hubris*, but Tyre's *oppression* of Jerusalem as the cause of the destruction of Tyre's beauty. In Ezek 26:2, Tyre comments "on/against Jerusalem" (על ירושלם) and rejoices: "Aha! The gateway of the

---

[1] E.g., Zimmerli, *Ezekiel*, 2:80, 95; Blenkinsopp, *Ezekiel*, 120; Block, *Ezekiel*, 2:86; Eichrodt, *Ezekiel*, 383; Gowan, *Man*, 69–92.

[2] Fohrer, *Ezechiel*, HAT 1.13 (Tübingen: Mohr Siebeck, 1955), 156.

[3] Greenberg, *Ezekiel 21–37*, 540, 544, 577, 593. Commenting specifically on Ezek 27, Greenberg maintains that the "the present condemnation of Tyre's boast of supplanting Jerusalem is not an outburst of patriotic petulance on Ezekiel's part, but an indictment of Tyre's soaring ambition to win hegemony over world trade" (540).

[4] This stereotypical accusation is used against Moab (Jer 48:29), Ammon and Moab (Zeph 2:10), Assyria (Zech 10:11), the Chaldeans (Isa 13:19), Egypt (Ezek 30:6, 18; 32:12), and Philistia (Zech 9:6). Cf. Corral, *Ezekiel's Oracles*, 5; Gowan, *Man*, 19–43.

peoples has been broken! She has been turned over to me! I will be satisfied! She has been laid waste" (האח נשברה דלתות העמים נסבה אלי אמלאה החרבה). Many commentators interpret "the gateway of the peoples" as referring to Jerusalem's city gates. Based on the whole verse, they further conclude that Tyre desires to profit from the destruction of Jerusalem.[5] On the other hand, Corral argues against this conventional identification of "the gateway" (דלתות),[6] and interprets the term as a designation of the Philistine seaports destroyed at the hands of Nebuchadnezzar.[7] Nevertheless, like the aforementioned commentators, Corral still maintains that Jerusalem's interests were in jeopardy by this act of destruction mentioned in 26:2. The ravaging of the Philistine seaports forced Judah's reliance upon Tyre for trade goods. Tyre's material wealth and opulence, which are described elaborately in chapters 27 and 28, are thus a result of its oppressive trading policies.[8] For all these exegetes, 26:2 becomes the crux of the prophecies against Tyre, representing the most direct evidence of Tyre's economic greed and extortion to maintain its own beauty. However, the tension between Tyre and Jerusalem is mentioned explicitly in only one verse (26:2), out of the seventy-six verses in Ezekiel's Tyre oracles. The rest of the Tyre oracles in Ezekiel do not highlight the oppression of Tyre against Judah. As Corral admits:

> Tyre is an exceptional case among the foreign nations condemned in these oracles [Ezekiel 25–32]. She never had territorial disputes with Judah, apparently she had no share in Jerusalem's destruction, she was not an unreliable political

---

[5] Kraetzschmar, *Das Buch Ezechiel*, HAT 3.1 (Göttingen: Vandenhoeck & Ruprecht, 1900), 203; Pohlmann, *Kapitel 20–48*, 378; Strong, "Ezekiel's Oracles," 173–74, 177; N. R. Bowen, *Ezekiel*, Abingdon Old Testament Commentaries (Nashville: Abingdon Press, 2010), 167–69.

[6] *Contra* Block, *Ezekiel*, 2:34, who suggests that the plural term refers to the city gates of Jerusalem, which consist of two doors and are treated as a single entity in the Hebrew text. Similarly, Premstaller translates the plural term as "Türflügel" (*Fremdvölkersprüche*, 53). Allen notes that the Targum paraphrased the "gateway" of Jerusalem as a market (*Ezekiel 20–48*, 75). Zimmerli justifies such a designation of Jerusalem by citing the Wiseman Chronicle that confirms either the political or economic pre-eminence of Jerusalem in the Levantine region during the sixth century BCE (*Ezekiel*, 2:614).

[7] Corral, *Ezekiel's Oracles*, 144. See, however, the critical review of Corral's interpretation by J. T. Strong, review of M. A. Corral, *Ezekiel's Oracles against Tyre: Historical Reality and Motivations*, *CBQ* 65 (2003): 431–32.

[8] Corral highlights the economic abundance of Tyre as indicated by the *Leitwort* רכלה "trade, merchandise" in 28:5, 16, 18; the root רכל "to trade" in 26:12; 27:3, 13, 14, 17, 20, 22, 24; 28:5, 16, 18; ערב "to exchange" in 27:9, 13, 17, 19, 25, 27, 33, 34; the noun עזבון "ware" in 27:12, 14, 16, 22, 27, 33; and the root סחר "to travel around, trade, exchange" in 27:12, 15, 16, 18, 21, 36 (*Ezekiel's Oracles*, 151–54, 157).

ally, and no obvious reason for rivalry, resentment, or anger is discernible in the Tyrian oracles.[9]

The economic affluence of Tyre in chapters 27 and 28, contrary to the opinions of Corral and others, is not presented as the result of oppressive gains, but voluntary endowments by the nations or YHWH. Furthermore, given that 26:2–6 is likely to be inserted later in order to provide a link to the proof-sayings in chapter 25, it becomes possible that this later inserted section stems from a different concern than that found in the other parts of the Tyre oracles.[10] Taking all these factors into consideration raises doubt as to whether the economic tension between Tyre and Judah is the dominant cause of the destruction of Tyre's perfect beauty.

Neither the hubris nor the economic oppression of Tyre sufficiently account for the extensive diatribe against Tyre's perfect beauty. A few scholars have provided means to look at this perfect beauty of Tyre through a third lens. They have noted that Ezekiel's prophecies that describe Tyre's beauty contain lexemes that can be linked to and aligned with other biblical passages describing Jerusalem. Though Greenberg belongs to the first camp of scholars who lay great stress on the hubris as the cause of divine retribution against Tyre's perfect beauty, his proposition about the connection between the perfect beauty of Tyre in 27:2 and that of Jerusalem in 16:14 will be useful for our subsequent discussion on the connections between the images of Tyre and Jerusalem.[11] Geyer, Gillmayr-Bucher, and more recently I. D. Wilson observe that the construction of the Tyrian ship in Ezek 27 is closely associated with the materials used for the Israelite temple and tabernacle.[12] Bogaert and R. R.

---

[9] Ibid., 57. In n. 154, he further notes that the only literary evidence for a military coalition in which Tyre was involved against Judah is in Ps 83:3–8. The Tyre oracles in Amos 1:9–10; Joel 4:4–8; Zech 9:2–4 are not as extensive as in Ezekiel. Furthermore, the Tyre oracle in Isa 23 does not accuse Tyre of oppressing Israel, but condemns Tyre for its hubris.

[10] In terms of form, both chapters 25 and 26 are structured as a proof-saying, with reason (יַעַן) and punishment (לָכֵן). Linguistically, the taunt הֶאָח in 26:2 brings to mind the taunt of Ammon against Israelite sanctuary in previous oracle (25:3). Another proof-saying appears in 28:1–10. Cf. Block, *Ezekiel*, 2:35; Zimmerli, *Ezekiel*, 2:34; Gosse, "Recueil," 543–44; Schwagmeier, "Untersuchungen," 264; K. Schöpflin, "Die Tyrosworte im Kontext des Ezechielbuches," in *Israeliten und Phönizier: Ihre Beziehungen im Spiegel der Archäologie und der Literatur des Alten Testaments und seiner Umwelt*, ed. M. Witte and J. F. Diehl, OBO 235 (Fribourg: Academic Press, 2008), 195.

[11] Greenberg, *Ezekiel 21–37*, 548. See a similar approach in Schwagmeier, "Untersuchungen," 267.

[12] Geyer, "Ezekiel 27," 105–26; S. Gillmayr-Bucher, "Ein Klagelied über verlorene Schönheit," in *"Wie schön sind deine Zelte, Jakob!" Beiträge zur Ästhetik des*

Wilson detect the linguistic connections between the precious stones of the Tyrian ruler's covering in Ezek 28:13 and the Israelite priestly breastplate in Exod 28:17–20 and 39:10–13.[13] These connections to the Israelite cult, temple, and priesthood are intriguing. Yet, these scholars do not explore more of the rhetorical significance of these connections within the literary context of the Tyre oracles.[14] Their studies are limited to independent chapters in Ezekiel.[15] As a result, their analyses are not synthesized and placed within the Tyre oracles systematically.

To remedy the situation, this chapter will delve into the rhetorical significance of these connections. First, I will examine the form and content of Ezek 26–28, highlighting the beauty motif featured most prominently in the two dirges (27:1–36; 28:11–19). Next, I will examine how this bears lexical allusions to the pre-exilic Israelite sanctuary and priestly splendor. Finally, I will analyze how these allusions influence the rhetorics of Ezekiel's prophecies. My argument is that the dirges exalt the perfect beauty of Tyre and its ruler, such that both exceed the glory of the pre-exilic Israelite temple and priesthood. With the sudden downfall of both the Tyrian city and its ruler, the oracles in Ezek 26–28 build up the suspense: If such an exalted beauty of Tyre is violable, can Jerusalem's temple and temple leadership escape the divine onslaught?

### 1. THE ALLOCATION OF THE PERFECT BEAUTY

The chronological formula in 26:1 (ויהי בעשתי עשרה שנה באחד לחדש "In the eleventh year, on the first day of the month...") marks the beginning of the

---

*Alten Testaments*, ed. A. Grund; Biblisch-Theologische Studien 60 (Neukirchen: Neukirchener Verlag, 2003), 72–99; I. D. Wilson, "The Metaphorical World of Ezek 27 in Ancient Judah," *ZAW* 125 (2013): 249–62, esp. 255–58.

[13] Bogaert, "Montagne," 131–53; idem, "Chérub," 29–38; Wilson, "Death," 211–18.

[14] E.g., Greenberg, *Ezekiel 21–37*, 548, and Schwagmeier, "Untersuchungen," 267, link the perfect beauty motif in Ezek 27 to Jerusalem's epithet in 16:54, but do not notice that Ezek 27 contain terminology related to the Israelite sanctuary. Despite observing the lexical allusions to the Israelite sanctuary in chapter 27, Geyer, "Ezekiel 27," 124, barely discusses the ideological functions of these semantic connections, and merely suggests that the shared terminology arises due to the similar architectural structures for the temples in Tyre and Jerusalem.

[15] For the studies focusing only on Ezek 28:11–19, see Bogaert, "Montagne," 131–53; idem, "Chérub," 29–38; Wilson, "Death," 211–18. For the studies focusing only on Ezek 27, see Geyer, "Ezekiel 27," 105–26; Wilson, "Metaphorical World," 249–62.

oracles against Tyre.[16] This chronological marker sets Ezek 26:1–28:26 apart from the previous unit at 24:1–25:17 and the following oracle concerning Egypt that begins at 29:1. Within the unit thus marked out, 26:1–21 and 28:1–10 are two proof-sayings, each of which begins with the messenger formula "and the word of YHWH came to me saying" (ויהי דבר יהוה אלי לאמר, 26:1; 28:1), and ends with the declaration formula "the declaration of the Lord YHWH" (נאם אדני יהוה, 26:21; 28:10). Both 27:1–36 and 28:11–19 bear the explicit label of "dirge" (קינה, 27:2; 28:12),[17] and both end with the "terror" (בלהות) induced by the fall of Tyre and that of the Tyrian king respectively (27:36; 28:19).[18] Taken as a whole, Ezek 26–28 consists of two proof-sayings and two dirges, which constitute an alternating pattern:

26:1–21 a proof-saying against Tyre, ending with נאם אדני יהוה
27:1–36 a dirge over Tyre, ending with the בלהות refrain
28:1–10 a proof-saying against Tyre's ruler, ending with נאם אדני יהוה
28:11–19 a dirge over Tyre's ruler, ending with the בלהות refrain[19]

While the proof-sayings (26:1–21; 28:11–19) are predominantly concerned with the reasons for and processes of divine judgment, the two dirges (27:1–36; 28:11–19) put Tyre's glory and splendor on center stage.

### 1.1. The Proof-Sayings

Little attention is paid to the past glory and splendor of Tyre and its ruler in the two proof-sayings (26:1–21; 28:1–10). Instead, the texts cast the limelight on its guilt and subsequent judgment. As in chapter 25, the accusations of Tyre in the proof-sayings of chapters 26 and 28 are provided by the reasons for judgment, signaled by the causal conjunction "because" (יען or יען אשר). These

---

[16] The chronological formula in 26:1 is the first to appear in the OAN within chapters 25–32, and also the first in Ezekiel to have the month missing. The LXX reads "twelfth year of the first day of the first month."

[17] Ezekiel deploys a funeral dirge as a proclamation of divine retribution (2:10; 19:1; 26:17; 27:2, 32; 28:12; 32:2; cf. Amos 5:1; 8:10; Jer 7:29; 9:10, 20). Elsewhere in 2 Sam 1:19–27; 3:33; 2 Chr 35:25, the funeral dirge is used in a literal sense, such that a person's physical death is chanted over. See further explications in Wilson, "Metaphorical Word," 253; Schöpflin, *Theologie*, 79; G. Fleischer, "קינה," *TDOT* 13:17–23.

[18] The בלהות refrain in Ezek 27:36; 28:19 reads: בלהות היית ואינך עד עולם. This differs from the more elaborate בלהות refrain in 26:21 that reads: בלהות אתנך ואינך ותבקשי ולא תמצאי עוד לעולם נאם אדני יהוה. See the explication in G. S. Goering, "Proleptic Fulfillment of the Prophetic Word: Ezekiel's Dirges over Tyre and Its Ruler," *JSOT* 36 (2012): 483–505, here 486.

[19] See Goering, "Fulfillment," 487.

reasons for judgment are then followed by the announcements of judgment, signaled by the conjunction "therefore" (לכן).

In the first proof-saying (26:1–21), Tyre is judged because of its mockery over Jerusalem and the broken "gateway of the peoples" (v. 2). As a result, a series of divine judgments, introduced by one conjunction (לכן) and two messenger formulas (כה אמר אדני יהוה "thus has the Lord YHWH declared"), are executed upon Tyre through the nations and Nebuchadnezzar king of Babylon (vv. 3–6, 7–14).[20] Tyre will become a plunder and transform into a "bare rock" (צחיח סלע, vv. 4, 14). Another two messenger formulas delineate two sections, which describe the impact of YHWH's judgment executed upon Tyre from both an earthly and a cosmic perspective (vv. 15–18, 19–21).[21] On earth, "all the princes of the sea" (כל נשיאי הים) will lift up a dirge and mourn for Tyre (v. 16). Cosmically speaking, Tyre will descend into the underworld, joining the "people of old" (עם עולם, v. 20). The whole judgment of Tyre is brought to an end with the solemn declaration formula, נאם אדני יהוה.[22]

The second proof-saying (28:1–10) does highlight the wisdom (חכמה) of the Tyrian prince (נגיד), but it only serves to confirm the prince's hubris and self-divinization that form the central reasons for judgment. The noun חכמה and its related form are atypical of Ezekiel's general vocabulary. However, they are concentrated in 28:3–5.[23] The wisdom of the prince is said to have

---

[20] Contrary to Wevers, *Ezekiel*, 200, the literary unit in vv. 7–14 is likely to be a *Fortschreibung* of the preceding unit in vv. 3–6, since the former specifies that the many nations (v. 3, גוים רבים) that are to come against Tyre are actually Nebuchadnezzar king of Babylon. M. Saur suggests that vv. 7–14 represent a cryptic account of the conquest of Tyre by Alexander the Great in the fourth century BCE ("Tyros im Spiegel des Ezechielbuches," in *Israeliten und Phönizier: Ihre Beziehungen im Speigel der Archäologie und der Literatur des Alten Testaments und seiner Umwelt*, ed. M. Witte and J. F. Diehl, OBO 235 [Fribourg: Academic Press, 2008], 167–72). For further explications of the semantic parallels between the two textual units and their redational relationship, see Gosse, "Recueil," 555–56; Block, *Ezekiel*, 2:38–39; Premstaller, *Fremdvölkersprüche*, 67; Pohlmann, *Kapitel 20–48*, 374–81.

[21] C. L. Crouch observes that "the announcement of the city's destruction is expressed in a mixed combination of historical and mythological language" ("Ezekiel's Oracles against the Nations in Light of a Royal ideology of Warfare," *JBL* 130 [2011]: 473–92, here 484).

[22] For a more detailed discussion of the structure of chapter 26 marked out by the formulaic language, see Block, *Ezekiel*, 2:33.

[23] Cf. 28:7, 12, 17a. The concentrated appearances of the wisdom motifs and the structural peculiarities in 28:3–5 prompt several commentators to read vv. 3–5 as the "alien" insertion into the proof-saying. See Wilson, "Death," 212; Fechter, *Bewältigung*, 160.

surpassed that of Daniel (v. 3).²⁴ With his wisdom, the prince has accumulated much wealth (vv. 4–5). Even so, that wisdom is quickly blamed as causing the haughtiness of the prince (ויגבה לבבך) in v. 5b, cf. גבה לבך in v. 2). Furthermore, v. 6, the *Wiederaufnahme* of v. 2, stresses the king's arrogant claim of possessing a god-like mind: "you compare your mind with the mind of God" ( תתך את לבבך כלב אלהים). Through this repetition, both verses (vv. 2, 6) form an *inclusio* and render the wisdom of the Tyrian prince described in between (vv. 3–5) as blameworthy.²⁵ Following the accusations, YHWH pronounces judgment over the prince via the prophet. Ezekiel predicts the corruption of the prince's wisdom and splendor by the "most ruthless of the nations" (עריצי גוים, v. 7),²⁶ who will bring the prince down to the pit, into the heart of the seas (v. 8). As in the first proof-saying, the oracle in 28:1–10 ends solemnly with the divine declaration formula—נאם אדני יהוה.

In short, the condemnations of Tyre and its ruler are explicitly accounted for and spelled out, but the motif of perfect beauty is nowhere to be seen in either of the proof-sayings. Besides the brief mention of the wisdom of the Tyrian prince, primary emphasis is placed not on the magnificence of Tyre and its ruler prior to the judgment, but on the processes of divine judgment and their aftermath.

## 1.2. THE DIRGES

It is only in the dirges in Ezek 27:1–36 and 28:11–19 that the perfect beauty of Tyre is described in detail. The dirges, unlike the aforementioned proof-

---

²⁴ The references to Daniel also appear in Ezek 14:14, 20. While Daniel in 28:3 emerges as a possessor of wisdom, Daniel in 14:14, 20 is considered a paragon of righteousness. דנאל in the book of Ezekiel has a different orthography in comparison to דניאל in the book of Daniel. On this basis, and given that the date of compostion of the book of Daniel is considered to be much later than the book of Ezekiel, older scholarship rejects identifying the Daniel in the book of Ezekiel with the wise protagonist in the book of Daniel, but correlates the former with *Dnil*, a righteous ruler, in the Ugaritic literature (e.g., Zimmerli, *Ezekiel*, 2:80). Nonetheless, recent scholars concur that Daniel in the book of Ezekiel might well have been a prototype of the main hero in the book of Daniel (e.g., Strong, "Ezekiel's Oracles," 209; H.-M. Wahl, "Noah, Daniel und Hiob in Ezechiel XIV 12–20 [21–3]: Anmerkungen zum traditionsgeschichtlichen Hintergrund," *VT* 42 [1992]: 542–53).

²⁵ Interestingly, K. L. Wong argues that the LXX version of Ezek 28:1–10, rather than the MT version, casts a more negative light on the prince of Tyre ("The Prince of Tyre in the Masoretic and Septuagint Texts of Ezekiel 28,1–10," in *Interpreting Translation: Studies on the LXX and Ezekiel in Honour of Johan Lust*, ed. F. García Martínez and M. Vervenne [Leuven: Leuven University Press, 2005], 447–61).

²⁶ עריצי גוים are identified as Nebuchadnezzar and his troop in Ezek 30:11. This expression also appears in Ezek 31:12; 32:12. Cf. קרית גוים עריצים in Isa 25:3.

sayings, focus on the affirmation, rather than the condemnation, of the splendor of Tyre and its ruler.

The first dirge, Ezek 27, compares Tyre to a powerful and magnificent merchant ship.[27] Following the brief introduction of Tyre's location in the middle of the sea and its trade (vv. 1–3a), YHWH exclaims: "O Tyre,[28] you have said 'I am perfect in beauty'" (צור את אמרת אני כלילת יפי, 27:3b).[29] This boasting is surprisingly not negated. In fact, the text is eager to pay homage to Tyre's beauty by placing the affirmation of Tyre's beauty in YHWH's mouth. Employing the combination of the roots כלל and יפה again in v. 4, YHWH testifies that the Tyrian builders and mercenaries from various countries aid to perfect the beauty of Tyre. As if one repetition is not enough, YHWH affirms this beauty yet again in v. 11 (כללו יפיך). The combination of כלל and יפה thus builds an *inclusio* for the first section of the dirge (vv. 3b–11), alerting the reader to the interior beauty of the Tyrian merchapt ship.[30] In the next section (vv. 12–25a), the keyword תרשיש in vv. 12, 25 forms another *inclusio*, outlining Tyre's external relationship with the trading partners from all around the world.[31] Tyre's trading partners come from a vast region that extends from Javan, Tubal, and Meshech in the northwest (v. 13) to Haran, Eden, and Assur in the northeast (v. 23). Bringing luxury goods into Tyre, these partners further augment its perfect beauty. After the two sections that elaborately describe the glory and splendor of the Tyrian ship, the verbs in v. 25b (ותמלאי ותכבדי) move the dirge into the third section (vv. 25b–36).[32] Here, the ship encounters its sudden demise, and many lament the lost beauty of Tyre.

The motif of perfect beauty, signaled by the combination of כלל and יפה, appears again in the second dirge (28:11–19). Here, the focus moves away from the city to the ruler of Tyre. Following the prophetic word formula that

---

[27] The Hebrew Bible reveals a close relationship between Tyre and ships. 1 Kgs 9:27 reports that Hiram king of Tyre assisted Solomon king of Israel in sailing the ships. In Isa 23 Tyre's destruction was bewailed by the ships of Tarshish that sailed from its port. Cf. J. A. Durlesser, *The Metaphorical Narratives in the Book of Ezekiel* (Lewiston: Mellen, 2006), 148–51.

[28] The LXX has a dative τῇ Σορ, which links the name to the preceding citation formula.

[29] Allen revocalizes אמרת אני in 27:3, so that the expression includes the "ship" אֳנִי (cf. 1 Kgs 9:26, 27; 10:11, 22; Isa 33:21) and reads: "you were called a ship" (*Ezekiel*, 2:80). For the attempt to delete אמרת as a later "interpretive element" and the shortening of the text to "you are a ship of perfect beauty" (אֶת אֳנִי כלילת יפי), see Eichrodt, *Ezekiel*, 378, 383; Zimmerli, *Ezekiel*, 2:41. Nevertheless, such an emended reading unnecessarily downplays the hubristic claim of Tyre.

[30] Durlesser, *Narratives*, 160.
[31] Ibid., 161.
[32] Ibid.

marks the beginning of a new section (ויהי דבר יהוה אלי לאמר, 28:11),[33] the prophet is commanded to lift up a dirge over the "king" (מלך) of Tyre.[34] In the first part of the dirge (vv. 12b–15a), the Tyrian king is addressed as a "seal of perfection" (חותם תכנית),[35] being praised as "full of wisdom" (מלא חכמה) and "perfect in beauty" (כליל יפי, v. 12).[36] The beauty of this royal figure is further elaborated by various kinds of precious stones that form his "covering" (מסכה, v. 13).[37] He is even identified as "the anointed covering cherub" living on the mountains of *Elohim* (v. 14).[38] In the second part of the dirge (vv. 15b–19),

---

[33] On the form-critical relation between Ezek 28:1–10 and 28:11–19, see Yaron, "Dirge," 45–49; Wilson, "Death," 211; Pohlmann, *Kapitel 20–48*, 390–91; G. Hölscher, *Hesekiel: Der Dichter und das Buch: Eine Literarkritische Untersuchung*, BZAW 39 (Giessen: Töpelmann, 1924), 140.

[34] The addressee here is called מלך, rather than נגיד as in the foregoing oracle (cf. 28:2). As such, Bogaert surmises that the מלך here refers to the divine patron of Tyre—Melkart ("Montagne," 136). Nevertheless, the common concerns for the ruler's trade in both the proof-saying and the dirge in Ezek 28 calls for an identification of the מלך with the נגיד. Also, מלך in Ezekiel always refers to an earthly king (Babylon in 17:12; 19:9; Egypt in 29:2–3; kings of the earth in 27:33; 28:17; 34:24; 37:25). See the arguments for the latter view in Block, *Ezekiel*, 2:103.

[35] While the vocalization of חותם in the MT indicates a masculine singular participle, the LXX and the Vulgate seem to understand the term as a construct noun, reading it as ἀποσφράγισμα and *signaculum* respectively. Within the Hebrew Bible, the noun denotes either seal-like stones engraved on priestly garments (cf. Exod 28:11, 21, 36; 39:6, 14, 30) or royal signets (Jer 22:24; Hag 2:23). תכנית, on the other hand, may derive from תכן connoting an ideal standard (cf. Ezek 43:10). Alternatively, some commentators amend the noun to תבנית "image, copy, pattern" (cf. Ezek 8:10; Exod 25:9, 40; 1 Chr 28:11, 12, 18, 19). For more explications, see D. E. Callender Jr., *Adam in Myth: Ancient Israelite Perspectives on the Primal Man*, HSS 48 (Winona Lake: Eisenbrauns, 2000), 92–97; H. M. Patmore, *Adam, Satan, and the King of Tyre: The Interpretation of Ezekiel 28:11–19 in Late Antiquity* (Leiden: Brill, 2012), 192–93; Fechter, *Bewältigung*, 185; M. Lynch, *Monotheism and Institutions in the Book of Chronicles: Temple, Priesthood, and Kingship in Post-exilic Perspective*, FAT 2/64 (Tübingen: Mohr Siebeck, 2014), 118, n. 164.

[36] מלא חכמה is missing in the LXX. Zimmerli considers the expression as a secondary insertion (*Ezekiel*, 2:82). However, it is noteworthy that the same juxtaposition of the wisdom (חכמתך) and beauty (יפעתך) motifs again appears in 28:17.

[37] The noun can either be derived from סוך "to anoint" (cf. Deut 28:40; Mic 6:15; Ezek 16:9; 2 Sam 12:20) or it can be derived from סכך "to cover" (cf. Exod 25:20; 37:9; 40:3; 1 Kgs 8:7; 1 Chr 28:18; Ezek 28:14, 16). The LXX thinks of it as referring to the act of binding or clothing (ἐνδέδεσαι). Cf. *HALOT* 1:746, 754; S. N. Bunta, "YHWH's Cultic Statue after 597/586 BCE: A Linguistic and Theological Reinterpretation of Ezek 28:12," *CBQ* 69 (2007): 222–41, esp. 237.

[38] The LXX does not identify the Tyrian king as the cherub, but suggests that the Tyrian king is "with the cherub" (μετὰ τοῦ χερουβ).

unrighteousness, sin, and violence have been found in the king of Tyre, such that he is cast away from the mountain of *Elohim*, turned into ashes, and exterminated forever.

Preceding the tragic destruction and downfall in the immediate future (*jetzt*, "now"), both dirges include extensive reminiscences of the glory and splendor of Tyre and its ruler (*einst*, "once"),[39] which are lacking in the proof-sayings. These concentrated appearances of the motif of beauty in the dirges about Tyre and its ruler thus warrant further investigation.

## 2. THE ALLUSIONS TO THE ISRAELITE SANCTUARY AND PRIESTHOOD

The dirges' interests in Tyrian glory and splendor point implicitly to the imagery of the pre-exilic Israelite sacral institutions described elsewhere in the Hebrew Bible. While Ezek 27 builds up extensive linguistic connections to the imagery of the Israelite tabernacle or temple found in the books of Exodus, Kings, and Chronicles, Ezek 28:11–19 contains semantic links to the imagery of the Israelite high priest depicted in Exod 28 and 39.

### 2.1. THE CONFLATION OF THE TABERNACLE AND FIRST TEMPLE IMAGES

First and foremost, the perfect beauty motif alerts the reader to an allusion to Jerusalem via the combination of כלל and יפה. The motif appears in 27:3–4, 11 and 28:12 to describe the beauty of both Tyre and its ruler. All other cases in which the combination appears concern Jerusalem (16:14, cf. 16:13, 25; Ps 50:2; Lam 2:15).[40] On this basis, Greenberg is among the first to compare Tyre's perfect beauty with that of Jerusalem.[41] By using the phrase "perfect in

---

[39] H. Jahnow views the thematic contrast between *einst* "once" and *jetzt* "now" as one of the characteristics of the קינה form (*Das hebräische Leichenlied im Rahmen der Völkerdichtung*, BZAW 36 [Gießen: Töpelmann, 1923], 99).

[40] With or without the complement of כלל, ten of the nineteen biblical occurrences of the noun "beauty" (יפי) are found in Ezekiel, referring not only to the beauty of Jerusalem, but also to the splendour of Tyre and its ruler, as well as to the glory of a tall cedar representing Assyria (16:14, 15, 25; 27:3, 4, 11; 28:7, 12, 17; 31:8). The other nine occurrences of the noun appear in Isa 3:24; 33:17; Ps 45:12; Prov 6:25; 31:30; Esth 1:11; Lam 2:15; Ps 50:2; Zech 9:17. Cf. Zimmerli, *Ezekiel*, 2:55; Block, *Ezekiel*, 2:51, 57.

[41] Greenberg, *Ezekiel 21–37*, 548. So also Premstaller, *Fremdvölkersprüche*, 82; Zimmerli, *Ezekiel*, 2:55; Block, *Ezekiel*, 2:57. Briefly, Fechter observes the motif of perfect beauty in both 27:3 and 28:12, but he does not notice its appearances in other oracles concerning Judah and Jerusalem in the rest of the Hebrew Bible (*Bewältigung*,

beauty," Ezek 27:3–4, 11 creates an intertextual link with Jerusalem's beauty in Ezek 16:14. Both Ps 50:2 and Lam 2:15 also use this expression to refer to Jerusalem; both texts are roughly contemporaneous with the book of Ezekiel.[42] Given the usage of this phrase in relation to Jerusalem, it is likely that Ezek 27 is alluding to this whole cultural tradition about Jerusalem, rather than just one specific instance.

Geyer provides another link between the beauty of Tyre and that of Jerusalem. He argues that the mechanical list of substances in 27:5–9 alludes to the Israelite sanctuary.[43] In this pericope, the substances enlisted from various countries, which are used for either the construction of the ship or the traded wares by Tyre, constitute the interior beauty of the merchant ship. While many commentators attempt to uncover a historical correlation between the nations named and the materials used for the construction,[44] Geyer focuses on literary influences and contends that more than thirty of these substances named in Ezek 27 are related to the temple, ark, or tabernacle.[45] Without denying his substantial thesis, some of the substances mentioned by Geyer, when read in isolation, are far too common without necessarily signifying a connection to the Israelite sanctuary. For instance, the term ברזל "iron" in Ezek 27:12, in Geyer's opinion, should be associated with the temple in 1 Chr 22:14, 16; 29:2; 2 Chr 2:6, 13.[46] But Geyer then admits that iron is also used in a variety of

---

121). The semantic links between the Tyre oracles and the prophecies concerning Jerusalem are more pronounced in the MT, while the terms used to describe the beauty of Jerusalem and that of Tyre are more varied in the LXX.

[42] S. Terrien dates Ps 50:2 to the pre-exilic time (*The Psalms: Strophic Structure and Theological Commentary* [Grand Rapids: Eerdmans, 2003], 399), but F.-L. Hossfeld and E. Zenger date the Psalm later to the post-exilic period (*Psalm 1–50*, NEchtB 29 [Würzburg: Echter Verlag, 1993], 309). Lam 2 is almost unanimously dated to post-587 BCE.

[43] Geyer, "Ezekiel 27," 105–26. His opinion is later followed by Bowen, *Ezekiel*, 165; Gillmayr-Bucher, "Klagelied," 88; Wilson, "Metaphorical World," 249–62.

[44] M. Saur, *Der Tyroszyklus des Ezechielbuches*, BZAW 386 (Berlin: de Gruyter, 2008), 185–97; idem, "Tyros im Spiegel des Ezechielbuches," in *Israeliten und Phönizier: Ihre Beziehungen im Spiegel der Archäologie und der Literatur des Alten Testaments und seiner Umwelt*, ed. M. Witte and J. F. Diehl, OBO 235 (Fribourg: Academic Press, 2008), 172–80; M. Liverani, "The Trade Network of Tyre According to Ezek. 27," in *Ah, Assyria ... ! Studies in Assyrian History and Ancient Near Eastern Historiography Presented to Hayim Tadmor*, ed. M. Cogan and I. Eph'al (Jerusalem: Magness Press, 1991), 65–79; I. M. Diakonoff, "The Naval Power and Trade of Tyre," *IEJ* 42 (1992): 168–93; Fohrer, *Ezechiel*, 154, 156; Pohlmann, *Kapitel 20–48*, 385, n. 59; Block, *Ezekiel*, 2:58–61; Greenberg, *Ezekiel 21–37*, 549–51; Wevers, *Ezekiel*, 206–7.

[45] Geyer, "Ezekiel 27," 119–25.

[46] Ibid., 120.

CHAPTER THREE 91

contexts within the Hebrew Bible: "Strangely, it was used for the sarcophagus of Og (Deuteronomy 3:11), but it is prohibited in the construction of altars (Deut. 27.5; Josh. 8.31; 1 Kings 6.7)."[47] Ezekiel 4:3 even uses the term twice to denote the warring context when Jerusalem was besieged, which is obviously unrelated to the sacred temple precinct. Since Geyer does not provide a criterion to clarify why the connections with 1 and 2 Chronicles, rather than those with Deuteronomy, Joshua, and Kings, are more appropriate to the hermeneutics of Ezek 27, the association between iron and temple becomes relatively arbitrary.

Concentrating on more limited but highly significant and distinctive terms within Ezek 27:3–11, I propose that this first section of the dirge conflates linguistic elements that characterize the tabernacle in the wilderness described in the priestly literature of the Pentateuch, the First Temple depicted in the book of Kings and Chronicles, and the Jerusalem temple alluded to in Ezek 16.

The ship-building materials in Ezek 27 correspond to the stately furnishing of the tabernacle described in the Pentateuch. The term קרש or הקרשים occurs once in Ezekiel (27:6) and over fifty times in Exodus and Numbers, but it does not occur elsewhere in the Hebrew Bible.[48] Exodus and Numbers employ קרשים exclusively to describe the long wooden acacia planks or frames with which the tabernacle was constructed.[49] The two distinctive terms—"blue" (תכלת) and "purple" (ארגמן)—are juxtaposed to describe the materials for ship covering in Ezek 27:7 (cf. vv. 16, 24). They appear side by side more than twenty times in Exodus, twice in Esther and Chronicles respectively, and once in Jeremiah.[50] Exodus uses the pair especially in the context of tabernacle offering and building as well as in reference to the priestly breastplate and ephod.[51] In a later tradition, in 2 Chronicles, the pair appears in the context of temple building. Even though the two terms are used in parallel in Jer 10:9 to denote the covering materials not of the tabernacle but of an idol, the context there remains cultic. The juxtaposed terms do appear twice in the book of Esther to describe the luxury enjoyed in the Persian palace, but Grossman

---

[47] Ibid.
[48] Exod 26:15, 16, 17, 18, 19 (2x), 20, 21 (2x), 22, 23, 25 (2x), 26, 27 (2x), 28, 29; 35:11; 36:20, 21, 22, 23, 24 (2x), 25, 26 (2x), 27, 28, 30, 31, 32, 33, 34; 39:33; 40:18; Num 3:36; 4:31. Noted by Kohn, *New Heart*, 58.
[49] Zimmerli, *Ezekiel*, 2:57.
[50] Exod 25:4; 26:1, 31, 36; 27:16; 28:5, 6, 8, 15, 33; 35:6, 23, 25, 35; 36:8, 35, 37; 38:18, 23; 39:1, 2, 3, 5, 8, 24, 29; 2 Chr 2:14; 3:14; Jer 10:9; Esth 1:6; 8:15.
[51] These Exodus passages are all listed as P in M. Noth, *A History of Pentateuchal Traditions*, trans. B.W. Anderson (Chico: Scholars Press, 1981), 267–71. For the shared technical terminology used by both P and Ezekiel, see Kohn, *New Heart*, 82.

suggests that the occurrences there presuppose the context of an Israelite temple, serving to highlight the contrast between the foreign palace and the Israelite sanctuary.[52] In summary, it is remarkable for a short section like 27:3–11 to contain two pairs of distinctive terms that appear elsewhere almost always in relation to the temple-/tabernacle-building context.

The materials and craftsmanship on board of the Tyrian ship in Ezek 27 further resemble those present in the construction of the First Temple in the books of Kings and Chronicles. In 27:5, the planks and mast of the Tyrian merchant ship are made out of cedar (ארז) from Lebanon and junipers (ברושים) from Senir.[53] In a majority of cases, the two terms—ארז and לבנון—occur together in 1 Kings and 2 Chronicles.[54] In distinction from the prophetic texts in Isa 14:8; 41:19, Ezek 31:8, and Zech 11:2, passages in 1 Kings and 2 Chronicles utilize the two terms exclusively in relation to Hiram king of Tyre, who supplied Solomon with the logs for temple building. As if to reinforce the link to the Israelite temple imagery, Ezek 27 further describes the crew on board of the Tyrian ship as חכמים (vv. 8b, 9a). Even though the term "wisdom" (חכמה) can appear in a wide range of contexts, the term in the sense of skill in technical matters appears almost exclusively in the contexts where the construction of the temple or the tabernacle are involved.[55] This calls to mind not only those wise builders of the tabernacle (Exod 28:3; 31:6; 35:10; 36:1, 2, 4, 8), but also the skillful temple artisans (1 Kgs 7:14; 1 Chr 22:15; 2 Chr 2:6, 12–13 [Eng. 2:7, 13–14]).[56] For instance, Hiram (Huram-abi), the temple artisan, is introduced as a skilled craftsman full of wisdom (חכמה, 1 Kgs 7:14; cf. איש חכם in 2 Chr 2:12–13 [Eng. 2:13–14]). In 1 Kgs 7:14, this Hiram/Huram-Abi has a Naphtalite mother, in 2 Chr 2:12–13 [Eng. 2:13–14], he has a Danite

---

[52] J. Grossman, *Esther: The Outer Narrative and the Hidden Reading* (Winona Lake: Eisenbrauns, 2011), 23–24. On the allusion of Esth 1:6 to the First Temple and Tabernacle, see also L. B. Paton, *A Critical and Exegetical Commentary on the Book of Esther* (Edinburgh: T&T Clark, 1908), 139. Moreeover, A. Koller, *Esther in Ancient Jewish Thought* (Cambridge: Cambridge University Press, 2014), 100, notes that the fortress of Susa in the book of Esther is called a בירה, which appears elsewhere in the Hebrew Bible only in 1 Chr 29 to denote the Jerusalem Temple.

[53] ברושים is a cognate to the Akkadian *burāšu*, while ארז in Akkadian is the semantic equivalent to *erēnu*. For the uses of cedar and juniper in Sennacherib's palace, see A. K. Grayson and J. Novotny, *The Royal Inscriptions of Sennacherib, King of Assyria (704–681 BC), Part 1* (Winona Lake: Eisenbrauns, 2012), 46. Within the Hebrew Bible, the two trees are often associated with the divine and royal might. For further explications, see Wilson, "Metaphorical World," 256.

[54] 1 Kgs 5:22, 24 [Eng. 5:8; 10]; 6:15, 18, 20, 34; 9:11; 2 Chr 2:7 [Eng. 2:8]. See also Isa 14:8; 41:19; Ezek 31:8; Zech 11:2.

[55] *HALOT* 1:314.

[56] Gillmayr-Bucher, "Klagelied," 89.

mother.⁵⁷ According to the biblical traditions, both Danites and Naphtalites have long standing connections with the region of Tyre and Sidon.⁵⁸ In both Chronicles and Kings, he has a Tyrian father. In light of this, a deep connection between temple and Tyre seems to be present in the Hebrew Bible, and it is likely for the editor, if not the author, of Ezek 27 to be aware of this traditional link when composing the glory of Tyre in the dirge.

Most interesting is that Ezek 27 contains temple language found in Ezek 16. In the latter chapter, Jerusalem is personified as the wife of YHWH and is characterized with a world-renowned beauty. The clothing of Lady Jerusalem in 16:9–14, as noted by Zimmerli, Block, and Galambush, employs the vocabulary that is used elsewhere only to describe the tabernacle in the wilderness.⁵⁹ The "fine leather" (תחש) in 16:10, for instance, is mentioned elsewhere only as the covering for the tabernacle and its cultic paraphernalia.⁶⁰ The juxtaposition of "fine linen" (שש) and "embroidered cloth" (רקמה) in the same verse of Ezek 16 appears exclusively in Exodus to describe the fabrics used for the wilderness tabernacle and the priestly garments.⁶¹ While the woman in Ezek 16:13 is fed with סלת, שמן, and דבש, Leviticus and Numbers employ the triad

---

⁵⁷ This brings the Huram-Abi in 2 Chronicles closer to Oholiab, the craftsman involved in the building of the tabernacle (cf. Exod 35:34). See Lynch, *Monotheism*, 125–26. For a discussion on Hiram/Huram's identity, see C. Sulzbach, "Nebuchadnezzar in Eden? Daniel 4 and Ezekiel 28," in *Stimulation from Leiden: Collected Communications to the XVIIIth Congress of the International organization for the Study of the Old Testament, Leiden 2004*, ed. H. M. Niemann and M. Augustin, BEATAJ 54 (Frankfurt am Main: Lang, 2006), 132–34.

⁵⁸ Cf. Judg 18:7, 27–30; see the discussion in R. B. Dillard, "The Chronicler's Solomon," *WTJ* 43 (1981): 289–300.

⁵⁹ Zimmerli, *Ezekiel*, 1:340–41; Block, *Ezekiel*, 1:485; Galambush, *Jerusalem*, 95.

⁶⁰ E.g., Exod 25:5; 26:14; 35:7, 23; 36:19; 39:34; Num 4:6, 8, 10, 11, 12, 14. The meaning of the term תחש is difficult to define, but the noun probably refers to either the tanned skin of a type of dophin, or a type of fine leather imported from Egypt. In Gen 22:24, it appears to be a place name or name of a territory. Cf. *HALOT* 2:1720–21; Galambush, *Jerusalem*, 95; Kohn, *New Heart*, 56.

⁶¹ Both שש and related forms of רקמה are juxtaposed in Exod 26:36; 27:16; 28:39; 35:35; 36:37; 38:18; 39:29. שש apppears 27 times in P (Exod 26:31, 36; 27:9, 16, 18; 28:5, 6, 8, 15, 39; 35:6, 23, 25, 35; 36:8, 16, 35; 38:9, 16, 18; 39:2, 3, 5, 8, 27, 28, 29) and 3 times in Ezekiel (16:10, 13 [Qere]; 27:7). It is also found in Gen 41:42 (E) and Prov 31:22. The feminine noun רקמה appears 12 times in the Hebrew Bible (Judg 5:30 [2x]; Ezek 16:10, 13, 18; 17:3; 26:16; 27:7, 16, 24; Ps 45:15; 1 Chr 29:2). For the predominantly cultic and secondarily royal connotation of רקמה in the Hebrew Bible, as well as its later usage in the eschatological contexts depicted in the Dead Sea Scrolls, see L. Lee, "רוקמה," *Theologisches Wörterbuch zu den Qumrantexten 3*, ed. H.-J. Fabry and U. Dahmen (Stuttgart: Kohlhammer, 2016), 643–45.

in reference to the offerings prescribed for the tabernacle.[62] Through these linguistic correpondences with the pre-exilic Israelite sanctuary, the perfect beauty of Jerusalem in Ezek 16 becomes justified on the basis that it is the dwelling place of YHWH.[63] What Zimmerli, Block, and Galambush do not notice is that the same section in Ezek 16 also shares terminology with chapter 27. In both chapters, the perfect beauty of both Tyre and Jerusalem are expressed through the combination of כלל and יפה.[64] Their shared beauty is further highlighted by another common lexeme, "splendor" (הדר, 16:13; 27:10). The embroidered fine linen (רקמה and שש) used to weave the sail of the Tyrian ship is also the clothing of Jerusalem, which symbolizes the Israelite tabernacle in Ezek 16.[65] Even outside the pericope in 27:3–11, we can find connections between chapters 27 and 16. Hence, the distinctive trade materials, דבש and שמן, offered by Judah and the land of Israel to Tyre in 27:17 also occur in 16:13, 19. In short, juxtaposing chapters 27 and 16 further strengthens the connections between the Tyrian merchant ship and the Israelite sanctuary.

Following the above survey, we observe a clear pattern of allusions: Ezek 27:3–11 employs terminology frequently and almost exclusively used elsewhere of the Israelite tabernacle or the Jerusalem temple. The pericope not only contains linguistic elements (קרש and תכלת // ארגמן) that appear almost exclusively in relation to the construction of the tabernacle in Pentateuch, it also incorporates lexemes (ארז // ברושים and חכמים) that occur frequently in relation to the building of the First Temple in the books of Kings and Chronicles. Even more remarkable are the shared locutions (רקמה; שש; הדר; כלל + יפה; דבש ושמן) describing both the Tyrian ship in Ezek 27 and the Jerusalem sanctuary in Ezek 16. This observation challenges Odell's comment that the terminology in Ezek 27 should be seen as referring to common trade goods in the ancient world, and that "not too much should be made of the sacral connections."[66] Our analysis does not deny that Ezek 27 can contain authentic

---

[62] E.g., Lev 2:7; Num 6:15; 7:13, 19; 8:8.

[63] Remarkably, the Targum explicitly links the terms in Ezek 16:9–13 to the cultic paraphernalia and tabernacle in the wilderness. Tg. Ps.-Jo. on Ezek 16:13, for instance, begins with YHWH's setting of the tabernacle in the midst of Jerusalem (ויהבית משכני ביניכון). Noted by M. Greenberg, "Ezekiel 16: Panorama of Passions," in *Love and Death in the Ancient Near East*, ed. J. H. Marks and R. M. Good (Guilford: Four Quarters Publication Company, 1987), 143–50, here 147–48.

[64] Within the book of Ezekiel, such a combination is found only in 16:14; 27:3–4, 11 and in another oracle concerning the Tyrian king in 28:12.

[65] Within the book of Ezekiel, the juxtaposition of שש and רקמה appears only in 16:10, 13 and 27:7, even though individual appearances of רקמה are found in 17:3 and 27:16, 24.

[66] Odell, *Ezekiel*, 346–47.

knowledge of certain nautical terminologies or trade networks.[67] Nonetheless, it is not possible to relegate all the terms as merely seafaring or trading materials.[68] The concentrated accumulation of specific terms, which appear elsewhere in the Hebrew Bible only in reference to the temple/tabernacle setting, strongly suggests that Ezek 27 draws from various Israelite temple or tabernacle elements, conflates them, reconfigures them, and infuses them into the imagery of the glorious ship of Tyre.

2.2. THE ENUMERATION OF THE JEWELS ON THE HIGH PRIESTLY PECTORAL

While the dirge in Ezek 27 correlates the image of Tyre with various images of the Israelite sanctuary, the dirge in Ezek 28 links the portrayal of the Tyrian king to that of the Israelite priesthood. The intention to draw such a comparison is first hinted at when the king is praised to be "full of wisdom" (מלא חכמה) and "perfect in beauty" (כליל יפי, 28:12). On the one hand, both the wisdom and beauty motifs, as noted in the previous section, appear in the dirge in Ezek 27 to characterize the skillful crew of Tyre and the splendid Tyrian ship. On the other hand, both of these motifs fit nicely into the Israelite temple/tabernacle context depicted elsewhere in the Hebrew Bible.

Moreover, the Tyrian king is located in "Eden, the garden of *Elohim*" (עדן גן אלהים, v. 13), which is later specified as on the "holy mountain of *Elohim*" (הר קדש אלהים, v. 14). Similar expressions are used to describe Mount Zion, on which the Jerusalem temple is situated. Mount Zion is called the "mountain of holiness/holy mountain,"[69] the "mountain of YHWH"[70] or the "mountain of God."[71] In this light, it becomes imaginable that the Tyrian king, possessing the wisdom and perfect beauty, being located in Eden and on the holy mountain, is someone closely related to the temple precinct.

---

[67] Cf. E. S. Krantz, *Des Schiffes Weg mitten im Meer*, ConBOT (Lund: Gleerup, 1982); Liverani, "Network," 65–79; Diakonoff, "Power," 168–93.

[68] Even Krantz, in her analysis of the terms ברושים and ארז, observes the frequent appearances of these terms in the sanctuary context of the Hebrew Bible (*Des Schiffes*, 154–55, 157).

[69] In Ps 2:6, the expression "my holy mountain" (הר קדשי) serves to qualify "Zion" (ציון). Similar expressions are found in Ps 3:5; 15:1; 43:3; 48:2; 99:9; Isa 11:9; 27:13; 56:7; 57:13; 65:11, 25; 66:20; Jer 31:23; Dan 9:16; 11:45; Joel 2:1; 3:21; Obad 16; Zeph 3:11; Zech 8:3. Cf. H. M. Patmore, "Did the Masoretes Get It Wrong? The Vocalization and Accentuation of Ezekiel XXVIII 12–19," *VT* 58 (2008): 245–57, esp. 252; idem, *Adam*, 201; Wilson, "Death," 215.

[70] Ps 24:3; Isa 2:3; 30:29; Mic 4:2. Cf. Patmore, "Masoretes," 253; idem, *Adam*, 201.

[71] The "mountain of God" refers to Horeb in texts such as Exod 4:27; 18:5; 24:13; 1 Kgs 19:8. Cf. Patmore, "Masoretes," 253; idem, *Adam*, 201.

Block refuses to associate the dirge in Ezek 28:11–19 with the Israelite sacral traditions,[72] but his objection is based on unnecessary polarization between the temple and Eden myths. Ezek 28:11–19, according to Block, mentions "Eden" and "the garden of *Elohim*," which belong "all either to Gen.1–3 or to extra-biblical mythologies."[73] On this basis, he argues that the association of the "holy mountain of *Elohim*," the "cherub," and the "stones of fire" with Jerusalem must be strained.[74] Nonetheless, the biblical traditions do attest an interweaving of the cult and creation. Hence, Wenham, in a landmark essay, posits the idea that the creation narrative in Gen 2–3 displays several lexical features appearing only or mainly in relation to the Israelite cultic sphere.[75] For instance, the verb used for YHWH's walking in the garden in Gen 3:8 is התהלך, and the same verb describes the divine presence in the tent sanctuaries (Lev 26:12; Deut 23:15; 2 Sam 7:6–7).[76] Also, related forms of the two verbs characterizing Adam's work—"to till it and keep it" (לעבדה ולשמרה, Gen 2:15—appear together elsewhere only with reference to the Levites' duties in guarding and ministering in the sanctuary (Num 3:7–8; 8:26; 18:5–6).[77] Furthermore, YHWH's clothing of Adam, employing the noun "garments" (כתנות) and the *hiphil* of "to clothe" (לבש, Gen 3:21), mirrors Moses's clothing of priests (Exod 28:41; 29:8; 40:14; Lev 8:13).[78] In addition to Gen 1–3, several psalmodic texts also envisage the temple in Jerusalem as mirroring the

---

[72] Block, *Ezekiel*, 2:111–12. So also Gowan, *Man*, 89–90: "This suggests that vss. 11–19 does not represent a description of the temple at Tyre with its priest-king, nor of the Jerusalem temple and its precincts, as others have thought."

[73] Block, *Ezekiel*, 2:111. So also Gowan, *Man*, 90: "It was the paradise myth in its peculiar Hebrew form which was the principle source of all the materials used here."

[74] Block, *Ezekiel*, 2:111.

[75] G. J. Wenham, "Sanctuary Symbolism in the Garden of Eden Story," *World Congress of Jewish Studies* 9 (1986): 19–25. For the temple background of Gen 1, see also U. Cassuto, *A Commentary on the book of Exodus* (Jerusalem: Magnes Press, 1967), 476; M. Weinfeld, "Sabbath, Temple, and the Enthronement of the Lord—the Problem of the Sitz im Leben of Genesis 1:1–2:3," in *Mélanges bibliques et orientaux en l'honneur de M. Henri Cazelles* (ed. A. Caquot and M. Delcor; Kevelaer: Butzon & Becker, 1981), 501–12; J. D. Levenson, *Creation and the Persistence of Evil* (Princeton: Princeton University Press, 1994), 78–87; B. Janowski, "Tempel und Schöpfung: Schöpfungstheologische Aspekte der priesterschriftlichen Heiligtumskonzeption," *Jahrbuch für biblische Theologie* 5 (1990), 37–69; M. S. Smith, *The Priestly Vision of Genesis 1* (Minneapolis: Fortress Press, 2010), 93; idem, *The Origins of Biblical Monotheism: Israel's Polytheistic Background and the Ugaritic Texts* (Oxford: Oxford University Press, 2001), 291.

[76] Wenham, "Sanctuary," 20.

[77] Ibid., 21.

[78] Ibid., 21–22.

cosmos. Like the garden of God, the temple is a place of paradisiacal abundance and the source of life-giving waters.[79] The river flowing in Eden is associated with a river whose source is in the temple.[80] Ps 78:69 draws a parallel between the building of the divine sanctuary and the creation of the world: "And he built his sanctuary like the heights, like the earth which he has founded forever."[81] Likewise, Ps 150:1 casts the divine sanctuary and the sky in *parallelismus membrorum*:

הללו אל בקדשו
הללוהו ברקיע עזו

Praise God in his sanctuary;
Praise him in the sky, his stronghold.[82]

There are strong intersections between creation and cult in the Hebrew Bible.[83] On this basis, the setting of the Tyrian king both in "Eden, the garden of *Elohim*" (Ezek 28:13) and on the "holy mountain of *Elohim*" (v. 14), along with the characterizations of the Tyrian king as "full of wisdom" and "perfect in beauty" (v. 12), does not preclude but rather reinforces the associations with the Israelite sacral traditions.[84]

The clearest evidence for the parallels between the Tyrian king and the Jerusalem priesthood is found in Ezek 28:13. There, the Tyrian king wears a covering made out of a selection of precious stones, which, as observed by Wilson and others, are reminiscent of the high priest's breastplate from Exod 28:17–20; 39:10–13.[85] The order of the stones from Exodus is as follows: אדם

---

[79] Ps 36:9–10; Gen 2:6–10. Cf. Newsom, "Maker," 202.

[80] Cf. Ps 46:5–6; Ezek 47:1–12; Zech 14:8; Joel 4:18. Cf. Ibid.

[81] Smith, *Origins*, 169.

[82] Ibid.

[83] Cf. the statement in Yaron, "Dirge," 40: "It can be proved that the Garden of Eden and the House of God are interchangeable and that according to the conception of the ancient Israelite believer, there was no difference between them."

[84] Interestingly, outside of the Hebrew Bible, several early Jewish writings not only conceive Eden as a sanctuary located in the land of Israel, in Jerusalem, or on/near Mount Moriah, but also designate Adam to be a priest in Eden. Hence, Adam in Jub. 3:27 assumes a priestly role to offer "a sweet-smelling sacrifice—frankincense, galbanum, stacte, and spices" at the gate of the Garden of Eden (cf. the Greek version of LAE 29:3). Also, Jub. 8:19 identifies the former Eden as "the Holy of Holies and the residence of the Lord" (cf. Jub. 4:26; Midr. Ps 92:6; Pesiq. Rab. 43:2; Pirqe R. El. 23; 31, etc.). For more detailed discussions of the reception history that binds both Eden and Temple imagery, see P. T. Lanfer, *Remembering Eden: The Reception History of Genesis 3:22–24* (Oxford: Oxford University Press, 2012), 127–57, esp. 135, 137, 140, 212.

[85] Wilson, "Death," 214; Fechter, *Bewältigung*, 165, 172–74; Callender, *Adam*, 102; Zimmerli, *Ezekiel*, 2:82; Greenberg, *Ezekiel 21–37*, 582.

"ruby," פטדה "topaz," ברקת "emerald," נפך "turquoise," ספיר "sapphire," יהלם "diamond," לשם "jacinth," שבו "agate," אחלמה "amethyst," תרשיש "beryl," שהם "onyx," ישפה "jasper."[86] Meanwhile, Ezek 28:13 shows the order of the stones engraved on the garments of the Tyrian king as such: אדם, פטדה, יהלם, תרשיש, שהם, ישפה, ספיר, נפך, and ברקת.[87] Patmore denies the parallels between the two lists, arguing that several of the stones also appear in other contexts.[88] Thus, פטדה, as he notes, appears in Job 28:19; תרשיש in Ezek 1:6; 10:9; Dan 10:6 (cf. Song 5:14); שהם in Gen 2:12; Exod 25:7; 28:9; 35:9, 27; 39:6; 1 Chr 29:2; נפך in Ezek 27:16.[89] Nonetheless, he ignores the fact that none of the biblical passages that he cites includes such an accumulation of shared precious stones as found in both Ezek 28 and Exod 28; 39. Linguistically, four out of the nine precious stones mentioned in MT Ezek 28:13 (אדם, יהלם, ישפה, ברקת) appear elsewhere only in Exod 28 and 39. Formally, both lists share a tripartite grouping.[90] Given the linguistic and formal similarities, the connections between the Tyrian king in Ezek 27 and the Israelite high priest in the two passages of Exodus become even more intertwined and tangible.

The direction of dependence between the list of jewels in Ezek 28 and that in the two Exodus passages is difficult to establish. Exod 28:17–20 is set in the larger priestly account that narrates YHWH's establishment of the tabernacle and its related service.[91] Like Exod 39:10–13, it enumerates twelve stones engraved upon the breastpiece of the high priest, which symbolize the twelve tribes of Israel—God's chosen people.[92] Now, if we allow the possibility that both passages of Exodus borrow and expand the list of stones engraved on the garment of the Tyrian king in Ezek 28:13, we will be lacking an account of motivation. After all, why would YHWH, in the middle of his instructions about the implementation of the sacred cultic service, require the

---

[86] Concerning the lack of agreement between the Greek gemstone names in the LXX and the Hebrew names in the MT, see J. A. Harrell, "Old Testament Gemstones: A Philological, Geological, and Archaeological Assessment of the Septuagint," *BBR* 21 (2011): 141–71, esp. 149–50. For the same lists of gemstones with the LXX, albeit in different orders, see Josephus, *J.W.* 5.233–34 and *Ant.* 3.165–68.

[87] For the tabulated comparison, see Premstaller, *Fremdvölkersprüche*, 110.

[88] Patmore, *Adam*, 195. Cf. Patmore's other statement: "Ezekiel is concerned to demonstrate the luxury of the setting; there is no need to assume a badly made allusions is at work here" ("Masoretes," 247).

[89] Patmore, *Adam*, 195.

[90] Wilson, "Death," 214.

[91] For the attempt to date Exod 28:17–20 in the late fifth or early fourth century BCE, see W. Zwickel, *Edelsteine in der Bibel* (Mainz: von Zabern, 2002), 48–49.

[92] For the understanding of high priestly precious stones as having evolved from the seal stones of the twelve tribes of Israel, see ibid., 45. For a picture of the reconstruction of the ancient Israelite high priest breastplate, see ibid., 32.

highest Israelite religious official to wear the garment of a non-Israelite monarch who had already been known to suffer a doomed fate? Alternatively, one could argue that both lists are parallel adaptations from a common archetypal source, such that both lists evolved independently without knowing each other.[93] However, this in turn creates new speculations about the existence of a source for which we have no evidence. Ultimately, the more plausible solution is that Ezek 28 is aware of the high priestly pectoral pictured in Exod 28 and 39. This is especially likely in light of the fact that there is a general agreement that the list of precious jewels in Ezek 28:13 represents a secondary element in the current dirge,[94] the insertion of which perhaps intends to invite a comparison between the pagan king and the Israelite high priest.[95]

This, however, is not to deny that there are indeed differences between the list of precious stones in Ezek 28:13 and that in Exod 28 and 39. Not only is the order of the stones in the two books different, some of the gems from the Exodus lists ("jacincth," "agate," and "amethyst") are missing from Ezek 28:13. As Bogaert and Patmore helpfully point out, it is the LXX, rather than the MT Ezekiel, that associates the Tyrian king more closely with the Israelite high priest envisaged in Exodus.[96] The LXX, contrary to the minuses and arrangement of the jewels in the MT Ezekiel, corresponds to the exact order of the precious stones from the high priest's pectoral in Exodus and lists all of them. Bogaert surmises that these tensions can be accounted for by the different literary profiles between the two versions.[97] According to his conjecture,

---

[93] E.g., H. R. Page Jr. suggests that Ezek 28:11–19 is derived from a myth of an astral rebellion without any links to Exodus (*The Myth of Cosmic Rebellion: A Study of Its Reflexes in Ugaritic and Biblical Literature*, VTSup 65 [Leiden: Brill, 1996], 148–58; cited in L.-S. Tiemeyer, "Zechariah's Spies and Ezekiel's Cherubim," in *Tradition in Transition: Haggai and Zechariah 1–8 in the Trajectory of Hebrew Theology*, ed. M. J. Boda and M. H. Floyd, LHBOTS 475 [New York: T&T Clark, 2008], 121, n. 62).

[94] Zimmerli, *Ezekiel*, 2:82, n. 13b; Eichrodt, *Ezekiel*, 389.

[95] Interestingly, even though the midrashic traditions do not identify the Tyrian king directly with the Israelite high priest, the traditions (e.g., Gen. Rab. 85:4) still associate the Tyrian figure close enough with Hiram I king of Tyre who helps to build the Solomonic temple in 1 Kgs 5–10 (cf. 2 Chr 2–9). See the discussions in Sulzbach, "Nebuchadnezzar," 132, esp. n. 22; Patmore, *Adam*, 26–35; idem, "Adam or Satan? The Identity of the King of Tyre in Late Antiquity," in *After Ezekiel: Essays on the Reception of a Difficult Prophet*, ed. A. Mein and P. M. Joyce, LHBOTS 535 (London: Bloomsbury, 2011), 64.

[96] Bogaert, "Montagne," 131–53; Patmore, "Adam," 62–63.

[97] According to Bogaert, "Montagne," 136, the LXX consistently presents the Tyrian figure as a human priest-king, the MT of Ezek 28:11–19 presents the figure as an angelic Cherub, who is to be identified with the patron god of Tyre, Melqart. See also idem, "Chérub," 33–34. On the other hand, Fechter suggests that the differences are

behind the oracle witnessed by the LXX stands an earlier version, which had been directed initially against the high priest of Jerusalem.[98] Later, this message of judgment was transformed into a dirge over the ruler of Tyre after the Judahites had found themselves in exile. This later form is now attested in the MT. The three missing stones and the different order of the stones in the MT version then represent this later attempt to obscure the allusion to the high priest.[99] In this manner, a priestly figure is transformed into a Tyrian figure. An earlier oracle of judgment against Israel has been "somewhat blurred in the final redaction" (quelque peu estempé dans la redaction finale) and turned into a message of consolation.[100]

Bogaert's account for the enumeration of the jewels in MT Ezek 28:13 thus helps clarify the differences between the MT Ezek 28 and the Exodus lists of jewels via the LXX version of Ezek 28, but his position is not without its problems. We concur that the editor if not the author of MT Ezek 28:11–19 could have imported the list of jewels as attested in the book of Exodus, but this does not automatically mean that the MT version is also dependent on the list of jewels found in the LXX. As argued persuasively by Richelle, various places in the MT version display a reading that is *difficilior* than the parallel sections in the LXX version, and it is thus likely that MT Ezek 28:11–19, rather than the LXX version, preserves a more original reading of the lament.[101] Furthermore, even if the editor if not the author of MT Ezek 28:11–19 could have sought to reduce the link to the high priest by removing some of the jewels and scrambling the order of the remaining ones in the verse, they strangely did not eliminate the priestly link completely. If, as Bogaert asserts, the target of divine retribution in the received MT Ezek 28:11–19 becomes solely concerned with the judgment of the Tyrian king, why should the allusions to the Israelite high priest be retained in the present MT version? The language and form of the list in MT Ezek 28:13 still bear strong resemblances to the high priestly pectoral mentioned in Exod 28 and 39. Patmore rightly

---

due to the fact that the editor or author of MT Ezek 28 quoted Exod 28 from memory rather than from direct citation (*Bewältigung*, 173–74).

[98] Bogaert, "Montagne," 141–47. So also T. Stordalen, *Echoes of Eden: Genesis 2–3 and Symbolism of the Eden Garden in Biblical Hebrew Literature*, CBET 25 (Leuven: Peeters, 2000), 334–48.

[99] Bogaert, "Montagne," 137; followed by J. Lust, "The Septuagint of Ezekiel according to Papyrus 967 and the Pentateuch," *ETL* 72 (1996): 131–37, here 133–34; idem, "Textual Criticism of the Old Testament and of the New Testament: Stepbrothers?" in *New Testament Criticism and Exegesis: Feschrift J. Delobel*, ed. A. Denaux, BETL 161 (Leuven: Leuven University Press, 2002), 15–31, here 23–24.

[100] Bogaert, "Montagne," 147.

[101] M. Richelle, "Le Portrait Changeant du Roi de Tyr (Ezéchiel 28.11–18) dans les Traditions Textuelles Anciennes," in *Phéniciens d'Orient et d'Occident. Mélanges Josette Elayi*, ed. A. Lemaire (Paris: Maisonneuve, 2014), 113–25, esp. 117–25.

argues: "If a scribe were prepared to remove three stones from the list and confuse the order, why would he not eliminate any possible confusion by changing the section entirely—or even removing it—so that no confusion with the high-priest's pectoral remained?"[102] Despite his questioning of Bogaert's position, Patmore strangely refuses to accept the parallels between the Tyrian royal in MT Ezek 28:11-19 and the priestly figure in Exod 28 and 39.[103] As I have argued, based on the unusual lexical parallels between MT Ezek 28:13 and Exod 28:17-20; 39:10-13, and given that the former text is more likely to be dependent on the latter texts, we must still insist that MT Ezek 28:11-19, even after the omissions and rearrangement, purposefully associates the Tyrian royal with the sacral imagery of the Israelite high priest. Therefore, Bogaert stands on shaky ground when he asserts that this rearrangement and transformation of Ezek 28:11-19 serves to console Israel with the destruction of the Tyrian king. To my mind, the imagery of the Israelite high priest still figures prominently in the received dirge, so that the message of destruction cannot be directed against the Tyrian king only, but must still evoke the memory of the Israelite high priest.

What Bogaert demonstrates and stresses correctly is that, in view of the differences between MT Ezek 28:13 and Exod 28:17-20; 39:10-13, as well as between MT Ezek 28:13 and LXX Ezek 28:13, the MT editor or author did not identify the Tyrian royal completely with the Israelite high priest, and must have a larger purpose in mind. The priestly and sacral elements contained especially in v. 13 cannot be the whole story of MT Ezek 28. We still have to take into account the other mythical elements, such as the imagery of cherub as well as the paradisiacal location, embodied by the Tyrian figure in 28:11-19. The extant differences between the MT and the LXX stimulate a need to explore the kind of rhetoric pursued by the Hebrew text of Ezek 28, which is different from the Greek version. What kind of rhetoric is envisaged in Ezek 28:11-19 when creating a Tyrian royal who resembles but is not completely identical with the Israelite high priest? This, in conjunction with the unsolved rhetoric of Ezek 27, forms our main task in the following section.

---

[102] Patmore, *Adam*, 156. Cf. Richelle, "Portrait," 118, who sees the list of jewels in the LXX as a result of later harmonization.

[103] Patmore suggests that the translator of LXX Ezek 28 has brrowed the list from LXX Exodus, while the MT Ezek 28 remains intact of any influence from the lists of high priestly jewels in the book of Exodus (*Adam*, 156, 195).

## 3. The Rhetorical Impact

Neither dirges in Ezek 27 and 28 is satisfied to present the perfect beauty of the Tyrian kingdom and Israelite sacral institutions in identical terms, but they integrate the allusions to the Israelite temple and priesthood in the rhetorical contexts that exalt the beauty of Tyre and its ruler over that of Jerusalem and its high priest. When even the grandiose Tyre and its king fail to escape the divine judgement and are destroyed *in toto*, the dirges in Ezek 27 and 28 become another form of judgment oracles implicating the inescapable doom of the Jerusalem temple and its priest.

### 3.1. The Foreboding Beauty

The portent of divine judgment has already been hinted at when both Tyre and its ruler are described at the outset as "perfect in beauty" (Ezek 27:3–4, 11; 28:12). As noted, this is an expression used most often to characterize Jerusalem (Ezek 16:14; Lam 2:15; Ps 50:2), and the Tyre oracles are likely to be aware of and allude to this imagery of Jerusalem. What we have not discussed is the contexts of judgment underlying these passages about the beauty of Jerusalem. These contexts, as will be argued, prove to be crucial in considering the rhetoric of the dirges over Tyre, since they provide a lens to view the tragic downfall of Tyre and its ruler in parallel to the catastrophe falling upon the sacral institutions and personnel in Jerusalem.

Commenting on the phrase "perfect beauty" in Ezek 27, Greenberg suggests a deliberate contrast between the beauty of Tyre and that of Jerusalem. However, his argument does not take into consideration the shared judgment contexts in the relevant passages both within and outside of Ezekiel. According to Greenberg, since all the other cases of the combination of כלל and יפה besides those from Ezek 27 and 28 are reserved for Jerusalem only, "perfect beauty" is a positive epithet, which properly belongs to Jerusalem.[104] Next, Greenberg claims that, since the utterance "You said" is the "preface of a blameworthy utterance" that is "frequent in Ezekiel's prophecies against the nations," Tyre's claim of perfect beauty in Ezek 27 must also be condemnatory.[105] Combining the above two considerations, and citing Rashi, Greenberg views Tyre's guilt in Ezek 27 as the appropriation of Jerusalem's epithet.[106] His argument, thus, contrasts the beauty between Tyre and Jerusalem, such that the latter, in comparison with the former, is accorded a more special, positive, and favorable status. Greenberg correctly observes the semantic links between the depicted beauty of Tyre and that of Jerusalem, but the contrast

---

[104] Greenberg, *Ezekiel 21–37*, 548.
[105] Ibid.
[106] Ibid.

between the two cities is not as great as he has suggested. Rather, in the passages about Jerusalem's perfect beauty, Zion is pictured either as the place of divine retribution or as the object that suffers the divine retribution (Ps 50:2; Lam 2:15; Ezek 16:14). As such, the contexts of divine judgment in these other passages, in which the combination of כלל and יפה appears, have already evinced a portent of the impending fall of Tyre's perfect beauty.

Despite stressing Zion as the perfect beauty, as the place where God shines forth (v. 2), the subsequent verses in Ps 50 emphasize rather the words of judgment issued by God in Zion to his gathered covenant people.[107] Ps 50 insists that even the people in the royal city—the perfect beauty—need to come under the divine judgment. Despite the fact that the judgment here carries a distinction, such that the "godly ones" will be preserved (v. 5, cf. v. 15), primary emphasis of the psalm is still placed on the retribution executed upon the wicked.[108] Psalm 50:4 is analogous to a trial scene, in which the heavens and earth are called forth to witness the judgment of God's people.[109] Having detailed the nature of God's justice (vv. 7–15), v. 16 directly challenges the wicked in accordance with God's covenant.[110] Psalm 50:17–20 then list out all the crimes committed by the wicked. The threat to those who forget God is subsequently spelled out in v. 22. In light of this literary context, the perfect beauty of Zion mentioned in Ps 50 must then be seen in the context of the justified judgment of God. The beauty of Zion is associated with the divine retribution against the wicked.

Even more radically, Lam 2 envisions the destruction of the whole of Jerusalem—the perfect beauty—without mentioning any distinction between the righteous and wicked. The wrath of YHWH consumes "all the habitations of Judah" (v. 2), slays "all that were pleasant to the eye" (v. 4), swallows up "all its palaces" (v. 5), destroys "his appointed meeting place" (v. 6), and rejects "his altar" (v. 7). Consequently, the former glory of Jerusalem becomes a laughing stock in the mouths of the passers-by (v. 15). The poem clearly alludes to Jerusalem's guilt (v. 14), and the dramatic downfall of Zion brings tension and doubt to YHWH's relation with the city. YHWH is presented consistently as the ultimate aggressor for this shattering beauty of Zion, such that the poet bewails: "YHWH has done what he purposed; he has accomplished his word which he commanded from days of old. He has thrown down without sparing, and he has caused the enemy to rejoice over you; he has exalted the

---

[107] For the tripartite structure of Ps 50 (vv. 1–6, 7–15, 16–23), see M. Oeming and J. Vette, *Psalm 42–89*, Neuer Stuttgarter Kommentar 13.2 (Stuttgart: Katholisches Bibelwerk, 2010), 63, Cf. H.-J. Kraus, *Psalms 1–59*, trans. H. C. Oswald, CC 1 (Augsburg: Augsburg Fortress, 1993), 488.

[108] Hossfeld and Zenger, *Psalm 1–50*, 308.

[109] Kraus, *Psalms 1–59*, 492. Cf. Deut 31:28; 32:1; Isa 1:2.

[110] Cf. Mic 6:3 and Jer 2:5.

might of your adversaries" (Lam 2:17).[111] The whole lament clearly presents the vulnerability of Zion's perfect beauty under divine judgment.

The reference to the perfect beauty of Jerusalem is also located in one of the grimmest passages within the book of Ezekiel.[112] Chapter 16 clarifies that the perfect beauty is not inherent in Jerusalem from the very beginning; 16:5 explicitly states that "You yourself were loathed on that day of your birth."[113] The beauty is a later endowment from YHWH, who claims to be its sole source (vv. 10–14). Nevertheless, Jerusalem becomes the unfaithful and adulterous wife of YHWH,[114] such that the endowment of the beauty upon Jerusalem is followed by an elaborate description of the reversal of the beauty (vv. 15–34), ending in the state in which Jerusalem began—in naked and bloodied abandonment. YHWH further chastises Jerusalem, by handing her over to her lovers to be exposed (v. 37), by putting blood upon her (v. 38), and by allowing her lovers to strip her of clothing and jewels (v. 39). In short, each step of Jerusalem's rise to perfect beauty is matched by a step in her decline.[115]

To summarize, Ps 50, Lam 2, and Ezek 16 anchor the motif of perfect beauty in various contexts of divine judgment. Ps 50 presents the perfect beauty as the place of divine judgment, while Lam 2 and Ezek 16 go to an extreme to assert the very destruction of that perfect beauty. Consequently, I cannot concur with Greenberg that the perfect beauty of Jerusalem is so positive that the dirges in Ezek 27 and 28 draw on this motif in order to contrast

---

[111] F. W. Dobbs-Allsopp, *Lamentations* (Louisville: John Knox Press, 2002), 78–90; R. B. Salters, *A Critical and Exegetical Commentary on Lamentations*, ICC (London: T&T Clark, 2010), 107; P. R. House, *Lamentations*, WBC 23B (Nashville: Nelson, 2004), 372.

[112] Eliezer b. Hyrcanus banned the public reading of Ezek 16 because it casts doubt on Israel's noble lineage (noted by Odell, *Ezekiel*, 184). Today, feminist scholars such as L. Day, "Rhetoric and Domestic Violence in Ezek 16," *BibInt* 8 (2000): 205–30; P. Day, "The Bitch Had It Coming to Her: Rhetoric and Interpretation in Ezekiel 16," *BibInt* 8 (2000): 231–54, look at Ezek 16 and focus on issues of gender, domestic violence, and pornography.

[113] Note the *inclusio* formed by the phrase "on the day of your birth" (ביום הולדת) in 16:4–5. Cf. Durlesser, *Narratives*, 110.

[114] For the biblical portrayal of Israel as the adulterous wife of YHWH, see Isa 1:21; Hos 4:12–15; 9:1; Jer 2:20–25. In the pentateuchal passages (e.g., Exod 24:14; Num 25:1–2; Judg 2:17; 8:27, 33), the Hebrew verb זנה "to whore" is used to describe the religious faithlessness of Israel. Cf. Galambush, *Jerusalem*, 20–23; Odell, *Ezekiel*, 182; Durlesser, *Narratives*, 104–7. For the comparison of the personified Jerusalem with the Mesopotamian and West Semitic cities, see M. E. Biddle, "The Figure of Lady Jerusalem: Identification, Deification and Personification of Cities in the Ancient Near East," in *The Biblical Canon in Comparative Perspective*, ed. K. L. Younger and W. W. Hallo, Scripture in Context 4 (Lewiston: Mellen, 1991), 172–87.

[115] So also Galambush, *Jerusalem*, 96–99.

it with Tyre's perfect beauty. Instead, the punitive overtone associated with the perfect beauty seems to implicate a common dire fate awaiting both Jerusalem and Tyre.

3.2. THE EXALTED GLORY

The parallels drawn between the perfect beauty of Tyre and that of Jerusalem take a surprising turn in the dirges of Ezek 27 and 28. The allusions to Jerusalem's sacral institution and personnel are placed in the literary contexts not only envisaging the beauty of both cities in identical terms, but also extolling the beauty of Tyre and its ruler in a more elaborate way that implicitly places the glory of the Jerusalem temple and its high priest in a subordinate position.

3.2.1. THE ALL-ENCOMPASSING TRADE LIST

That Tyre's splendour is even more superior than Jerusalem's is confirmed by the insertion of a trade list in the second section of the dirge in chapter 27 (vv. 12–25). Enclosed by the *Leitwort* תרשיש in vv. 12, 25, the list provides a record of Tyre's extensive trade network with other nations.[116] Each entry lists the name of the country dealers and the merchandise they bring in order to exchange for Tyre's products. Due to the distinctive cataloguing style that stands in contrast to the poetic ship metaphor in the surrounding passages, many commentators rightly recognize the trade list as a secondary intrusion into the present dirge.[117] What rhetorical function does such an editorial insertion into the original lament serve?

In my opinion, the trade list, having come after the rich allusions to the Israelite sanctuary in 27:3–11, serves to exalt the beauty of Tyre to an even higher level, and thus implicitly relativizes the temple beauty of Jerusalem. So great is the fame of Tyre's beauty that nations unheard or unseen of elsewhere in the Hebrew Bible, such as חלבון "Helbon" (v. 18),[118] צחר "Sahar" (v.

---

[116] Durlesser, *Narratives*, 154–55; Saur, *Tyroszyklus*, 68–69. The phrase "ships of Tarshish" (אניות תרשיש) appears in 1 Kgs 10:22; 22:49; Isa 2:16; 23:1, 14; 60:9; Ezek 27:25; Ps 48:8. This might indicate Tarshish as a land far away from the ancient Israelites, which can be reached only by the sea. Saur, *Tyroszyklus*, 198, associates Tarshish with the Greek Ταρτησσός or the Akkadian *adi māt Tarsisi*.

[117] Zimmerli, *Ezekiel*, 2:62–68; Eichrodt, *Ezekiel*, 382–84; Fuhs, *Ezechiel*, 148–50; Pohlmann, *Kapitel 20–48*, 388–89; Strong, "Ezekiel's Oracles," 196; Wevers, *Ezekiel*, 205.

[118] Besides the one occurrence in the book of Ezekiel, Helbon is mentioned in the inscriptions of Nebuchadnezzar. 1QapGen ar XXII, 10 mentions Helbon as lying in the north of Damascus. Cf. Saur, *Tyroszyklus*, 205.

18),[119] כלמד "Chilmad" (v. 23),[120] and כנה "Canneh" (v. 23),[121] bring their merchandise to exchange at Tyre's ports. So thorough is the influence of Tyre's beauty that it attracts nations from all directions. Many of these nations are mentioned in the Table of Nations in Gen 10.[122] In vv. 12–15 of the trade list, Tarshish, Javan, Tubal, Meschech, Beth-togarmah,[123] and the sons of Rhodes,[124] who are all Japhethites according to the Table of Nations, lie in the west and north of Tyre and form the outermost zone of the inhabited world known to ancient Israelite authors. Following this, vv. 16–18 reveal the innermost region toward the east of Tyre, including Aram (or Edom),[125] Damascus, Judah, and the land of Israel. Then vv. 19–22 list Uzal,[126] Dedan,[127] Arabia, Kedar, Raama, and Sheba, which lie in the southeast of Tyre. Finally, v. 23 mentions Mesopotamian Haran, Eden, and Assur in the north-east.[128] The extremes of west and east thus bind the list, and express Tyre's worldwide connections.

Most strikingly, Judah and the land of Israel are also included in the trade list of Tyre, as among the many traders who decorate the beauty of Tyre (v.

---

[119] The place cannot be localized with certainty. See ibid., 206.

[120] Several commentators consider this word corrupt. For the reading of כלמד as כל מדי "the whole of Media," as in the Targum, see Zimmerli, *Ezekiel*, 2:50; Saur, *Tyroszyklus*, 212.

[121] The place cannot be localized with certainty. See Saur, *Tyroszyklus*, 210.

[122] For the possible influence of the Table of Nations on Ezek 27, see P. C. Haldor, "The Tyrian Oracles in Ezekiel: A Study of Ezekiel 26:1–28:19" (PhD diss., Columbia University, 1970), 255; Odell, *Ezekiel*, 353; Greenberg, *Ezekiel 21–37*, 567.

[123] Tarshish also appears in Gen 10:4, Javan in Gen 10:2, 4, Tubal and Meschech in 10:2 (cf. v. 4), Beth-togarmah in 10:3. For further explications of these place names, see Saur, *Tyroszyklus*, 199.

[124] The MT of Ezek 27:15 reads דדן. The LXX reads Ῥοδίων. There is also a ר and ד confusion in Gen 10:4, 1 Chr 1:7. Given that Dedan is mentioned again in 27:20, it is more likely that the reading in Ezek 27:15 means רדן "Rhodes." Cf. Tov, *Textual Criticism*, 12–13; Saur, *Tyroszyklus*, 23, 202. For other identifications of this place name, see Block, *Ezekiel*, 2:74.

[125] Here, there is probably a ר and ד confusion, as in 27:15. Given that Damascus already represents Aram in 27:18, the noun in 27:16 probably refers to Edom (אדם). Cf. Saur, *Tyroszyklus*, 23, 202. For the view against this emendation, see Block, *Ezekiel*, 2:74.

[126] Cf. Gen 10:27. For the emendation of Ezek 27:19, from ויין מאוזל ודן to וודן ויין מאוזל, see A. Millard, "Ezekiel XXVII.19: The Wine Trade of Damascus," *JSS* 7 (1962): 201–3.

[127] Dedan appers in Gen 10:7 (// 1 Chr 1:9); Gen 25:3 (// 1 Chr 1:32); Isa 21:14, 16–17; Jer 25:23; Ezek 27:20; 38:13. Saur locates it in the south-west of Arabia (*Tyroszyklus*, 206).

[128] Cf. Block, *Ezekiel*, 2:81; Greenberg, *Ezekiel 21–37*, 567.

17).¹²⁹ This creates an impression that the material beauty of Tyre far exceeds that of the Jerusalem temple. The word נתן, which has been recurring in 16:15–34 to denote Jerusalem's throwing away of her beauty endowed by YHWH, also appears repeatedly in the commercial list in 27:12–24. This is a significant lexical link, since the root נתן used in both chapters appears in the unusual sense of payment. Both chapters use the root in a commercial sense—"to sell, exchange."¹³⁰ The direction of trading, however, is different for each city. In Ezek 16:31–34, Jerusalem voluntarily makes payment to other nations, even though she, as a harlot, should be the one who receives payment.¹³¹ In Ezek 27:12–24, Tyre, on the other hand, is the collector of the payments from all nations.¹³² In the trade list, Judah and the land of Israel (v. 17) are only two among many other groups of nations who pay homage to Tyre's commercial beauty. Reading chapters 16 and 27 together only sheds a more despicable light on Jerusalem, which voluntarily succumbs to please other nations rather than YHWH. The appearance of Judah and the land of Israel in the trade list does not enhance their own standing among the nations, but only aids to exalt and affirm the attractiveness of Tyre in Ezek 27.

All in all, the shared linguistic elements that evoke the Jerusalem temple imagery (27:3–11) are woven together with the impressive trade-list of Tyre (27:12–24). This trade-list not only affirms the alluring beauty of Tyre in the eyes of all nations from different directions, but also subsumes Judah and Israel under the dominating beauty of Tyre. By exalting the pagan beauty far beyond that of Jerusalem, Ezek 27 relativizes the perfect beauty of Jerusalem.

### 3.2.2. THE DIVINE CHERUB

While the trade list in Ezek 27:12–25a aggrandizes the beauty of Tyre over the glory of Jerusalem, the dirge in 28:11–19 exalts the beauty of the Tyrian royal over the splendour of the Israelite high priest. Endowed with wisdom

---

¹²⁹ For the juxtaposition of Judah and the land of Israel in this context, see Saur, *Tyroszyklus*, 203.

¹³⁰ Cf. Prov 31:24 where נתן parallels עשה "to make" and מכר "to sell." Joel 4:3 [Eng. 3:3] also displays a parallelism of נתן and מכר: ויתנו הילד בזונה והילדה מכרו ביין "They exchanged a boy for a harlot and sold a girl for wine." See Cooke, *Ezekiel*, 309; H. J. van Dijk, *Ezekiel's Prophecy on Tyre* (Rome: Pontifical Biblical Institute, 1968), 76.

¹³¹ In Ezek 16:31, 34, 41, נתן comes with אתנן, which are wages for sacral prostitution. Cf. Hos 2:14 [Eng. 2:12]; Deut 23:19 [Eng. 23:18]. The expression for sacral prostitution is applied metaphorically to Israel (Hos 9:1), Samaria (Mic 1:7), and Tyre (Isa 23:17–18). Cf. E. Lipinski, "נתן," *TDOT* 10:97.

¹³² In Ezek 27:12, 13, 14, 16, 17, 19, 22, the verb is combined with the preposition ב, meaning to "exchange for." Similar usage can be found in Lam 1:11; Joel 4:3 [Eng. 3:3]; 1 Kgs 5:24–25; 10:10, 13. Cf. Ibid., 10:98.

and perfect beauty, the Tyrian king wears a covering that strongly resembles the Israelite high priestly pectoral (vv. 12–13). Yet the text does not identify them completely. The next verse (v. 14; cf. v. 16) correlates the royal figure with an animate "cherub" (כרוב), placed on the "holy mountain of *Elohim*" (הר קדש אלהים). Thus, the Tyrian figure becomes comparable not only to a human priest, but also to a divine or semi-divine figure that potentially rivals YHWH himself.

The comparison of the Tyrian king with the cherub in the MT is rife with complexities. The vocalized MT reads v. 14 as follows:

| | |
|---|---|
| את כרוב ממשח הסוכך | You were the covering anointed cherub, |
| ונתתיך | and I brought you forth, |
| בהר קדש אלהים היית | on the holy mountain of *Elohim* you were, |
| בתוך אבני אש התהלכת | in the midst of fire stones you walked about. |

The LXX, contrary to the MT, does not envisage the king as a cherub, but distinguishes the king from the cherub, reading "I placed you beside the cherub on a holy mountain of *Elohim*" (μετὰ τοῦ χερουβ ἔθηκά σε ἐν ὄρει ἁγίῳ θεοῦ, 28:14; cf. v. 16).[133] Perusing the Hebrew text without the Masoretic vocalizations, Patmore has recently come up with a reading of v. 14 similar to the LXX, which does not perceive the Tyrian king as an anointed covering cherub.[134] Interestingly enough, he suggests that "Ezek xxviii 12–19 has been misread (deliberately or otherwise) by the scribe(s) who added the vocalization and accentuation."[135] According to Patmore, the Hebrew text, stripped of its vowels and cantillation marks, identifies the Tyrian king not as a cherub, but as a god (אלהים היית). For him, the text should be read as follows:

| | |
|---|---|
| כוננו את כרוב ממשח הסוכך | They established the covering anointed cherub. |
| ונתתיך בהר קדש | And I set you on the holy mountain. |
| אלהים היית | You were a god/divine being. |
| בתוך אבני אש התהלכת | In the midst of fire stones you walked about.[136] |

---

[133] The LXX seems to read את in v. 14 as a preposition "with" followed by the noun "cherub." There is also no mention of the "covering" of the cherub. Moreover, in v. 16, while the MT reads: "And I have destroyed you, O covering cherub, from the midst of the stones of fire" (ואבדך כרוב הסכך מתוך אבני אש), the LXX again interprets the cherub as a separate entity from the Tyrian king and reads: "And the cherub brought you out from the midst of the fiery stones" (καὶ ἤγαγέν σε τὸ χερουβ ἐκ μέσου λίθων πυρίνων). Cf. Bogaert, "Montagne," 134; Barr, "Cherub," 214–18.

[134] Patmore, *Adam*, 197–201; idem, "Masoretes," 245–57.

[135] Patmore, "Masoretes," 245.

[136] English translation modified from Patmore, *Adam*, 197; idem, "Masoretes," 254–55; idem, "Adam," 61. The first word cited above comes from the last word in

# CHAPTER THREE

Contrary to Patmore's syntactical rearrangement of Ezek 28:14, I still find merits in the current organization of the MT, which identifies the Tyrian figure as a cherub, and which allows the phrase ונתתיך to stand on its own, and which does not join the noun אלהים with the verb היית but places the noun in a construct relationship with the "holy mountain" (הר קדש). This preference for the MT is based on the following three considerations.

First of all, Patmore's re-vocalization of כוננו at the end of v. 13 as the active *polel* is not necessary.[137] The term can be understood well according to its current vocalization as a passive *polal*—"they were established" (כּוֹנָנוּ).[138] The grammatical subjects of this verb are likely to be "all the precious stones" (כל אבן יקרה) and "the gold of the workmanship of your tambourines and your pipes" (זהב מלאכת תפיך ונקביך) mentioned in the same verse.[139] The nine precious stones form the covering of the Tyrian king. The word תף appears about sixteen times in the Hebrew Bible. Except for the case in Ezekiel, both the singular and the plural forms of it always unambiguously denote "tambourine" or "tambourines."[140] The root נקב means "to bore," and so can designate a drilled thing that acts like a pipe.[141] Taken together, 28:13 can well convey that precious stones and musical instruments *were prepared* (כּוֹנָנוּ), in order to celebrate the day when the Tyrian figure was created (ביום הבראך). Patmore objects that the verb כון is not "for the trivial or frivolous," and it should not be used "to describe dressing up or musical instruments."[142] However, he does not explain why YHWH's adornment of a beautiful and wise royal with pre-

---

28:13. For other possibilities of reading the Hebrew consonantal text, see Yaron, "Dirge," 29.

[137] *Contra* Patmore, Adam, 198; idem, "Masoretes," 251.

[138] Admittedly the passive sense is rare in the Hebrew Bible. Elsewhere in the Hebrew Bible, it appears only in Ps 37:23 (*HALOT* 1:465). Nevertheless, the by-agent in Ps 37:23 refers to YHWH himself, which displays a contextual similarity with Ezek 28:14.

[139] According to the Masoretic vocalization, זהב concludes the list of precious stones. Given that gold is not a jewel, and that וזהב disrupts the three preceding groups of triplets, we will deviate slightly from the Masoretic reading and follow the LXX in connecting the term to the subsequent phrase (מלאכת תפיך ונקביך). Cf. Bunta, "Statue," 238; Patmore, "Masoretes," 248–49.

[140] Singular in Gen 31:27; Exod 15:20; 1 Sam 10:5; Job 21:12; Ps 81:3; 149:3; 150:4; Isa 5:12. Plural in Judg 11:34; 1 Sam 18:6; 2 Sam 6:5 (// 1 Chr 13:8); Isa 24:8; 30:32; Jer 31:4; Ezek 28:13. Cf. Callender, *Adam*, 106–7. For a list of other scholarly translations of this term, see D. Arbel, "Questions about Eve's Iniquity, Beauty, and Fall: The 'Primal Figure' in Ezekiel 28:11–19 and 'Genesis Rabbah' Traditions of Eve," *JBL* 124 (2005): 641–55, here 646–47.

[141] Cf. Callender, *Adam*, 106–7, followed by Arbel, "Questions," 647.

[142] Patmore, "Masoretes," 249. Cf. idem, *Adam*, 197.

cious stones, celebrated with grand music played by intricately made instruments on the day of the creation of the royal, should be seen as "trivial or frivolous." As Callender aptly points out, Job 15:7–8; 38:4–7 and Prov 8:31 imply that the creation of the primal man is an event that induces festivity and happiness on a grand cosmic scale.[143] The *polel* of כון, as Patmore also admits, generally has God as grammatical subject.[144] Following this, the *polal* of כון can well be a *passivum divinum*, indicating YHWH's special preparation of gifts showered upon the kingly creature. As such, there is no sufficient ground to dissociate כוננו from its current literary context in v. 13. The following את in v. 14 can then be logically read not as a direct definite object marker (אֵת), but as a second person singular pronoun (אַתּ) that begins a new sentence, identifying the king as the mythical creature: "you are the cherub" (את כרוב).[145]

Second, different from Patmore's syntactical understanding of ונתתיך, the Hebrew Bible does attest to a handful of instances where the verb can take a direct object alone, without the need to take an indirect object.[146] This is especially so when נתן denotes "to create," "to cause," or "to bring forth."[147] Prov 10:10 reads "he who winks the eye causes trouble" (קרץ עין יתן עצבת). Prov 13:10 asserts "by insolence comes nothing but strife" (רק בזדון יתן מצה). In both cases, the verbs derived from the root נתן, connote the sense of causation, and are paired with the direct objects—"trouble" and "strife" respectively—without taking any prepositional phrase or indirect object. Also, Num 14:4 describes that the rebellious Israelites in the wilderness desire to appoint (נתנה) a leader (ראש) for themselves. Again, the *qal* imperfect cohortative of נתן, in the sense of "to appoint, to set, to establish," is followed by the direct

---

[143] Callender, *Adam*, 107–9.

[144] Patmore cites 2 Sam 7:13; 1 Chr 17:12; Ps 9:8; Exod 15:7; Deut 32:6; Prov 3:19 ("Masoretes," 249).

[145] The Masoretic vocalization as אַתּ is peculiar, given that the subject is a male, rather than a female. Num 11:15; Deut 5:27 do use the feminine pronoun to denote a male subject. Cf. 1 Sam 24:19; Ps 6:4; Job 1:10; Eccl 7:22; Neh 9:6, where the *qere* אַתָּה corresponds to the *kethib* את. For this argument, see Patmore, *Adam*, 198, n. 53; Bunta, "Statue," 238; Greenberg, *Ezekiel 21–37*, 582; Barr, "Cherub," 215–16; Richelle, "Portrait," 121. Alternatively, Arbel, "Questions," 649–51, offers the following interpretation: This feminine form implies that the primal figure might have possessed female features, which in turn allow later traditions such as Gen. Rab. 18:1 to associate the primal figure with Eve.

[146] *Contra* Patmore, Adam, 200; idem, "Masoretes," 252, both of which state that "the verb "to set, give" (נתן) almost without exception takes a preposition to indicate the indirect object (e.g., על, אל, ל-, ב-)."

[147] E.g., נתן קול = to give forth sound: Exod 9:23; Num 14:1; 1 Sam 12:17–18; 2 Sam 22:14; Ps 18:14 [Eng. 18.13]; Jer 2:15; 4:16; 22:20; 25:30; 48:34; Lam 2:7; Joel 2:11; Amos 1:2; 3:4; Hab 3:10. נתן ריח = to emanate fragrance: Song 1:12; 2:13; 7:14 [Eng. 7:13]; Ezek 6:13. Cf. *HALOT* 1:733; E. Lipinski, *TDOT* 10:92.

object "a leader," without taking any prepositional phrase. In Ezek 36:8, Joel 2:22, Zech 8:12, and Ps 1:3, variant forms of נתן are used to describe the productive power of the land or the vine to give forth branches, fruits, or power.[148] In all these cases, different verbal forms of נתן possess the direct objects without being used in conjunction with any preposition. Perhaps the closest parallel to Ezek 28:14 is the phrase in 27:10, where the valiant men in the Tyrian ship are said to give and produce its splendour (המה נתנו הדרך). In light of all the above biblical examples, ונתתיך in Ezek 28:14 can stand quite independently on its own. Given the reference to "the day of your creation" (יום הבראך) in the previous verse, the expression ונתתיך can legitimately denote that YHWH has brought forth or caused to come into existence the Tyrian king, who is represented by the second masculine singular accusative pronominal suffix ך. In short, there is no need to attach an indirect object or a preposition after ונתתך in 28:14. Given the reference to creation in v. 13 (ביום הבראך), I propose to translate ונתתך in 28:14 as "and I created you" or "and I brought you forth."[149]

Third, in contrast to Patmore, I still find that the current vocalization of the MT, which places אלהים in a construct relationship to the "holy mountain" (הר קדש) in v. 14, fits the overall context of 28:11–19 better.[150] This is because the construct reading בהר קדש אלהים היית acts in parallel with בעדן גן אלהים היית in v. 13.[151] Morever, this construct reading as the "holy mountain of *Elohim*" in v. 14 corresponds to the construct reading in v. 16: מהר אלהים "from the mountain of *Elohim*." Patmore is correct that the combination of קדש, אלהים, and הר appears only rarely in the Hebrew Bible, but he dismisses the construct reading הר קדש אלהי in Dan 9:20 too easily.[152] Despite the fact that the date of

---

[148] Cf. Gen 4:12; Lev 26:20; Deut 11:17. With God as the grammatical subject, see Isa 43:20; Exod 9:23; Ps 105:32. Cf. *HALOT* 1:733; Lipinski, *TDOT* 10:92.

[149] This is in contrast to the common translation "and I *set/placed* you...," exemplified for instances in Bogaert, "Montagne," 134; Yaron, "Dirge," 29; Eichrodt, *Ezekiel*, 389; Zimmerli, *Ezekiel*, 1:85.

[150] Patmore rejects the Masoretic accentuation and insists that אלהים should be separated from בהר קדש, since "elsewhere in the Hebrew Bible the mountain is either "of Holiness" or "of God or Yahweh," never both." Patmore cites the appearances of "Mountain of Holiness" in Ps 2:6; 3:5; 15:1; 43:3; 48:2; 99:9; Isa 11:9; 26:13; 56:7; 57:13; 65:11, 25; 66:20; Jer 31:23; Dan 9:16; 11:45; Joel 2:1; 3:21; Obad 1:16; Zeph 3:11; Zech 8:3 "Mountain of God" in Exod 4:27; 18:5; 24:13; 1 Kgs 19:8; "Mountain of YHWH" in Ps 24:3; Isa 2:3; 30:29; Mic 4:2. However, he does observe the appearance of "the Holy Mountain of my God" (הר קדש אלהי) in Dan 9:20 (*Adam*, 201; "Masoretes," 252–53).

[151] So also A. Wood, *Of Wings and Wheels: A Synthetic Study of the Biblical Cherubim*, BZAW 385 (Berlin: de Gruyter, 2008), 67; Tiemeyer, "Zechariah's Spies," 108; Yaron, "Dirge," 31; Richelle, "Portrait," 122.

[152] Patmore, "Masoretes," 252; idem, *Adam*, 201.

composition of most of the book of Ezekiel might have been earlier than the book of Daniel, this does not definitively exclude the possibility that some of the lexical features in the former could have constituted the prototypes of the syntax found in the latter.[153] Taking all the foregoing into consideration, I thus insist on using the vocalizations of MT Ezek 28:14 as a basis for further interpretation, rendering its translation as follows: "You were the anointed cherub who covered, and I brought you forth, on the holy mountain of *Elohim* you were, in the midst of fiery stones you walked about."

The main problem of Patmore's argument is his insistence that the Masoretic presentation of the Tyrian king as a cherub counters the affirmation of the Tyrian king as a god.[154] It is my contention that the Masoretic identification of the Tyrian king with the cherub does not shy away from the possible divinity of the Tyrian king. Even if the MT does not directly present the Tyrian king as אלהים, the text still preserves the space of imagination for a human figure to transcend his humanity and attain a divine identity. This is all because the MT, as examined, understands the Tyrian king precisely *as* a cherub, and not *with* a cherub.

The majority of the biblical passages conceive the cherubim as the inanimate images decorating the fabrics of the tabernacle (Exod 26:1, 31; 36:8, 35), and adorning the interior of Solomon's temple (1 Kgs 6:23–29, 32, 35; 7:29, 36).[155] There are no detailed descriptions of the cherubim's appearance in these passages.[156] What can be ascertained from the descriptions of the Ark of the Covenant is that the cherubim are considered to be winged creatures (Exod 25:18–22; 37:7–9; Num 7:89; 1 Kgs 8:6–7; cf. 1 Kgs 6:23–29).[157] Apparently,

---

[153] Interestingly enough, the references to Daniel also appear in 28:3 (cf. 14:14, 20).

[154] Patmore, "Masoretes," 256.

[155] Cf. Ezek 41:18, 20, 25. Fifty-six out of the ninety-three occurrences of the lexeme כרוב in the Hebrew Bible appear in this kind of context. For the fuller statistics of this lexeme, see Wood, *Wings*, 8. For further explications, see also W. F. Albright, "What Were the Cherubim?" *BA* 1 (1938): 1–3; Tiemeyer, "Zechariah's Spies," 110; O. Keel, *Jahwe-Visionen und Siegelkunst: Eine neue Deutung der Majestätsschilderungen in Jes 6, Ez 1 und 10 und Sach 4*, SBS 84/85 (Stuttgart: Katholisches Bibelwerk, 1977), 15–45.

[156] See, however, the more comprehensive survey of the appearances of the cherubim in M. Metzger, *Königsthron und Gottesthron. Thronformen und Throndarstellungen in Ägypten und im Vorderen Orient im dritten und zweiten Jahrtausend vor Christus und deren Bedeutung für das Verständnis von Aussagen über den Thron im Alten Testament*, 2 vols., AOAT 15 (Kevalaer: Butzon und Berker, 1985), 1:311–12.

[157] For an explanation of the historical association of the cherubim with the Ark of the Covenant in the Jerusalem temple, see B. Janowski, "Keruben und Zion: Thesen zur Entstehung der Zionstradition," in *Ernten, was man sät: Feschrift für Klaus Koch*

the cherubim represent the divine presence, since the God of Israel is often designated as "he who dwells among the cherubim" (יושב הכרובים).[158] Even though the biblical texts in which this epithet appears might be dated later than the exile,[159] Albright and others have connected this divine epithet with the artistic representations of a king seated on a throne accompanied by the winged creatures, which were uncovered at Byblos, Hamath, and Megiddo, all dating between 1200 and 800 BCE.[160] More recently, Eichler argues from a grammatical point of view and suggests that this epithet ultimately seeks to identify "YHWH as a deity who dwells in a community of heavenly beings," which conveys a similar conception expressed in the scenes of theophany in 1 Kgs 22:19 and Isa 6:1–2.[161] Whether the cherubim are positioned as the sculpted images in the tabernacle and temple, or they are mentioned in the divine epithet, they are clearly conceived as supernatural beings standing in close proximity to the divine.[162]

What interests us most is several biblical presentations of the cherubim as animate heavenly beings who function as guardians or transporters.[163] Hence, the cherubim come alive in Gen 3:24, the setting of which, as in Ezek 28:13, points to Eden. There, the cherubim possess an apotropaic function. They are positioned in parallel with "the flame of the sword" (להט החרב), in order to guard (לשמר) the entrance to the Garden of Eden.[164] In yet another passage—

---

*zu seinem 65. Geburtstag*, ed. D. R. Daniels et al. (Neukirchen: Neukirchener Verlag, 1991), 231–64.

[158] There are only seven instances of this usage (1 Sam 4:4; 2 Sam 6:2; 2 Kgs 19:15; 1 Chr 13:6; Ps 80:1; 99:1; Isa 37:16). On this divine epithet, see Wood, *Wings*, 9–22; Albright, "Cherubim," 2; R. Eichler, "The Meaning of ישב הכרובים," *ZAW* 126 (2014): 358–71.

[159] F. Hartenstein, "Cherubim and Seraphim in the Bible and in the Light of Ancient Near Eastern Sources," in *Angels: The Concept of Celestial Beings—Origins, Development and Reception*, ed. F. V. Reiterer et al. (Berlin: de Gruyter, 2007), 155–88, here 160.

[160] Albright, "Cherubim," 1–2. For a fuller list of pictures of the sphinx-thrones, see *ANEP*, figs. 332, 456-59; Keel, *Jahwe-Visionen*, 32, figs. 15–17. Note that these scholars translate the epithet as "he who is seated upon the cherubim" and identify the cherubim as the winged sphinx. For a critical review of this position, see Eichler, "Meaning," 366; idem, "Cherub," 37.

[161] Eichler, "Meaning," 369–70.

[162] Cf. Barr, "Cherub," 220, who considers the cherub as "a semi-divine being or a divinely placed agent."

[163] Twenty eight out of the ninety three occurrences of the lexeme כרוב in the Hebrew Bible appear in this sense. Cf. Gen 3:24; 2 Sam 22:11 // Ps 18:11; Ezek 9:3; 10:1–9, 14–16, 18–20; 11:22; 28:14, 16. See Wood, *Wings*, 8.

[164] See D. Launderville, "Ezekiel's Cherub: A Promising Symbol or a Dangerous Idol?" *CBQ* 65 (2003): 165–83, here 167; Metzger, *Königsthron*, 1:309; Wood, *Wings*,

Ps 18:11 (= 2 Sam 22:11), the singular cherub appears as part of the storm theophany.[165] There, it possesses a locomotive function to transport the deity: "And He rode upon a cherub and flew."[166] The locomotive function of the cherubim comes forth most prominently in the book of Ezekiel. In chapters 8–11, the famous temple vision of Ezekiel envisages the cherubim as YHWH's throne carriers.[167] The wings of the cherubim are so powerful that the fluttering of these wings generates noise that is "like the voice of God Almighty when he speaks" (10:5). Being identified as the "living beings" (חיה) mentioned earlier in chapter 1, the cherubim, together with the wheels, rise up and form the vehicle that transports the divine glory (כבוד) to the prophet in Babylon (10:15, cf. vv. 20, 22).[168] Possessing the faces of a human, a lion, an ox, and an eagle, the cherubim embody superior intelligence and great ferocity (10:21; cf. 1:10).[169] Given that the Hebrew Bible contains numerous descriptions of the heavenly council, which consists of the sons of God,[170] his servants,[171] spirits,[172] and messengers,[173] the cherubim, as Tiemeyer rightly concludes, are most probably regarded as members of the divine council.[174]

---

51–61. For the Targumic renditions, which place the cherubim and the flame of the sword in a subordinate role assisting YHWH to guard the way to the tree of life, see R. Eichler, "When God Abandoned the Garden of Eden: A Forgotten Reading of Genesis 3:24," *VT* 65 (2015): 1–13.

[165] The riding of YHWH on a single cherub is comparable to Ezek 9:3; 10:4. This idea corresponds to the prevalent pictorial representations of Ancient Near Eastern gods standing or enthroned on their own beasts. See the pictures and explications in Keel, *Jahwe-Visionen*, 153–58; Hartenstein, "Cherubim," 160.

[166] See Wood, *Wings*, 84–95; Launderville, "Ezekiel's Cherub," 167; Metzger, *Königsthron*, 1:310.

[167] See Wood, *Wings*, 95–138; Hartenstein, "Cherubim," 173–78.

[168] The singular חיה in both cases is used as a collective. For the idea that Ezek 10:9–17 interprets the inaugural vision in Ezek 1:15–21, see D. J. Halperin, "The Exegetical Character of Ezek. X 9–17," *VT* 26 (1976): 129–41. For a comprehensive list of works that discuss the exegetical relationship between chapters 1 and 10, see Tiemeyer, "Zechariah's Spies," 111, n. 25. See also the explication in Zimmerli, *Ezekiel*, 1:232–33, 250.

[169] Contrary to the common assumption, Ezek 10:14 does not describe the four faces of the cherubim, but rather the four faces of the wheels. See Halperin, "Character," 138–39, who argues against Cooke, *Ezekiel*, 117; Zimmerli, *Ezekiel*, 1:25, 239–40.

[170] בני עליון in Ps 82:6; בני אלים in Ps 29:1; 89:7; בני האלהים in Job 1:6; 2:1; 38:7 (cf. Deut 32:8 in the LXX).

[171] משרתים in Ps 104:4; עבדים in Job 4:18; 44:26.

[172] הרוח in 1 Kgs 22:21. Cf. Job 4:15.

[173] מלאך מליץ in Job 4:18; 33:23.

[174] Tiemeyer, "Zechariah's Spies," 107.

This understanding of the cherub as a divine being is not restricted to the biblical traditions. The Mesopotamian traditions also contain mythological figures bearing the names *kāribu* and *kurību*, which are likely cognate with the Hebrew term כרובים.[175] According to *CAD* K, 216–217, *kāribu* is a participle of *karābu* ("to pray, to consecrate, to bless") used as an adjective denoting "a person performing a specific religious act," but it can also designate "a deity represented as making a gesture of adoration."[176] Following this, Wood understands the *kāribu* in one early Babylonian religious chronicle as "a descriptive word, modifying a god (or a statue of a god)," which is represented by the cuneiform sign DINGIR read as *ilu* "god." As such, the whole phrase is translated as "the praying deity."[177] However, both Glassner and Grayson read the cuneiform sign as the divine determinative.[178] As such, the *kāribu* can also be read as a proper noun, representing the name of a divine being (ᵈKa-ri-bu).[179] According to *CAD* K, 559, *kurību* is a noun meaning "representation of a protective genius [genie] with specific non-human features." In several Esarhaddon inscriptions, this figure bears the divine determinative, which indicates the figure's deified status.[180] The figure is listed with other apotropaic hybrid figures such as *lion*, *anzû*, and *laḫmu*.[181] Following this, a *kurību* prob-

---

[175] *AHw*, 1:449; *CAD*, 8:216–17, 559; Keel, *Jahwe-Visionen*, 16, n. 5; Hartenstein, "Cherubim," 158. Also consult the more extensive discussion of the etymology of כרובים in Wood, *Wings*, 143–55. Note, however, that F. A. M. Wiggermann thinks the *kurību* "is related with the Semitic word for raven (*gārib*), rather than with Akkadian *karābu*" ("Mischwesen. A. Philologisch. Mesopotamien," *RlA* 8:222–46, here 243).

[176] Cf. *HALOT*, 1:497.

[177] Wood, *Wings*, 152. The treatment of *kāribu* as a descriptive participle is also found in L. W. King, *Chronicles Concerning Early Babylonian Kings*, 2 vols. (London: Luzac, 1907), 2:84 (III, 16).

[178] For the different denotations of this cuneiform sign, see J. Huehnergard, *A Grammar of Akkadian*, HSS 45 (Atlanta: Scholars Press, 1997), 563.

[179] J.-J. Glassner, *Mesopotamian Chronicles*, WAW 19 (Atlanta: Society of Biblical Literature, 2004), 300 (51 iii 16); A. K. Grayson, *Assyrian and Babylonian Chronicles* (Locust Valley: Augustin, 1975; repr., Winona Lake: Eisenbrauns, 2000), 138. So also *CAD* K, 216.

[180] See E. Leichty, *The Royal Inscriptions of Esarhaddon, King of Assyria (680–669 BC)*, RINAP 4 (Winona Lake: Eisenbrauns, 2011), 136 (60:24'), 155 (77:10), (78:9), 161 (79:9), 175 (93:5); *CAD* K, 559; Wood, *Wings*, 141–56. For three distinct ways to identify deities in Akkadian texts, see M. B. Hundley, "Here a God, There a God: An Examination of the Divine in Ancient Mesopotamia," *AoF* 40 (2013): 68–107.

[181] For an overview of the Mesopotamian hybrid figures, see Wiggermann, "Mischwesen. A.," 8:222–46; A. Green, "Mischwesen. B. Archäologie. Mesopotamien," *RlA* 8:246–64, esp. 248, 253, 254, 256–57. For illustrations and explications

ably belongs to the same class of these apotropaic figures without being identical with them. It is unclear how the *kurību* looks. Wood notes that one text, describing an Assyrian prince's vision of the netherworld, envisages a monster with the head of *kurību*, but human hands and feet.[182] As Wood then conjectures, it is likely for the *kurību* to be "theriomorphic" or "therianthropic" rather than "anthropomorphic."[183] Wiggermann tentatively identifies the *kurību* as the hybrid creature—Griffin.[184] Hybrid figures in the ancient Near East, as explicated by Hundley, include "demons," "monsters," and "protective beings," which "partake of the divine nature."[185] We cannot assume that the ideological functions of *kāribu* and *kurību* correspond completely with those of the cherubim in the Hebrew Bible. Despite their other possible differences, the semi-divine or divine status seems to be a trait shared by these three categories of beings.

Taking into consideration all the above biblical and extra-biblical evidence, the Tyrian king, being identified as the animate cherub in Ezek 28:14 (cf. v. 16), can also be counted as a heavenly and even a divine being. The Tyrian royal is not merely a cherub, but the "anointed" (ממשח) cherub. Even though the precise meaning of ממשח is unclear, the term might be derived from the

---

of *lamassu* and *laḫmu*, see J. Black and A. Green, *Gods, Demons and Symbols of Ancient Mesopotamia: An Illustrated Dictionary* (Austin: University of Texas Press, 1992), 64–65, 115. For a more detailed examination of the *lamassu* as the protective deity, see Hundley, "God," 92–93. For the demonic feature and apotropaic function of *laḫmu*, see G. Mobley, *Samson and the Liminal Hero in the Ancient Near East*, LHBOTS 453 (London: Bloomsbury, 2006), 22–25.

[182] Wood, *Wings*, 154, cites W. von Soden, "Die Unterweltsvision eines assyrischen Kronprinzen," *ZA* 9 (1936): 1–31, here 16; *ANET*, 109.

[183] Wood, *Wings*, 154.

[184] Wiggermann, "Mischwesen. A.," 8:224, 241, 243. Many other scholars seek iconographical evidence to correlate the cherubim in the Hebrew Bible with the composite beings in the ancient Near East. Thus, Albright conjectures that the cherub is a composite being like "the winged sphinx or winged lion with human head" ("Cherubim," 2). So also E. Bloch-Smith, "Solomon's Temple: The Politics of Ritual Space," in *Sacred Time, Sacred Place: Archaeology and the Religion of Israel*, ed. B. Gittlen (Winona Lake: Eisenbrauns, 2002), 83–94, here 85, 88. Metzger further elaborates on and refines this hypothesis, claiming that the cherub, being identified with the winged sphinx, has the lion-dragon (*Löwendrachen*) as the ancestor. For further comparisons between the cherubim and the ancient Near Eastern composite beings, see Metzger, *Königsthron*, 1:312–25.

[185] Hundley, "God," 93–94. See also M. Hutter, "Demons and Benevolent Spirits in the Ancient Near East," in *Angels: The Concept of Celestial Beings—Origins, Development and Reception*, ed. F. V. Reiterer et al. (Berlin: de Gruyter, 2007), 21–34, esp. 23, 25–26, who suggests that "demons" or "protective spirits" are "divine beings of a lesser rank."

root משח "to anoint."[186] In the Hebrew Bible, the act of anointing usually marks the conferment of authority or the exaltation of status.[187] In accordance with this notion, Arbel helpfully suggests that "the reference to an 'anointed cherub' seems to be an alternative way of ranking the primal figure as a superior cherub among other cherubic beings."[188] The Tyrian royal is not merely a cherub, but "the covering" (הסוכך) cherub. The root סכך is also used in Exod 25:20; 37:9; 1 Kgs 8:7; 1 Chr 28:18 to describe the cherubim who flank the ark or the mercy seat on which God is supposed to be enthroned in the holy of holies.[189] To describe the Tyrian king as the cherub that protects the most intimate place of divine presence thus emphasizes the close proximity of the Tyrian king to the divine. Even if the Masoretes do not read אלהים היית in their division of Ezek 28:14, the *Leitwort* אלהים that occurs repetitively in the whole dirge (vv. 11–19) still plays tantalizingly with the idea of the possible divinity of the Tyrian king.[190] The term אלהים can be understood either in a generic sense as referring to any divine being, or as a proper noun referring to YHWH only.[191] Should we understand the cherub to be located in "the garden of *God*" or "the garden of *gods*" (v. 13)? Does the text mean to position the Tyrian figure on the "holy mountain of *God*" or "the holy mountain of *gods*" (vv. 14,

---

[186] See Greenberg, *Ezekiel 21–37*, 583; Zimmerli, *Ezekiel*, 2:85.

[187] E.g., Exod 29:29; Lev 4:3, 5, 16; 6:20; Ps 105:15; 132:10; 1 Sam 16:13; 2 Sam 2:4; 1 Kgs 19:16; 1 Chr 16:22. See D. Arbel, "'Seal of Resemblance, Full of Wisdom, and Perfect in beauty:' The Enoch/ Metatron Narrative of 3 Enoch and Ezekiel 28," *HTS* 98 (2005): 121–42, here 131, n. 27.

[188] Arbel, "Seal," 131.

[189] Miller, "Maelaek," 498–99; Wilson, "Death," 215; Yaron, "Dirge," 31–32.

[190] Cf. Ezek 28:13, 14, 16 (cf. אל and אלהים in 28:2, 6, 9). Previous scholarship, especially Pope, *El*, 97–103, has hypothesized that the appearances of אל in Ezek 28:2, 9 originated from the Ugaritic mythologies concerning the banishment of El from the mountains of gods to the deep of the seas. Also, it is interesting to note Rendtorff, who suggests that the term אל is not used as a proper noun exclusive to YHWH in some biblical texts. Rather, "אל kann also auch einen anderen Gott bezeichnen. Es bedeutet offenbar <Gott> in allgemeinen, eine <Gottheit>" (R. Rendtorff, "El als israelitische Gottesbezeichnung," *ZAW* 106 [1994]: 4–21, here 9, see the biblical examples cited in 11–12).

[191] Deuteronomy (cf. 1 Kgs 18) is one exemplary book that displays both the generic and the specific sense of the term. In order to eliminate such a confusion, when the term refers to YHWH specifically, a definite article is added so as to read האלהים. While the common Deuteronomic word אלהים, without the definite article, continues to be translated in a generic sense as "god" or "a god." See N. MacDonald, *Deuteronomy and the Meaning of "Monotheism*," 2nd ed., FAT 2/1 (Tübingen: Mohr Siebeck, 2012), 80. However, such a clear distinction does not always exist throughout the Hebrew Bible. See, for examples, the varied usages of this term in Exod 7:1; Zech 12:8; Ps 82:6. See also the detailed discussion in Rendtorff, "El," 14–21.

16)?¹⁹² Given the attested role of the animate cherub as part of the heavenly beings in the vicinity of God's presence, the dirge in Ezek 28:11–19 is enigmatic enough. Unlike the strong affirmation of the Tyrian ruler in Ezek 28:2 as a mere mortal (ואתה אדם ולא אל), the Tyrian king in 28:14 is ambiguously and inconclusively exalted to a god-like status, as a divine cherub.¹⁹³ By identifying the Tyrian king as a cherub, playing on the *Leitwort* אלהים, the dirge seems to exalt the foreigner to a divine being—a status higher than the mortal Israelite high priest.

### 3.3. THE DESTRUCTION *IN TOTO*

Daringly, the connections between the Tyrian ship and Jerusalem temple, between the Tyrian king and Israelite high priest are applied in specific sections of the two dirges, in order to relativize the beauty of pre-exilic Israelite sacral traditions and to exalt the glory of a pagan nation to an unprecedented height. Dramatically and abruptly, after the exaltation of the beauty, fame, and influence of Tyre and its ruler, both dirges move into the last sections that pronounce the fall and destruction of Tyre and its ruler *in toto*. We will see that the editor or author of Ezekiel, in the last sections of the two dirges, is bold enough to set up the fall of Tyre and its ruler from their material splendor in a way that brings suspense to the inexpressible fear for the doom of Jerusalem's temple and priestly glory.

### 3.3.1. THE FINAL BLOW BY THE EAST WIND

The demise of Tyre comes unexpectedly. In 27:26, the magnificent merchant ship epitomizing Tyre bears the brunt of the sudden attack of the east wind (רוח הקדים, v. 26). The reference to "the east wind" is characteristic of Ezekiel,¹⁹⁴ but all of these references within Ezekiel are concentrated only in two

---

¹⁹² The multiple possibilities for the translation of אלהים are perhaps best reflected in the English NASB and German *Herder Bibel*. While the KJV and *Luther Bibel* consistently translate the אלהים in Ezek 28 as "God" and "Gott" respectively; the NASB translates vv. 2, 9 as either "gods" or "god" with the rest of the occurrences of the term in the same chapter as "God." Similar mixed occurrences appear in the German *Herder Bibel*.

¹⁹³ On form-critical grounds, Ezek 28:1–10 and 28:11–19 are treated as two separate textual units. See Yaron, "Dirge," 45–49; Wilson, "Death," 211; Pohlmann, *Kapitel 20–48*, 390–91; Hölscher, *Hesekiel*, 140.

¹⁹⁴ Outside Ezekiel, the phrase רוח הקדים occurs only once in Exod 10:13; 14:21; Ps 48:7; Jer 18:17; and Jonah 4:8. All these cases specify that the east wind is a destructive force coming from God. Without the complement רוח or קדים can also stand alone as "east wind" as in Gen 41:6, 23, 27; Hos 12:2; 13:15; Job 15:2; 27:21; 38:24; Ps 78:26. Isa 27:8 attests to the construct form יום קדים.

Judah oracles and one Tyre oracle.[195] In Ezek 17:10 and 19:12, the east wind is predicted as the destructive force that blows against the southern kingdom Judah. Even though YHWH is not mentioned directly in these two verses, the source of the east wind is presumably divine (cf. 17:19).[196] When the east wind reappears in 27:26, YHWH is also not being mentioned explicitly. Nevertheless, in light of 26:3, 14, 19, where YHWH repeatedly acts as the active agent bringing down Tyre, it is only reasonable that the force behind the east wind in 27:26 is divine.[197] Given the distinctive appearances of the east wind in only the Tyre and Judah oracles within the book of Ezekiel, the destruction wreaked upon Tyre seems to be set deliberately in parallel to that upon Judah.

Following the sudden attack of the east wind, the complete cargo of Tyre, represented by the triad "wealth," "wares," and "merchandise," falls irreversibly into the midst of the seas (v. 27). This state of ruin is accompanied by the drowning of the "sailors," "pilots," "repairers of seams," "dealers in merchandise," "men of war," and all other "company" (v. 27). The impact of such a total destruction of Tyre can also be seen in 27:28–36. The pilots and sailors made up of many peoples all cry bitterly,[198] casting dust on their heads,[199] rolling in ashes,[200] plucking out their hairs,[201] and girding in sackcloth.[202] They will raise up a lament (קינה, v. 32) and mourn for the lost beauty of Tyre. These verses enlarge and intensify the reactions toward the fall of Tyre depicted in 26:15–17.[203] The end of chapter 27 links to the conclusion of chapter 26. More forcefully, chapter 27 affirms the real presence of the doom: Tyre is going to be destroyed tragically and completely, even though it possesses a perfect beauty that is universally recognized. At this point, the dramatic annihilation of Tyre raises an eerie prospect: If Tyre, which possesses a perfect

---

[195] Ezek 17:10; 19:12; 27:26. One distinctive feature of the use of the "east wind" in Ezekiel is that God is never mentioned directly as the agent.

[196] C. L. Crouch and C. A. Strine characterize the east wind in Ezek 17:10 as "a recognizable component of the divine arsenal, hostile to all life" ("Yahweh's Battle against Chaos in Ezekiel: The Transformation of Judahite Mythology for a New Situation," *JBL* 132 [2013]: 883–903, here 890).

[197] For the link between the east wind and the destructive power found, for instance, in Ps 48:7, see Eichrodt, *Ezekiel*, 384; Wevers, *Ezekiel*, 211. Haldor comments that the east wind in the Hebrew Bible "is held to be under the bidding of Yahweh" ("Tyrian Oracles," 242).

[198] The word מר or מרה "bitter, bitterness" appears three times in Ezek 27:30–31.

[199] Cf. Josh 7:6; Job 2:12; Lam 2:10

[200] Cf. Mic 1:10; Jer 6:26; 25:34.

[201] Cf. Ezek 7:18; Lev 21:5; Mic 1:16.

[202] Cf. Ezek 7:18; Esth 4:1.

[203] Premstaller, *Fremdvölkersprüche*, 89.

beauty far exceeding that of the Jerusalem temple, could be destroyed effortlessly by the divine east wind, how much more vulnerable would the small sanctuary in Judah be!

### 3.3.2. The Profanation of the Tyrian King

Having extolled the Tyrian king as a divine cherub, the dirge in Ezek 28:11–19 dramatically pronounces the retribution executed by YHWH upon the king. YHWH strangely accuses the Tyrian king of having "profaned the sanctuaries" (חללת מקדשיך, v. 18).[204] Due to the many sins of the king, YHWH casts him as profaned (ואחללך, v. 16). The double use of the verbal root חלל in both verses is especially striking, given that the object of punishment is a foreign king.[205]

Elsewhere in Ezekiel, the term חלל "to profane" is employed almost exclusively in the prophet's indictments against the Judahites.[206] Ezekiel uses this word mostly to describe *cultic offenses*, especially those committed by the people of Judah.[207] Thus, in Ezek 20, the so-called "revisionist history" of Israel, generations of the Israelites are accused of having profaned the holy name and Sabbaths of YHWH, breaking down the distinction between the holy and the common or profane.[208] Striking is the use of this word in describing YHWH's subsequent rejection of the Judahites. Ezekiel, as noted insightfully

---

[204] Within Ezekiel's OAN, the plural form of מקדש "sanctuary" appears only here in the Tyre oracle. Elsewhere in Ezekiel, it is used exclusively to refer to the Israelite cultic places (7:24; 21:7). At these two places, the Israelite sanctuaries are considered to be so abominable as to become the object of YHWH's defilement. Throughout Ezekiel and the Hebrew Bible, the singular form of מקדש refers almost always to the Israelite sanctuary or the related cultic contexts (except that Isa 16:12 refers to the Moabite sanctuary). E.g., Exod 25:8; 45:3, 18; 47:12; Lev 12:4; 16:33; 19:30; 20:3; 21:12, 23; 26:2, 31; Num 3:38; 10:21; 18:1; 19:20; Jer 41:41; Lam 1:10; Ezek 48:10; Amos 7:9, 13; Dan 11:31; 1 Chr 22:19; 2 Chr 20:8; 26:18; 29:21.

[205] Bogaert similarly states: "La conjunction de *hillèl* et de *miqdāš* en Éz 28,18 est particulièrement impressionnante" ("Montagne," 139–40).

[206] Within the Hebrew Bible, Ezekiel attests to the highest concentration of the related forms of this verbal root, which is comparably more numerous than the sixteen occurrences of חלל in the Holiness Code of Leviticus (18:21; 19:8, 12, 29; 20:3; 21:4, 6, 9, 12, 15, 23; 22:2, 9, 15, 32). Also see the occurrences in Isaiah (48:11; 53:5; 56:2, 6) and Jeremiah (25:29; 31:5; 34:16). A secondary meaning of this term is "to pierce." Ezekiel uses forms of this word to refer to the wounded or the dead in 6:4, 7, 13; 11:6, 7; 21:19, 30, 34; 26:15; 28:8, 9; 30:4, 11, 24; 31:17, 18; 32:20, 21, 22, 23, 24, 28, 29, 30, 31, 32; 35:8. For verification, see *HALOT*, 1:306–7; A. Mein, *Ezekiel and the Ethics of Exile*, Oxford Theological Monographs (Oxford: Oxford University Press, 2009), 154.

[207] See Ezek 13:19; 20:9, 13, 14, 16, 21, 22, 24, 39; 22:8, 16, 26; 23:38, 39; 25:3; 28:18; 36:20–23; 39:7; 44:7.

[208] Ezek 20:9, 13, 14, 16, 21, 22, 24, 39.

CHAPTER THREE 121

by Raitt, deploys the term חלל "to profane" in a similar sense to מאס "to reject."[209] YHWH is actively involved in the profanation of the Israelite sanctuaries. In Ezek 7:20–24, YHWH declares that he will send out his instruments of judgment to defile the sanctuary of Judah (צפוני).[210] The 3mp verbal form of חלל in vv. 21–22 indicates that the act of profanation is to be assigned to either the "foreigners" or the "wicked of the earth" or the "robbers." Meanwhile, the "worst of the nations" in v. 24 are held responsible for the profanation of the Israelite sanctuary. However, all of them are ultimately regarded as the instrument of YHWH's judgment, as indicated by the recurring 1cs verbal forms referring to YHWH's initiatives in vv. 20–22 and 24.[211] Even more shockingly, YHWH becomes the very perpetrator who profanes his own sanctuary in Judah: "Behold, I am about to profane (חלל) my sanctuary, the pride of your power, the desire of your eyes, and the delight of your soul" (24:21).[212] By naming the temple as the people's pride of power, desire of eyes, and delight of soul, this passage alludes to the Judahites' boast in the magnificence of the temple and possibly the exiles' insatiable longing for the glorious symbol of their former national pride and identity. That YHWH is the very executioner of the desecration of the sanctuary delivers a final blow to the popular theology of the impregnability of the temple, subsequently of Jerusalem, the capital city, and of Judah, the nation.[213]

Given the preponderant occurrences of the term in relation to Judah, חלל in 28:16, 18 most likely serves to align the profanation of the Tyrian ruler with the guilt of the Jerusalemite leadership. Despite being extolled as a divine cherub, YHWH stresses the created status of the Tyrian king (מיום הבראך in v. 15; cf. v. 13; ונתתיך in v. 14). The mortality of the king is further exemplified when he is cast on the ground (v. 17) and turned "to ashes on the earth" (v. 18).[214] The dirge ends in v. 19 with a threat that Tyre will become "a terror"

---

[209] T. M. Raitt, *A Theology of Exile: Judgment/Deliverance in Jeremiah and Ezekiel* (Philadelphia: Fortress Press, 1977), 68–74. According to him, such a sense of חלל as divine rejection also appears in Lam 2:2; Ps 89:33–34, 39; Isa 43:28; 47:6.

[210] For the understanding of צפוני "my treasured place" as the temple, or even more specifically, the holy of holies, see Cooke, *Ezekiel*, 82–83; Eichrodt, *Ezekiel*, 104; Mein, *Ezekiel*, 155; Zimmerli, *Ezekiel*, 1:21; Wevers, *Ezekiel*, 65. Meanwhile, Greenberg views it as referring to the land of Israel or the city of Jerusalem (*Ezekiel 1–20*,154).

[211] ונתתיו "and I will make it," ונתתי "And I will give it," והסבותי "And I will cause...to turn" והאתי "and I will bring," והשבתי "and I will make...cease."

[212] Cf. Mein, *Ezekiel*, 160.

[213] Cf. Block, *Ezekiel*, 1:792; Tooman, "Challenge," 498–514.

[214] For the resemblances between this description and the creation narratives in Gen 2:4; 3:19; 5:2, see Newsom, "Maker," 200–201; Arbel, "Seal," 128.

(בלהות)—the destruction and death commonly reserved for the wicked.[215] In the end, the comparison of the Tyrian figure to the Israelite high priest and a divine cherub is not to create a polarization between a particular perspective that is ultimately applicable to Jerusalem only and a more general perspective applicable to a mythological being only. Both images are needed in their received Masoretic form in order to highlight the fact that Jerusalem's leadership will not escape YHWH's judgment. The dirge raises the suspense: If the splendor and divinity of the Tyrian king cannot even help him to escape the fate of defeat and subordination under YHWH's sovereignty, can the Jerusalem temple leadership be spared from the divine retribution?

In the elegies of Tyre and its ruler, one finds intricately interwoven allusions to the Jerusalem temple and its priesthood (27:1–11; 28:12–13). These allusion are integrated in the literary contexts that display the pattern of exaltation and devastation. Through the exaltation of the Tyrian ship and king, as exemplified by the extensive trade network and the imagery of the divine cherub (27:12–25a; 28:14), the splendor once possessed by the Jerusalem temple and its high priest are dramatically relativized. Subsequently, the swift destruction wreaked upon the ship and king (27:25b–36; 28:12–19) bring suspense, anxiety, and apprehension towards the fate of the cultic sphere of Jerusalem: Can the Jerusalem temple and its priesthood survive the divine retribution? For now, the future outlook Ezekiel presents remains pessimistic.

---

[215] This feminine plural is a rare term, occurring three times in Ezekiel in relation to Tyre's demise (including 27:36; 28:19). Most of the time it appears in the psalmodic texts, referring to the destruction or death of the nations who plunder Israel (Isa 17:14) or the fate of the wicked (Ps 73:19; Job 18:11, 14; 24:17; 27:20; 30:15). See N. M. Sarna, "The Mythological Background of Job 18," *JBL* 82 (1963): 315–18, here 315; U. Cassuto, *The Goddess Anath: Canaanite Epics of the Patriarchal Age*, trans. I. Abrahams (Jerusalem: Magnes Press, 1971), 63; U. Rüterswörden, "King of Terrors," *DDD* 487.

# CHAPTER FOUR

# THE DEATH OF JUDAH IN EZEK 29–32

קינה היא ותהי לקינה

This is a lamentation, and has become a lamentation.

Ezek 19:14b

קינה היא וקוננוה בנות הגוים תקוננה אותה על מצרים ועל כל המונה תקוננה אותה נאם אדני יהוה

"This is a lamentation and they will chant it. The daughters of the nations will chant it. Over Egypt and over all her multitude they will chant it"—the declaration of the Lord YHWH.

Ezek 32:16

Egypt is the last foreign nation to receive a diatribe in Ezek 25–32. It alone commands four chapters of indictments, which constitute half of the oracles in Ezek 25–32.[1] The Egypt oracles are difficult to read, not only because of their length, but also due to their rich imagery, diverse themes, and motifs. In the first and last chapters of the Egypt oracles, Pharaoh is likened to a crocodile or a leonine monster (29:3; 32:2) stirring up turbulent waters. In the middle of the Egypt oracles, Pharaoh is compared to a cedar that grows monstrously high, such that it becomes "haughty in its loftiness" (31:10). The ultimate fate reserved for the monstrous Egypt is vividly visualized when Pharaoh's strong arm has been decisively broken by YHWH (30:20–26). The humiliating defeat of Pharaoh comes to a head when Pharaoh and his entourage are condemned to descend into the harrowing Sheol filled with the uncircumcised and the slain of the sword (32:17–32; cf. 31:15–18). Chaos monster,

---

[1] Oracles concerning Egypt are also found in Isa 19; Jer 43:8–13; 46; and Joel 4:19, but they are not as extensive as in Ezekiel.

precipitous cedar, broken arm, and gloomy Sheol all contribute to the portrayal of Egypt and its ruler as YHWH's inveterate enemy, who is alien and abnormal, to be cast aside and eliminated.

This chapter, however, aims to see through this sense of alienation, and points to a sense of familiarity, by showing that the image of Judah is embedded and repetitively alluded to in the series of oracles against Egypt. One peculiarity of the Egypt oracles is the presence of a large entourage accompanying Egypt. In the extensive slaughter, destruction, and annihilation pronounced throughout the oracles, alongside Egypt are the "fish of your Nile branches" (Ezek 29:4),[2] "Cush, Put, Lud, and all the mixed multitude, Kub, and the people of the covenant land" (30:5), the "noisy crowd" of Egypt (e.g., 31:2, 18; 32:18, 32), the "trees of Eden" (31:18),[3] and the "slain of the sword" (32:20–26, 28–32). All these accompany Egypt to face the divine judgment, even to encounter death in the netherworld. A question thus arises: Who is this multitude alongside Egypt? Almost all major studies on Ezekiel have found hints of the Judahites in the reference to "the people of the covenant land" (בני ארץ הברית, 30:5).[4] Yet, as far as my research reflects, no one has yet systematically explored the connection between this reference and the multiple appearances of the entourage of Egypt in the rest of Ezek 29–32. Nor has

---

[2] For the interpretation of the fish as the whole population of the inhabitants of Egypt (כל ישבי מצרים, 29:6), see Fuhs, *Ezechiel*, 2:160; Premstaller, *Fremdvölkersprüche*, 146; Block, *Ezekiel*, 2:138. Attention should be paid to the exegesis offered in Gunkel, *Schöpfung*, 75. Gunkel thinks that the fish of the Nile allegorically symbolize the supporters of Egypt (סמכי מצרים, 30:6) and all the helpers (כל עזריה, 30:8). More recently, Gunkel's position is also followed by Bowen, *Ezekiel*, 181; K. P. Darr, "The Book of Ezekiel," in *The New Interpreter's Bible: Introduction to Prophetic Literature*, ed. L. E. Keck (Nashville: Abingdon Press, 2001), 1405; S. K. Minj, *Egypt: The Lower Kingdom: An Exegetical Study of the Oracle of Judgment against Egypt in Ezekiel 29:1–16*, European University Studies 23 (Frankfurt am Main: Peter Lang, 2006), 75. Gunkel's position remains a viable possibility in that it highlights the centrality of the rhetoric against the Judeo-Egyptian alliance in Ezek 29:6–12. It pays sufficient attention to 29:16, which rules out any future alliance between Egypt and Israel. This anti-alliance rhetoric will be explored more fully in this chapter.

[3] Due to the reference to the trees' jealousy of the cedar and the fact that they are comforted by the descent of the cedar into Sheol (vv. 9, 16), some interpret those trees as the historical rival powers of Assyria (e.g., Block, *Ezekiel*, 2:188, 196; Greenberg, *Ezekiel 21–37*, 643). Eichrodt cautions against this view (*Ezekiel*, 426). Whether this records a historical rivalry or not, I am of the opinion that one should not overlook the fact that the text does emphasize the alignment of those trees in Eden with the cedar tree in that all of them are positioned inside the garden of God, and that all of them are ultimately condemned to the same fate of death.

[4] E.g., Zimmerli, *Ezekiel*, 2:130; Greenberg, *Ezekiel*, 2:622; Pohlmann, *Kapitel 20–48*, 414, n. 67; Fuhs, *Ezechiel*, 2:165; Block, *Ezekiel*, 2:160; Premstaller, *Fremdvölkersprüche*, 164.

anyone brought this reference in connection with the rationale of the divine judgment in the Egypt oracles. As will be argued, the indirect reference to the Judahites in 30:5 can be linked to the other references to the entourage of Egypt, so that the Egypt oracles indeed contain subtle allusions to Judah as among the entourage of Pharaoh.

Recognizing these allusions to Judah in the Egypt oracles, in my view, is crucial to understanding the rhetorical impacts of the unusual and variegated webs of linguistic connections between Ezekiel's prophecies concerning Egypt and Judah. Various commentators have observed these intricate connections. For instance, Vogels notes that Ezek 29:10–16 presents Egypt as undergoing dispersion and restoration, just like the exile of the house of Judah depicted elsewhere in Ezekiel's oracles.[5] Pohlmann acknowledges the shared dirge form and the common dendritic images in chapters 19 and 31, which target the Judahite princes and Pharaoh respectively.[6] Boadt further observes the many distinctive and unique words or expressions common to both the Egypt and Judah oracles in Ezekiel, which he judges to be "hardly an accidental coincidence."[7] What remains the subject of dispute is the literary impact generated by these intricate connections. Why do the Egypt oracles share so many verbatim correspondences with the Judah oracles? With the whole complex of Ezek 25–32 in view, Lyons speculates that the semantic links between the descriptions concerning the fate of the nations and that of Judah

---

[5] Cf. Ezek 29:12; 30:23, 26; 32:9 with 11:17; 20:34, 41; 28:25; 34:13; 36:24; 37:21. See Vogels, "Restauration de l'Égypte et Universalisme en Ez 29,13–16," *Bib* 53 (1972): 473–94, here 478.

[6] K.-F. Pohlmann, "Zur Frage nach ältesten Texten im Ezechielbuch – Erwägungen zu Ez 17, 19 und 31," in *Prophet und Prophetenbuch: Festschrift für Otto Kaiser zum 65. Geburtstag*, ed. V. Fritz, BZAW 185 (Berlin: de Gruyter, 1989), 150–72. Basing his argument on these shared literary features, Pohlmann suggests that Ezek 31* and Ezek 19 belong to the same redactional hand (161), and are concerned mainly with the fate of Jerusalem kingship (170). In his opinion, Ezek 17 is a later redaction and newer interpretation of the situation envisioned in chapter 19 (153, 167). A fuller discussion of his work will come later in this chapter.

[7] For the examples such as the usage of דליות "branches" in the Judah oracle (17:6, 7, 23) and the Egypt oracle (31:7, 9, 12) as well as the appearances of בין עבתים "among the interwoven foliage" in another Judah oracle (19:11) and the Egypt oracle (31:3, 11, 14), see Boadt, "Rhetorical Strategies," 194, 198. Without further analysis of the overall literary context where the lexical connections appear, Boadt comments briefly and tentatively that the common phraseology reflects "perhaps a lesson for Israel—a lesson now being played out before their very eyes. These kings and their fates are a foil against which Ezekiel will set a true theology of Israel's relationship to God in the presentation of chapters 33–48" (199).

exist because the nations have taken pleasure at Judah's fall.[8] Zimmerli and Block go even further to assert that some of these semantic links act to pass on comfort and consolation for a people who has experienced a similar disaster.[9] By contrast, Marzouk contends that the shared language between the Egypt and Judah oracles underscore "the similarities between Israel and Egypt in terms of their moral chaos and in terms of the judgment that falls upon them."[10]

After the examination of the allusions to Judah as Egypt's most intimate ally, we will evaluate each of the above positions with regard to the rhetorical functions of the verbatim correspondences between the Egypt and Judah oracles. My argument is that the allusions to Judah as among Egypt's most intimate allies aid the Egypt oracles to build up a logical treatise propounding one terrifying message, which suggests YHWH's readiness to bring down not only Egypt, but also Judah. It is only in a later vision (29:13–16), where the alignment between Egypt and Judah is no longer a possibility, that an ideal contrast between Egypt and the future house of Israel is highlighted.

Before elucidating the allusions to Judah and the rhetorical impacts generated by these allusions in more detail, let us first highlight how Ezekiel's prophecies shape Egypt as the monstrous enemy of YHWH.

---

[8] Lyons states: "It could be that insofar as the nations have taken pleasure at Israel's downfall (the result of divine punishment outlined in Leviticus 26), the fortunes of the nations have to a certain degree become linked in Ezekiel's mind with the fortunes of Israel" (*Law*, 122).

[9] Zimmerli makes the above statement with regard to the motif of the day of YHWH found in both Ezek 7 and 30 (*Ezekiel*, 2:135). Likewise, Block remarks: "Although they are in exile, far from the land of the covenant, they may take comfort in the knowledge that YHWH reigns supreme over all" (ibid., 2:171).

[10] Marzouk, *Egypt*, 118. While my study aligns with Marzouk's idea of a blurred boundary between Egypt and Israel, we differ in our approaches to the Egypt oracles in two main ways. First, Marzouk innovatively uses the theories from other social and ancient Near Eastern disciplines as a heuristic lens to read and inform the oracles against Egypt. My study, on the other hand, employs a more inductive approach to the biblical texts, focusing first on the Egypt oracles, before exploring the allusions to other biblical texts that are appropriated by the editors, if not the authors, of the Egypt oracles. Second, Marzouk pays more attention to the portrayals of Egypt as a monster in Ezek 29:1–16 and 32:1–16, 17–32, comparing them synchronically with the portrayals of Egypt's relation to Israel in Ezek 20 and 23. By contrast, I treat all the oracles against Egypt in chapters 29–32 more evenly, and I stress that the diachronic aspects of the Egypt oracles are equally important in shaping the message of the oracles.

## CHAPTER FOUR

### 1. THE SHAPING OF EGYPT AS YHWH'S ENEMY

In Ezek 29–32, Egypt or Pharaoh is metaphorically represented by or compared to three images. First, at the beginning and end of the Egypt oracles, Pharaoh is characterized as a monstrous תנים, which can be translated as either a "crocodile" or a "sea-monster/sea-dragon" (29:3–6a; 32:2–8). Second, sandwiched between the first and last chapters of the Egypt oracles is the imagery of the arm of Pharaoh that symbolizes Egypt's strength (30:20–26). Finally, the might of Pharaoh and his multitude is also portrayed via the monstrously tall cedar tree with its roots reaching deep into the waters and with its tops rising high above other trees (31:1–9). In what follows, we will observe how the strength and might embodied by each of these images are destroyed and shattered by YHWH, and thus put the enmity between YHWH and Egypt in the foreground.

#### 1.1. THE CROCODILE/DRAGON MONSTER

Ezekiel 29:1–6a and 32:1–8 identify Pharaoh as the תנים. In 29:3, after the chronological formula, which contextualizes the prophecy about one year after the beginning of the siege of Jerusalem "in the tenth year, in the tenth month, on the twelfth of the month" (cf. 1 Kgs 25:1 and Ezek 24:1), YHWH addresses Pharaoh as follows:[11]

> Behold, I am against you, O Pharaoh, the king of Egypt,[12]
> the great תנים who lies in the midst of his Nile branches,
> because he said: "My Nile[13] belongs to me and I made it for myself."

A second characterization of Pharaoh as the תנים appears in 32:2 as part of the last chapter of the Egypt oracles. The prophecy is contextualized by a chronological formula "in the twelfth year, in the twelfth month, on the twelfth day of the month," which dates after the fall of Jerusalem and after the message of the fall reached Ezekiel the prophet (cf. 33:21).[14] YHWH commands the prophet to lift up a dirge to Pharaoh the king of Egypt, saying:

---

[11] While YHWH addresses Pharaoh in the 2ms, the תנין that is likened to Pharaoh is addressed in the 3ms.

[12] The expression "the king of Egypt" (מלך מצרים) is missing in the LXX. See Block, *Ezekiel*, 2:135.

[13] In contrast to the MT, the LXX reads יארי as plural, translating it as οἱ ποταμοί, which is more consistent with the previous plural reference (יאריו "his Nile branches") in the same verse. Based on the principle of *lectio difficilior*, I will retain the MT reading in my translation. See Marzouk, *Egypt*, 162, n. 25.

[14] Instead of "the twelfth day of the month," the LXX has "the first day of the month" (μιᾷ τοῦ μηνὸς). See ibid., 161, n. 22.

You were like a lion of the nations,[15]
and you were like the תנים in the seas.
You burst forth in your rivers,
you stirred up water with your feet,
and you trampled their rivers.[16]

Taken as a whole, the first and last chapters of the Egypt oracles form an *inclusio*, such that the Egypt oracles begin and end with the comparison of Pharaoh to the תנים.

On its own terms, this Hebrew noun indicates a plural form of תן "jackal," but it should probably be a variant form of the singular noun תנין "crocodile/sea-monster/sea-dragon." Not only do the surrounding literary contexts of the two verses where the noun appears suggest an aquatic setting, but the verbs, adjective, possessive suffixes, and pronouns attributed to this creature are also singular.[17] Boadt further justifies this reading of תנין by citing examples of ם and ן confusion in Ezekiel.[18] For instance, in Ezek 33:26, the second masculine plural verb עשיתן is spelled with a ן rather than a ם and thus possibly shows Aramaic influence. Likewise, אתם in 13:20 displays a masculine form, but refers to the feminine plural noun "magic bands" (כסתות; cf. vv. 18, 20) of the female prophets.[19] 34:31 uses אתן as a masculine, while אין in 26:18 stands for איים. In light of the interchangeability between ם and ן elsewhere in Ezekiel, it becomes even more justifiable that the verse is comparing Pharaoh to

---

[15] The *niphal* of דמה "to be like" appears only here in the Hebrew Bible. Cf. Ezek 19:10, where the same root with a different stem occurs in a similar context.

[16] The LXX reads τοὺς ποταμούς σου "your rivers," which, with a 2ms pronominal suffix, is more consistent with the previous clauses in the same verse. The MT here has a 3mp pronominal suffix to the noun נהרות. On the principle of *lectio difficilior*, I retain the MT form in my translation. Cf. Marzouk, *Egypt*, 166, n. 47.

[17] Allen, *Ezekiel*, 2:102.

[18] L. Boadt, *Ezekiel's Oracles against Egypt: A Literary and Philological Study of Ezekiel 29–32* (Rome: Pontifical Biblical Institute, 1980), 26. Cf. M. K. Wakeman, *God's Battle with the Monster: A Study in Biblical Imagery* (Leiden: Brill, 1973), 75, n. 4.

[19] כסתות is considered to be an Akkadian loanword. M. C. A. Korpel prefers a derivation from *katāmu* ("to cover") and translates it as "covering nets" ("Avian Spirits in Ugarit and in Ezekiel 13," in *Ugarit, Religion and Culture: Proceedings of the International Colloquium on Ugarit, Religion and Culture, Edinburgh, July 1994. Essays Presented in Honour of Professor John C. L. Gibson*, ed. N. Wyatt et al., UBL 12 [Münster: Ugarit-Verlag, 1996], 99–113, here 103). For the understanding of the term as a derivation from *kasîtu* ("bondage," derived from the verb *kasû*, "to bind"), see J. Stökl, "The מתנבאות in Ezekiel 13 Reconsidered," *JBL* 132 (2013): 61–76, here 64.

התנין.²⁰ This reading is also supported by the ancient translations in the Targum (תנינא) and the LXX (τὸν δράκοντα).

Commentators debate the exact meaning of this תנין. At one end of the spectrum, most scholars such as Fechter, Fuhs, Kessler, Pohlmann, Boadt, and Guillaume consider the term in Ezek 29 and 32 as suffused with mythological overtones, referring to the mythical "monster" or "dragon."²¹ Yoder innovatively proposes that the expression התנים הגדול functions as a royal epithet, and traces its origin to the ancient Mesopotamian serpentine epithet—the Akkadian *ušumgallu* or the Sumerian UŠUMGAL—which literally means "great dragon," and which likewise serves to describe several monarchs in the ancient Near East.²² This mythological connotation of תנין is conveyed most clearly in Isa 27:1; 51:9; Ps 74:13–14 and Job 7:12, in which the תנין is set alongside other mythical creatures such as רהב, לויתן, or ים.²³ In all these texts, these creatures of the primeval ocean pose threats to the divine order, and the creator God is aroused to take up battle against them in order to establish his supreme hegemony.²⁴ As noted by Greenberg, the words such as "seas" (ימים) and "rivers" (נהרות) appearing in Ezek 32:2 "evoke the primeval water monsters whose uprising God crushed (e.g., Isa 51:9–10; Ps 74:13) but whose menace will not be finally removed until the eschaton (Isa 27:1)."²⁵ תנין as a dragon is also used to describe historical enemies like Nebuchadnezzar king

---

[20] For examples of interchange between *mem* and *nun* in Semitic languages, e.g., Akkadian, Ugaritic, Moabitic, Hebrew and Arabic, which may explain the confusion of *mem-nun* in Ezekiel, see Boadt, *Ezekiel's Oracles*, 26, n. 28.

[21] Fechter, *Bewältigung*, 228–30; Fuhs, *Ezechiel*, 2:159; Pohlmann, *Kapitel 20–48*, 406; Boadt, *Ezekiel's Oracles*, 26, 129, 131; P. Guillaume, "Metamorphosis of a Ferocious Pharaoh," *Bib* 85 (2004): 232–36, esp. 232–33; R. Kessler, *Die Ägyptenbilder der Hebräischen Bibel: Ein Beitrag zur neueren Monotheismusdebatte*, SBS 197 (Stuttgart: Katholisches Bibelwerk, 2002), 71.

[22] T. R. Yoder, "Ezekiel 29:3 and Its Ancient Near Eastern Context," *VT* 63 (2013): 486–96. For the ancient Near Eastern dragon motifs and traditions, see also C. Uehlinger, "Drachen und Drachenkämpfe im alten Vorderen Orient und in der Bibel," in *Auf Drachenspuren: Ein Buch zum Drachenprojekt des Hamburgischen Museums für Völkerkunde*, ed. B. Schmelz and R. Vossen (Bonn: Holos Verlag, 1995), 55–101.

[23] Uehlinger considers Leviathan (לויתן) and Rahab (רהב) as the same creature, albeit with two different names derived from the Canaanite and Mesopotamian cultures, respectively (*Drachen*, 76). According to him, the two names never appear next to each other in the Hebrew Bible. Only in Job 26:12–13 and 41, there is a differentiation between the two mythical creatures.

[24] For fuller discussions of the *Chaoskampf* in the Hebrew Bible, see Wakeman, *God's Battle*, 68-79; Marzouk, *Egypt*, 16–29, 70–114.

[25] Greenberg, *Ezekiel 21–37*, 651. However, Greenberg prefers to see the תנין in Ezek 29:3 as referring to a more mundane animal, i.e., "crocodile" (601–2).

of Babylon (Jer 51:34).²⁶ Understood as a sea-monster or sea-dragon, the תנין, as conceptualized by Levenson, functions like Leviathan, Amalek, and Gog as the "ancient and enduring opposition to the full realization of God's mastery, the opposition destined to be eliminated at the turn of the aeon."²⁷

At the other end of the spectrum, both Fohrer and Zimmerli posit a more naturalistic interpretation of the תנין as a "crocodile," and thus differentiate this understanding from the more mythological translation of "dragon."²⁸ At first blush, the claim of a non-mythological understanding of תנין seems probable in light of Exod 7:9–10, 12; Deut 32:33 and Ps 91:13, which juxtapose תנין with a "snake" (נחש, Exod 7:15) or "adder" (פתן, Exod 32:33 and Ps 91:13).²⁹ The reptilian form of תנין in Ezek 29:3–6a is also made more likely when it is used as a grammatical subject of the verbs such as "to lie down" (רבץ, 29:3) and "to trample" (רפס, 32:2). The creature is bedecked with "scales" (בקשקשתיך, 29:4). In addition, 29:3 contains a singular noun יאר that is commonly thought to be derived from an Egyptian root *i(t)rw* meaning "river" or "the Nile,"³⁰ which further supports the Egyptianization of the תנין and thus the translation "crocodile."

Even though we are ready to accept "crocodile" as a viable alternative translation of תנין, Marzouk rightly contends that describing Pharaoh as a crocodile does not strip תנין of its mythological connotations, since the crocodile is deified and worshipped in Egypt as Sobek.³¹ Being given the titles such as "Lord of the Floodwater," "Lord of the Foreshore," "Lord of the Marshland," and "Lord of the Nile," Sobek is presented as the protective deity over the Nile River.³² He is even identified as the son of Neith, a goddess personifying

---

²⁶ Note the mentioning of the sea (ים) and fountain (מקור) in Jer 51:36.

²⁷ Levenson, *Creation*, 38.

²⁸ Fohrer, *Ezechiel*, 166; Zimmerli, *Ezekiel*, 2:110–11. Note that Zimmerli considers the reference to תנין in 29:1–6a as naturalistic, while that in 32:2–8 as mythological (*Ezekiel*, 2:159).

²⁹ Note that Exod 7:8–13, in which תנין appears, and vv. 14–18, which refer to "the rod that was turned into a snake (נחש)," belong to two different literary strata. For the possible mythological connotations of תנין in Exod 7:9–10, 12 and Ps 91:13, see Guillaume, "Metamorphosis," 232–36; S. C. Jones, "Lions, Serpents, and Lion-Serpents in Job 28:8 and Beyond," *JBL* 130 (2011): 667–73.

³⁰ For this understanding, see Block, *Ezekiel*, 2:135; Fuhs, *Ezechiel*, 2:159; Zimmerli, *Ezekiel*, 2:110; T. O. Lambdin, "Egyptian Loan Words in the Old Testament," *JAOS* 73 (1953): 145–55, here 151.

³¹ Marzouk, *Egypt*, 159–60. See also H. Niehr, "תנין," *TDOT* 15:729; Bowen, *Ezekiel*, 180; P. Höffken, "Untersuchungen zu den Begründungselementen der Völkerorakel des Alten Testaments" (PhD diss., Reinischen Friedrich-Wilhelms-Universität, 1977), 223.

³² For a list of the water epithets of Sobek found in the Coffin Texts from the Middle Kingdom, see B. Altenmüller, *Synkretismus in den Sargtexten* (Wiesbaden:

the primordial water.³³ Moreover, Sobek is associated with royalty. In the Middle Kingdom (ca. 2055–1650 BCE), Sobek was fused with Horus, the falcon-headed god, who was the symbol of kingship with which the living Pharaohs were identified. The fusion results in a specific and standardized name: "Sobek of Shedet—Horus who resides in Shedet" (*sbk šdt ḥr ḥry-ib šdt*).³⁴ During the Twelfth and Thirteenth Dynasties, several rulers even took on the names such as Sobekhotep and Sobekneferu.³⁵ The god Amun explicitly employs the ferocity of a crocodile to characterize the might of Thutmose III (1479–1425 BCE) in front of his enemies: "I let them see your majesty as crocodile, master of terror in the water, unapproached."³⁶ Contrary to what Yoder asserts, the popularity of the cult of Sobek in Egypt persisted until the Greco-Roman period. Yoder claims that nine centuries separate Thutmose III's reign and the oracle in Ezek 32, and so Ezek 32 cannot possibly conceive Pharaoh as a crocodile god.³⁷ Yet, Bresciani cites a hymn from the Late Period (747–332 BCE), which is dedicated to Sobek and to Hor-Haroeris (Horus the Elder).³⁸ A pair of unnamed divine crocodiles were discovered to be the patron gods in the new Ptolemaic temple at Medinet Madi, while the Fayum crocodile

---

Harrassowitz, 1975), 185; F. Gomaᶜ, "Der Krokodilgott Sobek und seine Kultorte im Mittleren Reich," in *Studien zu Sprache und Religion Ägyptens: Zu Ehren von Wolfhart Westendorf, Bd. 2. Religion*, ed. F. Junge (Göttingen: Hubert & Co, 1984), 787–88.

³³ See Spell 317 (§510) in the Pyramid Texts from the Old Kingdom (ca. 2686–2181 BCE), the translation of which can be found in M. Lichtheim, *Ancient Egyptian Literature: The Old and Middle Kingdoms* (Berkeley: University of California Press, 1973), 40. For an explanation of the portrayal of Sobek in this spell, see M. Zecchi, *Sobek of Shedet: The Crocodile God in the Fayyum in the Dynastic Period* (Todi: Tau Education, 2010), 17; Altenmüller, *Synkretismus*, 186–87.

³⁴ For a fuller explanation of the usage of this epithet in the temple of Medinet Madi, see Zecchi, *Sobek*, 60–84, esp. 64, 67, 73–75. For the fusion of Horus and Sobek, see also Altenmüller, *Synkretismus*, 188.

³⁵ Sobekneferu is the daughter of Amenemhat III. Cf. Altenmüller, *Synkretismus*, 185.

³⁶ For an English translation of this hymn to Thutmose III, see M. Lichtheim, *Ancient Egyptian Literature: The New Kingdom* (Berkeley: University of California Press, 1976), 37.

³⁷ Yoder, "Ezekiel 29:3," 489. Yoder is correct to point out that "תנין as 'crocodile' lacks strong semantic backing and is found nowhere else in the HB," but we still cannot exclude the strong possibility of the conceptual borrowing in Ezekiel as a result of the prevalent Egyptian cult of Sobek that persisted until the Greco-Roman period.

³⁸ E. Bresciani, "Sobek, Lord of the Land of the Lake," in *Divine Creatures: Animal Mummies in Ancient Egypt*, ed. Salima Ikram (Cairo: American University in Cairo Press, 2005), 199–206, here 200–201. For the worship of Sobek in the Late Period, see also Zecchi, *Sobek*, 137–52.

deities possessing a wide array of names were also attested in the Greco-Roman period.³⁹ It is thus possible for Ezekiel to appropriate one of the most enduring ancient Egyptian symbols of Pharaoh in the oracles against Egypt, in order to issue an unsettling theological claim: Understood as a crocodile deity, Pharaoh in the two passages of Ezekiel rivals the divinity of YHWH and thus challenges the supreme authority of YHWH over the cosmos.

In this light, we need not differentiate too sharply between תנין as a chaotic sea-dragon and תנין as an Egyptian crocodile deity, since they essentially point to a single ideological function.⁴⁰ What unites these two conceptions of תנין is the challenge posed by this monster toward YHWH's supreme sovereignty. Picturing Pharaoh as the תנין thus foregrounds the deep-seated enmity between Pharaoh and YHWH.

The animosity between YHWH and Pharaoh is further reinforced by the surrounding literary contexts of both Ezek 29:3 and 32:2 that highlight the hubristic claims of Pharaoh. In 29:3b, the 3ms verb אמר introduces Pharaoh's direct speech. Pharaoh as the תנין claims to have made and possessed the Nile: "My Nile belongs to me and I made it for myself" (לי יארי ואני עשיתני).⁴¹ This proud claim (*Hoffartsmonolog*) forms a counterpart of YHWH's formulaic speech in Ezekiel: "I YHWH have spoken and acted" (אני יהוה דברתי ועשיתי).⁴² In this manner, Pharaoh's hubris clearly affronts YHWH's absolute sovereignty. In 32:2, the pompous status of Pharaoh reaches a climax, since he is compared to not only a mighty monster (תנין) in the seas, but also an energetic "young lion of the nations" (כפיר גוים; 32:2) on the land. The parallel imagery of both a lion and a sea-monster in v. 2 has caused confusions among the commentators. Most translate the *waw* conjunction as a disjunctive rather than a simple copula, necessitating a distinction between what Pharaoh claims to

---

³⁹ Bresciani, "Sobek," 202–3.

⁴⁰ For the understanding of the תנין as both a crocodile and a chaos monster, see Eichrodt, *Ezekiel*, 403; Premstaller, *Fremdvölkersprüche*, 144; Allen, *Ezekiel*, 2:105.

⁴¹ The quotations of the opponents' speech is a literary device used also in Isa 14:12–14; Ezek 26:2; 27:3. For a discussion of this literary technique in the prophetic literature, see E. F. Davis, "And Pharaoh Will Change His Mind (Ezekiel 32:31): Dismantling Mythical Discourse," in *Theological Exegesis: Essays in Honor of Brevard S. Childs*, ed. C. Seitz et al. (Grand Rapids: Eerdmans, 1998), 230–31.

⁴² Cf. Ezek 17:24; 22:14; 24:17; 36:36; 37:14. For the views that regard this proclamation of Pharaoh as superseding the sovereignty of YHWH as the creator, see Höffken, *Untersuchungen*, 208; Boadt, *Ezekiel's Oracles*, 30, 40–41; Minj, *Egypt*, 71–72. On the other hand, Fechter claims that the expression does not necessarily describe an act restricted only to YHWH's creation (*Bewältigung*, 240–41). More properly understood, Ezekiel employs the term עשה in relation to YHWH's acts of judgment (e.g., 5:8–10; 11:9). All in all, Fechter still shares with the others the opinion that this expression highlights the hubris of Pharaoh.

be (i.e., a lion) and what he actually is (i.e., a monster).⁴³ This is often based on the presupposition that the image of a lion is associated especially with royalty and is thus positive.⁴⁴ Indeed, several Pharaohs are described in the reliefs found in ancient Egypt as a "victorious lion," "a fierce-eyed lion," one who "fought like a lion," or "the lion with deep roar upon the mountaintops."⁴⁵ Nevertheless, Strawn points out that biblical evidence rarely attributes leonine characteristics to human kings.⁴⁶ Even if Ezek 19:1–9 does present the Judahite princes as lion cubs, the ultimate outcome is negative. More often than the human king, it is YHWH who appears to be associated with the lion motif.⁴⁷ Thus Ezekiel's association of the mortal Pharaoh with a lion can also bear a subversive connotation paralleling the defiant attitude toward YHWH embodied by the תנין. In fact, Lewis provides further ancient Near Eastern materials that present a ruler as both a lion and a dragon.⁴⁸ Associated with protection and royalty, the composite creature with leonine bodies and heads, yet long intertwined serpentine necks (serpopard) features most prominently at the back of the Narmer palette from Egypt.⁴⁹ Consequently, it is likely that

---

⁴³ So Fohrer, *Ezechiel*, 177; Eichrodt, *Ezekiel*, 432; Boadt, *Ezekiel's Oracles*, 129–30; Yoder, "Ezekiel 29:3," 488, n. 6; Marzouk, *Egypt*, 166, 169; and most English versions (e.g., CEV, NASB, ESV, NET, GNB, JPS). *Contra* the LXX, the Vulg., and NKJV.

⁴⁴ See esp. Boadt, *Ezekiel's Oracles*, 130–31.

⁴⁵ See Breasted, J. H., ed., *Ancient Records of Egypt: Historical Documents from the Earliest Times to the Persian Conquest*, 5 vols. (London: Histories and Mysteries of Man LTD., 1998), 3:200 (§465), 4:25 (§46), 468 (§921), 512 (§1005), cited in B. Strawn, *What is Stronger than a Lion: Leonine Image and Metaphor in the Hebrew Bible and the Ancient Near East*, OBO 212 (Fribourg: Academic Press Fribourg, 2005), 176, 177, 178, n. 170, 178, n. 271.

⁴⁶ Strawn, *Lion*, 54–58, 236–50.

⁴⁷ Cf. Job 10:16; 38:39–40; Isa 31:4; Jer 25:38; 49:19; 50:44; Hos 5:14; 11:10; 13:7–8; Amos 3:8. See also Strawn, *Lion*, 250–73; Boadt, *Ezekiel's Oracles*, 131.

⁴⁸ T. J. Lewis, "CT 13.33–34 and Ezekiel 32: Lion-Dragon Myths," *JAOS* 116 (1996): 28–47, esp. 28–38. He focuses especially on an Akkadian text (CT 13.33–34) found in the library of Ashurbanipal. In this text, most recently edited in W. G. Lambert, *Babylonian Creation Myths*, Mesopotamian Civilizations 16 (Winona Lake: Eisenbrauns, 2013), 361–65, the heroic Tishpak is commissioned to slay a monstrous creature, which is called both a "serpent" (*MUŠ*) and a "lion" (*labbu*). As such, Lewis considers this creature a "composite monster or dragon with leonine and serpentine attributes" (34, citing A. Heidel, *The Babylonian Genesis: The Story of Creation* [Chicago: The University of Chicago Press, 1951], 141; cf. "lion-serpent" in B. R. Foster, *Before the Muses: An Anthology of Akkadian Literature* [Bethesda: CDL Press, 2005], 488). Lewis also cites several biblical examples such as Ps 91:13; Isa 30:6; Amos 5:19; Job 41:26 to support his thesis.

⁴⁹ This Narmer Palette commemorates the victories of King Narmer (ca. 3100–2890 BCE). For the image, see Lewis, "Lion-Dragon Myths," 34–35.

Pharaoh in this context haughtily considers himself as not merely a sea-monster, but rather a mixture of two mighty creatures, both a lion of the nations and a monster in the sea. By merging the two images of a lion and a monster together, Pharaoh is said to extend his power over both the terrestrial and cosmic spheres.

Responding to these defiant and wildly inflated self-estimations of the monstrous creature, YHWH openly declares his enmity. In Ezek 29:3a (cf. 29:9a), YHWH initiates a speech duel: "Behold, I am against you, O Pharaoh, the king of Egypt" (הנני עליך פרעה מלך מצרים). Subsequently, a series of first-person verbs marks YHWH's declaration to inflict punishment upon his enemy. Hence, in vv. 4–5, YHWH asserts: "And I will put hooks in your jaws" (ונתתי חחים בלחייך),[50] "And I will make the fish of your Nile branches cling to your scales" (והדבקתי דגת יאריך בקשקשתיך),[51] "And I will bring you up out of the midst of your Nile branches" (והעליתיך מתוך יאריך), "And I will abandon you to the wilderness" (ונטשתיך המדברה אותך). YHWH further declares that "I have given you for food to the beasts of the land and to the birds of the sky" (לחית הארץ ולעוף השמים נתתיך לאכלה). This series of 1cs verbs, closed off by a recognition formula (וידעו כל ישבי מצרים כי אני יהוה, v. 6), reflects YHWH's strong determination to defeat his enemy. In Ezek 32:3, instead of using the hooks as in 29:4, YHWH vows to subdue the chaos monster by using a net, which can be a metaphor for death (cf. Qoh 9:12).[52] YHWH's judgment is announced with two terms for net (רשת and חרם) forming a *parallelismus membrorum*:

| ופרשתי עליך את רשתי | And I will throw my net over you |
| בקהל עמים רבים | With a company of many peoples[53] |
| והעלוך בחרמי | and they[54] will haul you up in my dragnet |

---

[50] Cf. Ezek 38:4. More discussion on the relation between these two verses is found in Chapter Four.

[51] The LXX attests to a singular reading for the Nile. Here, I follow the MT to render the translation plural: "The Nile branches."

[52] For more information about the connection between net and death, see A. A. Fischer, *Tod und Jenseits im Alten Orient und im Alten Testament*, Studien zu Kirche und Israel 7 (Neukirchen: Neukirchener Verlag, 2005), 133–34. The net motif also appears frequently in Ezek 12:13; 17:20; 19:8, 9; 32:3a, mainly "as a divine weapon and in contexts of divine punitive actions" (Bodi, *Erra*, 165). One positive reference to the net (משטח חרמים) does appear in 47:10, to describe the fertility of the living waters flowing from the temple (169).

[53] בקהל is missing in the LXX. Also, the LXX treats עמים רבים as the *nomen rectum* attached to the noun רשת.

[54] The LXX has YHWH as the grammatical subject, i.e., ἀνάξω.

CHAPTER FOUR 135

Subsequent to the capture of the monstrous king of Egypt, the anger vented by YHWH manifests itself on a cosmic level, such that YHWH pledges to "cover the heavens," "to darken their stars," "to cover the sun with a cloud," such that all luminaries upon the sky will no longer shine after YHWH's defeat of this monstrous Pharaoh, the king of Egypt (32:7–8).[55] The prediction of Egypt's bloodied defeat ends with a solemn declaration formula uttered by YHWH (נאם אדני יהוה, v. 8). In light of YHWH's intense verbal assaults, Pharaoh representing the whole of Egypt is considered as not only a foreign power but also a threat *par excellence* to YHWH's terrestrial and cosmic sovereignty.

1.2. THE BROKEN ARM

As in Ezek 29:1–6a and 32:1–8, dominant in 30:20–26 is the rivalry between YHWH and Pharaoh. The chronological formula at the beginning of this short prophecy in chapter 30 is dated to "the eleventh year, in the first month, on the seventh day of the month," which is three months after the prophecy in 29:1–16.[56] It is often thought that this is the time when Pharaoh Apries sought to relieve Jerusalem from the siege carried out by Nebuchadnezzar king of Babylon.[57] Ezek 30:21 responds to this situation by predicting YHWH's defeat of Pharaoh through the imagery of a broken arm:

> Son of man, I have broken the arm of Pharaoh, the king of Egypt.
> And behold, it has not been bound up, to produce healing by binding it with a bandage, so that it may become strong to wield the sword.

Remarkably, the singular noun "arm" (זרוע) and its plural form "arms" (זרעות) appear six times in this short oracle of merely seven verses.[58] Ezekiel not only depicts Pharaoh as having a broken arm, but also assigns the action of the breaking of Pharaoh's arm to YHWH (30:21–22).[59] Simultaneous to the

---

[55] Marzouk suggests that the cataclysmic catastrophe envisioned in this passage indicates that "Egypt is not just a political power; rather it plays a cosmological power in the reality of the exile" (*Egypt*, 199).

[56] P967 reads "tenth year."

[57] Cf. Jer 37:5–11. See also Block, *Ezekiel*, 2:175; J. K. Hoffmeier, "A New Insight on Pharaoh Apries from Herodotus, Diodorus and Jeremiah 46:17," *JSSEA* 11 (1981): 165–70; Eichrodt, *Ezekiel*, 420; Zimmerli, *Ezekiel*, 2:138; H. F. van Rooy, "Ezekiel's Prophecies against Egypt and the Babylonian Exiles," in *Proceedings of the Tenth World Congress of Jewish Studies. Division A. The Bible and Its World*, ed. D. Assaf (Jerusalem: World Union of Jewish Studies, 1990), 115–22, here 118.

[58] The text also refers three times to יד "hand" (30:22, 23, 25).

[59] Note that the verb in 30:21 is in perfect tense, while that in 30:22 is imperfect. As a result, Zimmerli thinks v. 21 "forms the kernel of the later expansion of the oracle as a whole" (*Ezekiel*, 2:138).

breaking of Pharaoh's arm, YHWH will strengthen the arms of the king of Babylon (30:24-25). The defeat of Pharaoh by YHWH through the strengthened arm of the Babylonian king leads to the dispersion of Egypt among the nations (30:23, 26).[60]

The imagery of Pharaoh's broken arm is especially startling when compared to the ancient Egyptian iconographic and Syro-Palestinian epigraphic materials. In the Egyptian culture, Pharaoh's bared arm is a symbol of strength. Keel presents a plethora of scenes, in which a Pharaoh holds the lock of his enemy in one hand, while the other hand is poised on high to bludgeon the man.[61] In order to describe the military strength of the Egyptian rulers, expressions related to the conquering arm (ḫpš) of Pharaoh, as observed by Hoffmeier, were in use ever since the Middle Kingdom (ca. 2055-1650 BCE), appearing more frequently in the New Kingdom (ca. 1550-1069 BCE), the Third Intermediate Period (1069-747 BCE), and even the Late Period (747-332 BCE).[62] Of particular interest is the Saitic Pharaoh, Apries (or Hophra, 589-570BCE), whose reign stands in chronological propinquity with the date formula stated in Ezek 30:20. His royal epithet "possessed of a muscular arm, strong armed man" (nb ḫpš) might have inspired the statement in Ezek 30:21. The references to both the "arm" and "sword" of Pharaoh in this verse of Ezekiel may be a type of wordplay on the epithet of Apries, since the Egyptian word ḫpš stands for both "sword" and "arm."[63] In addition to its representation of military strength, the arm of Pharaoh also lends legitimacy to royalty. Both

---

[60] The dispersion of the Egyptians here is expressed through the juxtaposition of the verbs זרה and הפיץ. Such a juxtaposition is characteristic of Ezekiel's descriptions of the deportations of both the Judahites and Egyptians. Cf. 5:2, 10, 12; 6:8; 11:16-17; 12:14-15; 20:23, 34, 41; 22:15, 19; 28:25; 29:12-13; 34:5, 6, 12, 13; 36:19, 24; 37:21; 39:27-28. For the possible influences of the Holiness Code and Deuteronomy on Ezekiel, see Gile, "Deuteronomy," 288-91.

[61] O. Keel, *Die Welt der altorientalischen Bildsymbolik und das Alte Testament: am Beispiel der Psalmen* (Zürich: Benziger, 1972), figs. 395, 397-402. Cf. J. K. Hoffmeier, "Some Egyptian Motifs Related to Warfare and Enemies and Their Old Testament Counterparts," in *Egyptological Miscellanies: A Tribute to Ronald James Williams*, ed. J. K. Hoffmeier and E. S. Meltzer, Ancient World 6 (Chicago: Ares Publishers, 1983), 57. See figs. 1, 4, 5 there. See also Block, *Ezekiel*, 2:175-176; Odell, *Ezekiel*, 386.

[62] J. K. Hoffmeier, "The Arm of God versus the Arm of Pharaoh in the Exodus Narratives," *Bib* 67 (1986): 378-87, esp. 380-85.

[63] K. S. Freedy and D. B. Redford, "The Dates of Ezekiel in Relation to Biblical, Babylonian and Egyptian Sources," *JAOS* 90 (1970): 462-85, here 482, followed by Hoffmeier, "Arm," 384, n. 72; idem, "Egypt as an Arm of Flesh: A Prophetic Response," in *Israel's Apostasy and Restoration*, ed. A. Gileadi (Grand Rapids: Baker, 1988), 91.

Görg and Hoffmeier point to the Amarna letters dated to the fourteenth century BCE to elucidate this scenario.[64] In his correspondence with the Egyptian royal court, Abduḫepa the ruler of Jerusalem gushes: "It was neither my father nor my mother, but the strong *arm* (*zu-ru-uḫ*) of the king that [p]laced me in the house of my father!"[65] Such an emphasis on the efficacy embodied by Pharaoh's arm motif in the ancient Near Eastern materials stands in especially sharp contrast with the restrained arm of Pharaoh in Ezek 30:20–26. It is reasonable to surmise that Ezek 30:20–26 could have been influenced by these ancient Near Eastern iconographic and epigraphic finds that straddle such a wide range of historical periods and geographical areas. Aware of the common mental image of Pharaoh's strong and victorious arm, Ezek 30:20–26 polemically reverses the image and transforms it into a broken and defeated arm.

The irony is not lost when Pharaoh becomes the enemy under the bludgeoning arm of YHWH. In Ezek 30:21–26, the first person singular verbs are pervasively used to highlight YHWH's action and initiative. Thus, YHWH breaks (שברתי, vv. 21, 22 [2x], 24) the arms of Pharaoh, makes the sword fall (הפלתי, v. 22) from Pharaoh's hand, and delivers his own sword (ונתתי את חרבי, v. 24; בתתי חרבי, v. 25) into the hand of the king of Babylon. In contrast to Pharaoh's broken arm, YHWH alone possesses the true strong arm by strengthening his instrument of judgment—the Babylonian king.[66] In fact, Ezek 20, a passage narrating the history of Israel since the exodus out of Egypt, applies the strong-arm motif to the "new exodus" context, where YHWH

---

[64] M. Görg, "'Der starke Arm Pharaos'—Beobachtungen zum Belegspektrum einer Metapher in Palästina und Ägypten" in *Hommages à François Daumas* (Montpellier: Université de Montpellier, 1986), 323–30, esp. 324–26; Hoffmeier, "Arm," 384–85. For the English translations of the relevant Amarna letters, see *ANET*, 487–88; *COS*, 3:287; W. L. Moran, *The Amarna Letters* (Baltimore: Johns Hopkins University Press, 1992), 326–32. For the Akkadian transliterations, see S. Izre'el, ed. "Amarna: The Amarna Texts," The Open Richly Annotated Cuneiform Corpus, http://oracc.museum.upenn.edu/contrib/amarna/corpus.

[65] In EA 288:13–15, Abduḫepa says: *ia-a-nu-mi* LU₂ AD.DA *a-ni ia-a-nu-mi* ⸢MI₂⸣ *um-mi-ia zu-ru-uḫ* LUGAL-*ri* KALAG.GA ⸢*ša*⸣-*ak*-⸢*na*⸣-[*an-ni*] *i-na* E₂ LU₂ ⸢AD⸣.DA.[A.NI]. See also EA 286:12; 287:27 and 288:14. According to *CAD* Z, 167, *zu-ru-uḫ* is only attested in the Amarna Tablets and no other Mesopotamian cuneiform text. This forms perhaps the strongest reason for seeing an Egyptian influence behind the Hebrew use of זרוע. See Hoffmeier, "Arm," 385. On the appropriate translation of the phrase *zu-ru-uḫ šarri dannu*, see Görg, "Arm," 324–25.

[66] The biblical passages generally employ the word "arm" to convey the symbolical meaning of strength and power. Cf. Job 35:9; Ps 44:4; 71:18; Prov 31:17. This is in addition to the literal sense as a human body part (e.g., Judg 15:14; Ezek 4:7; 13:30). Cf. *HALOT* 1:280.

brings the Israelites out of the exile only to punish them further in the wilderness.[67] As noted by Kreuzer, the two expressions—"mighty hand" (יד חזקה) and "outstretched arm" (זרוע נטויה)—are juxtaposed together and are supplemented by the expression of YHWH's outpouring wrath (חמה שפוכה) on his own people (20:33–34).[68] Thus, YHWH's arm connotes judgment for his people in Ezekiel. By contrast, the strong-arm motif appears in the pentateuchal traditions, especially in Exodus and Deuteronomy, to stress the salvific action of YHWH.[69] Narrating YHWH's mighty act in bringing the Israelites away from the oppression of Egypt, these pentateuchal texts use the strong-arm motif to express divine protection of the chosen people.[70] What unites the above biblical examples is the fact that the strong arm—in either the pentateuchal traditions or the book of Ezekiel—is consistently attributed to YHWH or YHWH's tool of judgment. The strong-arm motif conveys YHWH's power over his enemies, who can be either the foreigners or YHWH's own people. The biblical rhetoric is clear: YHWH is the only source of sovereignty and strength. As stated by Görg: "Die alttestamentliche Perspektive beläßt es nicht nur bei der Vorstellung vom Arm des Pharao, der zerbrochen wird. Ihr geht es darum, den Arm Jahwes als den alleinig „starken Arm "auszuweisen."[71] By attributing the breaking of Pharaoh's arm to YHWH, Ezek 30:20–26 aligns

---

[67] For the "new exodus" motif in Ezek 20, see S. Kreuzer, "Die Verwendung der Mächtigkeitsformel außerhalb des Deuteronomiums: Literarische und theologische Linien zu Jer, Ez, dtrG und P," *ZAW* 109 (1997): 369–84, here 380; A. Niccacci, "The Exodus Tradition in the Psalms, Isaiah and Ezekiel," *LASBF* 61 (2011): 9–35, here 29–34; Kohn, *New Heart*, 87.

[68] Kreuzer notes that חמה is typical of Ezekiel ("Verwendung," 380). Cf. 7:8; 9:8; 14:19; 20:8, 13, 21, 22; 30:15; 36:18. The noun appears elsewhere only in Jer 10:25 and Ps 79:6. In contrast to Jer 10:25 and Ps 79:6, Ezekiel nearly always applies the divine חמה to Israel or Jerusalem. See also P. Joyce, "Ezekiel 20:32–38: A Problem Text for the Theology of Ezekiel," in *Stimulation from Leiden: Collected Communications to the XVIIIth Congress of the International Organization for the Study of the Old Testament, Leiden 2004*, ed. H. M. Niemann et al. (Frankfurt am Main: Lang, 2006), 120; idem, *Ezekiel: A Commentary*, LHBOTS 482 (New York: T&T Clark, 2007), 152–53; Kohn, *New Heart*, 87.

[69] For the expression יד חזקה, see Exod 3:20; 6:1; 13:3, 9, 14, 16; 32:11; Deut 3:24; 4:34; 5:15; 6:21; 7:8, 19; 9:26; 11:2; 26:8; 34:12. For the expression זרוע נטויה, see Exod 6:6; Deut 4:34; 5:15; 7:19; 9:29; 11:2; 26:8. According to Kreuzer, the earliest attestations of the strong-arm motif, which he calls "die Mächtigkeitsformel" are to be found in Deut 26:8 and 5:15 ("Die Mächtigkeitsformel im Deuteronomium Gestaltung, Vorgeschichte und Entwicklung," *ZAW* 109 [1997]: 188–207).

[70] M. R. Akers surveys the presentation of the soteriological arm of YHWH in Ps 44:1–3; 77:11–20; 98; Isa 40–55; 51:4–8; 52:10; 53:1; 59; 63:4–5, 7–14 ("The Soteriological Development of the 'Arm of the Lord' Motif," *Journal for the Evangelical Study of the Old Testament* 2 [2014]: 29–48, here 33–48).

[71] Cf. Görg, "Arm," 329.

with the other biblical traditions and persuasively paints a more exalted and powerful status of YHWH in contrast to his adversary, Pharaoh.

1.3. THE CHTHONIC CEDAR

Two months after the prophecy issued in Ezek 30:20–26, and just a month before the fall of Jerusalem, "in the eleventh year, in the third month, on the first day of the month," the animosity between Pharaoh and YHWH boils up again (31:1).[72] This time Pharaoh the king of Egypt is dehumanized as a monstrously tall cedar, which was once a symbolism of the mighty kingdom of Assyria (v. 3).[73] With its top rising high up into the heavens, and with its roots sinking deep into the primordial source of water, the cedar provides shelter for all the birds, beasts, and nations on earth (vv. 3b–9). Introduced by the messenger formula (כה אמר אדני יהוה), an announcement of judgment is subsequently issued upon the cedar that has become proud and haughty (v. 10). The cedar will be given into the hands of the ruthless nations, being trampled and broken, such that it will become only a ruin for the birds and beasts to dwell upon (vv. 11–14). Set off by another messenger formula, YHWH dramatically announces the death of the tall cedar, predicting its plunge into Sheol or the

---

[72] Note that P967 reads the year in 30:20 and 31:1 as the "tenth year." Cf. Zimmerli, *Ezekiel*, 2:141; Gowan, *Man*, 95; Boadt, *Ezekiel's Oracles*, 94; van Rooy, "Ezekiel's Prophecies," 118; E. Haag, "Ez 31 und die alttestamentliche Paradiesvorstellung," in *Wort, Lied und Gottespruch: Beiträge zu Psalmen und Propheten: Festschrift für Joseph Ziegler*, ed. J. Schreiner (Würzburg: Echter Verlag, 1972), 171–78, here 171.

[73] Some prefer to read תאשור "cypress" in v. 3 instead of the MT's reference to אשור "Assyria" (Eichrodt, *Ezekiel*, 422; Boadt, *Ezekiel's Oracles*, 96; Zimmerli, *Ezekiel*, 2:141–42). These commentators claim that an initial ת on אשור, which has supposedly been dropped by pseudo-haplography after the final ה of the preceding word, must be restored. Such a textual restoration should yield תאשור "cypress," a suitable parallel to ארז "cedar" in the following phrase. Cf. Ezek 27:6. However, others correctly argue that such an emendation is not necessary (e.g., Odell, *Ezekiel*, 392, Stordalen, *Echoes*, 380, n. 9, 385). First, the other versions unanimously translate the Hebrew word as Assyria. Second, the generally personal use of מי invites comparison with a human, not a tree (cf. Greenberg, *Ezekiel*, 2:646–47). Third, the context of chapter 31 demands an imperial power such as Assyria with which Egypt could be compared. That Assyria is a suitable symbol of this imperial greatness is confirmed in the next oracle (32:22–32), which places Assyria at the head of the list of mighty nations descending into Sheol (cf. Block, *Ezekiel*, 2:184–85). Fourth, the parallel between Assyria and Egypt is also attested in Isa 19:23 and Zech 10:11. Fifth, historical evidence also records the alliance between Egypt and Assyria in resistance to the rising dominance of Babylon in the Levant during the second half of the seventh century (cf. Miller and Hayes, *History*, 446, 452). These five points account for the presence of Assyria in an Egypt oracle.

netherworld along with all the other trees of Eden, the uncircumcised, and those slain by the sword (vv. 15–18; cf. 32:17–32).[74]

According to Zimmerli, the poetic description of the world tree in vv. 3–8(9) "is free of any belittling tendency."[75] Likewise, Gowan claims that vv. 2–9 "offer no basis for saying about sin or judgment, the poem is wholly positive in tone."[76] For some, the negative judgment of the tree as hubristic and thus deserving the divine judgment in vv. 10–14 has only functioned as a secondary but not so successful connection between the positive allegory in vv. 2–9 and the harrowing journey of the tree to the underworld in vv. 15–18.[77] On stylistic grounds, the prosaic vv. 10–14 and vv. 15–18 describing the fall of the cosmic tree likely demonstrate their secondary nature. Still, all these commentators neglect the potentially subversive elements already lurking behind the poetic allegory. The comparison of Pharaoh and his entourage to an abnormally tall cedar drawing its nourishment from the deep has already cast the cedar in an ambiguous light from the very beginning of the oracle, such that the ensuing judgment leashed out later in vv. 10–14 and vv. 15–18 is already foreseeable in the poetic allegory in vv. 1–9.

Viewed in the ancient Near Eastern context, the portrayal of Pharaoh as a cedar in Ezek 31 potentially poses a challenge to YHWH's sole supremacy and divinity, and thus ultimately justifies YHWH's wrath to cut it down. Remarkable is the Egyptian association of a deceased Pharaoh with divinity via the link between a tree and Osiris, the god of the Netherworld. On the one hand, the deceased Pharaoh is regarded as a form of Osiris.[78] In the *Pyramid*

---

[74] Demarcated by the messenger formulas, and divided into three rough sections (vv. 2b–9, 10–14, 15–18), the literary structure of Ezek 31 is widely recognised among scholars. Cf. Block, *Ezekiel*, 2:178; Stordalen, *Echoes*, 384; Zimmerli, *Ezekiel*, 2:145; Gowan, *Man*, 94–95; Wevers, *Ezekiel*, 234; Boadt, *Ezekiel's Oracles*, 92–93.

[75] Zimmerli, *Ezekiel*, 2:147. Due to the Aramaisms in v. 5 and the sudden switch to the first person speech of YHWH in v. 9, Zimmerli considers the two verses to be secondary expansions within the poetic description of the world tree (145–146).

[76] Gowan, *Man*, 94. Cf. Allen, *Ezekiel 20–48*, 125.

[77] Zimmerli states: "It can be noticed in vv 10–14 that what is said about the fall has been added secondarily to the already completed image of the world tree, without there having been complete success in the attempt really organically to connect the tradition of the world tree with that of the journey of the lofty one to the underworld" (*Ezekiel*, 2:148). In his detailed text-critical analysis, Schweizer considers the reference to the pride and fall of the cedar in 31:7, 10–13 as a secondary expansion of the *Grundtext* (31:3–4, 6; "Der Sturz des Weltenbaumes [Ez 31]—Literarkritisch Betrachtet," *TQ* 165 [1985]: 197–213, here 210–11). Cf. F. Stolz, "Die Bäume des Gottesgartens auf dem Libanon," *ZAW* 84 (1972): 141–56, here 142.

[78] After the democratization of the afterlife in the Middle Kingdom, it is also possible for any decedent to be resurrected as Osiris. See A. El-Shahawy, *The Funerary*

*Texts* from the Old Kingdom (ca. 2686–2681 BCE), Osiris emerges as the "Lord of Dat (the Underworld),"[79] and dead Pharaohs are urged to sit "on the throne of Osiris" and thus rule over the realm of the dead.[80] During the New Kingdom period (ca. 1550–1069 BCE), the images of Osiris intertwined with dead Pharaohs, such that Osiris' insignia including the crook and frail were found inside the royal coffins, and the figures of the two sisters of Osiris—Isis and Nephthys—were placed at both ends of the sarcophagi of Pharaohs.[81] On the other hand, the death and resurrection of Osiris is also inextricably linked to the growth cycle of vegetation. In the Egyptian iconography, the face of Osiris is sometimes painted green, which possibly symbolizes vegetation and fertility.[82] In Budge's classic work entitled *The Gods of the Egyptians* comes a description of an iconography from the temple of Dendera, which depicts a Persea tree standing at the head of the mummied Osiris lying on his bier.[83] In Plutarch's *De Iside et Osiride* dated to the middle of the first century CE, Osiris' coffin has reached the shore of Byblos and a large tree subsequently grows around the coffin.[84] From this, Budge deduces that Osiris' "connection with the Persea-tree, and the legend which associates him with the Erica-tree, prove that at one time he was a tree-spirit, and that he absorbed the attributes of many tree-spirits both in the north and south of Egypt."[85]

---

*Art of Ancient Egypt: A Bridge to the Realm of the Hereafter* (Cairo: Farid Atiya Press, 2005), 73.

[79] J. G. Griffiths, *The Origins of Osiris and His Cult* (Leiden: Brill, 1980), 40. Cf. E. A. W. Budge, *The Gods of the Egyptians or Studies in Egyptian Mythology*, 2 vols. (London: Methuen & Company, 1904; repr., New York: Dover Publications, Inc., 1969), 2:115.

[80] Griffiths, *Origins*, 3. Cf. Budge, *Gods*, 2:130, who states: "From the Pyramid Texts we learn that the dead kings were already identified with Osiris."

[81] R. H. Wilkinson, *Die Welt der Götter im alten Ägypten: Glaube, Macht, Mythologie*, trans. T. Bertram (Darmstadt: Wissenschaftliche Buchgesellschaft, 2003), 63. For the pictures of the reliefs depicting the death and resurrection of Osiris, see Budge, *Gods*, 131–38.

[82] Wilkinson, *Götter*, 120. The same page shows the green-faced Osiris in the picture dated from the Nineteenth Dynasty (New Kingdom) found inside the grave of Nefertari. Cf. J. G. Griffiths, "Osiris," *LÄ* 4:623–33, here 628.

[83] Budge, *Gods*, 136, fig. 18.

[84] See Plutarch, *Isis and Osiris*, §15 (Babbitt, LCL). An English translation is also available in Budge, *Gods*, 189. While Babbitt's translation shows that the coffin landed "in the midst of a clump of heather," Budge considers that the coffin was washed up to the shore "in the branches of a bush of Tamarisk."

[85] Even though the narration of Plutarch does not specify which type of tree has grown around the coffin of Osiris, Budge relates the tree in Plutarch's story with the Erica-tree (*Osiris and the Egyptian Resurrection*, 2 vols. [London: Putnam's Sons, 1911], 1:19). Budge's opinion is also cited in C. Hays, "'There is Hope for a Tree:'

Osiris's association with trees is further supported by Hays. Helpfully summarizing Koemoth's *Osiris et les arbres*, Hays observes that the iconographic materials dated from the Ramesside era (1292–1069 BCE) onward often present the decedent in the form of Osiris enveloped within a tree, which symbolizes rebirth in the afterlife.[86] In another iconographic tradition, the Osirian decedent is buried underneath a tree-topped mound, which is "to be interpreted primarily as a place of rebirth for the deceased god buried in a crypt laid out beneath the mound."[87] Evident in the Osirian tradition is thus the association of the tree with the god of the netherworld, who is in turn linked to the death and resurrection of Pharaoh.

The Egyptian traditions could have exerted influences in the depiction of the tall cedar in Ezek 31. Not only does Plutarch's narration of the myth of Osiris mention the coffin of Osiris landed on the Levantine seacoast, "near the land of Byblos,"[88] but *djed*-pillar amulets, dated from the Late Bronze Age to the Hellenistic period and related to the Osirian afterlife religion, have also been found in the Levant.[89] Moreover, Hays points to the plethora of onomastic data supporting widespread worship of both Osiris and Isis in the Levant during the Iron Age and earlier.[90] It is thus possible for the Levantine seacoast to possess long-standing knowledge of the Egyptian myth of Osiris. All in all, the geographical and temporal propinquity could have created ideal conditions for the editors or authors of Ezek 31 to absorb, integrate, and reconfigure the symbol of the cosmic tree, so that the tall cedar represents the divine kingship of Pharaoh in the afterlife.

This possible conflation of omnifarious traditions in Ezek 31 thus builds up an imagery of a seditious cedar tree that dares to defy the political supremacy and cosmic control of YHWH.[91] As in the Mesopotamian imperial ideology, the monstrously tall cedar in chapter 31 exerts its political power to provide protection for "all great nations" (כל גוים רבים, v. 6).[92] Eager to assert his

---

Job's Hope for the Afterlife in the Light of Egyptian Tree Imagery," *CBQ* 77 (2015): 42–68, here 48.

[86] Hays, "Hope," 48–50.

[87] Ibid., 51, cites and translates it from P. Koemoth, *Osiris et les arbre: Contribution à l'étude des arbres sacrés de l'Égypte ancienne*, Aegyptiaca Leodiensia 3 (Liège: Centre Informatique de Philosophie et Lettres, 1994), 292–93.

[88] Plutarch, *Isis and Osiris*, §15. Cf. Hays, "Hope," 54.

[89] Ibid., 55.

[90] Ibid., 55–56.

[91] Stordalen comments that "this is a conflict between human and divine greatness, a story of human glory and due modesty" (*Echoes*, 388).

[92] *Contra* Boadt, *Ezekiel's Oracles*, 110, it is unclear if the expression גוים רבים necessarily denotes nations who are the enemy of God's people. Elsewhere in Ezekiel, the expression can refer to not only the pagan nations allied against Israel (38:23; 39:27), but also YHWH's tool of judgment against Tyre (26:3).

sovereignty over and above the imperial power of the tall cedar, YHWH proclaims that he himself has ordained the beauty of the cosmic cedar from the very beginning: "I made it beautiful with the multitude of its branches" (v. 9).[93] Ultimately, YHWH will summon "a chief of the nations" (איל גוים, v. 11) and "the ruthless of the nations" (עריצי גוים, v. 12) to bring down the mighty cedar tree.[94] Like Pharaoh who is able to transverse the boundaries of life and death in the Egyptian religion, the tree of Ezek 31 draws its source of life from "the deep" (תהום) and "many waters" (מים רבים; vv. 4–5, 7).[95] In the Hebrew Bible, the great deep and abundant waters are often mythological symbols of disorder and chaos,[96] which can be associated with the realm of death and cessation of life. In Gen 1, creation is marked by the absence of watery chaos (vv. 2, 6–7).[97] By contrast, the flood narrative reverses the process of creation, such that the divine annihilation of corrupted humanity is brought about through the waters gushing from the "great deep" (תהום רבה) and pouring from the "windows of heaven" (ארבי השמים; cf. Gen 6–8).[98] Viewed in this line of

---

[93] The sentence is missing in the LXX. The sudden switch to the first person address of YHWH also adds to the suspicion that this might be a later insertion into the poetic allegory. Cf. Zimmerli, *Ezekiel*, 2:143; Eichrodt, *Ezekiel*, 424; Wevers, *Ezekiel*, 237.

[94] איל means either "ram" or "leader." Cf. Ezek 17:13; 32:21; 39:18. The expression עריצי גוים appears in 7:21; 11:9; 28:7, 10; 30:11. Especially in 28:7 and 30:11–12, it is associated with זרים "the foreigners."

[95] Within the book of Ezekiel, and besides chapter 31, תהום appears only one more time in 26:19, where it is also juxtaposed with המים הרבים. By contrast, the same prophetic book attests to ten occurrences of מים רבים. Cf. Ezek 1:24; 17:5, 8; 19:10; 27:26; 31:5, 7, 15; 32:13; 43:2.

[96] E.g., the struggle against the insurgent waters (מים רבים) in Hab 3:13–15 is associated with the crushing of the head of the wicked. In Ezek 26:19, the great deep (תהום) and the abundant waters (מים רבים) are used in parallel with each other to represent the destructive forces engulfing Tyre. Cf. Isa 17:12–14; 51:9–10; Ps 77:17–18 [Eng. 77:16–17]; Ps 144:5–8. For further explications about the מים רבים as representation of the cosmic intransigent forces, see H. G. May, "Some Cosmic Connotations of *Mayim Rabbim*, 'Many Waters,'" *JBL* 74 (1955): 9–21; E.-J. Waschke, "תהום," *TDOT* 15:574–81, esp. 578–81.

[97] For the relationship between the water and netherworld/cessation of life in the Hebrew Bible, see D. Rudman, "The Use of Water Imagery in Descriptions of Sheol," *ZAW* 113 (2001): 240–44, here 243; P. S. Johnston, *Shades of Sheol: Death and Afterlife in the Old Testament* (Downers Grove: Intervarsity Press, 2002), 114–23; L. Lee, "Fiery Sheol in the Dead Sea Scrolls," *RevQ* 27/106 (2015): 249–70.

[98] B. M. Levinson, "A Post-Priestly Harmonization in the Flood Narrative," in *The Post-Priestly Pentateuch: New Perspectives on its Redactional Development and Theological Profiles*, ed. F. Giuntoli and K. Schmid (Tübingen: Mohr Siebeck, 2015), 113–23, here 117–18. To support this argument, Levinson also lists the following

biblical tradition, the cedar tree in Ezek 31 can be seen as a cosmic intransigent force, since it draws on the chaotic forces representing death from below to rejuvenate itself on earth.[99] In this manner, it brings to mind the aforementioned Egyptian tradition, where Pharaoh divinized as Osiris awaits his rejuvenation in the afterlife, which is symbolized via the tree on or around his coffin. Perhaps to combat this dismantled boundaries between life and death envisioned in the poetic allegory of Ezekiel, YHWH vows to cover "the deep" (תהום), withhold "the rivers" (נהרותיה),[100] and shut up "many waters" (מים רבים), so that the Pharaonic cedar will wither away and only be confined in "Sheol" (שאולה, v. 15). Recognizing the ancient Near Eastern context thus restores the subversive overtones to the Ezekialian image of the tree that could otherwise be perceived as merely positive. Throughout the Egypt oracles, Pharaoh is visualized not only as a chaos monster in opposition to YHWH's sovereignty, a broken arm defeated by YHWH's power, but also a chthonic cedar daring to transgress YHWH's boundaries of life and death. In a nutshell, Egypt represented by Pharaoh is YHWH's fiend *par excellence*.

## 2. The Allusions to Judah as Egypt's Ally

Apart from mentioning Pharaoh and Egypt, the oracles in Ezek 29–32 are further dotted with multiple references to Egypt's entourage. Alongside the Pharaonic monster are the other fish in the Nile (29:4). Just like Egypt, "Cush, Put, Lud, and all the mixed multitude, Libya and the people of the covenant land" will fall by the sword (30:5). The divine castigation is often addressed not only to Pharaoh, but also to "his multitude" (31:2, 18; 32:18, 20, 31, 32) and "his helpers" (32:21). Most startlingly, Judah seems to be present in the Egypt

---

works: H. Gunkel, *Genesis: Übersezt und erklärt*, 3rd ed., HKAT (Göttingen: Vandenhoeck & Ruprecht, 1917; reprinted, with indices by P. Schorlemmer, as 6th ed., 1964), 77, 144; U. Cassuto, *A Commentary on the Book of Genesis*, trans. I. Abrahams, 2 vols. (Jerusalem: Magnes, 1961–1964), 2:97; N. M. Sarna, *Understanding Genesis*, Heritage of Biblical Israel 1 (New York: Schocken, 1970), 55; M. Fishbane, *Text and Texture* (New York: Schocken, 1979), 33–34.

[99] Referring to the blessings mentioned in Gen 49:25 and Deut 33:13, Zimmerli characterizes the תהום in Ezek 31 more positively as a "tamed deep." Nevertheless, he also concedes that "the occurrence of תהום contains a reference to a power which surpasses the normal, everyday, earthly measure and still hints at the mythical power which once dared to enter into battle with the creator himself" (*Ezekiel*, 2:149). Cf. Waschke, *TDOT* 15:579–80.

[100] The third feminine singular possessive suffix attached to נהרות can refer to either the preceding שאול or תהום, since the latter two can be of feminine gender (cf. Isa 14:9; 28:10 for שאול; Gen 49:25; Ps 36:7 for תהום).

CHAPTER FOUR 145

oracles. Almost all major scholars of Ezekiel, including Zimmerli and Greenberg, have noticed hints of the Judahites' presence among the allies of Egypt in Ezek 30:5, in addition to two explicit references to "the house of Israel" in 29:6, 16.[101] Still, few have connected these references to the multiple appearances of the entourage in the rest of the Egypt oracles. Below, I propose to take into consideration the plurality of addressees and the multiple lexical connections built into the literary context of Ezek 29–32, and suggest that these chapters in Ezekiel contain explicit and not-so-explicit characterizations of Judah as among Egypt's closest allies.

2.1. THE CRUSHED REED TO THE HOUSE OF ISRAEL

One of the most explicit references to the "house of Israel" as Egypt's ally is found in Ezek 29:6b–9a.[102] Sandwiched between vv. 3–6a and vv. 9b–16, this proof-saying in vv. 6b–9a characterizes Egypt as a frail "staff of reed to the house of Israel." The proof-saying begins with a reason for judgment led by the conjunction "because" (יען), continues with a statement of judgment led by the conjunction "therefore" (לכן), and ends with a recognition formula (וידעו כי אני יהוה, v. 9a).[103]

On the one hand, the proof-saying represents a caesura from the surrounding literary context. The vulnerable and fragile reed depicted in vv. 6b–7 breaks the sustained focus on the powerful and hubristic Nile monster mentioned in the surrounding two verses (vv. 3, 9).[104] On the other hand, the proof-saying functions as a connecting point between the two sections in the surrounding literary context. The first part of the proof-saying with its second person masculine singular suffix has Pharaoh in view,[105] whereas the second

---

[101] See n. 4.

[102] Another reference to the "house of Israel" in Ezekiel's Egypt oracles is found in 29:16.

[103] Here I use the recognition formulas in vv. 6a, 9a, 16b as the endings and demarcation points for the three oracle units in 29:1–16. The opening of each oracle unit is different. The first begins with a messenger formula in v. 3. The second and the third begin with a judgment formula (יען...לכן) at vv. 6b, 9b. So also Vogels, "Restauration," 474; Kessler, Ägyptenbilder, 69; Premstaller, Fremvölkersprüche, 140–42; Zimmerli, Ezekiel, 2:106; Allen, Ezekiel, 2:103. Resorting to the Masoretic divisions, which place the messenger formula at the beginning of each oracle unit, H. F. van Rooy structures Ezek 29:1–16 differently into vv. 3–7, 8–12, 13–16 ("Parallelism, Metre and Rhetoric in Ezekiel 29:1–6," Semitics 8 [1982]: 90–105).

[104] Cf. אשר אמר לי יארי ואני עשיתני (v. 3) and יען אמר יאר לי ואני עשיתי (v. 9). See also the comment on vv. 6b–7 by Fechter, Bewältigung, 213: "Auch die Thematik ist neu, das jetzt verwendete Bild ein völlig anderes als das vorherige."

[105] Cf. vv. 6b–7. The MT reads היותם in v. 6b. The third masculine plural suffix refer to the "inhabitants of Egypt" mentioned in the preceding recognition formula (v.

part of the proof-saying with its second person feminine singular suffix has the whole land of Egypt in view.[106] In this way, the divine judgment on Pharaoh, which figures prominently in the first section of chapter 29 (cf. vv. 4–5), is brought in line with the divine depredation of the land of Egypt, which forms the focus in the third section of chapter 29 (cf. vv. 10–12).[107] Given the aforementioned change of imagery and conflation of literary styles, the proof-saying in vv. 6b–9a is likely a later insertion into vv. 3–6a and vv. 9b–12.[108] The aim of such an insertion is to qualify the power of Egypt by toning down the terrifying image of Pharaoh. Instead of being a powerful and mighty תנין, which claims to have made the Nile (vv. 3, 9b), Pharaoh in Ezek 29:6b–9a becomes merely a puny, fragile, and vulnerable reed to the "house of Israel."

This reed imagery clearly alludes to the political alliance between Egypt and Judah.[109] It also appears in Isa 36:6 (= 2 Kgs 18:21) in reference to the futility of Judah's hope in seeking political assistance from Egypt.[110] The verbal root שען often conveys a sense of politico-military reliance in the book of Isaiah.[111] In Isa 36:6, the root appears in the form of the expression משענת קנה. Apart from Isa 36 and the parallel passage in 2 Kgs 18, the expression only appears elsewhere in Ezek 29:6b.[112] In all of these passages, the extremely rare expression משענת קנה is combined with the verbal root רצץ "to break, to crush" and with a similar phrase conveying the act of leaning on.[113] A unique

---

6a). However, the LXX is more consistent with the following verse by translating היותם as the second person singular "you have become" (ἐγενήθης).

[106] Cf. vv. 8–9.

[107] Cf. Fechter, *Bewältigung*, 219. Note Fechter's argument that the Nile fish mentioned in v. 4 (ואת כל דגת יאריך) and v. 5 (ואת כל דגת יאריך) are later additions. In other words, he argues cogently that the first section of chapter 29 is an oracle unit that was originally directed at the Pharaoh and has only been expanded later to include the inhabitants of Egypt as the target of the divine castigation (221–22, 243–44).

[108] For a more detailed discussion of the literary dependence of 29:6b–9a on the elements present in 29:1–6a, 9b–12, see Fechter, *Bewältigung*, 213–23, 245–48.

[109] The Hebrew Bible often speaks of "the reed" (קנה) in connection with Egypt. E.g., in Job 40:15–24, the plant provides cover for the hippopotamus, which was once widespread along the Nile region. In Gen 41:5, 22 (E/JE), a single קנה appears in the dream of the Pharaoh (Noted by Lamberty-Zielinski, "קנה," *TDOT* 12:67). Cf. Isa 19:6; but see also 1 Kgs 14:15; Isa 35:7; Ps 68:31 [Eng. 68:30]).

[110] Noted also by Fuhs, *Ezechiel*, 2:160; Pohlmann, *Hesekiel*, 2:407; Premstaller, *Fremdvölkersprüche*, 146; Fechter, *Bewältigung*, 217, 222, 245–46; Zimmerli, *Ezekiel*, 2:112.

[111] Isa 10:20; 30:12; 31:1; cf. 2 Chr 16:7–8. Cf. Fechter, *Bewältigung*, 245.

[112] For the imagery of broken reed in other ancient Near Eastern literature, see Boadt, *Ezekiel's Oracles*, 38.

[113] Cf. הקנה הרצוץ "The bruised reed" in Isa 42:3, which describes YHWH's servant (*HALOT*, 2:1113).

set of linguistic connections can then be established between the two passages in Isaiah/2 Kings and Ezekiel.

Both passages display a similarly negative perception of the Egyptian help,[114] but the disastrous consequence of the alliance between Judah and Egypt is highlighted even more in Ezekiel. In the context of Sennacherib's campaign in Isa 36:6 (= 2 Kgs 18:21), Egypt is disparaged by the Assyrian Rabshakeh as a staff of reed that has already been broken (הרצוץ).[115] Even without Judah's seeking help from Egypt, the doom of Egypt has already been sealed. This thus renders not only Judah's, but also any man (איש)'s reliance on Egypt for its deliverance from the Assyrian onslaught absurd. By contrast, Ezek 29:6b–7 suggests that the reed will become broken (תרוץ) only when the house of Israel extends its hand to lean on the reed ("when they grasp you with the hand" and "when they lean on you").[116] Thus the significance of a political alliance between Judah and Egypt is stressed in this excerpt of Ezekiel. It is only when Judah relies on Egypt to withstand the Babylonian dominion that Egypt, as a staff of reed, will be crushed.[117]

In a nutshell, a comparison with the imagery of a frail reed in Isa 36:6 highlights the active role of Judah in Ezek 29:6b–7 in seeking the political alliance from Egypt, which will nevertheless fail to deliver national survival for the kingdom of Judah.

2.2. THE PEOPLE OF THE COVENANT LAND

After the explicit references to "the house of Israel" (בית ישראל, 29:6, 16) that has placed its confidence in Egypt, the next chapter of Ezekiel contains an intriguing reference to the "people of the covenant land" (בני ארץ הברית). In 30:5, "the people of the covenant land" are listed alongside Cush,[118] Put, Lud,

---

[114] The futility of the Egyptian help is also found in passages such as Hos 12:2; 2 Kgs 17:4; Isa 30:1–5; 31:1, 3; Jer 37:6–8.

[115] On the relation of Rabshakeh's speech to the wider biblical and ancient cultural milieus, see E. Ben Zvi, "Who Wrote the Speech of Rabshakeh and When," *JBL* 109 (1990): 79–92; P. Höffken, "Die Rede des Rabsake vor Jerusalem (2 Kön. xviii/Jes. xxxvi) im Kontext anderer Kapitulationsforderungen," *VT* 58 (2008): 44–55.

[116] The *Kethib* of the MT Ezek 29:7 attests to the form בכפך, while the *Qere* reads בכף. Different from the MT, The LXX has the 3mp pronominal suffix to the noun, i.e., χειρὶ αὐτῶν = בכפם. Cf. Zimmerli, *Ezekiel*, 2:112.

[117] The victory of the Babylonian onslaught is evident in the later oracle in 29:17–21, in which the Babylonian king is explicitly portrayed as YHWH's agent of judgment who deserves to be rewarded.

[118] The LXX reads here Πέρσαι, probably under the influence of 27:10 (noted by Block, *Ezekiel*, 2:157, n. 12). Cf. 29:10; 38:5. On Cush in the book of Ezekiel, see R. S. Sadler, *Can A Cushite Change His Skin? An Examination of Race, Ethnicity and Othering in the Hebrew Bible*, LHBOTS 425 (London: Bloomsbury, 2005), 99–107.

Kub,[119] and the "mixed rabble" (הערב). They are those who will fall with Egypt under the sword at "a time of *doom* for the nations" (עת גוים; cf. v. 3).[120] As pointed out by Zimmerli, it is rather peculiar that "the people of the covenant land" are particularly singled out from the other listed groups including the undifferentiated and generally termed "mixed rabble" (הערב).[121] Greenberg is quick to identify "the people of the covenant land" as "the coded epithet for Judah."[122] In what follows, we will justify the positions of Zimmerli and Greenberg with further evidence that suggests the "people of the covenant land" are indeed another allusion to the Judahites who serve as the allies of Egypt.

This proposition is made plausible in light of the usage of the term ברית. Within the book of Ezekiel, the term appears rather infrequently, but always at key junctures describing Judah's covenant with other nations and YHWH's covenant with the restored Israel.[123] ברית can connote either a politico-military treaty between the nations or a theological covenant with the divine. The term appears prominently in Ezek 17, referring to the treaty Zedekiah king of Judah has broken with Babylon in favor of Saite Egypt (vv. 13, 15, 16).[124] This breach of political treaty is further deemed as a betrayal of YHWH's covenant (v. 19). The theological meaning of ברית is reflected elsewhere in the book of Ezekiel, where the restored covenant inaugurated between YHWH and his people—Israel—is in view.[125] One constant factor unifying all these other passages of Ezekiel in which ברית appears is that Judah or the restored Israel are always involved as a covenantal partner. In the case of Ezek 30, a later expansion in vv. 6–8 clearly connects the "sons of the covenant land," along with the other nations, with "those who support Egypt"

---

[119] MT כוב "Kub" is not known. It may be a corruption for לוב "Libya." This is a reasonable deduction in light of the fact that the LXX ends the list with Λίβυες "Libyans," although elsewhere in Ezek 27:10; 38:5; Jer 46:9 (= LXX 26:9) the Greek term stands for פוט "Put." Cf. Zimmerli, *Ezekiel*, 2:123; Block, *Ezekiel*, 2:159.

[120] Eichrodt views the list of nations in v. 5 as merely a marginal gloss for the reference to כוש in v. 4 (*Ezekiel*, 414). However, the list of names in v. 5, to my mind, forms a crucial exposition of the "nations" (גוים) mentioned in v. 3.

[121] Zimmerli, *Ezekiel*, 2:130.

[122] Greenberg, *Ezekiel*, 2:622. So also Pohlmann, *Hesekiel*, 2:414; Fuhs, *Ezechiel*, 2:165; Block, *Ezekiel*, 2:160; Premstaller, *Fremdvölkersprüche*, 164.

[123] Cf. Ezek 17:13, 15, 16, 19; 16:59, 60, 62; 20:37; 34:25; 37:26 (2x); 44:7.

[124] The vassal treaty between Judah and Babylon is also evident in Ezek 21:28–34 [Eng. 21:23–29]; 29:14–16. Interestingly, the Greek version differs from the MT at Ezek 17:16 by characterizing the oath not as the political treaty with the Babylonian king, but as the covenant with YHWH. Cf. M. Tsevat, "The Neo-Assyrian and Neo-Babylonian Vassal Oaths and the Prophet Ezekiel," *JBL* 78 (1959): 199–204.

[125] Cf. Ezek 16:59, 60, 62; 20:37; 34:25; 37:26 (2x); 44:7.

CHAPTER FOUR                                                                149

(סמכי מצרים, v. 6) and "her [Egypt's] helpers" (עזריה, v. 8).[126] Several epigraphic materials provide the clues that the nations listed alongside Egypt were the mercenary troops of Egypt. According to Rassam Cylinder II:95–96, 111–115, Gyges of Lydia (לוד) was one ally of the Egyptian ruler—Psammetichus I—in the seventh century against the Assyrians.[127] When Nebuchadnezzar marched to Egypt, Put seems to have participated in the battle against Nebuchadnezzar.[128] Even though some modern translations such as *NASB* read with the Syriac version and render הערב as the Arabs,[129] the presence of the definite article indicates הערב is a common noun, referring to the non-native mercenary troops of Egypt.[130] Most of these nations mentioned in Ezek 30:5 are thus military allies of Egypt. On this basis, "the people of the covenant land" should probably be understood as related to Egypt in friendly politico-military terms.

The political alliance between Judah and Egypt is further justified by the subsequent list of names of Egyptian cities mentioned in 30:13–19. These names possibly allude to the presence of the Judahites who sought political refuge in Egypt during the rise of the Babylonian power.[131] The names of the Egyptian cities have caused considerable difficulties in interpretation, given several irregular repetitions with no geographical order in the enumeration of the cities.[132] Via a comparison with Mic 1:10–15, Blenkinsopp claims that

---

[126] For the secondary nature of vv. 6–8 in chapter 30, see Zimmerli, *Ezekiel*, 2:127.

[127] For an English translation of the relevant parts of the Rassam Cylinder, see D. D. Luckenbill, *Ancient Records of Assyria and Babylonia*, 2 vols. (Chicago: University of Chicago Press, 1926), 2:297–98, §§784–85, noted by Zimmerli, *Ezekiel*, 2:126; Block, *Ezekiel*, 2:159; Fuhs, *Ezechiel*, 2:165; Freedy and Redford, "Dates," 476–77.

[128] Zimmerli, *Ezekiel*, 2:104–5, 129.

[129] Cf. Ezek 27:21 and elsewhere.

[130] Cf. the mercenary troops of Egypt in Jer 25:20 and those of Babylon in Jer 50:37. For similar explications of this reference to הערב, see Zimmerli, *Ezekiel*, 2:129–130; Allen, *Ezekiel*, 2:113; Block, *Ezekiel*, 2:159; Greenberg, *Ezekiel*, 2:621; Wevers, *Ezekiel*, 228; Premstaller, *Fremdvölkersprüche*, 164.

[131] Jer 24:8 and 43–44 record fairly strong Jewish communities in Egypt since the first deportation in 587 BCE. Deut 17:16 implies that there were Israelite mercenaries in Egypt. A mercenary colony of Israelites is also known at Elephantine, an island on the Nile on Aswan during the sixth century BCE (*ANET*, 491–92). *Letter of Aristeas* 13 speaks of Psammetichus I having dispatched the Jewish troops to fight against the king of the Ethiopians. Possibly the Jews also participated in the campaign of Psammetichus II against Nubia (591 BCE). Cf. Pohlmann, *Hesekiel*, 2:414, n. 67; Zimmerli, *Ezekiel*, 2:130.

[132] See the perplexity voiced in Fohrer, *Ezechiel*, 172: "Das Wort macht zunächst einen verwirrenden Eindruck, da die angegebenen Namen unregelmäßig nach Unter- und Oberägypten führen." So also Zimmerli, *Ezekiel*, 2:131; Blenkinsopp, *Ezekiel*, 135; Greenberg, *Ezekiel*, 2:628. As a result, scholars often attribute vv. 13–19 with its

the list in Ezek 30:13–19 serves to convey the all-encompassing and ineluctable catastrophe coming upon Egypt.[133] The lists in Micah and Ezekiel may be comparable at a structural or a functional level, but the names in the former list remain lexically incomparable to those Egyptian cities mentioned in the latter text. A more fruitful solution, however, is offered by Zimmerli and Eichrodt, who compare the list in Ezek 30:13–19 with the Egyptian city names appearing in Jer 43–44.[134]

Through this comparison, several distinctive lexical correspondences are revealed. Jer 44:1 alone contains three of the eight different Egyptian city names enumerated in Ezek 30:13–19.[135] These are Pathros, Tahpanhes, and Memphis. Only in Jeremiah and Ezekiel do the three names appear together as a whole.[136] Moreover, both prophetic books give Tahpanhes a special significance. In Jer 43:7, 8–9, Tahpanhes is identified as the politically important place where "the house of Pharaoh" was located, and where the pro-Egyptian factions extended.[137] This is also the city, where the eponymous prophet proclaimed the triumph of Nebuchadnezzar and thus an anti-Egyptian message to the Judahites living in Egypt. The crucial significance of this Egyptian city is also evident in Ezek 30:18, when the destruction of all the Egyptian cities ends climactically with Tahpanhes. In comparison to other cities mentioned in vv. 13–19, this city alone receives a divine judgment that is intensified along cosmic lines encompassing the darkening of the sun and covering of the land with a cloud. The multiple correspondences of the city names coincide with a common historical situation reflected in both passages. In Jer 44:1, the three cities are identified as among the places where the Judahites sought refuge after the

---

opening messenger formula to a later layer in chapter 30. E.g., Fohrer asserts: "Das Wort, das sicherlich nicht von Ez stammt, sondern später hinzugefügt worden" (*Ezechiel*, 172). Pohlmann similarly states: "V.13–19 wirkt wie eine nachgetragene Spezifizierung und auch Steigerung der vorausgehenden recht pauschal gehaltenen Gerichtsworte" (*Hesekiel*, 2:416).

[133] Blenkinsopp, *Ezekiel*, 135. Cf. Odell, *Ezekiel*, 387.

[134] Zimmerli, *Ezekiel*, 2:124; Eichrodt, *Ezekiel*, 419. Contra Odell, *Ezekiel*, 287, who dismisses their comparison too easily: "Although some of the cities were known as places of Jewish refuge during Ezekiel's time (Jer 44:1), that is not the focus of the oracle."

[135] Jer 44:1–30 is an oracle unit introduced by the oracle reception heading at 40:1.

[136] Memphis (נֹף) in Ezek 30:13, 16; Jer 44:1; cf. Jer 2:16; 46:14, 19; Hos 9:6; Isa 19:13. Pathros (פתרוס) in Ezek 30:14; Jer 44:1, 15; cf. Isa 11:11; Ezek 29:14. Tahpanhes (תחפנחס) in Ezek 30:18; Jer 43:7, 8, 9; 44:1; cf. Jer 2:16; 46:14.

[137] The reference to the "house" or palace of Pharaoh in v. 9 is probably a reference to a royal building or secondary house of Pharaoh, for the capital of Egypt during this time was in Sais. See Fretheim, *Jeremiah*, 558; J. A. Thompson, *The Book of Jeremiah*, NIBCOT (Grand Rapids: Eerdmans, 2007), 670–71; McKane, *Jeremiah*, 2:1055.

Babylonian depredation of Jerusalem.[138] The literary complex in Ezek 30:1–19 is without a chronological formula, but the central section in vv. 10–12 explicitly presents Nebuchadnezzar as the divine tool of judgment against Egypt,[139] which is an image that likewise appears in 29:17–21 and 30:20–26. The end of chapter 29 predicts that Egypt is to become the reward given by YHWH to Nebuchadnezzar, since the king of Babylon "had no wages from Tyre for the labor that he had performed against it" (v. 18).[140] On the other hand, the end of chapter 30 reports the broken arm of Pharaoh and the strong arm of the king of Babylon, signifying the complete defeat of Egypt by Babylon. Deduced from these two surrounding passages, the oracle unit in 30:10–12 must then reflect the historical setting after the end of the siege of Tyre, and before the campaign that Nebuchadnezzar waged against Egypt in his thirty seventh year (568–567 BCE).[141] This roughly contemporaneous setting in Ezek 30 and Jer 43–44, along with the aforementioned common references to the Egyptian cities, highlights the possibility that the editors or authors of Ezek 30 knew of the situation in Egypt as reflected in Jer 43–44. They absorbed this information into a context of the divine judgment in order to rhetorically sever the hope of the Judahites to find political refuge in Egypt.

The text of chapter 30 is not solely concerned with the politico-military alliance between "the sons of the covenant land" and the Egyptians. The peculiar appearance of the גלולים in v. 13 points to a deeper problem: The religious affiliation between Judah and Egypt.[142] In v. 13, YHWH vows to annihilate the "dung gods" (גלולים) and the "empty gods" (אלילים) in the land of

---

[138] Cf. Nebuchadnezzar's capture of Jerusalem in Jer 39:1. See also Jer 43:1–7 for the decision made by the Judahite refugees to journey to Egypt and settle there.

[139] The pericope at 30:10–12 begins with a messenger formula ("Thus has the Lord YHWH declared") and ends with a declaration formula ("I YHWH have spoken").

[140] For the view that 29:17–20 is an update of the prediction about the complete destruction of Tyre recorded in 26:7–14, see A. S. Lawhead, "A Problem of Unfulfilled Prophecy in Ezekiel: A Response," *Wesleyan Theological Journal* 16 (1981): 15–19; T. Renz, "Proclaiming the Future: History and Theology in Prophecies against Tyre," *TynBul* 51 (2000): 17–58; N. D. Thompson, "A Problem of Unfulfilled Prophecy in Ezekiel: The Destruction of Tyre (Ezekiel 26:1–14 and 29:18–20)," *Wesleyan Theological Journal* 16 (1981): 93–106; D. Ulrich, "Dissonant Prophecy in Ezekiel 26 and 29," *BBR* 10 (2000): 121–41.

[141] *ANET*, 308b. See D. J. Wiseman, "Babylonia 605–539 B.C.," in *Cambridge Ancient History, Vol. 3, Part 2: The Assyrian and Babylonian Empires and Other States of the Ancient Near East, from the Eighth to the Sixth Centuries B.C.*, ed. J. Broadman et al., 2nd ed. (Cambridge: Cambridge University Press, 1991), 229–51, esp. 236, noted by L. C. Allen, *Jeremiah: A Commentary*, OTL (Louisville: Westminster John Knox, 2008), 440, n. 93.

[142] Peculiarly, the Greek version of Ezek 30:13 does not attest to the presence of the phrase והאבדתי גלולים. Uncertainties about the specific meaning of גלולים reigns, as

Egypt.¹⁴³ The appearance of the idols, especially the "dung gods," of the Egyptians is rather intriguing. Kessler observes instructively that Ezekiel never judges the foreign nations because of their idolatrous behavior.¹⁴⁴ Hence, the Egyptians' following their own idols would not have formed the main reason for YHWH to destroy the Egyptian "dung gods" and "empty gods." To my mind, the usage of the term גלולים suggests that the oracle in Ezek 30 is more related to Judah than to Egypt. The term גלולים is distinctive of the book of Ezekiel, such that thirty-nine out of forty-eight Hebrew Bible occurrences appear in this prophetic book.¹⁴⁵ It becomes Ezekiel's favorite term to denote the idolatry committed by Israel in the past and also in the exilic present.

In particular, Ezek 20 records Egypt as the very origin of the Israelite idolatry with the גלולים (vv. 7, 8).¹⁴⁶ According to this "revisionist history," both the Israelites and the Egyptians worship the same deities. The beginning of

---

the Septuagint translation of the Hebrew Bible exhibits little consistency in translating the term. Elsewhere in Ezekiel, the term is variously translated as εἴδωλα "idols," ἐνθυμήματά "thoughts, inventions, devices," ἐπιτηδεύματα "practices, habits," διανοήματα "thoughts, ideas," διάνοια "thoughts, intelligence," and βδελύγματα "abominations." Some scholars render גלולים with "*Scheissgötter*" or "dung gods". This is based on an argument from the etymology of גלל, which is related to both round stone and excrement. For more details, see D. Bodi, "Les *gillûlîm* chez Ezéchiel et dans l'Ancien Testament," *RB* 100 (1993): 481–510; J. F. Kutsko, *Between Heaven and Earth: Divine Presence and Absence in the Book of Ezekiel*, Biblical and Judaic Studies 7 (Winona Lake, Ind.: Eisenbrauns, 2000), 32–34; H. W. Wolff, "Jahwe und die Götter in der alttestamentlichen Prophetie," *EvT* 29 (1969): 397–416, here 407; H. D. Preuss, "גלולים," *TDOT* 3:1–5, esp. 2.

¹⁴³ The LXX has μεγιστᾶνας (= אילים) "great men," in parallel to the following נשיא. Here I follow the Hebrew to see the term as in parallel to גלולים. This is the only appearance of אלילים in Ezekiel. But it is a more common term for idolatry in First Isaiah. Of its eighteen biblical occurrences, אלילים occurs ten times in First Isaiah. Cf. Isa 2:8, 18, 20 (2x); 10:10, 11; 19:1, 3; 31:7 (2x). See Greenberg, *Ezekiel*, 2:624.

¹⁴⁴ Kessler comments on the Ezekiel's oracles against Egypt in general that "Dagegen spielt die Götterwelt Ägyptens in den Texten keine Rolle" (*Ägyptenbilder*, 80). Kessler further counters the opinion in Boadt, *Ezekiel's Oracles*, 170–71, by stating that "[e]r drückt sich aber missverständlich aus, wenn er darin eine Polemik gegen „the religious cults" der Nachbarn Israels sieht. Kulte werden gerade nicht thematisiert" (80, n. 41).

¹⁴⁵ Ezek 6:4, 5, 6, 9, 13 (2x); 8:10; 14:3, 4 (2x), 5, 6, 7; 16:36; 18:6, 12, 15; 20:7, 8, 16, 18, 24, 31, 39 (2x); 22:3, 4; 23:7, 30, 37, 39, 49; 30:13; 33:25; 36:18, 25; 37:23; 44:10, 12.

¹⁴⁶ Kessler claims that the idols of Egypt are in fact the Canaanite gods, which have been projected back to Egypt: "Es sind dies in Wahrheit gar keine ägyptischen Götter, sondern die Götter Kanaans, die nach Ägypten zurückprojiziert werden" (*Ägyptenbilder*, 119).

chapter 20 accuses the Israelites of defiling themselves the idols of Egypt (גלולי מצרים, vv. 7, 8). However, the very next reference to the idols becomes attached no longer to Egypt but rather to the first generation of the Israelites in the wilderness by utilizing the third person masculine plural suffixes (גלוליהם, cf. vv. 16, 18). The idols of the forefathers (גלולי אבותם, v. 24) finally transform into their own personal idols (גלוליכם, vv. 31, 39). Who is Egypt? Who is Israel? The distinction between them becomes blurred in light of the idolatrous relationship presented through this switch of pronominal suffixes in Ezek 20.[147] Given the prominent role of Egypt in Israel's aberration from YHWH, it is no wonder that the only appearance of the term in Ezekiel's OAN happens to be in this oracle concerning Egypt (30:13).[148] In light of the distribution and usage of גלולים in Ezekiel, it is more plausible that YHWH's destruction of the idols in the Egypt oracle serves a rhetorical purpose to eliminate the Judahite religious affiliation with Egypt.

Taken as a whole, the reference to "the people of the covenant land" (v. 5), who reside in the Egyptian cities commonly inhabited by the refugees from Judah (vv. 13–19), and who worship the idols such as "dung gods" and "empty gods" (v. 13), strongly hints at the presence of the Judahites in the land of Egypt. The people of Judah are affiliated not only militarily but also religiously with Egypt. Early interpretations of Ezek 30 must have also been informed by this understanding. More theologically explicit than the MT, the LXX translates "the sons of the covenant land" (בני ארץ הברית) as "the sons of my covenant" (καὶ τῶν υἱῶν τῆς διαθήκης μου).[149] The Targum associates the Hebrew place name of Thebes (נא; Ezek 30:14, 15, 16) with Alexandria, no doubt because of its great importance at a later time for the Jewish diaspora in Egypt.[150] In short, the prophet pronounces the demise of the nations, who had prostituted themselves by serving in Egypt's armies. Interpreting it either theologically or politically, the expression "the sons of the covenant land" affirms or leaves room for the presence of the elect people among the

---

[147] It is interesting to note at this point that the Septuagint translation of Ezek 20 employs less concrete and more pervasive terms, such as ἐνθυμήματα "thoughts, inventions, devices" (vv. 16, 24, 31) and ἐπιτηδεύματα "practices, habits" (vv. 7, 8, 28, 39), to translate גלולים. These more abstract interpretations of the term גלולים in the LXX present the idolatry as powerful enough to influence personal behavior and shape group identity. Cf. Premstaller, *Fremdvölkersprüche*, 167; Olley, *Ezekiel*, 363; Marzouk, *Egypt*, 184.

[148] For the complete occurrences of גלולים and other terminology of idolatry within Ezekiel, see Kutsko, *Heaven*, 29.

[149] For the Seleucid background of this Septuagint translation, see Olley, *Ezekiel*, 446.

[150] S. H. Levey, *The Targum of Ezekiel* (Edinburgh: T&T Clark, 1987), 88; Blenkinsopp, *Ezekiel*, 135; Zimmerli, *Ezekiel*, 2:134.

Egyptian mercenaries. Their presence does not avert the upcoming disastrous day of YHWH.

## 2.3. THE MULTITUDE

A more subtle hint that Judah is included among Egypt's allies can be sought in the appearance of the term המון in Ezek 29-32. It is significant that of the eighty-six occurrences of המון in the Hebrew Bible, nearly one-third is found in Ezekiel.[151] With thirteen occurrences, the term primarily characterizes Egypt.[152] Most of these occurrences appear in chapter 32, when Egypt goes down to Sheol and lies with the uncircumcised, the slain of the sword and other deceased nations. This term also characterizes Judah five times.[153] The rest of the occurrences in Ezekiel are used in association with the other foreign nations.[154] Based on this statistical consideration, Bodi rightly identifies the term as an important *Leitwort* in Ezekiel, especially in the Egypt oracles.[155]

The meaning of המון is helpfully classified by Bodi into three categories. The word can have the basic meaning of "noise, sound, rush, roar, murmur."[156] It can also have a quantitative meaning, designating "multitude, troops, crowd, horde, abundance, wealth."[157] Thirdly, it can signify the metaphorical sense

---

[151] Ezekiel uses the word twenty-seven times. Cf. A. Baumann, "המה," *TDOT* 3:414-18; G. Gerleman, "Die Lärmende Menge: Der Sinn des hebräischen Wortes Hamon," in *Wort und Geschichte: Festschrift für Karl Elliger zum 70. Geburtstag*, ed. H. Gese and H. P. Rüger; Kevelaer, AOAT 18 (Kevelaer: Butzon & Bercker, 1973), 71-75; Bodi, *Erra*, 119; Marzouk, *Egypt*, 119-21; Odell, *Ezekiel*, 69; idem, "The City of Hamonah in Ezekiel 39:11-16: The Tumultuous City of Jerusalem," *CBQ* 56 (1994): 479-89.

[152] Ezek 29:19; 30:4, 10, 15; 31:2, 18; 32:12 (2x), 16, 18, 20, 31, 32.

[153] Ezek 5:7; 7:11, 12, 13, 14.

[154] Ezek 39:11 (2x), 15, 16 (Gog of Magog); 32:24, 25 (Elam); 32:26 (Meshech-Tubal); 26:13 (Tyre); 23:42 (the multitude surrounding the promiscuous Oholibah and Oholah).

[155] Arguing against Fohrer, Bodi states: "We have rejected as arbitrary the approach which ... deletes 60% of all the occurrences of המון as glosses. The high statistical frequency of המון in Ezekiel indicates that one is dealing with an important catchword in the overall structure of the book" (*Erra*, 128).

[156] Amos 5:23; Isa 5:14; 13:4; 31:4; 32:14; Jer 3:23; 10:13; 47:3; 51:16, 42; 1 Sam 4:14; 14:19; 1 Kgs 18:41; Job 39:7; Dan 10:6. Cf. Ibid., 118.

[157] Gen 17:4, 5; Judg 4:7; 1 Sam 14:16; 2 Sam 6:19; 18:29; 2 Kgs 7:13 (2x); 25:11; Isa 5:13; 16:14; 29:5, 7, 8; 49:32; 60:5; Joel 4:15 [Eng. 3:14]; Ps 37:16; 42:5; Job 31:34; Qoh 5:9; Dan 11:10, 11 (2x), 12, 13; 1 Chr 29:16; 2 Chr 11:23; 13:8; 14:10; 20:2, 12, 15, 24; 31:10; 32:7. Cf. Ibid., 119; Gerleman, "Menge," 73.

of tumult, chaos, pomp, or arrogance.¹⁵⁸ Translators too often prefer one category of the meaning to the exclusion of the others. On the one hand, some German commentators such as Zimmerli and Eichrodt show a marked proclivity for the metaphorical meaning of המון. Almost without exception, they translate the term in Ezek 29–32 as *Gepränge*, "pomp," related to the hubris of Pharaoh.¹⁵⁹ On the other hand, the English Bible versions such as KJV, RSV, and NASB prefer the quantitative meaning of the term, rendering המון as "multitude" in most cases, and sometimes with "abundance" or "riches."¹⁶⁰ Like the aforementioned German commentators, Bodi also stresses the metaphorical meaning of the term, which, according to him, stands for "irreverence, hybris and insolence on the part of humans toward YHWH."¹⁶¹ For Bodi, המון in Ezekiel's oracles concerning Judah not only has the basic meaning of "noise, din," but also points to a deeper metaphorical meaning of human "hubris."¹⁶²

Bodi's understanding of המון through a metaphorical concept ("pride" or "hubris") invites a comparison between Judah and Egypt, both of which are often characterized as arrogant and tumultuous. A metaphorical rendition of Egypt's or Pharaoh's המון as "pomp" or "hubris" fits the following passages' characterizations of Egypt as arrogant and tumultuous. The monstrous Pharaoh claims to fashion the Nile himself (29:3). Pharaoh is further compared unfavourably to the cosmic tree that is towering on high (גבהת בקומה), and is proud of its height (ורם לבבו בגבהו, 31:10; cf. v. 14).¹⁶³ The parallelism between Egypt's המון and גאון in 32:12b confirms this metaphorical understanding of

---

¹⁵⁸ Cf. Ps 65:8, where YHWH "stills the roaring of the seas, the roaring of their waves, the tumult (המון) of the peoples." Likewise, Isa 17:12 uses the word in correlation with the chaos and uproar of the sea: "Ah, the roaring (המון) of many peoples, they roar (יהמיון) like the roaring (כהמות) of the sea! Ah, the roar of nations, they roar like the roaring of mighty waters!" Besides the book of Ezekiel, the Hebrew Bible attests to only a few examples of this metaphorical meaning. Cf. Bodi, *Erra*, 119, 128.

¹⁵⁹ With the exception of 32:12a, where a quantitative meaning of המון is taken up, Zimmerli adopts the metaphorical translation "pomp" in the Egypt oracles (*Ezekiel*, 2:117, 123, 125, 126, 141, 145, 156, 157, 163, 165, 169). Elsewhere in the book of Ezekiel, he translates the term either metaphorically (e.g., 5:7; 7:12–14) or quantitatively (e.g., "host" or "hordes" in 39:11, 15, 16). Eichrodt interprets the term in 29:19; 30:15; 32:31 quantitatively as "wealth" or "multitude," but still prefers the metaphorical meaning of the term as "pomp" at 31:2, 18; 32:12, 16, 18 (*Ezekiel*, 407, 413, 435, 422–23, 430–31, 435).

¹⁶⁰ E.g., Wevers renders all occurrences of המון as "wealth" or "multitude" (*Ezekiel*, 234, 239, 243–49).

¹⁶¹ Bodi, *Erra*, 128.

¹⁶² Ibid., 121–25, 128.

¹⁶³ The height and beauty of the tree seems to indicate a potential challenge to the supremacy of YHWH. Cf. Haag, "Ez 31" 172–73; Gowan, *Man*, 20–23.

המון as "hubris" or "pomp." As in the Egypt oracles, המון also plays an important role in characterizing the inhabitants of Jerusalem. In 5:7, Jerusalem's המון forms the reason for divine judgment and is defined by a comparison with that of the nations.[164] Defying God's statutes and ordinances, the city commits more turbulence and disorder than the other nations.[165] In 7:11–14, the oracle announcing the coming day of divine judgment also associates המון with the chaos and tumult of the capital city of Judah. The wrath of YHWH is called forth to contain the city's turbulence (כי חרון אל כל המונה; v. 12; cf. v. 14).[166] In 23:42, the המון caused by men who come from afar is brought into Jerusalem's precincts and has thereby increased the magnitude of the city's chaotic behaviour.[167] Overall, the uses of המון in the oracles against Jerusalem discussed above characterize Jerusalem and its inhabitants as chaotic and turbulent. Related passages such as Ezek 7:20; 16:49, 56 also reinforce this tumultuous image by accusing Judah of arrogance (גבה), pomp (גאון), satiety, and careless ease and thereby deserves YHWH's wrath. As such, the deployment of המון, understood metaphorically, underline the common state of disorder and hubris displayed by Judah and Egypt.[168]

Nevertheless, the above metaphorical understanding alone does not account for all of Ezekiel's Egypt oracles in which the term המון appears. The division between metaphorical and quantitative categories is in fact rather fluid in Ezekiel's oracles concerning Egypt. Without excluding the metaphorical sense like "hubris" or "pride," the immediate literary context more often demands a quantitative understanding of the term as "people, crowd, and multitude."[169] For instance, instead of focusing on the sole lone figure of Pharaoh, the oracle concerning the descent of the cedar into Sheol peculiarly also addresses Pharaoh's המון (31:2). Anxious that this plurality of addressees is not clear enough, this judgment ends with a repetition of the same vocabulary, depicting Pharaoh and המונו lying with other denizens of the netherworld

---

[164] *BHS* suggests an emendation to המרתכם, as a *hiphil* derived from מרה "to behave rebelliously," which is not necessary in light of the metaphorical meaning "turbulent" already embedded in המון.

[165] Odell, "City," 482–83; Marzouk, *Egypt*, 119–20.

[166] Odell, "City," 483–84. Even though a metaphorical meaning is preferred by Odell for Ezek 7:11–14, a quantitative rendition of המון as "wealth" and "multitude" is equally applicable in this particular pericope. Cf. Marzouk, *Egypt*, 120; Zimmerli, *Ezekiel*, 1:210; Greenberg, *Ezekiel*, 1:150.

[167] Odell, "City," 484.

[168] Cf. Marzouk, *Egypt*, 121.

[169] Cf. Gerleman, "Menge," 73–74, who states that המון in Ezekiel's Egypt oracles should be understood quantitatively as referring to a collective group consisting of various *peoples*, except those occurrences in 29:19 and 30:4, which speak of the collective consisting of various *material spoils*.

(31:18). As indicated by the interrogative phrase, אל מי "to whom," in the immediate context, Odell correctly weighs in with the remark that "personality traits are not usually addressed as subjects in oracles" and that "the chapter develops the metaphor of the greatness of the tree with reference to its allies (cf. vv. 6b, 12, 17)."[170] Therefore, it is more likely that המון in this particular passage denotes not only a metaphorical, but also a quantitative sense, referring to the multiple allies of Egypt. The same quantitative meaning should also be applied to the המון in 32:16, 18, 20, 31, 32, during Egypt's descent into the netherworld. Ezek 32:16 reads:

> This is a lamentation and they will chant it.[171]
> The daughters of the nations will chant it.
> Over Egypt and over all המונה they will chant it,"[172]
> —the declaration of the Lord YHWH.

In this verse, the המון is the object alongside Egypt to be lamented over. More appropriately, the המון, as an object of a funeral dirge, should be understood quantitatively as Egypt's allies. 32:18 also calls for the wailing over the המון of Egypt:

> Son of man, wail over המון מצרים,[173]
> and bring it down,[174]
> her and the daughters of the powerful nations,
> to the netherworld,
> with those who go down to the pit.

In the above verse, the המון is the very concrete object to be brought down. This is indicated by the third person masculine singular suffix attached to the imperative "bring down" (הוריד).[175] This object is further clarified and qualified by the subsequent phrase—"her and the daughters of the powerful nations"

---

[170] Odell, *Ezekiel*, 392.

[171] Instead of "they shall chant it," the LXX reads "you (singular) shall chant it" (θρηνήσεις), adding the prophet as another grammatical subject to perform the chanting. Cf. Zimmerli, *Ezekiel*, 2:157.

[172] The LXX differs from the MT by translating the המון metaphorically as an accusative singular ἰσχὺν, referring to the physical strength of Egypt.

[173] The LXX again translates the המון metaphorically as an accusative singular ἰσχὺν, referring to the physical strength of Egypt.

[174] The LXX translates the verb as the third person plural without the pronominal suffix: "they brought down" (καταβιβάσουσιν), treating Egypt and the dead nations as the direct object.

[175] To be noted, המון is a singular masculine noun.

(אותה ובנות גוים אדרם).[176] Again, the personality traits of Egypt are probably not the issue in v. 18. Furthermore, Ezek 32:31 characterizes Pharaoh's המון as "those slain by the sword" (חללי חרב) through the appositional placement.[177] The localization of Egypt's המון with the uncircumcised and the slain of the sword, as well as its designation as the recipient of lament and wailing demand and require a quantitative understanding of the term as "multitude."

Perceiving the term המון in this quantitative sense prompts further questions regarding not only a *characterization* but also an *identification* of this המון. Who exactly is then the המון in the Egypt oracles? The answer can only be answered tentatively. Given the judgment announced to the other nations associated with Egypt in chapters 30 and 31, this multitude is most plausibly identified as Egypt's allies. The exact enumeration of all of Egypt's allies is neither possible nor necessary. According to the book of Ezekiel, the most prominent ally of Egypt is Judah.[178] As analysed in the foregoing, this latter nation is also characterized by its "turbulence" (המון).[179] If this linguistic association is of any significance, Judah can then be counted as among the המון of Egypt. The metaphorical sense of pride and hubris is concretized and embodied by Judah, which in turn connects to and is identified with the המון of Egypt, understood now quantitatively as the "multitude." This quantitative meaning is nevertheless not devoid of the metaphorical connotation of pomp. In this light, Judah possibly becomes the bridge to understand both the metaphorical and the quantitative aspects of Egypt's המון.

2.4. THE CEDAR AND THE VINE

As already noted in the first part of this chapter, the presentation of a chthonic cedar in Ezek 31 is possibly influenced by the ancient Egyptian association of the tree with the death and resurrection of Osiris. It will be shown that the cedar in Ezek 31 reveals further familiarity with the biblical traditions. If the foregoing analyses concerning the broken staff of reed, the people of the covenant land, and the multitude point to a larger picture where Judah and Egypt are two entities in partnership, Ezek 31 goes even further to identify Judah in

---

[176] The reference to בנות גוים (vv. 16, 18) functions as a key phrase linking 32:17–32 to 32:1–16. Cf. Premstaller, *Fremdvölkersprüche*, 198.

[177] Cf. Ezek 32:20, 32.

[178] E.g., in 29:6b–9a, Egypt is portrayed as a political ally of Judah. For the portrayal of Egypt in Ezek 20 and 23 as the major influence on Judah's idolatry, see also Marzouk, *Egypt*, 125–52.

[179] For the distribution of the term in Ezekiel, see nn. 156–58. Marzouk correctly observes that "the word המון is used the most in association with Egypt (13 times) and Israel (5 times)" (ibid., 121).

the Egypt oracles by blending and blurring the identity of the cedar representing Egypt with the vine symbolizing Judah.[180]

Several biblical passages envision the tree as a symbolism of kingship.[181] The Anointed One by YHWH, for instance, is called "the Branch," comparable to "the shoot from the stem of Jesse."[182] The use of horticultural symbolism to denote the rivalry for kingship appears in Judg 9:8–15 and 2 Kgs 14:9 (// 2 Chr 25:18).[183] Moreover, Amos 2:9 employs the imagery of a cut-down tree as a symbol of divine judgment.[184] In Isa 16:6–11, which is an oracle passing judgment on pride and arrogance, a vine imagery is applied to a foreign nation Moab.[185] Still, none of the above dendritic images bear extensive lexical ties with the grand cedar in Ezek 31.[186]

The more extensive and distinctive lexical ties are to be found within Ezekiel. The grand cedar in Ezek 31 shares numerous unique or distinctive features with the tragic vine in chapters 15, 17, and 19.[187] The vine symbolizes the royal house of Judah,[188] which has been cast in such a miserable state that it will "completely wither" (17:10), be "plucked up in a fury" (19:12), and "be given to the fire for fuel" (15:6). Like the vine, the cedar is one tree accompanied by the many.[189] Both the vine and the cedar have twig (עָנָף),[190] branches

---

[180] Cf. Ezek 15:1–4; 17:1–24; 19:10–14.

[181] Cf. M. Metzger, "Zeder, Weinstock und Weltenbaum," in *Ernten, was man sät: Festschrift für Klaus Koch zu seinem 65. Geburtstag*, ed. D. R. Daniels, U. Gleßmer and M. Rösel (Neukirchen: Neukirchener Verlag, 1991), 197–229; Bertholet, *Hesekiel*, 109; Gowan, *Man*, 110–13.

[182] Jer 23:5; Zech 3:8; 6:12; Isa 11:1.

[183] Stordalen, *Echoes*, 164–166.

[184] Cf. Isa 10:18–19; 2:12–16. Gowan, *Man*, 111.

[185] Stordalen, *Echoes*, 177–178.

[186] E.g., Apart from the common reference to "cedars of Lebanon" (ארזי הלבנון), little semantic resemblances between Ezek 31 and the fable in Judg 9:8–15 exist. The pericope in Ps 80:9–14 shares several common motifs (e.g., גפן, שרש, ארז and עָנָף) with Ezek 31, but they also differ in some key terminology. While Ps 80:12 uses קציר and ינק to denote "branches" ad "shoots," Ezek 31 predominantly employs terms such as דלית, עבות and פארה. A later text in Dan 4:7–9 [Eng. 4:10–12], nevertheless, might have been influenced by the cosmic tree in Ezek 31. Cf. Sulzbach, "Nebuchadnezzar," 126–27.

[187] Noted also by Premstaller, *Fremdvölkersprüche*, 183; Boadt, "Rhetorical Strategies," 193–96, 198.

[188] Cf. Ps 80:9–14 [Eng. 80:8–13]; Isa 5:1–7. Vineyard imagery in the Hebrew Bible typically represents the relationship between YHWH and Israel.

[189] Ezek 15:2, 6; 31:4–5, 9.

[190] The singular absolute form appears within Ezekiel only at these three places: 17:8, 23; 31:3 (cf. ענפכם in 36:8). *HALOT* 1:858.

(דליותיו),[191] thick branches (עבתים),[192] and boughs (פארות).[193] All of their roots (שרש) are deep enough to be nourished by abundant waters (מים רבים).[194] None of these dendritic terms are applied in a later restoration oracle in Ezek 47:1–12, which presents a similar context where the trees sprouting by many waters.[195] The semantic connections among chapters 15, 17, 19, and 31 are thus more likely to be intentional. With these distinctive and even unique vocabulary clusters, the identity of the cedar in chapter 31 becomes intertwined with that of the rejected vine in chapters 15, 17, and 19.

With regard to the direction of dependence, it is appropriate to interpose a summary of Pohlmann's position with regard to chapters 17, 19, and 31. Pohlmann astutely observes that the vine symbolizing the king of Judah in 17:5–10 is more negatively evaluated than that in 19:10–14.[196] While the latter nourished by many waters raises itself majestically above the thick branches, the former rambles lowly and sprawls humbly toward a great eagle.[197] Whereas the reason for destruction of the majestic vine in chapter 19 remains shrouded in mystery, the lowly vine in chapter 17 earns its infamy specifically by turning away from the first great eagle and bending its roots to another great eagle.[198] Presenting a more explicit criticism of the Jerusalem kingship, Ezek 17:5–10, argues Pohlmann, signifies a later and deeper reflection on the destruction of Jerusalem than 19:10–14.[199]

Next, Pohlmann less convincingly discusses the relationship of the two aforementioned chapters with the Egypt oracle in chapter 31. For Pohlmann, the cedar in Lebanon mentioned in 31:3 is a more common motif related to

---

[191] Besides its occurrence in Ezek 17:6, 23; 19:11; 31:7, 9, 12, Jer 11:16 is the only other occurrence of this term within the Hebrew Bible. Cf. *HALOT* 1:222.

[192] The unique phrase על בין עבתים appears only at Ezek 19:11 and 31:3, 10, 14. Cf. *HALOT* 1:778.

[193] The term appears only in Ezek 17:6; 31:5, 8, 12, and 13. A similar yet dubious form appears in Isa 10:33. Cf. *HALOT* 2:909.

[194] In Ezek 17:5, 8; 19:10, the vine is planted by many waters. So is the cedar in Ezek 31:5, 7, 15. Cf. the danger and destruction imbued by this phrase in Ps 18:16; 29:3; 32:6; 77:19; 93:4; 144:7. For more explication of this expression, see Odell, *Ezekiel*, 240; May, "Cosmic Connotations," 9–21.

[195] Ezek 47:7, 12.

[196] Pohlmann, "Frage," 152–53.

[197] Compare and contrast especially Ezek 19:11 and 17:6.

[198] Cf. 17:7. Pohlmann comments on the destruction on the vine in Ezek 19:10–14: "Sein Geschick hing ab von Außeneinwirkungen, auf die er selbst keinen Einfluß nehmen konnte" ("Frage," 153). By contrast, he specifies the cause of destruction of the vine in Ezek 17:5–10, "daß er sich selbst falsch verhalten hat."

[199] Ibid., 154.

the elect status of Jerusalem or the kingship of Judah.[200] He further reconstructs an original version of Ezek 31,[201] which shares many literary motifs with chapter 19's depiction of the vine symbolizing the house of Judah.[202] The plants in both chapters, as he notes, have met their downfalls due to various external forces.[203] In Ezek 19:10–14, the fruitful vine is dried up by the east wind. In Ezek 31:3, 4a, the mighty cedar is cut down by the foreigners. Consequently, Pohlmann surmises, "daß Ez 31* ursprünglich zusammen mit Ez 19 überliefert worden ist, ja, daß beide Texte vielleicht sogar von ein und demselben Autor stammen."[204] Pohlmann suggests that the reconstructed text of Ezek 31 had first been directed against the Jerusalem kingship and was later adapted or "*umfunktioniert*" to be against Pharaoh.[205] According to Pohlmann, chapter 31* is like chapter 19 in that both lack theological reflection on the cause of the destruction of Jerusalem.[206] Only in chapter 17 is the downfall justified through the internal aberration of the vine.[207] The chapter shows a marked proclivity for Jehoiachin, the king of Judah who was banished to Babylon, on the one hand, and warns against the *volte-face* of Zedekiah, who sought the Egyptian help to resist Babylonian dominion, on the other.[208] Therefore, Pohlmann concludes that chapter 31* must have emerged earlier than chapter 17.

I agree with Pohlmann on the first but not the second point. Given its more specific reasoning for the destruction of the vine, Ezek 17 is more likely to be a later reflection on chapter 19 concerning the downfall of the kingship in Jerusalem. However, I am more sceptical of his attempt to place chapter 31* on a par with chapter 19 and to view chapter 17 as a reinterpretation of not only chapter 19 but also chapter 31*. The problem, to my mind, is twofold. First, Pohlmann does not explain why the sharing of literary motifs between chapters 19 and 31* necessarily renders the two passages contemporaneous. The cedar in Lebanon is a common motif not only in the biblical traditions, but also within the wider ancient Near Eastern milieu. As outlined by Stordalen, Lebanon timber emerges as a highly prized building material in both the

---

[200] Ibid., 155–56, 161. Cf. Jer 22:6, 20–23; Isa 10:34; Zech 11:1–3.

[201] Pohlmann reconstructs the original text, which consists of 31:2b, 3, 4a, 6aα, 12abα and 13a (ibid., 159).

[202] Pohlmann is mainly concerned with the shared literary motifs, and not the lexical connections (ibid., 159).

[203] Ibid., 160, cf. 153, 159.

[204] Ibid., 161.

[205] Ibid., 156.

[206] Ibid., 163. He perceives a great discrepancy between "*Tun*" and "*Ergehen*" in both chapters.

[207] Ibid., 154.

[208] Ibid., 164–69.

Mesopotamian and Ugaritic literature.[209] A depiction of the precious cedar is especially appropriate for the literary context of chapter 31, since the main subject under discussion is Egypt, which has the ability to rival YHWH and to seduce the Judahites politically. The general symbolic meaning of the cedar of Lebanon in the ancient Near East makes it difficult to jump to the conclusion that chapters 19 and 31* are contemporaneous. Placing chapter 31* before chapter 17 raises a second problem. As stated in the foregoing, Pohlmann posits the hypothesis that the main object of indictment had originally been the monarch in Jerusalem, but then shifted to Pharaoh king of Egypt.[210] Yet, Pohlmann does not account for the motivation of the change of addressee from Judah to Egypt in this later development of chapter 31. The more important question remains: Why should the characteristics initially belonging to the Jerusalem royal be transferred to a foreign ruler? Ezek 19 concentrates only on the fate of Judah, and thus does not provide a reason for the downfall of Egypt. On the other hand, chapter 17 explicitly refers to Zedekiah's treacherous treaty with Egypt. This likely supplied chapter 31 with a motivation for the downfall of the cosmic cedar.[211] With this consideration in mind, Pohlmann's assessment that chapter 17 is a reinterpretation of chapter 31* becomes less convincing.

More plausibly, the vine imagery in chapters 15, 17, and 19 serves as a template for the construction of the cedar imagery in chapter 31. From the above table, the cedar in the latter chapter is invested with all of the distinctive features applied to the vine in the former three chapters. Like the vine in chapter 15, the cedar is painted as a tree among many others. This is a motif found in neither chapter 17 nor chapter 19. Like the vine in chapter 17, the cedar grows in a "planting place" (מטע), which appears elsewhere only in Ezek 34:29, Isa 60–61, and Mic 1:6.[212] Only the vine in chapter 19 and the cedar in chapter 31 are said to possess the height to be exalted "among the thick branches" (בין עבתים). In this light, the more logical scenario is that chapter 31 descended from diverse traditions of the vine found in the other three chapters. The former conflated all the disparate elements found in the latter in order to enrich the imagery of the cedar. In this case, the monstrous cedar symbolizing Egypt was fashioned according to the vine representing Judah. The rhetorical impact

---

[209] Stordalen, *Echoes*, 163, cites *ANET*, 275, 291, 307; *KTU* 1.4 vi 18, 20; 1.17 vi 21; O. Loretz, "Cant 4,8 auf dem Hintergrund ugaritischer und assyrischer Beschreibungen des Libanons und Antilibanons," in *Ernten, Was man sät: Festschrift für Klaus Koch zu seinem 65. Geburtstag*, ed. D. R. Daniels, U. Gleßmer and M. Rösel (Neukirchen: Neukirchener Verlag, 1991), 131–41.

[210] Pohlmann, "Frage," 156.

[211] Cf. 17:15.

[212] Cf. *HALOT* 1:574.

is shocking enough to nullify the identity boundaries between Judah and Egypt in its received form. The Judahite soul is breathed into the very cedar of Egypt.

Following this direction of dependence, we are also in a better position to account for the motivation behind this identification of Egypt with Judah in chapter 31. Underlying this identification lurks a polemic against the conspiracy between Judah and Egypt.[213] Unlike Ezek 15 and 19, in which the motivation of divine judgment upon Jerusalem is not explicitly stated, chapter 17 vividly paints the Judahite king as seeking help from and sending envoys to Egpyt.[214] The prophecy in chapter 17 forthrightly condemns the defection of Zedekiah from the Babylonian sovereignty.[215] In response to this *volte-face*, the prophecy presages the withering of the vine, which symbolizes Zedekiah (vv. 9–10). Zedekiah will be brought under judgment and Egypt will prove itself to be an unreliable help (vv. 16–21). This negative portrayal of the alliance between the Judahite and the Egyptian monarchies supplies a motivation for the cedar in chapter 31 to embody attributes of the vine found in chapter 17. It further justifies the cedar's destruction and ultimate descent into Sheol.

Even though I insist that the cedar imagery in Ezek 31 is dependent on the vine imagery in chapter 17, I maintain that 17:22–24 is inserted later in response to the alignment envisioned in both 17:1–21 and 31:1–18.[216] The pessimistic blurring of identity generates another polemic, which exalts the exiles in Babylon to the position of the restored Israel, distinguishing them from the vine that has allied with Egypt and the cedar symbolizing Egypt. From 17:3–4 comes an implicitly favorable reference to the displacement of Jehoiachin, who is represented as the top of another cedar (צמרת הארז).[217] This reference later gives rise to an explicitly salvific pronouncement for the exiles in contrast to the non-exiles, and most importantly, in contrast to Egypt. The exaltation of the top of the divinely planted cedar in 17:22–24 stands diametrically

---

[213] For the historical setting of Ezek 17, see Zimmerli, *Ezekiel*, 1:361.

[214] Cf. 17:7, 15

[215] A common interpretation for this chapter is that Ezekiel contains no polemic against the Babylonian imperialism. Recently, Strine argues that the chapter contains a hidden polemic against Babylon, by asserting YHWH's superiority over and against Marduk, the patron god of Babylon (*Sworn Enemies*, 230–43).

[216] In terms of content and style, 17:22–24 resembles another restoration oracle in 16:53–58, 59–63. This unit in chapter 17 is marked off by the divine messenger formula (כה אמר אדני יהוה, v. 22). The previous units in 17:1–21 can exist quite independently without it. Therefore, this unit in vv. 22–24 is most likely a late insertion. On the late insertion of this verse, see Zimmerli, *Ezekiel*, 2:366–67.

[217] Odell notes that the text intriguingly casts a more favourable light upon Jehoiachin's exile into Babylon by designating Babylon as "the land of Canaan" (ארץ כנען, v. 4; *Ezekiel*, 209). Ps 137 laments that the exiles live as aliens in a strange land; but Ezekiel calls it the "land of Canaan," which, according to the Israelite traditions, is the land of promise.

opposite to the plumage of the cedar in chapter 31. The dissimilar fates stand out in light of several semantic features shared by the cedars in both chapters.[218] A comparison of both passages yields three observations concerning the verbatim correspondences. First, the Jehoiachin exiles in Babylon (chapter 17) as well as Pharaoh and his multitude (chapter 31) are all identified by the terms "cedar" and "Lebanon." Apart from 27:5 concerning the building material of the Tyrian ship, 17:3 and 31:3 contain the only two other occurrences of the combination of "cedar" and "Lebanon" in Ezekiel. Second, the shared reference to the cedar in Lebanon alone does not prove that both passages are related to one another. The cedar of Lebanon is cherished not only in the Israelite tradition, but also in the wider ancient Near Eastern milieu.[219] However, the appearances of a rare term צמרת "tree-top" bring the two pericopes even closer together (17:3, 22; 31:3, 10, 14). The term appears only at these two chapters in Ezekiel, in order to characterize Jehoiachin/Israel's future ruler and Assyria/Egypt respectively.[220] Third, the two cedars offer protection and shade to the birds and beasts (17:23; 31:6).[221] Overall, the lexical similarities between the two cedars are distinctive but more limited in scope in comparison to those between the vine in the Judah oracles and the cedar in the Egypt prophecy.

The shared phraseology brings the ultimate fates of both cedars into a sharper contrast. As Bowen nicely summarizes: "The language condemning Egypt is used positively in Ezekiel of Israel. God will plant a "lofty [or 'high'] cedar" where it will produce "boughs" in whose "shade" every kind of "bird" will "nest" (17:22–23)."[222] On the one hand, the cedar in Ezek 17 is finally raised high (vv. 22–24). On the other hand, the same type of tree in Ezek 31 who was initially towering on high (vv. 3, 10) will finally be brought down and descend into Sheol. In this light, a contrast is established not only between the Babylonian exiles and the people left in the land of Judah, but also between

---

[218] Cf. Bowen, *Ezekiel*, 195.

[219] In the Hebrew Bible, cedar in Lebanon does not necessarily refer to the specific house of Judah, but is more generally considered as a cherished and noble plant. It is the most cherished tree (1 Kgs 5:13[Eng. 4:33]), used for the construction of the temple and palace (1 Kgs 5:20 [Eng. 5:6]; 2 Sam 7:2; Jer 22:15). Due to its extraordinary beauty and strength, it is called the "cedar of God" (Ps 80:11) and "cedar of YHWH" (Ps 104:16). Cf. Haag, "Ez 31," 173.

[220] Boadt, "Rhetorical Strategies," 193–94.

[221] The MT 17:23 mentions only "birds of every kind" (כל צפור כל כנף), without mentioning the beast. By contrast, the LXX 17:23 juxtaposes πᾶν θηρίον "every beast" and πᾶν πετεινὸν "every bird." This makes LXX 17:23 a closer parallel to the LXX or the MT of 31:6.

[222] Bowen, *Ezekiel*, 195. Whereas Bowen correctly notices a contrast between the two *cedars* in Ezek 17 and 31, her exegesis nevertheless leaves the semantic resemblances between the *cedar* in Ezek 31 and the withering *vine* in Ezek 17 unexplained.

the Babylonian exiles and Egypt. In turn, this special status of the exiles who will become the restored Israel highlights and deepens the alignment between Egypt and Judah.

Returning to the question for the cedar at the beginning of chapter 31: "To whom are you like" (אל מי דמית)? The text offers no easy answer. The cedar in chapter 31 displays a much more fluid identity than is commonly recognized. It is Egypt comparable to Assyria of the past (31:3). Being lexically related to the exilic community awaiting future restoration (17:22–24), its ultimate annihilation nevertheless differs sharply from the promised restoration. A closer resemblance is perhaps found in the vine imagery representing the abandoned house of Judah (15:1–4; 17:3–10; 19:10–14). With the intertwining connections between the cedar and the abandoned vine, can we still differentiate who is Egypt and who is Judah?

Following the discussions in the previous four sections, we can conclude that Judah exists in the Egypt oracles with various degrees of concreteness. Explicitly, "the house of Israel" is named for putting its trust in Egypt (29:6) and it appears as the "covenant land" among the military allies of Egypt (30:5). More speculative, the tumultuousness displayed by Judah leads to its inclusion among the "multitude" (המון) of Pharaoh. Intricately, the characteristics of the vine symbolizing Judah in the other chapters of Ezekiel merge with the cedar of Assyria/Egypt in chapter 31. Taking all the evidence together, the shadow of Judah looms large in Ezekiel's indictments against Egypt.

## 3. THE RHETORICAL IMPACT

Armed with the above examination, we can better account for the fate of Egypt, which often bears unmistakable linguistic resemblances to the destiny of Judah. Why do such verbatim correspondences arise in both the Egypt and the Judah oracles? With the whole complex of Ezek 25–32 in view, Lyons ventures one solution. For him, the fortune of the nations and that of Judah intertwine with each other, since the nations have taken pleasure at Judah's fall.[223] Nevertheless, Lyons' comment appears to be overgeneralizing. His reasoning is not applicable to Egypt. Even though Ammon, Moab, and Tyre in particular are accused of issuing taunts and scorns against Judah,[224] nowhere else in Ezekiel is Egypt accused of this antagonistic role in relation to Judah.[225] Still,

---

[223] See n. 8. Cf. Lyons, *Law*, 122.

[224] Cf. Ezek 25:1–11; 26:2.

[225] Cf. Greenberg, *Ezekiel*, 2:611. Schwagmeier also states that "das Thema des Spottes gegen Israel (25,3.8.15; 26,2) spielt im gesamten Ägypten-Kontext keine Rolle" ("Untersuchungen," 269).

compared to other nations, Egypt alone is invested with such extensive lexical features that also characterize the Judah oracles. Therefore, it is difficult to concur with Lyons at this point that the lexical correspondences between the two groups of oracles are due to Egypt's pleasure at Judah's fall.

Alternatively, Zimmerli and Block suggest that the verbatim correspondences serve to pass on comfort and consolation for the Judahites. According to Zimmerli, the recurring motif of the "day of YHWH" in chapter 30 highlights the "profound consolation and comfort" for the people who have encountered a similar "day of YHWH" in chapter 7.[226] The shared motif, for Zimmerli, conveys the message that God judges beyond the land of Israel and beyond the exiles, with the ultimate aim of bringing all humans to recognize him.[227] Without commenting specifically on the motif, Block also shares Zimmerli's opinion, since he claims that chapter 30 offers hope to the exilic audience: "Although they are in exile, far from the land of the covenant, they may take comfort in the knowledge that YHWH reigns supreme over all."[228] Indubitably, that YHWH judges both Judah and Egypt in a highly similar fashion points to the portrayal of YHWH as the sole source of judgment.[229] Nevertheless, this appeal to the universality of YHWH does not explain why the judgment executed on Egypt needs to be interpreted as hopeful and comforting for Judah. In other words, why would Judah take solace in the judgment of Egypt when that judgment reverberates the painful and traumatic experience envisioned for Judah as well?

Lyons, Zimmerli, and Block do not pay sufficient attention to the political and religious alliance between Egypt and Judah. In contrast to the more optimistic reading from especially Zimmerli and Block, Pohlmann is closer to the mark with regard to the motif of the day of YHWH in chapter 30. Concerning the link between chapters 7 and 30, Pohlmann briefly remarks:

> Außerdem ist zu beachten, daß der zuständige Verfasser Formulierungen des Kontexts aufgenommen hat und sich offensichtlich auch an den Ausführungen zum Endgericht über das Land Israel in Ez 7 orientiert.[230]

In his opinion, the judgment over Judah and Egypt should be seen in alignment, such that the judgment upon Egypt goes against Judah as well. As will be argued, Pohlmann's insight can actually be extended to other parts of the Egypt oracles.

---

[226] See n. 9. Cf. Zimmerli, *Ezekiel*, 2:135.
[227] Cf. Ibid.
[228] See n. 9. Cf. Block, *Ezekiel*, 2:171.
[229] So also Lyons, *Law*, 122.
[230] Pohlmann, *Kapitel 20–48*, 414.

We have established that Ezek 29–32 perceives Egypt as the inveterate enemy of YHWH, and Judah exists as an intimate ally of Egypt. On this basis, it is only natural that the divine retribution meted out is shared by both nations.[231] The concocted lexical connections draw a parallel between the catastrophic ends of Egypt and Judah. Egypt shares with Judah the national destruction and death, the banishment into exile, and most surprisingly, the promise of restoration.

3.1. DESTRUCTION

The aforementioned history of alliance between Egypt and Judah in Ezek 29–32 explains the destruction of Egypt, which exhibits semantic similarities to the divine retribution on Judah depicted elsewhere in the book of Ezekiel.[232]

Ezekiel's references to punitive weapons such as sword and net elucidate the judgment shared between Egypt and Judah. Sword (חרב) is a common motif of punishment in the Hebrew Bible,[233] and the punishment by a sword figures prominently in the book of Ezekiel.[234] From this prophetic book come ninety-one occurrences of the noun חרב and its plural form. More than half of these occurrences (48x) are found in the oracles against Judah.[235] Another

---

[231] C. Grottanelli states: "any betrayal in favor of Yahweh's enemies must be punished in order to reconstruct harmony, and that violence must be exerted against the enemy but also against the sinful Israelites who have permitted that enemy to proper, or even to survive" ("The Enemy King is a Monster: A Biblical Equation," in *Kings and Prophets*, ed. idem [Oxford: Oxford University Press, 1999], 47–72, here 67).

[232] On the lexical connections between the oracles against Egypt and those against Judah, see also Premstaller, *Fremdvölkersprüche*, 146–50; Vogels, "Restauration," 478–79; Minj, *Egypt*, 103.

[233] E.g., Lev 26:33; Deut 32:41–42; 33:29; Judg 7:20; Isa 27:1; 34:5; 51:9; 66:16; Jer 12:12; 15:3; 21:7; 25:29, 38; 46:10; 47:6; 49:37; 50:16, 35; Amos 4:10; 7:9; 9:11; Zeph 2:12; Nah 2:14; Zech 13:7–9; Ps 7:12; 17:13. Noted by Bodi, *Erra*, 231, n. 3. For more details, see O. Eissfeldt, "Schwerterschlagene bei Hesekiel," in *Studies in Old Testament Prophecy*, ed. H. H. Rowley (Edinburgh: Clark, 1950), 73–81; Boadt, *Ezekiel's Oracles*, 40; Minj, *Egypt*, 80; Lyons, *Law*, 162–186; Vogels, "Restauration," 478–79.

[234] Ezekiel normally links the noun חרב to related forms of three verbal roots: "to come" (בוא, 5:17; 6:3; 11:8; 14:17; 29:8; 30:4; 32:11; 33:2, 3, 4, 6), "to fall" (נפל, 5:12; 6:11, 12; 11:10; 17:21; 23:25; 24:21; 25:13; 30:6, 17; 32:12, 22, 23, 24; 33:27; 39:23), and "to pierce" (חלל, usually as a construct combination with חרב, see 28:23; 31:17, 18; 32:20, 21, 22, 23, 24, 25, 26, 28, 29, 30, 31, 32; 35:8). Cf. Schöpflin, *Theologie*, 52; see Bodi, *Erra*, 231–46.

[235] 5:1, 2 (2x), 12 (2x), 17; 6:3, 8, 11, 12; 7:15 (2x); 11:8 (2x), 10; 12:14, 16; 14:17 (2x), 21; 16:40; 17:21; 21:8, 9, 10, 14 (2x), 16, 17, 19 (3x), 20, 24, 25, 33 (2x); 23:10, 25, 47 (plural); 24:21; 33:2, 3, 4, 6 (2x), 26, 27.

thirty times are in the Egypt oracles.²³⁶ The rest of the occurrences are scattered in the other oracles against the nations.²³⁷ As seen from the distribution, the divine retribution executed by a sword is preponderantly applied to Egypt and Judah. Moreover, the exact expression חרב מלך בבל "the sword of the king of Babylon" appears only twice within the book of Ezekiel: once in the Egypt oracle (32:11), and another time in the Judah oracle (21:24 [Eng. 21:19]). The Hebrew phrase מלך בבל appears not only in the context where judgments are carried out against foreign nations such as Tyre and Egypt,²³⁸ but also in several significant oracles against Judah.²³⁹ Schöpflin rightly suggests that the judgment by a sword upon foreign nations also implies judgment on the city of Jerusalem.²⁴⁰

The net constitutes another distinctive instrument of judgment in the book of Ezekiel. Within the Hebrew Bible, the net (רשת) is deployed as the instrument to catch wild animals,²⁴¹ or as a net design in the tabernacle and Solomon's temple.²⁴² Sometimes, the term figuratively designates the plots and devises of evil people.²⁴³ Within the book of Ezekiel, the term appears almost exclusively in the context of divine wrath, which is directed against the leader of Jerusalem (12:13), against Zedekiah, who broke the oath with the Babylonian king (17:20), and against the Judahite princes (19:8–9).²⁴⁴ Within the prophecies against foreign nations, רשת emerges only in the context of YHWH's defeat of the monstrous Pharaoh (32:3b).²⁴⁵ YHWH's execution of his judgment through the net thus links the fates of Judah and Egypt together.

---

²³⁶ 29:8, 30:4, 5, 6, 11, 17, 21, 22, 24, 25; 31:17, 18; 32:10, 11, 12, 20 (2x), 21, 22, 23, 24, 25, 26, 27 (plural), 28, 29, 30, 31, 32.

²³⁷ 25:13; 26:6, 8, 9 (plural), 11; 28:7 (plural), 23; 35:5, 8; 38:4 (plural), 8, 21 (2x); 39:23.

²³⁸ Ezek 29:18, 19; 30:10, 24, 25; 32:11. Note that the proper name "Nebuchadnezzar" (נבוכדראצר), appears only in the oracles against foreign nations, and not in the oracles against Judah. It corresponds to the Babylonian *Nabû-kudurrī-uṣur*, commonly interpreted as "O Nabu, protect my offspring." Cf. Block, *Ezekiel*, 2:40. Greenberg, *Ezekiel*, 2:532; D. S. Vanderhooft, *The Neo-Babylonian Empire and Babylon in the Latter Prophets*, HSM 59 (Atlanta: Scholars Press, 1999), 129.

²³⁹ Ezek 17:12; 19:9; 21:24, 26 [Eng. 21:19, 21]; 24:2.

²⁴⁰ Schöpflin states: "Wenngleich in den Völkerworten nicht Jerusalem das Gericht angesagt wird, scheint das kriegerische Gerichtsgeschehen, das auch diese Stadt betrifft, darin auf" (*Theologie*, 53).

²⁴¹ E.g., Prov 1:17. Cf. Bodi, *Erra*, 162.

²⁴² E.g., Exod 27:4–5; 38:4; 1 Kgs 7:17, 18, 20. Cf. Ibid.

²⁴³ E.g., Job 18:8–9; Prov 29:5; Pss 9:15; 9:16; 10:9; 25:15; 31:5; 35:7–8; 57:7; 140:6; Hos 5:1. Cf. Ibid.

²⁴⁴ The exception is the appearance of the term in Ezek 47:10. Cf. Ibid., 165.

²⁴⁵ The synonymous term חרם appears in the oracles against Tyre (26:5, 14), in order to denote not the divine tool of judgment, but the fisherman's net.

The onslaught of both Egypt and Judah, executed through either sword or net, is pictured as happening on "the day of YHWH," which becomes a literary motif binding the judgment of Egypt even closer to that of Judah. The phrase "the day of YHWH" (יום יהוה) appears sixteen times within the Hebrew Bible.²⁴⁶ Apart from these occurrences, variant forms exist in the Hebrew Bible, such that this day of divine intervention can even be proclaimed without mentioning the divine name.²⁴⁷ The day can also be characterized by the divine anger, accompanied by the cosmic and warring disasters, and reinforced by the emotions of those affected.²⁴⁸ Within Ezekiel, such a day appears in 13:5; but most prominently in 7:6–7, 9–10; 30:1–9, 13–19.²⁴⁹ Chapters 7 and 30 share several distinctive lexical features.²⁵⁰ Both chapters characterize the day as imminent (קרוב הים, 7:7; קרוב יום, 30:3).²⁵¹ The day is coming (הנה באה; 7:6, 10; 30:9). Similar to the judgment directed against the inhabitants of Jerusalem, the day of YHWH upon Egypt also entails a natural disaster, such that it is a "day of clouds, a time of doom for the nations" (30:3; cf. "tumult rather

---

²⁴⁶ Cf. Isa 13:6, 9; Ezek 13:5; Joel 1:15; 2:1, 11; 3:4; 4:14; Amos 5:18 (2x), 20; Obad 15; Zeph 1:7, 14 (2x); Mal 3:23. For different hypotheses about the original settings of "the Day of YHWH," see S. Mowinkel, "Jahves Dag," *NTT* 59 (1958): 1–56; G. von Rad, "The Origin of the Concept of the Day of Yahweh," *JSS* 4 (1959): 97–108; M. Weiss, "The Origin of the 'Day of the Lord'—Reconsidered," *HUCA* 37 (1966): 29–71. For the gaining of the eschatological meaning of יום יהוה in the Hebrew Bible, see Y. Hoffman, "The Day of the Lord as a Concept and a Term in the Prophetic Literature," *ZAW* 93 (1981): 37–50. Recent scholarly surveys of the motif within the Hebrew Bible include S. I. L. Norin, "Der Tag Gottes im Alten Testament: Jenseits der Spekulationen- was ist übrig?" in *Le jour du Dieu = Der Tag Gottes*, ed. Anders Hultgård et al., WUNT 245 (Tübingen: Mohr Siebeck, 2009), 33–42; W. Oswald, "Zukunftserwartung und Gerichtsankündigung: Zur Pragmatik der prophetischen Rede vom Tag Jhwhs," in *Le jour du Dieu = Der Tag Gottes*, ed. Anders Hultgård et al., WUNT 245 (Tübingen: Mohr Siebeck, 2009), 19–31; N. Wendebourg, *Der Tag des Herrn: Zur Gerichtserwartung im Neuen Testament auf ihrem alttestamentlichen und frühjüdischen Hintergrund*, WMANT 96 (Neukirchen: Neukirchener Verlag, 2003), 28–85.

²⁴⁷ E.g., יום ליהוה (Isa 2:12; Ezek 30:3); יום בא ליהוה (Zech 14:1); כיום מדין (Isa 9:3); ביום מצרים (Ezek 30:9); יום ירושלים (Ps 137:7). Cf. Hoffmann, "Day," 37; Norin, "Der Tag Gottes," 37, 38; Wendebourg, *Der Tag des Herrn*, 28–29.

²⁴⁸ E.g., יום נקם ליהוה (Isa 34:8); יום אף יהוה (Zeph 2:2; cf. Isa 13:9); יום עברת יהוה (Ezek 7:19; Zeph 1:18). Cf. Norin, "Der Tag Gottes," 36; Hoffman, "Day," 37; Wendebourg, *Der Tag des Herrn*, 28.

²⁴⁹ For a brief survey of the motif in Ezekiel, see Norin, "Der Tag des Herrn," 46–50.

²⁵⁰ Even though Norin recognizes the common motif of the day of YHWH in Ezek 7 and 30, he does not note the semantic parallels between the two chapters.

²⁵¹ Cf. קרוב יום יהוה "the day of YHWH is near" in Isa 13:6, Joel 1:15, 4:14, Obad 15, Zeph 1:7, 14.

than joyful shouting on the mountains" in 7:7). The day inaugurates YHWH's wrath and anger, such that the nations will come to "know that I am YHWH" (30:8; cf. 7:9).[252] This day further stirs up the emotions, fear, and anguish in the hearts of those inhabitants under punishments (30:4, 9, 16; cf. 7:17, 18). With these cosmic and emotional impacts, Egypt and Judah alike encounter the day of YHWH.[253] When the divine judgment comes upon Egypt, all the entourage including Judah are envisioned to fall like Egypt.

## 3.2. Exile

Amidst many lexical parallels between the Egypt and Judah oracles, of special significance is the language of exile. In the first two chapters of the Egypt oracles, the dispersion of the Egyptians among the nations after their fall in the hand of the Babylonian king is recounted several times.[254] The Egyptian banishment expressed through the two roots פוץ "to scatter"[255] and זרה "to disperse"[256] corresponds to the Judahite exile mentioned elsewhere in the book of Ezekiel. No other foreign nations in Ezekiel's oracles against the nations receive such a punishment.

It is likely that the threats of exile and dispersion in the Egypt oracles model after the same predictions in the Judah oracles. Overall, Ezekiel's deployment of the language of exile reflects a conflation and an expansion of the language of dispersion found in the pentateuchal materials. For instance,

---

[252] The motif of the day of YHWH is prominent especially in the prophetic books of the Hebrew Bible and designate YHWH's revelation and involvement in the world. Noted by Norin, "Der Tag Gottes," 39, 41; Wendebourg, *Der Tag des Herrn*, 28, 61–62.

[253] Oswald states: "Der Tag Jhwhs hat etwas Unerwartetes, man kann ihn nicht berechnen, niemand kann dem Gericht Gottes vorgreifen, niemand sich selbst sicher wähnen und meinen, nur andere würden dem Gericht verfallen" ("Zukunftserwartung," 29).

[254] Ezek 29:12; 30:23, 26 (cf. 32:9).

[255] Within Ezekiel, the related forms of פוץ appears in 11:16, 17; 12:15; 20:23, 34, 41; 22:15; 28:25; 29:12, 13; 30:23, 26; 34:5 (2x), 6, 12, 21; 36:19. In these cases, the term appears in the context of exile exclusively of Judah and Egypt. Outside Ezekiel, the term in *niphal* or *hiphil* also denotes exile (e.g., Deut 4:27; 28:64; 30:3). Cf. Neh 1:9; Isa 11:12; 24:21. For more explications, see H. Ringgren, "פוץ," *TDOT* 11:509–12.

[256] Out of its thirty-nine biblical occurrences, Ezekiel uses the *piel* verb זרה ten times (5:10, 12; 6:5; 12:14, 15; 20:23; 22:15; 29:12; 30:23, 26). The verb emerges in Ezekiel's descriptions of the divine act of judgment executed upon Israel and Egypt. For other appearances of the related forms of זרה, see Exod 32:20; Num 17:2; Lev 26:33; Isa 30:22, 24; 41:16; Ruth 3:2; Jer 4:11; 15:7; 31:10; 49:32, 36; 51:2; Ezek 5:2; Zech 2:2, 4; Pss 44:12; 106:27; 139:3; Job 18:15; Prov 1:17; 15:7; 20:8, 26; Mal 2:3; 1 Kgs 14:15. Cf. Marzouk, *Egypt*, 122; *HALOT* 1:280.

YHWH's threat to bring the nation Judah into exile is formulated as such: "I will scatter (והפיצותי) you among the nations, and I will disperse you (וזריתיך) through the countries, and I will consume your uncleanness from you" (22:15).[257] The same threat, which addresses the Egyptians, recurs in 30:26: "And I will scatter (והפצותי) the Egyptians among the nations, and I will disperse them among the lands."[258] Gile points out that Ezekiel always juxtaposes the verb זרה with the verb הפיץ to convey YHWH's act of dispersion.[259] He further demonstrates that the Deuteronomic passages about the dispersion, apart from chapter 29, consistently use the verb הפיץ.[260] On the other hand, the covenant curse in the Holiness Code employs the verb זרה and never הפיץ.[261] Therefore, Gile makes a cogent case that the scattering motif in Ezekiel represents a conflation of language derived from the Holiness Code on the one hand, and Deuteronomy on the other. Taking into consideration the volume of use in Ezekiel, the exilic language and imagery assigned to Judah alone far outweigh those attributed to Egypt. Vogels rightly claims that "C'est la formule très classique pour l'exil d'Israël."[262]

The Egypt oracles thus paraphrase the language ascribed to Judah in order to draw a parallel between the conditions of Egypt and Judah. The exile is reserved for Judah in the first part of the book of Ezekiel, which predicts the demise of Jerusalem. After these numerous predictions concerning the fall of the capital city of Judah, Egypt as the closest ally of Judah becomes the target of this judgment of exile. The ascription of this imagery to an ally only rhetorically affirms the certainty of the predictions concerning the exile of Judah. The imagery of exile indicates the demise of both Judah and Egypt.

3.3. DEATH

Even more daringly, the subsequent prophecies in Ezek 32 paint an imagery of death that not only announces the demise of Egypt but also creates apprehension toward the downfall of the kingdom of Judah.[263] The bleak motifs of dirge and netherworld, which are otherwise rarely discussed in detail in the

---

[257] Cf. Ezek 5:2, 10, 12; 6:8; 11:16–17; 12:14–15; 20:23, 34, 41; 22:15, 19; 28:25; 34:5, 6, 12, 13; 36:19, 24; 37:21; 39:27–28.

[258] Cf. Ezek 29:12–13; 30:23.

[259] Gile, "Deuteronomy," 288.

[260] Cf. Deut 4:27–28; 28:36–37, 41, 64; 29:23–27 [Eng. 29:25–28]. Cf. Ibid., 289–90.

[261] Ibid., 288–89, following Lyons, Law, 118, 183, compares Lev 26:33 with Ezek 5:2, 12; 12:14.

[262] Vogels, "Restauration," 478.

[263] Cf. Ezek 31:14, 15–18.

Hebrew Bible,[264] loom large in the prophecies against Egypt and climax at the end with an assemblage of denizens accompanying Egypt in the netherworld.[265]

The message of national demise is first proclaimed in the form of an elegy to Pharaoh (32:1–16), where the language and literary style closely resemble the dirge directed at the princes of Judah in chapter 19. Both laments share a unique form, building up an *inclusio* to embrace the content of destruction in the middle.[266] Similar to the funeral dirge lifted up over the princes of Israel in Ezek 19, the first half of chapter 32 begins with a command to the prophet to raise a lament (קינה, v. 2) and ends with a colophon, with its fourfold use of קנן/קנה (v. 16).[267] Both chapters deploy the imagery of lions (כפיר in 32:2; כפירים in 19:2) to symbolize the monarchs of Egypt and Judah. Despite the fact that the lion often symbolizes power and royalty in the ancient Near East, the texts in Ezekiel shy away from giving the metaphors any positive values.[268] All of the lions are to be captured by either net or hooks.[269] Such a close parallel in terms of form, language, and content invites a comparison between the announcement of the doom of Judah as a nation with that concerning Egypt.

This call to lament is not the only reminder of the death sentence announced to the nations. Ezekiel's last message concerning Egypt (32:17–32) also builds up both a temporal and a spatial suspense to the dire fate of the

---

[264] K. Schöpflin states: "Zunächst einmal fällt auf, dass Aussagen über das Totenreich in der hebräischen Bibel relative dünn gesät sind" ("Ein Blick in die Unterwelt (Jesaja 14)," *TZ* 58 [2002]: 299–314, here 300). For an overview of the death imagery and netherworld in the Hebrew Bible, see P. S. Johnston, "Death in Egypt and Israel: A Theological Reflection," in *The Old Testament in Its World*, ed. R. P. Gordon and J. C. de Moor, OtSt 52 (Leiden: Brill, 2005), 94–116, esp. 104–11; C. B. Hays, *Death in the Iron Age II and in the First Isaiah*, FAT 79 (Tübingen: Mohr Siebeck, 2011), 153–201; D. Alexander, "The Old Testament View of Life after Death," *Them* 11 (1986): 41–46; L. Wächter, "Unterweltsvorstellungen in Babylonien, Israel und Ugarit," *MIO* 15 (1969): 327–36.

[265] On death especially in relation to Ezek 32, see D. I. Block, "Beyond the Grave: Ezekiel's Vision of Death and Afterlife," *BBR* 2 (1992): 113–41; J. T. Strong, "Egypt's Shameful Death and the House of Israel's Exodus from Sheol (Ezekiel 32.17–32 and 37.1–14)," *JSOT* 34 (2010): 475–504; S. M. Olyan, "Unnoticed Resonances of Tomb Opening and Transportation of the Remains of the Dead in Ezekiel 37:12–14," *JBL* 128 (2009): 491–501.

[266] Odell, *Ezekiel*, 402; Block, *Ezekiel*, 2:198; Allen, *Ezekiel*, 2:130; Zimmerli, *Ezekiel*, 2:157. Ezekiel's laments over Tyre do not possess this envelope structure.

[267] Block, *Ezekiel*, 2:198.

[268] Cf. Strawn, *Lion*, 249–50.

[269] Ezek 19:4, 8, 9; 32:3.

house of Judah. The suspense stands out especially when this pericope in the MT is compared with its counterpart in P967.[270]

The MT and P967 of Ezek 32:17–32 depict different temporal horizons. P967 and other Septuagintal versions begin and end the list of nations with the giants (οι γιγαντες; 32:21, 27), who emerge elsewhere in Gen 6:4 as the product of the illicit sexual relationship between "the sons of God" and "the daughters of men."[271] The connection between the two episodes goes far deeper, since Ezek 32:27 characterizes the giants as "of old" (απ αιωνος), which is a phrase occurring elsewhere only in Gen 6:4.[272] As stated clearly in v. 27a in P967, "and they [the nations] were laid with the giants, the ones who fell from of old" (και εκοιμηθησαν μετα των γιγατων των πεπτωκοτων των απ αιωνος).[273] Ezek 32 in P967, along with other Greek versions, clearly connects the dead nations with the figures from the mythological past. The netherworld in the MT is occupied by not the primeval giants, but the mighty men (גבורים).[274] The MT characterizes the גבורים not as "of old" (מעולם, 32:27), but as a group in distinction "from the uncircumcised" (מערלים).[275] That is, MT Ezek 32:27a reads: "And they [the nations] will not lie with the mighty men, those who fell apart from the uncircumcised" ( ולא ישכבו את גברים נפלים מערלים).[276] This rendering of the MT coheres with the surrounding context where the denizens of the netherworld are repeatedly called the uncircumcised (ערלים), a term that reinforces the most shameful and impure status of the dead in chapter 32.[277] Without characterizing the warriors as "of old," the atmosphere of death in the MT netherworld exudes a flair of historical imminence.

---

[270] For an introduction of P967, see the discussion in Section 3.2 of Chapter One. For the P967 text of Ezek 32:17–32, see A. C. Johnson, et al., eds., *The John H. Scheide Biblical Papyri: Ezekiel*, Princeton University Studies in Papyrology 3 (Princeton: Princeton University Press, 1938), 168–69.

[271] Lilly, *Two Books*, 160–61, 166–67.

[272] Lust, "Divergences," 88; Lilly, *Two Books*, 192.

[273] Johnson, *Papyri*, 169.

[274] Note, however, that several scholars assert a connection between the recurrences of the participle נפלים in MT Ezek 32 and the Nephilim in Gen 6:4. See B. Doak, "Ezekiel's Topography of the (Un-)Heroic Dead in Ezekiel 32:17-32," *JBL* 132 (2013): 607-24, here 610, 622-23; E. G. Kraeling, "The Significance and Origin of Gen 6:1-4," *JNES* 6 (1947): 193-208, here 196-97; R. S. Hendel, "Of Demigods and Deluge: Toward an Interpretation of Genesis 6:1-4," *JBL* 106 (1987): 13-26, here 21-22; Block, *Ezekiel*, 2:228-29; idem, "Grave," 125; Eichrodt, *Ezekiel*, 436.

[275] *Contra* the emendation in Block, *Ezekiel*, 220.

[276] Cf. Lilly, *Two Books*, 165.

[277] The appearances of the uncircumcised in Ezek 32:17–32 are always paired with "the slain of the sword" (vv. 19, 21, 24, 25, 26, 28, 29, 30, 32). The "uncircumcised" also appear in 28:10 and 31:18, where even the Egyptians, the Edomites, and the Si-

As noted by Strong, "the two oracles in Ezekiel 32 both date to the final months of the Babylonian siege, a time when it must have been clear that Jerusalem would fall, as well as a time when the conditions within the city had arrived at their most horrific state."[278] Unlike P967, the death toll of the nations in the MT does not refer to an old myth but an imminent reality applicable also to the house of Judah.

The spatial arrangement of the denizens in both the MT and P967 of Ezek 32:17–32 also differ. P967 presents a shorter list of nations, concentrating only on Assyria (vv. 22–23) and Elam (vv. 24–27).[279] It also differentiates their leaders: the princes of Assyria (v. 29) and the princes of the north (v. 30).[280] Apart from the two aforementioned nations, no other foreign nations are named. The pericope on Elam in the papyrus is shorter than that in the MT.[281] On the other hand, the netherworld in the MT is a more crowded place.[282] In addition to Assyria (vv. 22–23) and Elam (vv. 24–27), the denizens include Meshech-Tubal (vv. 26–28).[283] The netherworld in the MT further houses the contiguous neighbours of Judah such as Edom (v. 29) and the Sidonians (v. 30). Consequently, the MT displays a geographical focus on the Levantine situation.[284] Lilly tentatively suggests that "the difference in geography between the two editions likely bespeaks different historical horizons against which the lament for Egypt is articulated."[285] While the focus on Elam and Assyria in P967 hints at the struggles between the two nations in the seventh century BCE, the references to Edom and the Sidonians in the MT suggest the Babylonian period when the two nations were active on the political

---

donians, who practiced the rite of circumcision, are called the uncircumcised. On circumcision in the ancient Near East, see Block, "Grave," 124, n. 68, who cites J. M. Sasson, "Circumcision in the Ancient Near East," *JBL* 85 (1966): 473–76; *ANET*, 326; Herodotus, *Histories*, 2:104; Josephus, *Ant.*, 8.10.3.

[278] Strong, "Death," 487.

[279] Lilly, *Two Books*, 162; Lust, "Divergences," 87; Olley, *Ezekiel*, 457.

[280] In v. 29, P967 reads: οι αρχοντες ασσουρ οι δοντες την ισχυν αυτου "The rulers of Assyria who gave his might." In v. 30, P967 further characterizes the "princes of the north" as παντες στρατηγοι ασσοουρ "all rulers of Assur." Cf. Johnson, *Papyri*, 169.

[281] Lilly, *Two Books*, 162; Olley, *Ezekiel*, 457.

[282] Lilly, *Two Books*, 162.

[283] In Ezek 27:13, the latter is treated as two separate nations—Meshech and Tubal, listed alongside Javan as the trading partners of Tyre. The two nations come to feature prominently in the eschatological battle in Ezek 38–39. Lust suggests that the MT inserts Meschech and Tubal in chapter 32, in order to present the enemies in the Gog oracles (chapters 38–39) not as eschatological but as historical figures ("Divergences," 87–88).

[284] Lilly, *Two Books*, 163.

[285] Ibid.

arena.²⁸⁶ In my view, the intention for including Edom and the Sidonians in the MT is to create a zooming-in effect that heightens the suspense about the dire fate of Judah. The Hebrew text shifts the limelight from the powerful nations in the north (Assyria, Elam, Meshech-Tubal) to the nations that are geographically closer to the kingdom of Judah. This, in turn, creates an encirclement of death, closing in to the target nation, Judah. Shortly after such a death sentence announced to Egypt, the demise of Jerusalem is declared (Ezek 33:21).

3.4. RESTORATION

So far, I have stressed that the fate suffered by Egypt is largely similar and almost identical to the kingdom of Judah. Both nations suffer a highly similar kind of downfall, which involves destruction, exile, and demise. Are their fates totally identical even after the demise and until the restoration, so that no difference ever exists between them?

To answer this question, we have to turn to Ezek 29:13–16, which proclaims an oracle of restoration to Egypt, and which is likely added later to its present context.²⁸⁷ In the oracle, Egypt will be restored after forty years of exile among the nations. YHWH will gather the Egyptians from the peoples (v. 13), turn the fortunes of Egypt (v. 14), give them a kingdom (vv. 14–15), and bring them to recognize YHWH as God (v. 16). This picture of restoration invites comparisons not only between Egypt and the restored Israel, but also between Egypt and other foreign nations such as Tyre, Ammon, Moab, Edom, and Philistia. An examination of the fate of the foreign nations, on the one hand, and that of the restored Israel, on the other, will act as a control in assessing the extent of the similarities between Egypt and Israel.

The restoration of Egypt contrasts with the fates of the other foreign nations appearing in Ezek 25–28. Why should Egypt alone receive a restoration that is not assigned to Tyre, Ammon, Moab, Edom, and Philistia? The oracles

---

²⁸⁶ Ibid., n. 77. Still, she cautions that "it is difficult to determine 'what actual political polemic is involved' for the Sidonians (צדני)."

²⁸⁷ Many have considered this section of the oracle, which is introduced by a new messenger formula ("For thus has the Lord YHWH declared") and a new concern for restoration, as a later addition. However, the extent of the addition remains controversial. Fechter considers vv. 13–16 as belonging to the third stage of expansion added after vv. 9b–11a, 12*, 16b (*Bewältigung*, 222–23). Alternatively, Pohlmann considers vv. 13–16 as being added together with vv. 9b–12 into chapter 29 such that "29,9b–16 dürfte das jüngste Stück im Komplex der Ägyptenworte sein" (*Kapitel 20–48*, 408–9).

concerning the neighboring nations of Judah all end with a note of destruction.[288] Ammon is sentenced to a fate not to be remembered among the nations.[289] Tyre faces the repeating curse, such that it will become terrors (בלהות), and fall into oblivion.[290] By contrast, Egypt suffers exile and death as a nation but ultimately receives restoration.[291] Why does the restoration oracle concerning Egypt appear in 29:13–16 at all, when none seems to be offered to the other foreign nations?[292]

Block helpfully provides a convincing solution based on the comparison between Ezek 29:16 and 28:24.[293] Both verses begin with the phrase "and it will never be again for the house of Israel" (ולא יהיה עוד לבית ישראל) and end with the recognition formula "then they will know that I am the Lord YHWH" (וידעו כי אני אדני יהוה). Ezekiel 28:24 makes clear that the foreign nations have taunted Judah and gloated over its destruction. Unlike the other nations, Egypt did not act so, but functioned as an "object of trust" for the house of Israel (29:16).[294] According to Block, this leaves YHWH free to pursue a different course with Egypt.[295] Egypt shares a relationship with the house of Israel that is not shared with the other foreign nations. Egypt is closer to Israel than the other nations. This understanding explains the destruction, exile, and death, which are uniquely shared between Egypt and Judah.

We must ask further if this intimacy between Egypt and Israel indicates YHWH's readiness to place the two nations on a par in the future restoration. A *prima facie* reading of Ezek 29:13–16 in light of the restoration oracles of Israel would seem to suggest so.[296] Detecting the small cluster of linguistic resemblances between the two groups of restoration oracles, Vogels charac-

---

[288] Marzouk, *Egypt*, 203.

[289] Cf. Ezek 25:10.

[290] Cf. Ezek 26:21; 27:36; 28:19.

[291] Cf. Ezek 29:13–16.

[292] Fuhs suggests that this restoration oracle in Ezek 29:13–16 is composed during the Jewish Diaspora in Egypt to tone down the harsh judgment given to Egypt in 29:1–12 (*Ezechiel*, 2:161–62). This suggestion brings us to a history behind the text, and he needs to provide more textual justification for this argument.

[293] Block, *Ezekiel*, 2:144.

[294] Note that the verbal root בטח "to trust, to be secure" appears twice in Ezek 28:16, in order to denote the restored Israel's security in the land granted by YHWH. Cf. Jer 2:37, where YHWH has rejected Assyria and Egypt as an object of trust for Judah. Rather, those who trust in YHWH are called the blessed (Jer 17:7). For further explications of the usage of this word in Ezekiel, see Marzouk, *Egypt*, 215; Minj, *Egypt*, 97.

[295] Block, *Ezekiel*, 2:144.

[296] Cf. the restoration oracles of Israel in Ezek 11:17–20; 20:34, 41; 28:25; 34:13; 36:24; 37:21.

terizes Ezek 29:13–16 as standing in line with some other "universalist" biblical texts such as Jonah, which advocate a more inclusive attitude to all Gentiles and nations.[297] The final purpose of the oracle, as he suggests, is to lead the nations through a religious conversion and recognition of YHWH's sovereignty over the nations' history.[298] For Vogels, the nations receive the benefits and have their own exodus experience. The outcome is a sense of belonging between YHWH and the nations, leading to the nations' recognition and submission, in addition to promising a restoration with new benefits.[299] However, it is doubtful if the kind of religious conversion of Egypt envisioned by Vogels really exists in 29:13–16. As noted in the previous discussion concerning the presence of "dung gods" (גלולים) in 30:13, the oracles against Egypt do not seem to center on the religious world of Egypt, unless it comes into contact with the idolatry of Israel.[300] Rather, the divine judgment executed through Babylon forms the focus of Ezekiel's oracles concerning Egypt.[301]

Minj's 2006 exegetical monograph on Ezek 29:1–16 follows, expands, and develops Vogels's "universalist" stance on 29:13–16.[302] In detail, he analyzes the significance and rhetorical function of the semantic and other literary resemblances between Ezekiel's restoration oracles for Egypt and Israel. He reads the linguistic and thematic connections as signifying not only judgment, but also salvation for both Egypt and Israel. Concerning the nature of salvation for these two nations, Minj differs from and goes even further than Vogels. For Vogels, YHWH demands Egypt to submit in a way different from the restored Israel, and so the restoration of Egypt must be distinguished from that of Israel.[303] By contrast, Minj assimilates the restoration of Egypt into that of

---

[297] Vogels, "Restauration," 482–83.

[298] Ibid., 482–83, 491.

[299] The above sentences are a rough paraphrase of Vogels, "Restauration," 493–94.

[300] Cf. Section 2.2 in Chapter Four.

[301] E.g., 29:17–21; 30:10, 24; 32:11. Kessler, *Ägyptenbilder*, 80.

[302] A similar "universalistic" interpretation of Ezek 29:13–16 can be found in P. E. Fitzpatrick, *The Disarmament of God: Ezekiel 38–39 in Its Mythic Context*, CBQMS 37 (Washington: Catholic Biblical Association of America, 2004), 154: "This regathering in the Oracle against Egypt presents the same theology of covenant as is presented in the texts on Israel. It is significant because it implies a shift to universalism. Yhwh directs the history of the nations as well." Likewise, Blenkinsopp compares the oracle in Ezek 29:13–16 with Jer 46:26 and Isa 19:18–25, such that the "blessing of Abraham will overflow Israel and descend on all peoples, a prophetic insight, often forgotten, which will be taken up by early Christianity" (*Ezekiel*, 131). See also B. F. Batto, *Slaying the Dragon: Mythmaking in the Biblical Tradition* (Louisville: Westminster John Knox, 1992), 165; L. Boadt, "Mythological Themes and the Unity of Ezekiel," in *Literary Structure and Rhetorical Strategies in the Hebrew Bible*, ed. L. J. de Regt et al. (Assen: Van Gorcum, 1996), 211–31, here 227.

[303] Vogels, "Restauration," 493.

Israel, such that "God deals with Egypt in the same way as with Israel. This places Egypt in a privileged place on par with Israel."[304] He justifies this reading with an examination of the deployment of the terms קבץ "to gather" and שוב שבות "to go into captivity" in 29:13–16. He stresses that קבץ is used elsewhere in the Hebrew Bible to denote salvation.[305] According to him, the same can be said about the usage of שוב שבות.[306] Then he quickly jumps to the conclusion that the usage of the same terms in 29:13–16 must also mean redemption for Egypt on a par with Israel.[307] He too easily dismisses the cases where the verbal forms of קבץ are used in the context of divine judgment on either Israel or the nations.[308] It is true that קבץ means salvation in two pericopes of Trito-Isaiah, which spell out a more inclusive attitude toward the foreigners.[309] However, the context of Ezekiel's oracles concerning Egypt is different. Ezekiel's polemic against any close relationship between Egypt and Judah makes it more speculative to conclude that קבץ in Ezek 29 allows the sort of inclusive attitude evident in Trito-Isaiah.

Vogels and Minj should be credited for their close attention to the semantic resemblances between the restoration oracles of Egypt and Israel. Their final conclusions, however, must be refined by examining the overall context of 29:13–16. Despite being a late insertion, 29:13–16 still demonstrates many

---

[304] Minj, *Egypt*, 187. He later claims that "Egypt is given the dignity of being one of God's people, similar to Israel, and placed beside her even as His dealing with Egypt becomes a paradigm for Israel's restoration and salvation" (213).

[305] קבץ occurs in the context of the salvation for Israel in Deut 30:3, 4; Ps 107:3; Isa 11:12; 31:10; 40:11; 43:5; 54:7; 56:8; Jer 23:3; 29:14; 31:8; 32:37; Ezek 11:17; 20:34; 20:41; 22:19; 28:25; 34:13; 36:24; 37:21; 39:27; Mic 2:12; 4:6; Zeph 3:19, 20; Zech 10:8, 10; Neh 1:9. In only three texts, it is used in the context to describe God's actions in favor of the *nations*: Isa 56:8; 66:18; Ezek 29:13. Cf. Ibid., 101–39.

[306] שוב כבות means "to restore from captivity." With people as the grammatical object, it occurs in Ezek 29:14 (the Egyptians); Jer 48:47 (Moab); Jer 49:6 (Ammon); Jer 49:39 (Elam); Jer 29:14 (the exiles); Zeph 2:7 (the remnant of the house of Judah); Jer 33:7 (Judah and Israel); Joel 4:1; Jer 31:23 (Jerusalem); Amos 9:14 (Israel); Jer 30:3 (Judah); Ps 85:2 (Jacob); Ezek 39:25 (Jacob and the house of Israel); Hos 6:11; Ps 14:7; 53:7; Deut 30:3; Zeph 3:20 (people in general). Cf. Ibid., 142.

[307] E.g., ibid., 133: "Israel remains God's chosen people; nonetheless, He extends the privilege of worshiping Him also to other nations, bringing them *on a par* with Israel" (italics mine).

[308] E.g., קבץ in Ezek 16:37; 22:20; Hos 8:10; Joel 4:2; Mic 4:12; Zeph 3:8. Cf. Ibid., 127–32.

[309] Isa 56:8; 66:18. Cf. C. Westermann, *Isaiah 40–66*, OTL (London: SCM Press, 1969), 296; J. Blenkinsopp, *Isaiah 56–66*, AB 198 (New York: Doubleday, 2003); B. S. Childs, *Isaiah*, OTL (Louisville: Westminster John Knox, 2001), 542; J. Kaminsky and A. Stewart, "God of All the World: Universalism and Developing Monotheism in Isaiah 40–66," *HTR* 99 (2006): 139–63.

shared locutions with the preceding pericopes in 29:1–12. The restoration oracle (vv. 13–16) is linked to the exile of Egypt among the nations (vv. 9b–12) through the connective כי. As noted by Vogels, the theme about false confidence is common to both v. 6b and v. 16, and there is the connecting motif of "forty years" at vv. 11, 12, 13.[310] All these indicate an editorial attempt to read 29:13–16 as continuing the polemic posited in 29:1–12, which is directed against the alliance between Judah and Egypt. It is Marzouk, who provides a more nuanced exegesis of the restoration oracle in 29:13–16.[311] As will be analyzed in detail below, Marzouk proposes that the restoration in vv. 13–16 does not promise a matching salvation for both Egypt and the restored Israel, but rather establishes an ideal geopolitical distance between Egypt and Israel in the newly restored era.

Upon closer examination, 29:13–16 marks the distinctions between Egypt and Israel in the future by creating the geographical and political distance between the two nations.[312] Geographically, YHWH will restore Egypt to its land of origin, Pathros (29:14). The name is derived from the Egyptian word *p'-t'-rs(y)* "the Southland."[313] In Isa 11:11, this land forms the southern part of ancient Egypt, lying between the Delta (מצרים) and Ethiopia (כוש).[314] As stated by Marzouk, the settling of Egypt to its southern part allows YHWH to create a greater geographical distance between Egypt and the Levant.[315] Politically, Egypt will become a "lowly kingdom" (ממלכה שפלה), so that it will no longer rule over the other nations (29:14b–15). The Hebrew word שפלה usually translated as "low" likely describes the minimization of Egypt's political status.[316] Minj argues that the expression "lowly kingdom" is devoid of any political connotation, and purely denotes the transformed character of Egypt, who will humbly accept YHWH's "sovereignty in His creation."[317] The same expression, however, occurs in Ezek 17:14 as a *terminus technicus* to denote

---

[310] Vogels, "Restauration," 475.
[311] Marzouk, *Egypt*, 204, 211–17.
[312] Ibid., 212.
[313] Ibid., 213; Block, *Ezekiel*, 2:143.
[314] The tripartite division of Egypt is similar to one of Esarhaddon's inscriptions (ca. 671 BCE), where the three aforementioned territories signify the totality of the Egyptian land under the reign of Taharaq. Esarhaddon designates himself as the "king of kings, king of Egypt, Pathros and Cush" (KUR.*mu-ṣur*, KUR. *pa-tu-ri-si u* KUR.*ku-si*). See Leichty, *Royal Inscriptions*, 145 (68:4–5); *ANET*, 290; Block, *Ezekiel*, 2:143, n. 76; Marzouk, *Egypt*, 213; Zimmerli, *Ezekiel*, 2:114.
[315] Marzouk, *Egypt*, 213.
[316] Ibid., 214.
[317] Minj, *Egypt*, 92–93.

the vassal status of Judah under the Babylonian imperialism.[318] As Minj concedes, 29:6–7 refers to some kind of political alliance between the house of Israel and Egypt.[319] It is thus more likely that the later insertion in 29:14b–15 seeks to counter the depicted alliance by positing a minimization of the political power of Egypt.[320]

The purpose for minimizing the geopolitical power of Egypt is clearly stated in 29:16. The first part of v. 16 reads: ולא יהיה עוד לבית ישראל למבטח מזכיר עון בפנותם אחריהם. The term מזכיר is a *hiphil* participle,[321] which stands as an apposition to מבטח "an object of trust." It is more likely that the former qualifies the latter. That is, the sentence should probably read: "No longer will it [Egypt] serve the house of Israel as an object of trust, *a reminder of iniquity* when they turned to them [Egyptians]."[322] Boadt offers an alternative translation: "No longer will it [Egypt] be an object of trust for the house of Israel, *but will be a reminder of the iniquity* when they turned to follow them [the Egyptians]."[323] According to this translation, Egypt will continue to haunt Israel, even after the restoration, by reminding them of their infidelity for following the Egyptians. In other words, even though Egypt will no longer be trusted by Judah, the boundary between Egypt and Judah will be reinforced by Israel's constant remembrance of their sinful alignment with Egypt in the past. This second translation aligns with the concept of restoration found in Ezek 16:59–63, where the motif of bringing the guilt to remembrance plays a central role. YHWH in chapter 16, argues Schwartz, restores the covenant with the Israelites, in order to force them to remember their past iniquities and feel the eternal remorse that the exile failed to bring about.[324] The same expression מזכיר עון also appears in Ezek 21:28 [Eng. 21:23], where the "capture

---

[318] Tsevat, "Vassal Oaths," 199–204; Premstaller, *Fremdvölkersprüche*, 149; Bowen, *Ezekiel* 182; Odell, *Ezekiel*, 375; Zimmerli, *Ezekiel*, 2:143–44

[319] Minj, *Egypt*, 93.

[320] The political connotation in the usage of ממלכה שפלה in vv. 14–15 does not need to refer to a specific vassal treaty between Egypt and Israel.

[321] More commonly, the term מזכיר qualifies a person whose job is a recorder (2 Sam 8:16; 20:24; 1 Kgs 4:3; 2 Kgs 18:18, 37; 1 Chr 18:15; 2 Chr 34:8; Isa 36:3, 22).

[322] This understanding is adopted in Minj, *Egypt*, 96, 203–5; Marzouk, *Egypt*, 214, 216; Zimmerli, *Ezekiel*, 2:109.

[323] Boadt, *Ezekiel's Oracles*, 48. This is also the translation of NKJV.

[324] B. J. Schwartz, "Ezekiel's Dim View of Israel's Restoration," in *The Book of Ezekiel: Theological and Anthropological Perspectives*, ed. M. S. Odell et al. (Atlanta: Society of Biblical Literature, 2000), 43–67. While Schwartz sees this bleak tone pervade in all of Ezekiel's restoration oracles, a more nuanced reading is provided by T. Ganzel, "The Descriptions of the Restoration of Israel in Ezekiel," *VT* 60 (2010): 197–211. According to Ganzel, while the restoration oracles in Ezek 11:14–21; 16:59–63; 20:33–44 maintain the anger of YHWH toward his people, the restoration oracles in

of the city of Jerusalem will function as an eternal sign and a reminder of the sin of the Israelites."[325] Contrary to the second translation, the first reading indicates that the restoration of Egypt will bring a new start for Israel, so that Egypt will no longer serve as a reminder of the Israelites' past faithlessness.[326] So great is the geopolitical distance created through the restoration of Egypt in 29:13–16 that the past will never be reiterated.

The recognition formula in the second part of v. 16 brings the restoration oracle to an end. Contrary to what Minj and Vogels assert, the recognition formula here does not signify the establishment of a covenantal relationship between YHWH and Egypt.[327] Rather the immediate literary context is one of warning and intimidation.[328] Elsewhere in the book of Ezekiel, the recognition formula often appears in a context where YHWH pledges to execute his punishments upon the nations.[329] By the same logic, the recognition formula in this oracle unit concerning Egypt does not signify an intimate relationship between Egypt and YHWH, but serves to highlight the acceptance of YHWH's might with trembling and trepidation.

The frightening aspect of this recognition formula becomes particularly evident when we compare the oracle unit with the other restoration oracles of Israel found in the book of Ezekiel.[330] Even though similar language and motifs of "gathering" and "settling" do exist between the restoration oracles of Egypt and Judah, these literary resemblances do not equalize salvation between Egypt and Israel. The immediate literary contexts of the passages concerning Israel's restoration reveal that the ultimate purpose of the restoration is to recover the relationship between YHWH and Israel, so that the people of Israel are filled with a new heart and new spirit from YHWH (11:17; 36:24), YHWH's holiness among his people is witnessed by the nations (20:41), Israel

---

Ezek 34; 36:16–38; 37:15–28; 39:21–29 present a genuinely optimistic outlook for the people of Israel.

[325] Marzouk, *Egypt*, 216; cf. Gen 41:9.

[326] Ibid.

[327] Cf. Eichrodt, *Ezekiel*, 406, who relates that "the assimilation of Egypt's destiny to that of Judah is a sign of how prophetic universalistic ideas of the pattern to be assumed by the nations of the world are breaking through, and of how all political vindictive feelings must be subordinated to those principles." A similar position is found in Zimmerli's explication of the use of the recognition formula throughout Ezekiel ("Knowledge," 88).

[328] *Contra* the aforementioned position of Eichrodt and Zimmerli, Strong argues that the recognition formula in Ezekiel's oracles against Egypt does not have the religious conversion of Egypt in mind. It is used in a context to amplify YHWH's power and might ("Recognition Formula," 130).

[329] E.g., Ezek 25:5, 7, 11, 14, 17; 26:6; 28:22, 26; 29:6, 9, 21; 30:8, 19, 26; 32:15.

[330] The promises of restoration to Israel include Ezek 11:17; 20:41; 28:25–26; 34:13; 36:24; 37:21–34.

will walk under the guidance of YHWH the good shepherd (34:13), and Israel is called YHWH's people and YHWH Israel's God (37:21–23). The so-called *Bundesformel* "they will be my people, and I will be their God" almost always accompany the restoration oracles of Ezekiel.[331] This kind of covenantal renewal for Israel stands in striking contrast with the promise of restoration to Egypt. Ezek 29:14 envisions a greater geographical distance between Egypt and Israel (v. 14). This distance is further reinforced by the diminishing political power of Egypt (v. 15). The ultimate purpose is to remove any residue of the Egyptian influence on the restored Israel (v. 16). The prophecy pronounces its hope, so that history will never repeat itself.

All in all, Ezek 29–32 exploits the intimate alliance between Egypt and Judah to sound the death knell of both nations. Egypt is first and foremost YHWH's inveterate enemy. Yet, Judah is repeatedly alluded to in Ezek 29–32 as among those in league with Egypt. The destruction, exile, and death sentenced for Judah's most intimate ally, Egypt, bears terrifying resemblances to the judgment pronounced to Judah. This explains why later interpreters were eager to announce a promise of restoration that does not place Egypt on a par with Israel (29:13–16). Rather, the restoration oracle magnifies the distance between Egypt and Israel, so as to extricate Israel from the past mire. Since Egypt had been Judah's most intimate ally, later interpreters were willing enough to insert glimpses of hope for no other foreign nations but Egypt alone. Nevertheless, this future restoration does not dominate the Egypt oracles. The destruction predicted for Egypt does not avert the upcoming doom of the kingdom of Judah. With the demise of Egypt comes the fall of the capital city of Judah. Closely following the collection of prophecies concerning Egypt, Ezek 33:21 reads: "In the twelfth year of our exile, in the tenth month, on the fifth day of the month, the fugitive from Jerusalem came to me, saying, 'The city has been struck down!'"

---

[331] Ezek 11:20; 14:11; 36:28; 37:23, 27. The *Bundesformel* and its variant forms are also attested in Hos 2:21–23; Jer 24:4–7; 30:18–32; 31:31–34; 32:36–41. Raitt considers it as "the single most important and effective way of expressing a new era in the God-Israel relationship" (*Theology*, 134). For a detailed analysis of the textual development of the *Bundesformel* within Ezekiel, see S. Petry, *Die Entgrenzung Jhwhs*, FAT 2/27 (Tübingen: Mohr Siebeck, 2007), 242–72.

# CHAPTER FIVE

# EXPLORING THE AFTERLIVES

ויהי בשתי עשׂרה שנה בעשׂרי בחמשה לחדש לגלותנו בא אלי הפליט מירושׁלם לאמר הכתה העיר.

And it came about in the twelfth year of our exile, in the tenth month, on the fifth of the month, the fugitive from Jerusalem came to me, saying, "The city has been struckdown."

Ezek 33:21

ואת־שם קדשי אודיע בתוך עמי ישראל ולא־אחל את־שם־קדשי עוד וידעו שגוים כי אני יהוה קדוש בישראל.

And my holy name I shall make known in the midst of my people Israel; and I shall not let my holy name be profaned any more. And the nations will know that I am YHWH, the holy one in Israel.

Ezek 39:7

This study has mapped a literary journey through Ezek 25–32, which is filled with vivid depictions of the dispossession of the lands contiguous to Judah, the destruction of the Tyrian mercantile empire, and the death of the monstrous Pharaoh and his entourage. A summary of what I have observed, discussed, and argued will emerge in the following section. After that, I will chart further repercurssions of this study by showing how some parts of the prophetic book can be better understood when perceived as comments on and responses to the message of judgment embedded in Ezek 25–32.

## 1. Summary

As observed in Chapter One, some commentators, generalizing the enmity between the nations and Judah, emphasize that the destruction of the nations in chapters 25–32 means the upcoming salvation of God's people. Others, presupposing the nations as judged according to a different standard of morality, render the judgment executed upon the nations irrelevant to that upon Judah. Such readings either too quickly anticipate the restoration promised to Israel in the later chapters of Ezekiel, or too neatly demarcate the boundary between Judah and the nations, and thereby unwarrantedly compound the dissimilitude or isolation of Ezek 25–32 within the rest of the book. The problem of such readings, as I have argued, becomes especially palpable when these chapters concerning foreign nations are compared with other biblical passages and the surrounding oracles concerning Judah. Appealing to the lexical allusions present within Ezekiel's oracles against the nations, the cataclysmic images of foreign nations in Ezek 25–32 converge and transform into a story that is also about the downfall of Judah. The corpus stresses the affinities between Judah and the nations. One way or another, all of these foreign nations mirror some characteristics of Judah and they all come under the divine punishments.

As examined in Chapter Two, the territories of two Transjordanian nations are made comparable to the Promised Land. The Ammonite and Moabite precincts, like the covenantal land, are called the "possession" (25:4, 10). These foreign lands produce "fruit" and "milk," which are agricultural products paired elsewhere to characterize the divine blessings offered to the Israelites (25:4). Collectively named "the glory of the land" (25:9), the Moabite cities lie in the region assigned conventionally to the Reubenites. In addition to their affinities with the Promised Land, these neighboring regions suffer the divine retribution, which is described in a manner resembling the language of judgment in Ezekiel's prophecies against Judah. YHWH's vengeance is poured out on Judah, Edom, and Philistia (25:14, 17; cf. 24:8). The punitive arm of YHWH strikes out against both Judah and the enemy nations (25:7, 13, 16; cf. 14:3, 17, 19, 21). Humans and beasts are cut off from not only the land of Judah, but also the territories of Edom, Philistia, and Ammon (25:7, 13, 16; cf. 14:3, 17, 19). The house of Judah gains no benefit from the acts of divine judgment, since the Ammonite and Moabite cities and lands are all to be handed over to the unidentified "sons of the east" (25:4, 9). Although a later layer of the text presents the people of Israel as the agent of divine judgment against Edom, the judgment ultimately serves not the territorial restoration of Israel, but the fulfilment of YHWH's wrath (25:14). Taken altogether, the oracles in Ezek 25 highlight not only territorial resemblances, but also shared judgment between Judah and its neighboring nations.

Describing the splendor and fame of Tyre's trade and monarch, Ezek 26–28 contains a similarly internalized perspective, which has formed the focus of Chapter Three. The dirge in Ezek 27 merges the imagery of the Israelite sanctuary and the magnificent Tyrian ship. Like the Jerusalem temple, the Tyrian ship is called the perfect beauty (27:3, 11; cf. 16:14). The construction of the Tyrian ship alludes to the wilderness tabernacle (e.g., Exod 25 and 26) and recreates the relations between Solomon and King Hiram of Tyre in building the First Temple (e.g., 1 Kgs 5). Equally noteworthy is the imagery of the precious jewelry worn by the Tyrian ruler in the dirge in 28:11–19. The object exhibits unmistakable links to the Israelite priestly pectoral in Exod 28:17–20 and 39:10–13. The beauty of Tyre and its ruler is not only equal to the splendor of the Israelite sacred cult; it is more than that. Tyre's beauty over Jerusalem's splendor is boldly exalted through the insertion of the trade list demonstrating Tyre's multi-national wealth (27:12–14). The Tyrian beauty captures the attention of the nations from all directions. Even Judah and the land of Israel are subsumed under this trade list, offering gifts to decorate the Tyrian mercantile beauty (27:17). The Tyrian king, being located in the divine garden, possesses primordial wisdom and perfect beauty (28:12–13). More than a mortal Israelite priest, the dirge paints the Tyrian ruler as an animate cherub, and thus tantalizingly raises him to a (near-) divine status (28:14). Following these exaltations, both dirges turn dramatically to predict a terrible future for Tyre and its ruler, which also links implicitly to Jerusalem's fate. When the Tyrian ship is shattered so easily by an east wind (27:26) and the Tyrian monarch is cast so decisively by YHWH as profaned (28:16), the dirges not only spell the doom of Tyre, but also raise a rhetorically eerie question: If the perfectly beautiful Tyre and its god-like wise ruler cannot withstand the divine judgment, can a small sanctuary and a mortal priest in Jerusalem survive? The literary context of Ezek 26–28 indicates a bleak prospect for the Jerusalem temple and its leadership.

Chapter Four has drawn our attention to Ezek 29–32, which directs the indictments at Egypt, Judah's strongest political ally in the resistance of the Babylonian hegemony (cf. 17:7, 15; 29:6, 16). Instead of lauding the help offered by Egypt, the oracles demonize this powerful ally of Judah, such that Egypt emerges as the inveterate enemy of YHWH. The text portrays Pharaoh as a chaos monster or a crocodile deity challenging YHWH's divine sovereignty (29:3–4; 32:2). Pharaoh is also a chthonic cedar drawing water from the cosmic deep (31:1–18). With his arm broken, Pharaoh ultimately becomes the defeated enemy of the Babylonian king, who acts as YHWH's agent of judgment (30:20–26). In light of the hostility between YHWH and Pharaoh, the intimate alliance between Egypt and Judah ever since the Israelite sojourn in Egypt (cf. Ezek 16, 20, 23) logically appears as a form of defiance against YHWH. The Judahites serve as military conscripts of Egypt and are thus deemed as traitors of YHWH's covenant (30:5). Symbolized as a cedar and a vine respectively, the two nations are presented as twins, sharing the same rebellious attitude toward YHWH (chapter 31; cf. chapters 15, 17, 19). Judah probably also exists among Egypt's multitude, lying with the slain of the sword and the uncircumcised (32:17–32). Exploiting the intimate relations between the two nations, the prediction of Egypt's doom conveys the most spine-chilling message concerning the survival of Judah as a nation. The language of divine retribution applied to both Egypt and Judah displays striking similarities. Both experience the catastrophic day of YHWH (30:2–3, 8–9; cf. 7:6–7, 9–10). Out of all nations, only Egypt and Judah are punished with exile (29:12; 30:23, 26; 32:9; cf. 5:10; 11:7; 12:15; 20:34; 22:15, 35; 36:19). They both face national collapses and demise (32:17–32 and 33:1–20, 21–22). Being an ally of Judah, Egypt is the only foreign nation that receives a promise of restoration (29:13–16; cf. 11:17–20; 20:34, 41; 28:25; 34:13; 36:24; 37:21). It is in this restoration oracle that we see a later attempt to widen the gap between the restored Israel and Egypt. The ideal picture painted by this restoration is such that Egypt will never interact politically with or even come close geographically to the restored Israel. From Ezekiel's perspective, the abandonment of past alignment with Egypt is essential for the national survival of the restored Israel.

As will be observed in the following, the attempts to parallelize and to polarize the relations between God's people and the foreign nations continue to unfold as we move to the rest of the book of Ezekiel.

## 2. Affirming the Oblique Judgement

The first kind of editorial response to the message of "oblique judgment" embedded in Ezek 25–32 can be glimpsed from the series of chronological formulas sprinkled in the eight chapters of prophecies against foreign nations. The literary significance of Ezekiel's chronological formulas stands out by a comparison with the other prophetic books. As noted by McKeating, neither in Isaiah nor in Jeremiah are dates deployed in the systematic way as in Ezekiel.[1] To be sure, Isaiah and Jeremiah contain dating of individual oracles. Isa 6:1 and 14:28 date the oracles more generally according to the end of the regnal year of the kings, while 7:1 sets the event more broadly "in the days of Ahaz."[2] The dates in Jeremiah's oracles are no more precise. They note the year or "the beginning of the reign of" a particular king,[3] and only incidentally

---

[1] H. McKeating, *Ezekiel*, OTG (Sheffield: JSOT Press, 1993), 62–63.

[2] Ibid., 62.

[3] For the passages that specify only the year, see Jer 1:2; 25:1; 32:1; 36:11; 45:1. For the passages that record "the beginning of the reign of" a particular king, see Jer 26:1; 27; 49:34. See also ibid.

refer to the month.⁴ The closer parallels to Ezekiel's dating system are to be found in the books of Haggai and Zechariah, both of which contain more precisely dated oracles.⁵ However, the time period covered by these oracles is not as extensive as those in Ezekiel. All the dates in Haggai occur in the second year of the Persian King Darius, that is, 520 BCE.⁶ The dates in Zechariah's prophecies range from the second to the fourth year of King Darius.⁷ By contrast, the dates in Ezekiel fall within a range of a twenty-two year period. Ezek 1:1 and 3:16 date their oracles to the fifth year, while 29:17 contains the latest chronological formula, which is dated to "the twenty-seventh year, in the first month, on the first of the month." Specific temporal statements occur thirteen times within Ezekiel.⁸ Seven of these appear in the OAN, especially in the prophecies concerning Egypt. In other words, more than half of the chronological formulas in Ezekiel appear in the OAN. In light of this, the systematic and extensive dating of the oracles in Ezekiel is unprecedented in the Hebrew Bible.

The significance of Ezekiel's chronological system has been more fully analyzed in Mayfield's 2010 monograph. Mayfield treats Ezekiel's temporal markers as a structural device that integrates chapters 25–32 with the surrounding passages concerning the fate of Judah.⁹ The focus of Mayfield's study remains synchronic by nature.¹⁰ However, many of Mayfield's ingenious insights can be strengthened by a diachronic awareness, as exemplified by scholars such as Zimmerli, Eichrodt, and Kutsch.¹¹ Appealing to the diachronic argument allows us to look at the two temporal markers at Ezek 24:1–2 and 33:21–22, which encircle chapters 25–32, as reflecting secondary placement. When read with these two temporal statements outside Ezekiel's OAN, the series of chronological formulas within the OAN becomes a structuring device linking the fate of the nations to the siege and fall of Jerusalem. In fact, the two markers at chapters 24 and 33 represent a later editorial effort to frame and affirm the message of "oblique judgment" in the prophecies against the foreign nations in Ezek 25–32.

---

⁴ Jer 28:1; 36:9; 41:1. See ibid.

⁵ Ibid., 63.

⁶ Hag 1:1, 15b; 2:10, 20. See ibid.

⁷ Zech 1:1, 7; 7:1. See ibid.

⁸ Ezek 1:1; 8:1; 20:1; 24:1; 26:1; 29:1, 17; 30:20; 31:1; 32:1, 17; 33:21; 40:1.

⁹ Mayfield, *Literary Structure*, 16, 169, 187.

¹⁰ Ibid., 15: "I attempt to bracket, in general, diachronic concerns in favour of examining the synchronic dimensions of the book of Ezekiel...It is simply a matter of scope that this study chooses to focus on synchronic questions."

¹¹ Zimmerli, *Ezekiel*, 1:9–16, 2:191–194; Eichrodt, *Ezekiel*, 336–37, 457–60; E. Kutsch, *Die chronologischen Daten des Ezechielbuches*, OBO 62 (Göttingen: Vandenhoeck & Ruprecht, 1985), 41–45, 61–63.

## 2.1. THE BEGINNING OF THE FATEFUL SIEGE

The temporal statement in Ezek 24:1–2 reads:

ויהי דבר יהוה אלי בשנה התשיעית בחדש העשירי בעשור לחדש לאמר בן אדם כתוב[12] לך את
שם היום את עצם היום הזה סמך מלך בבל אל ירושלם בעצם היום הזה

And the word of YHWH came to me in the ninth year, in the tenth month, on the tenth of the month, saying, "Son of man, write the name of the day, this very day. The king of Babylon has laid siege to Jerusalem on this very day."

This temporal statement differs from the other temporal statements in the book on two accounts.[13] First, in 24:1, the prophetic word formula ("And the word of YHWH came to me") precedes the date formula. The other date formulas in Ezekiel have either a date preceding the word formula,[14] or a date standing alone without the word formula.[15] Second, in 24:1, the noun "month" (חדש) is supplied before the ordinal number, "the tenth" (העשירי). Elsewhere in Ezekiel, the ordinal number stands alone without the noun חדש.[16]

A closer parallel to the date formula in Ezek 24:1 is found in 2 Kgs 25:1, which also records the blockade of Jerusalem by the Babylonian king. Not only do Ezek 24:1–2 and 2 Kgs 25:1 report the same date of the blockade, but both pericopes also place the noun חדש before the ordinal number.[17] In terms of content and style, the formulation in Ezek 24:1 then closely corresponds to the date formula in 2 Kgs 25:1.

Three explanations have been offered to account for the relationship between the date formulas in Ezek 24:1 and 2 Kgs 25:1. First, Fohrer surmises that the former serves as a template for the latter.[18] According to Fohrer, the date in Ezek 24:1 is original to the prophecy and belongs to the historical

---

[12] The *Qere* reads כתב.

[13] Noted also by Zimmerli, *Ezekiel*, 1:498–99; Kutsch, *Die chronologischen Daten*, 62.

[14] E.g., Ezek 26:1 reads: ויהי בעשתי עשרה שנה באחד לחדש היה דבר יהוה אלי לאמר. Cf. 29:1, 17; 30:20; 31:1; 32:1, 17.

[15] E.g., Ezek 8:1 reads: ויהי בשנה הששית בששי בחמשה לחדש, without any word formula preceding or following it. Cf. 1:1; 3:16; 20:1; 33:21; 40:1.

[16] E.g., Ezek 29:1 simply writes "on the tenth month" as בעשירי, without supplying the noun חדש.

[17] 2 Kgs 25:1 reads ויהי בשנת התשיעית למלכו בחדש העשירי בעשור לחדש, with the noun חדש coming before the ordinal number. Cf. Jer 52:4; 39:1. According to Fohrer, *Ezechiel*, 139, this date in Jeremiah is dependent on the corresponding date in 2 Kings.

[18] Fohrer, *Ezechiel*, 118, 139–40. A more comprehensive justification of his position can be found in idem, *Die Hauptprobleme des Buches Ezechiels*, BZAW 72 (Berlin: Töpelmann, 1952), 116–19.

setting when Nebuchadnezzar came up against Jerusalem.[19] That the same date formula appears in 2 Kgs 25:1, for Fohrer, can only be explained on the ground that 2 Kgs 25:1 presupposes the date formula in Ezek 24:1 and thus indicates an exilic rather than a pre-exilic origin at the earliest.[20] Contrary to Fohrer's deduction, the abnormalities of the date formula in Ezek 24:1 in comparison to the rest of the chronological statements in the same book speak against the originality of the date formula. It is thus more likely that the date formula in Ezek 24:1 adopts the style from 2 Kgs 25:1 rather than the other way around.

Alternatively, Zimmerli raises the possibility of the existence of an original date formula in Ezek 24:1, which had been integral to the chapter, and which was subsequently replaced by the date in 2 Kgs 25:1.[21] For Zimmerli, the significance of the beginning of the siege as a fast day in later traditions (cf. Zech 8:19) formed the reason for an editor to amend the style of the date in Ezek 24:1, so as to make it conform to the more precise date formula in 2 Kgs 25:1.[22] The prophet was further requested to write the date down (v. 2).[23] Apart from these two verses, the rest of the oracle never mentions the date again, let alone explains the action of the prophet. That is to say, the subsequent verses are rather self-explanatory even without the two preceding verses. As Greenberg comments: "Such confirmatory purpose and procedure are not even hinted at in the following oracle, hence we may doubt that originally its opening lines contained an exact date that would lead one to suppose them."[24] Zimmerli's hypothesis concerning a precursor of the date formula in Ezek 24:1 therefore remains speculative.

In comparison to the previous two propositions, the third explanation offered by Eichrodt seems more plausible. Eichrodt proposes that the date in

---

[19] Ibid., 118: "In Wirklichkeit wußte Ezechiel, daß Nebukadnezar auf dem Marsch nach Jerusalem war."

[20] Ibid., 139–40: "2 R 25₁ aber stammt, wie die Zählung der Monate zeigt, frühestens aus exilischer Zeit und geht auf Ez 24 ₁ f. oder gar auf die Sach 8 ₁₉ bezeugte Sitte des Trauertages zurück, die dann ihrerseits in Ez 24 ₁ begründet ist."

[21] Zimmerli, *Ezekiel*, 1:498–99.

[22] Ibid., 1:499. Cf. Freedy and Redford, "Dates," 468; Wevers, *Ezekiel*, 189.

[23] The prophets in Isa 8:1 and Hab 2:2 are also commissioned to write something down. Cf. Zimmerli, *Ezekiel*, 1:499; Schöpflin, *Theologie*, 326–27.

[24] Greenberg, *Ezekiel*, 2:496. So also Kutsch, *Die chronologischen Daten*, 62, who counters Zimmerli's hypothesis: "Allerdings ist die nachträgliche Änderung eines Datums, um ein nachfolgendes Jahwewort sekundär auf ein bestimmtes Ereignis zu beziehen, weniger wahrscheinlich." Similarly, N. Messel states: "Der Zweck wird nicht angezeigt, Ezechiel macht nachher von diesem Beweis keinen Gebrauch" (*Ezechielfragen* [Oslo: Jacob Dybwad, 1945], 19).

Ezek 24:1 is dependent on the date in 2 Kgs 25:1 and has been inserted secondarily into its current position.[25] Kutsch also shares this view.[26] However, both Eichrodt and Kutsch do not clarify the motivation of the editor to insert the chronological formula at this particular position in the book of Ezekiel. Eichrodt argues that the insertion simply serves "to make it [the date] seem still more impressive through its word-for-word agreement with the chronology given by an official historian."[27] He does not explain why the date must be given in this and not in another literary context within the book of Ezekiel.

Building on Mayfield's insights, I suggest that such an editorial insertion in Ezek 24 is motivated by both formal and thematic considerations. On the one hand, the insertion of 24:1–2 provides a *formal demarcation* for chapters 24 and 25 to be read together as one unit.[28] On the other hand, the insertion of the chronological formula provides a narrative setting that unites the *corresponding ideas and themes* across the two chapters.[29] In fact, the date formula indicates an editorial attempt to link the message of doom concerning Jerusalem (chapter 24) to the prophecies against Transjordan and Philistia (chapter 25).

Formally, the editorial insertion of the date formula in 24:1 signals a new boundary, which ends with another date formula in 26:1.[30] As such, both chapters 24 and 25 are sandwiched between the two date formulas. This formal

---

[25] Eichrodt, *Ezekiel*, 337.

[26] Kutsch, *Die chronologischen Daten*, 62.

[27] Eichrodt, *Ezekiel*, 337.

[28] Thus Mayfield states that "the two chapters—Ezekiel 24 and 25—are bound together as a literary unit with their common chronological formula" (*Literary Structure*, 158).

[29] Ibid., 163–64.

[30] The year number in the MT Ezek 26:1 is problematic to many commentators. Several other textual traditions differ from the year number in the MT. Codex Alexandrinus reads it as the "twelfth year" and P967 has the "tenth year." Only Codex Vaticanus follows the MT with the "eleventh year." For Zimmerli, *Ezekiel*, 2:26, 33–34, an editorial manipulation in the MT is possible here, since 26:1 spells the eleventh year as בעשתי עשרי, whereas the year number "eleven" is spelled as אחת עשרה elsewhere in Ezekiel (30:20; 31:1). For Fechter, *Bewältigung*, 87, the pre-fall year in the MT is impossible to the scene in Ezek 26, given that the narrative starting from v. 2 presupposes the fall of Jerusalem (cf. Wevers, *Ezekiel*, 147; Allen, *Ezekiel*, 73–75; Gosse, "Recueil," 554–57). In addition, this date formula is also the first in Ezekiel to have the month missing. All these indicate an editorial change in 26:1, but the scholars do not account for such an editorial manipulation. In my view, the desire to date the temporal marker in 26:1 to the year just before the fall indicates an attempt to use the prediction about the demise of Tyre as a poignant lens to observe the impending fall of Jerusalem. In addition, the missing month in MT Ezek 26:1 allows an ambiguous literary setting and thus avoids distinguishing between the fate of Tyre and that of

demarcation strengthens many existing lexical links between the two adjacent chapters. For instance, YHWH's threat to profane his sanctuary in 24:21 (מחלל את מקדשי) is fulfilled and presupposed in 25:3 (אמרך האח אל מקדשי כי נחל).[31] The divine retribution on Judah is also linked to that on Edom and Philistia by the *Leitwort* נקם (24:8; cf. 25:12–17).[32] The temporal markers at both ends of the designated textual unit thereby provide a concrete formal feature to group chapters 24 and 25 together and highlight the semantic parallels extant in both chapters.

Thematically, the editorial categorization of chapters 24 and 25 as a whole underscores the shared concerns about YHWH's judgment and election of Israel. The temporal marker in 24:1 reinforces the context of judgment common in both chapters. It is at this juncture that the news concerning the siege of Jerusalem is released (24:1–2).[33] Both chapters subsequently convey the demise of Jerusalem through a range of temporal perspectives.[34] The first subunit, in the form of a refutation speech, presents the city as a boiling pot and a bloody city, waiting to be judged (24:3–14). The second subunit announces through the death of Ezekiel's wife that the city will be destroyed (24:15–27). The third subunit presupposes the fall of the city through the gloating of the neighboring states (25:1–17).[35] Hence, the downfall of Jerusalem progresses through a range of temporal perspectives, from the beginning of the siege to the aftermath of the destruction.

Against this backdrop, the divine election of Jerusalem comes under severe scrutiny. In 24:3–5, the popular notion of election is presented.[36] The Jerusalemites liken themselves to the choice meat in the pot symbolizing their

---

Jerusalem too clearly. As such, a proleptic judgment against Tyre intertwines with the upcoming fall of Jerusalem.

[31] Premstaller, *Fremdvölkersprüche*, 36.

[32] Ibid., 44.

[33] For the dating of 24:1 to 15 January 588 BCE, see Greenberg, *Ezekiel*, 2:8; Kutsch, *Die chronologischen Daten*, 70; Allen, *Ezekiel*, 2:59; Zimmerli, *Ezekiel*, 1:498. For the dating to December 589 BCE, see Hölscher, *Hesekiel*, 126; Eichrodt, *Ezekiel*, 336.

[34] Mayfield, *Literary Structure*, 161–63.

[35] Contemporary scholars (e.g., Allen, *Ezekiel*, 2:66; Wevers, *Ezekiel*, 195; Zimmerli, *Ezekiel*, 2:11–12) focus on the historical date of composition of the oracles concerning the four nations in chapter 25, which should be after the destruction of Jerusalem. On the other hand, Mayfield suggests that whatever their compositional date, when chapter 25 is read with chapter 24, the "literary" date of the oracles is the beginning of the siege of Jerusalem (*Literary Structure*, 167). Such a literary date creates suspense and anticipation concerning the fall of Jerusalem.

[36] According to Block, "Cauldron," 12–37, Ezek 24:3b–5 is called the popular *Arbeitslied*.

city.[37] However, the subsequent verses present the prophetic imprecation of this false sense of election. Instead of being the choice meat, the Jerusalemites are compared to the scum (חלאתה) in the pot (v. 6).[38] Moreover, the temple as a common symbol of divine favour in ancient Israelite thought will suffer the fate of being torn down and destroyed. Schöpflin draws special attention to how the death of Ezekiel's wife embodies God's intention to destroy the people's temple, which is "the joy of their pride" (משוש תפארתם) and "the desire of their eyes (מחמד עיניהם, vv. 16, 21, 25; cf. 1 Kgs 20:6; Lam 2:4).[39] The corruption of the Jerusalemites and their failure in being God's elect lead to the inevitability of God's judgment upon the city. Ezek 25 continues to pose a challenge to Judah's election. After the fall of Jerusalem, the nations mock that "the house of Judah is like all the nations" (25:8).[40] They gloat over the profanation of the sanctuary (v. 3) and cheer maliciously over the desolation of the land of Israel (vv. 3, 6). As a whole, the chapter paints a scenario where the symbols of election—such as the land, the sanctuary, and the royal house of Judah—become devastated and an object of derision in the sight of the nations.

All in all, the insertion of the chronological formula at 24:1 highlights that both chapters 24 and 25 deal with the same issue of judgment and election. Ezek 24 challenges the inviolability of Jerusalem through YHWH's destroying power. Chapter 25 undermines this elect status of the house of Judah through the mockery of the contiguous kingdoms. The divine retribution that has been predicted for Jerusalem at the beginning of the siege in chapter 24 finds its fulfillment in chapter 25.

---

[37] See Ezek 11:3, where the Jerusalemites also use the imagery of pot and flesh to claim the inviolability and divine protection of Jerusalem (cf. v. 7).

[38] Many translate חלאתה as referring to the rust of the pot (Cf. *HALOT* 1:315, NASB, NAS). Nevertheless, Block notes that the copper does not rust ("Cauldron," 28–29). He suggests the term should instead be understood as referring to the "content of the pot, that is, the meat," the "putrid flesh," which symbolizes the residents of Jerusalem (29). Therefore, "her scum" is perhaps a better translation for חלאתה.

[39] Schöpflin compares the death of Ezekiel's wife in chapter 24 with Jer 16:2, 5 and Hos 1; 3, where the marriages of the prophets are being used as sign acts to denote YHWH's relationship with his own people (*Theologie*, 333). Ezek 16 and 23 also make use of the marriage metaphor to denote this relationship. In Ezek 24, YHWH's instruction for the prophet not to mourn for his dying wife means YHWH's rejection to be reconciled with his people and to avert the doom of Jerusalem. Cf. J. M. O'Brien, "God as (Abusing) Husband," in *Challenging the Prophetic Metaphor* (Louisville: Westminster John Knox, 2008), 63–76; D. Lipton, "Early Mourning? Petitionary Versus Posthumous Ritual in Ezekiel XXIV," *VT* 56 (2006): 185–202.

[40] Cf. Ezek 20:32, where the comparison between Judah and the other nations (גוים) is viewed derogatorily.

## 2.2. The Arrival of the Terrifying News

After the collection of prophecies against the nations in Ezek 25–32, another chronological statement appears in 33:21–22, which reads:

ויהי בשתי עשרה שנה בעשרי בחמשה לחדש לגלותנו בא אלי הפליט מירושלם לאמר הכתה העיר ויד יהוה היתה אלי בערב לפני בוא הפליט ויפתח את פי עד בוא אלי בבקר ויפתח פי ולא נאלמתי עוד

And it came about in the twelfth year of our exile,[41] in the tenth month,[42] on the fifth of the month that the fugitive from Jerusalem came to me, saying, "The city has been struck down." Now the hand of YHWH had been upon me in the evening, before the fugitive came. And he opened my mouth at the time he came to me in the morning; so my mouth was opened, and I was no longer speechless.

At first sight, the date formula in 33:21–22 is no different from those in 1:1; 26:1; 29:17; 30:20; 31:1; 32:1, 17. They are all structured as follows: ויהי + number of year with preposition ב + שנה + number of month with preposition ב + number of day with preposition ב + לחדש.[43] Like the dates in 1:2 (לגלותנו) and 40:1 (לגלות המלך יויכין), the date in 33:21 is recorded according to the year of exile.[44] That is to say, the date formula in chapter 33 stylistically fits the series of temporal markers in the book of Ezekiel.

Upon closer examination, the position of the chronological statement in chapter 33 exhibits a secondary nature. Ezek 33:21–22 appears abruptly in the midst of two discourses marked off by the prophetic word formula (33:1–20, 23–33).[45] In the first discourse, YHWH responds to the complaints about the justice of divine retribution (33:10, 17, 20), whereas the second portrays YHWH refuting the claim of land possession made by those who remain in the devastated land of Israel (33:24). It thus seems awkward for the news about the capture of Jerusalem to reach the exiles only in 33:21–22, when the surrounding discourses have already presupposed the catastrophe that befell Jerusalem. The arrival of the terrifying news in 33:21–22, argues Zimmerli, seems to be a more natural conclusion to 24:1–24, where the message about the doom of Jerusalem is predicted and symbolized through the death of the prophet's wife.[46] In fact, it is likely that a similar prophecy predicting the opening of the prophet's mouth was inserted in 24:25–27 after 33:21–22 had

---

[41] Some Greek manuscripts attest to a reading of "eleventh" year, which is closer to the post-fall date. LXX[88] reads "tenth" year. Noted by Block, *Ezekiel*, 2:253.

[42] The LXX reads "in the twelfth month" (ἐν τῷ δωδεκάτῳ μηνὶ).

[43] Fechter, *Bewältigung*, 237.

[44] Kutsch, *Die chronologischen Daten*, 10, 41; Zimmerli, *Ezekiel*, 2:192.

[45] Cf. "And the word of YHWH came to me saying" in 33:1, 23.

[46] Zimmerli, *Ezekiel*, 2:191.

been moved to its present location.⁴⁷ In other words, the current prophecy in 24:25–27 is a later replacement of the original pericope that has been moved to 33:21–22.

Given the secondary position of 33:21–22 within the present chapter, certain questions arise: Why should the arrival of the news concerning the fall of Jerusalem be postponed after the collection of prophecies against the foreign nations (chapters 25–32) and after an oracle that discusses the justice of YHWH's retribution of Jerusalem (33:1–20)? Why cannot it be retained at the end of chapter 24?

Mayfield insightfully suggests that the chronological formula at Ezek 33:21–22 works together with the temporal marker at 32:17 in order to formally bind together the prophecies in 32:17–32 and 33:1–20.⁴⁸ Despite his repeated exhortation to read the two textual units "as a unified whole" pivoting around the message of judgment,⁴⁹ his overall literary analysis still shows a proclivity to read the judgment of Egypt and that of Judah separately, rather than as connected. While admitting that the chronological markers formally bind the two textual units together, he still considers them as displaying different contents: "the two subnits of Ezekiel 32:17–33:20, with their *vastly different content*, are *read together as a unit*."⁵⁰ According to Mayfield, the judgment against Egypt is perhaps irrelevant to or even different from the divine punishment of Judah. His reading at this particular point suggests a dissociation of form and content. A more fruitful reading is to regard the temporal marker at 33:21–22 as a formal demarcation, which encourages reading the defense of divine justice to execute judgment on Jerusalem (33:1–20) as a natural conclusion to the oracles against Egypt that contain an oblique condemnation of the house of Judah (29:1–32:32).

Preceding the temporal marker in 33:21–22, there are six date formulas in the Egypt oracles.⁵¹ The six markers, along with the date formula in 33:21, demarcate six textual units. The temporal markers are not arranged according to the chronological order. The formulas at 29:1 (tenth year), 30:20 (eleventh year), and 31:1 (eleventh year) are dated immediately before the fall of Jeru-

---

⁴⁷ Ibid. Cf. Gosse, "Recueil," 535–38.

⁴⁸ Mayfield states that "this unit clearly continues the message of judgment even after the destruction" (*Literary Structure*, 184).

⁴⁹ Ibid., 182. For him, Ezek 33:1–20 "does not begin a new literary unit" and "the book does not provide any specific clues for a major division at the beginning of this chapter" (177). Citing Greenberg, he thinks that the content of judgment in 33:1–20 indicates that both 32:17–32 and 33:1–20 are brought structurally together in order to forge one final unit of judgment (186).

⁵⁰ Ibid., 171. Emphasis mine.

⁵¹ Ezek 29:1, 17; 30:20; 31:1; 32:1, 17.

salem. The formulas in 32:1 and 32:17 are dated after the time when the message concerning the fall of Jerusalem has come to the exiles (cf. 33:21).[52] The latest in the series of chronological formulas is found in 29:17, which sets the following oracle roughly sixteen years after the fall of Jerusalem.[53] This chronological disorder suggests that the Egypt oracles are arranged more in accordance with subject matter than with chronology.[54] In fact, the six textual units build a suspenseful narrative sequence, leading up into the judgment oracle concerning Jerusalem (33:1–20) and the climactic message concerning the collapse of this capital city (33:21).

The first textual unit in Ezek 29:1–16 begins by providing a *rationale* for the divine judgment against Egypt. The defiant attitude of Egypt towards YHWH's sovereignty and its alliance with Judah have led to the breach of the ideal separation between Egypt and Judah. The second textual unit in 29:17–30:19 describes the *process* of the divine judgment in destroying any alliance between Egypt and Judah.[55] From 29:17–21 comes the clarification that the tool of judgment deployed by YHWH to ravage Egypt is Nebuchadnezzar and his army.[56] The invasion by Nebuchadnezzar is pictured as divinely sanctioned and thus comparable to the day of YHWH (30:1–19, esp. vv. 10–12). The Babylonian incursion of Egypt vividly recalls YHWH's punishment upon Jerusalem, Ammon, and Tyre (21:23–37 [Eng. 21:18–32]; 29:17–21), where

---

[52] Kutsch, *Die chronologischen Daten*, 67: "So liegen die datierten Ägyptensprüche—abgesehen von 29,17–20—teils vor dem Beginn der Belagerung von Jerusalem (29,1; 30,20) bzw. bald nach deren Bekanntwerden bei den Exilierten (31,1), teils nach dem Eingang der Nachricht von der Eroberung der Stadt (32,1; 32,17)." Similarly, Zimmerli, *Ezekiel*, 2:104: "With the exception of the secondary addition in 29:17–21, they [Ezekiel's oracles against Pharaoh and against Egypt] are all to be dated in the time of the last siege of Jerusalem and the year immediately following."

[53] For Marzouk, *Egypt*, 42, this late date supports the claim that the prophet reconstructs a deeper level of relation between Egypt and Judah beyond a single historical event, beyond the sphere of political alliance. Historically and politically, Egypt has faded away from the scene of Judah's national life after 587 BCE. However, Egypt still relates theologically to the future fate of Israel in the imagination of the prophetic book. Similarly, for Mayfield, *Literary Structure*, 206, the insertion of this late date formula underscores the effectiveness of the divine judgment against Egypt despite the time lapsed.

[54] McKeating, *Ezekiel*, 68.

[55] Premstaller, *Fremdvölkersprüche*, 208: "29,17–21 konkretisiert die Drohung von V 1–16, indem die Vollstreckung des Gerichts an Ägypten dem Babylonierkönig Nebukadnezzar und seinen Truppen anvertraut wird."

[56] See R. Poser, *Das Ezechielbuch als Trauma-Literatur*, VTSup 154 (Leiden: Brill, 2012), 497; Zimmerli, *Ezekiel*, 2:120.

the Babylonian king also acts as an agent of divine judgment.[57] The third textual unit narrates the *outcome* of the divine judgment (30:20–26). King Nebuchadnezzar will emerge as the victor and Egypt, like Judah, will be exiled among the nations.[58] The last three literary units (31:1–18; 32:1–16; 32:17–33:20) employ a variety of mythical images such as a cosmic tree descending into Sheol, a creature embodying both a lion and a monster, and a busily occupied netherworld, respectively, to spell the doom of Egypt and its entourage. Within these mythical images varying allusions to the kingdom of Judah are embedded.[59]

In light of the intricate connections between Egypt and Judah in Ezek 29–32, it is not surprising that the storyline segues into the "doom prophecy" for the house of Judah in 33:1–20.[60] Greenberg observes that most scholars pay more attention to the more optimistic section in 33:23–33, while ignoring the message of judgment embedded in the first part of the same chapter (33:1–20). The significance of chapter 33, according to the *opinio communis*, lies mainly in its marking of the beginning of a new section of the book, "a new [post-fall] phase of Ezekiel's activity" as "pastor to individual exiles."[61] On the contrary, Greenberg rightly emphasizes that the style and many of the motifs of chapter 33 more closely resemble the judgment oracles in chapters 4–24 than the restoration and hope promised in chapters 34–48.[62] Hence, the watchman's motif in 33:1–9 parallels and recalls the commissioning of the prophet to issue judgment against Jerusalem in 3:16–21.[63] Meanwhile, 33:10–20 justifies the divine punishment of the wicked residents of Jerusalem by summarizing the relationship of sins and death in 18:1–32.[64] Reporting the demise of Jerusalem, the new chronological formula at 33:21–22 fulfills the doom prophecy sentenced to Jerusalem in 24:25–27 and ends the prophet's silence reported in

---

[57] See Vanderhooft, *Empire*, 129.

[58] For a fuller discussion, see Chapter Four, Section 3.2.

[59] For a fuller discussion, see Chapter Four, Sections 2.1, 2.2, 2.3, 2.4, 3.1, and 3.3.

[60] Greenberg, *Ezekiel*, 2:680: "Far from being a new phase of the prophet's mission, this oracle is the epilogue of his pre-fall mission as a prophet of doom. Nowhere in it is there so much as a hint that the lookout-prophet proclaims anything but doom."

[61] Ibid., 2:679, cites and counteracts the opinion in K. W. Carley, *The Book of Ezekiel: Commentary*, CBC 27 (Cambridge: Cambridge University Press, 1974), 218, 220. See also Hölscher, *Hesekiel*, 166; Cooke, *Ezekiel*, 366; Eichrodt, *Ezekiel*, 459–60; Fuhs, *Ezechiel*, 2:186; Blenkinsopp, *Ezekiel*, 150, who all share the opinion that 33:21 marks a new turn to salvation oracles in Ezekiel.

[62] Greenberg, *Ezekiel*, 2:675–79. He further remarks: "Ch. 33 is the last gasp of Ezekiel's pre-fall theology" (692). Cf. Odell, *Ezekiel*, 413; Zimmerli, *Ezekiel*, 2:183–89.

[63] Cf. Block, *Ezekiel*, 2:242.

[64] Cf. Ibid., 2:249, 251.

3:22–27.[65] Thus the formula climactically ends a narrative sequence with sustaining doom and judgment. Juxtaposing the divine retribution of Judah (33:1–20) with the doom of Judah's allies such as Egypt and other nations (29:1–32:32) further clarifies the logic of divine justice. It is precisely Judah's alignment with the other nations that leads to the demise of Judah as a nation. The demise of Egypt and its entourage becomes a poignant lens through which to observe the downfall of the kingdom of Judah.

In a nutshell, the two chronological statements in 24:1–2 and 33:21–22 represent the editorial attempts to link the OAN in chapters 25–32 more closely to the surrounding announcements of judgment in chapters 24 and 33. Through the juxtaposition of the fates of the nations with the siege and fall of Jerusalem, the editor(s) sought to reinforce the message of "oblique judgment," which had already been laid out within the collection of prophecies in chapters 25–32.

### 3. Transforming the Oblique Judgment

Despite the predominantly bleak message in Ezek 25–32, my previous analysis has shown some glimpses of hope for the restored Israel depicted in 29:13–16, so that it can turn away from the past disastrous alignment with the nations, and that an ideal separation between Israel and the nations can be created. The contrast between Israel and the nations generates a second type of editorial response in the latter parts of the book of Ezekiel. Two groups of oracles can be categorized under this second type of editorial response. They are the Mount Seir oracles in Ezek 35 and the Gog of Magog oracles in Ezek 38–39. By reusing the lexemes depicting the nations in chapters 25–32, chapters 35 and 38–39 transform the past alignments between Judah and the nations into a drastic contrast between the restored Israel and the nations.

---

[65] Even in the new textual unit of Ezek 33:21–33, the proclamations of judgment continue. As noted in ibid., 2:235, Ezek 33:23–29 summarizes the same charges of idolatry and abominations and announces the same judgment proclaimed in chapters 5–6, while also alluding to 11:14–21. Ezek 33:30–33 reflects 20:1–3, 31 and announces the fulfillment of the prediction of his audience's hardened hearts (2:3–7; 3:4–11). For Schöpflin, *Theologie*, 341–42, Ezek 33:30–32 depicts a transformed willingness of Ezekiel's audience to listen to the message (cf. 3:7) and thus proposes that 33:30–32 might already look forward to the salvation oracle coming in 36:26–27.

## 3.1. IN OPPOSITION TO THE MOUNTAINS OF ISRAEL

None of the passages in the book of Ezekiel displays an oracle against Mount Seir or Edom as full-fledged as chapter 35.[66] Seir appears as a marginal gloss alongside Moab in 25:8. From 25:12–14 comes a short and independent oracle against Edom, rebuking it for executing vengeance on the house of Judah. A brief reference to Edom appears in 32:29, where it is listed among a vast horde of dead nations in the netherworld, lying with the slain of the sword and the uncircumcised. It is only until chapter 35 that we have four elaborate oracles concerning the devastation of Mount Seir (vv. 3–4, 5–9, 10–13, 14–15).[67]

Zimmerli and Block have stressed the links between 35:1–15 and 36:1–15. The prophetic word formula in 35:1 resurfaces only later in 36:16.[68] Since this formula conventionally marks the beginning of a major oracle in Ezekiel,[69] Zimmerli remarks that 35:1–36:15 "is, therefore, against the chapter division of M [MT], to be regarded as a homogeneous unit."[70] Block further observes many lexical ties between both chapters.[71] For instance, the distinctive combination of "mountains" (הרים), "hills" (גבעות), "valleys" (גאות), and "ravines" (אפיקים) characterizes the terrain of both Seir and Israel (35:8; 36:4, 6). In Ezek 35, Mount Seir is portrayed as displaying the enmity (איבה, 35:5a) against the sons of Israel; it is the one who rejoices over the desolation of the land of Israel (שמח, שמחה, 35:14b–15), and who eagerly claims possession of

---

[66] On the basis of 35:15, Mount Seir and Edom can be used interchangeably. Klein suggests that Ezek 35's preference for the designation "Mount Seir" instead of "Edom" is probably determined by the editorial intention to form a parallelism with the "Mountains of Israel" in 36:1–15 (Klein, *Schriftauslegung*, 323; cf. Block, *Ezekiel*, 2:309). The identification of Edom with Seir can be seen in texts such as Gen 36:8, 9, 20, 21; Num 24:18; 2 Chr 25:11, 14. For a comprehensive analysis of Seir in the biblical texts, see Simian, *Nachgeschichte*, 273–90.

[67] The first and last oracles begin with a messenger formula "Thus has the Lord YHWH declared," while the second and third are the proof-sayings, each of which consists of a reason for judgment and an announcement of judgment. Cf. Pohlmann, *Kapitel 20–48*, 474; Dicou, *Edom*, 43. Note the division of the chapter into three sections (i.e., vv. 3b–4, 5–9, 10–15) in Lust, "Edom-Adam," 392.

[68] Ezek 36:16–21 begins with another prophetic word formula and displays a shift in focus, trying to account for the dispersion of Israel among the nations. Text critics commonly regard vv. 16–21 as distinctive from 36:1–15. Cf. Pohlmann, *Kapitel 20–48*, 474.

[69] E.g., Ezek 3:16b; 6:1; 7:1; 11:14; 12:1, 8, 17, 21, 26; 13:1; 14:2, 12; 15:1; 16:1; 17:1, 11; 18:1; 20:2; 21:1, 6, 13, 23; 22:1, 17, 23; 23:1; 24:1, 15, 20; 25:1; 26:1; 27:1; 28:1, 11, 20; 29:1, 17; 30:1, 20; 31:1; 32:1, 17; 33:1, 23; 34:1; 36:16; 37:15; 38:1. Cf. Schöpflin, *Theologie*, 57–66; Fechter, *Bewältigung*, 57–61; Mayfield, *Literary Structure*, 117–21.

[70] Zimmerli, *Ezekiel*, 2:232.

[71] Block, *Ezekiel*, 2:309–10.

the inheritance of Israel (וירשנוה, 36:10c). Likewise, in 36:2, the enemy (האיב) is the one who taunted the Mountains of Israel by exclaiming "Aha" (האח), and who claimed the Mountains of Israel as their own possession (מורשה). In short, both structural and lexical ties indicate attempts to read chapters 35 and 36 together.

Klein weighs in with a fresh insight, positing an original break between chapters 35 and 36. She argues that the present juxtaposition of both chapters is most likely not original.[72] While chapter 35 speaks explicitly against Mout Seir (vv. 2, 7, 15), chapter 36 directs a prophecy of judgment more generally against "the enemy" (האויב, v. 2), who is identified as the surrounding nations (הגוים אשר לכם מסביב, v. 7) or "the rest of the nations" (שארית הגוים, vv. 3, 4, 5).[73] The references to Edom in 35:15 and 36:5 appear to be later glosses to reinforce the connections between both chapters.[74] The multiple nations who taunt and mock the house of Israel, as Klein cogently argues, render Ezek 36 as originally connected to or dependent on the oracles against the Transjordan and Philistia in chapter 25.[75] The more specific and elaborate indictments against Edom in chapter 35 emerged later and were inserted before chapter 36, so that the destruction of Mount Seir has become a prelude to the restoration of the Mountains of Israel.[76]

In my view, Klein's thesis is insightful in that she provides a reading of Ezek 36 not only in relation to chapter 35, as Zimmerli and Block have emphasized, but also in relation to chapter 25. Her thesis posits a more direct connection between the OAN in chapter 25 and the restoration of the Mountains of Israel in chapter 36. Implicit and not fully developed in her thesis is the connection between Mount Seir in chapter 35 and the OAN in chapter 25. If we follow her redactional hypothesis that the restoration in chapter 36 is dependent on the scenarios depicted in chapter 25, and that chapter 35 is a later development dependent on chapter 36, we can then assume that the characterizations of Mount Seir in chapter 35 must have been influenced by or have been aware of the traditions of OAN in chapter 25 as well. In fact, Ezek 35 exhibits similarities to and further development of Ezek 25's ideology concerning the relationship between the nations and God's people.

---

[72] Klein, *Schriftauslegung*, 310–11.

[73] Ibid., 310.

[74] Ibid., 304–5, 310. See also Simian, *Nachgeshichte*, 115, 328, who thinks that the addition of the name Edom in 35:15 serves to clarify the name "Seir," which is otherwise seldomly used in the prophetic literature. The addition of the name Edom in 36:5, on the other hand, is dependent on 35:15 (352).

[75] Klein, *Schriftauslegung*, 311–12.

[76] Ibid., 311. A similar direction of dependence can be seen in the conclusion of Simian, *Nachgeschicte*, 355: "Sowohl Ez 36, 16–32 wie auch 35, 1–4, mit weniger Sicherheit Ez 6, selbstverständlich aber die ergänzenden Einheiten Ez 36, 33–36, 37–38 setzen Ez 36:1–11 voraus."

### 3.1.1. THE MAGNIFIED HOSTILITY

Ezekiel 35 magnifies the hostile *actions* of Mount Seir toward Israel. The enmity and tension between Judah and the nations that are blandly described in chapter 25 is transformed into a more concrete crime directed against the land of Israel in chapter 35. In this latter chapter, Edom or Mount Seir embodies the characteristics of other hostile nations to become Israel's enemy *par excellence*.

Of Mount Seir we read that it displays an "everlasting enmity" (איבת עולם, 35:5). Only Ezek 25:15 shares with 35:15 this Hebrew phrase.[77] Instead of the abstract accusation of the Philistines in chapter 25, the indictment against the "everlasting enmity" of Mount Seir in chapter 35 is more specific and concrete. In 25:15, the Philistines are accused of executing vengeance (נקם) with "everlasting enmity."[78] Yet the passage remains vague on the kind of vengeance in view. The object of the Philistines' enmity is also not specified. By contrast, 35:5 identifies Mount Seir and not the Philistines as the grammatical subject that executes the "everlasting enmity." YHWH directly holds Mount Seir accountable for its iniquity. Chapter 35 also specifies the object at which the enmity is directed. "The sons of Israel" are named concretely as suffering under the militancy of Mount Seir (35:5).[79] The animosity of Mount Seir toward the sons of Israel further manifests itself temporally. Mount Seir has executed its atrocity "in the time of their [of the sons of Israel] distress" and "at the time of the punishment of the end."[80] The latter expression appears elsewhere in Ezekiel in relation to the time when the kingdom of Judah fell prey to the Babylonian onslaught.[81] Mount Seir now becomes the villain who aggravates the dire situation of the sons of Israel.

Another instance exemplifying the intense hostility between Mount Seir and the sons of Israel comprises the former's desire to take possession of (וירשנוה, 35:10) the two lands belonging to the previous northern and southern

---

[77] Premstaller, *Fremdvölkersprüche*, 217. Cf. B. Gosse, "Ezéchiel 35–36,1–15 et Ezéchiel 6: La Désolation de la Montagne de Séir et le Renouveau des Montagnes d'Israël," *RB* 96 (1989): 511–17, here 514.

[78] For a fuller analysis of the oracle against the Philistines (Ezek 25:15–17), see Chapter Two, Section 1.5.

[79] Apart from 2:3; 4:13; 6:5; the expression "the sons of Israel" in Ezekiel almost always appears in a context that signifies a positive relationship between YHWH and his people (37:16, 21; 43:7; 44:9, 15; 47:22; 48:11).

[80] While the MT reads "at the time of their distress, at the time of the punishment of the end," the LXX conflates both prepositional phrases into one, reading "in a time of wickedness at the end." Cf. Block, *Ezekiel*, 2:311, n. 9.

[81] Cf. 21:30, 34 [Eng. 21:25, 29].

kingdoms,[82] which are envisioned together as the Mountains of Israel (הרי ישראל, 35:12).[83] The verb related to ירש links 35:10 to the other Ezekielian passages, including 25:4, 10, where the noun מורשה features prominently.[84] Yet, the deployment of the variant form of "to possess" (ירש) in chapter 35 differs from the usage of "possession" (מורשה) in chapter 25. As analysed in Chapter One, the noun מורשה appears in the oracles against the Transjordanian nations to stress the comparability between the foreign territories and the covenantal land.[85] In 25:4, 10, the territories of Ammon and Moab appear as the passive entities encroached by the sons of the east, just as the land of Judah fell prey to the Babylonian incursion. Alluding to Deut 2–3, Ezek 25 stresses that all lands, including that of Judah and those of the foreign nations, share the vanquished status under YHWH's sovereignty. This comparability is not at issue in chapter 35. Unlike Judah, Ammon, and Moab, Mount Seir does not passively suffer the incursion. The verbal form of ירש in 35:10 shows that Mount Seir actively carries out the encroachment. The object to be possessed is not the other foreign territories, but exclusively the land of Israel. The quotation in 35:10 peculiarly stresses the partition of the land: "two nations...two lands." Citing Gen 25:23, Olley thinks that this partition refers to the two countries, Edom and Judah.[86] However, the phrase in Ezek 35:10 is more probably comparable to the "two nations and two kingdoms" in Ezek 37:22 and the "two houses of Israel" in Isa 8:14.[87] That is to say, Ezek 35:10 considers the southern kingdom Judah and the northern kingdom Israel as two

---

[82] The LXX attempts to harmonize the 3fs suffix of וירשנוה with the previous reference to "the two nations and the two countries," stating: "and I [Mount Seir] will possess them [two nations and two countries]" (καὶ κληρονομήσω αὐτάς). So also the Targum and Syriac, as noted in Block, *Ezekiel*, 2:312.

[83] Within Ezekiel, the expression "the Mountains of Israel" (הרי ישראל) appears less frequently in the judgment oracles (6:2, 3; 19:9; 33:28) and more often in the restoration contexts (34:13, 14b; 35:12; 36:1, 2, 3, 4, 8; 37:22; 38:8; 39:2, 4, 17). Elsewhere in Ezekiel, the preferred locutions for the land of Israel are אדמת ישראל (e.g., 7:2; 11:17; 12:19, 22; 13:9; 18:2), אדמה (e.g 36:17, 24; 37:14, 21; 38:20; 39:26, 28), and ארץ (e.g., 6:14; 7:2, 7, 23, 27; 8:12, 17; 9:9). Cf. Klein, *Schriftauslegung*, 330; W. A. Tooman, "Transformations of Israel's Hope: The Reuse of Scripture in the Gog Oracles," in *Transforming Visions: Transformations of Text, Tradition, and Theology in Ezekiel*, ed. W. A. Tooman and M. A. Lyons, Princeton Theological Monograph Series (Eugene: Pickwick Publications, 2010), 61–62, n. 26.

[84] Besides the seven occurrences of the noun in Ezek 11:15; 25:4, 10; 33:24; 36:2, 3, 5, it appears elsewhere in the Hebrew Bible only in Exod 6:8 and Deut 33:4.

[85] See Chapter Two, Section 2.1.

[86] Olley, *Ezekiel*, 477. Cf. Lust, "Edom-Adam," 392.

[87] Zimmerli, *Ezekiel*, 2:235; Klein, *Schriftauslegung*, 303; Anderson, *Brotherhood*, 197, n. 87.

parts of Israel, and the emphasis of two highlights the greed of Mount Seir.[88] The subsequent 3fs suffix attached to the verb ירש, however, indicates that the two must be viewed as a single entity, the land of Israel. Unlike chapter 25, chapter 35 stresses the unique status of the land of Israel. Just as the Promised Land cannot be claimed as the possession of the Jerusalemites (11:15; 33:24), so it does not belong to Mount Seir or the rest of the nations (35:10; 36:2, 3, 5). It belongs solely to the regathered exiles (11:17; 36:12). The inviolability of the covenantal land is now reinforced by the qualification of the land as the indwelling of YHWH (יהוה שם היה, 35:10).[89] If chapter 35 had been aware of the alignment between the land of Judah and the foreign territories hinted by the use of מורשה in chapter 25, it then chose to reverse that alignment, highlighting the unique status of the covenantal land instead. This brings greater infamy to Mount Seir's aggressions in the land of Israel.

Mount Seir's *Schadenfreude* (שמחה) in the laying waste of the inheritance of the house of Israel provides a further glimpse into the escalating hostility (35:15). Apart from a closely related verse in 36:5, related forms of שמח also figure in 25:6 in the context of the malicious taunts and mockery of the land of Israel.[90] Upon closer examination, the focus of both chapters 25 and 35 with regard to *Schadenfreude* differs. In 25:6, Ammon clapped its hand, stamped its feet, and rejoiced (שמח) with all the spite in its soul (שאטך בנפש) over the devastated land of Israel.[91] The gesticulations of clapping hands and stamping feet echo the descriptions in Ezek 6:11; 21:19, 22 (Eng. 21:14, 17).[92] While the gestures in chapters 6 and 21 are associated with YHWH's wrath (חמה),[93]

---

[88] Greenberg, *Ezekiel*, 2:715.

[89] This qualification is likely to be a late insertion into 35:10. This is because a direct speech of YHWH constitutes the first part of 35:10, and the subsequent verse has YHWH speaking also in the first person. The reference to YHWH in the third person thus seems abrupt and possibly serves as a clarification that comes from a later hand. Cf. Zimmerli, *Ezekiel*, 2:226; Simian, *Nachgeschichte*, 107; Klein, *Schriftauslegung*, 303.

[90] The verb related to שמח also appears in 7:12 and 35:14, but only 25:6, 35:15, and 36:5 share the same context where the desolated land of Israel is rejoiced over by the nations.

[91] The Hebrew phrase "spite of soul" is distinctive of Ezekiel, appearing elsewhere only in 25:15 and 36:5.

[92] Both Ezek 6:11 and 21:20 [Eng. 21:15] also share the paralinguistic אח, which can be considered an exclamatory cry of grief. By contrast, the paralinguistic האח in 25:3 is associated with vindictive joy. For further explanations, see Friebel, *Sign-Acts*, 256; Block, *Ezekiel*, 1:674; Zimmerli, *Ezekiel*, 1:184–85.

[93] So Friebel, *Sign-Acts*, 301–3; Allen, *Ezekiel*, 1:89; Block, *Ezekiel*, 1:234–35. Interestingly, others emphasize that God's hand clapping conveys the divine triumphal glee. For the latter view, see Schöpflin, *Theologie*, 40–41; Bertholet, *Hesekiel*, 36;

the same gestures in chapter 25 are qualified by the Ammonites' light-hearted joy (שׂמח) and frivolous contempt (שׁאט).[94] By imitating the wrathful actions of YHWH and his prophet with gloating scorn, the Ammonites strike at the divine majesty. In chapter 25, YHWH's injured majesty becomes a more important issue than Israel's territorial interests and constitutes the reason for judgment executed on the Ammonites. On the other hand, in 35:14–15, the act of revilings over the desolated land of Israel is attributed to Mount Seir. For the first time in Ezekiel, the land of Israel is referred to as the "inheritance" (נחלה). The subsequent chapters of Ezekiel often use נחלה in a positive context, where the restored relationship between Israel and YHWH is in view.[95] The covenantal land in 35:15a is not only called an "inheritance;" it is further qualified as an inheritance belonging specifically to "the house of Israel." This attribution foregrounds Israel's territorial interests. In contrast to the gesticulations of the Ammonites in chapter 25, Mount Seir's actions in chapter 35 directly touch on the territorial interests of Israel.

Through these crucial lexical features shared by both chapters 25 and 35, we can better understand the force of later reinterpretation and transformation in the depictions of Mount Seir. As seen, Mount Seir transcends all the other foreign nations to become the adversary *par excellence*. The aggressions and mockery of the other nations in chapter 25 resurface in chapter 35. Only this time, all the hostile attributes of the nations are transferred to Mount Seir alone. Mount Seir takes on the roles and characteristics of the enemies of Judah, be they Ammon, Moab or Philistia.[96] In addition, the accusations levelled against Mount Seir in chapter 35 unfold more concretely and elaborately than the oracles found in chapter 25. Mount Seir is accused of directing the everlasting enmity against the sons of Israel during the time of divine punishment on the land of Judah, of claiming possession of the two lands and two countries belonging to the northern and the southern kingdoms of Israel, and of displaying the *Schadenfreude* over the desolated inheritance of the house of Israel. In all

---

Cooke, *Ezekiel*, 71; Fohrer, *Ezechiel*, 40; Fuhs, *Ezechiel*, 1:41; Greenberg, *Ezekiel*, 1:135.

[94] Gosse, "Ezéchiel 35-36,1–15," 514: "La différence vient de ce qu'au chapitre 6, le prophète s'est lamenté et qu'au chapitre 25, Ammon s'est réjoui."

[95] Cf. Ezek 36:12; 44:28; 45:1; 46:16; 47:14, 19, 22; 48:28, 29. נחלה in the construct form appears elsewhere most often in relation to the Promised Land. Cf. Num 16:14; Josh 13:23, 28, 14:3; 15:20; 16:8, 9; 18:20, 28; 19:1, 8, 9, 16, 23, 31, 39, 48; Jer 3:19.

[96] So Premstaller, *Fremdvölkersprüche*, 221: "Nach 25,12–15 wendet sich in c35 noch ein zweiter Spruch gegen Edom, welches hier in seinem Status von einem unter mehreren Feinden Judas quasi zum Feind schlechthin transformier wurde." On the transformation of Edom into a symbolic representation of the enemies of the restored Israel in the Hebrew Bible, see Cresson, "Condemnation," 125–48; Glazier-MacDonald, "Edom," 23–32.

this, the guilt of Mount Seir revolves around the territorial interests of the people of Israel.

### 3.1.2. THE MAGNIFIED DESOLATION

If the foregoing reasons for judgment center on the *hostile actions* of Mount Seir toward the Mountains of Israel, the subsequent announcements of judgment in Ezek 35 envision *a reversal of fortune* for the two. The judgment of Mount Seir is built upon the retribution executed on Edom and other foreign nations in chapter 25. In addition, the text magnifies Mount Seir's desolation by transferring the curses upon the Mountains of Israel in chapter 6 to the present chapter. Ultimately, Mount Seir in chapter 35 suffers a more severe punishment, especially when compared to the restoration of Israel in chapter 36.

Following Mount Seir's hostility and aggression against the house of Israel, YHWH vows to castigate it in a similar manner as he has promised to Edom in Ezek 25. In chapter 35, YHWH threatens to turn Mount Seir into a desolation (חרבה, 35:4), which is the same kind of threat directed at Edom in 25:13.[97] YHWH will stretch out his hand against Mount Seir (ונטיתי ידי עליך, 35:3) and cut off from the land all who pass through and return (והכרתי עבר ושב, 35:7).[98] This judgment of "cutting-off" and "stretching-hand" also features prominently in the divine judgment against Edom, Philistia, and Ammon (25:7, 13, 16).[99] Lastly, YHWH will enact his retribution on Mount Seir according to the latter's anger and jealousy vented at the house of Israel (ועשיתי כאפך וכקנאתך, 35:11).[100] The Hebrew clause distinctively echoes the anger and wrath of YHWH in 25:14 (ועשו באדום כאפי וכחמתי).[101] In short, the destruction of Edom in chapter 35 bears many continuities with that decreed upon the nations in chapter 25.

The divine wrath on Mount Seir in chapter 35 intensifies, as demonstrated by the text's reuse of several punitive elements delivered to the Mountains of

---

[97] In Ezekiel, the singular noun "a desolation" (חרבה) and its plural form are often used to describe the land of Judah after the divine judgment (5:14; 13:4; 26:2, 20; 33:24, 27; 36:4, 10; 38:8, 12), but they are also applied to characterize the land of Egypt (29:9, 10, 12; 30:12) or Edom/Mount Seir (25:13; 35:4). The verb appears in 6:6; 12:20; 19:7; 26:2, 19; 29:12; 30:7.

[98] The motif of the wiping out of all who pass through also appears in 14:15 and 33:28. Cf. Isa 34:10; 60:15; Jer 9:9, 11; Zeph 3:6, etc. Cf. Zimmerli, *Ezekiel*, 2:235.

[99] Noted also by Premstaller, *Fremdvölkersprüche*, 218.

[100] The LXX adds the dative pronoun "to you" (σοι) after the verb "I will do" (ποιήσω), in order to emphasize the intense anger of YHWH toward Mount Seir.

[101] Ezekiel assigns this and other similar expressions concerning wrath almost exclusively to YHWH. Cf. באפי in 13:13; באפי ובחמתי in 22:20. Cf. Simian, *Nachgeschichte*, 255; Premstaller, *Fremdvölkersprüche*, 219.

Israel in chapter 6.[102] This is not to deny that some parts of chapter 6 could have been influenced by chapter 35. For instance, YHWH's threat to Mount Seir that "I will stretch out my hand against you, and I will make you a desolation and a waste" (ונטיתי ידי עליך ונתתיך שממה ומשמה, 35:3; cf. 35:7) finds its almost exact parallel in 6:14.[103] But the motif of desolation seems to be less integral to chapter 6 than to chapter 35, since the noun "a desolation" (שממה) appears more frequently in the latter, for example, in vv. 3, 4, 5, 7, and 15.[104] The severity of the divine judgment is further reinforced by the announcement of YHWH to render Mount Seir "an everlasting desolation" (שממות עולם, 35:9). Therefore, the reference to the desolation of the Mountains of Israel at the end of chapter 6 might have been influenced by chapter 35. On the other hand, chapter 35 shows traces of later redaction that attempted to bring the chapter more in alignment with the oracle against the Mountains of Israel in chapter 6. For instance, in 6:3, the four-fold references to the "mountains" (הרים), "hills" (גבעות), "valleys" (גאות), and "ravines" (אפיקים) set the retribution scene for the Mountains of Israel.[105] 35:8b mentions only three of the above four—the hills (גבעתיך), valleys (גאותיך), and ravines (אפיקיך)—as the place of judgment for Mount Seir. Perhaps to align the verse even more closely with the four-fold references in 6:3, the editor added the reference to the mountains (הריו) into 35:8a. Still, the secondary nature of v. 8a is betrayed by the third person possessive suffix attached to the noun, which is incompatible with the second person possessive suffixes attached to the surrounding nouns.[106]

Another example also demonstrates the partial influence of chapter 6 on chapter 35. In 35:8, YHWH will fill Mount Seir with "its slain" (חלליו), or more specifically the "slain of the sword" (חללי חרב). This is the only verse in the chapter that relates the motifs of the slain and the sword with Mount Seir. Elsewhere in the chapter, the sword is mentioned only once in relation to the military actions of Mount Seir against the sons of Israel (35:5). By contrast,

---

[102] For an outline of the literary parallels between Ezek 6 and 35, see Gosse, "Ezéchiel 35–36,1–15," 512; Dicou, *Edom*, 45–46.

[103] Cf. Ezek 33:28, 29. Noted also by Dicou, *Edom*, 54; Klein, *Schriftauslegung*, 328; Gosse, "Ezéchiel 35–36,1–15," 513.

[104] The noun שממה mostly appears in the book of Ezekiel, i.e., 6:14; 12:20; 14:15 (מבלי עובר), 16; 15:8; 29:9, 10 (// חרב), 12; 33:28–29; 35:3–4, 7 (2x), 14–15; 36:34. Jeremiah also attests to a concentration of this noun (e.g., 4:27; 6:8; 9:10; 10:22; 12:10–11; 32:43; 34:22; 44:6; 49:2, 33; 50:13). Cf. Exod 23:29; Lev 26:33; Isa 1:7; Joel 4:19; Mic 7:13; Zeph 1:13; 2:4, 13; Mal 1:3.

[105] The four-fold references appear elsewhere only in Ezek 36:4, 6. Noted by Dicou, *Edom*, 44, 54; Klein, *Schriftauslegung*, 327; Simian, *Nachgeschichte*, 106; Gosse, "Ezéchiel 35–36,1–15," 512.

[106] Simian, *Nachgeschichte*, 111–12; Klein, *Schriftauslegung*, 302–3; Dicou, *Edom*, 54.

the motifs of the slain and the sword appear frequently in Ezek 6:1–7.[107] At the beginning of the judgment oracle, YHWH already announces that he will bring a sword to the mountains of Israel (6:3) and to make the slain fall in front of the idols (6:4). The motif of the slain even appears in conjunction with the recognition formula at the end of the textual unit (6:7).[108] Taken altogether, it is likely that some literary elements in chapter 6 have been incorporated into chapter 35, in order to magnify the severity of the doom of Mount Seir.

The magnitude of Mount Seir's desolation stands out especially when we compare Ezek 35 and 36. Neither chapter 6 nor chapter 25 envisions a territorial restoration for the house of Israel after the divine retribution.[109] By contrast, Ezek 36 clearly views the crimes of the nations and the divine blessings of the Mountains of Israel as standing in a causal relationship.[110] Having listed all the crimes of the nations committed against the Mountains of Israel (36:2–6), YHWH declares openly: "Surely the nations that are around you will bear their insult" (36:7). The ravage to be inflicted upon the nations signifies the beginning of the material compensation for the house of Israel. Subsequently, YHWH showers the mountains of Israel with elaborate promises of restoration, such that the Mountains of Israel will be covered with fruit and branches, and will be reinhabited with man and beast (36:8–12, 13–15). Apart from v. 7, the focus of chapter 36 remains not on the destruction of the nations, but the crimes of the nations and the subsequent restoration of Israel.

The most violent promises of destruction emerge only later in chapter 35, which conflates all the hostile nations mentioned in chapter 36 into one evil Mount Seir.[111] Ezek 35 deliberately highlights the differences between Mount

---

[107] Klein, *Schriftauslegung*, 328. Cf. Dicou, *Edom*, 54; Gosse, "Ezéchiel 35–36,1–15," 513.

[108] Ezek 6:1–7 can be seen as an independent textual unit, since its beginning is marked by the prophetic word formula ("And the word of YHWH came to me saying") and its end is signified by a recognition formula ("and you will know that I am YHWH").

[109] *Contra* M. H. Woudstra, "Edom and Israel in Ezekiel," *CTJ* 3 (1968): 21–35, here 28, who comments: "The similarity between the two Edom prophecies in Ezekiel [chapters 25 and 35] consists in the fact that both are meant to be a prelude to the future restoration of God's chosen people." In my view, the two chapters perform different functions. While Ezek 25 pours forth the imprecations on the nations to evoke and confirm the divine judgment against Judah, Ezek 35 deploys the destruction of Mount Seir as a contrast to the uplifting promises of restoration to the house of Israel. Cf. Lust, "Edom-Adam," 396.

[110] In 36:2–6, the crimes of the nations committed against the Mountains of Israel are first listed out. Subsequently, YHWH vows to pour out his wrath upon the nations (36:5–7).

[111] As already noted in the beginning of Section 2.1, chapter 35 is likely to be a later literary product with both chapters 25 and 36 in mind.

Seir and the Mountains of Israel. The cities of Mount Seir will be demolished and become uninhabited (עריך חרבה אשים, 35:4; cf. v. 9), while the cities of Israel will be inhabited and its waste places will be rebuilt (ונשבו הערים והחרבות תבנינה, 36:10b).[112] YHWH will cut off all living beings on the land of Mount Seir (והכרתי ממנו עבר ושב, 35:7), whereas the Mountains of Israel will be refilled with man and beast (והרביתי עליכם אדם ובהמה, 36:11).[113] Even though Mount Seir claims to have possessed the land of Israel (וירשנוה, 35:10),[114] the people of Israel will be the true possessor of that land (והולכתי עליכם אדם את עמי ישראל וירשוך, 36:12). "All Edom, all of it" (כל אדום כלה, 35:15) will receive divine retribution. By contrast, "all the house of Israel, all of it" (כל בית ישראל כלה, 36:10) will be repopulated and rebuilt.[115]

Indeed, Ezek 35 draws on various lexical features and literary motifs from chapters 6, 25, and 36. Through literary reuse and adaptation, chapter 35 transforms the rhetoric of chapter 25, so that the offences of Mount Seir consist more specifically of its violation of the territorial interests of the people of Israel. Whatever tension, conflict, and animosity between the nations and Judah that are only implicit or mute in chapter 25 become more full-blown in 35:1–15, where Mount Seir alone embodies all the characteristics applied formerly to Judah's oppressors.[116] So gravely considered is the offence of Mount Seir that the punishments inflicted upon it are derived not only from the curses on the nations in chapter 25, but also from the imprecations against the Mountains of Israel in chapter 6. Unlike previous oracles against the nations that highlight the shared punishment between Judah and the nations, the wholesale devastation of Mount Seir in chapter 35 marks the beginning of an elaborate restoration of the land of Israel in chapter 36. The conflation of omnifarious words and motifs effectively magnifies the evil and doom of Mount Seir.

### 3.2. NOT AN ALLY, BUT AN ENEMY

The Gog oracles in Ezek 38–39 attest to another full-blown conflict between the nations and the restored Israel. Gog in Ezek 38–39 is the "chief prince of Meshech and Tubal" (נשיא ראש משך ותבל, 38:2, 3). He is a foreign invader of

---

[112] Klein, *Schriftauslegung*, 310.

[113] Note also Ezek 25, where the cutting off motif always pairs the *hiphil* form of כרת "to cut off" with אדם ובהמה "man and beast."

[114] The quotations of Edom in Ezek 35:10; 36:2 bear resemblances to those of the inhabitants of Jerusalem in 11:15; 33:23. Cf. Lust, "Edom-Adam," 389.

[115] Cf. Lust, "Edom-Adam," 393.

[116] *Contra* Bartlett, "Edom," 20, who argues that Ezek 35 presents the view that "Edom is but one enemy among several of whom similar charges are made." I contend that Edom in Ezek 35 becomes not just *an* enemy, but *the* enemy who embodies the characteristics of previous fiends of Israel.

the restored Israel.[117] This invader is said to have orginated from the land of Magog (ארץ המגוג, 38:2).[118] He is accompanied by the other foreign nations, such as Persia, Cush, Lud, Meshech, and Tubal (38:1–5; 39:1).[119] All of them rise up to invade the land of Israel (38:8–9, 16). All of them are subsequently defeated (38:18–23). In the end, they are either left on the ground to be devoured by the birds of the sky and the beasts of the field (39:1–5, 17–20), or they are plundered and buried (39:8–10, 11–16).[120]

The Gog oracles in Ezek 38–39, like the prophecy against Mount Seir, appear to be a later addition to the book of Ezekiel. Tooman has cogently put forth three arguments to support this thesis.[121] First, the nature of the restoration presented in the Gog oracles differs from the surrounding chapters.[122] Ezek 38:8–12 presents a humble resettlement of Israel, the Mountains of Israel, "which were a continual waste" (v. 8). By contrast, the surrounding chapters portray the renewal of the Davidic monarchy (34), the prosperous land (36), the unified nation (37), and the glorious return of YHWH into the restored temple (40–48). Hence, in the Gog oracles emerges a tension, in which "only a small part of the restoration oracles has been fulfilled."[123] Second, the Gog

---

[117] The LXX and NASB translate ראש as another country name (Ρως, Rosh) alongside Meshech and Tubal. Nevertheless, the designation of ראש as a place name cannot be found elsewhere in the Hebrew Bible. Therefore, the two lexemes נשיא ראש should be read together as a title of Gog (cf. Num 10:4). Elsewhere in the Hebrew Bible, ראש also accompanies a noun to designate a title. E.g., כהן הראש (2 Kgs 25:18; Jer 52:24); הכהן הראש (Ezra 7:5; 2 Chr 31:10); and הכהן ראש (1 Chr 27:5). For the understanding of נשיא ראש as a title, see Tooman, *Gog*, 138, n. 6; Allen, *Ezekiel 20–48*, 199, n. 2b; Zimmerli, *Ezekiel*, 2:299; Hossfeld, *Untersuchungen*, 435; Fuhs, *Ezechiel*, 2:215; Pohlmann, *Hesekiel*, 2:505; Block, *Ezekiel*, 2:435; Premstaller, *Fremdvölkersprüche*, 235; C. Rösel, *JHWHs Sieg über Gog aus Magog. Ez 38–39 im Masoretischen Text und in der Septuaginta*, WMANT 132 (Neukirchen: Neukirchener Theologie, 2012), 130–31.

[118] מגוג usually appears without the definite article (Ezek 39:6; Gen 10:2; 1 Chr 1:5). The ה is perhaps a locative ה attached to the previous noun ארץ. Therefore, the MT of Ezek 38:2 understands Magog as a place of origin for Gog.

[119] These subordinates of Gog also appear as the trading partners of Tyre or the entourage of Egypt in Ezek 27:10; 30:5; 32:26.

[120] Based on the prophetic word formula, the messenger formula, the recognition formula and other formulaic language, we can divide the Gog oracles into the following sections: 38:1–9, 10–13, 14–16, 17, 18–23; 39:1–5, 6–7, 8–10, 11–13, 14–16, 17–20, 21–22, 23–24, 25–29. For a fuller analysis of the structure in the Gog oracles, see Block, *Ezekiel*, 2:431–32; B. Biberger, *Endgültiges Heil innerhalb von Geschichte und Gegenwart: Zukunftskonzeptionen in Ez 38–39, Joel 1–4 und Sach 12–14*, BBB 161 (Göttingen: Vandenhoek & Ruprecht, 2010), 38–39.

[121] Tooman, *Gog*, 72–83.
[122] Ibid., 73–75.
[123] Ibid., 75.

oracles interrupt the logical flow from Ezek 37:24–29 to Ezek 40–48.[124] Summarizing the restoration in chapters 34–37 and referring to "my sanctuary" and "dwelling place," the pericope 37:24–29 indicates YHWH's promise to dwell among his people. This forms a logical bridge to the vision of the restored temple in Ezek 40–48, but Ezek 38–39 "stands between the oracles of restoration (chs 34–37) and the vision of their enactment (chs 40–48)."[125] The tension and interruption created by the Gog oracles can perhaps be explained by the oracles' mobility in different manuscript traditions, which constitutes the third argument of Tooman's thesis.[126] As noted in Chapter One, P967, being the earliest Greek witness to Ezekiel, places chapter 37 after chapters 38–39 instead of before as in the MT.[127] This mobility of the Gog oracles thus heightens the likelihood that the Gog oracles are a self-contained textual unit that "was added to the book of Ezekiel toward the end of its literary evolution."[128] In my view, the postexilic setting of the Gog oracles (e.g., 38:8, 11) implies that these oracles have emerged later than the oracles against Egypt, which mainly contain the exilic literary settings and the exilic chronological formulas. The evidence for the late insertion of the Gog oracles into the prophetic book is on the whole cumulative and convincing.

Being a later insertion, the Gog oracles display many reuses of the language found in the rest of the book of Ezekiel.[129] It will be observed that Gog and his entourage display literary attributes previously assigned to not only Judah's enemies, but also Judah's political allies, especially Egypt. The present construction of Gog in Ezek 38–39 constitutes another later editorial attempt to reinterpret Ezek 25–32 and to polarize the nations and the restored Israel.

### 3.2.1. THE PREVIOUS ALLY

Some biblical scholars seek historical identifications of the enigmatic figure Gog. Gog has been identified as Gyges king of Lydia, *Gâgi* the Assyrian

---

[124] Ibid., 75–76.

[125] Ibid., 76. Noting the absence of the reference to נשיא, David, or shepherd in the Gog oracles, Bøe concludes that "the whole emphasis [in the Gog oracles] is on the direct intervention by God himself from heaven" (*Gog and Magog: Ezekiel 38–39 as a Pre-Text for Revelation 19, 17–21 and 20, 7–10*, WUNT 2/135 [Tübingen: Mohr Siebeck, 2001], 110–11).

[126] Tooman, *Gog*, 77–83.

[127] See Chapter One, Section 3.2.

[128] Tooman, *Gog*, 82.

[129] For an overview of the lexical features reused by the Gog oracles, see Fitzpatrick, *Disarmament*, 74–81; Tooman, *Gog*, 39-64; idem, "Transformations," 52–53.

prince, or *Gaga* the Syrian territory.¹³⁰ Astour links Gog's invasion of the land of Israel with Umman-manda's incursion of Naram-Sin's kingdom.¹³¹ More recently, Strine has identified Gog of Magog as a veiled reference to the Babylonian deity, Marduk. None of these propositions yields any consensus.¹³² A growing number of commentators now recognize Gog in Ezek 38–39 as a literary composite figure derived from a wide array of written sources within the Hebrew Bible.¹³³ A more vexing issue, then, is how best to understand the literary connections between the Gog oracles and the other biblical texts.

Commenting on the semantic links between the Gog oracles and Ezekiel's OAN in particular, Tooman minimizes their exegetical values. He does not consider "the OAN to be anything more for the author of GO [the Gog oracles] than a quarry for Ezekiel's locutions."¹³⁴ He thinks that "there is no interpretation, reapplication, or updating of Ezekiel's OAN in GO [the Gog oracles]."¹³⁵ The lexical connections, for him, represent the Gog oracles' effort "to mirror Ezekiel's idiolect and to create cohesion between his new composition and the wider book of Ezekiel, nothing more."¹³⁶ However, the verbatim correspondences between the Gog oracles and Ezek 25–32 form too specific a pattern, so as to suggest an intention that goes beyond creating mere literary consistency.

Galambush should be credited for observing precise semantic connections between the portrayals of Gog in Ezek 38–39 and Nebuchadnezzar in the rest

---

¹³⁰ Cf. Bøe, *Gog*, 91–99; Biberger, *Heil*, 42–43; Fitzpatrick, *Disarmament*, 85–88; Rösel, *Sieg*, 312–16; J. Lust, "Gog," *DDD* 373–75.

¹³¹ M. C. Astour, "Ezekiel's Prophecy of Gog and the Cuthean Legend of Naram-Sin," *JBL* 95 (1976): 567–79.

¹³² C. A. Strine, "Chaoskampf against Empire: YHWH's Battle against Gog (Ezekiel 38–39) as Resistance Literature," in *Divination, Politics, and Ancient Near Eastern Empires*, ed. A. Lenzi and J. Stökl, ANEM 7 (Atlanta: Society of Biblical Literature, 2014), 87–108.

¹³³ So Klein, *Schriftauslegung*, 128–32; Tooman, *Gog*, 133; idem, "Transformations," 50–110. Rösel states the differences between the historical identification and rhetorical function: "Die entscheidende Frage für den Text selbst ist nicht die Identifikation dieser Gestalt, sondern ihre Funktion für die Heiligung des JHWH-Namens vor den Völkern und die endgültige Verhältnisbestimmung zwischen JHWH, dem wiederhergestellten Israel und den Völkern" (*Sieg*, 323).

¹³⁴ Tooman, *Gog*, 132.

¹³⁵ Ibid., 133.

¹³⁶ Ibid. Cf. His earlier statement that the "reuse of antecedent Scripture" is "to supplement Ezekiel in an effort to harmonize the book with a wider body of traditional religious literature, literature found in today's canon within the Torah, Prophets, and Psalms" (35, 37).

of Ezekiel.[137] Nebuchadnezzar was the Babylonian king, who conquered Judah and destroyed the Jerusalem temple in the sixth century BCE. He is said to be a king of kings whom YHWH has brought up "from the north" (מצפון) against Judah and other nations.[138] The Babylonian king is accompanied by a "host" (קהל),[139] which consists of "many peoples" (עמים רבים).[140] They capture "spoil" and "plunder" (ושלל שללה ובזז בזה).[141] In nearly identical terms, Gog is described as the foe "from the remote parts of the north" (מירכתי צפון),[142] who commands a "host" (קהל) made up of "many peoples" (עמים רבים).[143] Like Nebuchadnezzar, Gog also engages in capturing "spoil" and seizing "plunder" (לשלל שלל ולבז בז).[144] Equally interesting is that the mustering of Gog by YHWH (38:3–9) and the scheming of Gog against the vulnerable people (38:10–12) correspond to the advancement of Nebuchadnezzar upon Kedar and Hazor in Jer 49:28–32.[145] The depictions of Nebuchadnezzar and Gog are so similar that Galambush identifies Gog as a cipher for the Babylonian king Nebuchadnezzar.[146] As stated by Galambush, the prophet exiled to Babylon must have written the Gog oracles in order to convey a "veiled polemic" against Nebuchadnezzar, Judah's oppressor.[147]

The strength of Galambush's argument derives from the concrete lexical links she observes between Nebuchadnezzar and Gog, but I will not go as far as her in arguing that "Gog *is* Nebuchadnezzar, the same 'foe from the north' who has commanded the most terrible of nations throughout the book of Ezekiel."[148] I acknowledge that the writer(s) of Ezek 38–39 could have drawn inspiration from the portrayals of the Babylonian king to shape Gog, but did not identify the latter with the former. In my view, Gog's portrayal is not only inspired by the language applied to Nebuchadnezzar, but is also drawn from many other sources concerning the foreign nations in the book of Ezekiel.

---

[137] J. Galambush, "Necessary Enemies: Nebuchadnezzar, YHWH and Gog in Ezekiel 38–39," in *Israel's Prophets and Israel's Past: Essays on the Relationship of Prophetic Texts and Israelite History in Honor of John H. Hayes*, ed. B. E. Kelle and M. B. Moore, LHBOTS 446 (London: Bloomsbury, 2006), 254–65, here 259.

[138] 26:7. Cf. ἀπὸ βορρᾶ in LXX 23:24. Cf. Galambush, "Necessary Enemies," 259.

[139] 16:40; 23:24, 46, 47; 26:7; 32:3.

[140] 26:7; 32:3; cf. 23:24; 26:3.

[141] 26:12; 29:19.

[142] 38:15; 39:2. Cf. 38:6.

[143] 38:6, 9, 15, 22; 39:12.

[144] 38:12, 13.

[145] For the citation of the lexical correspondences such as חשב, לבטח, ברית, and דלתים, see Galambush, "Necessary Enemies," 260.

[146] Ibid: "Just as the Babylonian monarch was YHWH's tool with which to punish the people, so now he will be the tool by which YHWH glorifies his name."

[147] Ibid., 258.

[148] Ibid., Emphasis mine.

As Klein correctly argues: "Die vielfachen Referenzen zeigen, dass Gog mit Zügen gezeichnet wird, die vor allem in Ez 25–32, aber auch in der Bildrede Ez 23 zur Beschreibung der Assyrer, Babylonier und Ägypter verwendet werden."[149] Klein is commendable in observing wider sources of inspiration for the Gog oracles. However, she seems to lump all nations together as the enemies of Judah. Commenting on the lexical connections between the Gog and the Egypt oracles, Klein states: "Allerdings spricht gerade die Häufung der Stichwortverbindungen in 38,4f. dafür, dass hier bewusst auf *vorgegebene Feindedarstellungen* zurückgegriffen wird, um Gog auf diese Weise Züge verschiedenster *Gegner* zu verleihen."[150] If this remark does not clarify which enemies (*Gegner*) she has in mind, her comment in the next page makes it clear: "Die Bezüge häufen sich dabei in der Fortschreibung 38,1–9, so dass vermutet werden kann, dass diese Ergänzung unter anderem die Angleichung Gogs an *die vorhergehenden Feindbilder* intendiert. Die Feindmacht Gog mit den ihn begleitenden Völkern erscheint damit als eine Personifikation aller *Feinde, die Israel im Buch Ezechiel gegenüberstehen*, wobei allerdings die Herleitung des Namens Gog ungeklärt bleiben muss."[151] In other words, she understands all foreign nations in the book of Ezekiel, without any exception, as the former enemies of Israel.

Contrary to Tooman's hypothesis, the semantic links between the Gog oracles and Ezekiel's other prophecies against the nations do not merely serve to "create cohesion between his new composition and the wider book of Ezekiel,"[152] but are also imbued with further exegetical values. Whereas Galambush and Klein understand Gog as a veiled reference to Israel's former enemies, be they Nebuchadnezzar or other foreign nations, I maintain that the semantic links between the Gog oracles and Ezekiel's OAN encourage connecting Gog and his entourage in Ezek 38–39 to not only Judah's enemies, but also Judah's political allies, especially Egypt.[153]

In the beginning of the prophecy against Gog (38:3–4a), the antihero is introduced in a way that is especially similar to the passage surrounding the monstrification of Pharaoh (29:3–4). With a duel formula "Behold, I am against you" (הנני עליך or הנני אליך), YHWH opens his speech to both Pharaoh

---

[149] Klein, *Schriftauslegung*, 131. In her conclusion, she suggests: "Gestalt Gogs gewissermaßen ein Kompendium der Fremdvölker im Buch, so dass er als der historische Feind *katexochen* erscheint" (371).

[150] Ibid., 130. Emphasis mine.

[151] Ibid., 131. Emphasis mine.

[152] Cf. Tooman, *Gog*, 133.

[153] Scholars have noted the extensive textual connections between the Egypt oracles and the Gog pericopes, but they seldom discuss the rhetorical significance of these connections in detail, let alone see these connections as a reformulation of the identity of Israel's former ally. Cf. Biberger, *Heil*, 67–68; Klein, *Schriftauslegung*, 128; Batto, *Dragon*, 157; Boadt, *Ezekiel's Oracles*, 176; Fitzpatrick, *Disarmament*, 154.

and Gog (29:3; 38:3).¹⁵⁴ In addition, YHWH vows to put hooks in their jaws (בלחייך, 29:4a; 38:4a). The term חח for "hook" and its related forms are rare in the Hebrew Bible.¹⁵⁵ The singular form appears in Exod 35:22 to denote one of the offerings to YHWH. In Isa 37:29 and 2 Kgs 19:28, God threatens to place a hook on the invading Assyrians. The plural forms of the same noun, apart from 2 Chr 33:11, are found in Ezek 19:4, 9; 29:4; and 38:4.¹⁵⁶ Only Ezek 29:4 and 38:4 share the combination of the verbal root נתן, the plural noun חחים, and the prepositional phrase בלחייך.¹⁵⁷ The phrase "And I will put hooks in your jaws" (ונתתי חחים בלחייך) is absent in LXX Ezek 38:4. This adds to the suspicion that the phrase in MT 38:4 is a later gloss, dependent on 29:4.¹⁵⁸ The reuse of this unique combination helps construct unmistakable resemblances between Gog and Israel's former ally Pharaoh.

The links between Pharaoh and Gog deepen when the host of other nations surrounding Gog is taken into consideration. Gog is addressed as the chief prince of Meshech and Tubal (נשיא ראש משך ותבל, 38:2, 3; 39:1).¹⁵⁹ Gomer and Beth-togarmah from the remote parts of the north also join the entourage of Gog (38:6).¹⁶⁰ So far all these aforementioned nations are situated north of Israel. Of significance are the three countries in the south of Israel – Paras, Cush, and Put (פרס כוש ופוט)—who are mentioned as part of the entourage of Gog (38:5).¹⁶¹ The use of the third person plural in reference to Gog and his entourage in this verse contrasts with the second person singular addresses in the surrounding verses. Therefore, the reference to the three southern nations is likely a later insertion. Zimmerli and Wevers are puzzled by the insertion of these nations; as Wever comments: "Nor does the list make good sense."¹⁶² Meanwhile, Zimmerli asserts that "they basically have no business in the army

---

¹⁵⁴ This expression appears thirteen times in Ezekiel (5:8; 13:8; 21:8; 26:3; 28:22; 29:3, 10; 30:22; 34:10; 35:2; 36:9; 38:3; 39:1). All these appearances are in a context of divine judgment. See also the more sporadic usage of this expression in Jer 23:30, 31, 32; 50:31; 51:25; Nah 2:14; 3:15. Cf. Simian, *Nachgeschichte*, 178–79.

¹⁵⁵ Fechter, *Bewältigung*, 231; Batto, *Dragon*, 157.

¹⁵⁶ *HALOT* 1:305. The occurrence in 2 Chr 33:11 is with different vocalizations.

¹⁵⁷ For other lexical connections between Ezek 38–39 and Ezek 29:4–5, see Tooman, *Gog*, 151.

¹⁵⁸ Allen, *Ezekiel*, 2:200; Crane, *Restoration*, 146; Zimmerli, *Ezekiel*, 2:284; Block, *Ezekiel*, 2:436–37; Olley, *Ezekiel*, 497.

¹⁵⁹ Meshech and Tubal also figure in Ezek 27:13; 32:26.

¹⁶⁰ Besides Ezek 38:6, Gomer only appears in Gen 10:2–3 // 1Chr 1:5–6, where he appears as the first son of Japhet. Beth-Togarmah appears in Ezek 27:14. In Gen 10:3, Togarmah is a son of Gomer and thus a grandson of Japheth (cf. 1 Chr 1:6).

¹⁶¹ For Block, *Ezekiel*, 2:440, Paras is equivalent to the Egyptian Pathros, the latter of which is mentioned in 29:17. Likewise, for Eichrodt, *Ezekiel*, 381, behind Paras in Ezek 27:10 lies "some still unidentified African tribe."

¹⁶² Wevers, *Ezekiel*, 287.

of these wild, warrior tribes who are capable of waging their own wars."[163] Contrary to their opinions, I suggest that the insertion of "Paras, Cush, and Put" not only enriches the military strength of Gog,[164] but also aligns the entourage of Gog with Israel's former allies. These inserted nations appear elsewhere in the book of Ezekiel as the traditional allies of Tyre and Egypt (cf. 27:10; 30:5). They help multiply the wealth of Tyre and provide military support for Egypt. As argued in Chapters Two and Three, Judah, along with these nations, is also listed among the helpers and allies of Egypt (27:17; 30:5). As such, the inserted nations represent those who formerly stood in the same line with Judah; but now, they stand beside Gog in order to come up against the land of Israel.

Strikingly, the clothing and weapons of Gog's entourage in 38:4b–5 recall Israel's former foreign lovers who appear in chapter 23.[165] The references to horses and horsemen (סוס ופרשים),[166] the splendidly attired (לבשי מכלול) army,[167] the weapons including buckler and shield (צנה ומגן)[168] are all found in both chapters. That Ezek 38:4b–5 intends to allude to Israel's former lovers is strengthened by its pattern of enumeration. As Tooman observes, Ezek 23:12 describes Assyria as those who are splendidly attired (לבשי מכלול), and as horsemen riding on horses (פרשים רכבי סוסים).[169] On the one hand, Ezek 38:4b–5 tactfully inverts this order, so that Gog's army consists of the three elements in the following order: Horses (סוסים), horsemen (פרשים), and those who are splendidly attired (לבשי מכלול).[170] It transfers the attributes of Israel's former lovers to Gog's present army, encouraging the identification of the latter with the former.[171]

Even the subsequent fate of Gog and his allies mirrors the destiny of Pharaoh and his entourage. The divine retribution on Gog is said to be happening

---

[163] Zimmerli, *Ezekiel*, 2:306.

[164] The inserted nations, along with the nations mentioned in 38:2–3, 6, form an enclosure: 38:2 Meshech (N); 38:2 Tubal (N); 38:5 Paras (E); 38:5 Cush (SW); 38:5 Put (W); 38:6 Gomer (N); 38:6 Beth-togarmah (N). Noted by Bøe, *Gog*, 107. Block argues that since the aforementioned nations are distant peoples, the description in Ezek 38–39 is of a "universal conspiracy" (*Ezekiel*, 2:441).

[165] Cf. Tooman, *Gog*, 152. Cf. Klein, *Schriftauslegung*, 129.

[166] Ezek 38:4b; 23:6, 12, 23.

[167] Ezek 38:4b; 23:12. These are the only two occurrences of the noun "completeness, perfection" (מכלול) in the Hebrew Bible. The LXX of Ezek 38:4b translates the phrase as "dressed in breastplates" (ἐνδεδυμένους θώρακας), and thus makes the military imagery more explicit. Cf. Block, *Ezekiel*, 2:437, n. 53; Tooman, *Gog*, 152, n. 63.

[168] Ezek 38:4b; 23:24.

[169] Tooman, *Gog*, 152.

[170] Ibid.

[171] Ibid., 153.

"on that day" (ביום ההוא).¹⁷² Apart from this, the phrase characterizes YHWH's judgment on Egypt (29:21; 30:9) and appears nowhere else in the book of Ezekiel.¹⁷³ In 30:9, this day is qualified as "the day of Egypt" (יום מצרים). This is the day when the allies of Egypt will come under the divine retribution, and when widespread fear and anguish will fall upon Cush. Like Egypt, Gog will be judged "on that day" (ביום ההוא). In 38:18, the day is qualified as the one "when Gog comes against the land of Israel" (ביום בוא גוג על אדמת ישראל).¹⁷⁴ It is also the day when YHWH will direct his "fury" (חמה), "anger" (אף),¹⁷⁵ "zeal" (קנאה), and "wrath" (עברה) against Gog.¹⁷⁶ In 38:19, the phrase ביום ההוא appears again to introduce a series of war, pestilence, and natural disasters that will plague Gog and the accompanying people.¹⁷⁷ Later in 39:8, 11, the day also marks the death and burial of Gog. In short, the day, which recalls the judgment on Pharaoh and his allies, now inaugurates the divine retribution befalling Gog and his allies.

The posthumous treatment of the bodies of Gog and his army further aligns the fate of Gog with the end of Pharaoh. In 39:4–5, YHWH threatens to cast Gog and his army in the open field (על פני השדה תפול),¹⁷⁸ such that they will be devoured by every kind of carrion birds and wild animals (לעיט צפור כל כנף וחית השדה נתתיך לאכלה). Ezekiel 39:17–20 further elaborates on this devouring

---

¹⁷² Ezek 38:10, 14, 18, 19; 39:8, 11. Ezek 39:13 mentions the victory of Israel over Gog as the day when YHWH will glorify himself (והיה להם לשם יום הכבדי). Ezek 39:22b combines the recognition formula with the phrase מן היום ההוא והלאה.

¹⁷³ *Contra* Tooman, *Gog*, 65, who suggests the phrase is only found in the Gog oracles. The fact is that the phrase figures prominently in Ezek 30, which is one of the oracles against Egypt. A similar motif about the day of YHWH also appears in Ezek 7, which announces the divine judgment against Judah.

¹⁷⁴ Cf. Ezek 38:10, 14.

¹⁷⁵ באפי is missing in the LXX 38:18b. Cf. Rösel, *Sieg*, 227.

¹⁷⁶ As noted in ibid., n. 471, the juxtaposition of קנאה, חמה, and אף are found in Ezek 5:13; Prov 27:4. The juxtaposition of קנאה, חמה, and עברה are found in Ps 90:9, 11; Prov 14:35–15:1; Lam 2:2–4; Ezek 22:20–21. Only Ezek 38:18b–19a attests to the juxtaposition of the four anger terms. For Biberger, *Heil*, 62, the concentrated appearances of the terms relating YHWH's emotions here as "einzigartig" in the Hebrew Bible.

¹⁷⁷ Cf. Ezek 38:19b–22. For Pohlmann, *Ezechiel*, 115, the pericope 38:18–23 is the latest redactional layer within the book of Ezekiel, as it introduces the divine judgment with cosmic significance that displays an apocalyptic *Tendenz*.

¹⁷⁸ According to Klein, *Schriftauslegung*, 128, the phrase על פני השדה תפול only appears in the Egypt and the Gog oracles and nowhere else in Ezekiel, even though פני שדה also appears in Lev 14:7, 53; 17:5; 19:16; 1 Sam 14:25; Jer 9:21. Cf. Biberger, *Heil*, 67, n. 261.

of the corpses by the animals by turning it into a feast of YHWH.[179] This treatment distinctively parallels the abandoned status of Pharaoh's monstrous body in the wilderness, which is also devoured by the beasts of the earth and the birds of the sky (לחית הארץ ולעוף השמים נתתיך לאכלה, 29:5; cf. 32:4–5). The gruesome dismemberment of bodies thus binds the total defeat of Pharaoh and Gog together.

The ultimate localization of the bodies of Gog and his allies recalls the position of Pharaoh and his entourage in the netherworld. The root קבר appears seven times altogether in 39:11–16, in order to describe the death of Gog. The concentrated appearances of this *Leitwort* evoke the terrifying descent of Egypt and other nations into the graves of the netherworld (קברת, 32:17–32, esp. vv. 22–26).[180] The name of the valley where Gog is buried is named Hamon-gog (המון גוג),[181] which forms an *inclusio* to the pericope in 39:11–15 (16). This name appears throughout Ezek 29–32 to describe the turbulent crowd who accompany Pharaoh.[182] Especially in chapter 32, the term appears no less than eight times.[183] Just like "Gog and all his המון" (39:11), so "Pharaoh/Egypt and all his המון" will also be dead.[184] The ultimate demise of Gog and his allies draws attention to the demise of Pharaoh and his entourage.

Taken as a whole, the cumulative lexical links draw the connections between Gog and Judah's allies, especially Egypt, close together. Through the tactful use of distinctive language, Ezek 38–39 infuses the attributes of Pharaoh into the great antihero Gog, the former appearing throughout Ezekiel as the dominant ally of the kingdom of Judah. The Gog oracles encourage the readers to identify the hordes of Gog with Egypt's allies and Israel's former lovers. The subsequent day of divine judgment, the bloody consumption of the bodies of Gog's army, and the bleak burial of Gog and his host all vividly recall the fate reserved for Pharaoh and his entourage, who were once Judah's allies.

---

[179] Cf. Zeph 1:7; Isa 34:6–8; Block, *Ezekiel*, 2:473. Logically, the event in Ezek 39:17–20 should come before the scene depicted in vv. 11–16. After the animals have devoured the flesh of Gog's host, the people of the land bury the bones left. For further explications, see Biberger, *Heil*, 78; Fitzpatrick, *Disarmament*, 99, n. 91.

[180] Klein, *Schriftauslegung*, 130–31. Another place where this Hebrew root is used frequently is in 37:12–13, and nowhere else in Ezekiel.

[181] For B. P. Irwin, "Molek Imagery and the Slaughter of Gog in Ezekiel 38–39," *JSOT* 65 (1995): 93–112, here 96; Block, Ezekiel, 2:469, the place name for Gog's interment גיא המון גוג (39:11) is a word play on גיא הנם, where the Judahites are buried. For further discussions on the burial place of Gog, see Biberger, *Heil*, 72, n. 277.

[182] See the discussion in Chapter Four, Section 2.3.

[183] Ezek 32:12, 16, 20, 25, 26, 31, 32.

[184] Cf. Ezek 31:2, 18; 32:16, 31, 32.

## 3.2.2. The Present Enemy

Despite all the aforementioned similarities to Egypt and the other allies of Judah, Gog now appears as the *primus* enemy, who wages war on the restored Israel. The opposition between Gog and Israel manifests in three main ways. First, it is displayed through the geographical position of Gog in relation to the land of Israel. Second, it is reflected through the aggressions of Gog against Israel. Third, it is shown through the contrasting ends of Gog and Israel.

We know very little about the specific geographical location of Gog. We are familiar with nations such as Egypt and Tyre, who, being near to Judah, had major impacts on Judah's political, cultural, and socio-economic life. By contrast, all we know about Gog is that it is an egregious invader from the north, who lives far away from Israel.[185] In 38:6, one of Gog's allies, Beth-togarmah, is from the "remote parts of the north" (ירכתי צפון). Later in 38:15, Gog is depicted as leading an army out of "the remote parts of the north" (ירכתי צפון). In 39:2, YHWH raises up Gog from the "remote parts of the north" (ירכתי צפון). Throughout the text, the place of origin of Gog is firmly anchored in the north. Ezekiel's characterization of the foe as coming from the north of Israel shapes Gog as a threat to the Zion theology. This is comparable to Jer 6:22–23, where a great nation is aroused to attack the "daughter Zion." Like Gog in Ezekiel, the ominous war machine in the book of Jeremiah is identified as coming "from the north land" (מארץ צפון), "from the remote parts of the land" (מירכתי ארץ). On this basis, Klein speculates that the enemy-from-the-north motif in the Gog oracles is dependent on Jer 6:22–23, the oldest text in which this motif appears.[186] On the other hand, Tooman objects to this association, arguing that Jer 6:22–23 does not attest to the exact locution ירכתי צפון, but reads: "a people has come *from the north land* (מארץ צפון), and a great nation will be aroused *from the remote parts of the land* (מירכתי ארץ)."[187] For him, a closer parallel is to be found in Isa 14:4b–21, which deploys the exact locution ירכתי צפון to characterize the "mountain of assembly," on which the

---

[185] B. S. Childs suggests that the enemy from the north depicted in Ezek 25–32 is essentially a "human enemy on the plane of history," while the enemy from the north in Ezek 38–39 becomes the trans-historical "representative of the cosmic powers of returned chaos" ("Enemy from the North and the Chaos Tradition," *JBL* 78 [1959]: 187–98, here 196). So also Zimmerli, *Ezekiel*, 2:303; Fitzpatrick, *Disarmament*, 87; A. Lauha, *Zaphon: Der Norden und die Nordvölker im Alten Testament*, AASF B 49.2 (Helsinki: Suomalainen Tiedeakatemia, 1943), 70.

[186] Klein, *Schriftauslegung*, 139. Cf. Biberger, *Heil*, 46–47, 55, 66; Childs, "Enemy," 190–95; W. L. Holladay, *Jeremiah 1: A Commentary on the Book of the Prophet Jeremiah Chapters 1–25*, Hermeneia 22 (Philadelphia: Fortress Press, 1986), 42–43.

[187] Tooman, *Gog*, 176.

hubristic tyrant sits.[188] In my view, Klein's proposition to relate Ezekiel's use of the enemy-from-the-north motif to Jer 6 is more persuasive. Isa 14 conceptualizes the north as the seat of the deity. This divine throne in the north will make the tyrant in Isa 14 "like the Most High" (v. 14).[189] The hubris of the tyrant, however, is not the issue in Jer 6 and Ezek 38–39.[190] By contrast, both of the latter passages conceptualize the north as the place, where the threat against Zion or the Mountains of Israel arises.[191] In Jer 6, Zion is where the divine seat is supposedly located, and it stands diametrically opposite to the north. Likewise, several passages in Ezekiel present צפון as the direction from which the invaders of Israel descend.[192] In particular, Ezek 39:2 characterizes Gog as originating "from the remote parts of the north" (מירכתי צפון), to come up "against the Mountains of Israel" (על הרי ישראל). The parallelism formed by these two prepositional phrases strengthens the opposition between Gog and Israel. Given that the historical enemies of the northen kingdom Israel and the southern kingdom Judah, be they Assyrians, Aramaeans, or Babylonians, came from the north, it is not surprising that both Jer 6 and Ezek 38–39 envision the north as the direction of the threat to God's people.[193] In light of this, I concur with Klein that Jer 6, rather than Isa 14, is a better *Vorlage* for Ezek 38–39. As in Jer 6, the north in Ezek 38–39 signifies a hazard to the Mountains of Israel.

---

[188] Ibid., 171, 175–76.

[189] Cf. Ps 48:1b–3.

[190] Cf. Rösel, *Sieg*, 317–18: "Die Verwendung des Motivs ירכתי צפון in Ez 38–39 lässt demnach über die bloße Wendung hinaus keine inhaltlichen Gemeinsamkeiten mit Jes 14,13 oder Ps 48,3 erkennen." So also Lauha, *Zaphon*, 53.

[191] Cf. the enemies from the north against Israel in Isa 14:31; Jer 1:13–15; 4:6; 6:1, 22; 10:22; 13:20; 15:12; Hab 1:5–11; Joel 2:20. See also the enemies from the north against other nations in Jer 46:6, 10, 20, 24; 47:2; 50:3, 9, 41; 51:48.

[192] צפון in Ezekiel appears in 1:4; 8:5; 21:9; 26:7; 32:30; 38:6, 15, 39:2; 40:19, 20, 23, 35, 44, 46; 41:11; 42:1 (2x), 2, 4, 11, 13, 17; 44:4; 46:9; 47:17 (2x); 48:16, 30. In 26:7, the north is the direction from which Nebuchadnezzar descends; 32:30 presents the chiefs of the north as the once mighty power who inspired terror on earth. In 9:2, the פקדות are summoned by God from the north to slay the inhabitants of Jerusalem. On the other hand, another strand of literature relates the north as the seat of the deity (e.g., 1:4; 44:4). Cf. Tooman, *Gog*, 171, n. 149.

[193] Cf. E. Lipinski, "צפון," *TDOT* 12: 435–43, here 441; M. Roncace, "North, Enemy from the," *New Interpreter's Dictionary of the Bible* 4:282; Rösel, *Sieg*, 316–20. Apart from these historical considerations, the enemy-from-the-north motif also contains a mythological aspect. In the Ugaritic texts, Mount Zaphon is the seat of Baal, who shot his poisonous arrows at his enemies. Therefore, Zaphon is also associated with terror and horror. For the Ancient Near Eastern background of the expression ירכתי צפון, see Fitzpatrick, *Disarmament*, 106–7. Bibeger, *Heil*, 46–47.

The depicted aggressions carried out by Gog further highlight the opposition between Gog and Israel. One of Ezekiel's prophecies against Egypt presents Pharaoh as a vulnerable broken reed to the house of Judah (29:6–7). Underlying this imagery, the political or military support offered by Egypt to Judah is presumed.[194] Egypt's crime thus does not consist in its attacking of Judah. By contrast, Gog's attack of the Mountains of Israel stands out in 38:8–9. As if one repetition is not enough to emphasize the crime of Gog, 38:16 again takes up the impending presence of Gog against Israel with verbatim correspondences.[195] Both aforementioned pericopes predict that Gog will come up against the restored land of Israel "in the latter years" (באחרית השנים, 38:8) or "in the latter days" (באחרית הימים, 38:16).[196] Gog will come upon YHWH's people and YHWH's land "like the storm" (כשאה, 38:9) and "like the cloud, covering the land" (כענן לכסות הארץ; 38:9, 16).[197] The noun "storm" (שאה) is associated elsewhere in the Hebrew Bible with the devastation or desolation of the land.[198] To advance like a cloud further evokes the action of the ominous enemy from the north in Jer 4:3 (כענן יעלה), or the divine retribution on Egypt in Ezek 30:18 (ענן יכסה).[199] All these terms add to the destructive overtone of Gog's actions. In the *Wiederaufnahme*, Israel is called YHWH's people (עמי ישראל, 38:14, 16; 39:7),[200] who dwell in YHWH's land (ארצי, 38:16). The link of God-people-land is made explicit in these Gog passages.[201] Taken altogether, Gog's sinister advance places him in opposition to YHWH's people and YHWH's land.

The antagonism between Gog and Israel comes to a head when the death of one eventuates in the restoration of another. From the perspective of Ezekiel, the demise of Egypt also sounds the death knell of the kingdom of Judah (32:1–33:22).[202] Even though Egypt will be deprived of any political influence

---

[194] For a fuller discussion, see Chapter Four, Section 2.1.

[195] Cf. Tooman, *Gog*, 156.

[196] The expression "in the latter days" is common in the Hebrew Bible. Cf. Gen 49:1; Num 24:14; Deut 4:30; 31:29; Isa 2:2; Jer 23:20; 30:24; 48:47; 49:39; Dan 10:14; Hos 3:5; Mic 4:1. In the Aramaic Dan 2:28, an equivalent phrase באחרית יומיא appears. For a comprehensive overview of the scholarly debates concerning the exact meaning of אחרית, see Biberger, *Heil*, 55–57; Tooman, *Gog*, 94–97.

[197] The LXX treats the verb תהיה as superfluous. Here, we follow the MT, linking it to the expression "like the cloud covering the land," while categorizing the two foregoing verbs (תבוא, ועליתה) into two separate clauses. Cf. Allen, *Ezekiel 20–48*, 200, n. 9a.

[198] Job 30:3, 14; 38:27; Isa 6:11; Zeph 1:15.

[199] Rösel, *Sieg*, 193.

[200] The names "Israel" and "Jacob" also appear in 39:9, 23, 25, 29. Of significance, the names "Judah" and "Jerusalem" are not used. Noted in Bøe, *Gog*, 108.

[201] Olley, *Ezekiel*, 500; Biberger, *Heil*, 59.

[202] For a fuller discussion, see Chapter Four, Section 3.3.

on Israel and will be placed at a greater geographical distance from Israel, the former, like the latter, also receives a promise of restoration (29:13–16).[203] The contrast between the two nations is not as great as the difference between the fates of Gog and Israel in Ezek 38–39. In the latter chapters, the demise of Gog is directly juxtaposed with the restoration of Israel.[204] Israel will rise phoenix-like from this frightening experience to become enriched by the spoil of the fallen enemies.[205] The day has come for a reversal of Israel's fate. The text clearly captures this reversal through the verbal parallelism between 38:10–13 and 39:10.[206] In Ezek 38:10–12, YHWH first reveals Gog's inner mind, which devises a plan, aiming "to capture spoil" (לשלל שלל) and "to seize plunder" (לבז בז) from the inhabitants of Israel.[207] In v. 13, the other nations such as "Sheba and Dedan and the traders of Tarshish with all its magnates" also scrutinize Gog's intention "to capture spoil" (הלשלל שלל) and "to seize plunder" (הלבז בז).[208] Ironically, the next chapter reveals that the inhabitants of Israel will be the people who capture spoil (ושללו את שלליהם) and seize plunder (ובזזו את בזזיהם) from Gog's host (39:9–10). As noted, the two *figurae etymologicae* involving the roots בזז and שלל reinforce the contrasting fates of Gog and Israel. The plundered now become the plunderers.[209] The very end of the Gog oracles zooms into the fate of Israel (39:23–29).[210] Here the defeat of Gog is related to the restoration of Israel in two respects. First, YHWH's triumphant defeat of Gog and his allies prove that the exile was not the result of YHWH's inability to protect his people, but rather a punishment for Israel's

---

[203] For a fuller discussion, see Chapter Four, Section 3.4.

[204] M. Nobile remarks that the Gog oracles are "die Radikalisierung der Orakel gegen die Völker" or "die Fortsetzung die Klimax von Ezechiel 25–32" ("Beziehung zwischen Ez 32,17–32 und der Gog-Perikope (Ez 38–39) im Lichte der Endredaktion," in: *Ezekiel and His Book: Textual and Literary Criticism and Their Interrelation*, ed. J. Lust, BETL 74 [Leuven: Leuven University Press, 1985], 257).

[205] Cf. Astour, "Ezekiel's Prophecy," 568.

[206] A similar reversal appears in 35:15, where Mount Seir will become a שממה, since it has taunted Israel as a שממה. Cf. Rösel, *Sieg*, 263; Biberger, *Heil*, 72.

[207] The combination of the two verbs (בזז and שלל) appears in Ezek 26:12; 29:19; 38:12, 13; 39:10. Outside Ezekiel, it occurs only in Isa 10:6: לשלל שלל ולבז בז.

[208] While the LXX reads the plural of כָּפָר "village" (αἱ κῶμαι; cf. Josh 18:24; 1 Sam 6:18; Song 7:12; 1 Chr 27:25), the Masoretic vocalization renders the noun as derived from כפיר, meaning "young lion." In 32:2 כפיר גוים is used as a designation of royalty. Thus, for Block, *Ezekiel*, 2:449, the noun in 38:13 means the magnates, the leading merchants.

[209] Biberger, *Heil*, 72: "Die jenigen, die ausgezogen sind, um Beute zu machen, werden nun ausgeplündert von denen, die sie ausplündern wollten." Cf. Bøe, *Gog*, 117.

[210] For various approaches to the delimitation of Ezek 39:21–29, see K. L. Wong, "The Masoretic and Septuagint Texts of Ezekiel 39,21–29," *ETL* 78 (2002):130–47, here 130–31; Fitzpatrick, *Disarmament*, 100–101; Klein, *Schriftauslegung*, 112–14.

iniquities and transgressions (vv. 23–24).[211] Second, the elimination of Gog marks the turning point of Israel's fate. Whereas Nebuchadnezzar's invasion of Judah signifies the exile of God's people, Gog's invasion of Israel ultimately fails and signifies YHWH's willingness to re-establish Israel in their own land (vv. 25–29). With the destruction of the enemies, Israel will be gathered into their own land, and YHWH "will not hide my face from them any longer" (v. 29).[212] The promise of restoration to Israel is thus a direct outcome of the preceding destruction of Gog and his allies.

At the end, identifying Gog with only Israel's former enemies hardly draws sufficient attention to the alliance and the intimate relation between Judah and the nations depicted elsewhere in the book of Ezekiel. Whoever composed the Gog oracles must have been aware of the deep alignment between Judah and the other nations, so that Gog is also made to embody characteristics and attributes assigned previously to Judah's other foreign lovers, especially Egypt. The role of Gog, however, differs from these allying nations. He is shaped as an invader from the distant north, a trope that is often associated with the enemies of Israel in the Hebrew Bible. Central to the oracles are the aggressions carried out by Gog against Israel. The destruction and death of Gog and his hordes inaugurate a new era, when Israel will again live securely within the land endowed by YHWH. In a nutshell, Ezekiel's Gog oracles draw from onminfarious biblical elements and themes, so that all foreign historical nations, whether friends or foes, are all combined and transformed into a metahistorical symbol of chaos or evil, standing in opposition to YHWH and the restored Israel in the eschatological era.

All the aforementioned passages, be they the chronological markers in 24:1–2 and 33:21–22 or the prophecies against Mount Seir and Gog in chapters 35 and 38–39, betray their secondary nature within the book of Ezekiel. Their late origins, however, do not dictate that they respond to Ezek 25–32 in the same way. On the one hand, the insertion of the date about the beginning of the siege of Jerusalem in 24:1–2 allows the shared divine judgment of Jerusalem and the neighbouring nations in chapters 24 and 25 come to a sharper focus. In a similar vein, the inserted temporal marker in 33:21–22, which marks the end of the siege and the arrival of the news of the fall of Jerusalem, binds the death of Egypt (32:17–32) and Judah (33:1–20) together. Both chronological markers thus affirm and deepen the link between Judah and the foreign nations, by embracing the oracles concerning the doom of the nations with the announcements of the demise of the capital city of Judah.

On the other hand, Ezek 35 and 38–39, deeply anxious of this alignment between Judah and the nations, reconstruct another vision, where the divine retribution on Mount Seir and Gog completely turns the message of "oblique

---

[211] Tooman, *Gog*, 191.
[212] This hiding-face motif in v. 29 corresponds to that appearing in vv. 23, 24.

judgment" in Ezek 25–32 on its head, such that the restoration of Israel is now heralded via the eradication of the nations. Both chapters 35 and 38–39 contribute to the transformations of the role and fate of the nations, such that all the foreign nations now stand in an absolute contrast to the restored Israel. Underlying this polarization, nevertheless, is a poignant recognition of the past alignment. Ezekiel 35 incorporates the curse that was once announced to the mountains of Israel in chapter 6. YHWH's retribution on Gog and his allies in Ezek 38–39 recalls the terrifiying punishment decreed against Egypt and Judah's other foreign allies. The eagerness for the oracles to polarize the nations and Israel reflects the anxiety of past alignment between the nations and Judah, which comes to the fore in Ezek 25–32. In short, both the affirmation and transformation of the "oblique judgment" message in the rest of the book of Ezekiel shed light on the lively debates about the relationship between the foreign nations and God's people. As will be seen in the next few pages, the debates continue to unfold in the early biblical interpretations and modern scholarly discussions.

# EPILOGUE

## IMPLICATIONS OF THE STUDY

העיר משׂחקת מחבואים בין שמותיה ירושלים, אל־קודס, שלם, ג׳רו, ירו, לוחשת: יבוס, יבוס,
יבוס. בחשכה. בוכה בגעגועים: אליה קפיטולינה, אליה, אליה. היא באה אל כל אחד הקורא לה
בלילה לבדו. אך אנו יודעים מי בא אל מי.

The city plays hide-and-seek among her names: Yerushalayim, al-Quds, Salem, Jeru, Yeru, Whispering [her first, Jebusite name]: Yevus, Yevus, Yevus, in the dark. She weeps with longing: Ælia Capitolina, Ælia, Ælia. She comes to anyone who calls her at night, alone. But we know who comes to whom.

Yehuda Amichai

This study bears two main implications for the scholarly discourse about Ezekiel's OAN. First, this study potentially builds a foundation for further research on how the relationship between God's people and the nations continues to play out in the history of the interpretation of Ezekiel's OAN. Several early reception materials of Ezek 25–32 do not display positive attitudes toward the foreign nations. Instead, these reception materials mirror the demonization of foreign nations and the polarization of nations and Israel, which have already begun in Ezekiel's oracles against Gog and Seir. The Targumic translation of Ezek 32:17–32 transforms the contrast between the netherworld and the land of the living in the MT into a contrast between the foreign territory and the land of Israel. Instead of following MT Ezek 32:23, which accuses Assyria of "spreading terror in the land of the living," the Targumic translation accuses Assyria and its entire army of exercising "tyrannical dominion over the land of Israel."[1] Patmore also notes a similar trend, where

---

[1] For the English translation of this Aramic excerpt, see H. S. Levey, *The Aramaic Bible: The Targums: Vol. 13: The Targum of Ezekiel* (Edinburgh: T&T Clark, 1987), 91–93. For other peculiarities of the Targum of Ezekiel, see idem, "The Targum of Ezekiel," *HUCA* 46 (1975): 139–58.

the early rabbis and church fathers demonized the Tyrian ruler in Ezek 28 as the egoistic foreigner or Satan.[2] Extant in these texts is thus a binary contrast between the elect and the nations.

Meanwhile, one Qumran text strengthens the message of oblique judgment to the house of Judah in Ezek 25. According to Strugnell, the text in 4Q177 (*Catena*) II, 14 contains a citation of Ezek 25:8: "The house of Israel and Judah is like all the peoples."[3] This is a mockery issued to the house of Judah by Moab and Seir. In the Qumran text, "the house of Israel and Judah" most likely refers to the Qumran community, the elect.[4] The identity of the speaker of this taunt is perplexing. It is odd that, in this Qumran text, the names of Moab and Seir are not mentioned at all. Steudel observes that compared to 1QpHab, which renders the hostile foreign powers easily recognizable, the roles of the foreign peoples in 4Q177 are relatively pale.[5] The "congregation of those looking for easy interpretations" (II, 12) is usually understood to be the Pharisees, the internal Jewish enemies of the Qumran community.[6] As such, 4Q177 likely reconfigures the statement uttered by Moab and Seir in Ezek 25:8, so that it represents the internal strife among various Jewish groups. Without being named, the foreign nations in 4Q177 function as a symbol of the wicked, who are now identified with the internal enemies, standing in opposition to the righteous elect, that is, the Qumran community.

---

[2] See the discussions of b. Hul. 89a and Origen's *Homilies on Ezekiel* in Patmore, *Adam*, 29–30, 60–64.

[3] J. Strugnell, "Notes ne marge du volume V des <Discoveries in the Judaean Desert of Jordan>," *RevQ* 26 (1970): 163–276, here 243–45, cited in A. Steudel, *Der Midrasch zur Eschatologie aus der Qumrangemeinde (4QMidrEschat a.b): Materielle Rekonstruktion, Textbestand, Gattung und traditionsgeschichtliche Einordnung des durch 4Q174 ("Florilegium") und 4Q177 ("Catena A") repräsentierten Werkes aus den Qumranfunden*, STDJ 13 (Leiden: Brill, 1994), 78, 98. For an English translation of this Qumran text, see *DSSSE* 1:365.

[4] In 4Q177 II 7 is a reference to "the sons of the light" (בני האור); in the reconstructed II 10, 13 are references to "the men of the Community" (אנשי היחד). The terminology is typically used to describe the community members in Qumran. So D. Dimant, "The Apocalyptic Interpretation of Ezekiel at Qumran," in *Messiah and Christos: Studies in the Jewish Origins of Christianity*, ed. I. Gruenwald et al., TSAJ 32 (Tübingen: Mohr Siebeck, 1992), 31–51, here 39; Steudel, *Midrasch*, 167–69.

[5] See Steudel, *Midrasch*, 168, even though she reconstructs II, 14, so that it reads "they are the peoples/the nations on the last days" [המה העמים/הגוים באחרית הימים].

[6] G. J. Brooke, "Catena," in *Encyclopedia of the Dead Sea Scrolls*, ed. L. H. Schiffman and J. C. VanderKam, 2 vols. (Oxford: Oxford University Press, 2000), 1:121–22, here 121: "The enemy mentioned in Psalm 13.5 is identified with the Seekers after Smooth Things and then interpreted through Ezekiel 25.8." דורשי החלקות also appears in 4Q169 3–4 I, 7 to represent the internal enemies of the community members. Cf. S. Tzoref, *The Pesher Nahum Scroll from Qumran: An Exegetical Study of 4Q169*, STDJ 53 (Leiden: Brill, 2004), 87–163; Steudel, *Midrasch*, 168.

The above examples provide snippets of the wide spectrum of attitudes towards the foreign nations within the early reception materials of Ezek 25–32. The OAN in Ezek 25–32 augment the significance of the collapse of Judah, so that the people who once lived in Judah realize the disintegration of previous boundary markers, and notice how similar the other nations are to Judah itself. This recognition of similarities pulls later texts in different directions to search for further refinements of future identity. This quest for identity is not only evident in the reception materials of the OAN. As helpfully demonstrated by Tzoref, the Qumran materials also display diverse attitudes toward the foreigners. Jubilees outrightly excludes Ishmael and Esau from the patriarchal blessings, so that both are subject to cursed eradications, whereas the treatment of the non-elect in 4Q252 is more ambiguous and less harsh by comparison.[7] Donaldson and Nickelsburg argue cogently that even in the literature that demonstrates the most exclusive understanding of the elect as in 1 Enoch, individual passages still include the nations in the worship of Israel's God in the last days and the foreigners within the sphere of eschatological blessings.[8] Despite the generally negative assessment of the Gentiles, several rabbinic texts, according to Kaminsky, present a more lenient attitude towards the foreign nations.[9] The fluid and diverse interpretations of the foreign nations and foreigners within and beyond the Second Temple Period await further explorations. It will be useful for future studies to connect this study about the development of Ezekiel's OAN with other early interpretations of biblical traditions.

A second implication of this study concerns the common scholarly assumption that all OAN are xenophobic, particularistic, and intolerant. In 1941, in his *Introduction to the Old Testament*, Pfeiffer issued a classic statement concerning the OAN in the Hebrew Bible in general:

---

[7] S. Tzoref, "Covenantal Election in 4Q252 and Jubilees' Heavenly Tablets," *DSD* 18 (2011): 74–89. For further details about the different roles taken by the foreign nations in the Qumran, see A. C. Hagedorn and S. Tzoref, "Attitudes to Gentiles in the Minor Prophets and in Corresponding Pesharim," *DSD* 20 (2013): 472–509, esp. 489–509.

[8] Cf. 1 *En.* 10:21–11:2; 48:4–5; 50:2–3; 90:30–38; 91:14; 100:6; 105:1–2; T. L. Donaldson, *Judaism and the Gentiles: Jewish Patterns of Universalism (to 135 CE)* (Waco: Baylor University Press, 2008), 77–97; G. W. E. Nickelsburg, "The We and the Other in the Worldview of 1 Enoch, the Dead Sea Scrolls and Other Early Jewish Texts," in *The "Other" in Second Temple Judaism*, ed. D. C. Harlow et al. (Grand Rapids: Eerdmans, 2011), 262–78, here 270.

[9] J. S. Kaminsky, "Israel's Election and the Other in Biblical, Second Temple, and Rabbinic Thought," in *The "Other" in Second Temple Judaism*, ed. D. C. Harlow et al. (Grand Rapids: Eerdmans, 2011), 23–29, esp. 23–25.

Although such anathemas against the heathen were inaugurated by Amos..., they reflect on the whole not the moral indignation of the great pre-exilic prophets but rather the nationalism of the "false prophets" and of later Jews chafing for centuries under alien rule. The masses did not rise to the idealistic universalism of a Second Isaiah, nor even to the friendly attitude of toleration of foreigners that animates the books of Ruth and Jonah. Ardently nationalistic and fanatically intolerant, postexilic Jews found some relief by gleefully anticipating divine vengeance on their enemies and oppressors.[10]

This statement judges all the OAN as "nationalistc" and "fanatically intolerant" by setting this collection of prophecies over and against the more "universalistic" Second Isaiah. Pfeiffer assigns all the OAN to the "false prophets." Only those in accord with Second Isaiah's universalistic inclusion of all nations in the eschatological salvation can be called "true prophecy." This exaltation of Second Isaiah persists to the present day. Vorländer deploys YHWH's salvation of Israel and the whole world in Isa 43:10–13 to define monotheism, claiming that Second Isaiah is the "Kronzeuge für den alttestamentlichen Monotheismus."[11] This glorification of Second Isaiah is further popularized by Armstrong's *A History of God*, where the book of Isaiah is portrayed as the defining literature of the Israelite monotheism. Drawing on Isa 19:24–25 and 46:1, Armstrong purports that YHWH in Isaiah "had become the symbol of a transcendent reality that made narrow interpretations of election seem petty and inadequate."[12] All these claims demonstrate that the "universal" participation in eschatological salvation, as pictured in Second Isaiah, becomes the touchstone to define and evaluate both election and monotheism of the ancient Israelites.[13] But does Second Isaiah represent the purely universalistic prophecy? Is it the most suitable yardstick to measure and characterize all the OAN in the Hebrew Bible?

---

[10] Pfeiffer, *Introduction*, 443. Pfeiffer's definition of Second Isaiah encompasses chapters 40–66 (cf. 415–16).

[11] H. Vorländer, "Der Monotheismus Israels als Antwort auf die Krise des Exils," in *Der Einzige Gott: Die Geburt des biblischen Monotheismus*, ed. B. Lang (München: Kösel, 1981), 84–113, here 93. He thinks that universalism is the defining consequence of monotheism and, with the rise of monotheism during the exile, as attested in literature such as Second Isaiah and deuteronomistic texts, the particular Yahwism has transformed into a universal world religion (108–10).

[12] K. Armstrong, *A History of God: From Abraham to the Present: The 4000 Year Quest for God* (London: Mandarin, 1994), 74–76. See, however, J. S. Kaminsky, *Yet I Loved Jacob: Reclaiming the Biblical Concept of Election* (Nashville: Abingdon Press, 2007), 152, who argues that Israel's election is not dissolved even when Isa 19 speaks of Gentile inclusion.

[13] For the Enlightenment embracement of the soteriological and ethical "universalism" and its influence in biblical scholarship, see J. Blenkinsopp, "Yahweh and Other Deities: Conflict and Accommodation in the Religion of Israel," *Int* 40 (1986):

Brett, Kaminsky, Stewart, and MacDonald rightly contend that the putative universalism in Second Isaiah is not straightforward.[14] On the one hand, Second Isaiah proclaims the servant figure to be "light of the nations" such that God's "salvation may reach the end of the earth" (49:6; cf. 42:6); and the "nations" and "islands" will hope for the *torah* and salvation of YHWH (42:4; 44:5). On the other hand, Second Isaiah envisions nations in a more subservient role to Israel.[15] The nations will come to Israel in chains (45:14) and foreign kings will lick the dust of Israel's feet (49:23). Certainly, some of the contradictory passages can be explained by a historical approach, attributing the new openness to the foreigners in Isa 56:1–8 and 66:18–24, for instance, to a Third rather than a Second Isaiah.[16] Nevertheless, Kaminsky argues that even within the fairly unified Second Isaiah, contradictory exclamations are placed right next to one another. In Isa 45:22–23, for example, YHWH promises salvation to all nations, but the very next verses proclaim humiliation to the nations who were once responsible for the humbling of Israel (45:24b–25).[17] Zion, according to Brett and MacDonald, remains the focus of the eschatological visions in Second Isaiah, such that these visions should be seen as "nationalist-universalist rather than internationalist,"[18] and that "Land and temple are certainly reconfigured in the post-exilic period, but neither is erased."[19] In short, while Second Isaiah does include some universal elements within its eschatological vision, this vision is not devoid of particular aspects; Zion's centrality is not dissolved as a result of the universalism. Second Isaiah's presentations of God's/Israel's relation to the nations are, thus, much more complex and require careful qualifications within their own literary context.

This problematization of the "universalistic" Second Isaiah brings us back to Pfeiffer's evaluation of all OAN in the Hebrew Bible. While Pfeiffer

---

354–66, here 360–62; Kaminsky, *Jacob*, 1–3; J. D. Levenson, "The Universal Horizon of Biblical Particularism," in *Ethnicity and the Bible*, ed. M. G. Brett, BibInt 19 (Leiden: Brill, 1996), 143–69, here 157.

[14] M. G. Brett, "Nationalism and the Hebrew Bible," in *The Bible in Ethics*, JSOTS 207 (Sheffield: Sheffield Academic Press, 1995), 136–63, esp. 151–57; Kaminsky, *Jacob*, 137–58; Kaminsky and Stewart, "Universalism," 139–63; N. MacDonald, "Monotheism and Isaiah," in *Interpreting Isaiah: Issues and Approaches*, ed. D. G. Firth and H. G. M. Williamson (Downers Grove: IVP Academic, 2009), 43–61.

[15] According to D. W. Van Winkle, "The Relationship of the Nations to YHWH and to Israel in Isaiah 40–55," *VT* 35 (1985): 446–58, in Second Isaiah the universal salvation of the nations exists simultaneously with the nations' submission to Israel. Noted also by Kaminsky and Stewart, "Universalism," 139, n. 1.

[16] Kaminsky and Stewart, "Universalism," 155–62.

[17] Kaminsky, *Jacob*, 149.

[18] Brett, "Nationalism," 154, 155.

[19] MacDonald, "Monotheism," 55.

measures the biblical OAN against Second Isaiah, and judges the former as "nationalistic" and "intolerant," my examination of the rhetorical functions of Ezek 25–32 reveals a remarkably inclusive picture, imbued with insightful self-reflection.[20] When we approach Ezek 25–32 within its own literary context, when we allow the yardstick of Second Isaiah to drop away, another kind of universal picture becomes apparent in the putatively exclusivist Ezek 25–32. The kind of participation of the nations in Israel's eschatological worship of YHWH, as envisioned in the book of Isaiah, does not need to be the only type of universal element in Israel's religion. An alternative voice calls out from Ezek 25–32, asking to recognize the shared flaws, frailty, and brokenness among the nations, conveying an internalized perspective that unites all nations to Judah. This picture is not a glorious salvation as in Second Isaiah. Nonetheless, it speaks of another universality—a universal vulnerability. Ezekiel's OAN, therefore, presents a picture that stands in tension with Pfeiffer's evaluation of the OAN as representing the national zeal of later Jews, necessarily intolerant to the Gentiles, and xenophobic toward the foreign nations.

This universal brokenness within Ezekiel in no way allows a simple purgation of Israel's particular identity within the texts. After all, the recognition of shared brokenness is achieved by drawing on particular characteristics attributed to each individual nation. Hence, according to Ezekiel, only the lands of Transjordan and Philistia are comparable with the territory of Judah; only the commercial empire of Tyre most vividly mirror the glory of the Jerusalem temple; and only the covenant of Egypt is seductive enough to cause Judah to stray away from YHWH. All nations are different from each other in their own ways. The characteristics of each foreign nation are not equivalent to all the features of Judah. Yet, various characteristics of the nations can interweave to mirror Judah's unique identity, the notion of which deepens and matures upon interaction and comparison. This internalization fuels further transformations of self-identity. For Ezek 38–39, the recognition of past alignment with the other foreign nations generates an eagerness to create a new reality, where a new land and nation stands securely away from the former enemies or allies.

---

[20] A few studies concerning OAN have similarly questioned the classification of biblical OAN as simply "nationalistic." See, for instance, G. R. Hamborg, "Reasons for Judgement in the Oracles against the Nations of the Prophet Isaiah," *VT* 31 (1981): 145–59; Davis, "Mythical Discourse," 224–39. Raabe proposes that the OAN in the Hebrew Bible presents a variety of rhetorical functions rather than promising salvation to Israel ("Why," 236–57). His later article on Ezekiel's OAN, nevertheless, presumes singularly that the OAN functions to restore Israel's fortune ("Transforming the International Status Quo: Ezekiel's Oracles against the Nations," in *Transforming Visions: Transformations of Text, Tradition and Theology in Ezekiel*, ed. W. A. Tooman and M. A. Lyons, Princeton Theological Monograph Series 127 [Eugene: Pickwick Publications, 2010], 187–207).

The recognition of the commonality with the others, therefore, does not exclude Israel's own identity, but deepens it.

This study can best be concluded via one playful poem of Yehuda Amichai:[21]

> The city plays hide-and-seek among her names: Yerushalayim, al-Quds, Salem, Jeru, Yeru, Whispering [her first, Jebusite name]: Yevus, Yevus, Yevus, in the dark. She weeps with longing: Ælia Capitolina, Ælia, Ælia. She comes to anyone who calls her at night, alone. But we know who comes to whom.

Like the city that has changed its name throughout the history, Ezekiel's prophecies against the nations have also undergone textual developments that continue to unfold in subsequent reception materials. The different names attached to the city are analogous to the diverse textual traditions responding to Ezekiel's prophecies. We will certainly do no good to harmonize all these particular names, but I do think that the discovery of differences can benefit from the recognition of commonality. Coming from different perspectives, the various names ultimately describe the same city. Just like the city in Amichai's poem, Ezek 25–32 is teaching a poignant lesson about this recognition of commonality amidst differences.

---

[21] For the most recent English translation, see Yehuda Amichai, "Jerusalem, 1967," in *The Poetry of Yehuda Amichai*, ed. Robert Alter (New York: Farrar, Straus and Giroux, 2015), 81–89, here 84.

# BIBLIOGRAPHY

Aharoni, Y. *Arad Inscriptions: Judean Desert Studies*. Jerusalem: Israel Exploration Society, 1981.
———. "The Negeb of Judah." *IEJ* 8 (1958): 26–38.
Aḥituv, S. *Echoes from the Past: Hebrew and Cognate Inscriptions from the Biblical Period*. Translated by A. F. Rainey. Carta Handbook. Jerusalem: Carta, 2008.
Akers, M. R. "The Soteriological Development of the 'Arm of the Lord' Motif." *Journal for the Evangelical Study of the Old Testament* 2 (2014): 29–48.
Albertz, R. *Die Exilszeit: 6. Jahrhundert v. Chr. Biblische Enzyklopädie 7*. Stuttgart: Kohlhammer, 2001.
Albright, W. R. "The Seal of Eliakim and the Latest Preexilic History of Judah, with Some Observaions on Ezekiel." *JBL* 51 (1932): 77–106.
———. "What Were the Cherubim?" *BA* 1 (1938): 1–3.
Alexander, D. "The Old Testament View of Life after Death." *Them* 11 (1986): 41–46.
Allen, L. C. *Ezekiel 20–48*. WBC 29. Waco: Word Books, 1990.
———. *Jeremiah: A Commentary*. OTL. Louisville: Westminster John Knox, 2008.
Altenmüller, B. *Synkretismus in den Sargtexten*. Wiesbaden: Harrassowitz, 1975.
Amichai, Y. "Jerusalem, 1967." Pages 81–89 in *The Poetry of Yehuda Amichai*. Edited by R. Alter. New York: Farrar, Straus and Giroux, 2015.
Anderson, B. A. *Brotherhood and Inheritance: A Canonical Reading of the Esau and Edom Traditions*. LHBOTS 556. New York: T&T Clark, 2011.
Anderson, G. A. "Ezekiel 28, the Fall of Satan, and the Adam Books." Pages 133–47 in *Literature on Adam and Eve: Collected Essays*. Edited by G. A. Anderson et al. SVTP 15. Leiden: Brill, 2000.
Arbel, D. "Questions about Eve's Iniquity, Beauty, and Fall: The 'Primal Figure' in Ezekiel 28:11-19 and 'Genesis Rabbah' Traditions of Eve." *JBL* 124 (2005): 641–55.
———. "'Seal of Resemblance, Full of Wisdom, and Perfect in Beauty': The Enoch/Metatron Narrative of 3 Enoch and Ezekiel 28." *HTR* 98 (2005): 121–42.
Armstrong, K. *A History of God: From Abraham to the Present: The 4000 Year Quest for God*. London: Mandarin, 1994.
Assis, E. "Why Edom? On the Hostility towards Jacob's Brother in Prophetic Sources." *VT* 56 (2006): 1–20.

Astour, M. C. "Ezekiel's Prophecy of Gog and the Cuthean Legend of Naram-Sin." *JBL* 95 (1976): 567–79.
Avi-Yonah, M., and B. Oded. "Moab." Pages 399–404 in vol. 2 of *Encyclopaedia Judaica*. Edited by M. Berenbaum and F. Skolnik. 2nd ed. 22 vols. Detorit: Macmillan Reference USA. 2007.
Bach, R. *Die Aufforderungen zur Flucht und zum Kampf im alttestamentlichen Prophetenspruch*. WMANT 9. Neukirchen: Neukirchener Verlag, 1962.
Bartlett, J. R. "Edom and the Fall of Jerusalem, 587 B.C." *PEQ* 114 (1982): 13–24.
———. "The Moabites and Edomites." Pages 229–258 in *Peoples of Old Testament Times*. Edited by D. J. Wiseman. Oxford: Clarendon Press, 1973.
Barr, J. "'Thou Art the Cherub:' Ezekiel 28:14 and the Post-Ezekiel Understanding of Genesis 2–3." Pages 213–23 in *Priests, Prophets and Scribes: Essays on the Formation and Heritage of Second Temple Judaism in Honour of Joseph Blenkinsopp*. Edited by E. Ulrich et al. JSOTSup 149. Sheffield: JSOT Press, 1992.
Batto, B. F. *Slaying the Dragon: Mythmaking in the Biblical Tradition*. Louisville: Westminster John Knox Press, 1992.
Becker, J. "Erwägungen zur Ezechielischen Frage." Pages 137–49 in *Künder des Wortes: Beiträge zur Theologie der Propheten*. Edited by L. Ruppert et al. Würzburg: Echter, 1982.
Beentjes, P. C. "Oracles against the Nations, a Central Issue in the 'Latter Prophets.'" *Bijdr* 50 (1989): 203–9.
Bentzen, A. "The Ritual Background of Amos 1:2–2:16." *OtSt* 8 (1950): 85–99.
Ben Zvi, E. "Othering, Selfing, 'Boundarying' and 'Cross-Boundarying' as Interwoven with Socially Shared Memories: Some Observations." Pages 20–40 in *Imagining the Other and Constructing Israelite Identity in the Early Second Temple Period*. Edited by E. Ben Zvi and D. V. Edelman. LHBOTS 456. London: Bloomsbury, 2014.
———. "Who Wrote the Speech of Rabshakeh and When?" *JBL* 109 (1990): 79–92.
Berges, U. F. *The Book of Isaiah: Its Composition and Final Form*. Translated by M. C. Lind. Sheffield: Sheffield Phoenix Press, 2012.
Bertholet, A. *Hesekiel*. HAT 1.13. Tübingen: Mohr Siebeck, 1936.
Bewer, J. A. *The Book of Ezekiel in the Authorized Version with Introductions and Critical Notes*. 2 vols. Harpers Annotated Bible 9. New York, N.Y.: Harper, 1954.
Biberger, B. *Endgültiges Heil innerhalb von Geschichte und Gegenwart: Zukunftskonzeptionen in Ez 38–39, Joel 1–4 und Sach 12–14*. BBB 161. Göttingen: Vandenhoek & Ruprecht, 2010.
Biddle, M. E. *Deuteronomy*. SHBC 4. Macon: Smyth & Helwys, 2003.
———. "The Figure of Lady Jerusalem: Identification, Deification and Personification of Cities in the Ancient Near East." Pages 173–94 in *The Biblical Canon in Comparative Perspective*. Edited by K. L. Younger and W. W. Hallo. Scripture in Context 4. Lewiston: Mellen, 1991.
Black, J., and A. Green. *Gods, Demons and Symbols of Ancient Mesopotamia: An Illustrated Dictionary*. Austin: University of Texas Press, 1992.
Blenkinsopp, J. *Ezekiel*. IBC. Louisville: Westminster John Knox, 1990.
———. *Isaiah 56–66*. AB 198. New York: Doubleday, 2003.

———. "Yahweh and Other Deities: Conflict and Accommodation in the Religion of Israel." *Int* 40 (1986): 354–66.
Bloch-Smith, E. "Solomon's Temple: The Politics of Ritual Space." Pages 83–94 in *Sacred Time, Sacred Place: Archaeology and the Religion of Israel*. Edited by B. Gittlen. Winona Lake: Eisenbrauns, 2002.
Block, D. I. "Beyond the Grave: Ezekiel's Vision of Death and Afterlife." *BBR* 2 (1992): 113–41.
———. "Bny 'Mwn: The Sons of Ammon." *AUSS* 22 (1984): 197–212.
———. *The Book of Ezekiel*. NICOT. 2 vols. Grand Rapids: Eerdmans, 1997, 1998.
———. "Ezekiel's Boiling Cauldron: A Form-Critical Solution to Ezekiel XXIV 1–14." *VT* 41 (1991): 12–37.
Boadt, L. *Ezekiel's Oracles against Egypt: A Literary and Philological Study of Ezekiel 29–32*. BibOr 37. Rome: Pontifical Biblical Institute, 1980.
———. "Mythological Themes and the Unity of Ezekiel." Pages 211–31 in Literary Structure and Rhetorical Strategies in the Hebrew Bible. Edited by L. J. de Regt et al. Assen: Van Gorcum, 1996.
———. "Rhetorical Strategies in Ezekiel's Oracles of Judgment." Pages 182–200 in *Ezekiel and His Book: Textual and Literary Criticism and Their Interrelation*. Edited by J. Lust. BETL 74. Leuven: Leuven University Press, 1986.
Bodi, D. *The Book of Ezekiel and the Poem of Erra*. OBO 104. Freiburg: Universitätsverlag, 1991.
———. "Les gillûlîm chez Ezéchiel et dans l'Ancien Testament." *RB* 100 (1993): 481–510.
Bogaert, P.-M. "Le Chérub de Tyr (Ez 28, 14.16) et l'Hippocampe de ses Monnaies." Pages 38–51 in *Prophetie und geschichtliche Wirklichkeit im alten Israel*. Edited by R. Liwak et al. Stuttgart: Kohlhammer, 1991.
———. "Montagne Sainte, Jardin d'Éden et Sanctuaire (Hiérosolymitain) dans un Oracle d'Ézéchiel contre le Prince de Tyr (Éz 28,11–19)." *Homo Religiosus* 9 (1983): 131–53.
Botterweck, G. J., and H. Ringgren, eds. *Theological Dictionary of the Old Testament*. Translated by D. E. Green. 15 vols. Grand Rapids: Eerdmans, 1974–2006.
Bowen, N. R. *Ezekiel*. Abingdon Old Testament Commentaries. Nashville, Tenn.: Abingdon Press, 2010.
Bøe, S. *Gog and Magog: Ezekiel 38–39 as a Pre-Text for Revelation 19, 17–21 and 20, 7–10*. WUNT 2/135. Tübingen: Mohr Siebeck, 2001.
Braulik, G. *Deuteronomium: 2. 16,18–34,12*. NEchtB 28. Würzburg: Echter-Verlag, 1992.
Breasted, J. H., ed. *Ancient Records of Egypt: Historical Documents from the Earliest Times to the Persian Conquest*. 5 vols. London: Histories and Mysteries of Man LTD., 1998.
Bresciani, E. "Sobek, Lord of the Land of the Lake." Pages 199–206 in *Divine Creatures: Animal Mummies in Ancient Egypt*. Edited by Salima Ikram. Cairo: American University in Cairo Press, 2005.
Brett, M. G. "Nationalism and the Hebrew Bible." Pages 136–63 in *Bible in Ethics*. JSOTS 207. Sheffield: Sheffield Academic Press, 1995.

Brooke, G. J. Catena, in: Pages 121–22 in vol. 1 of *Encyclopedia of the Dead Sea Scrolls*. Edited by L. H. Schiffman and J. C. VanderKam. 2 vols. Oxford: Oxford University Press, 2000.
Brown, K. "Temple Christology in the Gospel of John: Replacement Theology and Jesus as the Self-Revelation of God." Master diss., Trinity Western University, 2010.
———. *The Vision in Job 4 and Its Role in the Book: Reframing the Development of the Joban Dialogues*. FAT 2/75. Tübingen: Mohr Siebeck, 2015.
Budd, P. J. *Numbers*. WBC. Waco: Word, 1984.
Budge, E. A. W. *The Gods of the Egyptians or Studies in Egyptian Mythology*. 2 vols. London: Methuen & Company, 1904. Repr., New York: Dover Publications, Inc., 1969.
———. *Osiris and the Egyptian Resurrection*. 2 vols. London: Putnam's Sons, 1911.
Bunta, S. N. "Yhwh's Cultic Statue after 597/586 B.C.E.: A Linguistic and Theological Reinterpretation of Ezekiel 28:12." *CBQ* 69 (2007): 222–41.
Byron, J. "Abel's Blood and the Ongoing Cry for Vengeance." *CBQ* 73 (2011): 743–56.
Callender Jr., D. E. *Adam in Myth: Ancient Israelite Perspectives on the Primal Man*. HSS 48. Winona Lake: Eisenbrauns, 2000.
———. "The Primal Man in Ezekiel and the Image of God." SBLSP (1998): 606–25.
Carley, K. W. *The Book of the Prophet Ezekiel: Commentary*. CBC 27. Cambridge: Cambridge University Press, 1974.
Caspari, C. P. "Jesajanische Studien. I. Jeremia ein Zeuge für die Aechtheit von Jes. C. 34." *Zeitschrift für die gesammte lutherische Theologie und Kirche* 4 (1843): 1–73.
Cassuto, U. *A Commentary on the Book of Exodus*. Translated by I. Abrahams. Jerusalem: Magnes Press, 1967.
———. *A Commentary on the Book of Genesis*. Translated by I. Abrahams. 2 vols. Jerusalem: Magnes Press, 1961, 1964.
———. *The Goddess Anath: Canaanite Epics of the Patriarchal Age*. Translated by I. Abrahams. Jerusalem: Magnes Press, 1971.
Childs, B. S. "Enemy from the North and the Chaos Tradition." *JBL* 78 (1959): 187–98.
———. *Exodus*. OTL. Philadelphia: The Westminster Press, 1974.
———. *Isaiah*. OTL. Louisville: Westminster John Knox, 2001.
Christensen, D. L. *The Transformations of the War Oracle in Old Testament Prophecy: Studies in the Oracles against the Nations*. HDR 3. Missoula: Scholars Press, 1975.
Clines, D. J. A. *The Esther Scroll: The Story of the Story*. JSOTSup 30. Sheffield: JSOT Press, 1984.
Cooke, G. A. *A Critical and Exegetical Commentary on the Book of Ezekiel*. ICC. Edinburgh: T&T Clark, 1951.
Corral, M. A. *Ezekiel's Oracles against Tyre: Historical Reality and Motivations*. BibOr 46. Roma: Pontifical Biblical Institute, 2002.
Crane, A. S. *Israel's Restoration: A Textual-Comparative Exploration of Ezekiel 36–39*. VTSup 122. Leiden: Brill, 2008.

Cresson, B. C. *The Condemnation of Edom in Postexilic Judaism*. Pages 125–48 in *The Use of the Old Testament in the New and Other Essays: Studies in Honor of William Franklin Stinespring*. Edited by J. M. Efird. Durham: Duke University Press, 1972.
Crouch, C. L., and C. A. Strine. "Yahweh's Battle against Chaos in Ezekiel: The Transformation of Judahite Mythology for a New Situation." *JBL* (2013): 883–903.
Crouch, C. L. "Ezekiel's Oracles against the Nations in Light of a Royal ideology of Warfare." *JBL* 130 (2011): 473–92.
Darr, K. P. "The Book of Ezekiel." Pages 1073–1607 in *The New Interpreter's Bible: Introduction to Prophetic Literature*. Edited by L. E. Keck. Nashville: Abingdon Press, 2001.
Davis, E. F. "And Pharaoh Will Change His Mind (Ezekiel 32:31): Dismantling Mythical Discourse." Pages 224–39 in *Theological Exegesis: Essays in Honor of Brevard S. Childs*. Edited by C. Seitz et al. Grand Rapids: Eerdmans, 1998.
Day, L. "Rhetoric and Domestic Violence in Ezekiel 16." *BibInt* 8 (2000): 205–30.
Day, P. "The Bitch Had It Coming to Her: Rhetoric and Interpretation in Ezekiel 16." *BibInt* 8 (2000): 231–54.
Dearman, J. A. "Historical Reconstruction and the Mesha Inscription." Pages 155–210 in *Studies in the Mesha Inscription and Moab*. Edited by J. A. Dearman. ABS 2. Atlanta: Scholars Press, 1989.
De Troyer, K. *The End of the Alpha Text of Esther: Translation and Narrative Technique in MT 8:1–17, LXX 8:1–17, and at 7:14–41*. SCS 48. Atlanta: Society of Biblical Literature, 2000.
Diakonoff, I. M. "The Naval Power and Trade of Tyre." *IEJ* 42 (1992): 168–93.
Dicou, B. *Edom, Israel's Brother and Antagonist: The Role of Edom in Biblical Prophecy and Story*. JSOTSup 169. Sheffield: JSOT Press, 1994.
Dietrich, W. "Rache: Erwägungen zu einem alttestamentlichen Thema." *EvT* 36 (1976): 450–72.
Dillard, R. B. "The Chronicler's Solomon." *WTJ* 43 (1981): 289–300.
Dimant, D. "The Apocalyptic Interpretation of Ezekiel at Qumran." Pages 31–51 in *Messiah and Christos: Studies in the Jewish Origins of Christianity*. Edited by I. Gruenwald et al. TSAJ 32. Tübingen: Mohr Siebeck, 1992.
Ditommaso, L. *The Dead Sea: New Jerusalem Text: Contents and Contexts*. TSAJ 110. Tübingen: Mohr Siebeck, 2005.
Doak, B. "Ezekiel's Topography of the (Un-) Heroic Dead in Ezekiel 32:17–32." *JBL* 132 (2013): 607–24.
Dobbs-Allsopp, F. W. *Lamentations*. Louisville: John Knox Press, 2002.
Dobbs-Allsopp, F. W. et al. *Hebrew Inscriptions: Texts from the Biblical Period of the Monarchy with Concordance*. New Haven: Yale University Press, 2005.
Donaldson, T. L. *Judaism and the Gentiles: Jewish Patterns of Universalism (to 135 CE)*. Waco: Baylor University Press, 2008.
Driver. S. R. *An Introduction to the Literature of the Old Testament*. New York: Charles Scribner's Sons, 1891. Repr., Gloucester: Peter Smith, 1972.
Durlesser, J. A. *The Metaphorical Narratives in the Book of Ezekiel*. Lewiston: Mellen, 2006.

Eichler, R. "The Meaning of ישב הכרובים." *ZAW* 126 (2014): 358–71.

———. "When God Abandoned the Garden of Eden: A Forgotten Reading of Genesis 3:24." *VT* 65 (2015): 1–13.

Eichrodt, W. *Ezekiel: A Commentary*. Translated by C. Quin. OTL. Philadelphia: The Westminster Press, 1970.

Eissfeldt, O. "Schwerterschlagene bei Hesekiel." Pages 73–81 in *Studies in Old Testament Prophecy*. Edited by H. H. Rowley. Edinburg: T&T Clark, 1950.

El-Shahawy, A. *The Funerary Art of Ancient Egypt: A Bridge to the Realm of the Hereafter*. Cairo: Farid Atiya Press, 2005.

Fechter, F. *Bewältigung der Katastrophe: Untersuchungen zu ausgewählten Fremdvölkersprüchen im Ezechielbuch*. BZAW 208. Berlin: de Gruyter, 1992.

Fensham, F. C. "Common Trends in Curses of the Near Eastern Treaties and *Kudurru*-Inscriptions Compared with Maledictions of Amos and Isaiah." *ZAW* 75 (1963): 155–75.

Fisch, S. *Ezekiel: Hebrew Text and English Translation with an Introduction and Commentary*. London: Soncino Press, 1964.

Fischer, A. A. *Tod und Jenseits im Alten Orient und im Alten Testament*. Studien zu Kirche und Israel 7. Neukirchen: Neukirchener Verlag, 2005.

Fischer, G. "Jer 25 und die Fremdvölkersprüche: Unterschiede zwischen hebräischem und griechischem Text." *Bib* 72 (1991): 474–99.

Fishbane, M. *Biblical Interpretation in Ancient Israel*. Oxford: Clarendon Press, 1985.

———. *Text and Texture*. New York: Schocken, 1979.

Fistill, U. *Israel und das Ostjordanland: Untersuchungen zur Komposition von Num 21, 21–36,13 im Hinblick auf die Entstehung des Buches Numeri*. ÖBS 30. Frankfurt am Main: Lang, 2007.

Fitzpatrick, P. E. *The Disarmament of God: Ezekiel 38–39 in Its Mythic Context*. CBQMS 37. Washington, D. C.: Catholic Biblical Association of America, 2004.

Fohrer, G. *Die Hauptprobleme des Buches Ezechiel*. BZAW 72. Berlin: Töpelmann, 1952.

———. *Ezechiel*. HAT 1.13. Tübingen: Mohr Siebeck, 1955.

———. "Prophetie und Magie." *ZAW* 78 (1966): 25–47.

Foster, B. R. *Before the Muses: An Anthology of Akkadian Literature*. Bethesda: CDL Press, 2005.

Frankel, D. *The Land of Canaan and the Destiny of Israel*. Siphrut 4. Winona Lake: Eisenbrauns, 2011.

Freedy, K. S., and D. B. Redford. "The Dates in Ezekiel in Relation to Biblical, Babylonian and Egyptian Sources." *JAOS* 90 (1970): 462–85.

Fretheim, T. E. *Jeremiah*. SHBC 15. Macon: Smyth & Helwys, 2002.

Friebel, K. G. *Jeremiah's and Ezekiel's Sign-Acts*. JSOTSup 283. Sheffield: Sheffield Academic Press, 1999.

Fuhs, H. F. "Ez 24: Überlegungen zu Tradition und Redaktion des Ezechielbuches." Pages 266–82 in *Ezekiel and His Book*. Edited by J. Lust. BETL 74. Leuven: Leuven University Press, 1986.

———. *Ezechiel 1–24*. NEchtB 7. Würzburg: Echter-Verlag, 1984.

———. *Ezechiel 25–48*. NEchtB 22. Würzburg: Echter-Verlag, 1988.

Fujita, S. *The Temple Theology of the Qumran Sect and the Book of Ezekiel: Their Relationship to Jewish Literature of the Last Two Centuries B.C.* Ann Arbor: Univ. Microfilms, 1983.
Galambush, J. *Jerusalem in the Book of Ezekiel.* SBLDS 130. Atlanta: Scholars Press, 1992.
———. "Necessary Enemies: Nebuchadnezzar, Yhwh and Gog in Ezekiel 38–39." Pages 254–265 in *Israel's Prophets and Israel's Past: Essays on the Relationship of Prophetic Texts and Israelite History in Honor of John H. Hayes.* LHBOTS 446. Edited by B. E. Kelle and M. B. Moore. London: Bloomsbury, 2006.
Ganzel, T. "The Descriptions of the Restoration of Israel in Ezekiel." *VT* 60 (2010): 197–211.
García Martínez, F. "New Jerusalem." Pages 606–10 in vol. 2 of *Encyclopedia of the Dead Sea Scrolls.* Edited by L. H. Schiffman and J. C. VanderKam. 2 vols. Oxford: Oxford University Press, 2000.
———. "New Jerusalem at Qumran and in the New Testament." Pages 277–89 in *The Land of Israel in Bible, History and Theology: Studies in Honour of E. Noort.* Edited by J. van Ruiten and J. C. de Vos. VTSup 124. Leiden: Brill, 2009.
———. "The 'New Jerusalem' and the Future Temple of the Manuscripts from Qumran." Pages 180–213 in *Qumran and Apocalyptic: Studies on the Aramaic Texts from Qumran.* STDJ 9. Leiden: Brill, 1992
García Martínez, F., and E. J. C. Tigchelaar, eds. *Dead Sea Scrolls Study Edition.* 2 vols. Leiden: Brill, 1997–1998.
Gerleman, G. "Die Lärmende Menge: Der Sinn des hebräischen Wortes Hamon." Pages 71–75 in *Wort und Geschichte: Festschrift für Karl Elliger zum 70. Geburtstag.* Edited by H. Gese and H. P. Rüger. AOAT 18. Kevelaer: Butzon & Bercker 1973.
Gertz, J. C. "Kompositorische Funktion und literarhistorischer Ort von Deuteronomium 1–3." Pages 103–23 in *Deuteronomistischen Geschichtswerke.* BZAW 365. Berlin: de Gruyter, 2006.
Geyer, J. B. "Ezekiel 27 and the Cosmic Ship." Pages 105–26 in *Among the Prophets: Language, Image and Structure in the Prophetic Writings.* Edited by P. R. Davies and D. J. A. Clines. JSOTSup 144. Sheffield: JSOT Press, 1993.
———. "Mythology and Culture in the Oracles against the Nations." *VT* 36 (1986): 129–45.
Gile, J. "Deuteronomy and Ezekiel's Theology of Exile." Pages 287–306 in *For Our Good Always: Studies on the Message and Influence of Deuteronomy in Honor of Daniel I. Block.* Edited by J. S. DeRouchie et al. Winona Lake: Eisenbrauns, 2013.
———. "Ezekiel 16 and the Song of Moses: A Prophetic Transformation?" *JBL* 130 (2011): 87–108.
Gillmayr-Bucher, S. "Ein Klagelied über verlorene Schönheit." Pages 72–99 in *"Wie schön sind deine Zelte, Jakob!": Beiträge zur Ästhetik des Alten Testaments.* Edited by A. Grund. Biblisch-Theologische Studien 60. Neukirchen-Vluyn: Neukirchener Verlag, 2003.
Glassner, J.-J. *Mesopotamian Chronicles.* WAW 19. Atlanta: Society of Biblical Literature, 2004.
Glatt-Gilad, D. A. "The Re-Interpretation of the Edomite-Israelite Encounter in Deuteronomy II." *VT* 47 (1997): 441–55.

Glazier-McDonald, B. "Edom in the Prophetical Corpus." Pages 23–32 in *You Shall Not Abhor an Edomite for He Is Your Brother: Edom and Seir in History and Tradition*. Edited by D. V. Edelman. ABS 3, Atlanta: Scholars Press, 1994.

Görg, M. "'Der Starke Arm Pharaos'—Beobachtungen zum Belegspektrum einer Metapher in Palästina und Ägypten." Pages 323–30 in *Hommages à François Daumas*. Montpellier: Université de Montpellier, 1986.

Goering, G. S. "Proleptic Fulfillment of the Prophetic Word: Ezekiel's Dirges over Tyre and Its Ruler." *JSOT* 36 (2012): 483–505.

Gomaᶜ, F. "Der Krokodilgott Sobek und seine Kultorte im Mittleren Reich." Pages 787–88 in *Studien zu Sprache und Religion Ägyptens: Zu Ehren von Wolfhart Westendorf, Bd. 2. Religion*. Edited by F. Junge. Göttingen: Hubert & Co. 1984.

Gordon, R. P. "The Ideological Foe: The Philistines in the Old Testament." Pages 22–36 in *Biblical and Near Eastern Essays*. Edited by C. McCarthy. JSOTSup 375. London: T&T Clark International, 2004.

Gosse, B. "Ezéchiel 35–36,1–15 et Ezéchiel 6 : La Désolation de la Montagne de Séir et le Renouveau des Montagnes d'Israël." *RB* 96 (1989): 511–17.

———. "Le Recueil d'Oracles contre les Nations d'Ezéchiel XXV-XXXII dans la Rédaction du Livre d'Ezéchiel." *RB* 93 (1986): 535–62.

Gottwald, N. K. *All the Kingdoms of the Earth: Israelite Prophecy and International Relations*. Minneapolis: Fortress Press, 2007.

Gowan, D. E. *When Man Becomes God: Humanism and "Hybris" in the Old Testament*. PTMS 6. Eugene: Pickwick Publications, 1975.

Grayson, A. K. *Assyrian and Babylonian Chronicles*. Locust Valley: Augustin, 1975. Repr., Winona Lake: Eisenbrauns, 2000.

Grayson, A. K. and J. Novotny. *The Royal Inscriptions of Sennacherib, King of Assyria (704–681 BC), Part 1*. Winona Lake: Eisenbrauns, 2012.

Green, A. "Mischwesen. B. Archäologie. Mesopotamien." *RlA* 8:246–64.

Greenberg, M. *Ezekiel 1–20: A New Translation with Introduction and Commentary*. AB 22. Garden City: Doubleday, 1983.

———. *Ezekiel 21–37: A New Translation with Introduction and Commentary*. AB 22A. Garden City: Doubleday, 1997.

———. "Ezekiel 16: Panorama of Passions." Pages 143–50 in *Love and Death in the Ancient Near East: Essays in Honor of Marvin H. Pope*. Edited by J. H. Marks and R. M. Good. Guilford: Four Quarters Publication Company, 1987.

———. "What Are Valid Criteria for Determining Inauthentic Matter in Ezekiel?" Pages 123–35 in *Ezekiel and His Book: Textual and Literary Criticism and Their Interrelation*. Edited by J. Lust. BETL 74. Leuven: Leuven University Press, 1986.

Griffith, F. L. *Catalogue of the Demotic Papyri in the John Rylands Library*. 3 vols. Manchester: Manchester University Press, 1909.

Griffiths, J. G. "Osiris." Pages 623–33 in vol. 4 of *Lexikon der Ägyptologie*. Edited by W. Helck, E. Otto, and W. Westendorf. Wiesbaden: Harrassowitz, 1975–1992.

———. *The Origins of Osiris and His Cult*. Leiden: Brill, 1980.

Grossman, J. *Esther: The Outer Narrative and the Hidden Reading*. Siphrut 6. Winona Lake: Eisenbrauns, 2011.

Grottanelli, C. "The Enemy King is a Monster: A Biblical Equation." Pages 47–72 in *Kings and Prophets*. Edited by C. Grottanelli. Oxford: Oxford University Press, 1999.
Guillaume, P. "Metamorphosis of a Ferocious Pharaoh." *Bib* 85 (2004): 232–36.
Gunkel, H. *Genesis: Übersezt und erklärt*. 3rd ed. HKAT. Göttingen: Vandenhoeck & Ruprecht, 1917. Repr., with indices by P. Schorlemmer, as 6th ed., 1964.
———. *Schöpfung und Chaos in Urzeit und Endzeit*. Göttingen: Vandenhoeck und Ruprecht, 1921.
Haag, E. "Ez 31 und die alttestamentliche Paradiesvorstellung." Pages 171–78 in *Wort, Lied und Gottesspruch: Beiträge zu Psalmen und Propheten, Festschrift für Jeseph Ziegler*. Edited by J. Schreiner. FB 2. Würzburg: Echter Verlag, 1972.
Hagedorn, A. C. "Looking at Foreigners in Biblical and Greek Prophecy." *VT* 57 (2007): 432–48.
———. *Die Anderen im Spiegel: Israels Auseinandersetzung mit den Völkern in den Büchern Nahum, Zefanja, Obadja und Joel*. BZAW 414. Berlin: de Gruyter, 2011.
Hagedorn, A. C., and S. Tzoref, "Attitudes to Gentiles in the Minor Prophets and in Corresponding Pesharim." *DSD* 20 (2013): 472–509.
Haldor, P. C. "The Tyrian Oracles in Ezekiel: A Study of Ezekiel 26:1–28:19." PhD diss., Columbia University, 1970.
Haller, M. "Edom im Urteil der Propheten." Pages 109–17 in *Vom Alten Testament: Karl Marti zum 70. Geburtstage Gewidmet*. Edited by K. Budde. BZAW 41. Gießen: Töpelmann, 1925.
Hallo, W. W. and K. L. Younger, Jr., eds. *The Context of Scripture*. 3 vols. Leiden: Brill, 1997, 2000, 2002.
Halperin, D. J. "The Exegetical Character of Ezek. X 9–17." *VT* 26 (1976): 129–41.
Hamborg, G. R. "Reasons for Judgement in the Oracles against the Nations of the Prophet Isaiah," *VT* 31 (1981): 145–59.
Haran, M. "An Archaic Remnant in Prophetic Literature." *BIES* 13 (1946/47): 7–15.
Harrell, J. A. "Old Testament Gemstones: A Philological, Geological, and Archaeological Assessment of the Septuagint." *BBR* 21 (2011): 141–71.
Hartenstein, F. "Cherubim and Seraphim in the Bible and in the Light of Ancient Near Eastern Sources." Pages 155–88 in *Angels: The Concept of Celestial beings—Origins, Development and Reception*. Edited by F. V. Reiterer et al. Berlin: de Gruyter, 2007.
Hayes, J. H. "The Oracles against the Nations in the Old Testament: Their Usage and Theological Importance." PhD diss., Princeton Theological Seminary, 1964.
———. "The Usage of Oracles against Foreign Nations in Ancient Israel." *JBL* 87 (1968): 81–92.
Hays, C. B. *Death in the Iron Age II and in the First Isaiah*. FAT 79. Tübingen: Mohr Siebeck, 2011.
———. "'There is Hope for a Tree:' Job's Hope for the Afterlife in the Light of Egyptian Tree Imagery." *CBQ* 77 (2015): 42–68.
Heidel, A. *The Babylonian Genesis: The Story of Creation*. Chicago: The University of Chicago Press, 1963.

Helbig, J. *Intertextualität und Markierung: Untersuchungen zur Systematik und Funktion der Signalisierung von Intertextualität.* Beiträge zur neueren Literaturgeschichte 3.141. Heidelberg: Winter, 1996.

Hendel, R. S. "Of Demigods and the Deluge: Toward an Interpretation of Genesis 6:1–4." *JBL* 106 (1987): 13–26.

Herrmann, J., *Ezechiel.* KAT 11. Leipzig: Deichert, 1924.

Hillers, D. R. *Treaty-Curses and the Old Testament Prophets.* Sacra scriptura antiquitatibus orientalibus illustrata 16. Roma: Pontifical Biblical Institute, 1964.

Holladay, W. L. *Jeremiah 1: A Commentary on the Book of the Prophet Jeremiah Chapters 1–25.* Hermeneia 22. Philadelphia: Fortress Press, 1986.

Hölscher, G. H. *Hesekiel: Der Dichter und das Buch.* BZAW 39. Gießen: Töpelmann, 1924.

Höffken, P. "Die Rede des Rabsake vor Jerusalem (2 Kön. xvii/Jes. xxxvi) im Kontext anderer Kapitulationsforderungen" *VT* 58 (2008): 44–55.

———. "Untersuchungen zu den Begründungselementen der Völkerorakel des Alten Testaments." PhD diss., Rheinischen Friedrich-Wilhelms-Universität, 1977.

Hoffman, Y. "From Oracle to Prophecy: The Growth, Crystallization and Disintegration of a Biblical *Gattung*." *JNSL* 10 (1982): 75–81.

———. "The Day of the Lord as a Concept and a Term in the Prophetic Literature." *ZAW* 93 (1981): 37–50.

Hoffmeier, J. K. "A New Insight on Pharaoh Apries from Herodotus, Diodorus and Jeremiah 46:17." *JSSEA* 11 (1981): 165–70.

———. "Egypt as an Arm of Flesh: A Prophetic Response." Pages 79–97 in *Israel's Apostasy and Restoration.* Edited by A. Gileadi. Grand Rapids: Baker, 1988.

———. "Some Egyptian Motifs Related to Warfare and Enemies and Their Old Testament Counterparts." Pages 53–70 in *Egyptological Miscellanies: A Tribute to Ronald James Williams.* The Ancient World 6. Chicago: Ares Publishers, 1983.

———. "The Arm of God versus the Arm of Pharaoh in the Exodus Narratives." *Bib* 67 (1986): 378–87.

Hossfeld, F.-L. *Untersuchungen zu Komposition und Theologie des Ezechielbuches.* FB 20. Würzburg: Echter, 1977.

Hossfeld, F.-L. and E. Zenger. *Psalm 1–50.* NEchtB 29. Würzburg: Echter Verlag, 1993.

House, P. R. *Lamentations.* WBC 23B. Nashville: Nelson, 2004.

Huehnergard, J. *A Grammar of Akkadian.* HSS 45. Atlanta: Scholars Press, 1997.

Hundley, M. B. "Here a God, There a God: An Examination of the Divine in Ancient Mesopotamia." *AoF* 40 (2013): 68–107.

Hutter, M. "Demons and Benevolent Spirits in the Ancient Near East." Pages 21–34 in *Angels: The Concept of Celestial Beings—Origins, Development and Reception.* Edited by V. Reiterer et al. Berlin: de Gruyter, 2007.

Huwyler, B. *Jeremia und die Völker: Untersuchungen zu den Völkersprüchen in Jeremia 46–49.* FAT 20. Tübingen: Mohr Siebeck, 1997.

Irwin, B. P. "Molek Imagery and the Slaughter of Gog in Ezekiel 38 and 39." *JSOT* 65 (1995): 93–112.

Izre'el, S, ed. "Amarna: The Amarna Texts." The Open Richly Annotated Cuneiform Corpus. http://oracc.museum.upenn.edu/contrib/amarna/corpus.

Jackson, K. P. "The Language of the Mesha<sup>c</sup> Inscription." in *Studies in the Mesha Inscription and Moab*. Edited by J. A. Dearman. ABS 2. Atlanta: Scholars Press, 1989.
Jahnow, H. *Das hebräische Leichenlied im Rahmen der Völkerdichtung*. BZAW 36. Gießen: Töpelmann, 1923.
Janowski, B. "Keruben und Zion: Thesen zur Entstehung der Zionstradition." Pages 231–64 in *Ernten, Was Man Sät*. Edited by D. R. Daniels, U. Gleßmer, M. Rösel. Neukirchen: Neukirchener Verlag, 1991.
———. "Tempel und Schöpfung: Schöpfungstheologische Aspekte der priesterschriftlichen Heiligtumskonzeption." *Jahrbuch für biblische Theologie* 5 (1990): 37–69.
Japhet, S. *From the Rivers of Babylon to the Highlands of Judah: Collected Studies on the Restoration Period*. Winona Lake: Eisenbrauns, 2006.
Johnston, A. C., H. S. Gehman, and E. H. Kase, Jr., eds. *The John H. Scheide Biblical Papyri: The Hohn H. Scheide Biblical Papyri: Ezekiel*. Princeton University in Papyrology 3. Princeton: Princeton University Press, 1938.
Johnston, P. S. "Death in Egypt and Israel: A Theological Reflection." Pages 94–116 in *The Old Testament in Its World*. Edited by Robert P. Gordon and J. C. de Moor. OtSt 52. Leiden: Brill, 2005.
———. *Shades of Sheol: Death and Afterlife in the Old Testament*. Downers Grove: Intervarsity Press, 2002.
Jones, B. C. *Howling over Moab: Irony and Rhetoric in Isaiah 15–16*. SBLDS 157. Atlanta: Scholars Press, 1996.
Jones, G. H. "An Examination of Some Leading Motifs in the Prophetic Oracles against Foreign Nations." PhD diss., University of Wales, 1970.
Jones, S. C. "Lions, Serpents, and Lion-Serpents in Job 28:8 and Beyond." *JBL* 130 (2011): 667–73.
Joosten, J. *People and Land in the Holiness Code: An Exegetical Study of the Ideational Framework of the Law in Leviticus 17–26*. VTSup 67. Leiden: Brill, 1996.
Joyce, P. M. *Ezekiel: A Commentary*. LHBOTS 482. London: Bloomsbury, 2007.
———. "Ezekiel 20.32–38: A Problem Text for the Theology of Ezekiel." Pages 119–23 in *Stimulation from Leiden: Collected Communications to the XVIIIth Congress of the International Organization for the Study of the Old Testament, Leiden 2004*. Edited by H. M. Niemann et al. BEATAJ 54. Frankfurt am Main: Lang, 2006.
Kaminsky, J. S. "Israel's Election and the Other in Biblical, Second Temple, and Rabbinic Thought." Pages 17–30 in *The "Other" in Second Temple Judaism*. Edited by D. C. Harlow et al. Grand Rapids: Eerdmans, 2011.
———. *Yet I Loved Jacob: Reclaiming the Biblical Concept of Election*. Nashville: Abingdon Press, 2007.
Kaminsky, J. S., and A. Stewart. "God of All the World: Universalism and Developing Monotheism in Isaiah 40–66." *HTR* 99 (2006): 139–63.
Keel, O. *Die Welt der altorientalischen Bildsymbolik und das Alte Testament: am Beispiel der Psalmen*. Zürich: Benziger, 1972.
———. *Jahwe-Visionen und Siegelkunst: Eine neue Deutung der Majestätsschilderungen in Jes 6, Ez 1 und 10 und Sach 4*. SBS 84/85. Stuttgart: Katholisches Bibelwerk, 1977.

Kessler, R. *Die Ägyptenbilder der Hebräischen Bibel: Ein Beitrag zur neueren Monotheismusdebatte*. SBS 197. Stuttgart: Katholisches Bibelwerk, 2002.
King, L. W. *Chronicles Concerning Early Babylonian Kings*. 2 vols. London: Luzac, 1907.
Klein, A. *Schriftauslegung im Ezechielbuch: Redaktionsgeschichtliche Untersuchungen zu Ez 34–39*. BZAW 391. Berlin: de Gruyter, 2008.
Koehler, L., W. Baumgartner, and J. J. Stamm. *The Hebrew and Aramaic Lexicon of the Old Testament*. Translated and edited under the supervision of M. E. J. Richardson. 5 vols. Leiden: Brill, 1994–2000.
Koemoth, P. *Osiris et les arbre: Contribution à l'étude des arbres sacrés de l'Égypte ancienne*. Aegyptiaca Leodiensia 3. Liège: Centre Informatique de Philosophie et Lettres, 1994.
Kohn, R. L. *A New Heart and a New Soul: Ezekiel, the Exile and the Torah*. JSOTSup 358. London: Sheffield Academic Press, 2002.
Koller, A. *Esther in Ancient Jewish Thought*. Cambridge: Cambridge University Press, 2014.
Konkel, M. *Architektonik des Heiligen: Studien zur zweiten Tempelvision Ezechiels (Ez 40–48)*. BBB 129. Berlin: Philo, 2001.
Koopmans, W. T. "Poetic Reciprocation: The Oracles against Edom and Philistia in Ezek. 25:12–17." Pages 113–22 in *Verse in Ancient Near Eastern Prose*. Edited by J. C. de Moor et al. AOAT 42. Kevelaer: Butzon & Becker, 1993.
Korpel, M. C. A. "Avian Spirits in Ugarit and in Ezekiel 13." Pages 99–113 in *Ugarit, Religion and Culture: Proceedings of the International Colloquium on Ugarit, Religion and Culture, Edinburgh, July 1994: Essays Presented in Honour of Professor John C. L. Gibson*. Edited by N. Wyatt et al. Ugaritisch-biblische Literatur 12. Münster: Ugarit-Verlag, 1996.
König, F. E. "Gibt es 'Zitate' im Alten Testament?" *NKZ* 28 (1908): 734–46.
Kraeling, E. G. "The Significance and Origin of Gen. 6:1–4." *JNES* 6 (1947): 193–208.
Kraetzschmar, R. *Das Buch Ezechiel: Übersetzt und erklärt von Richard Kraetzschmar*. HAT 3.1. Göttingen: Vandenhoek & Ruprecht, 1900.
Krantz, E. S. *Des Schiffes Weg Mitten im Meer, Beiträge zur Erforschung der nautischen Terminologie des Alten Testaments*. ConBOT. Lund: Gleerup, 1982.
Kraus, H.-J. *Psalms 1–59*. Translated by H. C. Oswald. CC 1. Augsburg: Augsburg Fortress, 1993.
Kreuzer, S. "Die Mächtigkeitsformel im Deuteronomium Gestaltung, Vorgeschichte und Entwicklung." *ZAW* 109 (1997): 188–207.
———. "Die Verwendung der Mächtigkeitsformel außerhalb des Deuteronomiums: Literarische und theologische Linien zu Jer, Ez, Dtrg und P." *ZAW* 109 (1997): 369–84.
Kutsch, E. *Die chronologischen Daten des Ezechielbuches*. OBO 62. Göttingen: Vandenhoeck & Ruprect, 1985.
Lambdin, T. O. "Egyptian Loan Words in the Old Testament." *JAOS* 73 (1953): 145–55.
Lambert, W. G. *Babylonian Creation Myths*. Mesopotamian Civilizations 16. Winona Lake: Eisenbrauns, 2013.

Lanfer, P. T. *Remembering Eden: The Reception History of Genesis 3:22–24*. Oxford: Oxford University Press, 2012.
Lauha, A. *Zaphon: Der Norden und die Nordvölker im Alten Testament*. AASF B 49.2. Helsinki: Suomalainen Tiedeakatemia, 1943.
Launderville, D. "Ezekiel's Cherub: A Promising Symbol or a Dangerous Idol?" *CBQ* 65 (2003): 165–83.
Lawhead, A. S. "A Problem of Unfulfilled Prophecy in Ezekiel: A Response." *Wesleyan Theological Journal* 16 (1981): 15–19.
Lee, L. "Fiery Sheol in the Dead Sea Scrolls," *RevQ* 27/106 (2015): 249–70.
———. "רוקמה Colorful Weaving, Embroidery." *Theologisches Wörterbuch zu den Qumrantexten* 3: 643–45.
Leichty, E. *The Royal Inscriptions of Esarhaddon, King of Assyria (680–669 BC)*. Winona Lake: Eisenbrauns, 2000.
Lemaire, A. "Edom and the Edomites." Pages 225–44 in *The Books of Kings: Sources, Composition, Historiography and Reception*. Edited by André Lemaire and Baruch Halpern. VTSup 129. Leiden: Brill, 2010.
Levenson, J. D. *Creation and the Persistence of Evil*. Princeton: Princeton University Press, 1994.
———. "The Universal Horizon of Biblical Particularism." Pages 143–69 in Ethnicity and the Bible. Edited by M. G. Brett. BibInt 19. Leiden: Brill, 1996.
Levey, S. H. *The Aramaic Bible: The Targums: Vol. 13: The Targum of Ezekiel*. Edinburgh: T&T Clark, 1987.
———. "The Targum to Ezekiel." *HUCA* 46 (1975): 139–58.
Levine, B. A. *Numbers: A New Translation with Introdcution and Commentary*. 2 vols. AB 4, 4A. New York: Doubleday, 1993, 2000.
Levinson, B. M. "A Post-Priestly Harmonization in the Flood Narrative." Pages 113–23 in *The Post-priestly Pentateuch: New Perspectives on its Redactional Development and Theological Profiles*. Edited by F. Giuntoli and K. Schmid. Tübingen: Mohr Siebeck, 2015.
———. *Deuteronomy and the Hermeneutics of Legal Innovation*. New York: Oxford University Press, 1997.
———. *Legal Revision and Religious Renewal in Ancient Israel*. Cambridge: Cambridge University Press, 2008.
Lewis, T. J. "CT 13.33–34 and Ezekiel 32: Lion-Dragon Myths." *JAOS* 116 (1996): 28–47.
Lichtheim, M. *Ancient Egyptian Literature: The New Kingdom*. Berkeley University of California Press, 1976.
———. *Ancient Egyptian Literature: The Old and Middle Kingdoms*. Berkeley: University of California Press, 1973.
Lilly, I. A. *Two Books of Ezekiel: Papyrus 967 and the Masoretic Text as Variant Literary Editions*. VTSup 150. Leiden: Brill, 2012.
Lipschits, O. *The Fall and Rise of Jerusalem: Judah under Babylonian Rule*. Winona Lake: Eisenbrauns, 2005.
Lipton, D. "Early Mourning? Petitionary Versus Posthumous Ritual in Ezekiel XXIV." *VT* 56 (2006): 185–202.

Liverani, M. "The Trade Network of Tyre according to Ezekiel 27." Pages 65–79 in *Ah, Assyria...! Studies in Assyrian History and Ancient Near Eastern Historiography Presented to Hayim Tadmor*. Edited by Mordecai Cogan and Israel Eph'al. ScrHier 33. Jerusalem: Magness Press, 1991.

Lohfink, N. "Darstellungskunst und Theologie in Dtn 1,6–3,29." *Bib* 41 (1960): 105–34.

———. "Dtn 12,1 und Gen 15,18: Das dem Samen Abrahams geschenkte Land als der Geltungsbereich der deuteronomischen Gesetze." Pages 183–210 in *Die Väter Israels*. Edited by M. Görg. Stuttgart: Katholisches Bibelwerk, 1989.

Loretz, O. "Cant 4,8 auf dem Hintergrund ugaritischer und assyrischer Beschreibungen des Libanons und Antilibanons." Pages 131–41 in *Ernten, Was man sät: Festschrift für Klaus Koch zu seinem 65. Geburtstag*. Edited by D. R. Daniels, U. Gleßmer, and M. Rösel. Neukirchen: Neukirchener Verlag, 1991.

———. "Der Wohnort Els nach ugaritischen Texten und Ez 28,1–2.6–10." *UF* 21 (1989): 259–67.

Luckenbill, D. D. *Ancient Records of Assyria and Babylonia: Historical Records of Assyria from Sargon to the End*. 2 vols. Chicago: University of Chicago Press, 1926.

Lust, J. "Edom-Adam in Ezekiel, in the MT and LXX." Pages 387–401 in *Studies in the Hebrew Bible, Qumran, and the Septuagint Presented to Eugene Ulrich*. Edited by P. W. Flint et al. VTSup 101. Leiden: Brill, 2006.

———. "Exodus 6,2–8 and Ezekiel." Pages 209–24 in *Studies in the Book of Exodus: Redaction-Reception-Interpretation*. BETL 126. Edited by M. Vervenne. Leuven: Leuven University Press, 1996.

———. "Ezekiel 36–40 in the Oldest Greek Manuscript." *CBQ* 43 (1981): 517–33.

———. "Ezekiel's Utopian Expectations." Pages 403–19 in *Flores Florentino: Dead Sea Scrolls and Other Early Jewish Studies in Honour of Florentino Garcia Martinez*. Supplements to the Journal for the Study of Judaism 122. Edited by A. Hilhorst et al. Leiden: Brill, 2007

———. "Gog גוג." Pages 373–75 in *Dictionary of Deities and Demons in the Bible*. Edited by K. van der Toorn et al. 2nd ed. Leiden: Brill, 1999.

———. "Magog מגוג." Pages 535–37 in *Dictionary of Deities and Demons in the Bible*. Edited by K. van der Toorn et al. 2nd ed. Leiden: Brill, 1999.

———. "Major Divergences between LXX and MT in Ezekiel." Pages 83–92 in *The Earliest Text of the Hebrew Bible: The Relationship between the Masoretic Text and the Hebrew Base of the Septuagint Reconsidered*. Edited by A. Schenker. SCS 52. Atlanta: Society of Biblical Literature, 2003.

———. "Messianism in LXX-Ezekiel: Towards a Synthesis." Pages 417–30 in *The Septuagint and Messianism*. Edited by M. A. Knibb. Leuven: Peeters, 2006

———. "The Septuagint of Ezekiel according to Papyrus 967 and the Pentateuch." *ETL* 72 (1996): 131–37.

———. "Textual Criticism of the Old Testament and of the New Testament: Stepbrothers?" Pages 15–31 in *New Testament Criticism and Exegesis: Its Significance for Exegesis: Essays*. Edited by A. Denaux. BETL 161. Leuven: Leuven University Press, 2002

———. "The Use of Textual Witnesses fort he Establishment of the Text: The Shorter and Longer Texts of Ezekiel: An Example: Ez 7." Pages 7–20 in *Ezekiel and His Book: Textual and Literary Criticism and Their Interrelation*. Edited by J. Lust. BETL 74. Leuven: Leuven University Press, 1986.
Lynch, M. *Monotheism and Institutions in the Book of Chronicles: Temple, Priesthood, and Kingship in Post-exilic perspective*. FAT 2/64. Tübingen: Mohr Siebeck, 2014.
Lyons, M. A. *From Law to Prophecy: Ezekiel's Use of the Holiness Code*. LHBOTS 507. New York: T&T Clark, 2009.
———. "Marking Innerbiblical Allusion in the Book of Ezekiel." *Bib* 88 (2007): 245–50.
MacDonald, N. *Deuteronomy and the Meaning of "Monotheism."* 2nd ed. FAT 2/1. Tübingen: Mohr Siebeck, 2012.
———. "Edom and Seir in the Narratives and Itineraries of Numbers 20–21 and Deuteronomy 1–3." Pages 83–104 in *Deuteronomium—Tora für eine neue Generation*. Edited by G. Fischer et al. Wiesbaden: Harrasowitz, 2011
———. "Monotheism and Isaiah." Pages 43–61 in *Interpreting Isaiah: Issues and Approaches*. Edited by D. G. Firth and H.G.M. Williamson. Downers Grove: IVP Academic, 2009.
Machinist, P. "Biblical Traditions: The Philistines and Israelite History." Pages 53–83 in *The Sea Peoples and Their World: A* Reassessment. Edited by E. D. Oren. University Museum Monograph 108. Philadelphia: University of Pennsylvania Museum, 2000.
Malamat, A. "The Kingdom of Judah between Egypt and Babylon: A Samll State within a Great Power Confrontation." *ST* 44 (1990): 65–77.
Margulis, B. B. "Studies in the Oracles against the Nations." PhD diss., Brandeis University, 1966.
Martens, K. "'With a Strong Hand and an Outstretched Arm:' The Meaning of the Expression byd ḥzqh wbzrw' nṭwyh." *SJOT* 15 (2001): 123–41.
Marzouk, S. A. *Egypt as a Monster in the Book of Ezekiel*. FAT 2/76. Tübingen: Mohr Siebeck, 2015.
May, H. G. "Some Cosmic Connotations of Mayim Rabbim." *JBL* 74 (1955): 9–21.
Mayfield, T. D. *Literary Structure and Setting in Ezekiel*. FAT 2/43. Tübingen: Mohr Siebeck, 2010.
McKane, W. *A Critical and Exegetical Commentary on Jeremiah*. 2 vols. ICC. Edinburgh: T&T Clark, 1986.
McKeating, H. *Ezekiel*. OTG. Sheffield: JSOT Press, 1993.
Mein, A. *Ezekiel and the Ethics of Exile*. Oxford Theological Monographs. Oxford: Oxford University Press, 2001.
Mendecki, N. "Postdeuteronomistische Redaktion von Ez 28, 25–26?" *BN* 73 (1994): 66–73.
Mendenhall, G. E. "The 'Vengeance' of Yahweh" Pages 69–104 in *The Tenth Generation: The Origins of the Biblical Tradition*. Baltimore: Johns Hopkins University Press, 1976.
Messel, N. *Ezechielfragen*. SNVAO HF 1. Oslo: Jacob Dybwad, 1945.
Metzger, M. *Königsthron und Gottesthron. Thronformen und Throndarstellungen in Ägypten und im Vorderen Orient im dritten und zweiten Jahrtausend vor Christus*

*und deren Bedeutung für das Verständnis von Aussagen über den Thron im Alten Testament*. 2 vols. AOAT 15. Kevalaer: Butzon und Berker, 1985.

———. "Zeder, Weinstock und Weltenbaum." Pages 197–229 in *Ernten, Was Man Sät: Festschrift für Klaus Koch zu seinem 65. Geburtstag*. Edited by D. R. Daniels, U. Gleßmer, and M. Rösel. Neukirchen: Neukirchener Verlag, 1991.

Milgrom, J. *Numbers: The Traditional Hebrew Text with the New JPS Translation. JPS Torah Commentary*. Philadelphia: Jewish Publication Society of America, 1990.

Millard, A. "Ezekiel XXVII.19: The Wine Trade of Damascus." *JSS* 7 (1962): 201–3.

Miller, G. D. "Intertextuality in Old Testament Research." *Currents in Biblical Research* 9 (2011): 283–309.

Miller, J. E. "The Maelaek of Tyre (Ezekiel 28,11–19)." *ZAW* 105 (1993): 497–501.

Miller, J. M. "Moab and the Moabites." Pages 1–40 in *Studies in the Mesha Inscription and Moab*. Edited by J. A. Dearman. ABS 2. Atlanta: Scholars Press, 1989.

Miller, J. M., and J. H. Hayes. *A History of Ancient Israel and Judah*. 2nd edition. London: SCM Press, 2006.

Miller, P. D. "The Wilderness Journey in Deuteronomy: Style, Structure, and Theology in Deuteronomy 1–3." Pages 572–92 in *Israelite Religion and Biblical Theology: Collected Essays*. JSOTSup 267. Sheffield: Sheffield Academic Press, 2000.

Minj, S. K. *Egypt: The Lower Kingdom: An Exegetical Study of the Oracle of Judgment against Egypt in Ezekiel 29, 1–16*. European University Studies 23. Frankfurt am Main: Peter Lang, 2006.

Mizrahi, N. "The Songs of the Sabbath Sacrifice and Biblical Priestly Literature: A Linguistic Reconsideration." *HTR* 104 (2011): 33–57.

Mobley, G. *Samson and the Liminal Hero in the Ancient Near East*. LHBOTS 453. London: Bloomsbury, 2006.

Moran, W. L., ed. *The Amarna Letters*. Baltimore: Johns Hopkins University Press, 1992.

Morgenstern, J. "The Mythological Background of Psalm 82." *HUCA* 14 (1939): 111–14.

Mowinckel, S. "Jahves Dag." *NTT* 59 (1958): 1–56.

———. *The Psalms in Israel's Worship*. Translated by D. R. Ap-Thomas. 2 vols. Oxford: Blackwell, 1962.

Newsom, C. A. "A Maker of Metaphors: Ezekiel's Oracles against Tyre." Pages 191–204 in "*The Place is Too Small for Us:*" *The Israelite Prophets in Recent Scholarship*. Edited by R. P. Gordon. Sources for Biblical and Theological Study 5. Winona Lake: Eisenbrauns, 1995.

———. *Songs of the Sabbath Sacrifice: A Critical Edition*. HSS 27. Atlanta: Scholars Press, 1985.

Niccacci, A. "The Exodus Tradition in the Psalms, Isaiah and Ezekiel." *LASBF* 61 (2011): 9–35.

Nickelsburg, G. W. E. "The We and the Other in the Worldview of 1 Enoch, the Dead Sea Scrolls and Other Early Jewish Texts." Pages 262–78 in *The "Other" in Second Temple Judaism*. Edited by D. C. Harlow et al. Grand Rapids: Eerdmans, 2011.

Nobile, M. "Beziehung zwischen Ez 32,17–32 und der Gog-Perikope (Ez 38–39) im Lichte der Endredaktion." Pages 255–59 in *Ezekiel and His Book: Textual and*

*Literary Criticism and Their Interrelation.* Edited by J. Lust. BETL 74. Leuven: Leuven University Press, 1985.

Norin, S. I. L. "Der Tag Gottes im Alten Testament: Jenseits der Spekulationen - Was ist übrig?" Pages 33–42 in *Le Jour de Dieu = Der Tag Gottes*. Edited by Anders Hultgård et al. WUNT 245. Tübingen: Mohr Siebeck, 2009.

Noth, M. *A History of Pentateuchal Traditions.* Translated by B. W. Anderson. Chico: Scholars Press, 1981.

Nurmela, R. "The Growth of the Book of Isaiah Illustrated by Allusions in Zechariah." Pages 245–59 in *Bringing out the Treasure: Inner Biblical Allusion in Zechariah 9-14.* Edited by M. J. Boda and M. Flyod. LHBOTS 370. London: Bloomsbury, 2003.

Nysse, R. W. "Keeping Company with Nahum: Reading the Oracles against the Nations as Scripture." *WW* 15 (1995): 412–19.

O'Brien, J. M. "Edom as (Selfish) Brother." Pages 153–74 in *Challenging Prophetic Metaphor: Theology and Ideology in the Prophets.* Louisville: Westminster John Knox, 2008.

———. "God as (Abusing) Husband." Pages 63–76 in *Challenging Prophetic Metaphor: Theology and Ideology in the Prophets.* Louisville: Westminster John Knox, 2008.

Oded, B., and L. I. Rabinowitz. "Ammon, Ammonites." Pages 83–87 in vol. 2 of *Encyclopaedia Judaica.* Edited by M. Berenbaum and F. Skolnik. 2nd ed. 22 vols. Detroit: Macmillan Reference USA. 2007.

Odell, M. S. "The City of Hamonah in Ezekiel 39:11–16: The Tumultuous City of Jerusalem." *CBQ* 56 (1994): 479–89.

———. "Creeping Things and Singing Stones: The Iconography of Ezekiel 8: 7–13 in Light of Syro-Palestinian Seals and the Songs of the Sabbath Sacrifice." Pages 195–210 in *Images and Prophecy in the Ancient Eastern Mediterranean.* Edited by M. Nissinen and C. E. Carter. FRLANT 233. Göttingen: Vandenhoeck & Ruprecht, 2009.

———. *Ezekiel.* SHBC 16. Macon: Smyth & Helwys, 2005.

Oeming, M., and J. Vette. *Psalm 42–89.* Neuer Stuttgarter Kommentar 13.2. Stuttgart: Katholisches Bibelwerk, 2010.

Olley, J. W. *Ezekiel: A Commentary Based on Iezekiēl in Codex Vaticanus.* Septuagint Commentary Series 7. Leiden: Brill, 2009.

Olyan, S. M. "Unnoticed Resonances of Tomb Opening and Transportation of the Remains of the Dead in Ezekiel 37:12–14." *JBL* 128 (2009): 491–501.

Oswald, W. "Zukunftserwartung und Gerichtsankündigung: Zur Pragmatik der prophetischen Rede vom Tag Jhwhs." Pages 19–31 in *Le Jour de Dieu = Der Tag Gottes.* Edited by Anders Hultgård et al. WUNT 245; Tübingen: Mohr Siebeck, 2009.

Otto, E. *Deuteronomium 1–11.* Freiburg im Breisgau: Herder, 2012.

Page Jr., H. R. *The Myth of Cosmic Rebellion: A Study of Its Reflexes in Ugaritic and Biblical Literature.* VTSup 65. Leiden: Brill, 1996.

Patmore, H. M. "Adam or Satan? The Identity of the King of Tyre in Late Antiquity." Pages 59–69 in *After Ezekiel: Essays on the Reception of a Difficult Prophet.* Edited by A. Mein and P. M. Joyce. LHBOTS 535. London: Bloomsbury, 2011.

———. *Adam, Satan, and the King of Tyre: The Interpretation of Ezekiel 28:11–19 in Late Antiquity*. Jewish and Christian Perspectives Series 20. Leiden: Brill, 2012

———. "Did the Masoretes Get It Wrong? The Vocalization and Accentuation of Ezekiel XXVIII 12–19." *VT* 58 (2008): 245–57.

———. "The Shorter and Longer Texts of Ezekiel: The Implications of the Manuscript Finds from Masada and Qumran." *JSOT* 32 (2007): 231–42.

Paton, L. B. *A Critical and Exegetical Commentary on the Book of Esther*. Edinburgh: T&T Clark, 1908.

Paul, S. M. "Amos 1:3-2:3: A Concactenous Literary Pattern." *JBL* 90 (1971): 397–403.

———. *Amos: A Commentary on the Book of Amos*. Hermeneia. Minneapolis: Fortress Press, 1991.

Peels, H. G. L. *The Vengeance of God: The Meaning of the Root NQM and the Function of the NQM-Texts in the Context of Divine Revelation in the Old Testament*. OtSt 31. Leiden: Brill, 1995.

Petersen, D. L. "The Oracles against the Nations: A Form-Critical Analysis." SBLSP (1975): 39–61.

Petry, S. *Die Entgrenzung Jhwhs*. FAT 2/27. Tübingen: Mohr Siebeck, 2007.

Pfeiffer, R. H. *Introduction to the Old Testament*. New York: Harper, 1941.

Pitard, W. T. "Amarna *ekēmu* and Hebrew 'Naqam.'" *Maarav* (1982): 5–25.

Plutarch. *Moralia, Volume V: Isis and Osiris*. Translated by F. C. Babbitt. Loeb Classical Library. Cambridge: Harvard University Press, 1936.

Pohlmann, K.-F. *Das Buch des Propheten Hesekiel (Ezechiel): Kapitel 20–48*. ATD 22,2. Göttingen: Vandenhoeck & Ruprecht, 2001.

———. *Ezechiel: Der Stand der theologischen Diskussion*. Darmstadt: Wissenschaftliche Buchgesellschaft, 2008.

———. *Ezechielstudien: Zur Redaktionsgeschichte des Buches und zur Frage nach den ältesten Texten*. BZAW 202. Berlin: de Gruyter, 1992.

———. "Zur Frage nach ältesten Texten im Ezechielbuch - Erwägungen zu Ez 17,19 und 31." Pages 150–72 in *Prophet und Prophetenbuch: Festschrift für Otto Kaiser zum 65. Geburtstag*. Edited by V. Fritz. BZAW 185. Berlin: de Gruyter, 1989.

Pope, M. H. *El in the Ugaritic Texts*. VTSup 2. Leiden: Brill, 1955.

Popović, M. "Prophet, Book and Texts: Ezekiel, Pseudo-Ezekiel and the Authoritativeness of Ezekiel Traditions in Early Judaism." Pages 227–51 in *Authoritative Scriptures in Ancient Judaism*. Edited by M. Popović. JSJSup 141. Leiden: Brill, 2010.

Porten, B. "The Identity of King Adon." *BA* 44 (1981): 36–52.

Poser, R. *Das Ezechielbuch als Trauma-Literatur*. VTSup 154. Leiden: Brill, 2012.

Premstaller, V., *Fremdvölkersprüche des Ezechielbuches*. FB 104. Würzburg: Echter, 2005.

Preuss, D. *Deuteronomium*. EdF 164. Darmstadt: Wissenschaftliche Buchgesellschaft, 1982.

Raabe, P. R. "Transforming the International Status Quo: Ezekiel's Oracles against the Nations." Pages 187–207 in *Transforming Visions: Transformations of Text, Tradition and Theology in Ezekiel*. Edited by W. A. Tooman and M. A. Lyons.

Princeton Theological Monograph Series 127. Eugene: Pickwick Publications, 2010.

———. "Why Prophetic Oracles against the Nations?" Pages 236–57 in *Fortunate the Eyes That See: Essays in Honor of David Noel Freedman in Celebration of His Seventieth Birthday*. Edited by A. B. Beck et al. Grand Rapids: Eerdmans, 1995.

Rad, G. von. "The Origin of the Concept of the Day of Yahweh." *JSS* 4 (1959): 97–108.

Raitt, T. M. *A Theology of Exile: Judgment/Deliverance in Jeremiah and Ezekiel*. Philadelphia: Fortress Press, 1977.

Reinhartz, A. *Scripture on the Silver Screen*. Louisville: Westminster John Knox, 2003.

Rendtorff, R. "El als israelitische Gottesbezeichnung: Mit einem Appendix: Beobachtungen zum Gebrauch von האלהים." *ZAW* 106 (1994): 4–21.

———. "Genesis 15 im Rahmen der theologischen Bearbeitung der Vätergeschichten." Pages 74–81 in *Werden und Wirken des Alten Testaments: Festschrift für Claus Westermann*. Edited by R. Albertz et al. Göttingen: Vandenhoeck & Ruprecht, 1980.

Renz, T. "Proclaiming the Future: History and Theology in Prophecies against Tyre." *TynBul* 51 (2000): 17–58.

Reventlow, H. G. *Das Amt des Propheten bei Amos*. FRLANT 80. Göttingen: Vandenhoeck & Ruprecht, 1962.

———. *Wächter über Israel: Ezechiel und seine Tradition*. BZAW 82. Berlin: Töpelmann, 1962.

Richelle, M. "Le Portrait Changeant du Roi de Tyr (Ezéchiel 28.11–18) das les Traditions Textuelles Anciennes." Pages 113–25 in *Phéniciens d'Orient et d'Occident. Mélanges Josette Elayi*. Edited by A. Lemaire. Paris: Maisonneuve, 2014.

Rösel, C. *Jhwhs Sieg über Gog aus Magog: Ez 38–39 im masoretischen Text und in der Septuaginta*. WMANT 132. Neukirchen: Neukirchener Theologie, 2012.

Rom-Shiloni, D. "Ezekiel as the Voice of the Exiles." *HUCA* 76 (2005): 1–45.

Roncace, M. "North, Enemy from the." Page 282 in vol. 4 of *The New Interpreter's Dictionary of the Bible*. Edited by K. D. Sakenfeld. 5 vols. Nashville: Abingdon Press, 2009.

Rooy, H. F. van. "Parallelism, Metre and Rhetoric in Ezekiel 29:1–6." *Semitics* 8 (1982): 90–105.

———. "Ezekiel's Prophecies against Egypt and the Babylonian Exiles." Pages 115–22 in *Proceedings of the Tenth World Congress of Jewish Studies. Division A. The Bible and Its World*. Edited by D. Assaf. Jerusalem: World Union of Jewish Studies, 1990.

Rudman, D. "The Use of Water Imagery in Descriptions of Sheol." *ZAW* 113 (2001): 240–44.

Rudnig, T. A. *Heilig und Profan: Redaktionskritische Studien zu Ez 40–48*. BZAW 287. Berlin: de Gruyter, 2000.

Rütersworden, U. "King of Terrors." Pages 486–88 in *Dictionary of Deities and Demons in the Bible*. Edited by K. van der Toorn et al. 2nd ed. Leiden: Brill, 1999.

Sadler, R. S. *Can a Cushite Change His Skin? An Examination of Race, Ethnicity and Othering in the Hebrew Bible*. LHBOTS 425. London: Bloomsbury, 2005.

Salters, R. B. *A Critical and Exegetical Commentary on Lamentations*. ICC. London: T&T Clark, 2010.
Sarna, N. M. "The Mythological Background of Job 18." *JBL* 82 (1963): 315–18.
———. *Understanding Genesis*. Heritage of Biblical Israel 1. New York: Schocken, 1970.
Sasson, J. M. "Circumcision in the Ancient Near East." *JBL* 85 (1966): 473–76.
Saur, M. *Der Tyroszyklus des Ezechielbuches*. BZAW 386; Berlin: de Gruyter, 2008.
———. "Tyros im Spiegel des Ezechielbuches." Pages 165–89 in *Israeliten und Phönizier: Ihre Beziehungen im Spiegel der Archäologie und der Literatur des Alten Testaments und seiner Umwelt*. Edited by M. Witte and J. F. Diehl. OBO 235. Fribourg: Academic Press, 2008.
Scatolini, S. S. "Ezek 36, 37, 38 and 39 in Papyrus 967 as Pre-Text for Re-Reading Ezekiel." Pages 331–57 in *Interpreting Translation*. BETL 192. Leuven: Leuven University Press, 2005.
Schipper, B. U. *Israel und Ägypten in der Königszeit: Die kulturellen Kontakte von Salomo bis zum Fall Jerusalems*. OBO 170. Freiburg: Universitätsverlag, 1999.
Schmid, K. "The Book of Ezekiel." Pages 451–65 in *T&T Clark Handbook of the Old Testament*. Edited by J. C. Gertz et al. Translated by J. Adams-Maßmann. New York: T&T Clark International, 2012.
———. "The Book of Jeremiah." Pages 431–50 in *T&T Clark Handbook of the Old Testament*. Edited by J. C. Gertz et al. Translated by J. Adams-Maßmann. New York: T&T Clark International, 2012.
Schöpflin, K. "Ein Blick in die Unterwelt (Jesaja 14)." *TZ* 58 (2002): 299–314.
———. "Die Tyrosworte im Kontext des Ezechielbuches." Pages 191–213 in *Israeliten und Phönizier: Ihre Beziehungen im Spiegel der Archäologie und der Literatur des Alten Testaments und seiner Umwelt*. Edited by M. Witte and J. F. Diehl. OBO 235. Fribourg: Academic Press, 2008.
———. *Theologie als Biographie im Ezechielbuch: Ein Beitrag zur Konzeption alttestamentlicher Prophetie*. FAT 36. Tübingen: Mohr Siebeck, 2002
Schultz, R. L. *The Search for Quotation: Verbal Parallels in the Prophets*. JSOTSup 180. Sheffield: Sheffield Academic Press, 1999.
Schwagmeier, P. "Untersuchungen zu Textgeschichte und Entstehung des Ezechielbuches in masoretischer und griechischer Überlieferung." PhD diss., Universität Zürich, 2004.
Schwally, F. "Die Reden des Buches Jeremia gegen die Heiden XXV, XLVI–LI." *ZAW* 8 (1888): 177–217.
Schwartz, B. J. "Ezekiel's Dim View of Israel's Restoration." Pages 69–95 in *The Book of Ezekiel: Theological and Anthropological Perspectives*. Edited by M. S. Odell et al. Atlanta: Society of Biblical Literature, 2000.
Schweizer, H. "Der Sturz des Weltenbaumes (Ez 31)—Literarkritisch Betrachtet." *TQ* 165 (1985): 197–213.
Seeligmann, I. L. "Voraussetzungen der midraschexegese." Pages 150–81 in *Congress Volume: Congress of the International Organization for the Study of the Old Testament, Copenhagen 1953*. VTSup 1. Leiden. Brill, 1953.

Seiler, S. "Intertextualität." Pages 275–93 in *Lesarten der Bibel: Untersuchungen zu einer Theorie der Exegese des Alten Testaments*. Edited by H. Utzschneider and E. Blum. Stuttgart: Kohlhammer, 2006.
Sharp, C. J. "'Take another Scroll and Write:' A Study of the LXX and the MT of Jeremiah's Oracles against Egypt and Babylon." *VT* 47 (1997): 487–516.
Simian, H. *Die theologische Nachgeschichte der Prophetie Ezechiels*. FB 14. Würzburg: Echter Verlag, 1974.
Smend, R. *Der Prophet Ezechiel*. Kurzgefasstes exegetisches Handbuch zum Alten Testament 8. Leipzig: S. Hirzel Verlag, 1880.
Smith, M. S. *The Origins of Biblical Monotheism: Israel's Polytheistic Background and the Ugaritic Texts*. Oxford: Oxford University Press, 2001.
———. *The Priestly Vision of Genesis 1*. Minneapolis: Fortress Press, 2010.
Soden, W. von. "Die Unterweltsvision eines assyrischen Kronprinzen." *ZA* 9 (1936): 1–31.
Sommer, B. D. *A Prophet Reads Scripture: Allusion in Isaiah 40–66*. Contraversions: Jews and Other Differences. Stanford: Stanford University Press, 1998.
———. "Exegesis, Allusion and Intertextuality in the Hebrew Bible: A Response to Lyle Eslinger." *VT* 46 (1996): 479–89.
Spieckermann, H. "From Biblical Exegesis to Reception History." *Hebrew Bible and Ancient Israel* 3 (2012): 327–50.
Steudel, A. *Der Midrasch zur Eschatologie aus der Qumrangemeinde (4QMidrEschat a.b): Materialle Rekonstruktion, Textbestand, Gattung und traditionsgeschichtliche Einordnung des durch 4Q174 ("Florilegium") und 4Q177 ("Catena A") repräsentierten Werkes aus den Qumranfunden*. STDJ 13. Leiden: Brill, 1994.
Stordalen, T. *Echoes of Eden: Genesis 2–3 and Symbolism of the Eden Garden in Biblical Hebrew Literature*. CBET 25. Leuven: Peeters, 2000.
Stökl, J. "The מתנבאות in Ezekiel 13 Reconsidered." *JBL* 132 (2013): 61–76.
Stolz, F. "Die Bäume des Gottesgartens auf dem libanon." *ZAW* 84 (1972): 141–56.
Strawn, B. A. "Comparative Approaches: History, Theory, and the Image." Pages 117–42 in *Method Matters: Essays on the Interpretation of the Hebrew Bible in Honor of David L. Petersen*. Edited by J. M. LeMon and K. H. Richards. SBLRBS 56. Atlanta: Society of Biblical Literature, 2009.
———. *What Is Stronger than a Lion? Leonine Image and Metaphor in the Hebrew Bible and the Ancient Near East*. OBO 212. Fribourg: Academic Press Fribourg, 2005.
Strine, C. A. "Chaoskampf Against Empire: YHWH's Battle Against Gog (Ezek 38–39) As Resistance Literature." Pages 87–108 in *Divination, Politics and Ancient Near Eastern Empires*. Edited by A. Lenzi and J. Stökl. ANEM 7. Atlanta: Society of Biblical Literature, 2014.
———. *Sworn Enemies: The Divine Oath, the Book of Ezekiel, and the Polemics of Exile*. BZAW 436. Berlin: de Gruyter, 2013.
Strong, J. T. "Egypt's Shameful Death and the House of Israel's Exodus from Sheol (Ezekiel 32.17–32 and 37.1–14)." *JSOT* 34 (2010): 475–504.
———. "Ezekiel's Oracles against the Nations within the Context of His Message." PhD diss., Union Theological Seminary of Virginia, 1993.

———. "Ezekiel's Use of the Recognition Formula in His Oracles against the Nations." *PRSt* 22 (1995): 115–34.

———. Review of M. A. Corral, *Ezekiel's Oracles against Tyre: Historical Reality and Motivations*. *CBQ* 65 (2003): 431–32.

Strugnell, J. "Notes ne marge du volume V des <Discoveries in the Judaean Desert of Jordan>," *RevQ* 26 (1970): 163–276.

Sulzbach, C. "Nebuchadnezzar in Eden? Daniel 4 and Ezekiel 28." Pages 125–36 in *Stimulation from Leiden: Collected Communications to the XVIIIth Congress of the International Organization for the Study of the Old Testament, Leiden 2004*. Edited by H. M. Niemann and M. Augustin. BEATAJ 54. Frankfurt am Main: Lang, 2006.

Sweeney, M. A. "The Assertion of Divine Power in Ezekiel 33:21–39:29." Pages 156–72 in *Form and Intertextuality in Prophetic and Apocalyptic Literature*. FAT 45. Tübingen: Mohr Siebeck, 2005.

Talmon, S. "1043–2220 (MasEzek) Ezekiel 35:11–38:14." Pages 59–75 in *Masada VI: The Yigael Yadin Excavations 1963–1965: Hebrew Fragments from Masada*. Jerusalem: Israel Exploration Society and the Hebrew University of Jerusalem, 1999.

Terrien, S. *The Psalms: Strophic Structure and Theological Commentary*. The Eerdmans Critical Commentary. Grand Rapids: Eerdmans, 2003.

Thompson, J. A. *The Book of Jeremiah*. NIBCOT. Grand Rapids: Eerdmans, 2007.

Thompson, N. D. "A Problem of Unfulfilled Prophecy in Ezekiel: The Destruction of Tyre (Ezekiel 26:1–14 and 29:18–20)." *Wesleyan Theological Journal* 16 (1981): 93–106.

Tiemeyer, L.-S, "Zechariah's Spies and Ezekiel's Cherubim." Pages 104–27 in *Tradition in Transition: Haggai and Zechariah 1-8 in the Trajectory of Hebrew Theology*. Edited by M. J. Boda and M. H. Floyd. LHBOTS 475. London: Bloomsbury, 2008.

Tigchelaar, E. "Notes on the Ezekiel Scroll from masada (MasEzek)." *RevQ* 22/86 (2005): 268–75.

Tooman, W. A. "Ezekiel's Radical Challenge to Inviolability." *ZAW* 121 (2009): 498–514.

———. *Gog of Magog*. FAT 2/52. Tübingen: Mohr Siebeck, 2011.

———. "Transformation of Israel's Hope: The Reuse of Scripture in the Gog Oracles." Pages 50–110 in *Transforming Visions: Transformations of Text, Tradition, and Theology in Ezekiel*. Edited by W. A. Tooman and M. A. Lyons. Princeton Theological Monograph Series. Eugene: Pickwick Publications, 2010.

Torrey, C. C. *Pseudo-Ezekiel and the Original Prophecy*. YOSR 18. New Haven: Yale University Press, 1930.

Tov, E. "The Literary History of the Book of Jeremiah in the Light of Its Textual History." Pages 211–37 in *Empirical Models for Biblical Criticism*. Edited by J. H. Tigay. Philadelphia: University of Pennsylvania Press, 1985.

———. "The Lucianic Text of the Canonical and Apocryphal Sections of Esther: A Rewritten Biblical Book." *Textus* 10 (1982): 1–25.

———. *Textual Criticism of the Hebrew Bible*. Minneapolis: Fortress Press, 1992.

———. *The Greek and Hebrew Bible: Collected Essays on the Septuagint*. VTSup 72. Leiden: Brill, 1999.

Tsevat, M. "The Neo-Assyrian and Neo-Babylonian Vassal Oaths and the Prophet Ezekiel." *JBL* 78 (1959): 199–204.
Tzoref, S. "Covenantal Election in 4Q252 and Jubilees' Heavenly Tablets." *DSD* 18 (2011): 74–89.
———. *The Pesher Nahum Scroll from Qumran: An Exegetical Study of 4Q169.* STDJ 53. Leiden: Brill, 2004.
Uehlinger, C. "Drachen und Drachenkämpfe im alten Vorderen Orient und in der Bibel." Pages 55–101 in *Auf Drachespuren: Ein Buch zum Drachenprojekt des Hamburgischen Museums für Völkerkunde.* Edited by B. Schmelz and R. Vossen. Bonn: Holos Verlag, 1995.
Ulrich, D. R. "Dissonant Prophecy in Ezekiel 26 and 29." *BBR* 10 (2000): 121–41.
———. "Proleptic Intrusions of the Final Judgment in Ezekiel's Oracles against the Nations." PhD diss., Westminster Theological Seminary, 1996.
Ulrich, E. "Multiple Literary Editions: Reflections toward a Theory of the History of the Biblical Text." Pages 99–120 in *Dead Sea Scrolls and the Origins of the Hebrew Bible.* Grand Rapids: Eerdmans, 1999.
Vanderhooft, D. S. *The Neo-Babylonian Empire and Babylon in the Latter Prophets.* HSM 59. Atlanta: Scholars Press, 1999.
Van Dijk, H. J. *Ezekiel's Prophecy on Tyre: <Ez. 26, 1–28, 19>: A New Approach.* BibOr 20. Rome: Pontifical Biblical Institute, 1968.
Van Winkle, D. W. "The Relationship of the Nations to YHWH and to Israel in Isaiah 40–55," *VT* 35 (1985): 446–58.
Vieweger, D. *Die literarischen Beziehungen zwischen den Büchern Jeremia und Ezechiel.* BEATAJ 26. Frankfurt am Main: Peter Lang, 1993.
Vittmann, G., *Der demotische Papyrus Rylands 9.* Ägypten und Altes Testament 38. Wiesbaden: Harrassowitz, 1998.
Vogels, W. "Restauration de l'Égypte et Universalisme en Ez 29, 13–16." *Bib* 53 (1972): 473–94.
Vorländer, H. "Der Monotheismus Israels als Antwort auf die Krise des Exils." Pages 84–113 in Der Einzige Gott: Die Geburt des biblischen Monotheismus. Edited by B. Lang. München: Kösel, 1981.
Wächter, L. "Unterweltsvorstellungen in Babylonien, Israel und Ugarit." *MIO* 15 (1969): 327–36.
Wahl, H.-M. "Noah, Daniel und Hiob in Ezechiel XIV 12–20 (21–3): Anmerkungen zum traditionsgeschichtlichen Hintergrund." *VT* 42 (1992): 542–53.
Wakeman, M. K. *God's Battle with the Monster: A Study in Biblical Imagery.* Leiden: Brill, 1973.
Weinfeld, M. "Sabbath, Temple, and the Enthronement of the Lord - the Problem of the *Sitz im Leben* of Genesis 1:1–2:3." Pages 501–12 in *Mélanges Bibliques et Orientaux en l'Honneur De M. Henri Cazelles.* Edited by A. Caquot and M. Delcor. AOAT 212. Kevelaer: Butzon & Becker, 1981.
Weiss, M. "The Origin of the 'Day of the Lord'—Reconsidered." *HUCA* 37 (1966): 29–71.
———. "The Pattern of the 'Execration Texts' in the Prophetic Literature." *IEJ* 19 (1969): 150–157.

Wendebourg, N. *Der Tag des Herrn: Zur Gerichtserwartung im Neuen Testament auf Ihrem alttestamentlichen und frühjüdischen Hintergrund.* WMANT 96. Neukirchen: Neukirchener Verlag, 2003.

Wenham, G. J. "Sanctuary Symbolism in the Garden of Eden Story." Pages 19–25 in *Proceedings of the Ninth World Congress of Jewish Studies. Division A: The Period of the Bible.* Jerusalem: World Union of Jewish Studies, 1986.

Westermann, C. *Isaiah 40-66.* OTL. London: SCM Press, 1969.

———. *Grundformen Prophetischer Rede.* 5th ed. BEvT 31. München: Kaiser, 1978.

Wevers, J. W. *Ezekiel.* The Century Bible. London: Nelson, 1969.

Widengren, G. *Sakrales Königtum im Alten Testament und im Judentum.* Franz-Delitzsch Vorlesungen 1952. Stuttgart: Kohlhammer, 1955.

———. "Early Hebrew Myths and Their Interpretation." Pages 165–76 in *Myth, Ritual, and Kingship.* Edited by S. H. Hooke. Oxford: Clarendon Press, 1958.

Wiggermann, F. A. M. "Mischwesen. A. Philologisch. Mesopotamien." *RIA* 8:222–46.

Wilkinson, R. H. *Die Welt der Götter im alten Ägypten: Glaube, Macht, Mythologie.* Translated by T. Bertram. Darmstadt: Wissenschaftliche Buchgesellschaft, 2003.

Williamson, H. G. M. "The Concept of Israel in Transition." Pages 141–61 in *The World of Ancient Israel.* Edited by R. E. Clements. Cambridge: Cambridge University Press, 1989.

Wilson, I. D. "The Metaphorical World of Ezekiel 27 in Ancient Judah." *ZAW* 125 (2013): 249–62.

Wilson, R. R. "The Death of the King of Tyre: The Editorial History of Ezekiel 28." Pages 211–18 in *Love and Death in the Ancient Near East: Essay in Honor of Marvin H. Pope.* Edited by J. H. Marks. Guilford: Four Quarters, 1987.

Wiseman, D. J. "Babylonia 605–539 B.C." Pages 229–51 in *Cambridge Ancient History, Vol.3, Part 2: The Assyrian and Babylonian Empires and Other States of the Ancient Near East, from the Eighth to the Sixth Centuries B.C.* Edited by J. Broadman et al. 2nd ed. Cambridge: Cambridge University Press, 1991.

———. *Nebuchadrezzar and Babylon: Schweich Lectures in Biblical Archaeology.* Oxford: Oxford University Press, 1983.

Wold, D. J. "The Kareth Penalty in P: Rationale and Cases." SBLSP 1 (1979): 1–25.

Wolff, H. W. "Jahwe und die Götter in der alttestamentlichen Prophetie." *EvT* 29 (1969): 397–416.

Wood, A. *Of Wings and Wheels: A Synthetic Study of the Biblical Cherubim.* BZAW 385. Berlin: de Gruyter, 2008.

Wong, K. L. "The Masoretic and Septuagint Texts of Ezekiel 39,21–29," *ETL* 78 (2002): 130–47.

———. "The Prince of Tyre in the Masoretic and Septuagint Texts of Ezekiel 28,1–10." Pages 447–61 in *Interpreting Translation: Studies on the LXX and Ezekiel in Honour of Johan Lust.* Edited by F. García-Martínez and M. Vervenne. BETL 192. Leuven: Leuven University Press, 2005.

Woudstra, M. H. "Edom and Israel in Ezekiel." *CTJ* 3 (1968): 21–35.

Yaron, K. "The Dirge over the King of Tyre." *ASTI* 3 (1964): 28–57.

Yoder, T. R. "Ezekiel 29:3 and Its Ancient Near Eastern Context." *VT* 63 (2013): 486–96.

Young, I. "The Dead Sea Scrolls and the Bible: The View from Qumran Samuel." *ABR* 62 (2014): 14–30.

Zecchi, M. *Sobek of Shedet: The Crocodile God in the Fayyum in the Dynastic Period*. Todi: Tau Education, 2010.

Zimmerli, W. *A Commentary on the Book of the Prophet Ezekiel*. Hermeneia. 2 vols. Philadelphia: Fortress Press, 1979, 1983.

———. "Das Phänomen der 'Fortschreibung' im Buche Ezechiel." Pages 174–91 in *Prophecy: Essays Presented to Georg Fohrer on His Sixty-Fifth Birthday 6 September 1980*. Edited by J. A. Emerton. Berlin: de Gruyter, 1980.

———. "Die Eigenart der prophetischen Rede des Ezechiel." *ZAW* 66 (1954): 1–26.

———. *Grundriß der alttestamentlichen Theologie*. Theologische Wissenschaft 3. Stuttgart: Kohlhammer, 1972.

———. "Knowledge of God According to the Book of Ezekiel." Pages 29–98 in *I Am Yahweh*. Edited by W. Brueggemann. Translated by D. W. Stott. Atlanta: John Knox Press, 1982.

Zunz, L. "Bibelkritisches." *ZDMG* 27 (1875): 676–88.

Zwickel, W. *Edelsteine in der Bibel*. Mainz: von Zabern, 2002.

# ANCIENT SOURCES INDEX

HEBREW BIBLE/OLD TESTAMENT
Genesis
  1–2        41
  1–3        96
  1:6–8     41
  1:7–8     41
  1:9        41
  1:9–10    41
  1:11–12   41
  1:14–18   41
  1:20       41
  1:29–30   41
  2–3        96
  2:6–10    97
  2:7        41
  2:12       98
  2:15       96
  3:8        96
  3:21       96
  3:24       113
  4:10       72
  4:12       111
  6–8        143
  6:4        173
  10:2       106, 208
  10:2–3    213
  10:3       213
  10:4       106
  10:7       106
  14:18–20   19
  15         64–65
  15:3       64
  15:4       64
  15:7       64
  15:8       64
  17:4       154
  17:5       155
  22:24      93
  25:23      201
  26:10      59
  27:28      68
  27:39      68
  29:1       55
  31:27      109
  36:8       198
  36:9       198
  36:20      198
  36:21      198
  41:5       146
  41:6       118
  41:22      146
  41:23      118
  41:27      118
  41:42      93
  49:1       219
  49:25      144

Exodus
  3:8        68
  3:17       68

| | | | |
|---|---|---|---|
| 3:20 | 138 | 25:5 | 48, 93 |
| 4:27 | 95, 111 | 25:7 | 98 |
| 6:1 | 138 | 25:8 | 120 |
| 6:2–8 | 65 | 25:9 | 88 |
| 6:6 | 138 | 25:18–22 | 112 |
| 6:8 | 64, 77 | 25:20 | 88, 117 |
| 7:5 | 73 | 25:40 | 88 |
| 7:8–13 | 130 | 26 | 42, 185 |
| 7:9–10 | 130 | 26:1 | 91, 112 |
| 7:12 | 130 | 26:14 | 48, 93 |
| 7:14–18 | 130 | 26:15 | 91 |
| 7:15 | 130 | 26:16 | 91 |
| 7:19 | 73 | 26:17 | 91 |
| 8:1 | 73 | 26:18 | 91 |
| 8:2 | 73 | 26:19 | 91 |
| 8:13 | 73 | 26:20 | 91 |
| 9:22 | 73 | 26:21 | 91 |
| 9:23 | 110–11 | 26:22 | 91 |
| 10 | 106 | 26:23 | 91 |
| 10:12 | 73 | 26:25 | 91 |
| 10:13 | 118 | 26:26 | 91 |
| 10:21 | 73 | 26:27 | 91 |
| 10:22 | 73 | 26:28 | 91 |
| 13:3 | 138 | 26:29 | 91 |
| 13:5 | 68 | 26:31 | 91, 93, 112 |
| 13:9 | 138 | 26:36 | 48, 91, 93 |
| 13:14 | 138 | 27:4–5 | 168 |
| 13:16 | 138 | 27:9 | 93 |
| 14:16 | 73 | 27:16 | 48, 91, 93 |
| 14:21 | 118 | 27:18 | 93 |
| 14:26 | 73 | 28 | 5, 89, 98–101 |
| 14:27 | 73 | 28:3 | 92 |
| 15:7 | 110 | 28:5 | 91, 93 |
| 15:9 | 64 | 28:6 | 91, 93 |
| 15:14–15 | 27 | 28:8 | 91, 93 |
| 15:20 | 109 | 28:9 | 98 |
| 18:5 | 95, 111 | 28:11 | 88 |
| 23:29 | 205 | 28:13 | 98, 101 |
| 24:13 | 95, 111 | 28:15 | 91, 93 |
| 24:14 | 104 | 28:17–20 | 19, 20, 83, 97–98, 101, 185 |
| 25 | 185 | | |
| 25:3 | 106 | 28:21 | 88 |
| 25:4 | 91 | 28:33 | 91 |

| | | | |
|---|---|---|---|
| 28:36 | 88 | 36:35 | 91, 93, 112 |
| 28:39 | 48, 93 | 36:37 | 48, 91, 93 |
| 28:41 | 96 | 37:7–9 | 112 |
| 29:8 | 96 | 37:9 | 88, 117 |
| 29:29 | 117 | 38:4 | 168 |
| 31:6 | 92 | 38:9 | 93 |
| 32:11 | 138 | 38:16 | 93 |
| 32:20 | 170 | 38:18 | 48, 91, 93 |
| 32:33 | 130 | 38:23 | 91 |
| 33:4 | 68 | 39 | 5, 89, 98–100 |
| 34:6 | 43 | 39:1 | 91 |
| 35:6 | 91, 93 | 39:2 | 91, 93 |
| 35:7 | 48, 93 | 39:3 | 91, 93 |
| 35:9 | 98 | 39:5 | 91, 93 |
| 35:10 | 92 | 39:6 | 88, 98 |
| 35:11 | 91 | 39:8 | 91, 93 |
| 35:22 | 212 | 39:10–13 | 19, 20, 83, 97, |
| 35:23 | 48, 91, 93 | | 98, 101, 185 |
| 35:25 | 91, 93 | 39:14 | 88 |
| 35:27 | 98 | 39:24 | 91 |
| 35:34 | 93 | 39:27 | 93 |
| 35:35 | 48, 91, 93 | 39:28 | 93 |
| 36 | 42 | 39:29 | 48, 91, 93 |
| 36:1 | 92 | 39:30 | 88 |
| 36:2 | 92 | 39:33 | 42, 91 |
| 36:4 | 92 | 39:34 | 93 |
| 36:8 | 91–93, 112 | 40:3 | 88 |
| 36:16 | 93 | 40:14 | 96 |
| 36:19 | 93 | 40:18 | 42, 91 |
| 36:20 | 91 | 45:3 | 120 |
| 36:21 | 91 | 45:18 | 120 |
| 36:22 | 91 | 47:12 | 120 |
| 36:23 | 91 | | |
| 36:24 | 91 | Leviticus | |
| 36:25 | 91 | 2:7 | 94 |
| 36:26 | 91 | 4:3 | 117 |
| 36:27 | 91 | 4:5 | 117 |
| 36:28 | 91 | 4:16 | 117 |
| 36:30 | 91 | 6:20 | 117 |
| 36:31 | 91 | 8:13 | 96 |
| 36:32 | 91 | 12:4 | 120 |
| 36:33 | 91 | 14:7 | 215 |
| 36:34 | 9 | 14:53 | 215 |

| | | | |
|---|---|---|---|
| 16:33 | 120 | 4:8 | 48, 93 |
| 17–26 | 74 | 4:10 | 48, 93 |
| 17:4 | 75 | 4:11 | 93 |
| 17:5 | 215 | 4:12 | 93 |
| 17:9 | 75 | 4:14 | 93 |
| 17:10 | 74–75 | 4:31 | 42, 91 |
| 17:13 | 71 | 6:15 | 94 |
| 18:21 | 120 | 7:13 | 94 |
| 19:8 | 120 | 7:19 | 94 |
| 19:12 | 120 | 7:89 | 112 |
| 19:16 | 215 | 8:8 | 94 |
| 19:29 | 120 | 8:26 | 96 |
| 19:30 | 120 | 10:4 | 208 |
| 20:3 | 74, 120 | 10:21 | 120 |
| 20:5 | 54, 74 | 11:15 | 110 |
| 20:6 | 74 | 13:2 | 69 |
| 20:24 | 68 | 13:16–17 | 69 |
| 21:4 | 120 | 13:21 | 69 |
| 21:6 | 120 | 13:25 | 69 |
| 21:12 | 120 | 13:27 | 67–68, 77 |
| 21:15 | 120 | 13:32 | 69 |
| 21:23 | 120 | 14:1 | 110 |
| 22:2 | 120 | 14:6–7 | 69 |
| 22:9 | 120 | 14:34 | 69 |
| 22:15 | 120 | 14:36 | 69 |
| 22:32 | 120 | 14:38 | 69 |
| 26 | 126 | 14:8 | 68 |
| 26:2 | 120 | 14:24 | 64 |
| 26:12 | 96 | 16:13–14 | 68 |
| 26:20 | 111 | 16:14 | 203 |
| 26:22 | 73, 75 | 17:2 | 170 |
| 26:25 | 72 | 18:1 | 120 |
| 26:31 | 120 | 18:5–6 | 96 |
| 26:33 | 38, 75, 167, 170–71, 205 | 19:20 | 120 |
| | | 20 | 67 |
| 26:38 | 73 | 20:14–21 | 67 |
| 27:28 | 75 | 21 | 11 |
| | | 21:13 | 70 |
| Numbers | | 21:15 | 70 |
| 3:7–8 | 96 | 21:21–31 | 71 |
| 3:36 | 42, 91 | 21:24 | 70 |
| 3:38 | 120 | 21:27 | 11 |
| 4:6 | 48, 93 | 21:27–30 | 11 |

| | | | |
|---|---|---|---|
| 21:27–35 | 70 | 6:3 | 68 |
| 22:36 | 70 | 6:21 | 138 |
| 23–24 | 11 | 7:8 | 138 |
| 24:10 | 56 | 7:13 | 68 |
| 24:14 | 219 | 7:19 | 138 |
| 24:18 | 198 | 9:26 | 138 |
| 25:1–2 | 104 | 9:29 | 138 |
| 31:3 | 60 | 11:2 | 138 |
| 32:37–38 | 70–71 | 11:9 | 68 |
| 32:38 | 69 | 11:17 | 111 |
| 33:44 | 70 | 12:15 | 69 |
| 33:49 | 69 | 12:22 | 69 |
| 33:53 | 64 | 14:4 | 69 |
| | | 15:22 | 69 |
| Deuteronomy | | 17:14 | 57 |
| 1:8 | 66 | 17:16 | 149 |
| 1:21 | 66 | 23:15 | 96 |
| 1:25 | 67 | 23:19 | 107 |
| 1:33 | 69 | 23:22–24 | 44 |
| 1:39 | 66 | 26:8 | 138 |
| 2 | 67 | 26:9 | 68 |
| 2–3 | 66–67, 201 | 26:15 | 68 |
| 2:2–8 | 67 | 27:3 | 68 |
| 2:5 | 66 | 27:5 | 91 |
| 2:9 | 66 | 28:36 | 34, 58 |
| 2:12 | 66–67 | 28:36–37 | 171 |
| 2:19 | 66 | 28:40 | 88 |
| 2:21 | 66 | 28:41 | 171 |
| 2:22 | 66 | 28:64 | 34, 38, 58, 170–71 |
| 2:24 | 66 | | |
| 2:26–37 | 70–71 | 29:23–27 | 171 |
| 2:31 | 66 | 30:3 | 170, 178 |
| 3:11 | 55, 91 | 30:4 | 178 |
| 3:12 | 66 | 31:20 | 68 |
| 3:18 | 66 | 31:28 | 103 |
| 3:20 | 66 | 31:29 | 219 |
| 3:24 | 138 | 32:1 | 103 |
| 4:27 | 38, 170 | 32:6 | 110 |
| 4:27–28 | 34, 58, 171 | 32:8 | 66 |
| 4:30 | 219 | 32:8 LXX | 114 |
| 4:34 | 138 | 32:33 | 130 |
| 5:15 | 138 | 32:41–42 | 167 |
| 5:27 | 110 | 32:43 | 72 |

| | | | | |
|---|---|---|---|---|
| 33:1 | 65 | | Judges | |
| 33:2 | 66 | | 1:19 | 64 |
| 33:2–5 | 65 | | 1:27 | 64 |
| 33:3 | 66 | | 2:17 | 104 |
| 33:4 | 64–66 | | 4:7 | 154 |
| 33:6–25 | 65 | | 5:30 | 93 |
| 33:13 | 144 | | 6:3 | 55 |
| 33:26–29 | 65 | | 6:33 | 55 |
| 33:29 | 167 | | 7:12 | 55 |
| 34:12 | 138 | | 7:20 | 167 |
| | | | 8:10 | 55 |
| Joshua | | | 8:24–28 | 19 |
| 5:6 | 68 | | 8:27 | 104 |
| 7:6 | 119 | | 8:33 | 104 |
| 8:7 | 64 | | 9:8–15 | 159 |
| 8:31 | 91 | | 10:6 | 54 |
| 12:3 | 69–71 | | 11 | 54 |
| 13:17 | 69–71 | | 11:12–28 | 70 |
| 13:19–20 | 70–71 | | 11:34 | 109 |
| 13:20 | 69 | | 15:7 | 60 |
| 13:23 | 203 | | 15:14 | 137 |
| 13:28 | 203 | | 18:7 | 93 |
| 14:3 | 203 | | 18:27–30 | 93 |
| 15:8 | 58 | | | |
| 15:10–11 | 58 | | Ruth | |
| 15:20 | 203 | | 3:2 | 170 |
| 16:8 | 203 | | | |
| 16:9 | 203 | | First Samuel | |
| 17:12 | 64 | | 2:7 | 64 |
| 18:12–13 | 58 | | 4:4 | 113 |
| 18:16 | 58 | | 4:14 | 154 |
| 18:18–19 | 58 | | 6:18 | 220 |
| 18:20 | 203 | | 8:5 | 57 |
| 18:24 | 220 | | 8:20 | 57 |
| 18:28 | 203 | | 10:5 | 109 |
| 19:1 | 203 | | 12:17–18 | 110 |
| 19:8 | 203 | | 14:16 | 154 |
| 19:9 | 203 | | 14:19 | 154 |
| 19:16 | 203 | | 14:24 | 19 |
| 19:23 | 203 | | 14:25 | 215 |
| 19:31 | 203 | | 14:34 | 19 |
| 19:39 | 203 | | 14:35 | 19 |
| 19:48 | 203 | | 14:47 | 54 |

| | | | |
|---|---|---|---|
| 16:13 | 117 | 6:7 | 91 |
| 18:6 | 109 | 6:15 | 42, 92 |
| 18:25 | 60 | 6:18 | 42, 92 |
| 18:41 | 154 | 6:20 | 42, 92 |
| 24:13 | 72 | 6:23–29 | 112 |
| 24:13b | 62 | 6:32 | 112 |
| 24:14 | 11 | 6:34 | 42, 92 |
| 24:19 | 110 | 6:35 | 112 |
| | | 7:14 | 92 |
| Second Samuel | | 7:17 | 168 |
| 1:19–27 | 84 | 7:18 | 168 |
| 2:4 | 117 | 7:20 | 168 |
| 2:18 | 69 | 7:29 | 112 |
| 3:33 | 84 | 7:36 | 112 |
| 6 | 19 | 8:6–7 | 112 |
| 6:2 | 113 | 8:7 | 88, 92, 117 |
| 6:5 | 109 | 9:11 | 42 |
| 6:19 | 154 | 9:26 | 87 |
| 7:2 | 164 | 9:27 | 87 |
| 7:6–7 | 96 | 10:10 | 107 |
| 7:13 | 110 | 10:11 | 87 |
| 8:11b–12 | 54 | 10:13 | 107 |
| 8:16 | 180 | 10:22 | 87, 105 |
| 12:20 | 88 | 11:33 | 54 |
| 12:26 | 55 | 14:15 | 146, 170 |
| 12:27 | 55 | 18 | 117 |
| 17:27 | 55 | 19:8 | 95, 111 |
| 18:29 | 154 | 19:16 | 117 |
| 20:24 | 180 | 20:6 | 192 |
| 22:11 | 113–14 | 20:11 | 11 |
| 22:14 | 110 | 20:28 | 11–12 |
| | | 22:19 | 113 |
| First Kings | | 22:21 | 114 |
| 4:3 | 180 | 22:49 | 105 |
| 5 | 185 | 25:1 | 127 |
| 5–10 | 99 | | |
| 5:3 | 69 | Second Kings | |
| 5:10 | 55 | 1:1 | 70 |
| 5:13 | 42, 164 | 3:4 | 70 |
| 5:20 | 164 | 3:5 | 70 |
| 5:22 | 42, 92 | 7:13 | 154 |
| 5:24 | 42, 92 | 9:7 | 72 |
| 5:24–25 | 107 | 11:12 | 56 |

| | | | |
|---|---|---|---|
| 14:9 | 159 | 2:6 | 90, 92 |
| 17:4 | 147 | 2:7 | 42, 92 |
| 18:18 | 180 | 2:12–13 | 92 |
| 18:21 | 34, 42, 146–47 | 2:13 | 90 |
| 18:37 | 180 | 2:14 | 91 |
| 19:15 | 113 | 3:14 | 91 |
| 19:28 | 212 | 11:23 | 154 |
| 23:13 | 54 | 13:8 | 154 |
| 24:1–2 | 28 | 14:10 | 154 |
| 24:2 | 26–28, 54 | 16:7–8 | 146 |
| 25:1 | 188–90 | 20:2 | 154 |
| 25:4–5 | 26 | 20:8 | 120 |
| 25:11 | 154 | 20:12 | 154 |
| 25:18 | 208 | 20:15 | 154 |
| | | 20:24 | 154 |

First Chronicles

| | | | |
|---|---|---|---|
| 1:5 | 208 | 25:11 | 198 |
| 1:5–6 | 213 | 25:14 | 198 |
| 1:6 | 213 | 25:18 | 159 |
| 1:9 | 106 | 26:18 | 120 |
| 1:32 | 106 | 29:12 | 120 |
| 13:6 | 113 | 31:10 | 154, 208 |
| 13:8 | 109 | 32:7 | 154 |
| 16:22 | 117 | 33:11 | 213 |
| 17:12 | 110 | 34:8 | 180 |
| 18:11 | 54 | 35:25 | 84 |
| 18:15 | 180 | | |

Ezra

| | |
|---|---|
| 2:57 | 69 |
| 7:5 | 208 |
| 9:12 | 64 |

| | |
|---|---|
| 22:14 | 90 |
| 22:15 | 92 |
| 22:16 | 90 |
| 22:19 | 120 |
| 27:5 | 208 |
| 28:11 | 88 |
| 28:12 | 88 |
| 28:17 | 88 |
| 28:18 | 88, 117 |
| 28:19 | 88 |
| 29 | 92 |
| 29:2 | 90, 93, 98 |
| 29:16 | 154 |

Nehemiah

| | |
|---|---|
| 1:9 | 170, 178 |
| 4:1 | 29 |
| 7:59 | 69 |
| 9:6 | 110 |

Esther

| | |
|---|---|
| 1:6 | 91–92 |
| 1:11 | 89 |
| 4:1 | 119 |
| 8:15 | 91 |

Second Chronicles

| | |
|---|---|
| 2–9 | 99 |

| Job | | |
|---|---|---|
| 1:3 | 55 | |
| 1:6 | 114 | |
| 1:10 | 110 | |
| 2:1 | 114 | |
| 2:12 | 119 | |
| 4:15 | 114 | |
| 4:18 | 114 | |
| 7:12 | 129 | |
| 10:16 | 133 | |
| 13:26 | 64 | |
| 15:2 | 118 | |
| 15:7–8 | 110 | |
| 16:18 | 72 | |
| 18:8–9 | 168 | |
| 18:15 | 170 | |
| 21:12 | 109 | |
| 26:12–13 | 129 | |
| 26:41 | 129 | |
| 27:21 | 118 | |
| 27:23 | 56 | |
| 28:19 | 98 | |
| 30:3 | 219 | |
| 30:14 | 219 | |
| 31:34 | 154 | |
| 33:23 | 114 | |
| 35:9 | 137 | |
| 38:4–7 | 110 | |
| 38:7 | 114 | |
| 38:24 | 118 | |
| 38:27 | 219 | |
| 38:39–40 | 133 | |
| 39:7 | 154 | |
| 39:25 | 55 | |
| 40:15–24 | 146 | |
| 41:26 | 133 | |
| 44:26 | 114 | |

| Psalms | | |
|---|---|---|
| 1:3 | 111 | |
| 2:6 | 95, 111 | |
| 3:5 | 95, 111 | |
| 6:4 | 110 | |
| 7:12 | 167 | |
| 9:8 | 110 | |
| 9:15 | 168 | |
| 9:16 | 168 | |
| 10:9 | 168 | |
| 14:7 | 178 | |
| 15:1 | 95, 111 | |
| 17:13 | 167 | |
| 18:11 | 113–14, 122 | |
| 18:14 | 110, 122 | |
| 18:16 | 160 | |
| 24:3 | 95, 111 | |
| 24:17 | 122 | |
| 25:15 | 168 | |
| 27:20 | 122 | |
| 29:1 | 114 | |
| 29:3 | 160 | |
| 30:15 | 122 | |
| 31:5 | 168 | |
| 32:6 | 160 | |
| 35:7–8 | 168 | |
| 35:9 | 68 | |
| 35:21 | 55 | |
| 35:25 | 55 | |
| 36:7 | 75, 144 | |
| 36:8 | 68 | |
| 37:16 | 154 | |
| 37:23 | 109 | |
| 40:16 | 55 | |
| 42:5 | 154 | |
| 43:3 | 95, 111 | |
| 44:1–3 | 138 | |
| 44:4 | 137 | |
| 44:12 | 170 | |
| 45:12 | 89 | |
| 45:15 | 93 | |
| 46:2–4 | 9 | |
| 46:5–6 | 97 | |
| 46:7–8 | 9 | |
| 47:1–12 | 97 | |
| 47:2 | 56 | |
| 48:1b–3 | 217 | |
| 48:2 | 95, 111 | |

| | | | |
|---|---|---|---|
| 48:3 | 217 | 89:33–34 | 121 |
| 48:7 | 118–19 | 89:39 | 121 |
| 48:8 | 105 | 90:9 | 215 |
| 50 | 104 | 91:13 | 130, 133 |
| 50:1–6 | 103 | 93:4 | 160 |
| 50:2 | 41, 43, 89–90, 102–3 | 98 | 138 |
| | | 98:8 | 56 |
| 50:4 | 103 | 99:1 | 113 |
| 50:5 | 103 | 99:9 | 95, 111 |
| 50:7–15 | 103 | 104:2 | 41 |
| 50:15 | 103 | 104:4 | 114 |
| 50:16 | 103 | 104:8 | 41 |
| 50:16–23 | 103 | 104:14 | 41 |
| 50:17–20 | 103 | 104:16 | 164 |
| 50:22 | 103 | 104:25 | 41 |
| 53:7 | 178 | 104:29 | 41 |
| 57:7 | 168 | 104:30 | 41 |
| 64:12 | 68 | 105:15 | 117 |
| 65:8 | 155 | 105:32 | 111 |
| 65:10 | 68 | 106:27 | 170 |
| 68:22 | 59 | 107:3 | 178 |
| 68:31 | 146 | 110:4 | 19 |
| 71:18 | 137 | 132:10 | 117 |
| 73:19 | 122 | 136:5 | 41 |
| 74:13 | 129 | 136:6 | 41 |
| 74:13–14 | 129 | 136:7–9 | 41 |
| 77:11–20 | 138 | 137 | 163 |
| 77:17–18 | 143 | 137:3 | 28 |
| 77:19 | 160 | 139:3 | 170 |
| 78:26 | 118 | 140:6 | 168 |
| 78:69 | 97 | 144:5–8 | 143 |
| 79:6 | 138 | 144:7 | 160 |
| 79:10 | 62 | 149:3 | 109 |
| 80:1 | 113 | 149:7 | 60, 72 |
| 80:9–14 | 159 | 150:1 | 97 |
| 80:11 | 164 | 150:4 | 109 |
| 80:12 | 159 | | |
| 81:3 | 109 | Proverbs | |
| 82:6 | 114 | 1:17 | 168, 170 |
| 83:1–8 | 27 | 3:19 | 110 |
| 83:3–8 | 82 | 6:5 | 69 |
| 85:2 | 178 | 6:25 | 89 |
| 89:7 | 114 | 8:31 | 110 |

| | | | |
|---|---|---|---|
| 10:10 | 110 | 2:16 | 105 |
| 13:10 | 110 | 2:18 | 152 |
| 14:4 | 110 | 2:20 | 152 |
| 14:35–15:1 | 215 | 3:24 | 89 |
| 15:7 | 170 | 4:2 | 69 |
| 20:8 | 170 | 5:1–7 | 159 |
| 20:26 | 170 | 5:12 | 109 |
| 27:4 | 215 | 5:13 | 154 |
| 29:5 | 168 | 5:14 | 154 |
| 31:17 | 137 | 6:1 | 186 |
| 31:22 | 93 | 6:1–2 | 113 |
| 31:24 | 107 | 6:11 | 219 |
| 31:30 | 89 | 7:1 | 186 |
| | | 8:1 | 189 |
| Ecclesiastes | | 8:14 | 201 |
| 5:3–4 | 44 | 9:3 | 169 |
| 5:9 | 154 | 9:12 | 61 |
| 7:22 | 110 | 9:13 | 74 |
| 9:12 | 134 | 10:7 | 74 |
| | | 10:10 | 152 |
| Song of Songs | | 10:11 | 152 |
| 1:12 | 110 | 10:18–19 | 159 |
| 2:9 | 69 | 10:20 | 146 |
| 2:13 | 110 | 10:33 | 160 |
| 2:17 | 69 | 10:34 | 161 |
| 5:14 | 98 | 11:1 | 159 |
| 7:12 | 220 | 11:9 | 95, 111 |
| 7:14 | 110 | 11:11 | 150, 179 |
| 8:14 | 69 | 11:12 | 170, 178 |
| | | 11:14 | 55, 58, 62 |
| Isaiah | | 11:14–21 | 180 |
| 1–32 | 25 | 13–23 | 1, 2 |
| 1–39 | 25 | 13:1 | 2 |
| 1:2 | 103 | 13:2 | 2 |
| 1:7 | 205 | 13:4 | 154 |
| 1:21 | 104 | 13:6 | 43, 169 |
| 1:21–26 | 72 | 13:9 | 169 |
| 1:24 | 72 | 13:14 | 69 |
| 2:2 | 219 | 13:19 | 80 |
| 2:3 | 95, 111 | 14 | 2, 217–18 |
| 2:8 | 152 | 14:4b–21 | 217 |
| 2:12 | 169 | 14:8 | 42, 92 |
| 2:12–16 | 159 | 14:9 | 144 |

| | | | |
|---|---|---|---|
| 14:12–14 | 132 | 27:8 | 118 |
| 14:13 | 217 | 27:13 | 95 |
| 14:14 | 217 | 28:5 | 69 |
| 14:22 | 74 | 28:10 | 144 |
| 14:28 | 2, 186 | 29:5 | 154 |
| 14:31 | 218 | 29:7 | 154 |
| 15–16 | 10, 27, 70 | 29:8 | 154 |
| 15:1 | 2 | 30:1–5 | 147 |
| 16:6–11 | 159 | 30:6 | 133 |
| 16:14 | 154 | 30:12 | 146 |
| 16:59–63 | 180 | 30:22 | 70 |
| 17:1 | 2 | 30:24 | 170, 219 |
| 17:12 | 55 | 30:29 | 95, 111 |
| 17:12–14 | 143 | 30:32 | 109 |
| 17:14 | 122 | 31:1 | 146 |
| 19 | 123 | 31:4 | 133, 154 |
| 19:1 | 2, 152 | 31:7 | 152 |
| 19:3 | 152 | 31:10 | 178 |
| 19:6 | 146 | 32:14 | 154 |
| 19:13 | 150 | 33:17 | 89 |
| 19:18–25 | 177 | 33:21 | 87 |
| 19:23 | 139 | 34 | 2 |
| 19:24–25 | 226 | 34–35 | 25 |
| 20:33–34 | 180 | 34:5 | 167 |
| 21:1 | 2 | 34:5–8 | 59 |
| 21:2b | 2 | 34:6–8 | 215 |
| 21:5b | 2 | 34:10 | 204 |
| 21:11 | 2 | 35:3–4 | 62 |
| 21:13 | 2 | 35:7 | 146 |
| 21:14 | 106 | 36 | 42, 146 |
| 21:16–17 | 106 | 36–39 | 25 |
| 22:1 | 2 | 36:3 | 180 |
| 23 | 82, 87 | 36:6 | 34, 42, 146, 147 |
| 23:1 | 2, 105 | 36:22 | 180 |
| 23:14 | 105 | 37:16 | 113 |
| 23:17–18 | 107 | 37:29 | 212 |
| 23:20 | 219 | 40–52 | 25 |
| 24–27 | 25 | 40–55 | 138 |
| 24:8 | 109 | 40–66 | 226 |
| 24:21 | 170 | 40:11 | 178 |
| 25:3 | 86 | 41:16 | 170 |
| 26:13 | 111 | 41:19 | 92 |
| 27:1 | 129, 167 | 42:3 | 146 |

| | | | |
|---|---|---|---|
| 42:4 | 227 | 63:7–14 | 138 |
| 42:6 | 227 | 65:11 | 95, 111 |
| 43:5 | 178 | 65:25 | 95, 111 |
| 43:10–13 | 226 | 66:16 | 167 |
| 43:20 | 111 | 66:18 | 178 |
| 43:28 | 121 | 66:18–24 | 227 |
| 44:5 | 227 | 66:20 | 95, 111 |
| 44:16 | 55 | | |
| 45:14 | 227 | Jeremiah | |
| 45:22–23 | 227 | 1:2 | 186 |
| 45:24b–25 | 227 | 1:2–10 | 15 |
| 47:6 | 121 | 1:13–15 | 37, 218 |
| 48:11 | 120 | 2–3 | 37 |
| 48:47 | 219 | 2:5 | 103 |
| 49:32 | 155 | 2:8 | 37 |
| 49:6 | 227 | 2:15 | 110 |
| 49:23 | 227 | 2:16 | 150 |
| 49:32 | 154 | 2:17 | 104 |
| 49:39 | 219 | 2:20–25 | 104 |
| 51:4–8 | 138 | 2:26 | 37 |
| 51:8–10 | 22 | 2:30b | 37 |
| 51:9 | 167 | 2:37 | 176 |
| 51:9–10 | 129, 143 | 3:19 | 69, 203 |
| 52:10 | 138 | 3:20 | 69 |
| 53:1 | 138 | 3:23 | 154 |
| 53:5 | 120 | 3:29 | 70 |
| 54:7 | 178 | 4:3 | 219 |
| 55:2 | 56 | 4:6 | 37, 218 |
| 56:1–8 | 227 | 4:9 | 37 |
| 56:2 | 120 | 4:11 | 170 |
| 56:6 | 120 | 4:16 | 110 |
| 56:7 | 95, 111 | 4:23–28 | 44 |
| 56:8 | 178 | 4:27 | 205 |
| 57:13 | 95, 111 | 5:9 | 60, 71 |
| 59 | 138 | 5:10 | 2 |
| 60–61 | 162 | 5:12–14 | 37 |
| 60–62 | 25 | 5:29 | 60, 71 |
| 60:5 | 154 | 5:30–31 | 37 |
| 60:9 | 105 | 6 | 217–18 |
| 60:15 | 204 | 6:1 | 37, 218 |
| 60:16 | 67 | 6:4 | 120 |
| 63:1–4 | 59 | 6:4–6 | 2 |
| 63:4–5 | 138 | 6:7 | 120 |

| | | | |
|---|---|---|---|
| 6:8 | 205 | 21:7 | 167 |
| 6:12 | 74 | 21:10 | 54 |
| 6:13 | 120 | 21:19 | 120 |
| 6:13–15 | 37 | 21:30 | 120 |
| 6:14 | 205 | 21:34 | 120 |
| 6:22 | 37, 218 | 22:6 | 161 |
| 6:22–23 | 217 | 22:15 | 164 |
| 6:26 | 119 | 22:20 | 110 |
| 7:29 | 84 | 22:20–23 | 161 |
| 8:11 | 37 | 22:24 | 88 |
| 9:8 | 71 | 23:3 | 178 |
| 9:9 | 60, 204 | 23:5 | 159 |
| 9:10 | 84, 205 | 23:9 | 69 |
| 9:11 | 204 | 23:9–32 | 37 |
| 9:20 | 84 | 23:30 | 212 |
| 9:21 | 74, 215 | 23:31 | 212 |
| 9:25 | 54 | 23:32 | 212 |
| 10:9 | 91 | 23:33–40 | 37 |
| 10:13 | 154 | 24:4–7 | 182 |
| 10:22 | 37, 205, 218 | 24:8 | 149 |
| 10:25 | 138 | 25:1 | 186 |
| 11:5 | 68 | 25:13 | 25 |
| 11:6 | 120 | 25:15–38 | 25 |
| 11:7 | 120 | 25:19–23 | 54 |
| 11:16 | 160 | 25:20 | 149 |
| 11:20 | 71 | 25:23 | 106 |
| 12:10–11 | 205 | 25:29 | 120, 167 |
| 12:12 | 167 | 25:30 | 110 |
| 13:19 | 69 | 25:34 | 119 |
| 13:20 | 37, 218 | 25:38 | 133, 167 |
| 14:13–17 | 37 | 26:1 | 186 |
| 15:3 | 167 | 26:9 LXX | 148 |
| 15:6 | 74 | 26:15 | 120 |
| 15:7 | 170 | 27 | 186 |
| 15:12 | 37, 218 | 27:1 | 28, 129 |
| 15:15 | 71, 72 | 27:3 | 26–27, 30 |
| 16:2 | 192 | 27:4–8 | 26 |
| 16:5 | 192 | 28:1 | 28, 69, 187 |
| 17:7 | 176 | 28:4 | 69 |
| 18:17 | 118 | 28:8 | 120 |
| 20:10 | 71 | 28:9 | 120 |
| 20:12 | 71 | 29:14 | 178 |
| 21:5 | 74 | 30:3 | 178 |

| | | | |
|---|---|---|---|
| 30:4 | 120 | 44:11 | 54 |
| 30:11 | 120 | 44:15 | 150 |
| 30:18–32 | 182 | 45 | 25 |
| 30:24 | 120 | 45:1 | 186 |
| 31:4 | 109 | 46 | 123 |
| 31:5 | 120 | 46–51 | 1, 4, 11 |
| 31:8 | 178 | 46:3–6 | 2 |
| 31:10 | 170 | 46:6 | 37, 218 |
| 31:23 | 95, 111, 178 | 46:9 | 148 |
| 31:31–34 | 182 | 46:9–10 | 2 |
| 32 LXX | 25 | 46:10 | 37, 71–72, 167, 218 |
| 32:1 | 186 | | |
| 32:22 | 68 | 46:14 | 150 |
| 32:36–41 | 182 | 46:19 | 150 |
| 32:37 | 178 | 46:20 | 37, 218 |
| 32:43 | 75, 205 | 46:24 | 37, 218 |
| 33:7 | 178 | 46:26 | 177 |
| 34:16 | 120 | 47:1 | 29 |
| 34:22 | 205 | 47:2 | 37, 218 |
| 35:8 | 120 | 47:3 | 154 |
| 36:9 | 187 | 47:6 | 167 |
| 36:11 | 186 | 48 | 10, 70 |
| 36:29 | 74, 75 | 48:1–47 | 27 |
| 37:3–10 | 36 | 48:6–8 | 2 |
| 37:5–11 | 31, 135 | 48:7 | 27 |
| 37:6–8 | 147 | 48:23 | 69 |
| 37:7–8 | 32 | 48:28 | 2 |
| 37:19 | 37 | 48:29 | 80 |
| 39:1 | 151, 188 | 48:34 | 110 |
| 40:11 | 28, 54 | 48:45–46 | 11 |
| 40:11–12 | 26–27 | 48:47 | 178 |
| 41:1 | 187 | 49:2 | 26, 55, 205 |
| 41:15 | 26 | 49:6 | 178 |
| 41:41 | 120 | 49:8 | 2 |
| 43:1–7 | 151 | 49:14–15 | 2 |
| 43:7 | 150 | 49:19 | 133 |
| 43:8–9 | 150 | 49:28 | 55 |
| 43:8–13 | 123 | 49:28–29 | 2 |
| 43–44 | 149–51 | 49:28–32 | 211 |
| 44:1 | 150 | 49:30 | 2 |
| 44:1–30 | 150 | 49:31–33 | 2 |
| 44:6 | 205 | 49:32 | 170 |
| 44:7 | 74 | 49:33 | 205 |

| | | | |
|---|---|---|---|
| 49:34 | 186 | 2:2–4 | 215 |
| 49:36 | 170 | 2:4 | 103, 192 |
| 49:37 | 167 | 2:5 | 103 |
| 49:39 | 178 | 2:7 | 103, 110 |
| 50:3 | 37, 218 | 2:10 | 119 |
| 50:8–10 | 2 | 2:14 | 103 |
| 50:9 | 37, 218 | 2:15 | 41, 43, 56, 89–90, 102–3 |
| 50:13 | 205 | | |
| 50:14–15 | 2 | 4:21–22 | 28 |
| 50:15 | 60, 71 | | |
| 50:16 | 2, 167 | Ezekiel | |
| 50:21–23 | 2 | 1 | 114 |
| 50:26–27 | 2 | 1–24 | 13, 18, 39, 51 |
| 50:28 | 71 | 1–39 | 47 |
| 50:29–30 | 2 | 1:1 | 187–88, 193 |
| 50:31 | 212 | 1:2 | 193 |
| 50:35 | 167 | 1:4 | 218 |
| 50:41 | 37, 218 | 1:6 | 98 |
| 50:44 | 133 | 1:10 | 114 |
| 51:2 | 170 | 1:15–21 | 114 |
| 51:3–4 | 2 | 1:24 | 143 |
| 51:5 | 59 | 1:27 | 42 |
| 51:6 | 2, 71 | 1:28 | 42 |
| 51:9 | 129 | 1:27–28 | 41 |
| 51:11 | 71 | 2:3 | 200 |
| 51:11–12 | 2 | 2:3–7 | 197 |
| 51:16 | 154 | 2:10 | 84 |
| 51:25 | 74, 212 | 3:4–11 | 197 |
| 51:27–29 | 2 | 3:6 | 15 |
| 51:34 | 130 | 3:7 | 197 |
| 51:34–47 | 72 | 3:16 | 187–88 |
| 51:36 | 71–72, 130 | 3:16–21 | 196 |
| 51:42 | 154 | 3:16b | 198 |
| 51:45 | 2 | 3:22–27 | 197 |
| 51:48 | 37, 218 | 4–7 | 39 |
| 52:4 | 188 | 4–24 | 196 |
| 52:24 | 208 | 4:3 | 91 |
| | | 4:7 | 137 |
| Lamentations | | 4:13 | 200 |
| 1:10 | 120 | 5–6 | 197 |
| 1:11 | 107 | 5:1 | 167 |
| 2 | 104 | 5:2 | 136, 167, 170–71 |
| 2:2 | 103, 121 | 5:7 | 154, 155, 156 |

| | | | |
|---|---|---|---|
| 5:8 | 212 | 7:18 | 119, 170 |
| 5:8–10 | 132 | 7:19 | 169 |
| 5:10 | 136, 170–71, 186 | 7:20 | 156 |
| 5:12 | 74, 136, 167, 170–71 | 7:20–24 | 121 |
| | | 7:21 | 143 |
| 5:13 | 215 | 7:21–22 | 121 |
| 5:14 | 204 | 7:23 | 201 |
| 5:17 | 167 | 7:24 | 55, 120 |
| 6 | 199, 202, 205, 207, 221 | 7:27 | 201 |
| | | 8–11 | 114 |
| 6:1 | 198 | 8:1 | 187–88 |
| 6:1–7 | 206 | 8:2 | 41–42 |
| 6:2 | 54, 201 | 8:5 | 218 |
| 6:3 | 167, 201, 205–6 | 8:10 | 88, 152 |
| 6:4 | 120, 152, 206 | 8:12 | 201 |
| 6:5 | 152, 170, 200 | 8:17 | 201 |
| 6:6 | 152, 204 | 9:2 | 218 |
| 6:7 | 120, 206 | 9:3 | 113–14 |
| 6:8 | 136, 167, 171 | 9:8 | 138 |
| 6:9 | 152 | 9:9 | 201 |
| 6:11 | 56, 167, 202 | 10 | 114 |
| 6:11–12 | 74 | 10:1–9 | 113 |
| 6:12 | 56, 167 | 10:4 | 114 |
| 6:13 | 110, 120, 152 | 10:5 | 114 |
| 6:14 | 73–74, 201, 205 | 10:9 | 98 |
| 7 | 125, 166, 169 | 10:9–17 | 114 |
| 7:1 | 198 | 10:14 | 114 |
| 7:2 | 201 | 10:14–16 | 113 |
| 7:6 | 170 | 10:15 | 114 |
| 7:6–7 | 169, 186 | 10:18–20 | 113 |
| 7:7 | 169–70, 201 | 10:20 | 114 |
| 7:8 | 138 | 10:21 | 114 |
| 7:9 | 170 | 10:22 | 114 |
| 7:9–10 | 169, 186 | 11:3 | 192 |
| 7:10 | 170 | 11:5 | 64 |
| 7:11 | 154 | 11:5–12 | 72 |
| 7:11–14 | 156 | 11:6 | 120 |
| 7:12 | 154, 156, 202 | 11:7 | 120, 186, 192 |
| 7:12–14 | 155 | 11:8 | 167 |
| 7:13 | 154 | 11:9 | 132, 143 |
| 7:14 | 154, 156 | 11:10 | 167 |
| 7:15 | 74, 167 | 11:12 | 58 |
| 7:17 | 170 | 11:14 | 198 |

| | | | |
|---|---|---|---|
| 11:14–21 | 197 | 14:8–9 | 74 |
| 11:15 | 64–65, 77, 201–2, 207 | 14:9 | 74 |
| | | 14:11 | 182 |
| 11:16 | 170 | 14:12 | 198 |
| 11:16–17 | 136, 171 | 14:12–20 | 73, 75 |
| 11:17 | 65, 125, 170, 178, 181, 201–2 | 14:12–23 | 73–74 |
| | | 14:13 | 51, 74–75 |
| 11:17–20 | 176, 186 | 14:14 | 86, 112 |
| 11:20 | 182 | 14:15 | 204–5 |
| 11:22 | 113 | 14:16 | 205 |
| 12:1 | 198 | 14:17 | 74, 75, 167, 184 |
| 12:8 | 198 | 14:19 | 74–75, 138, 184 |
| 12:13 | 55, 134, 168 | 14:20 | 86, 112 |
| 12:14 | 167, 170–71 | 14:21 | 74–75, 167, 184 |
| 12:14–15 | 136, 171 | 14:21–23 | 76 |
| 12:15 | 75, 170, 186 | 14:22 | 37 |
| 12:16 | 74, 167 | 15 | 159–60, 162–63, 186 |
| 12:17 | 198 | | |
| 12:19 | 201 | 15–19 | 39 |
| 12:20 | 204–5 | 15:1 | 198 |
| 12:21 | 198 | 15:1–4 | 159, 165 |
| 12:22 | 201 | 15:1–8 | 74 |
| 12:26 | 198 | 15:2 | 159 |
| 12:26–28 | 48 | 15:6 | 159 |
| 13:1 | 198 | 15:8 | 205 |
| 13:4 | 204 | 16 | 5, 37, 42, 48, 93–94, 104, 107, 185, 192 |
| 13:5 | 169 | | |
| 13:8 | 212 | | |
| 13:9 | 201 | 16:1 | 198 |
| 13:13 | 204 | 16:4–5 | 104 |
| 13:17 | 54 | 16:5 | 104 |
| 13:18 | 128 | 16:9 | 88 |
| 13:19 | 120 | 16:9–14 | 93 |
| 13:20 | 128 | 16:10 | 48, 93–94 |
| 13:30 | 137 | 16:10–14 | 104 |
| 14 | 5, 73–78 | 16:12 | 120 |
| 14:1–11 | 73, 75 | 16:13 | 42, 89, 93–94 |
| 14:2 | 198 | 16:14 | 41–43, 79, 82, 89–90, 94, 102–3, 185 |
| 14:3 | 152, 184 | | |
| 14:4 | 152 | | |
| 14:5 | 152 | 16:15 | 89 |
| 14:6 | 152 | 16:15–34 | 104, 107 |
| 14:7 | 152 | 16:18 | 93 |

| | | | |
|---|---|---|---|
| 16:19 | 42, 93 | 17:14 | 179 |
| 16:25 | 89 | 17:15 | 31, 34, 148, 162, 185 |
| 16:26 | 34 | | |
| 16:27 | 34 | 17:16 | 55, 148 |
| 16:28 | 34 | 17:16–21 | 163 |
| 16:29 | 34 | 17:19 | 119, 148 |
| 16:31 | 107 | 17:20 | 55, 134, 168 |
| 16:31–34 | 107 | 17:21 | 167–68 |
| 16:34 | 107 | 17:22 | 163–64 |
| 16:36 | 152 | 17:22–23 | 164 |
| 16:37 | 104, 178 | 17:22–24 | 163–65 |
| 16:38 | 104 | 17:22 LXX | 37 |
| 16:39 | 104 | 17:23 | 125, 159, 164 |
| 16:40 | 168, 211 | 17:23 LXX | 37, 164 |
| 16:41 | 107 | 17:24 | 132 |
| 16:49 | 156 | 18:1 | 198 |
| 16:53–58 | 163 | 18:1–32 | 196 |
| 16:56 | 156 | 18:2 | 201 |
| 16:57 | 59, 61–62 | 18:6 | 152 |
| 16:59 | 148 | 18:12 | 152 |
| 16:59–63 | 163, 180 | 18:15 | 152 |
| 16:60 | 148 | 19 | 125, 159–63, 172 |
| 16:62 | 148 | 19:1 | 84 |
| 17 | 21, 159–64, 186 | 19:1–9 | 133 |
| 17:1 | 198 | 19:2 | 172 |
| 17:1–21 | 163 | 19:4 | 172, 213 |
| 17:1–24 | 159 | 19:7 | 204 |
| 17:2–12 | 11 | 19:8 | 134, 172 |
| 17:3 | 93–94, 164 | 19:8–9 | 168 |
| 17:3–10 | 159, 165 | 19:9 | 55, 88, 134, 168, 172, 201, 213 |
| 17:3 LXX | 37 | | |
| 17:4 | 163 | 19:10 | 143, 160 |
| 17:5 | 143, 160 | 19:10–14 | 159, 160–61, 165 |
| 17:5–10 | 160 | 19:11 | 125, 160 |
| 17:6 | 125, 160 | 19:12 | 119, 159 |
| 17:7 | 125, 185 | 19:14b | 123 |
| 17:8 | 143, 159 | 20 | 21, 120, 126, 137–38, 152–53, 158, 185 |
| 17:8–9 | 68 | | |
| 17:9–10 | 163 | | |
| 17:10 | 119, 159 | 20:1 | 187–88 |
| 17:11 | 198 | 20:1–3 | 197 |
| 17:12 | 55, 88, 168 | 20:2 | 198 |
| 17:13 | 143, 148 | 20:5–9 | 22 |

| | | | |
|---|---|---|---|
| 20:6 | 68 | 21:16 | 167 |
| 20:7 | 34, 152–53 | 21:17 | 167, 202 |
| 20:7 LXX | 153 | 21:19 | 55, 56, 120, 167, 202 |
| 20:8 | 138, 152–53 | | |
| 20:8 LXX | 153 | 21:20 | 167, 202 |
| 20:9 | 120 | 21:21 | 55 |
| 20:13 | 120, 138 | 21:22 | 56, 202 |
| 20:14 | 120 | 21:23 | 18, 198 |
| 20:15 | 68 | 21:23–28 | 26, 34 |
| 20:16 | 120, 152–53 | 21:24 | 167 |
| 20:16 LXX | 153 | 21:25 | 55, 167 |
| 20:18 | 152–53 | 21:26 | 168 |
| 20:21 | 120, 138 | 21:28 | 180 |
| 20:22 | 120, 138 | 21:28–34 | 148 |
| 20:23 | 69–70, 136, 170–71 | 21:30 | 120, 200 |
| | | 21:33 | 33, 167 |
| 20:24 | 120, 152–53 | 21:33–35a | 34 |
| 20:24 LXX | 153 | 21:33–37 | 16–17, 195 |
| 20:28 LXX | 153 | 21:34 | 120, 200 |
| 20:31 | 152–53, 197 | 22:3 | 152 |
| 20:31 LXX | 153 | 22:1 | 198 |
| 20:32 | 34, 57–58, 192 | 22:4 | 59, 69, 152 |
| 20:33 | 75 | 22:14 | 132 |
| 20:33–34 | 138 | 22:15 | 75, 136, 170–71, 186 |
| 20:34 | 125, 136, 170–71, 176, 178, 186 | | |
| | | 22:17 | 198 |
| 20:37 | 148 | 22:19 | 136, 171, 178 |
| 20:39 | 120, 152–53 | 22:20 | 178, 204 |
| 20:39 LXX | 153 | 22:20–21 | 215 |
| 20:41 | 125, 136, 170–71, 176, 178, 181, 186 | 22:23 | 198 |
| | | 22:35 | 186 |
| | | 23 | 21, 34, 37, 126, 158, 185, 192, 211, 214 |
| 21 | 202 | | |
| 21:1 | 198 | | |
| 21:2 | 18, 54 | 23:1 | 198 |
| 21:6 | 198 | 23:1–4 | 22 |
| 21:7 | 18, 54, 120 | 23:6 | 214 |
| 21:8 | 167, 212 | 23:7 | 152 |
| 21:8–9 | 73 | 23:10 | 167 |
| 21:9 | 167, 218 | 23:12 | 214 |
| 21:10 | 167 | 23:23 | 214 |
| 21:13 | 198 | 23:24 | 211, 214 |
| 21:14 | 167, 202 | 23:24 LXX | 210 |

| | | | |
|---|---|---|---|
| 23:25 | 167 | | 200–204, 206–7, |
| 23:30 | 152 | | 221, 224 |
| 23:37 | 152 | 25–28 | 175 |
| 23:39 | 55, 152 | 25–29 | 38 |
| 23:42 | 154, 156 | 25–32 | 1, 3, 4–5, 7–8, |
| 23:46 | 211 | | 12–14, 16–17, |
| 23:47 | 167, 211 | | 22–23, 25, 32, |
| 23:49 | 152 | | 35–36, 38–40, |
| 24 | 5, 7, 8, 71, 77, | | 43–46, 50, 52, |
| | 187, 190, 192– | | 81, 84, 123, 125, |
| | 94, 197, 221 | | 165, 183–84, |
| 24:1 | 5, 127, 187–92, | | 186–87, 193–94, |
| | 198 | | 197, 209, 211, |
| 24:1–2 | 187–88, 190–91, | | 217, 221, 223, |
| | 197, 221 | | 225, 228–29 |
| 24:1–24 | 193 | 25:1 | 18, 53, 198 |
| 24:1–25:17 | 84 | 25:1–3a | 63 |
| 24:2 | 36, 55, 168, 189 | 25:1–5 | 38, 58 |
| 24:3–5 | 192 | 25:1–7 | 34 |
| 24:3–14 | 72, 191 | 25:1–11 | 165 |
| 24:3b–5 | 191 | 25:1–17 | 191 |
| 24:6 | 192 | 25:2 | 54 |
| 24:6–8 | 72 | 25:2–3a | 53 |
| 24:7 | 71 | 25:2b | 63 |
| 24:8 | 71–72, 184, 191 | 25:3 | 18, 33, 51, 54, |
| 24:15 | 198 | | 63, 77, 82, 165, |
| 24:15–27 | 191 | | 191–92, 202 |
| 24:16 | 192 | 25:3b | 54–55 |
| 24:17 | 132 | 25:3b–4 | 63 |
| 24:20 | 198 | 25:3b–5 | 54, 63 |
| 24:21 | 18, 55, 121, 167, | 25:4 | 52, 60, 64–65, |
| | 167, 191–92 | | 67–68, 77, 184, |
| 24:25 | 192 | | 201 |
| 24:25–27 | 14, 194, 196 | 25:4–5 | 54–55 |
| 24:26–27 | 37 | 25:4b | 67 |
| 25 | 2, 4, 5, 8, 13, 14, | 25:5 | 56, 61, 181 |
| | 15, 16, 18, 33, | 25:6 | 51, 54, 56, 61, |
| | 39, 51–53, 57, | | 63, 77, 192, 202 |
| | 59, 61–64, 67, | 25:6–7 | 56, 63, 73 |
| | 69, 71, 73–79, | 25:7 | 52, 54, 56, 62– |
| | 82, 84, 184, 190, | | 63, 73–74, 181, |
| | 192–93, 199, | | 184, 204 |

| | | | |
|---|---|---|---|
| 25:8 | 18, 33, 51, 54, 58, 63, 77, 165, 192, 198, 224 | 26:1 P967 | 190 |
| | | 26:1–16 | 2 |
| | | 26:1–21 | 84–85 |
| 25:8–11 | 57, 63 | 26:1–28:19 | 14 |
| 25:9 | 58, 68, 77, 184 | 26:1–28:26 | 84 |
| 25:9–11 | 54, 58 | 26:1b–5a | 38–39 |
| 25:10 | 52, 58, 60, 64–65, 68, 77, 176, 184, 201 | 26:2 | 34, 55, 80–82, 85, 132, 165, 204 |
| | | 26:2–6 | 82 |
| 25:11 | 181 | 26:3 | 85, 119, 142, 211–12 |
| 25:11b | 58 | | |
| 25:12 | 33, 51, 54, 59, 71, 77 | 26:3–6 | 85 |
| | | 26:4 | 85 |
| 25:12–14 | 35, 57–60, 198 | 26:5 | 168 |
| 25:12–15 | 203 | 26:6 | 181 |
| 25:12–17 | 63, 72–73, 77–78, 191 | 26:7 | 37, 55, 74, 210–11, 218 |
| 25:13 | 51, 62–63, 73, 75, 167, 184, 204 | 26:7–14 | 36, 38, 85, 151 |
| | | 26:12 | 211, 220 |
| 25:13–14 | 52, 54, 59 | 26:13 | 74, 154 |
| 25:14 | 60–61, 71–72, 77, 181, 184, 204 | 26:14 | 85, 119, 168 |
| | | 26:15 | 120 |
| 25:14a | 60 | 26:15–17 | 119 |
| 25:14b | 60 | 26:15–18 | 80, 85 |
| 25:14c | 61 | 26:16 | 74, 85, 93 |
| 25:15 | 33, 51, 54, 61, 62–63, 71, 77, 165, 200 | 26:17 | 84 |
| | | 26:18 | 128 |
| | | 26:19 | 119, 143, 204 |
| 25:15–17 | 58, 61, 200 | 26:19–21 | 85 |
| 25:16 | 62–63, 73–74, 184, 204 | 26:20 | 85, 204 |
| | | 26:21 | 84, 176 |
| 25:16–17 | 52, 54, 62 | 27 | 2, 5, 19, 38–39, 42–43, 81–82, 87, 89, 90–95, 98, 101–2, 104–7, 119, 185 |
| 25:17 | 61, 71–72, 76–78, 181, 184 | | |
| 25:17a | 62 | | |
| 25:17b | 60 | 27:1 | 198 |
| 26 | 82, 84–85, 119 | 27:1–3a | 87 |
| 26–32 | 16 | 27:1–11 | 122 |
| 26–28 | 4–5, 14, 16, 41, 79, 83–84, 185 | 27:1–36 | 83–84, 86 |
| | | 27:2 | 82, 84 |
| 26:1 | 36, 83–84, 187–88, 190, 193, 198 | 27:3 | 42, 80, 87, 89, 132, 185 |
| 26:1 LXX | 190 | | |

| | | | |
|---|---|---|---|
| 27:3–4 | 41, 43, 89–90, 94, 102 | 27:24 | 42, 91, 93–94 |
| | | 27:24 LXX | 37 |
| 27:3–11 | 91–92, 94, 105, 107 | 27:25 | 81, 87, 105, 220 |
| | | 27:25b | 87 |
| 27:3b | 79, 87 | 27:25b–36 | 87, 122 |
| 27:3b–4 | 79 | 27:26 | 79, 118–19, 143, 185 |
| 27:3b–11 | 87 | | |
| 27:4 | 87, 89 | 27:27 | 81, 119 |
| 27:4–25a | 79 | 27:28–36 | 80, 119 |
| 27:5 | 92 | 27:30–31 | 119 |
| 27:5–9 | 90 | 27:32 | 84, 119 |
| 27:6 | 42, 91, 139 | 27:33 | 81, 88 |
| 27:7 | 42, 91, 93–94 | 27:34 | 81 |
| 27:8b | 92 | 27:36 | 81, 84, 122, 176 |
| 27:9 | 81 | 28 | 2, 5, 17, 19, 20, 81–82, 84, 95, 98–100, 102, 104–5, 224 |
| 27:9a | 92 | | |
| 27:10 | 94, 111, 147, 208, 213–14 | | |
| 27:11 | 41, 43, 87, 89, 90, 94, 102, 185 | 28 LXX | 101 |
| | | 28:1 | 84, 198 |
| 27:12 | 81, 87, 90, 105, 107 | 28:1–10 | 15, 17, 20, 82, 84–86, 88, 118 |
| 27:12–14 | 185 | 28:2 | 80, 86, 88, 117, 118 |
| 27:12–15 | 106 | | |
| 27:12–24 | 107 | 28:3 | 86, 112 |
| 27:12–25 | 105 | 28:3–5 | 85–86 |
| 27:12–25a | 80, 87, 107, 122 | 28:4–5 | 86 |
| 27:13 | 81, 87, 107, 174, 213 | 28:5 | 81 |
| | | 28:5b | 81 |
| 27:14 | 107, 213 | 28:6 | 86, 117 |
| 27:15 | 81, 106 | 28:7 | 85–86, 89, 143 |
| 27:16 | 42, 81, 91, 93–94, 98, 106–7 | 28:8 | 86, 120 |
| | | 28:9 | 117–18, 120 |
| 27:16–18 | 106 | 28:10 | 84, 143, 173 |
| 27:17 | 34, 42, 81, 93, 107, 185, 214 | 28:11 | 88, 198 |
| | | 28:11–19 | 19, 38–39, 83, 84, 86–89, 96, 99, 100–101, 107, 109, 111, 117–18, 120, 185 |
| 27:18 | 81, 105–6 | | |
| 27:19 | 81, 106–7 | | |
| 27:19–22 | 106 | | |
| 27:20 | 106 | | |
| 27:21 | 81, 149 | 28:12 | 41, 79, 84–85, 88–89, 95, 97, 102 |
| 27:22 | 107 | | |
| 27:23 | 87, 106 | | |

| | | | |
|---|---|---|---|
| 28:12–13 | 108, 122, 185 | 29:1–5 | 38 |
| 28:12–19 | 108, 122 | 29:1–6a | 127, 130, 135, 146 |
| 28:12b–15a | 88 | | |
| 28:13 | 19–20, 79, 83, 88, 95, 97–101, 109–11, 113, 117, 121 | 29:1–12 | 176, 179 |
| | | 29:1–16 | 16, 126, 135, 145, 177, 195 |
| | | 29:1–32:32 | 194, 197 |
| 28:13 LXX | 101 | 29:2 | 54 |
| 28:14 | 88, 95, 97, 108–13, 116–18, 121–22, 185 | 29:2–3 | 88 |
| | | 29:3 | 123, 127, 129, 130, 132, 145–46, 155, 212 |
| 28:14 LXX | 108 | | |
| 28:15 | 121 | 29:3–4 | 185, 212 |
| 28:15b–19 | 88 | 29:3–6a | 127, 130, 145 |
| 28:16 | 81, 88, 108, 113, 116–17, 120–21, 176, 185 | 29:3–7 | 145 |
| | | 29:3a | 134 |
| | | 29:3b | 132 |
| 28:16 LXX | 108 | 29:4 | 124, 130, 134, 144, 146, 213 |
| 28:16–18 | 79 | | |
| 28:17 | 88–89, 121 | 29:4–5 | 134, 146, 213 |
| 28:17a | 85 | 29:4a | 212 |
| 28:18 | 81, 120–21 | 29:5 | 146, 215 |
| 28:19 | 84, 121–22, 176 | 29:6 | 34, 124, 134, 145, 147, 165, 181, 185 |
| 28:20 | 198 | | |
| 28:20–24 | 24 | | |
| 28:21 | 54 | 29:6–7 | 180, 218 |
| 28:22 | 181, 212 | 29:6–12 | 124 |
| 28:23 | 167 | 29:6a | 145 |
| 28:24 | 24, 61, 176 | 29:6b | 145 |
| 28:24–26 | 12, 24 | 29:6b–7 | 42, 145, 147 |
| 28:25 | 24, 125, 136, 170–71, 176, 178, 186 | 29:6b–9a | 145–46, 158 |
| | | 29:7 | 147 |
| | | 29:8 | 73, 167–68 |
| 28:25–26 | 24, 39 | 29:8–12 | 145 |
| 28:26 | 61, 181 | 29:9 | 145, 181, 204–5 |
| 29 | 42, 129, 151, 178 | 29:9a | 134, 145 |
| 29–32 | 4, 5, 8, 14, 21–22, 123–24, 126–27, 144–45, 154–55, 167, 182, 185, 196, 216 | 29:9b | 145–46 |
| | | 29:9b 11a | 175 |
| | | 29:9b–12 | 146, 175, 179 |
| | | 29:9b–16 | 145, 175 |
| | | 29:10 | 147, 204–5, 212 |
| 29:1 | 36, 84, 187–88, 194–95, 198 | 29:10–12 | 146 |
| | | 29:10–16 | 125 |

| | | | |
|---|---|---|---|
| 29:11 | 179 | 30:6 | 80, 124, 149, 167 |
| 29:12 | 75, 125, 170, 175, 179, 186, 204–5 | 30:6–8 | 148 |
| | | 30:7 | 204 |
| | | 30:8 | 124, 149, 181 |
| 29:12–13 | 136, 171 | 30:8–9 | 186 |
| 29:13 | 170, 175, 178–79 | 30:9 | 169–70, 214–15 |
| 29:13–16 | 126, 145, 175–79, 181–82, 186, 197, 219 | 30:10 | 15, 55, 154, 168, 177 |
| | | 30:10–12 | 151, 195 |
| 29:13–16a | 39 | 30:11 | 86, 120, 143, 168 |
| 29:14 | 150, 178–79, 182 | 30:11–12 | 143 |
| 29:14–15 | 175 | 30:12 | 204 |
| 29:14–16 | 148 | 30:13 | 150–53, 177 |
| 29:14b–15 | 179 | 30:13–19 | 149–50, 153, 169 |
| 29:15 | 182 | 30:14 | 150, 153 |
| 29:16 | 145, 147, 175–76, 180–82, 185 | 30:15 | 15, 138, 153–55 |
| | | 30:16 | 150, 153, 170 |
| 29:16b | 145, 175 | 30:17 | 167–68 |
| 29:17 | 36, 187–88, 193–94, 198, 213 | 30:18 | 80, 150, 219 |
| | | 30:19 | 181 |
| 29:17–20 | 30, 151, 195 | 30:20 | 136, 139, 187–88, 193–95, 198 |
| 29:17–21 | 147, 151, 177, 195 | | |
| | | 30:20–26 | 123, 127, 135, 137–39, 151, 185, 196 |
| 29:17–30:19 | 195 | | |
| 29:18 | 30, 55, 151, 168 | | |
| 29:19 | 15, 55, 154–56, 168, 211, 220 | 30:21 | 135, 137 |
| | | 30:21–22 | 135 |
| 29:21 | 181, 214 | 30:21–26 | 137 |
| 30 | 126, 135, 151–53, 158, 166, 169 | 30:22 | 135, 137, 168, 212 |
| 30–32 | 38 | 30:23 | 75, 125, 135–36, 170–71, 186 |
| 30:1 | 198 | | |
| 30:1–9 | 169 | 30:24 | 55, 120, 137, 168, 177 |
| 30:1–19 | 151, 195 | | |
| 30:2–3 | 186 | 30:24–25 | 136 |
| 30:3 | 148, 169–70 | 30:25 | 55, 135–37, 168 |
| 30:4 | 15, 120, 154, 156, 167–68, 170 | 30:26 | 125, 136, 170–71, 181, 186 |
| 30:5 | 123–25, 144, 147, 149, 153, 165, 168, 185, 208, 214 | 31 | 16, 21, 125, 139–40, 142, 144, 158–63, 165, 186 |
| | | 31:1 | 36, 139, 187–88, 193–95, 198 |
| 30:5 LXX | 147 | | |

| | | | |
|---|---|---|---|
| 31:1–9 | 127, 140 | 31:17 | 120, 156, 167, 168 |
| 31:1–18 | 159, 185, 196 | 31:18 | 15, 120, 124, 144, 154–56, 167–68, 173, 216 |
| 31:2 | 15, 124, 143–44, 154–56, 216 | | |
| 31:2–9 | 140 | 32 | 2, 129, 131, 154, 171, 174, 216 |
| 31:2b | 161 | | |
| 31:2b–9 | 140 | 32:1 | 36, 187–88, 193–95, 198 |
| 31:3 | 125, 139, 159–61, 164–65 | | |
| 31:3 LXX | 37 | 32:1–8 | 127, 135 |
| 31:3–4 | 140 | 32:1–16 | 126, 172, 196 |
| 31:3–8 | 140 | 32:1–33:22 | 219 |
| 31:3b–9 | 139 | 32:2 | 84, 123, 127, 129–30, 132, 172, 185, 220 |
| 31:4–5 | 143, 159 | | |
| 31:4a | 161 | | |
| 31:5 | 140, 143, 160 | 32:2–8 | 127, 130 |
| 31:6 | 140, 142, 164 | 32:3 | 134, 172, 211 |
| 31:6–7 | 143 | 32:3a | 134 |
| 31:6aα | 161 | 32:3b | 168 |
| 31:6b | 157 | 32:4–5 | 215 |
| 31:7 | 125, 140, 143, 160 | 32:7–8 | 135 |
| | | 32:8 | 135 |
| 31:8 | 42, 89, 92, 160 | 32:9 | 126, 170, 186 |
| 31:8 LXX | 37 | 32:10 | 168 |
| 31:9 | 124–25, 140, 143, 159 | 32:11 | 55, 167–68, 177 |
| | | 32:12 | 15, 80, 86, 154–55, 167–68, 216 |
| 31:10 | 123, 139, 155, 160, 164–65 | | |
| | | 32:12b | 155 |
| 31:10–13 | 140 | 32:13 | 143 |
| 31:10–14 | 140 | 32:15 | 181 |
| 31:11 | 125, 143 | 32:16 | 15, 123, 154–55, 157–58, 172, 216 |
| 31:11–14 | 139 | | |
| 31:12 | 86, 125, 143, 156, 160 | 32:17 | 36, 187–88, 193–95, 198 |
| 31:12abα | 161 | 32:17–32 | 123, 126, 140, 158, 172–74, 185–86, 194, 216, 221, 223 |
| 31:13 | 160 | | |
| 31:13a | 161 | | |
| 31:14 | 125, 155, 160, 164, 171 | | |
| | | 32:17–33:20 | 194, 196 |
| 31:15 | 143–44, 160 | 32:18 | 124, 144, 154–55, 157–58 |
| 31:15–18 | 123, 140, 171 | | |
| 31:16 | 124 | 32:19 | 173 |

| | | | |
|---|---|---|---|
| 32:20 | 120, 144, 154, 157–58, 167–68, 216 | 33:1 | 193, 198 |
| | | 33:1–9 | 196 |
| | | 33:1–20 | 186, 193–97, 221 |
| 32:20–26 | 124 | 33:2 | 167 |
| 32:21 | 120, 143–44, 167–68, 173 | 33:3 | 167 |
| | | 33:4 | 167 |
| 32:21 P967 | 173 | 33:6 | 167 |
| 33:21–22 | 194, 221 | 33:10 | 193 |
| 32:22 | 120, 167–68 | 33:10–20 | 196 |
| 32:22–26 | 216 | 33:12–13 | 14 |
| 32:22–23 P967 | 174 | 33:17 | 193 |
| | | 33:20 | 193 |
| 32:22–32 | 139 | 33:21 | 5, 36, 127, 175, 182–83, 187–88, 193–95 |
| 32:23 | 120, 167–68, 223 | | |
| 32:24 | 120, 154, 167–68, 173, 201 | | |
| | | 33:21–22 | 37, 186–87, 193–94, 196–97, 221 |
| 32:24–26 | 48 | | |
| 32:24–27 P967 | 174 | 33:21–33 | 197 |
| | | 33:21 LXX | 37 |
| 32:25 | 154, 167–68, 173, 216 | 33:23 | 193, 198, 207 |
| | | 33:23–29 | 197 |
| 32:26 | 154, 167–68, 173, 208, 213, 216 | 33:23–33 | 196 |
| | | 33:24 | 64–65, 77, 193, 202, 204 |
| 32:27 | 168, 173 | 33:25 | 152 |
| 32:27 P967 | 173 | 33:26 | 128, 167 |
| 32:28 | 120, 167–68, 173 | 33:27 | 74, 167, 204 |
| 32:28–32 | 124 | 33:28 | 201, 204 |
| 32:29 | 120, 167–68, 173, 198 | 33:28–29 | 205 |
| | | 33:30–32 | 197 |
| 32:29 P967 | 174 | 33:30–33 | 197 |
| 32:30 | 120, 167–68, 173, 218 | 34 | 181, 208 |
| | | 34–37 | 45, 209 |
| 32:30 P967 | 174 | 34–48 | 196 |
| 32:31 | 120, 144, 154–55, 157–58, 167–68, 216 | 34:1 | 198 |
| | | 34:5 | 136, 170–71 |
| | | 34:6 | 136, 170–71 |
| 32:32 | 120, 124, 144, 154, 157–58, 167–68, 173, 216 | 34:10 | 212 |
| | | 34:12 | 136, 170–71 |
| | | 34:13 | 125, 136, 171, 176, 178, 181–82, 186, 201 |
| 33 | 7, 8, 37, 187, 196–97 | | |
| 33–48 | 13, 125 | 34:14b | 201 |

| | | | |
|---|---|---|---|
| 34:21 | 170 | 35:15a | 203 |
| 34:24 | 88 | 36 | 39, 199, 206–8 |
| 34:25 | 148 | 36–39 | 39 |
| 34:25–30 | 24, 39 | 36:1 | 201 |
| 34:29 | 162 | 36:1–11 | 199 |
| 34:31 | 128 | 36:1–15 | 198 |
| 35 | 2, 5, 8, 16–17, 33, 57, 59, 197–202, 204–7, 221 | 36:1–23 | 48 |
| | | 36:2 | 55, 64–65, 199, 201–2, 207 |
| 35–36 | 59 | 36:2–3 | 65, 77 |
| 35:1–4 | 199 | 36:2–5 | 65 |
| 35:1–15 | 198, 207 | 36:2–6 | 206 |
| 35:1–36:15 | 198 | 36:3 | 64, 199, 201–2 |
| 35:2 | 54, 198, 212 | 36:4 | 198–99, 201, 204–5 |
| 35:2–9 | 57 | | |
| 35:3 | 73, 204–5 | 36:5 | 35, 61, 64, 77, 199, 201–2 |
| 35:3–4 | 198, 205 | | |
| 35:3b–4 | 198 | 36:5–7 | 206 |
| 35:4 | 204–5, 207 | 36:6 | 198, 205 |
| 35:5 | 59, 61, 200, 205 | 36:7 | 199, 206 |
| 35:5–9 | 198 | 36:8 | 111, 159, 201 |
| 35:5a | 198 | 36:8–12 | 206 |
| 35:6 | 59 | 36:9 | 212 |
| 35:7 | 73, 198, 204–5, 207 | 36:9–10 | 97 |
| | | 36:10 | 204, 207 |
| 35:8 | 120, 167, 198 | 36:10b | 207 |
| 35:8a | 205 | 36:10c | 199 |
| 35:8b | 205 | 36:11 | 207 |
| 35:9 | 205, 207 | 36:12 | 65, 202–3, 207 |
| 35:10 | 59, 65, 200–202, 207 | 36:13 | 15 |
| | | 36:13–15 | 206 |
| 35:10–13 | 198 | 36:16 | 198 |
| 35:10–15 | 198 | 36:16–18 | 181 |
| 35:11 | 59, 204 | 36:16–21 | 198 |
| 35:11–38:14 | 49 | 36:16–32 | 199 |
| 35:12 | 201 | 36:17 | 201 |
| 35:13 | 59 | 36:18 | 138, 152 |
| 35:14 | 202 | 36:19 | 75, 136, 170–71, 186 |
| 35:14–15 | 198, 203, 205 | | |
| 35:14b–15 | 198 | 36:23a | 49 |
| 35:15 | 35, 198, 199, 200, 202, 205, 207, 220 | 36:23bβ–38 | 48 |

| | | | |
|---|---|---|---|
| 36:24 | 125, 136, 171, 176, 178, 181, 186, 201 | 38:4a | 212 |
| | | 38:4b | 214 |
| | | 38:4b LXX | 214 |
| 36:25 | 152 | 38:4b–5 | 214 |
| 36:26–27 | 197 | 38:5 | 147, 213 |
| 36:28 | 182 | 38:6 | 37, 211, 213, 217–18 |
| 36:33–36 | 199 | | |
| 36:34 | 205 | 38:8 | 201, 204, 208–9, 219 |
| 36:36 | 132 | | |
| 36:37–38 | 199 | 38:8–9 | 208, 218 |
| 37 | 49, 208–9 | 38:8–12 | 208 |
| 37:1–14 | 49 | 38:9 | 211, 219 |
| 37:12–13 | 216 | 38:10 | 214–15 |
| 37:14 | 132, 201 | 38:10–12 | 211, 220 |
| 37:15 | 198 | 38:10–13 | 208, 220 |
| 37:15–28 | 181 | 38:11 | 209 |
| 37:16 | 200 | 38:12 | 204, 211, 220 |
| 37:21 | 125, 136, 171, 176, 178, 186, 200–201 | 38:13 | 106, 211, 220 |
| | | 38:13 LXX | 220 |
| | | 38:14 | 214–15, 219 |
| 37:21–23 | 182 | 38:14–16 | 208 |
| 37:21–34 | 181 | 38:15 | 37, 211, 217–18 |
| 37:22 | 201 | 38:16 | 208, 218–19 |
| 37:23 | 152, 182 | 38:17 | 208 |
| 37:24–29 | 209 | 38:18 | 214–15 |
| 37:25 | 88 | 38:18–23 | 208, 215 |
| 37:25–28 | 39 | 38:18b–19a | 215 |
| 37:26 | 148 | 38:18b LXX | 215 |
| 37:27 | 182 | 38:19 | 214–15 |
| 38–39 | 2, 4–5, 8, 13, 16–17, 48–49, 174, 197, 207–10, 212–14, 216–19, 221, 228 | 38:19b–22 | 215 |
| | | 38:20 | 201 |
| | | 38:22 | 211 |
| | | 38:23 | 142 |
| | | 39:1 | 208, 212–13 |
| 38:1 | 198 | 39:1–5 | 208 |
| 38:1–5 | 208 | 39:2 | 37, 211, 217–18 |
| 38:1–9 | 208, 212 | 39:4 | 201 |
| 38:2 | 54, 207–8, 213 | 39:4–5 | 215 |
| 38:3 | 207, 212–13 | 39:6 | 208 |
| 38:3–4a | 212 | 39:6–7 | 208 |
| 38:3–9 | 211 | 39:7 | 183, 201, 219 |
| 38:4 | 134, 212–13 | 39:8 | 214–15 |
| 38:4 LXX | 213 | 39:8–10 | 208 |

| | | | |
|---|---|---|---|
| 39:9 | 219 | 42:4 | 218 |
| 39:9–10 | 220 | 42:11 | 218 |
| 39:10 | 220 | 42:13 | 59, 218 |
| 39:11 | 154–55, 214–16 | 42:17 | 218 |
| 39:11–13 | 208 | 43:2 | 143 |
| 39:11–16 | 208, 215–16 | 43:7 | 200 |
| 39:12 | 211 | 43:10 | 88 |
| 39:13 | 214 | 44:4 | 218 |
| 39:14–16 | 208 | 44:7 | 148 |
| 39:15 | 154–55 | 44:9 | 200 |
| 39:16 | 154–55 | 44:10 | 152 |
| 39:17 | 201 | 44:12 | 152 |
| 39:17–20 | 208, 215 | 44:15 | 200 |
| 39:18 | 143 | 44:28 | 203 |
| 39:21–22 | 208 | 44:29 | 59 |
| 39:21–29 | 181 | 45:1 | 203 |
| 39:22b | 214 | 46:9 | 218 |
| 39:23 | 167, 219 | 46:16 | 203 |
| 39:23–24 | 208, 220 | 46:20 | 59 |
| 39:23–29 | 24, 220 | 47:1–12 | 160 |
| 39:25 | 178, 219 | 47:7 | 160 |
| 39:25–29 | 39, 208, 220 | 47:12 | 160 |
| 39:26 | 201 | 47:10 | 134, 168 |
| 39:27 | 142, 178 | 47:13–48:29 | 71 |
| 39:27–28 | 136, 171 | 47:14 | 203 |
| 39:28 | 201 | 47:17 | 218 |
| 39:29 | 219–20 | 47:18 | 34 |
| 40–48 | 47–48, 208–9 | 47:19 | 203 |
| 40:1 | 187–88, 193 | 47:22 | 200, 203 |
| 40:2 | 34 | 48:10 | 120 |
| 40:19 | 218 | 48:11 | 200 |
| 40:20 | 218 | 48:16 | 218 |
| 40:23 | 218 | 48:28 | 203 |
| 40:35 | 218 | 48:29 | 203 |
| 40:39 | 59 | 48:30 | 218 |
| 40:44 | 218 | | |
| 40:46 | 218 | Daniel | |
| 41:11 | 218 | 2:28 | 219 |
| 41:18 | 112 | 4:7–9 | 159 |
| 41:20 | 112 | 8:9 | 69 |
| 41:25 | 112 | 9:16 | 95, 111 |
| 42:1 | 218 | 9:20 | 111 |
| 42:2 | 218 | 10:6 | 98, 155 |

| | | | |
|---|---|---|---|
| 10:14 | 219 | 4:13 | 2 |
| 11:10 | 154 | 4:14 | 169 |
| 11:11 | 154 | 4:15 | 154 |
| 11:12 | 154 | 4:18 | 97 |
| 11:13 | 154 | 4:19 | 123, 205 |
| 11:16 | 69 | | |
| 11:31 | 120 | Amos | |
| 11:41 | 69 | 1–2 | 1, 2, 9, 11, 12, 24, 54 |
| 11:45 | 69, 95, 111 | 1:2 | 110 |
| Hosea | | 1:2–2:16 | 9 |
| 1 | 192 | 1:5 | 74 |
| 2:14 | 107 | 1:8 | 74 |
| 2:21–23 | 182 | 1:9–10 | 82 |
| 3 | 192 | 2:1–3 | 27 |
| 3:5 | 219 | 2:3 | 74 |
| 4:12–15 | 104 | 2:9 | 159 |
| 5:1 | 168 | 3:4 | 110 |
| 5:8 | 2 | 3:8 | 133 |
| 5:14 | 133 | 4:10 | 167 |
| 6:11 | 178 | 5:1 | 84 |
| 8:10 | 178 | 5:18 | 169 |
| 9:1 | 104, 107 | 5:19 | 133 |
| 9:6 | 150 | 5:20 | 169 |
| 11:10 | 133 | 5:23 | 154 |
| 12:2 | 118, 147 | 7:9 | 120, 167 |
| 13:7–8 | 133 | 7:13 | 19, 120 |
| 13:15 | 118 | 8:10 | 84 |
| | | 9:11 | 167 |
| Joel | | 9:14 | 178 |
| 1:15 | 43, 169 | | |
| 2:1 | 95, 111, 169 | Obadiah | |
| 2:11 | 110, 169 | 1 | 2 |
| 2:20 | 218 | 1:16 | 111 |
| 2:22 | 111 | 11:13–14 | 28 |
| 3:4 | 169 | 15 | 169 |
| 3:21 | 95, 111 | 16 | 95 |
| 4 | 2, 13 | 17 | 64 |
| 4:1 | 178 | 19 | 62 |
| 4:2 | 178 | | |
| 4:3 | 107 | Jonah | |
| 4:4–8 | 82 | 4:8 | 118 |
| 4:9–12 | 2 | | |

| Micah | |
|---|---|
| 1:6 | 162 |
| 1:7 | 107 |
| 1:10 | 119 |
| 1:10–15 | 149 |
| 1:16 | 119 |
| 2:12 | 178 |
| 4:1 | 219 |
| 4:2 | 95, 111 |
| 4:6 | 178 |
| 4:12 | 178 |
| 4:13 | 2 |
| 5:9–14 | 74 |
| 6:3 | 103 |
| 6:15 | 88 |
| 7:13 | 205 |

| Nahum | |
|---|---|
| 1:1 | 2 |
| 1:14 | 74 |
| 2:13 | 74 |
| 2:14 | 167, 212 |
| 3:15 | 212 |
| 3:19 | 56 |

| Habakkuk | |
|---|---|
| 1:1 | 2 |
| 1:5–11 | 218 |
| 2:2 | 189 |
| 3:10 | 110 |
| 3:13–15 | 143 |

| Zephaniah | |
|---|---|
| 1:3 | 74–75 |
| 1:7 | 169, 215 |
| 1:13 | 205 |
| 1:14 | 169 |
| 1:15 | 219 |
| 1:18 | 169 |
| 2–3 | 1 |
| 2:2 | 169 |
| 2:4 | 205 |
| 2:6–7 | 62 |
| 2:7 | 178 |
| 2:8–9 | 55 |
| 2:10 | 80 |
| 2:12 | 167 |
| 2:13 | 205 |
| 3:6 | 74, 204 |
| 3:8 | 178 |
| 3:11 | 95, 111 |
| 3:19 | 178 |
| 3:20 | 178 |

| Haggai | |
|---|---|
| 1:1 | 187 |
| 1:15b | 187 |
| 2:10 | 187 |
| 2:20 | 187 |
| 2:23 | 88 |

| Zechariah | |
|---|---|
| 1:1 | 187 |
| 1:7 | 187 |
| 2:2 | 170 |
| 2:4 | 170 |
| 2:8 | 75 |
| 3:8 | 159 |
| 6:12 | 159 |
| 7:1 | 187 |
| 8:3 | 95, 111 |
| 8:12 | 111 |
| 8:19 | 189 |
| 9 | 1 |
| 9:1 | 2 |
| 9:2–4 | 82 |
| 9:6 | 80 |
| 9:7 | 62 |
| 9:17 | 89 |
| 10:8 | 178 |
| 10:10 | 178 |
| 10:11 | 80, 139 |
| 11:1–3 | 161 |
| 11:2 | 92 |
| 13:7–9 | 167 |
| 14 | 13 |

| | | | |
|---|---|---|---|
| 14:1 | 169 | 40 | 27 |
| 14:8 | 97 | | |

*KTU*
1.4 vi 18, 20   162
1.17 vi 21   162

Malachi
1:3   205
2:3   170
3:23   169

Lachish
3   32

EGYPTIAN AND MESOPOTAMIAN TEXTS

CT 13
33–34   133

Mesha
lines 9–10   70
line 30   70

EA 288
13–15   137
14   137

APOCRYPHA AND PSEUDEPIGRAPHA

1 Esdras
4:42–46   28

EA 286
12   137

1 Maccabees
10:83–84   29
11:4   29

EA 287
27   137

1 Enoch
10:21–11:2   225
48:4–5   225
50:2–3   225
90:30–38   225
91:14   225
100:6   225
105:1–2   225

Papyrus Rylands
IX, 14:16–19   31

Pyramid Texts
Spell 317   131

RINAP 4
60:24'   115
68:4–5   179
77:10   115
78:9   115
79:9   115
93:5   115

Jubilees
3:27   97
4:26   97
8:19   97

Life of Adam and Eve
29:3   97

WAW 19
51 iii 16   115

DEAD SEA SCROLLS
1QapGen ar
XXII, 10   105

WEST SEMITIC INSCRIPTIONS
Arad
24   27

1QpHab   224

4Q169
 3–4 I, 7 224

4Q177
 II, 7 224
 II 10 224
 II, 12 224
 II, 13 224
 II, 14 224

4Q252 225

ANCIENT JEWISH WRITERS
Josephus, *Against Apion*
 1.21 30

Josephus, *Jewish Antiquities*
 3.165–68 98
 10.180–85 27

Josephus, *Jewish War*
 5.233–34 98

NEW TESTAMENT
John
 1:14 43

GRECO-ROMAN LITERATURE
Herodotus, *History*
 2.157 29
 2.159 29

Plutarch, *Isis and Osiris*
 §15 141

RABBINIC WORKS AND TARGUMIM
b. Hul.
 89a 224

b. Sanh.
 89a 37

Gen. Rab.
 18:1 110
 85:4 99

Midr. Ps
 92:6 97

Pesiq. Rab.
 43:2 97
Pirqe R. El.
 23 97
 31 97

Tg. Ps.-Jo.
 Ezek 16:13 94
 Ezek 32:23 223

EARLY CHRISTIAN WRITINGS
*Theopilus to Antolycus*
 2.35 37

# MODERN AUTHORS INDEX

Aharoni, Y. 27–28
Aḥituv, S. 27, 32
Akers, M. R. 138
Albertz, R. 2, 10, 13, 25, 52, 65
Albright, W. R. 36, 112–13, 116
Alexander, D. 172
Allen, L. C. 18, 36, 52, 57, 59, 64, 81, 87, 128, 132, 140, 145, 149, 151, 172, 190–91, 202, 208, 213, 219
Altenmüller, B. 130–31
Amichai, Y. 223, 229
Anderson, B. A. 66, 201
Anderson, G. A. 20
Arbel, D. 109–10, 117, 121
Armstrong, K. 226
Assis, E. 28, 59
Astour, M. C. 210, 220
Avi-Yonah, M. 27, 70
Bach, R. 2
Bartlett, J. R. 27, 29, 207
Barr, J. 20, 108, 110, 113
Batto, B. F. 177, 212
Becker, J. 15
Beentjes, P. C. 3
Bentzen, A. 9–10

Ben Zvi, E. 22, 147
Berges, U. F. 25
Bertholet, A. 60, 159, 202
Bewer, J. A. 18, 52
Biberger, B. 208, 210, 212, 215–17, 219–20
Biddle, M. E. 65–66, 104
Black, J. 116
Blenkinsopp, J. 31, 36, 52, 80, 149–50, 177–78, 196, 226
Bloch-Smith, E. 116
Block, D. I. 12, 16, 19, 24, 34, 48, 52, 54–57, 69–72, 74, 76, 80–82, 85, 88–90, 93–94, 96, 106, 121, 124, 126–27, 130, 135–36, 139–40, 147–49, 166, 168, 172–74, 176, 179, 191–93, 196, 198–202, 208, 213–16, 220
Boadt, L. 3, 16, 21, 36, 39–40, 125, 128–29, 132–33, 139–40, 142, 146, 152,

|  |  |  |  |
|---|---|---|---|
| | | 159, 164, 167, 177, 180, 212 | Diakonoff, I. M. 90 |
| | | | Dicou, B. 28 |
| Bodi, D. | | 61, 134, 152, 154–55, 167–68 | Dietrich, W. 62, 71 |
| | | | Dillard, R. B. 93 |
| Bogaert, P.-M. | | 20, 39, 82–83, 88, 99–101, 108, 111, 120 | Dimant, D. 224 |
| | | | Ditommaso, L. 47 |
| | | | Doak, B. 173 |
| Bowen, N. R. | | 81, 90, 124, 130, 164, 180 | Dobbs-Allsopp, F. W. 27–28, 32, 104 |
| Bøe, S. | | 209–10, 214, 219–20 | Donaldson, T. L. 225 |
| | | | Driver, S. R. 15 |
| Braulik, G. | 66 | | Durlesser, J. A. 87, 104–5 |
| Breasted, J. H. | 133 | | Eichler, R. 113–14 |
| Bresciani, E. | 131–32 | | Eichrodt, W. 13, 24–25, 31, 34, 52, 55, 57–58, 60, 64, 69–70, 74–75, 80, 87, 99, 105, 111, 119, 121, 124, 132–33, 135, 139, 143, 148, 150, 155, 173, 181, 187, 189–91, 196, 213 |
| Brett, M. G. | 227 | | |
| Brooke, G. J. | 224 | | |
| Brown, K. | 43, 46 | | |
| Budd, P. J. | 11 | | |
| Budge, E. A. W. | 141 | | |
| Bunta, S. N. | 88, 109–10 | | |
| Byron, J. | 72 | | |
| Callender, D. E. | 20, 88, 97, 109–10 | | |
| Carley, K. W. | 196 | | |
| Caspari, C. P. | 43 | | Eissfeldt, O. 167 |
| Cassuto, U. | 96, 122, 144 | | El-Shahawy, A. 140–41 |
| Childs, B. S. | 74, 132, 178, 217 | | Fechter, F. 2–3, 7–8, 24, 38, 39, 54–55, 57, 68, 71, 85, 88, 89, 97, 99, 129, 132, 145–47, 175, 190, 193, 198, 213 |
| Christensen, D. L. | 2, 10–12, 23 | | |
| Clines, D. J. A. | 40 | | |
| Cooke, G. A. | 36, 55, 60, 107, 114, 121, 196, 203 | | |
| Corral, M. A. | 16, 28–32, 80–82 | | Fensham, F. C. 10 |
| Crane, A. S. | 48–50, 213 | | Fisch, S. 70 |
| Cresson, B. C. | 28, 203 | | Fischer, A. A. 134 |
| Crouch, C. L. | 85, 119 | | Fischer, G. 25, 67 |
| Darr, K. P. | 124 | | Fishbane, M. 45, 144 |
| Davis, E. F. | 132, 228 | | Fistill, U. 11 |
| Day, L. | 104 | | Fitzpatrick, P. E. 177, 210, 212, 216–18, 220 |
| Day, P. | 104 | | |
| Dearman, J. A. | 27, 70 | | Fohrer, G. 10, 14, 80, 90, 130, 133, 149– |
| De Troyer, K. | 46 | | |

|   |   |   |   |
|---|---|---|---|
|  | 50, 154, 188–89, 203 | Grayson, A. K. | 92, 115 |
|  |  | Green, A. | 115–16 |
| Foster, B. R. | 133 | Greenberg, M. | 15–16, 29, 33, 52–53, 55, 62, 70, 80, 82–83, 89–90, 94, 97, 102, 104, 106, 110, 117, 124, 129, 139, 148–49, 152, 156, 165, 168, 189, 191, 194, 196, 202–3 |
| Frankel, D. | 64, 66 |  |  |
| Freedy, K. S. | 136, 149, 189 |  |  |
| Fretheim, T. E. | 36, 150 |  |  |
| Friebel, K. G. | 56, 202 |  |  |
| Fuhs, H. F. | 13, 19, 25, 30, 52, 55, 59–60, 64, 72, 105, 124, 129–30, 146, 148–49, 176, 196, 203, 208 |  |  |
| Fujita, S. | 47 | Griffith, F. L. | 31 |
| Galambush, J. | 47–48, 93–94, 104, 210–11 | Griffith, J. G. | 141 |
|  |  | Grossman, J. | 91–92 |
| Ganzel, T. | 180 | Grottanelli, C. | 167 |
| García Martínez, F. | 47, 49, 86 | Guillaume, P. | 129 |
|  |  | Gunkel, H. | 19, 124, 144 |
| Gerleman, G. | 154, 156 | Haag, E. | 139, 155, 164 |
| Gertz, J. C. | 3, 25, 66 | Hagedorn, A. C. | 2, 10, 24, 225 |
| Geyer, J. B. | 2, 39–40, 82–83, 90–91 | Haldor, P. C. | 106, 119 |
|  |  | Haller, M. | 28 |
| Gile, J. | 26, 34, 38, 40–41, 43, 73, 75, 136, 171 | Hallo, W. W. | 104 |
|  |  | Halperin, D. J. | 114 |
|  |  | Hamborg, G. R. | 228 |
| Gillmayr-Bucher, S. | 82, 90, 92 | Haran, M. | 10–11 |
|  |  | Harrell, J. A. | 98 |
| Glassner, J.-J. | 115 | Hartenstein, F. | 113–15 |
| Glatt-Gilad, D. A. | 66–67 | Hayes, J. H. | 10, 26–27, 29, 31–32, 139, 211 |
|  |  | Hays, C. B. | 141–42, 172 |
| Glazier-McDonald, B. | 28, 203 | Heidel, A. | 133 |
|  |  | Helbig, J. | 41–42 |
| Görg, M. | 67, 137–38 | Hendel, R. S. | 173 |
| Goering, G. S. | 84 | Herrmann, J. | 19 |
| Gomaᶜ, F. | 131 | Hillers, D. R. | 10 |
| Gordon, R. P. | 21, 61, 172 | Holladay, W. L. | 217 |
| Gosse, B. | 19, 36, 52, 55, 82, 85, 190, 194, 200, 203, 205–6 | Hölscher, G. H. | 118, 191, 196 |
|  |  | Höffken, P. | 130, 132, 147 |
| Gottwald, N. K. | 10, 55, 64 | Hoffman, Y. | 10, 23, 169 |
| Gowan, D. E. | 33, 80, 96, 139–40, 155, 159 | Hoffmeier, J. K. | 135–37 |
|  |  | Hossfeld, F.-L. | 53, 103, 208 |

| | | | |
|---|---|---|---|
| House, P. R. | 104 | Lanfer, P. T. | 97 |
| Huehnergard, J. | 115 | Lauha, A. | 217–18 |
| Hundley, M. B. | 115–16 | Launderville, D. | 113–14 |
| Hutter, M. | 116 | Lawhead, A. S. | 151 |
| Huwyler, B. | 2 | Lee, L. | 93, 143 |
| Irwin, B. P. | 216 | Leichty, E. | 115, 179 |
| Izre'el, S. | 137 | Lemaire, A. | 28, 100 |
| Jackson, K. P. | 70 | Levenson, J. D. | 96, 130, 227 |
| Jahnow, H. | 89 | Levey, S. H. | 154, 223 |
| Janowski, B. | 96, 112 | Levine, B. A. | 11 |
| Japhet, S. | 65 | Levinson, B. M. | 41, 45, 143 |
| Johnston, P. S. | 143, 172 | Lewis, T. J. | 133 |
| Jones, B. C. | 2 | Lichtheim, M. | 131 |
| Jones, G. H. | 2, 9 | Lilly, I. A. | 48–50, 173–75 |
| Jones, S. C. | 130 | Lipschits, O. | 26, 29–32 |
| Joosten, J. | 74 | Lipton, D. | 192 |
| Joyce, P. M. | 99, 138 | Liverani, M. | 90, 95 |
| Kaminsky, J. S. | 178, 225–27 | Lohfink, N. | 65–67 |
| Keel, O. | 112–15, 136 | Loretz, O. | 19, 162 |
| Kessler, R. | 129, 145, 152, 177 | Luckenbill, D. D. | 149 |
| King, L. W. | 115 | Lust, J. | 3, 15, 48–50, 59, 64–65, 72, 86, 100, 173–74, 198, 201, 206–7, 210, 220 |
| Klein, A. | 37, 45, 48, 198–99, 201–2, 205–7, 210, 212, 214–18, 220 | | |
| | | Lynch, M. | 88, 93 |
| Koemoth, P. | 142 | Lyons, M. A. | 38, 40–41, 71, 73, 75, 125–26, 165–67, 171, 201, 228 |
| Kohn, R. L. | 38, 64, 73, 91, 93, 138 | | |
| Koller, A. | 92 | | |
| Konkel, M. | 48 | MacDonald, N. | 67, 117, 227 |
| Koopmans, W. T. | 59 | Machinist, P. | 29–30, 62 |
| | | Malamat, A. | 31 |
| Korpel, M. C. A. | 128 | Margulis, B. B. | 2, 10–11 |
| König, F. E. | 43 | Martens, K. | 73 |
| Kraeling, E. G. | 173 | Marzouk, S. | 21–22, 31, 36, 39–40, 126–130, 133, 135, 154, 156, 158, 170, 176, 179–81, 195 |
| Kraetzschmar, R. | 81 | | |
| Krantz, E. S. | 95 | | |
| Kraus, H.-J. | 103 | | |
| Kreuzer, S. | 138 | | |
| Kutsch, E. | 187–91, 193, 195 | May, H. G. | 143, 160 |
| Lambdin, T. O. | 130 | Mayfield, T. D. | 13, 187, 190–91, 194–95, 198 |
| Lambert, W. G. | 133 | | |

| | | | |
|---|---|---|---|
| McKane, W. | 25, 150 | Olley, J. W. | 68, 153, 174, 201, 213, 219 |
| McKeating, H. | 186, 195 | | |
| Mein, A. | 99, 120–21 | Olyan, S. M. | 172 |
| Mendecki, N. | 24 | Oswald, W. | 169–70 |
| Mendenhall, G. E. | 71 | Otto, E. | 66 |
| | | Page Jr., H. R. | 99 |
| Messel, N. | 189 | Patmore, H. M. | 49–50, 88, 95, 98–101, 108–112, 223–24 |
| Metzger, M. | 112–14, 116, 159 | | |
| Milgrom, J. | 11 | | |
| Millard, A. | 106 | Paton, L. B. | 92 |
| Miller, G. D. | 41, 43–44 | Paul, S. M. | 9–11 |
| Miller, J. E. | 117 | Peels, H. G. L. | 60, 71–72 |
| Miller, J. M. | 26–27, 29, 31–32, 70–71, 139 | Petersen, D. L. | 9, 24, 50 |
| | | Petry, S. | 182 |
| Miller, P. D. | 66–67 | Pfeiffer, R. H. | 4, 225–28 |
| Minj, S. K. | 124, 132, 167, 176–181 | Pitard, W. T. | 71–72 |
| | | Pohlmann, K.-F. | 16, 38, 73, 76, 81, 85, 88, 90, 105, 118, 124–25, 129, 146, 148–49, 150, 160–62, 166–67, 175, 198, 208, 215 |
| Mizrahi, N. | 47 | | |
| Mobley, G. | 116 | | |
| Moran, W. L. | 137 | | |
| Morgenstern, J. | 20 | | |
| Mowinckel, S. | 9 | | |
| Newsom, C. A. | 21, 47, 97, 121 | | |
| Niccacci, A. | 138 | | |
| Nickelsburg, G. W. E. | 225 | Pope, M. H. | 19–20, 117 |
| | | Popović, M. | 50 |
| Nobile, M. | 220 | Porten, B. | 29 |
| Norin, S. I. L. | 169–70 | Poser, R. | 195 |
| Noth, M. | 91 | Premstaller, V. | 3, 16–17, 38, 55, 57, 64, 73, 81, 85, 89, 98, 119, 124, 132, 145–46, 148–49, 153, 158–59, 167, 180, 191, 195, 200, 203–4, 208 |
| Notvotny, J. | 92 | | |
| Nurmela, R. | 38 | | |
| Nysse, R. W. | 4, 7 | | |
| O'Brien, J. M. | 29, 59, 192 | | |
| Oded, B. | 26–27, 70 | | |
| Odell, M. S. | 30, 34, 40, 47, 53, 55, 70, 94, 104, 106, 136, 139, 150, 154, 156–57, 160, 163, 172, 180, 196 | | |
| | | Preuss, D. | 66, 152 |
| | | Raabe, P. R. | 2, 228 |
| | | Rabinowitz, L. I. | 26–27 |
| | | Rad, G. von | 169 |
| | | Raitt, T. M. | 121, 182 |
| | | Redford, D. B. | 136, 149, 189 |
| Oeming, M. | 103 | Reinhartz, A. | 76 |

| | | | |
|---|---|---|---|
| Rendtorff, R. | 64, 117 | Stordalen, T. | 100, 140, 142, 159, 162 |
| Renz, T. | 151 | | |
| Reventlow, H. G. | 18, 69, 74 | Stökl, J. | 128, 210 |
| Richelle, M. | 100–101, 111 | Stolz, F. | 140 |
| Rösel, C. | 208, 210, 215, 218–20 | Strawn, B. A. | 50, 133, 172 |
| | | Strine, C. A. | 64–65, 119, 163, 210 |
| Rom-Shiloni, D. | 65 | | |
| Roncace, M. | 218 | Strong, J. T. | 3, 8, 19, 31, 38–39, 52, 54, 61, 64, 68, 73, 81, 86, 105, 172, 174, 181 |
| Rooy, H. F. van. | 135, 139, 145 | | |
| Rudman, D. | 143 | | |
| Rudnig, T. A. | 47 | | |
| Rüterswörden, U. | 122 | | |
| Sadler, R. S. | 147 | Strugnell, J. | 224 |
| Salters, R. B. | 104 | Sulzbach, C. | 93, 99, 159 |
| Sarna, N. M. | 122, 144 | Sweeney, M. A. | 25 |
| Sasson, J. M. | 174 | Talmon, S. | 49 |
| Saur, M. | 85, 90, 105–7 | Terrien, S. | 90 |
| Scatolini, S. S. | 48–49 | Thompson, J. A. | 150 |
| Schipper, B. U. | 31–32 | Thompson, N. D. | 151 |
| Schmid, K. | 3, 25, 143 | Tiemeyer, L.-S. | 99, 111–12, 114 |
| Schöpflin, K. | 54, 56, 82, 84, 167–68, 172, 189, 192, 197–98, 202 | Tigchelaar, E. | 49 |
| | | Tooman, W. A. | 40–42, 48, 121, 201, 208–10, 212, 214–15, 217–19, 221, 228 |
| Schultz, R. L. | 37, 40–41, 43 | | |
| Schwagmeier, P. | 18, 37, 39, 49, 53, 55, 82–83, 165 | Torrey, C. C. | 15 |
| | | Tov, E. | 25, 46, 106 |
| Schwally, F. | 4 | Tsevat, M. | 148, 180 |
| Schwartz, B. J. | 180 | Tzoref, S. | 224–25 |
| Schweizer, H. | 140 | Uehlinger, C. | 129 |
| Seeligmann, I. L. | 45 | Ulrich, D. R. | 9, 151 |
| Seiler, S. | 40 | Ulrich, E. | 20, 46 |
| Sharp, C. J. | 25 | Vanderhooft, D. S. | 168, 196 |
| Simian, H. | 73, 198–99, 202, 204–5, 213 | Van Dijk, H. J. | 16, 107 |
| | | Van Winkle, D. W. | 227 |
| Smend, R. | 15 | | |
| Smith, M. S. | 96–97 | Vette, J. | 103 |
| Soden, W. von | 116 | Vieweger, D. | 37 |
| Sommer, B. D. | 40–41, 43–44 | Vittmann, G. | 31 |
| Spieckermann, H. | 45–46 | Vogels, W. | 125, 145, 167, 171, 177–79, 181 |
| Steudel, A. | 224 | | |
| | | Vorländer, H. | 226 |

| | | | |
|---|---|---|---|
| Wächter, L. | 172 | | 130, 135, 139– |
| Wahl, H.-M. | 86 | | 40, 143–50, 154– |
| Wakeman, M. K. | 128–29 | | 57, 163, 166, |
| Weinfeld, M. | 96 | | 172, 179–81, |
| Weiss, M. | 10, 169 | | 187–91, 193–96, |
| Wendebourg, N. | 169–70 | | 198–99, 201–2, |
| Wenham, G. J. | 96 | | 204, 208, 213–4, |
| Westermann, C. | 3, 65, 178 | | 217 |
| Wevers, J. W. | 34, 36, 60, 62, | Zunz, L. | 15 |
| | 76, 85, 90, 105, | Zwickel, W. | 98 |
| | 119, 121, 140, | | |
| | 143, 149, 155, | | |
| | 189–91, 213 | | |
| Widengren, G. | 19 | | |
| Wiggermann, | | | |
| F. A. M. | 115–16 | | |
| Wilkinson, R. H. | 141 | | |
| Williamson, | | | |
| H. G. M. | 54, 227 | | |
| Wilson, I. D. | 82–84 | | |
| Wilson, R. R. | 20, 39, 83, 85, | | |
| | 88, 90, 92, 95, | | |
| | 97–98, 117–18 | | |
| Wiseman, D. J. | 27, 30, 151 | | |
| Wold, D. J. | 74 | | |
| Wolff, H. W. | 152 | | |
| Wood, A. | 111–16 | | |
| Woudstra, M. H. | 206 | | |
| Yaron, K. | 19, 39, 88, 97, | | |
| | 109, 111, 117–18 | | |
| Yoder, T. R. | 129, 131, 133 | | |
| Young, I. | 46 | | |
| Younger, K. L. | 104 | | |
| Zecchi, M. | 131 | | |
| Zimmerli, W. | 14–16, 24, 29– | | |
| | 31, 33–37, 48, | | |
| | 54–58, 60, 62– | | |
| | 63, 69–71, 73– | | |
| | 74, 80–82, 86– | | |
| | 89, 91, 93–94, | | |
| | 97, 99, 105–6, | | |
| | 111, 114, 117, | | |
| | 121, 124, 126, | | |

www.ingramcontent.com/pod-product-compliance
Lightning Source LLC
Chambersburg PA
CBHW021355290426
44108CB00010B/248